Commitment to Unity

Commitment
to Unity W. Kent Gilbert

A History
of the Lutheran Church in America

FORTRESS PRESS
PHILADELPHIA

To the long line of people
who formed and were the
Lutheran Church in America

Photographs on pp. 131, 176, 183, 252, 289, 316, 360, 405, and 503 are used with permission of *The Lutheran.*

Photographs on pp. xx, 26, 30, 37, 42, 52, 71, 130, 143 (bottom), 211 (top), 232, 338, 393, 399, 430, and 435 are from ELCA Archives.

Photographs on pp. 143 (top), 211 (bottom), 292 (bottom), and 504 are used with permission of ELCA Commission for Communication.

Photograph on p. 168 is used with permission of ELCA Office for Communication.

Illustration on p. 535 is by Bernhard Sperl.

Library of Congress Cataloging-in-Publication Data

Gilbert, W. Kent.
Commitment to unity.
Includes index.
1. Lutheran Church in America—History. 2. Christian union—Lutheran Church in America—History. 3. Lutheran Church—United States—History. 4. United States—Church history. I. Title.
BX8048.2.G55 1988   284.1'33'09   88–45239
ISBN 0–8006–0891–7

2518F88   Printed in the United States of America   1–891

CONTENTS

Abbreviations   vii

Introduction by H. George Anderson   xi

Preface   xv

1. Immigration and Americanization   1

2. Moving Toward Merging   67

3. Growing Together   121

4. Old Problems and New Strategies   197

5. Challenges, Victories, and Changes   279

6. Reaching Out to Others   387

7. To the Present and into the Future   475

Appendixes:

A. The Constitution of the Lutheran Church in America   565

B. Background Studies Relating to the History of the
Lutheran Church in America and Its Predecessor Bodies   581

C. Officers of the Lutheran Church in America   585

D. Synodical Presidents/Bishops of the Lutheran Church in
America   587

E. Chief Executives of Churchwide Agencies of the
Lutheran Church in America   593

Index   597

ABBREVIATIONS

ABL	Association of Black Lutherans
ACC	Approved Constitution for Congregations
ACS	Approved Constitution for Synods
AELC	American Evangelical Lutheran Church (Danish) 1953–62
	Association of Evangelical Lutheran Churches 1976–87
ALC	American Lutheran Church 1930–60
	The American Lutheran Church 1960–87
BAM	Board of American Missions
BCECV	Board of College Education and Church Vocations
BEM	Baptism, Eucharist and Ministry
BPE	Board of Parish Education
BPen	Board of Pensions
BPub	Board of Publication
BSM	Board of Social Ministry
BTE	Board of Theological Education
BWM	Board of World Missions
CCA	Commission on Church Architecture
CCC	Committee on Church Cooperation
CCMGI	Consulting Committee on Minority Group Interests
CCP	Commission on Church Papers
CCWCS	Consulting Committee on Women in Church and Society
CFS	Commission on Function and Structure
CNLC	Commission for a New Lutheran Church
COE	Commission on Evangelism
COS	Commission on Stewardship
CW	Commission on Worship

CWA	Churchwide Agencies
CYA	Commission on Youth Activities
CYM	Commission on Youth Ministry
DAG	Designated Advance Giving
DMNA	Division for Mission in North America
DPL	Division for Professional Leadership
DPS	Division for Parish Services
DWME	Division for World Mission and Ecumenism
ECM	Executive Council Minutes
ELC	Evangelical Lutheran Church
ELCA	Evangelical Lutheran Church in America
ELCC	Evangelical Lutheran Church of Canada
ELCIC	Evangelical Lutheran Church in Canada
EM	Educational Ministry
ILCW	Inter-Lutheran Commission on Worship
JCLU	Joint Commission on Lutheran Unity
LCA	Lutheran Church in America
LCA-BL	Lutheran Church in America Bylaws
LCAC	Lutheran Church in America Constitution
LCA-CS	Lutheran Church in America-Canada Section
LCAM	Lutheran Church in America Minutes
LCMS	Lutheran Church-Missouri Synod
LCUSA	Lutheran Council in the USA
LCW	Lutheran Church Women
LIRS	Lutheran Immigration and Refugee Service
LLM	Lutheran Laymen's (Laity) Movement
LSTC	Lutheran School of Theology at Chicago
LWA	Lutheran World Action
LWF	Lutheran World Federation
LWM	Lutheran World Ministries
LWR	Lutheran World Relief
M	Used as a suffix for "Minutes" throughout
NCCCUSA	National Council of the Churches of Christ in the USA
NLC	National Lutheran Council
OAF	Office for Administration and Finance
OB/S	Office of the Bishop and the Secretary
OC	Office for Communications
ORP	Office for Research and Planning
PLMD	Parish Life and Ministry Development

PRT	Press, Radio and Television
RVOG	Radio Voice of the Gospel
UELC	United Evangelical Lutheran Church
ULCA	United Lutheran Church in America
WCC	World Council of Churches

INTRODUCTION

IT'S NEVER TOO EARLY TO WRITE HISTORY OR to learn from it. The observations of eyewitnesses and participants have immense value, both in themselves and as resources for later historians. Although one may be able to see more widely from a distance, one loses the whiff and tang of life among the events.

The following account of the history of the Lutheran Church in America benefits from the fact that its author was a key figure in the story he tells. As Executive Secretary of the LCA's Board of Parish Education and later as Executive Director of its Division for Parish Services, he exercised widening responsibility for programs that involved congregational stewardship, worship, education, evangelism, and service. His position and experience also placed him on the LCA's Cabinet of Executives, where his good sense and tactical skill helped to shape decisions that would eventually be made by others. This account, therefore, has the authority of an "insider" behind it, and its extensive notes will guide those who come later to rich veins of documentation which they can mine on their own.

What does this account tell us? What difference has the Lutheran Church in America made to the history of Christianity? Are there any elements of church life in North America that would not exist if there had been no LCA?

The most obvious answer is that at least the LCA's successor body, the Evangelical Lutheran Church in America, owes its existence to the unremitting efforts of its parent. The LCA actively worked for its own demise. Its constitution required it to "strive for the unification of all Lutherans within its boundaries in one church and to take constructive measures leading thereto." Conventions of the LCA repeatedly made that mandate their own as they authorized committees to seek organic union with sister Lutheran bodies. As Dr. Gilbert points out in his preface, "Commitment to Unity" seems an apt description for the spirit that permeated the LCA and that finally led to the formation of the Evangelical Lutheran Church in America in 1987. Undoubtedly, wider Lutheran union would have come in time, but the active role of the LCA made it happen at least a decade sooner.

The LCA also provided leadership to wider movements toward Christian unity. Its presidents played key roles in ecumenical organizations. Dr. Fry earned the epithet "Mr. Protestant" for his contributions to the formation of the National Council of Churches and the World Council of Churches, and his contributions to those organizations continued unabated during the early years of the LCA. Dr. Marshall became a trusted adviser to ecumenical organizations because of his organizational and financial abilities. Bishop Crumley forged a vital personal link between the LCA and leaders of Orthodox communions and the Roman Catholic Church, reestablishing bonds that had been broken since the Reformation. All of these leaders also provided strong theological resources for the ecumenical movement at a time when other leaders had become embroiled in purely programmatic concerns.

Other theological contributions to ecumenism came from the clergy of the LCA. When the Second Vatican Council opened the possibility for theological discussion with other Christian bodies, it was the Executive Director of the National Lutheran Council, Paul Empie, who seized that opportunity and organized a series of dialogues between Lutherans and Roman Catholics in the United States —a pattern that was soon adopted internationally and duplicated widely within North America. William Lazareth helped to shape the path-finding document on *Baptism, Eucharist and Ministry* during his work as Director of the WCC's Secretariat for Faith and Order. Although these were the contributions of individuals, the LCA actively shared their priorities and supported their efforts.

In its own structure the LCA provided a unique example to the rest of American Christianity. The structure originated in compromises between the national polities of its Swedish, Danish, and Finnish parents on the one hand, and the more regional polity of the United Lutheran Church in America on the other. The resulting hybrid structure was surprisingly balanced for so large a church. By comparison with its sister Lutheran bodies, which were slightly smaller in size, the LCA was less centralized and was able to maintain a high level of local involvement in decision making without sacrificing unity. This unique distribution of power proved highly successful in building consensus, so that actions of LCA churchwide conventions were widely accepted by congregations.

During the decade of the 1970s, when its sister Lutheran bodies suffered schism or conflict from their conservative wings and many other denominations split, the LCA preserved unity. How did this happen? Certainly its participative structure helped; but a more subtle reason lay in the extensive educational effort which had accompanied the introduction of the Long-Range Program of Parish Education in 1964. Parish school teachers from all over the country were taught to use contemporary biblical scholarship to interpret the Bible in a way consistent with the Lutheran Confessions. When battles between literalism and liberalism split other denominations in the 1970s, the leaders of LCA congregations were those same former teachers who had learned that there was another alternative. Their refusal to panic over biblical issues enabled the LCA to ride out the storm and in fact to move forward with a new series of studies linking Word and witness.

In its twenty-five years the LCA produced many additional achievements, records, and contributions. In the following pages they will emerge against the background of some of the stormiest years in American social history. The how and the why of that story is told in a manner that will evoke memories in those who lived through it and interest in those who learn of it here for the first time.

H. GEORGE ANDERSON

PREFACE

SOME LONG-FORGOTTEN TEACHER IN MY HIGH school years gave those of us who happened to be awake at the moment some inkling of relativity by explaining the way train whistles change their pitch as an engine sweeps past and the sound fades in the distance. As I worked on this manuscript, it seemed to me a parable of how difficult and even presumptuous it is to try to write "a history" as the events themselves are still speeding by and hurtle us into an unknown future. Surely, the passage of time and the phenomenon of distance will change the pitch, the tone, of recent happenings so that those with the chance for reflection will perceive these happenings in other ways.

Why bother then to attempt writing the story of the Lutheran Church in America now, when it may, no, certainly will be interpreted quite differently in three or four decades? To plead that I was asked to do so is a feeble excuse. Even to argue that I don't expect to be doing a great deal of writing, say in the year 2017, isn't very satisfying.

Apart from my own fascination with the subject, however, there have been two things that tempted me to plunge into the unsettled dust of the LCA's passing in an attempt to chronicle something of what happened during the quarter century of its life. One was strong encouragement by three of the church's most respected historians, who shall remain nameless to protect their innocence, that even someone who had spent all of those years laboring in the salt mines as a church executive could provide significant insights into history. The other was the recognition that in spite of the perils involved in viewing the contemporary scene, historians with the impeccable credentials of an E. Clifford Nelson or a Sydney E. Ahlstrom had brought their religious histories as close to the present moment as possible. As Nelson put it, "There is, therefore, a certain audacity and excitement in writing contemporary history, especially when one undertakes the task in full cognizance of the risk that the results may be vulnerable."[1]

It is, of course, even more risky when one has had only a modicum of training at the graduate level in methods of historical research. There is scant satisfaction in the fact that the professional historians disagree among themselves about the craft. I did, initially, find some comfort in reading Carl L. Becker's provocative essay "Everyman His Own Historian," until I found that other notable historians, such as Oscar Handlin and C. Vann Woodward, found in this view the seeds of a popular relativism that could threaten the integrity of the record.[2] But there have been some helpful guideposts provided by experienced writers as one explores the labyrinth of sources that compose the raw material of LCA history and the way predecessor bodies helped shape its character and purpose.

The title *Commitment to Unity* was not in my mind when the research began. It emerged as a thread that seemed to run through so much that the LCA did. This theme has at least two dimensions.

One is the sociological change that has occurred in every wave of Lutheran immigration from European homelands to North America. The immigrants have almost always attempted to preserve their own ethnic and cultural purity as a necessary part of preserving their religious identity. But the longer these folk lived in this polyglot land, that kind of ethnic insularity became less viable, and they gradually opened the doors of their churches to others. Sometimes, of course, it was the other way around, and the doors were opened to them. In 1714 it was Aree Van Guinea, a Black freedman from Dutch Guiana, who literally opened the doors of his Raritan Valley home in New Jersey so that Justus Falckner could hold a service there for immigrants from the Palatinate. The first child baptized that day was a little Black girl, and the congregation founded is now the oldest in that state.[3]

The sad thing, however, was that for so long many of our forebears thought there was something intrinsically German or Danish or Swedish or Finnish about being Lutheran. The reality was that by the time the LCA was formed in 1962, it was like a huge mixed salad of virtually every kind of people who ever came to these shores. Lately, we have been discovering that each part lends its distinctive flavor to the whole without necessarily sacrificing its individual character.

It has taken some wrenching social changes through the years to stamp out pockets of prejudice against people of color or people of languages other than English, and even to afford women the recognition and opportunities they have always deserved. Progress toward this kind of unity within the body of Christ has been agonizingly slow and still has a long road to travel toward realization.

The second dimension of the theme has been unity among the various Lutheran families themselves. That vision goes back at least to the time of Henry Melchior Muhlenberg. So often, however, when a merger did occur, it was watched with a wary eye by others. And there was often the suspicion that a body, such as the United Lutheran Church, which invited all other groups that accepted the Lutheran Confessions to join with it, would fail the litmus test of orthodoxy because of its very inclusiveness. The LCA itself suffered the same fate for a long while. Its pursuit of Lutheran unity, to say nothing of its ecumenical thrust, sometimes led the church into unproductive byways and ecclesiastical cul-de-sacs that meant retracing steps and trying other ways. But now a more inclusive Evangelical Lutheran Church in America is being born, and its future is in God's hands.

There is always the danger, as Barbara Tuchman reminds us in *Practicing History,* of allowing a theme to alter the true shape of the historical landscape. "I visualize the 'large organizing idea' as one of those iron chain mats pulled by a tractor to smooth over a plowed field," she writes. "I see the professor climbing up on the tractor and away he goes, pulling behind his large organizing idea over the bumps and furrows of history until he has smoothed it out to a nice, neat, organized surface—in other words, into a system."[4] Not being a professor *or* a professional historian, I think I have left enough knobs and angles and rough edges poking through the unity theme that anyone with the interest can take hold and reorganize the LCA story in another pattern. Indeed, I feel confident in believing someone will.

The list of those who have helped me in various ways as this volume was written is lengthy. Historians H. George Anderson and Robert H. Fischer not only coached me on procedures in the early going but also reviewed the manuscript itself. Significant insights came from lengthy interviews with persons such as historian and former LCA executive E. Theodore Bachmann; Bishop James R. Crumley, Jr.; world mission executive Gerald E. Currens; former

Secretary of both the LCA and ULCA George F. Harkins; Lutheran Church Women executive Kathryn E. Kopf; former archivist of cooperative Lutheranism Helen Knubel; former Augustana Seminary professor Paul M. Lindberg; former President of the Augustana Lutheran Church and first Secretary of the LCA Malvin H. Lundeen; Assistant to the LCA Bishop and Coordinator for the ELCA Transition Team Dorothy J. Marple; former LCA President Robert J. Marshall; LCA Secretary Reuben T. Swanson; authority on world missions David L. Vikner; and former President of the Suomi Synod Raymond W. Wargelin.

Others who reviewed the manuscript in whole or part were Martin E. Carlson, former Augustana executive and Assistant to both Presidents Franklin Clark Fry and Robert J. Marshall; Howard A. Christensen, a leader of the American Evangelical Lutheran Church and later an LCA synodical bishop; and Lloyd E. Sheneman, executive director of the Division for Professional Leadership of the LCA. The manuscript has benefited from the practiced editorial eyes of Harold W. Rast, director and senior editor of Fortress Press; Frank W. Klos, Jr., editorial director of the Division for Parish Services of the LCA; and his predecessor, Donald R. Pichaske. Lois Geehr was responsible for the meticulous copyediting.

Persons who graciously cooperated in digging through records and supplying essential documents included Arvid E. Anderson, director of research for DPS; Sonia E. Lind, administrative assistant to the LCA secretary; Sister Frieda Gatzke, directing deaconess of the LCA Deaconess Community; Alice M. Kendrick, director of the LCUSA records and information center, and her able assistant Miriam Wolbert; Craig J. Lewis, director of the Department of Theological Education of DPL; John M. Mangum, former editor and director of planning for the Division for World Mission and Ecumenism of the LCA; Leonard A. Sibley, director of the LCA Department of Planning, Research and Evaluation; Robert R. Strohl, who has managed the congregational data system for the LCA; and Associate Archivist of the LCA, Elisabeth Wittman, and her staff.

The committee who conceived and initiated the LCA History Project consisted of William P. Cedfeldt, Robert W. Endruschat, Harold W. Rast, and Reuben T. Swanson.

A special word of appreciation is due to the AAL for its generous grant towards the LCA History Project. Not only has this grant supported the research and writing of the manuscript but also the publication and distribution of the book itself to pastors and lay leaders of the church. The AAL has demonstrated by its many grants through the years its support of both the church's present mission and the preservation of the Lutheran heritage in this country.

In many ways, the largest measure of my gratitude goes to my wife, Libby, who not only read every word of every draft and permitted the piles of documents to invade almost every spare inch of our home but also encouraged me even when it meant postponing that long-promised and longer-deferred retirement we plan to share together.

W. KENT GILBERT

NOTES

1. E. Clifford Nelson, ed., *The Lutherans in North America* (Philadelphia: Fortress Press, 1975), x.

2. Carl L. Becker's "Everyman His Own Historian" was presented as a speech to the American Historical Association in 1931. It is reprinted in Robin W. Winks, ed., *The Historian as Detective* (New York: Harper & Row, 1968), 5–23. See also C. Vann Woodward, "American Attitudes Toward History" in *Historian as Detective,* 38, and Oscar Handlin, *Truth in History* (Cambridge, Mass.: The Belknap Press of Harvard University Press, 1979), 411–13.

3. Michael L. Cobbler, "Useful Lives, Black Lutherans in Ministry Past and Present," *LCA Partners* (April/May 1984): 11.

4. Barbara W. Tuchman, *Practicing History, Selected Essays* (New York: Alfred A. Knopf, 1981), 255.

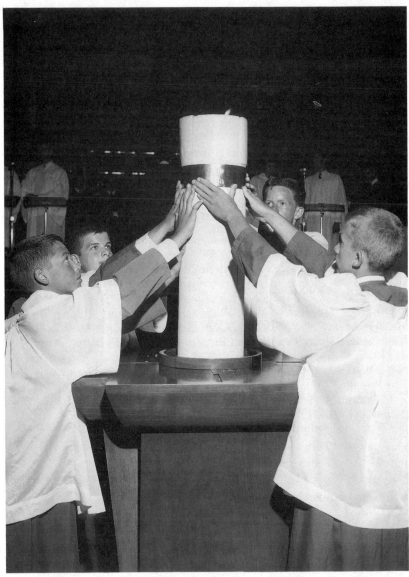

Candlelighting ceremony at the opening session of the constituting convention of the LCA

Chapter **1** | # IMMIGRATION AND AMERICANIZATION

IT WAS A MOVING MOMENT ON THE MORNING of June 28, 1962, when seven thousand people gathered in Cobo Hall, Detroit, to celebrate the formation of the Lutheran Church in America. Slowly, four lighted quarter candles were brought together to form one huge candle and a single flame. For those who watched, that joining symbolized more than the merging of four ecclesiastical organizations into a new church body. It also meant the blending of four rich Lutheran traditions rooted in Denmark, Finland, Germany, and Sweden. It underscored that in many ways the history of Lutheranism in North America has been the story of immigrants—their hopes, their beliefs, their customs, and their experiences through the years in the new land.

It is easy to forget that, apart from the comparatively small number who are descendants of native North Americans, all the rest of the population of the United States and Canada are of immigrant stock who came to these shores within the last three and one-half centuries.[1] Each wave of newcomers brought with them the cultures of their homelands. Indeed, as Abdel Ross Wentz put it, "the early settlements were like footnotes to European history. The nations of Europe in the seventeenth and eighteenth centuries were not only diverse in faiths, political attitude, and manners, but were also internally most varied. This pattern was transplanted to America and elaborated."[2]

Although the formation of the LCA created the largest Lutheran body in North America, the four groups which came together did not look upon this as the end of the quest for unity. The people at Cobo Hall seemed to have a much broader vision. The preamble to the constitution makes this clear. "Remembering the prayer of our Lord Jesus Christ that His disciples might be one as He and the Father are

1

one, and believing that His Spirit is ever leading His people toward unity in the household of God, we of the American Evangelical Lutheran Church, the Augustana Evangelical Lutheran Church, The Finnish Evangelical Lutheran Church of America, and The United Lutheran Church in America, persuaded that the time has come when His unifying power should be manifested through a united profession of faith by these churches and through forms of fellowship which will make for a more effective stewardship of His gifts to us, adopt this constitution to govern our common life in Him and our united witness to Him, praying that He who is the Lord of the Church may thereby lead us toward a more inclusive union of all Lutherans on this continent."[3] This commitment to unity has been a continuing motif in the LCA's history and does much to explain its many efforts toward inter-Lutheran cooperation through the years.

THE EARLY YEARS

The story which led to the LCA, however, begins with the diverse streams of immigrants who came to the New World. Although there had been Lutherans among early attempts at colonization, all of these efforts failed. Around 1528 there were Lutherans reported among a group sent by a German banking house to what is now Venezuela, but the scheme collapsed. In 1564 French Huguenots founded Fort Caroline in what is now Florida, but the colonists were massacred the following year by the Spanish. The leader of the Spanish forces, Peter Menendez, is said to have justified this barbarous act by claiming, "I do this not as to Frenchmen but as to Lutherans [*Luteranos*]."[4] To sixteenth-century Spaniards, all Protestants were "Lutherans." In all probability, the victims were actually Calvinists, but the myth of the Lutherans in Florida still persists.

In 1619 Jens Munk led a Danish expedition to Hudson Bay. A Lutheran pastor, Rasmus Jensen, was the chaplain. After a terrible winter almost the whole company, including Jensen, died of sickness and hunger. Only Munk and two other survivors made their way back to Denmark the following year.

The earliest permanent Lutheran settlers may have been among colonists sent to New Netherlands in 1623 and 1625 by the Dutch West India Company. But there does seem to be evidence that by the 1630s at least some were among the Dutch colonists.[5] Because they suffered severe religious repression at the hands of the Reformed establishment in the colony, the Lutherans were unable to form a congregation until 1649, when they petitioned fellow Lutherans in Amsterdam for a pastor. It was not until 1657 that John Ernest Gutwasser was sent, but the authorities never permitted him to preach or conduct services.[6] When the British seized the colony in 1664, a greater degree of religious freedom was allowed, and Lutheran congregations began to flourish.[7]

The first Lutheran congregations in the New World, therefore, were established when Sweden succeeded in founding a colony along the banks of the Delaware River in 1638. The settlers themselves were not only from Sweden but also Finland, which at that time was a part of Sweden. The first governor, Peter Minuit,[8] was instructed to provide for worship according to the Augsburg Confession, and in 1639 Reorus Torkillus came as pastor. When Peter Minuit lost his life at sea, Peter Hollander was sent as governor. He was succeeded by Johan Printz, a four-hundred-pound giant of a man who was called "Big Tub" (or probably more accurately translated "Big Guts") by the Indians.[9]

Printz brought with him John Campanius, a pastor who would soon be noted for his translation of *Luther's Small Catechism* into the language of the Lenape Indians. During the four years before Torkillus's death and during the tenure of Campanius, log churches were built in what are now Wilmington, Tinicum, and Philadelphia.[10] In 1655 the Dutch seized the colony, but the governor at that time insisted as a condition of surrender that the Lutherans be permitted one pastor. The man who remained was a Finn, Lars Lock, who continued to serve even long after the English ousted the Dutch in 1664.[11]

The lot of the handful of Lutherans in North America in the seventeenth century was extremely difficult. They were widely scattered, used languages foreign to the English colonies, and never had a dependable supply of pastors. In fact, from 1691 until 1697 there was not a single Lutheran minister on the continent.[12] The task of keeping the congregations going fell to laymen who refused to give up despite the absence of help from their mother countries. Finally in 1697, the Church of Sweden sent Andrew Rudman and Eric Bjork to Philadelphia and Wilmington, where within a few years historic Gloria Dei (Old Swedes) and Trinity churches were built. In the years that followed, the few congregations along the Delaware and the Hudson were interrelated by the fact that pastors sometimes moved from one colony to another. But the Lutherans were few. Indeed, it is estimated that there were only about two thousand of a wide range of ethnic backgrounds in the whole of North America in 1700.

Following the American Revolution, the Swedish church sent no more pastors to America. By 1787 virtually all Swedish congregations were using English, and an agreement was reached that pastors could be either Lutheran or Episcopalian. "The way was thus prepared for the immediate de facto and the later de jure transfer of the Swedish Lutheran parishes to the Protestant Episcopal Church."[13]

Beginning in 1683, however, a new group, the Germans, were entering the colonies. Their first settlement was in Germantown, now a part of Philadelphia. Beset by problems in their homeland and attracted by the promise of freedom in William Penn's colony, the Germans began to arrive in droves. Germany itself was not really a nation at that time but a collection of duchies and principalities ravaged by the Thirty Years' War and religious strife. It was from this source, however, that the strength of Lutheranism grew in North America during the next century and a half.

In order to appreciate the merging of traditions in the LCA, it is helpful to follow the story of the four ethnic Lutheran streams— German, Swedish, Danish, and Finnish—in the intervening years. They arrived in different waves of immigration, but they shared a common confession. The longer they were in North America, of course, the more they became a part of the culture. None of them remained ethnic isolates. Eventually, each received people of many backgrounds into membership. Their unique heritages, however, were reflected in the merger.

THE GERMANS: SOURCES OF THE ULCA

The United Lutheran Church in America was the most heterogeneous of the four bodies that formed the LCA. After more than three centuries of immigration, its ranks included a Slovak synod, an Icelandic synod, a Caribbean synod (largely Hispanic and Black), a Finnish conference, a Hungarian conference, as well as members from virtually every group that ever made its way to the shores of North America. However, the ULCA's earliest origins and its greatest numbers are directly traceable to the Germans.

The first large influx of German Lutherans came from the Palatinate in Southwestern Germany when severe weather, the aftermath of war, and religious persecution led thousands to leave their home-

lands. In 1708 Joshua Kocherthal, a Lutheran minister, led a group
of fifty-five Palatines to what is now Newburgh, New York. Two years
later he returned with three thousand more.[14] In order to pay for
their passage, the Palatines agreed to produce tar and ship masts for
the British navy. The newcomers, who were settled on the frontiers
of the New York colony, were also intended by the government to
be a buffer against the French and Indians. Most of the Germans,
however, had been farmers and became unhappy with their lot.
Many resettled in the Mohawk Valley, and others worked their way
south along the rivers and streams to a spot near Reading, Pennsylvania.[15]

Richard Wolf describes this period of introduction of Lutheranism
in America as "chaotic" and points out two consequences: "Many
Lutherans fell prey to 'vagabond preachers,' lapsed from church
membership, or joined other denominations. . . . A second consequence was of greater importance for the future of the Lutheran
church in America. Lutherans who wished to retain their Lutheran
affiliation here learned that it was not to be the relatively easy state-
church affiliation they had known in Germany. Here they would
have to work out their own problems, make their own decisions,
gather their own congregations, secure their own clergymen, effect
their own organizations, and pay their own way. Little financial help
could be anticipated from Germany, and repeated appeals for pastors went unfulfilled. Here they would have to relate themselves to
a far wider range of denominational alignments, involving more
divergent theological positions and patterns of polity and worship
than they had ever met in the homeland. The adjustment was not
quick and easy; it held the potential threat that the Lutheran church
might never prosper here in America."[16]

The relatively few Lutheran congregations were widely scattered
and frequently without pastors, which caused a problem of oversight.
The first attempt to form an organization of congregations was made
by Wilhelm Berkenmeyer in New York in 1735, but the effort
failed.[17] The task of creating the first synod in North America, therefore, fell to Henry Melchior Muhlenberg, a young pastor from the
north German state of Hannover.

Ecclesia Plantanda

In 1734 lay leaders of congregations in Philadelphia, Trappe, and
New Hanover jointly petitioned the pietist foundation in Halle, Saxony, for financial help and pastors. Finally in 1742, the foundation

selected Muhlenberg and sent him to help the struggling parishes. After an arduous voyage, he landed in Charleston, South Carolina. From there he went to Ebenezer, Georgia, to visit the Lutheran religious refugees from Salzburg, Austria, who had established a thriving community and strong congregation.[18] While in the South, Muhlenberg was greatly disturbed by the practice of slavery and wrote in his journal, "This is a horrible state of affairs, which will entail a severe judgment."[19]

Continuing his journey to Pennsylvania, Muhlenberg discovered the congregations he was sent to serve were in disarray because of the influence of Count Zinzendorf, leader of the Bohemian Brethren, who had claimed to be "Evangelical Lutheran Inspector and Pastor at Philadelphia."[20] He also had to contend with an incompetent, itinerant preacher named Valentine Kraft.[21] He quickly put things in order, however, and set about strengthening the congregations.

Muhlenberg thought of the church in the New World as *ecclesia plantanda* (the church being planted)—in contrast to the established church *(ecclesia plantata)* of his European homeland.[22] His vision went beyond his own parishes, and Lutherans throughout the colonies began to seek his leadership in dealing with problems. He traveled tirelessly and maintained correspondence with pastors and congregations everywhere he went.

Together with two other pastors, Muhlenberg developed a common liturgy which was submitted to other pastors for approval in April 1748. In August he took the most important step in his career. He invited six pastors and twenty-four laymen from ten congregations to meet with him at St. Michael's in Philadelphia to approve the liturgy and form a synod. Both tasks were accomplished. Interestingly, the laymen said they had no objection to the liturgy "except the public service lasts too long, especially in the cold winter."[23] The new synod itself in time became the Ministerium of Pennsylvania. It was a crucial step in building an organization that could deal with the rising tide of immigration. In 1749 alone more than twelve thousand Germans landed in Philadelphia, and by 1771 there were eighty-one Lutheran congregations in Pennsylvania and nearby states.[24]

The infant synod, however, faced several serious problems. First, many of the German immigrants were impoverished and desperately in need of help to survive. In describing the situation in Pennsylvania, Henry Eyster Jacobs comments, "Germans were decoyed from their homes by conscienceless agents . . . who, by fabulous

Henry Melchior Muhlenberg

stories of the wealth to be acquired and the easy terms by which passage could be secured, enticed unsuspecting immigrants into signing papers in an unknown language, not only committing them and their children to slavery, but sometimes separating husband and wife, parents and children."[25] It is estimated that between one-half and two-thirds of those who came from 1720 to 1725 were such indentured servants, or "redemptioners."[26]

Second, the synod initially had little real power. Although there was provision for an "overseer," a post soon filled by Muhlenberg himself, many practical problems emerged as the synod grew.[27] Finally in 1781, the synod adopted a constitution which gave the body the ambitious name of "The Evangelical Lutheran Synod of North America."[28] This landmark document had many important features, such as its confessional basis and the vesting of the authority for ordination in the synod. Political factors in the new nation led to revision of the synod's constitution in 1792. The synod, now called "The Evangelical Lutheran Congregations in Pennsylvania and Adjacent States," seated lay delegates with voice and vote equal to clergy, a practice which has persisted to the present day. Abdel Ross Wentz summarizes the situation succinctly, "The organization of Lutherans rested on democratic principles expressed in a constitution that safeguarded the independence of the congregations and the rights of the individual pastor and layman. Lutherans had now given complete expression in their corporate life to the fact that they are American."[29]

Third, the number of congregations and ministers was never equal to the opportunities provided by the flood of immigrants. By 1790 the number of nominal Lutherans in the United States had grown to about 120,000 of which possibly only one-seventh were related to congregations.[30] The situation was aggravated by the fact that during the Revolutionary War and immediately following it many loyalist and neutral Germans moved to Canada. While early German settlements in Canada had been largely in Nova Scotia, the flow from the United States was now into "Upper Canada" (present-day Ontario). At the same time, the Lutherans were following the frontier westward in the United States. Both lay persons and clergy for these settlements came from Lutheran centers in the East. As H. George Anderson has noted, "Some of these centers were so drained of their human resources that they would never recover."[31]

Fourth, the doctrinal integrity of Lutheranism in the young nation came into question. A wave of rationalism had swept across Europe and for a time influenced the church in North America.[32] The 1792 version of the Ministerium constitution eliminated all references to the Lutheran Confessions. This change was in part due to a concern on the part of some Lutheran leaders for making the constitution more palatable to their Reformed neighbors during a period of unionism.

Fifth, use of the German language in worship and church affairs became an issue. Like Lutheran immigrants of other nationalities, many Germans felt that there was an essential link between using their language and preserving their cultural and religious identity in English-speaking America. In 1805 the Pennsylvania Ministerium took an action forbidding the use of any language except German in synodical business.[33] The struggle over whether to use English or German continued with divisive results.[34]

As early as the 1780s, it became apparent that the Lutheran congregations were too far-flung to be comprehended within a single synod. Under the leadership of John Christopher Kunze, pastor of the United German Lutheran Churches in New York City, nine ministers in New York and New Jersey formed a new synod at Albany in October 1786. The new body, named the "New York Ministerium," made provision for lay representatives from congregations at synodical meetings. These lay delegates had full voting powers on all matters except approval of candidates for ordination and examination of ministers whose conduct or doctrinal positions were in question. This was different from the practices at that particular time in Pennsylvania, where the synod was also called a "ministerium."[35]

Between 1803 and 1829 seven more synods came into being: North Carolina, Ohio, Maryland-Virginia, Tennessee, South Carolina, West Pennsylvania, and Virginia. The formation of these new and separate synods posed a new problem, the possibility of fragmentation and isolation instead of Lutheran unity. As widely varied practices began to develop, it suggested to some leaders "the need for closer union and co-operation among the synods."[36]

The General Synod

In 1819 the Pennsylvania Ministerium proposed a plan (Plan Entwurf) for a central union of all synods in the United States. The plan met with much opposition. On October 22, 1820, however, representatives from the Pennsylvania, New York, North Carolina, and

Maryland-Virginia synods met in Hagerstown, Maryland, to draw up a constitution for a General Synod. While the constitution did not grant as much power to the general body as some had hoped, it did provide for planning seminaries and mission institutions; aid for poor ministers, their widows and orphans; the creation of a treasury; and the role of common agent in dealing with other denominations. This key stance on interdenominational affairs set the pattern for all Lutheran bodies in the future.[37]

Within a year all synods but the New York Ministerium had ratified the constitution, and the General Synod held its first convention at Frederick, Maryland. Because of internal pressures, the Pennsylvania Ministerium, which had pushed formation of the general body, withdrew in 1823 and did not rejoin until 1853. The General Synod, however, not only survived but also drew together many of the strands of the Muhlenberg tradition.[38]

Apart from seeking to provide defenses against unionism and rationalism, the General Synod had as a high priority establishing a seminary to supply the need for pastors in the United States and raise the educational standards for their preparation. Up until this time, ministers had been prepared by an apprenticeship system in which they studied with established pastors. Although doctrinal foundations were not explicit in the synod's constitution, this shortcoming was remedied when a seminary was established at Gettysburg, Pennsylvania, in 1826. As Richard Wolf has pointed out, "Acceptance of the Augsburg Confession was part of the pledge required of professors by the seminary constitution."[39] Samuel Simon Schmucker, who had been a principal figure in preserving the General Synod in its early years, was named the professor and later president.[40] Although the Lutheran seminary at Gettysburg was not the first attempt at forming such an institution in the New World, it is the only one which has survived to this day.[41]

The new seminary soon had to deal with a thorny problem. Few students who came had had a "classical" education as preparation. To remedy this, the General Synod established Pennsylvania College (later named "Gettysburg College") in 1832 as a separate institution about a mile from the seminary campus. Charles Philip Krauth was named as president.[42]

Although Schmucker had been a champion of doctrinal integrity, he was aware of changing theological currents. In 1855, he and some colleagues issued "The Definite Synodical Platform." This document sought rapprochement among American Protestants by a recension of the Augsburg Confession. It was a mistaken judgment as to how far Lutheranism need go in adapting to its American environment. This movement, which was labeled "American Lutheranism," provoked widespread controversy. Eventually, Schmucker himself abandoned this extreme position, and "American Lutheranism" withered. As Wentz comments, "It was the registered conviction of the great host of Lutherans in America that Lutheranism can live and flourish in this country without giving away its own spirit or adulterating its own original life and character. The future of the Lutheran Church in America was to belong to the conservative type of Lutheranism."[43] It is unfortunate that Schmucker, who contributed so much to the development of Lutheranism in North America, is often remembered primarily for a passing point of view which he outgrew.

Fragmentation

In some respects, however, the forces that would lead to a fragmentation among Lutherans in North America were already at work. Again, immigration played a crucial role. Lutherans poured into North America from the 1830s through the balance of the century. As Sydney Ahlstrom has put it, "No Protestant communion was so thoroughly transformed by the later nineteenth-century immigration as was the Lutheran. Three million immigrants came from the diverse provinces of Germany, perhaps a half of them at least vaguely Lutheran, 1.75 million from Scandinavia, nearly all of them at least nominally Lutheran, and a heavy scattering of others from Finland, Iceland, and various parts of the Austro-Hungarian empire. They settled in every section of the country, in cities and on farms, but, of course, overwhelmingly in the North."[44]

The immigrants not only reintroduced the language problem for those synods that were becoming largely English speaking but also brought a new conservative influence. There had been a revival of Lutheran confessionalism in Europe which spread into existing congregations in the East and dominated the formation of new synods in the Midwest. The establishment of the "German Evangelical Lutheran Synod of Missouri, Ohio, and Other States" in 1847 was a prime example. The synodical makeup of North America was never to be the same.[45]

Meanwhile, two ruptures occurred in the mid-nineteenth century which destroyed the hopes that the General Synod would preserve a unity among those in the Muhlenberg tradition. First, the Civil War precipitated the withdrawal of five southern synods to form the "General Synod of the Evangelical Lutheran Church in the Confederate States of America." Although it was hoped that the end of hostilities would bring a restoration of unity between Southern and Northern Lutherans, a second division of the church in the North frustrated that hope.[46]

Two major points of tension existed between the Pennsylvania Ministerium and the General Synod. One was concern about centralization of authority in a general body. The Ministerium regarded a general church body as an advisory conference "whose decisions required the ratification of the synods."[47] Proponents of a strong central church did not agree.[48] This same issue has plagued Lutherans in North America to this day.

The other problem was a concern about the doctrinal stance of the General Synod. In 1864 the General Synod admitted the Franckean Synod to membership. The constitution of this small group in western New York did not acknowledge the Augsburg Confession. The Ministerium's delegates withdrew from the General Synod meeting in order to report their protest about admission of the Franckean group at the next meeting of the Ministerium the following year. Adding fuel to the fire was a decision in 1864 by the Ministerium to start a new seminary in Philadelphia and take away some of the faculty and student body from Gettysburg. Although the Ministerium contended that neither action was meant to sever relations with the General Synod or Gettysburg Seminary, this was the practical result.

In 1866 the Ministerium went a giant step further. It issued a call to all Lutheran synods, congregations, and ministers in the United States and Canada which confessed the Unaltered Augsburg Confession to attend a convention in Reading, Pennsylvania, on December 12–14 to form a new general body. The following year eleven synods chose full membership, and the General Council was born. The General Synod was dealt a devastating blow but managed to survive and flourish.[49]

Relating Once More

Although it would take a half century before the three bodies in the Muhlenberg tradition would unite again, it was not long before overtures began to be made. In 1873 the General Synod passed a resolution suggesting exchange of delegates with "other Evangelical

Lutheran bodies in the United States."[50] The General Council countered with a proposal for a colloquium for all Lutherans who accepted the Unaltered Augsburg Confession. Both the General Synod and the General Synod, South accepted, and the first "Free Lutheran Diet" was held in Philadelphia in 1877. Although these meetings were not attended by official delegates, they provided an arena in which the Lutherans could once more talk with one another.

Despite its small size, the General Synod, South (later renamed the United Synod, South) played an important role in the eventual rapprochement of the three bodies. In 1876 it proposed developing a common form of worship for all English-speaking congregations. Both the General Council and the General Synod agreed to participate. By 1888 the Common Service was approved and became the basis for worship in the English language for the bulk of Lutherans in North America. The General Synod South then proposed developing a complete worship book and hymnal, which led to the *Common Service Book* of 1917. There is no doubt that cooperation in worship matters was a major factor in eventual merger.[51]

Gradually old animosities diminished. There was now some cooperation in women's, men's, and youth work as well as in home and foreign missions. Finally in 1895 the three bodies began to send fraternal delegates to one another's conventions. It seemed that the road to reunion was beginning to open, but there were still lingering doubts in the General Council and the United Synod, South about the General Synod.[52] They were concerned that the General Synod was still infected by the "American Lutheranism" of S. S. Schmucker. Although the leaders of the General Synod held that their adherence to the Augsburg Confession was basic evidence of their Lutheranism, they were willing to accede to some of the General Council's requests in the interests of unity. The synod "affirmed the Bible to *be* the Word of God and incorporated the pledge to the unaltered Augsburg Confession and acknowledgment of the other confessional writings into its constitution. That action not only paved the way for eventual merger but also placed all Lutherans in America, for the first time, on virtually the same confessional basis."[53]

Catalysts to Union

Two diverse events at last provided catalysts to help bring the three groups from the Muhlenberg tradition closer together. One was the United States' entry into World War I. The other was the four hun-

dredth anniversary of the Reformation. As Fred W. Meuser has put
it, "The combination of a great religious celebration and the wrenching experience of the Great War catapulted Lutherans into twen-
tieth-century American society. In the process of reconciling
conflicting national loyalties, confronting irrational hostility, reaffirming a spiritual heritage, and reacting to the new demands for
quick response Lutherans began to see themselves, their inner
bonds, their strengths and weaknesses, their great potential, in a new
light. . . . Theologically, there was little change, but the self-aware-
ness and the spirit of the church has never been the same."[54]

As early as 1909, the General Council invited all other Lutheran
bodies to join in celebrating the quadricentennial of Luther's posting
of the Ninety-five Theses in 1517. The refusal of the Midwestern
Lutherans to participate meant that only the three "Eastern Lutheran" groups were left to mount the event. The plans were ambitious. There were to be joint Lutheran worship services, lectures,
publications, a special offering—all designed to heighten awareness
of the Lutheran heritage. Inevitably, many of these arrangements
took on a Germanic flavor.

Suddenly on April 6, 1917, a scant eight months before the celebration was to occur, the United States declared war on Germany. Just
as suddenly, an anti-German mood swept through the country. Frequently, Scandinavian and other ethnic groups also suffered prejudice because the Lutherans were linked with Germany in the public
mind. Pastors were accused of having taken an oath of allegiance to
the Kaiser. Some were tarred and feathered by irate citizens. Lutheran schools which taught German were attacked.[55] The hysteria
at times bordered on the ridiculous. In the attempt to purge society
of every German influence, even sauerkraut was renamed "liberty
cabbage." In fairness it must be said that prior to United States
involvement in the war, many Lutheran writers and leaders had
been outspokenly anti-British and pro-German. This quickly
changed, however, as the Lutheran church bodies themselves declared their loyalty to the nation. There were two important out-
comes of this turbulent period: the dramatic shift to the use of
English in congregations and the growing realization that a rich
confessional heritage was not synonymous with or dependent upon
ethnic backgrounds.[56]

While the war changed the tenor of the four hundredth anniversary celebration itself, the committee had arrived independently at

a crucial recommendation on April 18, 1917—just twelve days after the United States declared war. The crowning symbol of the jubilee, the committee declared, should be a decision to reunite the General Synod, the General Council, and the United Synod, South. Interestingly, it was the lay members of the committee who pressed for organic union. The churches warmly welcomed this initiative. Actions by the three bodies followed swiftly. On November 11, 1918, the day of the armistice in Europe, the three general bodies each held their final meetings in New York. On November 14 the first convention of the United Lutheran Church in America was called to order, and the reunion had become a reality.[57]

Even on the night before the constituting convention began, however, the merger hung in the balance. Many of those at the constituting convention assumed that the first president would be Theodore E. Schmauk, the outstanding theologian and leader of the General Council. There was still a basic tension between the view of those in the General Synod who wanted a strong central church body and those in the General Council who advocated more synodical control. As Abdel Ross Wentz describes the situation, "This issue between age-old synodism and the new churchism was so keen in the Pennsylvania Ministerium that, the evening before the actual consummation of the merger . . . when it became fairly apparent that a General Synod man would be elected president of the new body, it required a long night session of the Ministerium for leaders like Drs. Jacobs and Weller and Keiter to persuade their delegation to acquiesce and participate in the act of organization the next day."[58]

The delegates did indeed elect a president from the General Synod, Frederick H. Knubel.[59] Knubel had come to prominence as the president of the inter-Lutheran Commission for Soldiers' and Sailors' Welfare, which had played such an important role during the war. He was known as a man of great spiritual depth, diplomacy, and executive ability. His skill in bringing the new church through the difficult period which followed proved the choice to be a wise one.[60]

The ULCA at the outset, of course, was far from being fully unified. The forty-five member synods represented a variety of different practices and histories, and their territories overlapped each other like a crazy quilt. Some were quite small and had unusual names like "Olive Branch" and "Holston."[61] Others like the venerable Ministerium of Pennsylvania were huge by comparison. While all forty-five "were placed on the same doctrinal basis, committed to the same general practices, and brought to conduct their general benevolence missionary operations through the same general boards," Wentz notes, "it was soon clear that the United Lutheran Church would not be truly united until synodical sections were drawn into more compact units in their respective territories."[62] These negotiations stretched out over four decades. In fact, it was not until 1954 that the Central Pennsylvania Synod and the Ministerium of Pennsylvania straightened out their boundaries. Meanwhile, two linguistic synods, Slovak-Zion and Icelandic, were admitted on a nongeographical basis in 1920 and 1942 respectively.[63]

The stance of the ULCA toward Lutheran unity was clearly set forth in the preamble to its constitution which stated, "We . . . now invite and until such end be attained continue to invite all Evangelical Lutheran congregations and synods, one with us in the faith, to unite with us, upon the terms of this constitution, in one general organization."[64] The new million-member body also made clear that it intended a real and permanent organic union. In the view of Meuser, "The ULCA's polity, from the outset, did not share the assumption of most other Lutherans that only the congregation was truly 'church,' or that each congregation must retain full independence over against supracongregational structures, or that the general body was merely 'advisory' to the congregations. This merger gave to the general body and its boards and commissions powers greater than those of its own predecessor bodies or the other Lutheran synods."[65] And yet in many ways, the ULCA was and remained a federation of synods rather than the monolithic structure perceived by others.[66] But the basic direction regarding organic Lutheran unity had been set that would influence ULCA relations and merger negotiations with other Lutheran bodies from that time forward.

Legacy of Two Centuries

For all their internal squabbles and often reluctant adaptation to the American scene, the Germans had brought a solid legacy of accomplishment to the ULCA.

Education. From the time of Martin Luther, Lutherans had recognized education as a necessity for a healthy church and society. Long before public education became the norm in North America, Lutheran pastors and parishioners established their own schools alongside their churches. During the colonial period more than a hundred parish schools were founded, but these often were plagued by the difficulty of finding capable teachers. When public schools were introduced in the early nineteenth century, some congregations continued their own schools for a while, but there were few left within the ranks of the ULCA when it was formed. Catechetics, however, had maintained a central place in parish education, and the Sunday school was almost universal.[67]

The German Lutherans were also deeply interested in higher education. An educated clergy was and continues to be a hallmark of Lutheranism. As early as 1797, a bequest by John Christopher Hartwick, an eccentric Lutheran clergyman, resulted in the formation of a seminary in New York State. After a history fraught with difficulties, Hartwick Seminary closed in 1941.[68] As noted earlier, Gettysburg Seminary was founded in 1826 and still continues, as do other early institutions such as Philadelphia and Southern. Other seminaries, such as Hamma (now part of Trinity), Chicago (now part of the Lutheran School of Theology at Chicago), and Northwestern (now part of Luther Northwestern), merged with other schools of theology in later years. The high watermark in number of seminaries was reached in the 1950s with twelve.[69] Colleges were also important to the Lutherans who formed the ULCA. By the Civil War, twenty had been founded of which ten still are in existence today.[70]

Publications. Closely allied with the concern for education was the interest the Germans had in publishing. The first enduring periodical, the *Evangelisches Magazin,* appeared in 1811. It was a quarterly sponsored by the Pennsylvania Ministerium and edited by J. H. C. Helmuth of Philadelphia.[71] In 1806 the Henkel Press was established in New Market, Virginia, and began to publish a series of books in English including translations of Luther's Catechism and the entire Book of Concord.

At first the general bodies did not have their own publishing house, but that changed in 1855 when the Lutheran Publication Society was formed as an auxiliary to the General Synod. When the General Council was established in 1867, it provided in its constitution for a board of publication.[72] By the time the ULCA was formed, the Lutherans were publishing a wide variety of books, periodicals, tracts, hymnals, and parish education materials.

Missions. True to Muhlenberg's concern for the planting of the church, the Germans were deeply committed to missions both at home and abroad. Initially, home missions were largely efforts by individual pastors. As the tide of settlement swept westward in the United States and Canada, the stronger synods developed fairly efficient mission enterprises. The New York Ministerium, for example, set up a Committee on Home Missions and a missionary fund. Persons like the legendary Ernest Lewis Hazelius traveled all over northern New York and Upper Canada helping infant congregations.[73] The General Synod went through a period when the work was carried on by mission societies, but in 1869 the General Synod became the first of the Lutheran general bodies to assume responsibility for the mission enterprises of its member synods. By the time the ULCA was fully operative, however, great strides had been made, and many hundreds of new congregations had been started.[74]

Among the less effective aspects of home mission work, however, was the often stumbling effort to minister to non-Caucasians in the population. For example, following the Civil War, pressure mounted in the South to find ways to adjust the earlier practice of baptizing slaves and having them attend the congregations of their owners. The North Carolina Synod at first resolved " 'that we retain the same relation to the freedmen as we have heretofore done,' and congregations continued to make provision for the seating of Negro members when the annual sale of pews occurred. But turmoil and unrest in the ensuing years made continuing cooperation difficult."[75] Finally, the strategy which prevailed was to assist Blacks to set up their own congregations with their own pastors.

After a process of examination, some Blacks were licensed to preach, and in 1878 D. J. Koontz was ordained. According to H. George Anderson, "Koontz, 'called the only ordained colored Lutheran minister in the world,' preached at conference and synod meetings, but he was still not allowed to attend synod or vote."[76] Actually, Koontz was not the first Black to be ordained in North America. That distinction, apparently, belonged to Jehu Jones, who had been a member of St. John's Lutheran Church in Charleston, South Carolina. Although Jones had intended to be a missionary to Africa, he ended up in Philadelphia. There he started the first Black Lutheran congregation on the mainland in 1836.[77]

Financial support for the mission work to be done in North Carolina was not forthcoming, however. In 1889 the Black pastors asked permission to form their own synod, which took the name "The Alpha Synod of the Evangelical Lutheran Church of Freedmen in America." In response to a request for help from the fledgling synod, the Missouri Synod stepped into the breach with support and soon set up a combination high school, normal school, and seminary to meet the needs. As Anderson has put it, "The plan of the southern General Synod thus proved workable, but only by those who were willing to invest in its success."[78]

In the area of foreign missions, much of the initial effort by North Americans was on a nondenominational basis. In 1810 the American Board of Commissioners for Foreign Missions was established in Boston and within fifty years had sent 328 missionaries overseas.[79] The German Lutherans took a different tack, however, and set up their own mission societies and later assigned responsibility for foreign work to church boards.[80] The first American missionary was John Christian Frederick Heyer, who was commissioned October 5, 1841, by the Pennsylvania Ministerium society and dispatched to the Telugu area of India. A small, wiry man of forty-eight, possessed of great zeal and boundless energy, "Father" Heyer traveled through the high country from village to village until he selected Guntur as the site for his mission. It was not an ideal spot geographically, but on July 21, 1842, he made the choice, and American Lutheran mission work was born.[81]

Heyer's career was remarkable. He had the vision to establish schools which began to develop a native leadership that is so essential for a successful mission enterprise.[82] Thinking to retire in 1857 at age sixty-four, Heyer returned to the United States but was soon called to begin home mission work in Minnesota. In 1869 he was greatly disturbed to learn that the General Synod contemplated turning over the India field to the Church Missionary Society in England. At a meeting of the Pennsylvania Ministerium, the seventy-seven-year-old missionary pled with the synod to assume responsibility for the work and said that if no one else was prepared to make the twelve-thousand-mile trip, he would volunteer himself.

"Someone jumped to his feet and asked, 'Will Father Heyer tell us how soon that will be?'

"Stooping to the floor, Heyer picked up his ever present valise. Holding it so all could see, he replied, 'I am ready *now!*' "[83] Heyer won his point and within weeks was on his way to India again.

Just as the wives of pastors so often labored side by side with their husbands in North America, this was the case with many missionary families. One woman who should be noted was Lorena Gunn. Her husband died of consumption while serving in Guntur. Instead of returning home, Lorena Gunn remained to operate a girls' school and became the first regularly called woman missionary among American Lutherans.[84]

One of the towering figures in world missions was Dr. Anna Kugler, the first woman medical missionary in India. A graduate of the Women's Medical College in Philadelphia, Dr. Kugler arrived in India in 1883 and, with the exception of a few brief home leaves, labored there until her death in 1930.[85] Because she was a woman, she could care for the Hindu women's health needs, which no male doctor could do because of the caste system.[86] One of the persons she treated was the wife of the Rajah of Ellore. In gratitude Rajah Bhujanga Rao gave Dr. Kugler's hospital in Guntur an inn to provide lodging for relatives of patients. After becoming a convert to Christianity, the scholarly Brahmin spent ten years translating the New Testament into Telugu. In 1924 he wrote Anna Kugler, "The little insight I possess in the spiritual realm is directly due to the influence that your life work is exerting upon me."[87]

At least in part due to the example of these pioneers, foreign mission work continued to grow, and by the time the ULCA came into being, fields had been established not only in India but also in Japan, Liberia, Argentina, and British Guiana.[88]

At the same time, a new kind of social concern began to take shape at home. During the nineteenth century there had been an upsurge of interest in humanitarian work in European churches which spread across the Atlantic. It became the forerunner of certain types of "social ministry" concerns among Lutherans in North America today. The outstanding proponent of such work on this continent was William Alfred Passavant, who founded the first Lutheran hospital in Pittsburgh in 1849 to care for sick and wounded veterans of the Mexican War. In the years that followed, he was responsible for establishing an amazing number of hospitals, homes for the aged, orphanages, and other institutions of mercy that ministered to the needs of thousands.[89]

Closely allied to social welfare work in Germany was the deaconess movement that had been started at Kaiserswerth in 1833 by Pastor Theodor Fliedner and his wife Fredericke. Passavant had heard of the movement and persuaded Fliedner to send four sisters to help in the infirmary, which became the Passavant Hospital. In 1884 seven other German deaconesses, led by Sister Marie Krueger, were brought to Philadelphia by John D. Lankenau, a Lutheran philanthropist. Their task was to put in order the struggling German Hospital. Soon a motherhouse was established in Philadelphia and later a second in Baltimore. From these two centers came a stream of deaconesses who served in hospitals, schools, homes, inner mission agencies, and congregations in every part of the ULCA and its predecessor bodies.[90]

Interestingly, the deaconesses came from many different places. For example, Sister Emma Francis, the first Black deaconess, was born on the island of St. Kitts. After studying in Germany, she was commissioned to work as a missionary for the Danish Church at the Ebenezer Home for Orphaned Girls on St. Croix in 1908. When the Virgin Islands became part of the United States, she was received as a deaconess by the Philadelphia Motherhouse. After helping to organize a congregation for West Indians in Harlem, which became the large Transfiguration Lutheran Church, she returned to St. Croix to resume supervision of the Ebenezer Home.[91]

Although pastors, missionaries, deaconesses, teachers, and other full-time servants of the church played key roles in the centuries leading to the ULCA, their commitment was matched by dedicated laity who remained loyal to their Lutheran heritage in trying circumstances. Adam Keffer, of Vaughan, Ontario, will serve as an example. After his congregation had been without a pastor for more than fifteen years, Keffer set out in the spring of 1849 to seek help. He walked barefoot more than 250 miles to Klecknersville, Pennsylvania, to plead his cause before the Pittsburgh Synod. Impressed, the synod determined to look into the matter, but nothing happened. The following year Keffer, footsore and exhausted, was back again asking for a pastor. This time Charles F. Diehl was dispatched to minister to the people who would not desert their heritage or take no for an answer.[92]

All in all, the history of the Germans in the Muhlenberg tradition seemed like a long, long march that took them this way and that, coming together and then separating before they found one another again in 1918. For the newly formed ULCA, the decades that followed were ones marked by consolidation, growth, and clarification of its identity.

At the same time, it was a period in which the various Lutheran

Anna Kugler

Sister Emma Francis

bodies in North America were seeking closer rapport with one another in ways that eventually led to key mergers. Before dealing with that part of the story, however, it is important to examine how those in the Swedish, Danish, and Finnish traditions became major actors in the drama of Lutheranism on this continent.

THE SWEDES: SOURCES OF AUGUSTANA

"Our song of jubilee must in part be sung in a minor key, because of what might have been but was not," wrote P. O. Bersell in 1948 when the Augustana Lutheran Church marked the one hundredth anniversary of the first congregation which was to become part of the Augustana Synod in 1860. "We are about to enter our second century as a Church. It might as well have been our fourth century as the oldest American Lutheran Church."[93] On a more positive note, however, the growth of the Augustana Lutheran Church from that first congregation of five families to a church body with almost 630,000 baptized members in 1962 was little short of phenomenal.

It is ironic that the most historic Lutheran church buildings, which the Swedes had built along the Delaware in the seventeenth century, were lost to another denomination at about the same time that a new wave of Swedish immigration began in the nineteenth century. As was pointed out earlier in this chapter, the Church of Sweden had all but abandoned the Swedish congregations in the New World after the American Revolution. Nor was direct help forthcoming when the nineteenth-century immigrants strove to establish Lutheran congregations in their new homeland.[94]

Exodus

Conditions seemed ripe for an exodus from Sweden in the 1800s. The country had lost its hold on Finland in 1809. A French marshal, Jean Baptiste Jules Bernadotte, was elected the ruler in 1810. A new constitution promised greater freedom to the people, but suffrage was based on property rights, and there was little recognition for the common people. Economic pressures were building that threatened the livelihood of farming families. Compulsory military service for men and limited rights for women contributed to unrest. Factors such as these encouraged approximately one and one-half million Swedes to come to America between 1840 and the beginning of World War I. It was a staggering loss of people for a country the size of Sweden.[95] But come they did, lured by "America fever" with its promises of free land and the democratic aura of a country where even the humblest man can stand upright and be called "Mister."

Coming as they did from a nation where the church was established by law and supported by the state, the Lutheran immigrants found themselves in a free but highly competitive religious environment.[96] "Here every religious institution was strictly on its own, since there were no guarantees undergirding its future well-being. Each was free to poach on the precincts of another, proselyting wherever possible and gaining advantage over rival groups by whatever means the laws of the land and the restrictions of conscience would allow. In some respects it must have seemed to many a newcomer to these shores that he had suddenly been plunged into a kind of religious jungle where survival depended upon the law of tooth and claw."[97]

Parishes and Pastors

The founding of the first congregation which eventually became a part of the Augustana Synod was a story of sheer determination by Swedish laypersons staunchly loyal to their Lutheran heritage in the midst of the strange religious environment of America. In 1845 a small group of immigrants led by Peter Kassel founded a settlement along the banks of the Skunk River in Jefferson County, Iowa. Their early years in New Sweden were plagued with difficulties, including many fatal illnesses. In 1848, however, a handful of people, who had been meeting for devotions in various homes, urged Magnus Håkanson, a devout shoemaker, to act as their pastor. Although he was untrained, Håkanson agreed. The sacraments were administered, services were conducted, and the little flock functioned de facto as a congregation. In 1850 Håkanson was granted an ecclesiastical license by the Joint Synod of Ohio. When the Augustana Church celebrated its jubilee in 1948, the congregation at New Sweden was acknowledged to be the first parish.[98]

The person who is thought of as the "founding father" of the Augustana Synod, however, was Lars Paul Esbjörn, a pastor in Oslätt-fors in Sweden. Esbjörn was caught up in the enthusiasm for immigration to America that affected so many Swedes in mid-nineteenth century, when glowing reports of marvelous opportunities in the New World were circulated in the Old Country. The Church of Sweden took a dim view of its people and pastors emigrating but reluctantly allowed Esbjörn to maintain his ministerial status while

Lars Paul Esbjörn

making it clear that he could not expect financial help. On June 29, 1849, he set sail with 146 persons who were not quite sure where they would end up in America. In New York the remnants of the party who had survived the sixty-eight-day voyage came under the influence of an unscrupulous land agent. The agent painted a rosy picture of Andover, Illinois, which he described as a beautiful town on the banks of a river plied by steamboats.[99]

The gullible immigrants agreed to go to Andover and set out up the Hudson River and across the Erie Canal by barge for the Great Lakes. The barge was filthy, and the party was swept by disease. Esbjörn's infant son died of cholera, and the pastor himself arrived in Chicago critically ill. At last, the party made its way to Andover only to find that the "beautiful city" was a few ramshackle houses and the "river," a creek meandering through a swamp.[100] During the early days, Esbjörn's own determination to stay was tested, but his wife, Amalia, was a source of strength for him. Less than three years after their arrival, the "Mother of the Augustana Lutheran Church" died and was buried in "an 84-cent casket made from boards meant for the steeple of the little Andover church."[101]

The plight of Esbjörn and his people became so desperate that he applied to the American Home Mission Society in New York for aid. The society agreed to grant him $300 per year, but the conditions were severe. Influenced by revivalism, the society insisted that no one could be received into the congregation unless he proved that he had been "born again." Baptism or transfer from the Church of Sweden was not enough.[102]

Paths to Cooperation

Fortunately, in 1850 William A. Passavant, the missions pioneer from Pittsburgh, and W. M. Reynolds, president of Capital University, Columbus, Ohio, were touring the area around Andover. Passavant arranged for financial help and for Esbjörn to travel through the eastern part of the country to lay the needs of the Scandinavian Lutherans before congregations and leaders. One Lutheran celebrity who was moved by the appeal was Jenny Lind, the famous singer, who gave $1,500 to the cause. Esbjörn returned to Illinois from his travels with about $3,000, which provided for constructing the first church buildings the Swedes had in the Midwest.[103]

Convinced that the future of Lutheranism lay with cooperation, Esbjörn helped to form a Mississippi Conference, which included the

Swedish congregations, in the newly created Northern Illinois Synod in 1851. Other pastors arrived from Sweden to expand the work, notably Tufve Hasselquist, Erland Carlsson, Jonas Swensson, and O. C. T. Andrén. Others were trained in Sweden but ordained in America. Eric Norelius was a prime example.[104]

The Swedes remembered all too clearly, however, the fate of the congregations along the Delaware which had depended upon a supply of pastors from Sweden. They were determined to find a way to educate their own ministers in America.[105] For this reason they entered wholeheartedly into synodical plans to have a Scandinavian professorship at Illinois State University in Springfield. The "university" was a small Lutheran school, originally located in Hillsboro, that was intended to train pastors and teachers. A struggle between conservative Lutherans and the exponents of "American Lutheranism" in the Northern Illinois Synod was already underway, however, and the new professorship simply served to focus the tensions.[106]

Esbjörn, who had been chosen as the Scandinavian professor in 1858, became concerned about the weak position of the Northern Illinois Synod regarding the Augsburg Confession. Increasingly disillusioned about the situation, he wrote to his friend Norelius that he regarded the period as a "Babylonian Captivity" and suggested that the Scandinavians set up their own school in Chicago.[107] Finally, having been accused of insubordination by William Reynolds, president of Illinois State University, Esbjörn quit his post in disgust on March 30, 1860, and urged the Scandinavian students to leave the university. Esbjörn moved his family to Chicago, and seventeen of the twenty Scandinavian students at the university followed him.[108]

A New Church Is Born

Esbjörn's resignation brought to a head a smoldering dissatisfaction on the part of the Scandinavians with the doctrinal position and practices of the General Synod. The Scandinavian Conference not only supported Esbjörn at its meeting a few weeks later but voted for a special session on June 5 at Jefferson Prairie, near Clinton, Wisconsin, to form a new synod.[109] Forty-nine congregations, thirty-six Swedish and thirteen Norwegian, were represented by twenty-five pastors and fifteen laymen at the meeting. They had before them the draft of a constitution which made clear that the new synod's doctrinal position would be based on the *Confessio Augustana,* or

Unaltered Augsburg Confession. The Scandinavian Evangelical Lutheran Synod of North America was approved, and Hasselquist was elected first president. A seminary was authorized, and Esbjörn was selected as the professor.[110]

Within less than a year the nation would be plunged into a civil war. It was hardly an auspicious time to launch a new church body, but the Scandinavians forged ahead, determined that their unique religious heritage would be preserved in spite of great difficulties. G. Everett Arden describes the situation of the birth of the Augustana Synod and the underlying reasons for it with helpful clarity in his official history of the church.[111] The founding of the Synod was obviously an act of faith and courage.

The Augustana Synod evidently had made an inspired choice, however, in its first president. In the words of one writer, "Hasselquist was the most versatile and the ablest leader in the annals of Swedish-American Lutheranism. In accounting for any major policy adopted by the Swedish Lutheran Church in the first four decades of its existence, the historian must reckon with this God-fearing son of Skåne. . . . He wielded an influence that placed the stamp of pietism and Low-Church forms so indelibly on the Augustana Synod, that it occupied a unique place among Lutheran synods. He knew the problems and limitations of a church that depended for its support upon a transplanted population, and he anticipated the day when the propagation of the Gospel in America, through the medium of a foreign language, would be over. As educator and ecclesiastical statesman, his orientation in the American environment was remarkably rapid."[112]

Augustana Seminary was maintained in Chicago for three years under Esbjörn's leadership, but a decision was made in 1862 to move the school to Paxton, Illinois, a mere dot on the map in the middle of the prairie. Esbjörn resigned as professor and left for Sweden to raise funds for the school. Hasselquist agreed to serve in his absence. Although he was quite successful in garnering funds for the seminary and even obtained five thousand books for the library as a gift from the king, Esbjörn never returned.[113] Hasselquist remained as professor and president until 1891. Meanwhile, the institution was expanded to include a college and was moved to Rock Island in 1875.[114] It would be hard to overestimate the influence that Hasselquist had on the Synod through his students during his long tenure. He was not a dogmatician but had a practical bent rooted in a "childlike and

Tufve Nilsson Hasselquist

Scripture-centered faith."[115] He produced in turn a number of skillful practical churchmen in the Augustana Church.

Moving in Broader Circles

Although relations were for the most part amicable between the Swedes and Norwegians in the Augustana Synod, it was not long before Norwegian nationalism began to assert itself. In 1866 a newspaper was started, *Den Norske Lutheraner,* which served to deepen a Norwegian consciousness. The synodical convention in 1868 took two major actions which foreshadowed division. One was authorization of a Norwegian professorship at the seminary, and the other was appointment of a committee to consider dividing the Synod along national lines. August Weenaas of Norway, called as the Norwegian professor, immediately began to criticize the synod as "a Swedish communion with a Norwegian annex."[116] At the 1869 convention, the Norwegians requested the privilege of establishing their own college and seminary. The school, soon located at Marshall, Wisconsin, had Weenaas as its head. The Swedes were careful neither to encourage the Norwegians' withdrawal nor to stand in their way. Finally, at the 1870 synodical meeting, the Norwegians voted to leave and form the Norwegian-Danish Augustana Synod. The parting was achieved peacefully and without acrimony.[117] The separation did allow those who remained in Augustana to concentrate more directly on meeting the needs of Swedish immigrants in the years that followed.

Another significant step taken in 1870 was the Augustana Synod's decision to join the recently formed General Council. The Augustana group had concerns over such matters as the General Council's stand on membership in lodges, but they did seek the wider fellowship on the basis of doctrinal agreements.[118] Not everything about Council membership was to prove satisfactory, however. Augustana did not view itself as simply a geographical district of a national body. It already had its own publishing house, colleges, a seminary, home mission program, and a sense of responsibility to minister to Scandinavians wherever they were to be found.[119]

Home missions, as it turned out, became one of the areas of friction between Augustana and the General Council. Originally, Augustana's concern had been almost exclusively for mission work among Swedish immigrants. The Council's home mission work among English-speaking people, therefore, posed little problem. As it became more evident that English would become a major language for Augustana people and as the General Council expanded its work into the upper Midwest, tensions mounted. An agreement known as the "Lancaster Compromise" was reached at the 1882 convention of the Council which ruled that wherever a congregation was formed "out of material from existing churches" both pastor and congregation should belong to the synod of which the mother congregation was a member.[120] In 1891, however, the Council admitted the Synod of the Northwest, made up largely of congregations on the territory of Augustana's Minnesota conference. The Augustana Synod regarded this as a violation of agreements and withdrew the following year from further home mission work with the Council. This eventually paved the way for Augustana to establish its own English missions.[121] A real shift in direction was underway. By 1908 an Association of English Churches was formed within Augustana. This led to the preparation of English-language materials, including a hymnal and liturgy based upon the Common Service.[122]

Seminary education also became a source of irritation. In 1869 the General Council proposed a seminary in Chicago to serve its congregations in the Midwest and invited Augustana to be a part of the endeavor. At that time the Synod did not foresee a problem with a seminary for English-speaking students only 175 miles from its own school. By 1887, however, when the Chicago seminary loomed as a reality, Augustana urged the General Council not to proceed. In fact, a group in the Synod proposed in 1899 that the Council give the land it had acquired in Chicago as a new campus for Augustana Seminary. The General Council in turn suggested that it would provide two acres of the parcel so that the two seminaries could be built side by side. The Synod was not ready to accept those terms, and the General Council opened its new school in 1891. The event was "not an occasion for unmixed rejoicing in the Swedish Lutheran household," according to one observer.[123]

Augustana's break with the Council finally came in 1918 over the impending merger that would form the United Lutheran Church. Despite support for the merger by Augustana's president and vice-president, the Synod voted to withdraw from the Council and to resume an independent status. Both the actions taken by the Augustana Synod and the Council's response were gracious. The General Council's resolution indeed expressed "the hope that the Augustana Synod may soon determine to enter into organic union with The

United Lutheran Church and aid in the formation of one American Lutheran Church."[124] The next long step on that road, however, was not to be taken for another forty-four years, although Augustana would demonstrate its inter-Lutheran and ecumenical interests in other ways.

Internal Issues

Two major internal issues disturbed the unusually smooth course of the Augustana Synod after the withdrawal of the Norwegians. One was a theological controversy which emanated from a wing of the Swedish revival movement. The principal leader of the Swedish revival had been a lay preacher, Carl Olof Rosenius. Although there were many different strands of the movement, these pious folk generally opposed the strong traditionalism and institutionalism of the Church of Sweden and sought a spiritual freedom based on "the Word of God alone."[125] Because of their emphasis on winning souls, they were often referred to as "Mission Friends."

A young cobbler, Carl August Björk, who had been caught up in the movement, emigrated from Sweden to the United States in 1864 and became a member of Magnus Håkanson's congregation in Swede Bend, Iowa. He became a lay preacher and rallied a group to the "Mission Friends" point of view. When a new pastor, C. J. Malmberg, was called to Swede Bend, he sought to reach an understanding with the Björk faction, but they chose to form a "Mission Society" that would promote their form of revivalism. The Mission Society movement soon began to spread to other parishes.[126]

The problem became even more serious with the importing of the books and ideas of Paul P. Waldenström, a Church of Sweden pastor and a former follower of Rosenius. Waldenström, who had parted company with Rosenius, attacked Lutheran confessional theology, particularly in denying the objective nature of Christ's atonement. In 1876 Johann G. Princell, a recently ordained Augustana pastor, began to promote such theological concepts. This disruptive influence led to his suspension from the ministry.

The debate over Waldenström's views continued, and in 1885 forty-nine congregations, mostly from the Augustana Synod, formed the Swedish Evangelical Mission Covenant of America with Björk as the first president. In Eugene L. Fevold's judgment, "The most obvious effect of the Waldenström controversy on the Augustana Synod was the removal of dissident elements and the emergence of another denominational competitor for the allegiance of Swedish immigrants."[127]

The other issue which had to be fought through in Augustana was one of polity. As the Synod grew by leaps and bounds, it seemed in danger of disunity bred by parochialism. The original constitution defined the Synod as ordained pastors and the lay delegates of congregations. In 1879 the Synod adopted a constitutional change which defined the Synod as the congregations related to it. Congregations would be represented at conventions by the pastor and a lay delegate. In the view of G. Everett Arden, "With the adoption of this proposal the pendulum had swung to the opposite extreme, relegating the ministerial office to a delegatory status only, while making the congregation, as such, the constitutive element of the Synod. This was tantamount to outright congregationalism."[128]

The congregational polity, however, was not enough to satisfy those who were out to weaken the central church. Led by Peter Sjöblom of Minnesota, these forces proposed in 1880 that the Synod be redefined as made up of the conferences related to it. This was sectionalism with a vengeance. The highly respected T. N. Hasselquist and Eric Norelius combined their influence to defeat this "states' rights" move.[129] The following year, Sjöblom started a movement to have the Minnesota Conference withdraw from Augustana and set up its own synod. His allies deserted him, however, and Sjöblom abandoned the plan.[130]

The controversy about parochialism and sectionalism continued to simmer. In 1888 President Erland Carlsson pointed out the dangers of the trend toward decentralization in his final report to the Synod. Finally in 1893 a new synodical constitution was adopted which defined the Synod as consisting of pastors and congregations. It also made clear that the Synod was not subordinate to the conferences.[131] This stance on synodical polity was to become a crucial ingredient in all merger discussions in the future.

Ending an Era, Beginning a New

The decades of the twentieth century were times of dramatic transition for Augustana. The Synod convention at Duluth in 1911 in a symbolic way marked the ending of an era. Eric Norelius, now seventy-eight and the last link with the pioneer period, stepped down as president. In the words of the editor of *Augustana*, "The sons of the pioneers are being challenged to prove their mettle."[132] While the process of Americanization had been going on for many years, the period which included World War I hastened the change to a truly indigenous church. What is more, Augustana had become a church with sufficient history to look back with satisfaction upon many accomplishments and ahead with confidence and strength.

Home mission concern helped to transform Augustana from a regional entity to a continent-wide church. During the late nineteenth century, Augustana was the most aggressive of the Scandinavian groups in the East, establishing strong congregations in New York State and New England.[133] Others were founded on the West Coast and in the Southwest. Augustana also began to push into Canada and in 1913 established a Canada Conference.[134] The Synod had been cooperating with the General Council in its foreign mission field in India and in 1895 sent Charlotte Swensson there as its first woman missionary. Interestingly, when she returned to the United States on furlough in 1900, she became the first woman ever to address an Augustana Synod Convention.[135]

In 1917 the Augustana Mission Society decided to open a mission in the Sudan. World War I intervened, however, and it was not until 1920 that Ralph D. Hult was sent to begin the work. Shortly thereafter, the Leipzig Mission Society requested help with its orphaned field in the Kilimanjaro District of Tanganyika, and Augustana agreed to transfer its missionaries there. When the German missionaries were able to return, the Augustana workers moved west to the Iramba Province where they began an extensive program.[136] Other Augustana mission fields included China, Japan, Hong Kong, Taiwan, and Uruguay.[137]

A powerful impetus for mission work came from the Women's Missionary Society, which was founded in 1892 by Emmy Evald, the daughter of pioneer pastor Erland Carlsson. She served for forty-three years as president and initiated much of the innovative work among women.[138] Women also played a significant role in inner missions and education through the diaconate, which had its center in Omaha.[139]

Education was a dominant concern of the Swedes. Not only did they establish a college and seminary in 1860; they also founded other colleges, such as Gustavus Adolphus at St. Peter, Minnesota; Bethany at Lindsborg, Kansas; and Upsala at East Orange, New Jersey.[140] Nor was education neglected in the parish. Parochial schools were important in the early days, and catechetical instruction was always basic, but later Sunday schools, vacation schools, camps, and a wide variety of new forms of parish education were added.[141] It was this passion for Christian education that led Augustana into far-reaching cooperation with other Lutheran church bodies, particularly in the 1940s and 1950s. It was one harbinger of greater unity to come.

THE DANES: SOURCES OF THE AELC

It was not surprising that the Danes, being a seafaring people, would try their luck at finding a northwest passage to the Orient, as did other European nations. In 1619 King Christian IV sent a two-ship expedition led by Jens Munk to search for this fabled passage. Although they set sail from Copenhagen on May 9, Munk's little band of sixty-five men found their way blocked by ice when they reached Frobisher Bay in what is now Canada. Heading south and west, they arrived in Hudson Bay, where Munk decided to set up a camp to wait out the coming winter. He boldly claimed the area for Denmark and named it Nova Dania.[142]

Rasmus Jensen had been sent along as the expedition's chaplain, and it was he who is credited with conducting the first Lutheran worship services in North America. The winter proved to be a terrible ordeal. Hunger, cold, and disease began to take their toll. Pastor Jensen cared for the sick before he, too, became desperately ill. Despite his weakness he preached from his sick bed until he died February 20. Captain Munk himself continued to conduct the worship. Finally in June, only Munk and two crew members were alive, but somehow they managed to set sail in the smaller of their two vessels and arrived in Norway September 21. The captain at last made his way to Denmark on Christmas Day, 1620.

Although the king hoped to send Munk back to form a settlement the following year, the captain was too ill to go. The plan was abandoned. Enok Mortensen wrote sadly, "Thus the Danish people missed their chance to build a permanent settlement in the new world."[143] But that was not the end of the story. A scattering of individual Danish immigrants did come to the North American mainland in the following years, even though it would be two and one-half centuries before the Danes came in significant numbers.

A generation later, Danish colonists did come to what is now the Virgin Islands. Beginning in 1665 the Danish church began to send a long series of pastors to minister to the settlers. The islands were

Emmy Carlsson Evald

known as the Danish West Indies and were governed by Denmark until they were sold to the United States in 1917. At that time there were some three thousand Lutherans living on the islands. Some were of Danish descent, but most were Blacks.[144]

The Surge of the Sixties

Various factors account for the fact that prior to 1860 only about five thousand Danish immigrants were recorded as having come to the United States. In fact, between 1820 and 1830 only 189 Danes came to America.[145] Denmark itself had suffered devastating reversals as a result of siding with Napoleon in his war with England. The British had bombarded Copenhagen and seized the Danish fleet in 1807. In the final peace terms, Denmark was required as punishment to cede the island of Helgoland to the British and Norway to Sweden. With her overseas trade completely destroyed, Denmark entered a depression and finally went bankrupt in 1813.[146] By contrast, the rapid increase in population in the first half of the nineteenth century, which had led to mass emigrations from Norway and Sweden, did not affect Denmark until the 1860s because many of the new workers were absorbed by rapid industrialization and the opening of new farmlands in western Denmark.[147]

From the 1860s to the 1920s was a different story. In these years, about one hundred thousand Danes made their way to the New World. Some were fleeing from unemployment and severe economic conditions. Many young men were seeking to escape military conscription by Prussia, which had seized Schleswig and Holstein after Denmark's defeat in the war of 1864.[148] Political unrest and a new spirit of independence at home made the more adventurous susceptible to glowing reports from friends who had already gone to America. With a kind of wry humor, they reasoned, "If they who emigrated and whom we have known well, neither drowned in the ocean, were plundered, shot or hanged, and neither have burned to death nor frozen, why should we not follow them?"[149]

The Religious Background

Christianity had come to Denmark nearly a thousand years before the Danish church crossed the Atlantic in the nineteenth century. According to Johannes Knudsen, "When the American nation was born, the Danish church was an old established state institution, stagnant in official and archaic forms and with Rationalism and Traditionalism fighting a battle of dead bones."[150] In the 1800s a spiritual awakening that had begun in Germany swept through Denmark. The movement was led by men like Bishops J. P. Mynster and H. L. Martensen. When the absolute monarchy in Denmark was replaced by a constitutional form of government, the state church became a folk church. As one historian assessed the changes, "The scathing criticism of Søren Kierkegaard helped the church clean house, and . . . revival movements burst forth sporadically."[151]

The person who was most responsible for keeping the revival movement within the church was Bishop N. F. S. Grundtvig.[152] He was concerned that the Danish church was on the verge of extinction because of indifference. The only signs of life seemed to be "godly gatherings" of lay people in the rural areas, and these meetings were opposed by the church. In his own spiritual struggles, Grundtvig came to what was called "the matchless discovery." "It dawned on me in a blessed moment," he wrote, "that the matchless witness which I had searched for sounded as a voice from heaven in the Apostolic Creed at baptism."[153] Grundtvig was branded a heretic on the grounds that he had abandoned Lutheran doctrine and denied the authority of the Scriptures. Actually, he believed "the Bible to be the source of Christian enlightenment but not of Christianity itself; for it is the church which has created the Bible, and not the Bible which has created the church. . . . With prophetic insight Grundtvig saw, as the secret of the church, that our Lord Jesus Christ himself is present as the Living Word in the Christian congregation."[154]

In rejecting Pietism, Grundtvig emphasized that human living was created and willed by God. As a result he was concerned for both the spiritual and cultural awakening of the people. This led Grundtvig to develop an adult education movement based upon folk schools which would have widespread influence. A great hymnwriter, he also left a rich heritage in this field.[155] It was the Grundtvigian tradition which was to be reflected in America by the American Evangelical Lutheran Church.

Another movement, however, arose in Denmark which would eventually lead to a division among the Danish churches in North America. Organized in 1853 by a group of pietistic laymen, it was originally known as "The Association for Inner Mission in Denmark."[156] In 1861 it was renamed the "Society for Inner Mission" and came under the influence of the great revivalist preacher Vilhelm Beck. As Fevold explains, "The emphasis in this movement was upon repentance, conversion, and a personal experience of faith."[157] It championed orthodoxy and rigid standards of conduct, which inevitably resulted in tensions with the Grundtvigians. The society placed great emphasis on lay preaching and was highly successful in its mission work, establishing hundreds of chapels throughout Denmark.[158] Although Beck had shared many of Grundtvig's views regarding the church, he became increasingly biblicistic in his own approach and critical of Grundtvig's concept of the Word of God.

In the words of Enok Mortensen, "The Church of Denmark may be symbolized as a great cathedral. In the nave are found the faithful worshippers of the center *(hojkirkelige)*. They are the conservative element, often deeply but always unobtrusively pious. The two revival movements of the 19th century are found in the side-aisles: Grundtvigianism on the left, the Inner Mission on the right. And outside, sometimes in close proximity, often at some distance, are the masses of people, baptized and confirmed and indisputably members of the Church but whose relationship to it is strangely impersonal and tenuous."[159] The folk church, however, seemed sufficiently broad to encompass the whole spectrum.

The Church Moves to North America

Until the 1870s, the new Danish immigrants tended to find their spiritual home in the Norwegian Church. This was understandable since the Danes and the Norwegians had a joint monarchy for four centuries and shared many traditions. "It is thus not strange that the first Danish immigrant pastor worked among the Norwegians, nor to put it another way, that one of the first two Norwegian pastors in the Middle West was a Dane."[160] He was Claus L. Clausen, a pastor in Muskego, Wisconsin, who together with three other ministers formed the Norwegian Evangelical Church in America in 1851.

Clausen, however, continued to have a specific concern for the Danish immigrants and in 1869 visited Denmark where he urged that mission work be undertaken among the Danes in America. Working together, the Inner Mission people and the followers of Grundtvig formed a commission which sent three men to America in 1871 to investigate the field. They were the Rev. A. C. L. Grove-Rasmussen, Rasmus Andersen (a student), and Anders Sixtus Nielsen (a lay preacher). Grove-Rasmussen returned in time to Denmark, but both Nielsen and Andersen remained and were later ordained.

Two other Danish ministers soon came to America. Both had missionary experience. Niels Thomsen had served as a missionary in India, and Adam Dan, a gifted leader, had taught orphans in Jerusalem. Together with Nielsen and Andersen, they met in Neenah, Wisconsin, on September 9, 1872, and formed a Church Mission Society. It was not intended that the society would be a church because the four men expected to maintain ties with the church in Denmark. The doctrinal position was stated as being in full agreement with the confessions of the mother church. The group also planned a paper, *Kirkelig Samler* (Church Gatherer), which began publication in October. Dan served as both the editor of the paper and first president of the society.[161]

At its convention in 1874, the new society took the first steps that would eventually lead to its becoming a church but still maintained that it was really part of the Danish Folk Church. Growth was rapid, and by 1878 there were sixty-eight congregations and seventeen ministers. At the same time there was a growing hope that there might be a free and independent church body. At the society's convention in 1878 the die was cast and the name changed to "The Danish Evangelical Lutheran Church in America." At first the church was unwilling to adopt a constitution, perhaps because of opposition from the Society for Advancement of the Gospel Among the Danes in America, which was based in Denmark. A year later, however, the new church adopted a constitution that provided for governance by a president, two trustees, and an annual convention of congregational delegates. "In reality, this was a *declaration of independence*" from the committee in Denmark, although that group continued to send pastors to America for many years.[162] A. S. Nielsen was elected president for a one-year term but also "ordainer," a post that was to be for life.[163]

Schism

Although formation of the Danish Evangelical Lutheran Church in America seemed at first to have brought Grundtvigians and Inner Mission people into a harmonious relationship, the seeds of a schism had already been sown. Two issues, which had been imported from Denmark along with the immigrants, kept rising to the surface. One was the persistent question, as Knudsen pointed out, "of the interpretation of the Bible or rather the matter of determining the Christian authority. . . . The other point of controversy was the question as to whether or not Christian people could have general

Adam Dan

cultural interests and should participate in a cultural life or whether they, in a pietistic emphasis, should withdraw from that life."[164] Issues of this depth could be accommodated within the broad range of views that existed in the Danish Folk Church. Within the "free church" setting in the New World, however, there was less tolerance of differences.[165]

Some of the first signs of trouble were rather subtle. In 1881 the new editor of *Kirkelig Samler* suddenly dropped the word "folkelig" from the subtitle of the paper. Previously, the wording had been "For Christian and *folkelig* Enlightenment and Edification on the Basis of the Faith." The following year the next editor changed the masthead further to read "Lutheran Periodical for Christian Enlightenment and Edification." According to Mortensen, "Here, the essential differences between the Inner Mission and the Grundtvigian were for the first time defined and accentuated; for the word *folkelig* emanated from Grundtvig's views and is, basically, the antonym of the word *pietistic.*"[166]

This issue of Pietism came more directly to a head in the formation of the Danish Folk Society in 1887 by Pastor F. L. Grundtvig, the son of the famous bishop. The purpose of the society was ostensibly to preserve and augment Danish traditional values. The organization grew rapidly, but many saw in it the characteristics of a secret society and an agency to promote Grundtvig's churchly views. "Intended to embrace and unite all Danes in a common cause, [the society] became instead a divisive factor that engendered dissension and strife."[167]

The focal point of much of the doctrinal tension was centered in the infant seminary that the church had established in a defunct folk school at West Denmark, Wisconsin, in 1887. The seminary was started in a sincere effort to assure the Danes a steady supply of indigenously trained pastors. Pastor Thorvald Helveg, a university graduate from Denmark, was chosen as president. Since many regarded Helveg as a disciple of Grundtvig, the president himself insisted that a second teacher be chosen who represented the Inner Mission tradition. The choice was Pastor P. S. Vig, the son of a poor farmer. Vig had attended the folk school at Askov but later came under the influence of a revivalist preacher who had been influenced by Dwight L. Moody.[168]

Helveg and Vig differed sharply on the question of whether the Bible was the Word of God. Helveg took the Grundtvigian position that the Apostles' Creed was the basic confession of the Christian church and that the church had produced the Scriptures rather than the other way around. Vig was adamant about the Bible being literally inspired and "the only norm and source of Christian faith and life."[169] Supporters rallied around both men. Finally the tensions became so great that in 1891 the church convention asked the two professors to resign and closed the seminary.[170]

Although there were repeated efforts to resolve the differences between the Grundtvigians and the Inner Mission forces, the break finally came in 1894. At the 1893 convention in Racine, the Danish Church adopted without dissent a new constitution designed to solve the biblical question. "But unfortunately a motion was passed, also without objection," Mortensen noted, "that *pastors or congregations who will not sign the synod's constitution within three months cannot belong to the synod.*' "[171] By the deadline on February 15, 1894, only forty-one of fifty-six ministers and forty out of 119 congregations had signed. Acrimony among members and litigation over property rights were widespread. The lasting result was a dissolution of the fragile ties that had bound the folk church together.[172]

Two other factors had paved the way for the schism. During the 1893 convention, a group calling itself the "Association for Evangelical Danes in America" had been formed within the church. In the fall of 1894, this group together with about one-third of the synod's congregations and pastors seceded to organize the Danish Evangelical Lutheran Church of North America [the "North Church"]. Earlier a number of congregations and pastors of the Norwegian-Danish Conference had also withdrawn from that body. Within two years, these two groups would form the United Evangelical Lutheran Church in America, a body that ultimately became part of the American Lutheran Church almost six decades later.[173]

The Danish Church After 1894

After the Inner Mission groups had withdrawn, the remnant of the Danish Evangelical Lutheran Church moved to establish its own seminary and college at Grand View, Des Moines, Iowa. By October 1895 the first building of the school was partially completed, and the following year the first student was enrolled. In 1897 Rasmus Vestergaard, of Denmark, was elected the first president. Beginning modestly in the character of a folk school, Grand View College in 1924 became a two-year college and in 1975 had an accredited four-year baccalaureate program. The seminary program was the primary source for pastors in the church through the years until it joined the Chicago Lutheran Seminary at Maywood and then became part of the merger which formed the Lutheran School of Theology at Chicago in 1962.[174]

True to its Grundtvigian roots, the Danish Church emphasized baptismal grace, nurture, and fellowship rather than conversion experiences and pietism. Their celebration of life in this world earned the Danish Church members the sobriquet "the happy Danes." In contrast, the UELC came to be known rather unjustly as "the gloomy Danes." Many in the Danish Church tradition would agree with the observation of one observer, "Only in a very broad and general way do these appellations fit. The AELC tradition is perhaps that of the 'abundant life' as expressed in a gay conviviality, in the lilt of song, in the fellowship of the folk-dance, in the sumptuously-spread coffee table. (Detractors have called coffee and kringle the Grundtvigian sacraments!) But we Danes have no corner on the happiness market."[175]

The Danish Church in America was congregational in character and resisted centralization. Perhaps, according to Fevold, "The desire to perpetuate its Danish heritage—linguistic, cultural, and religious—resulted in the retention of its Danish character longer than its sister synod and delayed Americanization."[176] There was a certain isolationist flavor within the synod, which may have been due in part to the fact that so many pastors had been born and educated in Denmark. They encouraged such unusual practices as seeking to establish Danish colonies in order to expand the church.[177] Vacation schools, folk schools, and youth groups all became ways of perpetuating the Danish language and culture.[178] In the view of one writer, the Danish Church "was one of the last immigrant churches to accept and change to the English language. . . . English finally took precedence during the 1930s, but it wasn't until the '40s that the AELC [as it was later called] ordained its first pastor of non-Danish descent."[179] In 1936 the Church elected Alfred Jensen president, a position he held until 1960. Jensen proved to be a farsighted leader. As early as 1946 and again in 1952, he raised questions about Danish exclusivity and urged starting congregations on an all-English basis.[180]

In 1953 the Church acknowledged its changing mission to serve all people by dropping "Danish" from its title and becoming the American Evangelical Lutheran Church.[181] The AELC had paid dearly, however, for clinging so long to its Danish roots. As historian Johannes Knudsen put it, "By attrition we were gradually not only losing members to other churches but we were losing congregations. Many of our congregations were small groups that had received a certain support because they had an ethnic background. Now that the ethnic background was gone, or we were in a situation where it didn't matter any longer, the attempt to keep these small congregations proved more and more difficult. Let me mention, for instance, the Eastern District—New England, New York, New Jersey—where we at one time had eleven churches. By the time we were merged this number had by attrition dwindled down to three."[182]

Although it had long clung to its ethnic background, the AELC also had an ecumenical side. It belonged to the National Lutheran Council; the National Council of Churches of Christ in the USA, where C. Arild Olsen, an AELC member, was for many years executive secretary of the Division of Life and Work; and the World Council of Churches.[183] The AELC also joined in inter-Lutheran work on the *Service Book and Hymnal* and the Long-Range Program of Parish Education. In 1955 the AELC convention had a proposal before it to become a nongeographical synod of the ULCA. Although the vote was 157 to 124 in favor of affiliation, the motion failed for lack of a two-thirds majority.[184] Later, Johannes Knudsen, who had favored the proposal, talked with Franklin Clark Fry, president of the ULCA, expressing his regret at the decision. Fry's reply was, "Never mind, Joe. Now you can join Augustana and the United Lutheran Church in an effort to create a new church."[185]

The Danish Church had supported foreign mission work with gifts since the late nineteenth century, but in 1913 the synod formally adopted the field in Santal, India, as a special cause. It was not until 1920, however, that the church sent Dagmar Miller as its first missionary.[186] The fact that she was a woman was important because foreign missions were high on the concerns of women in the synod. In 1908 a dozen women and two pastors had founded *Danske Kvinders Missionsfond* (Women's Mission Society) at the time that the synod convention was being held, although women were not technically eligible to be delegates. The first president was Mrs. Jens Gregersen. Recognition of women had been slow in coming. Mortensen notes wryly, "During the first thirty years of the synod's history, it was tacitly assumed that women, like children, should be seen and not heard."[187] In fact, the constitution of 1903 made it clear that synod delegates were to be males only. It caused something of a stir, therefore, when the congregation in Nysted, Nebraska, chose Thyra Dorf, the wife of its pastor, to be a delegate to the Racine convention. Perhaps because they were conscious of the growing suffrage movement, the male delegates quietly ignored a motion to bar her from voting, and Thyra Dorf became the first female representative, even though the all-male clause in the constitution wasn't changed until 1912.[188]

Although small in numbers, the AELC contributed greatly to the leadership of the LCA when it came into being. Two of its pastors in time became synodical bishops: Howard Christensen in Michigan and Herluf Jensen in New Jersey. Others such as Johannes Knudsen, Axel Kildegaard, and Daniel Martensen were seminary professors. Erling Jensen, who had been a professor at Iowa State University and senior physicist for the Atomic Energy Commission, became president of Muhlenberg College. Others became staff of churchwide agencies. Still others were staff of synods, agencies, and institutions. An even longer list could be compiled, but the evidence is clear that the "Happy Danes" brought a rich legacy of human resources to the new church.

THE FINNS: SOURCES OF THE
SUOMI SYNOD

In one sense, the Finns were among the earliest Lutheran immigrants to North America, but in another they were among the latest. When the Swedish expedition landed in Delaware in 1638, Finland had been a part of Sweden for nearly five centuries. Finland was not, however, a subject province of Sweden. According to historian John H. Wuorinen, Finland was "an integral part of the kingdom, whose inhabitants were 'native Swedes' in the eyes of the law, possessing the same rights and privileges as were enjoyed by the inhabitants of the Swedish part of the kingdom. Law and the administration of justice, religious life, education, and governmental and administrative organization were institutionalized in both parts of the kingdom according to patterns which had gradually evolved in the course of a common history extending over several centuries."[189]

By the time that the Dutch had taken control of the Swedish colony, it is estimated that about four hundred immigrants had been settled in New Sweden. The exact number who were Finns is difficult to say because all names were recorded in Swedish.[190] However, it is generally believed that the majority were Finnish.[191] It is known that, because of the difficulty in getting people to volunteer to go to the New World, provincial governors were sometimes told to use force. In 1641 the Swedish Royal Council ordered one governor to seize the Finns guilty of destroying forests in his district and hold them for shipment to America on the next ship.[192]

Influx in the 1800s

With the Dutch and later the English occupation of Delaware, the Finnish immigration to the colony ended in any significant sense. It was not until the time of the Civil War that the first wave of what were to be thousands of Finnish immigrants came to North America.[193] Finland was then a part of Russia, which had wrested control of the country from Sweden in 1809. Many factors contributed to the exodus: the end of traditional industries such as tar burning in the forests, an agrarian and industrial revolution, severe economic conditions, the institution of compulsory military service, and the tactics of unscrupulous "immigrant runners."

The new arrivals were quick to report to those who remained in the homeland the wonders and prosperity of North America. One report said, "The residents of the Ii-parish in 1866 learned from one such letter that 'in America even the grain grows up in a week, that peas there rotted at the base of trees, and that the supply of red wine flowing from between cracks in the cliffs never became exhausted, not even by drinking it.' "[194] Lured by such promises, thousands crossed the Atlantic, but many returned to Finland homesick or disappointed. According to one estimate, some 243,000 Finns came to the United States and another 60,000 to Canada by 1918.[195] The largest concentrations in the United States were in Michigan, Minnesota, Massachusetts, New York, and Washington.[196] The "copper country" of Upper Michigan tended to be the center of Finnish settlements and, therefore, of the church.

To the immigrants, language was a vital link to a folk culture which they had cherished in the Old Country. During the centuries that Finland was controlled by Sweden, the official language of the country was Swedish. Finnish was the language of the vast majority of the common people for whom Swedish was a foreign tongue. When Finland was ceded to Russia, there was genuine alarm that if Russian became the new official language, there would be no hope of preserving either Finnish or the dream of an autonomous Finland.[197]

J. V. Snellman, a philosopher and respected statesman, was the leader of the long struggle to raise the status of Finnish to the recognized language of the country. "During the 1840's," writes Eino Jutikkala, "the entire educated class felt the impact of his ideas. Some opposed them, either because they believed a change of language presented too many difficulties or because they doubted the ability of the Finns to create and maintain a culture of their own. These doubts were largely swept away in the enthusiasm that followed the publication (in 1835 and 1849) of the folk-epic *Kalevala*, compiled by Elias Lonnrot from ancient folk poems taken down from the lips of country people. A large number of educated people did begin to speak Finnish, with varying degrees of proficiency, in their homes, and the foundation of a Finnish-speaking educated class was laid."[198]

Adjusting to a New Land

For the immigrants of the latter half of the nineteenth century, the rising national consciousness in Finland, the new pride in language, and rapidly shifting economic conditions in the homeland were all factors in their adaptation to their new setting. But there was more. Most were of poor peasant stock who had to struggle for economic survival. Their tendency at first was to withdraw from conflict with American society and to try to preserve their own values. They often settled in ethnic enclaves where they were looked upon as foreigners in the same way that other late arrivals from southern and eastern Europe were viewed.[199] Indeed, it was not until Finland obtained independence from Russia in 1920 that many Americans began to think of the Finns as a people in their own right and not as Russians.[200]

Forming a wide variety of organizations, ranging from temperance societies to labor groups, was one way that Finns developed a sense of belonging. Often these various groups were in conflict with one another. As Hoglund explains the situation, "Among the promoters of organizations were nationalists who emphasized ethnic consciousness. They declared that Finnish nationalism or culture could survive in America. By transmitting the language, customs, and patterns of thought which supposedly were Finnish, they expected that their children would acquire the parental culture. Through the language, said one writer, children had access to the 'Finnish mind.' If there were schools to teach the language, he added, the future of Finnish nationality was assured in America."[201] For socialists, however, language and nationalism were barriers to their goals.

The Church in America

For those to whom religion had been a vital part of their lives, the church seemed a natural place to turn in this strange land. But the question became, "What church?" There were three distinct organizations, each with a relatively small following: the Laestadian Movement, the Church of Finland, and the Evangelical Movement.[202]

The "Laestadian" group was named for Lars Levi Laestadius, a pastor in northern Sweden and Finland. The group was revivalistic in character and relied heavily on lay preachers. In 1867 a congregation composed of Norwegians, Swedes, and Finns was formed in Hancock, Michigan. In time, the Norwegian-American pastor excommunicated the Laestadian element for what he regarded as un-Lutheran beliefs. In 1872 the group organized its own congregation under a lay preacher, Salomon Korteniemi. The group chose the name of "Finnish Apostolic Lutheran Church." The strictly congregational polity adopted in their constitution formed the basis for other Laestadian-type congregations in later years. The distinguishing characteristic of the group, however, was the practice that confession had to be "en voce" to the congregation which held the "power of the keys."[203] Some Laestadian congregations would finally form a national body, the Apostolic Lutheran Church, in 1928.[204]

The Finns who were the forerunners of those who helped to form the Lutheran Church in America were first organized in Calumet, Michigan. Along with Swedes, Norwegians, and a few Danes, they were served by a Norwegian pastor, Nils E. Boe. Because he felt that he could not minister effectively to the Finns in their own language, Boe wrote a letter to Finland pleading that these people should have their own pastor.[205] The response to the appeal came from the Finnish Missionary Society in Helsinki, which sent Alfred E. Backman, who was the first Lutheran pastor to come from Finland since colonial times.[206] Backman served the Finns in Calumet and nearby Quincy from 1876 until 1881. He was one of approximately one hundred men dispatched by the Missionary Society to further development of Lutheran work among the Finns. Unfortunately, most stayed for only a few years, and the need for an indigenous clergy became apparent.

In 1885 John K. Nikander arrived in the Upper Peninsula of Michigan and during his long ministry became the patriarch of Finnish Lutherans in North America. Along with three other pastors and sixteen laymen, he helped form the Finnish Evangelical Lutheran Church (Suomi Synod) in 1890. Nikander served as its president until his death in 1919. The road to the future for the new church body, however, was not easy. The first constitution of the church was viewed with suspicion by some because it seemed to centralize authority and to give too much power to the clergy. Nikander himself had reservations about the constitution, and by 1896 it had been thoroughly revised. In the view of Douglas J. Ollila, the new form emphasized "synodical polity, which maintained a careful balance between the power of the clergy and that of the laity, provided the framework for thoroughly democratic procedures, and emphasized the role of the local congregation."[207]

There were those, however, who were not reconciled to the direction of the Suomi Synod. In 1898 some of those who were dissatisfied organized the Finnish American National Evangelical Lutheran Church as an alternative to the Suomi Synod. According to Fevold, "Theological differences appear not to have been a factor at the time. Early in its career the National Church identified itself with the Evangelicals and the Gospel Society of Finland."[208] In 1964 it merged with the Lutheran Church-Missouri Synod.

Providing an Indigenous Clergy

One lesson that the Finns had learned from the experiences of the early settlers along the Delaware was that they could not depend on a supply of ministers from Finland. Indeed, in the nineteenth century there was a shortage of pastors in the home country, and they were released reluctantly to work in America.[209] Some way, obviously, was needed to train ministers in this country who would be attuned to both the particular needs of the immigrants and the social conditions in America.

Prior to the formation of the Suomi Synod, other Lutheran bodies sought to provide a ministry to the Finns. One notable example was the Augustana Synod. In 1873 J. J. Hoikka immigrated to the United States and two years later entered Augustana College. Following college and seminary, he was ordained by the Augustana Synod and became the first pastor prepared in this way with the purpose of serving Finns in mind. He was called by the Home Mission Board of

Jacob Johansson Hoikka, Kaarlo Tolonen, Juho Kustaa Nikander, three of the founding pastors of the Suomi Synod

the synod to serve a Swedish congregation in Astoria, Oregon, and to do mission work among the Finns. During his work on the West Coast and in Michigan, he established twenty-three Finnish congregations with the understanding that they would join a Finnish Lutheran synod when one was organized.[210]

At its constituting convention in 1890, the Suomi Synod authorized the formation of a college and two years later selected Hancock, Michigan, as a "temporary" location. It was not until September 1896, however, that the college was opened in rented quarters. J. K. Nikander was selected as the first rector, and its first building was dedicated in 1900. As Arnold Stadius described the purpose of the school, "The founders of Suomi College, none of whom had passed through the public school system in America, planned the new college to preserve the Finnish religion, heritage and culture, in the academic framework they knew from Finland. Nikander and his fellow pastors envisioned a faculty of dedicated Christian men and women who would pass on to the Finnish youth of the New World the values of the Old."[211]

In September 1896, eleven students were enrolled in "Suomi Opisto," the Finnish school. By the end of the first semester there were seven girls and fifteen boys. The plan was to have seven levels in the school. By 1906, however, Stadius notes, "The program was for all practical purposes limited to a six-year format, with classes three through six being the equivalent of high school grades nine through twelve, and the first two classes being the elastic, catch-all classes of the Preparatory Department."[212] The Preparatory Department was intended for those pupils aged nine or above who were handicapped by not being able to handle either English or Finnish.

In the fall of 1904, seven young men who had completed the entire program at the college became the first students of the seminary. The program was planned for two years and emphasized the usual range of theological subjects, including Greek and Hebrew. There were initially three men on the faculty: Pastors Nikander, Johannes Back of Hancock, and Alfred Gröning of Atlantic. The seminary continued as a separate department of the college until 1958 when it merged with the ULCA seminary at Maywood, Illinois.[213]

Suomi College continued to be an important source of leadership for the synod but did not offer credits beyond the secondary level until 1923. At that time the Preparatory Department was phased out and a Junior College established. Enrollment was hampered some-

what by the widespread perception that the school was exclusively
Finnish. The change to English actually was underway not only in
the college but also in the synod, although the transition would take
years. Articles continued to appear in Finnish language newspapers
during the 1920s, however, criticizing the use of English in the
classes.[214] The change was inevitable in spite of the opposition. In
fact, by 1955 even the minutes of the synod were published entirely
in English.

The Changing Suomi Scene

The Suomi Synod itself was changing in other ways. The death of its
patriarch, Dr. Nikander, in 1919 was symbolic of the ending of the
church's pioneering period. He was succeeded as head of the college
and on an interim basis as president of the church by John Wargelin,
who was one of the first graduates of the college in 1904 and the
seminary in 1906. Although born in Finland, he was brought to
America at an early age and used English as though he had been born
in the United States.[215]

World War I and restrictive immigration laws brought a virtual
end to the influx of Finnish immigrants into the United States. By
1929 the quota for the whole country of Finland had been reduced
to 569 in the United States. For a time, therefore, most immigrants
were diverted to Canada.[216] Meanwhile, the "first-comers" of the
1860s and 1870s were dying out, and those born in America put
down deep roots in this society. Children were seen as the key to
the future and the preservation of the Finnish heritage. Sunday
schools and other organizations attracted children in great numbers. As Hoglund indicates, "In the three major Lutheran groups it
was reported that their memberships were the largest ever and
that about one-third of their members were under thirteen years.
With few exceptions the young members had also been born in
America."[217]

The Suomi Synod was also beginning to forge links with other
Lutheran bodies. Because the synod had no unified budget at that
time, home missions efforts were severely restricted by financial
problems. About 1920 the consistory of the synod sent a letter to the
ULCA's Board of American Missions requesting aid. The board responded positively and for a decade provided grants-in-aid to struggling Suomi congregations as well as assistance to students at Suomi
Seminary.[218] As the world sank into a financial depression, the board

indicated that it could only continue this help if Suomi became an affiliated synod of the ULCA. In 1931 the consistory submitted the proposal to the congregations of the synod, but it was defeated, although not by an overwhelming majority.[219] A decision was reached in 1931, however, to turn over to the ULCA all of Suomi's mission work in Canada which the synod was having great difficulty sustaining.[220]

As Raymond Wargelin points out, "Up until about the 1950's the ULCA was the only Lutheran body that provided the hospitality of calling men out of the Suomi Synod, particularly those who had gone into graduate work, into the service of ULCA colleges and seminaries."[221] Among these persons were T. A. Kantonen at Hamma Divinity School, V. K. Nikander at Wagner College, Walter Kukkonen and Karlo Keljo at Chicago Seminary, J. W. Heikkinen at Gettysburg Seminary, Bernhard Hillila who was dean at Hamma, and Toivo Harjunpaa at Pacific Lutheran Seminary. Dr. Kantonen, who was the first professor born of Finnish stock to become a teacher of theology in a non-Suomi seminary, was a prolific writer and set as one of his goals bringing the riches of Finnish theological thought to the American scene.[222]

Cooperation with other Lutherans was by no means confined to the ULCA. During World War I, Suomi had participated in the Soldiers' and Sailors' Relief efforts. In the mid-1930s the Suomi Synod affiliated with the National Lutheran Council, which opened new horizons of cooperation. In the area of worship, the use of English began to expand. It was a natural step, therefore, when the Augustana Synod published its hymnal in English for many Suomi congregations to adopt it as a source of hymns for their own services. The traditional Finnish liturgy had been translated into English and was used widely, although some congregations had begun using the Common Service in the 1930s. When the time came, Suomi entered into the inter-Lutheran project to produce the *Service Book and Hymnal* in 1957. The "red book" was welcomed without difficulty in most Suomi congregations.[223] Similarly, Suomi entered wholeheartedly into the joint Long-Range Program for Parish Education undertaken by the churches which formed the LCA.

It would be fair to say that this stream of the Finnish tradition had moved from the status of an immigrant people to that of full partnership in American Lutheranism and American society. And yet there was no disposition to forsake the rich heritage which their forebears had brought from the mother country. When the LCA was formed in 1962, more than a hundred Suomi congregations opted to form a linguistic conference to enrich the life of the new church body. Moreover, as was true of the AELC, Suomi contributed a number of leaders to the life of the LCA itself beyond what might have been expected from its size. These included synodical officials, churchwide staff, college and seminary professors, LCUSA staff, and agency executives.[224]

HYPHENATED PEOPLE

With the bitter memories of World War I fresh in people's minds, President Woodrow Wilson declared, "There are a great many hyphens left in America. For my part I think the most un-American thing in the world is a hyphen."[225] For many persons through the years the idea that someone could be legitimately a "Swedish-American" or a "German-Canadian" has been an anomaly that might be tolerated but hardly celebrated. After all, the New World was supposed to be a "melting pot" where the vestiges of ethnic origins were absorbed within some sort of new amalgam. Others have seen America as more of a "salad bowl" where the individual ingredients lend their flavor to the whole without losing completely their original qualities.[226]

Horace M. Kallen, however, takes issue with President Wilson's narrow view and celebrates the hyphens in peoples' lives: "Hyphenation as such is a fact which permeates all levels of life. A man is at once a son and a husband, a brother and a friend . . . a citizen of a state and a member of a church. . . . But it is absurd to lose sight of the truth that the hyphen unites very much more than it separates. . . . Culture is nothing more than spiritual hyphenation."[227] From this perspective, it is recognized that each ethnic group in a polyglot nation joins hands with its ancestors in another place and another time to bring into another age the richness of a heritage.

The Germans, the Swedes, the Danes, and the Finns, who called themselves Lutheran, had to learn the importance of this lesson during the decades that brought them together in a new church body. What still remained as unfinished business was to apply the same insight with the same understanding to God's children from myriad other backgrounds.

NOTES

1. "I once thought to write a history of the immigrants in America," wrote Oscar Handlin in 1951. "Then I discovered that the immigrants *were* American history." Quoted by Sydney E. Ahlstrom in *A Religious History of the American People* (New Haven and London: Yale University Press, 1972), 515.

2. Abdel Ross Wentz, *A Basic History of Lutheranism in America* (Philadelphia: Muhlenberg Press, 1955), 3.

3. *Constitution and Bylaws of the Lutheran Church in America, 1984,* 3.

4. Theodore G. Tappert, "The Church's Infancy," in *The Lutherans in North America,* ed. E. Clifford Nelson (Philadelphia: Fortress Press, 1975), 3.

5. Lars P. Qualben, *The Lutheran Church in Colonial America* (New York: Thomas Nelson & Sons, 1940), 127. Qualben states, "In New Amsterdam the Lutheran group grew steadily and became very cosmopolitan in its makeup, for it included Germans, Norwegians, Danes and Dutch." Qualben cites colonial records to indicate that Scandinavian Lutherans were in New Amsterdam as early as 1630 or 1631.

6. Tappert, "Church's Infancy," 7–8.

7. A. R. Wentz, *Basic History,* 6–7.

8. Minuit had originally been governor of New Netherlands under the Dutch.

9. *The Encyclopedia Americana,* 1965, vol. 22, p. 618.

10. William J. Finck gives an account of these events in *Lutheran Landmarks and Pioneers in America* (Philadelphia: United Lutheran Publication House, 1913), 30–37.

11. Tappert, "Church's Infancy," 10–11; A. R. Wentz, *Basic History,* 10–11.

12. Tappert, "Church's Infancy," 13.

13. Ibid., 20.

14. Ahlstrom, *Religious History,* 254. See also Howard B. Furer, *The Germans in America, 1607–1970* (Dobbs Ferry, N.Y.: Oceana Publications, 1973), 3.

15. Tappert, "Church's Infancy," 23–24.

16. Richard C. Wolf, *Documents of Lutheran Unity in America* (Philadelphia: Fortress Press, 1966), 4.

17. Harry J. Kreider, *History of the United Lutheran Synod of New York and New England* (Philadelphia: Muhlenberg Press, 1954), xvii, 10–12.

18. A. R. Wentz, *Basic History,* 39.

19. *The Journals of Henry Melchior Muhlenberg,* trans. Theodore G. Tappert and John W. Doberstein (Philadelphia: Muhlenberg Press, 1942), 1:58.

20. Wolf, *Documents,* 10.

21. Henry Eyster Jacobs, *A History of the Evangelical Lutheran Church in the United States* (New York: Charles Scribner's Sons, 1893), 196–218.

22. See Tappert, "Church's Infancy," 56.

23. Wolf, *Documents,* 24.

24. Ahlstrom, *Religious History,* 258–59.

25. Jacobs, *History,* 235–36.

26. Ibid., 26.

27. Ahlstrom, *Religious History,* 258. Some historians have referred to the position filled by Muhlenberg as "superintendent."

28. Wolf, *Documents,* 25–29.

29. A.R. Wentz, *Basic History,* 54.

30. Tappert, "Church's Infancy," 36–38. See also A. R. Wentz, *Basic History,* 44. Wentz estimates there were only about forty Lutheran ministers in the whole country when Muhlenberg died in 1787.

31. H. George Anderson, "The Early National Period," in *The Lutherans in North America,* ed. Nelson, 101.

32. Jacobs, *History,* 309–18. A. R. Wentz, *Basic History,* 73–74, also summarizes the doctrinal problems of the period.

33. A. R. Wentz, *Basic History,* 76.

34. Anderson gives an excellent summary of the language problem in "Early National Period," 95–99.

35. Kreider gives a detailed analysis of the formation of the new synod in *History,* 14–32.

36. Wolf, *Documents,* 43.

37. Anderson, "Early National Period," 120.

38. See A. R. Wentz, *Basic History,* 78–82. See also Wolf, *Documents,* 43–94; and Jacobs, *History,* 357–63.

39. Wolf, *Documents,* 45.

40. The fullest account of Samuel Simon Schmucker and his influence on American Lutheranism is in Abdel Ross Wentz, *Pioneer in Christian Unity: Samuel Simon Schmucker* (Philadelphia: Fortress Press, 1967).

41. The effort to establish Hartwick Seminary in New York is recounted in Kreider, *History,* 37–40.

42. Anderson, "Early National Period," 129.

43. A. R. Wentz, *Basic History,* 143–44. August R. Suelflow and E. Clifford Nelson give a summary of the "American Lutheran" controversy in "Following the Frontier," in *The Lutherans in North America,* ed. Nelson, 217–27. See also Wolf, *Documents,* 98–105.

44. Ahlstrom, *Religious History,* 756.

45. See Wolf, *Documents,* 179–98; and A. R. Wentz, *Basic History,* 116–22.

46. See Wolf, *Documents,* 118–41. A. R. Wentz, *Basic History,* chap. 20, gives a thorough review of these events. See also Jacobs, *History,* 451–55.

47. Jacobs, *History,* 468.

48. A. R. Wentz, *Basic History,* 155–56.

49. These events are described in detail in Jacobs, *History,* 455–70; Wolf, *Documents,* 137–52; A. R. Wentz, *Basic History,* 149–56; and Suelflow and Nelson, "Frontier," 230–36.

50. Wolf, *Documents,* 247.

51. See ibid., 252–59. See also Eugene L. Fevold, "Coming of Age," in *The Lutherans in North America,* ed. Nelson, 333–34; and A. R. Wentz, *Basic History,* 232–34.

52. It should be emphasized, however, that the process of dealing with complex issues did not come quickly or easily. As Wolf describes the situation, "These years between 1862 and 1919 were confused and difficult years for the Lutherans in America, filled with controversy, disunity, and division. Yet within these years Lutherans found their awareness of the bases of unity more important that the elements that made for disunity." See Wolf, *Documents*, 117.

53. Fred W. Meuser, "Facing the Twentieth Century, 1900–1930" in *The Lutherans in North America*, ed. Nelson, 375.

54. Ibid., 391.

55. It is estimated that in worship 80 percent of Lutherans used one of some thirty languages that were their mother tongues prior to World War I. The figures ranged from 5 percent for the United Synod South to 92 percent for the General Council and 99 percent for the Norwegian Synod. See E. Clifford Nelson, *The Rise of World Lutheranism, an American Perspective* (Philadelphia: Fortress Press, 1982), 49–50.

56. Meuser gives a concise description of these developments, "Twentieth Century," 396–403. See also E. Clifford Nelson, *Lutheranism in North America 1914–1970* (Minneapolis: Augsburg Publishing House, 1972), 3–10.

57. A. R. Wentz, *Basic History*, 282–83.

58. A. R. Wentz, "In the Beginning," *ULCA Yearbook, 1962*, 8.

59. Originally, Knubel had not been a delegate to the meeting. Amos John Traver reported in "Years of Growth," *ULCA Yearbook, 1962*, 9, "The night before the sessions began, I was asked by my good friend E. F. Eilert if I would be willing to step aside and permit Dr. Frederick H. Knubel to take my place on the delegation. Mr. Eilert said there was good reason to believe that Dr. Knubel might be elected president of the new church. So I enjoyed a choice seat at the press table during the convention."

60. See Meuser, "Twentieth Century," 376; and Frederick K. Wentz, *Lutherans in Concert* (Minneapolis: Augsburg Publishing House, 1968), 11–12.

61. *ULCA Minutes, 1918,* 5–8, lists the names and dates of origin of the member synods at the time of merger.

62. A. R. Wentz, *Basic History*, 287.

63. The story of the Slovaks and Icelanders is told in Richard C. Wolf, *Lutherans in North America* (Philadelphia: Lutheran Church Press, 1965), 92; and in Todd Nichol, *All These Lutherans* (Minneapolis: Augsburg Publishing House, 1986), 41–42.

64. Wolf, *Documents*, 272.

65. Meuser, "Twentieth Century," 376–77.

66. As Abdel Ross Wentz pointed out in his later writings, President Franklin Clark Fry saw the Augustana Lutheran Church model of centralization of authority in the church-at-large as preferable to the ULCA's federative character. This became Fry's stance during the negotiations that led to the formation of the LCA and a concentration of authority at the churchwide level in that body. See Wentz's memo in Robert H. Fischer, ed., *Franklin Clark Fry. A Palette for a Portrait*, a supplementary number of *The Lutheran Quarterly* 24 (1972):101–5.

67. See Tappert, "Church's Infancy," 75; and Anderson, "Early National Period," 138–39.

68. Richard W. Solberg, *Lutheran Higher Education in North America* (Minneapolis: Augsburg Publishing House, 1985), 41–43, 297.

69. A. R. Wentz, *Basic History,* 295.

70. Solberg, *Higher Education,* 52. Solberg's book is the most thorough and up-to-date treatment of the whole field of Lutheran higher education available.

71. A. R. Wentz, *Basic History,* 90–91.

72. Suelflow and Nelson, "Frontier," 208–9.

73. Anderson, "Early National Period," 112–14.

74. A. R. Wentz, *Basic History,* 107–9, 295.

75. Hugh George Anderson, *Lutheranism in the Southeastern States 1860–1886, a Social History* (Paris: Mouton, 1969), 210.

76. Ibid., 215.

77. Jeff C. Johnson, "Black Lutherans in the New World, Myths and Realities," *The Cresset* 47, no. 4 (February 1984):11. See also Paul G. McCullough et al., *A History of the Lutheran Church in South Carolina* (Columbia, S.C.: South Carolina Synod, 1971), 268–70.

78. Anderson, *Lutheranism in Southeastern States,* 217.

79. See Ahlstrom, *Religious History,* 859; and E. Theodore Bachmann, *They Called Him Father* (Philadelphia: Muhlenberg Press, 1942), 116–17.

80. Suelflow and Nelson, "Frontier," 200–2.

81. Bachmann, *Father,* 144–46.

82. Ibid., 206.

83. Ibid., 305.

84. Ibid., 213–14.

85. A full record of Anna Kugler's work is in her diaries, which are preserved in the Archives of the Lutheran Church in America at the Lutheran School of Theology, Chicago.

86. Lani L. Johnson, *Led by the Spirit, a History of Lutheran Church Women* (Philadelphia: Lutheran Church Women, 1980), 18–19.

87. From a letter dated May 16, 1924, in the LCA Archives.

88. Meuser, "Twentieth Century," 369–70. See also David L. Vikner "LCA in World Mission 1842–1942," in *Background Papers to the Document —Call to Global Mission* (New York: DWME, 1982), 160.

89. Suelflow and Nelson, "Frontier," 197–98.

90. A thorough treatment of the LCA deaconess movement is contained in Frederick S. Weiser, *To Serve the Lord and His People* (Gladwyne, Pa.: Deaconess Community of the Lutheran Church in America, 1984).

91. Cecelia R. Wilson, "Sister Emma Francis, First Black Deaconess in American Lutheran History," *Illinois Lutheran,* (January–February 1986):5.

92. Suelflow and Nelson, "Frontier," 202–3. The 1984 LCA convention in Toronto was the last attended by delegates of the three Canadian synods which were about to join the new Lutheran church body in Canada. As a memento, the Canada Section presented the LCA with a statuette of Adam Keffer.

93. From *A Century of Life and Growth,* quoted in Daniel Nystrom, ed., *A Family of God* (Rock Island: Augustana Press, 1962), 1.

94. See G. Everett Arden, *Augustana Heritage* (Rock Island: Augustana Press, 1963), 2; and A. R. Wentz, *Basic History,* 194–95.

95. Oscar N. Olson, *The Augustana Lutheran Church in America* (Rock Island: Augustana Book Concern, 1950), 1–6. See also A. R. Wentz, *Basic History,* 194–95.

96. At one time it was estimated that sixteen different religious groups were competing for members among Swedish immigrants. (From an unpublished study by Martin E. Carlson at the University of Chicago Divinity School, 1943.)

97. Arden, *Augustana,* 17.

98. Ibid., 22–25.

99. In time, "The path to Illinois became a highway for multitudes of Swedes, and that State was to the Swedish immigration what Wisconsin was to the Norwegians." Kendric Charles Babcock, *The Scandinavian Element in the United States* (New York: Arno Press and the New York Times, 1969), 54. Chicago at one point had the third largest Swedish population of any city in the world. See ibid., 50.

100. The journey of Esbjörn's party is described more fully in Arden, *Augustana,* 27–32; Olson, *Augustana Church,* 48–55; and Suelflow and Nelson, "Frontier," 165–68.

101. Charlotte Odman, "The Mother of the Augustana Synod," in *A Family of God,* ed. Daniel Nystrom (Rock Island: Augustana Press, 1962), 141.

102. Arden, *Augustana,* 32–35. See also Olson, *Augustana Church,* 108.

103. Arden, *Augustana,* 36–37.

104. A. R. Wentz, *Basic History,* 130–31; Arden, *Augustana,* 38–43.

105. It should be noted that the Swedes were intensely interested in education in general. Illiteracy was almost unknown in Sweden by the end of the nineteenth century. This interest carried over into the New World. See Babcock, *Scandinavian Element,* 109–10.

106. Arden, *Augustana,* 51–59.

107. Ibid., 65.

108. Arden, *Augustana,* 68–70; Suelflow and Nelson, "Frontier," 191; Olson, *Augustana Church,* 279–85.

109. Arden, *Augustana,* 73.

110. See Conrad Bergendoff, "How the Augustana Church Came to Be," in *Augustana Annual* (Rock Island: Augustana Book Concern, 1960), 41–47; and Suelflow and Nelson, "Frontier," 191–92.

111. See Arden, *Augustana,* 71–94.

112. George M. Stephenson, "Religion," in *Swedes in America,* ed. Adolph B. Benson and Naboth Hedin (New Haven: Yale University Press, 1938), 131–32.

113. Ernst W. Olson, "Colleges," in ibid., 156–58.

114. Ibid., 158–61. See also Solberg, *Higher Education,* 187–88.

115. Arden, *Augustana,* 99, 101.

116. Ibid., 138.

117. Ibid., 139–42; and Suelflow and Nelson, "Frontier," 193.

118. A. R. Wentz, *Basic History*, 200–1.

119. Arden, *Augustana*, 153.

120. See *Minutes of the General Council, 1882*, 41.

121. Arden, *Augustana*, 158.

122. A. R. Wentz, *Basic History*, 204–5.

123. Quoted from Stephenson, *Religious Aspects of Swedish Immigration* (Minneapolis: 1932), by Arden, *Augustana*, 155.

124. Wolf, *Documents*, 280–81.

125. Arden, *Augustana*, 160. Arden gives a thorough account of the whole theological crisis in Augustana in his volume, pp. 160–88.

126. Fevold, "Coming of Age," 327.

127. Ibid., 328. See also Arden, *Augustana*, 188. Arden stated, "The events connected with the emergence of the Mission Friends movement in America constituted the greatest crisis ever faced by the Augustana Church. This experience had both a deleterious as well as a salutary effect upon the Synod." He regarded as salutary the clarification of Augustana's theology in a way that deepened its confessional consciousness and the fact that the controversy "served to purge the Synod of dissident elements."

128. Arden, *Augustana*, 193.

129. Fevold, "Coming of Age," 326.

130. Arden, *Augustana*, 194.

131. Arden, *Augustana*, 194–97; and A. D. Mattson, *Polity of the Augustana Synod* (Rock Island: Augustana Book Concern, 1941), 93–96.

132. Quoted in Arden, *Augustana*, 231.

133. Fevold, "Coming of Age," 260.

134. Meuser, "Twentieth Century," 367.

135. Burnice Fjellman, "Women in the Church," in *Centennial Essays*, ed. Emmer Engberg (Rock Island: Augustana Book Concern, 1961), 215.

136. G. A. Brandelle, "The Progress of the Augustana Synod," in *After 75 Years, 1860–1935* (Rock Island: Augustana Book Concern, 1936), 17–19.

137. See Arden, *Augustana*, 356–58.

138. See Nystrom, *Family of God*, 143–49.

139. Fjellman, "Women," 209–10.

140. Solberg, *Higher Education*, 177–204. Solberg gives an excellent summary of the history of Augustana institutions of higher education.

141. See Arden, *Augustana*, 106–10; and Nystrom, *Family of God*, 202–6.

142. Enok Mortensen, *The Danish Lutheran Church in America* (Philadelphia: Board of Publication, Lutheran Church in America, 1967), 19–20. Mortensen's book was commissioned in 1963 by the Danish Special Interest Conference of the LCA as the official history of the American Evangelical Lutheran Church.

143. Ibid., 21. Mortensen, of course, was speaking of a settlement on the North American mainland.

144. Tappert, "Church's Infancy," 4.

145. Paul C. Nyholm, *The Americanization of the Danish Lutheran Churches in America* (Copenhagen: Institute for Danish Church History, 1963), 67.

146. See Mortensen, *Danish Church,* 10.

147. Solberg, *Higher Education,* 249.

148. Babcock, *Scandinavian Element,* 63.

149. Quoted by Mortensen, *Danish Church,* 38, a brochure by R. Sørenson cited by P. S. Vig, *Danske i Amerika* (Minneapolis: 1908), 346.

150. Johannes Knudsen, "The Danish Lutheran Church in America," in Johannes Knudsen and Enok Mortensen, *The Danish-American Immigrant, Phases of His Religion and Culture* (Published by the authors, Grand View College, Des Moines, 1950), 6.

151. Ibid., 6.

152. Johannes Knudsen's *Danish Rebel* (Philadelphia: Muhlenberg Press, 1955) is a definitive biography and interpretation of Grundtvig.

153. Quoted by Mortensen, *Danish Church,* 11–12, from Grundtvig's book *Kirkespejlet* (The Church Mirror).

154. Ibid., 12.

155. See ibid., 13–16. See also Knudsen, "Danish Lutheran Church," 7.

156. See Mortensen, *Danish Church,* 15. "Inner Mission" in the Danish parlance referred to work within the homeland as contrasted with mission work overseas.

157. Fevold, "Coming of Age," 268.

158. Knudsen, "Danish Lutheran Church," 7. See also Mortensen, *Danish Church,* 16.

159. Mortensen, "Our Father's Church We Build," in Knudsen and Mortensen, *Danish-American Immigrant,* 5.

160. Knudsen, "Danish Lutheran Church," 8.

161. Mortensen provides a detailed account of this formative period in *Danish Church,* 28–48.

162. Nyholm, *Americanization,* 91–95.

163. Knudsen, "Danish Lutheran Church," 11.

164. Interview of Johannes H. V. Knudsen by Robert H. Fischer in *The Oral History Collection of the Archives of Cooperative Lutheranism* (New York: LCUSA), 1979, 25–26.

165. Mortensen, "Our Father's Church We Build," 9.

166. Ibid.

167. Mortensen, *Danish Church,* 91.

168. Ibid., 94–103. See also Solberg, *Higher Education,* 253–54.

169. Mortensen, *Danish Church,* 100.

170. Solberg, *Higher Education,* 254.

171. Mortensen, *Danish Church,* 116.

172. Ibid., 117.

173. Fevold, "Coming of Age," 269–71. There is speculation that the 1894 schism might never have occurred if the group that left the Norwegian-

Danish Conference had been willing to join the mainstream of Danish Lutheranism. See also Mortensen, *Danish Church*, 119.

174. Solberg, *Higher Education*, 254–56. See also Ernest D. Nielsen, "The Church's Concept of Grand View College Through the Years," in *The AELC, Phases of Its History and Heritage*, 26–35. See also Mortensen, *Danish Church*, 127–42.

175. Verner Hansen, "The Happy Danes," *ULCA Yearbook, 1962*, 25.

176. Fevold, "Coming of Age," 271.

177. Hansen, *ULCA Yearbook 1962*, 23. See also Babcock, *Scandinavian Element*, 63.

178. Nyholm, *Americanization*, 272–73.

179. Axel Kildegaard, "Those Happy Danes," in *America's Lutherans* (Columbus: Wartburg Press, 1958), 50.

180. Mortensen, *Danish Church*, 239–40.

181. Ibid., 240–41.

182. Interview with Knudsen, *The Oral History Collection*, LCUSA Archives, 1979, 30.

183. Mortensen, *Danish Church*, 220, 250, 254, 259.

184. Ibid., 254–55.

185. Interview with Knudsen, *The Oral History Collection*, LCUSA Archives, 1979, 29.

186. Mortensen, *Danish Church*, xiii.

187. Ibid., 162.

188. See *Annual Report* (of the Danish Evangelical Lutheran Church), 1902, 3. See also *Dannevirke*, July 17, 1912.

189. John H. Wuorinen, *The Finns on the Delaware 1638–1655* (New York: Columbia University Press, 1938), 9.

190. Ibid., 51.

191. Tappert, "Church's Infancy," 5.

192. Wuorinen, *Finns*, 57. Actually, the Finns had been invited to colonize an extensive wilderness area and granted the right to clear land by burning. Eventually, the land became significant for mining and population growth. See also Amandus Johnson, *The Swedes in America, 1638–1900* (Philadelphia: Lenape Press, 1914), 143–44.

193. Tappert, "Church's Infancy," 272. See also Jacob W. Heikkinen, *The Story of the Suomi Synod* (Published 1986), 5–7. This volume is the published history of the Suomi Synod commissioned by the (Suomi) Finnish Special Interest Conference of the Lutheran Church in America.

194. Reino Kero, "The Background of Finnish Emigration," in *The Finns in North America*, ed. Ralph J. Jalkanen (Hancock: Michigan State University Press, 1969), 59.

195. John Wargelin, *The Americanization of the Finns* (Hancock: Finnish Lutheran Book Concern, 1924), 54–68.

196. A. William Hoglund, *Finnish Immigrants in America* (Madison: University of Wisconsin Press, 1960), 187.

197. Eino Jutikkala, "Toward Independence: A Survey of the History of Finland to 1920," in *The Finns in North America,* ed. Jalkanen, 14–15.

198. Ibid., 15.

199. Carl E. Waisenen, "The Social Problems of the Finns in America," in *The Finns in North America,* ed. Jalkanen, 199–207.

200. Hoglund, *Immigrants,* 125.

201. Ibid., 123.

202. Tappert, "Church's Infancy," 273.

203. This practice is described in a series of letters by J. K. Nikander and other pioneer pastors in *Dear Uncle,* a translation from the Finnish by Raymond W. Wargelin (New York Mills, Minn.: Parta Printers, 1984).

204. Tappert, "Church's Infancy," 273. See also David T. Halkola, "Finnish-Language Newspapers in the United States," in *The Finns in North America,* ed. Jalkanen, 90.

205. Interview with Raymond W. Wargelin, *The Oral History Collection,* LCUSA Archives, 1983, 130–31. Wargelin, prior to his oral history interview, had prepared a lengthy audiotape recording detailing much of the Suomi Synod history. The transcript is included with the interview material.

206. Fevold, "Coming of Age," 274.

207. Douglas J. Ollila, Jr., "The Suomi Synod in Perspective," in *The Finns in North America,* ed. Jalkanen, 193.

208. Fevold, "Coming of Age," 275.

209. Arnold Stadius, "Suomi College and Seminary," in *The Finns in North America,* ed. Jalkanen, 101.

210. Interview with Raymond Wargelin, *The Oral History Collection,* LCUSA Archives, 1983, 135–36.

211. Stadius, "Suomi College and Seminary," 95.

212. Ibid., 96.

213. Ibid., 115.

214. Ibid., 103–8.

215. Ibid., 106.

216. Hoglund, *Immigrants,* 139.

217. Ibid., 142.

218. Interview with Raymond Wargelin, *The Oral History Collection,* LCUSA Archives, 1983, 153. See also Heikkinen, *Suomi Synod,* 213.

219. Interview with Raymond Wargelin, *The Oral History Collection,* LCUSA Archives, 1983, 154.

220. Ibid., 155–56. See also *ULCA Minutes, 1930,* 414–15; and *1932,* 44, 85.

221. Ibid., 157.

222. Taito A. Kantonen, "Finnish Theology on the American Scene," in *The Finns in North America,* ed. Jalkanen, 183.

223. Interview with Raymond Wargelin, *The Oral History Collection,* LCUSA Archives, 1983, 171.

224. Raymond W. Wargelin, the last president of the Suomi Synod, has completed a study of the contributions that Suomi pastors made to the LCA through the years until 1986 (Source, *Suomi-Synod Ministerium, 1876–1962,* manuscript in LCA Archives).

225. From a speech at St. Paul, Minnesota, September 9, 1919, quoted by Nystrom, *Family of God,* 35.

226. See Carl N. Degler, *Out of Our Past* (New York: Harper & Row, 1962), 290.

227. Horace M. Kallen, *Culture and Democracy in the United States* (New York: Boni and Liveright, 1924), 62–64, quoted in Nystrom, *Family of God,* 35.

Chapter 2 | # MOVING TOWARD MERGING

THE FORTY-FOUR YEARS FROM THE FORMA-
tion of the United Lutheran Church to the creation of the Lutheran
Church in America spanned a period of unprecedented change in
human history. It was a time of new mobility, from automotive travel
to jet airliners to the exploration of space. Warfare moved from
trenches and horse-drawn artillery to panzer divisions, massive
bombing raids, and the atomic age. Communication systems soon
advanced to include radio and television. Knowledge expanded at an
exponential rate, and the invention of the computer promised even
faster growth. The political scene shifted dramatically with the emergence of new world powers and the birth of new nations. Oppressed
peoples in many parts of the globe began to demand a role in their
own future. Traditional moral values were under attack, and basic
institutions such as the family began to unravel.

Writers in fields ranging from science to politics to religion detected in the deep-wrenching changes sweeping over society por-
tents of an even more unsettling future. In 1960 economist Robert
L. Heilbroner described the events which come at us daily as
"charged with surprise and shock. When we think back over the past
few years what strikes us is the suddenness of its blows, the unan-
nounced descent of its thunderbolts. Wars, revolutions, uprisings
have burst upon us with terrible rapidity. Advances of science and
technology have rewritten the very terms and conditions of the
human contract with no more warning than the morning's headlines, but seem to have done so behind our backs, while we were
not looking. These recurring shocks of contemporary history throw
a pall of chronic apprehension over our times. . . . All conspire to
make of our encounter with history a frightening and disorienting
ordeal."[1]

PREDECESSOR BODIES OF THE LUTHERAN CHURCH IN AMERICA

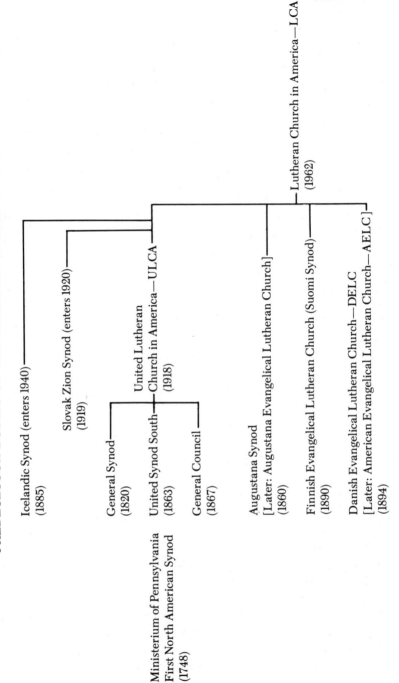

Icelandic Synod (enters 1940)
(1885)

Slovak Zion Synod (enters 1920)
(1919)

United Lutheran
Church in America—ULCA
(1918)

General Synod
(1820)

United Synod South
(1863)

General Council
(1867)

Ministerium of Pennsylvania
First North American Synod
(1748)

Augustana Synod
[Later: Augustana Evangelical Lutheran Church]
(1860)

Finnish Evangelical Lutheran Church (Suomi Synod)
(1890)

Danish Evangelical Lutheran Church—DELC
[Later: American Evangelical Lutheran Church—AELC]
(1894)

Lutheran Church in America—LCA
(1962)

The church, of course, was not immune to the shifting currents around it. In his *A Religious History of the American People,* Sidney Ahlstrom gives a thorough analysis of the interplay of religious and societal forces during the four decades with which we are concerned here. Ahlstrom suggests that the period itself can be divided for the purpose of discussion into three segments: "The Twenties: From Armistice to the Crash," "The Thirties: From the Crash to Pearl Harbor," and "World War II and the Postwar Revival."[2] Although it is not possible to do more than allude to the historic happenings in these decades that form the background of our own story, it will be helpful to use similar categories in examining the events leading up to the birth of the LCA.

FROM WAR TO DEPRESSION

World War I had been by virtually every measure the most widespread and costly in history. About sixty-five million persons had been mobilized; thirteen million, killed; twenty-two million, wounded; and seven million, permanently disabled. It is estimated that at least as many civilians as military died from causes such as disease and starvation, raids and massacres. Economic losses and the long-term results in society were incalculable.[3]

Britain seemingly emerged from World War I as a dominant force in the world, but there already were signs that its colonial empire was heading for decline. Germany, weighed down by reparation demands and overwhelming inflation, was sliding toward revolution in its political and social structures. Russia, wracked by its own revolution, was slowly shaping itself into a force that would eventually make it one of the two leading powers in the world. The United States seemed to have retreated into a posture of isolation that could not long be maintained. Meanwhile, in the Far East, Japan was emerging as a new power with colonial ambitions.

The twenties were a time of abrupt economic shifts. After a brief postwar recession, there followed a period of fragile economic growth and unwarranted optimism. Then came the crash which plunged the world into the Great Depression. Relentlessly, the stage was being set for another terrible war, the greatest the world had ever known.

THE LUTHERAN CHURCH IN THE TWENTIES

During World War I, almost all Lutheran bodies in the United States joined forces in the National Lutheran Commission for Soldiers' and Sailors' Welfare to minister to service personnel and deal with government agencies.[4] The success of this cooperative effort seemed to surprise most Lutherans and make them aware of their combined strength. Frederick H. Knubel, who chaired the commission, foresaw that there were other urgent needs that went beyond the commission's authority that required concerted action.[5] These included representation in Washington to counter efforts to ban the use of German even in worship, the need for new missions in booming communities near defense industries, and the probability that Lutherans in postwar Europe would be in desperate need of assistance.[6]

Knubel and T. E. Schmauk, president of the General Council, issued invitations to meet in Harrisburg, Pennsylvania, on July 17, 1918, ostensibly to follow through on an earlier suggestion that a "national council or committee representing the entire Lutheran Church as far as possible" be formed. Events moved quickly, and on September 6 representatives of the General Synod, the General Council, the Joint Synod of Ohio, Synod of Iowa and Other States, the Augustana Synod, the Norwegian Lutheran Church, the Norwegian Lutheran Free Church, and the Danish Lutheran Church met in Chicago to deal with specific proposals (the United Synod, South sent a letter indicating its great interest). The church presidents "took action—without waiting for the approval of their church bodies—to establish the National Lutheran Council."[7]

The purposes for the new organization included (1) gathering uniform statistical information about Lutheran church bodies; (2) providing publicity particularly when the churches spoke together on an issue; (3) representing the churches in relationships with outside entities and informing the constituency about specific needs; (4) dealing with or creating agencies to deal with problems arising from war or other emergencies; (5) coordinating activities and agencies of the churches to deal with problems arising from social, economic, intellectual, or other developments affecting religious life; (6) fostering Christian loyalty and maintaining a proper relationship between church and state with correlated but distinct functions.[8] Interestingly, the original wording used "Lutheran Church" in the singular in stating purposes, although the council was not thought of as synon-

Frederick H. Knubel

ymous with a church. At the same time, it was made clear that nothing was to compromise the confessional position of any member body.

One of the first practical tasks which faced the Council was relief work among European Lutherans who were suffering from the devastating aftershocks of World War I. Since regular budgets of the church bodies were so meager, a special appeal for $500,000 was launched in 1919 and another for $1,800,000 in 1920. One of the most poignant messages came in the form of a poster that showed a mother, child in arms, seated in the ruins of their home. Below were the words "Tired of Giving? You don't know what it is to be tired."[9]

The Council sent J. A. Morehead, who was on leave from the presidency of Roanoke College, to Europe in 1920 to administer its relief work. At first, relief efforts were directed mostly to Lutherans in Poland, France, and Germany. After the terrible winter of 1921–22, however, the Council expanded its work to try to help the four million Lutherans in Russia. All in all, the Council spent nearly eight million dollars and collected thousands of tons of clothing and food for relief in its first decade—an impressive accomplishment when translated into present-day economic terms.[10] Gradually, however, as the flush of success in these cooperative efforts faded, American Lutherans like other churches became weary with this kind of well-doing. Even their leaders' attention began to focus on other pressing matters. The satisfying overseas effort did have a salutary effect within the Council itself during its early rocky years. Frederick K. Wentz concludes, "Without this overseas program the NLC would have expired in its infancy."[11]

Tensions Within the National Lutheran Council

The United Lutheran Church from its inception had been identified with "Eastern Lutheranism." This concept, in the minds of midwesterners, carried with it the stigma of liberalism and the suspicion of not being fully committed to doctrinal purity. Most midwestern churches in the Council, therefore, often leaned toward the conservatism of Missouri and the Synodical Conference but at the same time were willing to work with the ULCA in practical matters. The midwestern bodies wanted the Council's work limited to *res externae* (external matters) rather than *res internae* (internal matters). Their intention was to make limited cooperation possible without requiring agreement on all doctrinal points. The ULCA's position, as stated by Knubel, was that this was an improper use of terms from the Lutheran Confessions. He insisted on scriptural grounds that "there are no *res externae* in the life of the Christian and the Church."[12]

One issue that precipitated an early crisis revolved around whether the churches in the Council recognized one another's ministries so that comity arrangements could be worked out in home missions. According to Fred W. Meuser, "The United Lutheran Church was ready. The Norwegians and the Midwestern Germans were not, at least not without further checking into the position of the United Lutheran Church on questions they considered crucial."[13] Although the ULCA was unhappy about the implications, it agreed to participate in a "Joint Committee to confer on questions of doctrine and practice, with a view to coordination of their home mission and other work."[14] H. G. Stub, president of the Norwegian Lutheran Church of America, had made the proposal through a fear of unionism "because joint home mission work was hardly cooperation in 'externals.' "[15]

Four papers had been commissioned for presentation at a meeting of the committee in March 1919 to set forth the views of the United Lutheran Church, the Norwegian Lutheran Church, and the Ohio and Iowa Synods. In addition, Knubel was asked to prepare a paper on "The Essentials of the Catholic Spirit in the Church." The paper read by Stub, of the NLCA, was made the subject of discussion, while time pressure made it necessary to delay discussion of Knubel's paper as well as one on "Constructive Lutheranism" by Henry Eyster Jacobs of the ULCA until the next meeting.[16]

Stub's paper, which became known as the "Chicago Theses," set forth a position which E. Clifford Nelson terms "exclusive confessionalism" that was representative of Midwest Lutheranism.[17] It stressed that the Old and New Testaments were "the inspired and inerrant Word of God,"[18] a phrase that was to become a crucial issue in Lutheran unity discussions for decades. In addition, it regarded as a matter of principle that Lutherans would worship in their own churches, avoid pulpit and altar fellowship with non-Lutherans, and not hold membership in societies that had "religious exercises, from which the name of the triune God or the name of Jesus . . . is excluded, or which teaches salvation through works."[19] Knubel and Jacobs objected to this exclusivism, but the theses were applauded as excellent by Missouri's official journal, *Lehre und Wehre*.[20] "As far as the Chicago Theses were concerned," Meuser points out, "the Mid-western synods hoped they might become official statements of all the consulting bodies. However, because they knew that the United Lutheran Church was opposed in principle to making full coopera-tion dependent upon new statements of doctrinal agreement, they did not press for official adoption in their own churches. They re-ceived official status only when the Minneapolis Theses (1925), of which they became a part, were adopted by most of the Midwestern synods later in the decade."[21]

At the conclusion of the March 1919 meeting, a committee com-posed of Knubel, Stub, and Schmauk was requested to review the paper on the "catholic spirit" and report at a later meeting of the full committee on doctrine and practice. When Schmauk became criti-cally ill, his place was taken by Charles M. Jacobs, a professor at the Lutheran Seminary in Philadelphia. Jacobs wrote the final draft of the report which Knubel supported and Stub did not.[22] The report was discussed at a conference in Chicago, March 11–12, 1920. The point of view taken in the paper was one of "ecumenical confession-alism"[23] that stressed the catholic nature of the Lutheran Confes-sions. Despite Knubel's and Jacobs' urgings that the guidance given by the paper was needed in the many interchurch situations that were emerging, the committee adjourned without approving "The Essentials of the Catholic Spirit." The Joint Committee on Doctrine and Practice was allowed to expire quietly. It was clear that two theological positions would have to exist side by side in the National Lutheran Council if its other major purposes were to be achieved.[24]

Drawing Lines—Forming Alliances

While the cessation of the conferences on doctrine and practice in a sense moved the arena of discussion outside of the National Lu-theran Council, the process of clarifying the positions of the midwest-ern synods and the United Lutheran Church continued unabated. What occurred in the next decade was important not only for the total spectrum of Lutheranism in North America but also specifically for those groups that would later form the Lutheran Church in America.

The United Lutheran Church had not been dissuaded by events from its concern for a statement on church relations. At its second biennial convention in Washington, October 1920, the ULCA adopt-ed unanimously a "Declaration of Principles Concerning the Church and Its External Relations" that reproduced the Knubel-Jacobs document almost in its entirety.[25] The declaration began with a description of the church as one, holy, catholic, and apostolic, and emphasized the definition in the Augsburg Confession that the church is present wherever "the Gospel is rightly taught and the Sacraments are rightly administered." It asserted that it is the responsibility of every group of Christians calling itself a church to describe its relationships with other churches in the spirit of catholicity:

1. To declare unequivocally what it believes concerning Christ and His Gospel, and to endeavor to show that it has placed the true interpretation upon that Gospel and to testify definitely and frankly against error.

2. To approach others without hostility, jealousy, suspicion or pride, in the sincere and humble desire to give and receive Christian service.

3. To grant cordial recognition of all agreements which are discovered between its own interpretation of the Gospel and that which others hold.

4. To cooperate with other Christians in works of serving love . . . insofar as this can be done without surrender of its interpretation of the Gospel, without denial of conviction, and without suppression of its testimony as to what it holds to be the truth.[26]

The declaration goes on to reiterate the position in the ULCA Constitution about seeing no doctrinal barrier to complete cooperation and organic union with other bodies which accept the Lutheran Confessions. It also defines prerequisites for organic union with other Protestant churches as well as for participation in cooperative movements with other Protestant bodies. Finally, it warns against movements and organizations injurious to the Christian faith. This section addresses the much-disputed matter of "lodges" or "secret societies" in terms of "doctrines and principles" which contradict basic Christian truths.

As Charles M. Jacobs, one of the authors, pointed out, there had been serious problems in the past because there had been no such statement of principles among American Lutherans. "Unless the principles are defined," he declared, "the policy of the Church will be dictated by something else than principle—by sentiment, by prejudice, by consideration of ecclesiastical politics and diplomacy. In other words, the Church is almost sure to embark on a career of opportunism. In politics opportunism is a weakness; in the Church it is a sin."[27] Although not all ULCA leaders would have used Jacobs' language in expressing their views, they voted for a clearly ecumenical stance at the 1920 convention. Known generally as "The Washington Declaration," the statement became the policy to which the ULCA adhered throughout its life in relationships with other church bodies and organizations.

Meanwhile, the midwestern Lutherans were beginning to articulate what they hoped would be a "middle ground" between the ULCA and the strongly conservative Synodical Conference.[28] It must be remembered that this was the time of bitter battles between Fundamentalists and Modernists, climaxed by the spectacle of the Scopes trial that dealt with teaching evolution in the public schools.[29] While Lutherans had always been deeply concerned about the place of the Scriptures in the life of the church, they did not participate directly in the Fundamentalist-Modernist battle.[30] They could hardly have been oblivious, however, to what was going on around them. Just what was meant by "biblical inerrancy," therefore, assumed a new urgency for definition.

Although the leaders of the Norwegian Lutheran Church, Ohio Synod, Iowa Synod, and Augustana had agreed as early as 1920 to seek closer relationships among their synods, it was not until 1925 that first steps were taken in this direction by convening a colloquy in Minneapolis. Augustana was not represented at the colloquy, but the Buffalo Synod was. The main product of the conference was the Minneapolis Theses, which were intended not only as the basis for cooperation but also, in Meuser's view, "at key points as a witness against the United Lutheran Church."[31]

The very first affirmation of the theses was that the signatories accepted "without exception all the canonical books of the Old and New Testaments as a whole, and in all their parts, as the divinely inspired, revealed, and inerrant Word of God."[32] The Lutheran symbols were also to be accepted without reservation and without "exception or limitation in all articles and parts, no matter whether a doctrine is specifically cited as a confession or incidentally introduced for the purpose of elucidating or proving some other doctrine."[33] Although it was acknowledged that there are Christians in every denomination, church fellowship which ignored doctrinal differences was rejected as "unionism, pretense of union that does not exist."[34] On the lodge question, it was agreed that pastors who belonged to any anti-Christian society could not be tolerated. The synods which accepted the theses were to "recognize each other as truly Lutheran" and could enter into pulpit and altar fellowship with one another.

There were two major organizational entities related to the Minneapolis Theses. One was the American Lutheran Church; the other, the American Lutheran Conference.[35]

The American Lutheran Church came into being in 1930 as a result of lengthy negotiations among the Joint Synod of Ohio, the Iowa Synod, and the Buffalo Synod. Once more the question of defining inerrancy was a sticking point. In fact, the merger was almost aborted by an Iowa Synod action to separate the key words "inspired and inerrant" in the constitution.[36] The theological leader of Iowa, J. Michael Reu, had opposed this section of the Minneapolis Theses on which the constitution was based. As E. Clifford Nelson points out, "After two years of controversy, an official 'Appendix' interpreting the constitutional article on Scripture was approved. This action placed the new church in the position of affirming inerrancy of 'the original texts' and recognized the present Bible 'as substantially identical with the original texts and as the only inspired and inerrant authority. . . .' "[37] With this hurdle surmounted, the merger took place August 11, 1930.

The American Lutheran Conference was created also in 1930 as a federation rather than a merged church. In addition to the newly formed ALC, it included the Norwegian Lutheran Church, Lutheran Free Church, United Danish Lutheran Church, and Augustana. The Conference was aimed at mutual counsel concerning the faith, life, and work of the church, and cooperation in such matters as allocation of home mission fields, elementary and higher Christian education, inner mission work, student work in state schools, foreign missions, joint publishing, and exchange of professors among seminaries.[38] Not all of these purposes were achieved, but the Conference did provide an arena during its twenty-four-year existence where churches with a wide variety of languages and traditions learned to know one another and work closely together.[39]

According to Abdel Ross Wentz, however, "The distinctive mission of the American Lutheran Conference is not easy to find. The secretary of the Conference once said that the new movement was originally 'conceived as largely a defensive alliance, created for the purpose of protecting its members against possible aggression by the

United Lutheran Church and the Synodical Conference.' "[40] In light of this intention by most of the members of the Conference, Augustana's position was an interesting one. Although it had affirmed the Minneapolis Theses, Augustana's Committee on Church Unity was busily at work with a similar group from the ULCA aimed at closer cooperation between these two churches. In G. Everett Arden's judgment, "The endeavor to face, as it were, in two directions at once was perhaps ingenuous and naive, but even in these early stages of inter-Lutheran relationships, Augustana assayed the role of intermediary, hoping to become a bridge across which rapprochement between 'exclusive confessionalism' and 'ecumenical confessionalism' might be achieved."[41] This "bridge" stance on the part of Augustana was an important factor as various steps were taken that led in time toward formation of the Lutheran Church in America.

FROM DEPRESSION TO WAR

In retrospect, the Great Depression that smashed the economies of North America and Europe in the 1930s can be recognized as the result of forces at work for a decade. The settlements imposed on Germany and the other central powers after World War I were crushing burdens that could not be endured. The seeming prosperity in the United States and the allied countries was unsustainable. Ironically, few people paid much attention to the fact that by the mid-twenties a depression was already under way among American farmers, who were caught in a price squeeze and were going bankrupt by the thousands.[42] Speculators continued to bid up prices of equities as though the upward spiral would continue forever, but on October 24, 1929, the New York Stock Market collapsed. Thirteen million shares, a huge sum for those times, were dumped on the market in one day.[43] Paper fortunes were lost, and people at last realized that something was terribly wrong with the economy.

As historian Sydney Ahlstrom describes the times, "The Crash came as a shock to many Americans—like a 'firebell in the night' to denizens of an allegedly fireproof building. . . . But there was no mistaking the Great Depression as actuality. . . . The national income dropped from $83 billion in 1929 to $40 billion in 1932, while the number of unemployed began to approach fifteen million in 1933."[44] People who lived through the suffering of those days find it virtually impossible to communicate the horror of the experience or why they still bear deep psychological scars. Some contradictions in the ability to cope with needs seemed bizarre but, unfortunately, still have their global parallels today. There was abundant food around, but literally millions faced starvation; warehouses full of clothing while many were ill-clad; countless empty houses while people existed in squatters shacks.[45] The government seemed paralyzed by events.

In November 1932 the Democratic party was swept into power. Within a period of one hundred days after his inauguration in 1933, President Franklin Delano Roosevelt sent fifteen major messages to Congress and pushed through a series of measures that changed dramatically and irrevocably the role of government in dealing with social and economic problems.[46] A beginning had been made, but the way back to economic health would be long and painful.

The year 1933 was a decisive one in Europe as well, for it was then that Adolf Hitler came to power and Germany became a Nazi state. Building a strong industrial base and a modern military machine, he extended German control to the demilitarized Rhineland and Austria. Internal opposition was suppressed, and Western powers, such as England and France, intimidated. Jews were shipped off to concentration camps, and eventually six million were exterminated in the Holocaust. In September 1935 Hitler declared that the Nazi state held supremacy over the Evangelical (Protestant) Church. "The Reich Bishop was shorn of his authority. . . . In 1937 it was made a crime to contribute money to the Confessional Synod or any other church group not approved by the minister of church affairs."[47]

In spite of nonaggression pacts, Hitler's armies invaded Poland on September 1, 1939. Two days later Great Britain and France declared war. Only twenty-five years and one month after the outbreak of the First World War, Europe plunged into the Second World War.[48] Russia took the opportunity to seize Eastern Poland and later invaded Finland before Germany at last turned its forces against the Soviets. Italy delayed declaring war until France was prostrate. Japan, which had long since seized Manchuria and was pushing through China, had already made the conflict global by siding with Germany.

Canada, of course, had been drawn into the war on the side of the Allies,[49] but the United States was at first ostensibly neutral, although it had begun to rebuild its military forces and assisted Britain through a "Lend-Lease" program. "Then on Sunday, 7 December, 1941, a Japanese decision brought America's indecision to an end." Ahlstrom writes, "The New York Philharmonic Symphony's broadcast of Schubert's *Unfinished Symphony* was interrupted by the solemn announcement that Pearl Harbor had been treacherously attacked. America was at war—and the Depression decade passed into history."[50]

The Lutheran Church in the Depression

For the Lutheran church bodies, however, the Depression years had been a time of severe testing that left them ill-prepared in many ways to meet the strains that would come with another war. Congregations that had overbuilt during boom times were suddenly confronted with unmanageable debt burdens. Some even resorted to withholding contributions that had been given for benevolence.[51] One by-product of the financial crunch was that churches were forced to centralize many functions that had been more widely dispersed. For example, President P. O. Bersell moved in 1935 to make Minneapolis the administrative center of the Augustana Synod.[52]

Cost cutting at all levels, while painful, did bring some benefits. For example, the ULCA, which had been burdened with thirteen seminaries at merger, reduced the number to ten. The loss of members in many mainline denominations led to the view that there had been a depression in religion as well as in the economic area. The larger Lutheran bodies, such as Augustana and the ULCA, however, managed to sustain a slow if not spectacular growth throughout the thirties.[53]

Perhaps the most dramatic development was the effort of the churches to alleviate human suffering. The thirties brought to a focus the sluggish movement of Lutherans toward involvement in social issues. As Abdel Ross Wentz has pointed out in a chapter on "Lutherans Discover the Human Race," it was not until well into the twentieth century that Lutheran leaders had "anything to say about the industrial and economic situations that produced the major social problems of the time. . . . Their emphasis was upon the regeneration of the individual soul. Sin and evil referred to theology and there was no social ethics. Their reliance was mainly upon institutions of mercy and human repair."[54]

Ambrose Hering, superintendent of the Lutheran Inner Mission Society of New York, was one of the first Lutherans to see not only the need for direct relief work by the churches but also a different kind of social consciousness. "The planned society which this period of business upheaval will unquestionably usher in," he said, "will need the highest religious idealism. Unrestrained individualism and class privilege must be replaced by an inclusive brotherhood and . . . zest for the common welfare."[55]

The situation led the Lutheran bodies to work more closely together in such areas as home missions because of the sheer waste of uncontrolled ecclesiastical competition. In addition, although the National Lutheran Council was severely limited by budget shortages, it did set up a Committee on Social Trends in 1933, made a survey of the hodgepodge of three hundred inner mission agencies, and in 1938 created a Department of Welfare to coordinate this crucial work.[56]

Trying Again for Unity

Although the United Lutheran Church was still smarting from the formation of the American Lutheran Conference as a counterpoise to it in the NLC, it made another overture toward Lutheran unity at its 1934 convention. Known as the "Savannah Declaration," this statement reiterated the position that the fact that the various Lutheran bodies all subscribed to the same Confessions provided "a firm basis on which to unite in one Lutheran Church in America and that there is no doctrinal reason why such a union should not come to pass."[57] The Savannah convention went on to direct President Knubel to invite all the other bodies "to confer with us with a view to establishment of closer relationships between them and ourselves."[58] Both the Missouri Synod and the American Lutheran Church accepted the invitation to meet for conversations.

Two meetings with Missouri simply served to harden the lines of separation between it and the ULCA. Missouri rested its position on the 1932 "Brief Statement" which declared that the Scriptures were verbally inspired and "that they contain no errors or contradictions, but they are in all their parts and words the infallible truth, also in those parts which treat of historical, geographical, and other secular matters."[59] The United Lutheran Church position "saw the Scriptures as the human instrument whereby God communicated his Word, the gospel. Moreover, Christ was seen as the Word because he is God's gospel or message to men."[60] *The Lutheran Witness*, official organ of Missouri, promptly published an editorial accusing the ULCA of denying that the Bible is the Word of God.[61] When the committee met again in 1938, it was obvious that further efforts were futile. Following this session, Missouri took an action indicating willingness to continue discussions but stating, "These negotiations must not be interpreted as implying that the Synod has changed its position in any of the doctrines discussed or that we are approaching doctrinal agreement with the U.L.C.A."[62] There were no more meetings.

Discussions between the ALC and the ULCA went on for nearly four years but fared little better than those with Missouri. The ULCA's objective was organic union; ALC hoped for no more than pulpit and altar fellowship. In the end, neither goal was realized.[63] At the first meeting in February 1936, President C. C. Hein of the ALC proposed that the Minneapolis Theses be the basis of discussion. Knubel objected, feeling that this would prevent any real progress. A compromise was reached in which it was agreed to concentrate on the issues of lodge membership by clergy, inspiration of the Scriptures, fellowship with non-Lutherans, and ecclesiastical discipline.

The crucial sticking point again proved to be the view of the Scriptures. The ALC reiterated its concept of inerrancy; the ULCA urged a Christocentric view. Papers and prolonged debates at several meetings brought no real solution. Finally, it was agreed that each commission would report to its own convention in 1938. Each convention in turn adopted a statement which underscored the position of its own commissioners.[64]

The ULCA statement, known as "The Baltimore Declaration," was essentially the position paper prepared by C. M. Jacobs for the discussions with ALC. The Declaration stated forthrightly that "the only rule and standard, according to which all dogmas and teachers are to be judged, are nothing else than the prophetic and apostolic Scriptures of the Old and New Testaments."[65] It went on to state that the authority of the Scriptures comes from the fact that they are the Word of God. The term "Word of God," however, is used in more than one way in the Confessions and the Scriptures themselves. "In its most real sense, the Word of God is the Gospel, *i.e.*, the message concerning Jesus Christ. . . . In and through this Gospel the Holy Spirit comes to men, awakening and strengthening their faith, and leading them into lives of holiness."[66] In a wider sense the Word of God is his self-revelation that reaches its fullness and completion in the life and work of Jesus Christ. "The whole revelation of God to men which reached completion in Christ . . . is faithfully recorded and preserved in the Holy Scriptures, through which alone it comes to us. We therefore accept the Scriptures as the infallible truth of God in all matters that pertain to His revelation and our salvation."[67]

The statement continued by explaining in precise language that the Scriptures are a unity centering in Christ, and although they have "their more important and their less important parts . . . the whole body of Scripture in all its parts is the Word of God . . . inspired by God."[68] Although the Declaration did not define the mode of inspiration, it affirmed that the Scriptures are the spring from which God's saving power flows, the only source of doctrine, and the only rule and norm for Christian faith and life. The complete statement became the formulation of the ULCA's position on the Scriptures that would be both a source of difference with as well as a basis for negotiation with other Lutheran bodies in the future.

Meanwhile, at its 1938 convention the American Lutheran Church had issued its own statement known as "The Sandusky Declaration." Based on Reu's earlier paper, it was intended to summarize a number of different points that had been covered in conversations with the Missouri Synod and, therefore, included items other than the one on "Scripture and Inspiration." The declaration was consistent with the Minneapolis Theses and stated that "by virtue of inspiration, i.e., the unique operation of the Holy Spirit by which He supplied to the Holy writers contents and fitting word . . . the separate books of the Bible constitute an organic whole without contradiction or error."[69] ALC had hoped that this total statement would lead to fellowship with the Missouri Synod, but this did not happen; nor did it help to bridge the gulf between ALC and the United Lutheran Church.[70]

The last act of the drama of ALC and ULCA came in the drafting of "The Pittsburgh Agreement" in 1939. Knubel, eager to see something come of all the years of discussion, agreed to the compromise wording "the separate books of the Bible are related to one another, and taken together, constitute a complete, errorless, unbreakable whole of which Christ is the center."[71] Reu wanted to know if this went beyond the Baltimore Declaration, and Knubel said that he believed it did.[72] The hoped-for agreement resulted in a storm of protest in the ULCA. Herbert Alleman, Old Testament professor at Gettysburg Seminary, wrote a lengthy critique in *The Lutheran Church Quarterly* in which he said, "The Articles constitute what is called the Pittsburgh *Agreement.* They had better be called the Pittsburgh *Disagreement. . . .* We are not one in this matter, and it is hypocrisy to deny it."[73]

When the document was presented to the 1940 ULCA convention, strong opposition developed from those delegates who felt that the church's position had been compromised too much. Among those who spoke against the agreement was a young pastor from Akron, Ohio, Franklin Clark Fry, who was destined to become president four years later. The convention finally adopted the statement but added the proviso that it was to be understood in light of the Washington Declaration (1920), the Savannah Declaration (1934), and the Baltimore Declaration (1938), and not the other way around.[74] Even though ALC also approved the Pittsburgh articles, it did not declare pulpit and altar fellowship with the ULCA. There the matter would rest for a long while as ALC turned more toward Missouri and the Norwegian Lutheran Church.[75]

In the background of all that had happened, it should be recognized that significant trends in biblical and theological thought were underway in both the United Lutheran Church and the Augustana Synod. In the ULCA, a generation of seminarians had studied under such men as C. M. Jacobs and Henry Offermann at Philadelphia, E. E. Flack at Hamma, and A. R. Wentz, Raymond T. Stamm, and H. C. Alleman at Gettysburg, all of whom held a Christocentric view of the Scriptures that was open to higher criticism.[76] Something of the same was occurring at Augustana Seminary, where the death or retirement of some of the old guard faculty members opened the way for such forward-looking thinkers as Conrad Bergendoff, A. D. Mattson, and Eric H. Wahlstrom.[77] These developments helped to lay the groundwork for greater rapport between the United Lutheran Church and Augustana in the years that lay ahead.

GLOBAL CONFLICT—GLOBAL CHANGE

At the time, World War I had seemed to show the ultimate lengths to which humanity could go in inflicting death and destruction. World War II, however, eclipsed those horrors with massed air raids on civilian targets that reduced whole cities to rubble, systematic genocide waged by the Nazis against six million Jews, and the incredible carnage wrought when an atomic bomb was dropped on Hiroshima, August 6, 1945, and three days later when a second bomb fell on Nagasaki.

The end of hostilities came swiftly at the last in both Europe and Asia. Before his reported suicide in a Berlin bunker on May 1, Adolf

Hitler named Grand Admiral Karl Doenitz his successor.[78] Six days later, an emissary of Doenitz surrendered all of the forces of the Third Reich in a little schoolhouse at Reims.[79] Two days after the first atomic bomb was dropped, the Soviet Union, which had maintained neutrality in the Pacific, declared war on Japan. On August 10 the Japanese sued for peace through the Swiss and Swedish governments, and the formal surrender was signed on the battleship *Missouri* in Tokyo harbor on September 2, 1945. As Walter Langsam points out, "Six years and a day had elapsed since the outbreak of the bloodiest and costliest war in history."[80]

The task of rebuilding a shattered world was awesome. A report by the United Nations Relief and Rehabilitation Administration estimated in 1944 that a half billion people in thirty-five countries in Europe and Asia were under the Axis Powers' yoke and were facing semistarvation. In Europe alone there were some thirty million displaced persons. It was estimated that one million French were in Germany at the war's end and that it would take one train every hour, every day for eight months just to move that number.[81]

Dramatic changes in leadership occurred during the final months of the war. Roosevelt died suddenly and was succeeded by Harry Truman as president. Winston Churchill, who had led Britain throughout the war, was ousted as prime minister in a Labor Party victory that brought Clement Attlee into office.

Peace was soon supplanted by the Cold War between the United States and Russia. Most of Eastern Europe was swept into the Soviet camp. The world map was being redrawn as the colonial strength of Britain and France began to crumble. Communist armies were on the march in China, and in a few years, Chiang Kai-shek's government collapsed and moved its headquarters to the island of Taiwan. The United States and its allies were embroiled once again in an Asian conflict when North Korean troops invaded South Korea on June 25, 1950.[82] An uneasy truce was finally negotiated in Korea in 1953 after Dwight D. Eisenhower became president of the United States.

Other deep changes were occurring in the fabric of North American society. Following two decades of depression in the United States, the postwar years brought new affluence. In Sydney Ahlstrom's words, "Along with these economic changes came an equally momentous transformation in the balance, structure, and dynamics of American life. By 1950 two-thirds of the American population had moved into metropolitan regions. In a great crescendo of migration, Negroes and Puerto Ricans moved into the inner cities. Orchards, woods, and open fields yielded to the bulldozer to accommodate an expansion of suburban population that was three times greater than that of the central cities."[83]

Revival or "Religion in General"?

As so often is the case, war once again produced a resurgence of interest in religion in the United States and Canada. This "revival," however, seemed qualitatively different from those surges of spiritual reawakening that had been characteristic in the past. Martin Marty, writing in the late 1950s, declared, "The present revival has brought with it some highly novel features which do not conform to the pattern of the past. For one thing, as a nation we are reaching a point of near-saturation as far as religious interest goes. And the religion is largely so inoffensive that the pendulum of reaction is not likely to swing very far. . . . For this is an utterly new thing: a revival that goes not against the grain of the nation but with it; a revival that draws its strength from its safe residence in the mores of the nation."[84]

The fact that this phenomenon was often branded as "shallow" did not alter the fact that it had to be taken seriously as a shift towards what Marty called a "maturing national religion."[85] In Ahlstrom's view, it was a "new form of patriotic piety that was closely linked to the 'cold war.' . . . There seemed to be a consensus that personal religious faith was an essential element in proper patriotic commitment. In all of these modes, religion and Americanism were brought together to an unusual degree."[86] As Marty so rightly foresaw, this *religion-in-general* signaled the beginning of a post-Protestant era. "The religious complex which has the most to lose in this process," he wrote, "is Protestantism, because Protestantism had the greatest investment in the religious situation that has lately been supplanted."[87]

On the surface, of course, the churches seemed to be flourishing. Membership figures surged. Sunday schools were packed with children of the postwar baby boom and often had to go to two or even three sessions to accommodate the numbers. Freed from prewar debt, many congregations entered upon extensive building programs. New congregations were established rapidly in the expanding suburbs.[88] Some denominations began to be apprehensive about the decline in inner-city congregations, however, and slowly recognized the urgency of ministering to nonwhites who were moving into these areas.[89]

The fragility of the new religiosity, however, became all too apparent. "Yet with new multitudes entering their portals, almost unbidden, the churches muffed their chance," Ahlstrom explains. "Put more analytically, the so-called revival led to a sacrifice of theological substance, which in the face of the harsh new social and spiritual realities of the 1960's left both clergy and laity demoralized and confused. A loss of confidence occurred. Quantifiable aspects of the situation (church membership, attendance, and giving; seminary enrollments; demissions from the clergy, etc.) began to register decline. Thinkers who for some years—or decades—had been speaking of the 'death of God' and of a 'post-Christian era' began to be heard. Forces of cultural change, subtle, pervasive, and ineluctable—far less tangible than wars, depressions, and political campaigns—were altering the moral and religious ethos."[90]

The Lutherans and the Times

It was against the background of these shifts in society, the political sphere, and the religious climate that the Lutheran churches themselves were undergoing major changes that would lead within two decades to major realignments and mergers. The earlier tendency to concentrate home mission work on their own linguistic group, so characteristic of midwestern Lutheran bodies particularly, changed dramatically after the war. Lutherans began new missions with enthusiasm. According to Nelson, "At its peak the mission program produced one new congregation every 54 hours!"[91] Even though the Lutheran churches were not impervious to some of the undesirable aspects of the fifties revival, their efforts at evangelism were based firmly upon a doctrinal and catechetical emphasis.[92]

There were significant shifts among the leaders who had guided the churches through the tortuous paths since World War I. In 1944 Frederick H. Knubel, the only president the ULCA had known, was badly weakened by a series of small strokes and was doubtful about continuing to serve.[93] The convention, perhaps recognizing the situation, elected Franklin Clark Fry, a young pastor from Akron, Ohio, its president on the fourth ballot.[94] Fry was a forceful leader with an analytic mind, a prodigious memory, boundless energy, and an acerbic wit.[95] In time he became a legendary figure in Lutheranism and world Christianity.

Shifts in leadership were occurring also in the other Lutheran bodies that would eventually form the LCA. P. O. Bersell, who had led Augustana since 1935, left office in 1951 and was succeeded by Oscar A. Benson. Although Alfred Jensen had been president of the Danish church (AELC) since 1936, the office was made full time in 1942.[96] John Wargelin became president of the Suomi Synod in 1950 and was succeeded by his son Raymond in 1955.

Other significant developments were also changing the landscape of Lutheranism. These should be mentioned because of their impact on the way various bodies would relate to one another in the early sixties.

Worship. One far-reaching change in congregational life was in the area of worship. In 1944 the ULCA convention directed its president to invite all Lutheran bodies in the United States and Canada to join in developing a common hymnal. Augustana and the American Lutheran Church promptly accepted. The Commission on the Hymnal held its first meeting in June 1945 with an appointee of the president of the Evangelical Lutheran Church in attendance as an observer. Later the ELC along with the UELC, AELC, Suomi, and the Lutheran Free Church joined fully in the effort.

"That first meeting," writes Edward T. Horn III, "reminded one of nothing so much as twenty strange dogs released on the same block! There was much sniffing, and no one was quite sure of anyone else. There was great fear that voting on all questions would be by blocs, and it was only when the ULCA delegation split down the middle on many questions that this fear was dissipated."[97]

The "strange dogs" did get along remarkably well, however, and by 1946 those on the hymnal commission were joined by another Commission on a Common Liturgy. Both commissions were chaired by Luther D. Reed, a noted liturgical scholar on the faculty of Philadelphia Seminary.[98] The road to achieving a book that would be common for more than two-thirds of the Lutherans in North America was a long one, but by March 1958 the *Service Book and Hymnal* was a reality. Within a decade there were 2,750,000 copies of the new book in print.[99]

There can be no doubt that the use of common forms of worship in congregations has played a significant role throughout history in drawing the people of separate Lutheran church bodies closer together. This had been the case with the Common Service, and it was to be true of this new effort. When that happens, it is usually only a matter of time before various ecclesiastical machines begin to mesh their gears in new ways.

Parish Education. A second area of cooperation which affected congregations directly was Christian education. As early as 1940, the Parish and Church School Board (renamed Board of Parish Education in 1952) of the ULCA had projected a new series of Sunday school materials. The parallel boards of Augustana and the American Lutheran Church soon expressed interest in making this a joint effort. The cooperative project was authorized in 1942 with Theodore Finck, of the ULCA, as the chief editor.[100] The product, *The Christian Growth Series,*[101] marked the first time that these bodies had produced materials in full color. The series, however, was educationally conservative and interpreted the Bible quite literally.[102] It did, however, develop a mutual confidence among the three boards and their publishing houses that continued to be a factor throughout the remaining life of Augustana, the ULCA, and the ALC.

In 1953 the ULCA board undertook a "unified study" of its total educational program. Paul Vieth, an outstanding religious education professor at Yale Divinity School, led the study. The result was a document produced in 1954 entitled *Parish Education: A Statement of Basic Principles and a Program of Christian Education.* The seminal idea in the report was that the church should begin planning at once a coordinated program for parish education that would serve long-range needs. In 1955 work began on the Long-Range Program of Parish Education.[103] When it soon became apparent that the ALC and Augustana were interested in cooperation, an invitation was issued to all churches in the National Lutheran Council to join in the project. All eight bodies accepted, and in 1957 a joint staff picked up the work at the point of developing age-group objectives.

By midyear the Evangelical Lutheran Church, over the strong protests of the American Lutheran Board of Parish Education, insisted that those bodies which would ultimately form the new TALC (The American Lutheran Church[104]) should withdraw and produce a curriculum attuned to that emerging body's needs.[105] The church bodies that would form the LCA continued the program which became known as "The LCA Parish Education Curriculum." It provided the congregations of the new church with the first Protestant curriculum that had coordinated closely the efforts of every educational arm of the parish: Sunday church school, vacation church

school, weekday church school, catechetics, school of religion, family
life education, leadership education, as well as church camps and
summer schools. In time more than 90 percent of LCA congregations
used the program, which proved to be a unifying factor among Lutherans in a highly mobile society.[106]

Higher Education. Higher education was a third area where dramatic changes took place in this period. World War II decimated the
number of male students in regular college programs. Many Lutheran schools, however, were able to survive the financial crunch by
serving as centers for various military training programs. The V-12
Navy program, for example, provided Muhlenberg College with
some $426,000 of its $671,000 budget in 1943–44.[107]

During the years following World War II and the Korean conflict,
the colleges were inundated with returning veterans who were
studying under the "GI Bill of Rights." Physical facilities and faculties
had to be increased drastically almost overnight. But this was only
the beginning. As Richard Solberg indicates, "Close behind followed
a surge of new public policy, setting off waves of educational legislation that rolled through American society for the next 40 years. In
1948 President Truman's Commission on Higher Education proclaimed a new goal: 'higher education for all.' With this it became
national policy that Jacksonian rather than Jeffersonian principles
would henceforth govern access to American collegiate education, as
had long been true in the public schools of the land."[108]

The Lutheran church bodies responded to the need with highly
successful appeals for millions of dollars to expand their colleges. By
the late 1950s Carthage College had been moved from Illinois to a
spectacular new site on the shores of Lake Michigan at Kenosha,
Wisconsin. A new pattern of cooperative ownership began when
ALC, ELC, ULCA, Augustana, and UELC formed a joint corporation
to establish California Lutheran College, which opened in Thousand
Oaks in 1961.[109] But infusions of government funds were often necessary to cope with expanding needs. With government money, however, there are likely to come government expectations. Stung by
Russian success in launching the first space satellite, the United States
passed the National Defense Education Act in 1958. According to
Solberg, "The very title of the act announced that higher education
was to be used as an instrument of public policy needs, for the
furtherance of national manpower needs, for defense, and the
achievement of foreign policy goals."[110]

It was obvious that Lutheran colleges were changing in size, in composition of their student bodies, and often in the close-knit sense of community that had prevailed on small campuses in the past. But Lutheran educators were concerned also about maintaining standards of quality and the liberal arts tradition that had been characteristic of their institutions. Fortunately, there was already a mechanism for examining some common problems cooperatively.[111] The National Lutheran Education Conference had been created in 1910 as a forum for Lutheran college and seminary executives. By 1958 the conference set up its own headquarters in Washington with Gould Wickey as its executive. "His leadership promised strength and stability for the Lutheran Educational Conference and its 64 member institutions as they entered the stormy decade of the 60s."[112]

World Missions. Foreign mission work was an area in which the parent bodies of the Lutheran Church in America had long had a variety of cooperative arrangements. When the Augustana Synod became a member of the General Council in 1870, it assumed responsibility for the work in progress in Rajahmundry, India. Enthusiasm for this mission actually came when the Rev. and Mrs. A. B. Carlson went as the Synod's first missionaries to India under the auspices of the Council.[113] The AELC had been involved in the Santal field in India since 1913.[114] In 1920 the Lutheran Church of China was constituted with synods related to both the Augustana Lutheran Church and the United Lutheran Church as well as to other North American bodies and European mission societies.[115] Augustana, Suomi, and the ULCA all cooperated in the Japan Evangelical Lutheran Church.[116] Further cooperative work within the National Lutheran Council and the Lutheran World Federation were important in developing relationships.

World War II brought with it a dramatic change in world missions. It signaled the end of the century-long period in which the North American and European churches, as David Vikner notes, "sent a steady stream of *missionary personnel* to Africa, Asia, and South America. . . . As children of their time, these missionaries accepted their role of 'bearing the white man's burden.' They cooperated with colonial authorities, and at times accepted their protection."[117] Although the disintegration of colonialism had begun in World War I, the 1940s brought about a radical shift toward the emergence of newly independent nations. These nations often had artificially aligned borders and single-party, authoritarian regimes. The Western "sending churches" soon found themselves dealing with what has been called "The Younger Church Stage" of world missions.

During the twenty-five years between 1943 and 1968, the mission agencies were faced with a host of new issues. According to Nelson, these included such questions as, "How could indigenization be speeded? . . . In the face of new nationalism, how could 'younger churches' escape the stigma of being outposts of Western 'imperialism' and rise above the charge of being little more than 'ecclesiastical Western colonies'? What was the relation of the 'western' missionary to the younger churches? Was he really needed any longer?"[118] As all of the mission churches that became related to the LCA achieved full autonomy, it became necessary to redefine their relationship to the North American church. In the case of ULCA, its Board of Foreign Missions adopted a policy statement in 1958 that "called for the turning over of all mission-related programs, institutions, and properties to the national churches; the dissolution of the mission agencies; and the assurance of financial support if requested and available."[119]

A further example of how events precipitated cooperation in world missions arose from the ousting of missionaries from the People's Republic of China when the Communists took over the country in the 1950s. China had once been the largest of all Lutheran fields with more than a thousand missionaries from fourteen societies in 1926.[120] Many of the North American Lutheran missionaries went to Hong Kong and Taiwan where the Evangelical Lutheran Church of Hong Kong and the Taiwan Lutheran Church were formed in 1954. Others went to Japan where they related to the JELC.[121] These close relationships were significant for the mission boards of the LCA predecessor bodies.

Inter-Lutheran and Ecumenical Agencies

World War II and the years that followed were marked by an increase in the importance of the National Lutheran Council and the formation of new entities, such as the Lutheran World Federation, the Canadian Lutheran Council, the National Council of Churches of Christ in the USA, and the World Council of Churches. Only a few highlights can be provided here.

National Lutheran Council. The Council, along with its companion agency Lutheran World Relief and its highly successful Lutheran World Action appeals, spearheaded the relief and resettlement tasks so urgently needed after the war. Ralph Long, the farsighted executive of the Council; Paul Empie, director of LWA and later executive director of the NLC itself; Franklin Clark Fry, president of LWR, and Clarence Krumbholz and Bernard A. Confer, LWR administrators, were major figures in these efforts. The results were phenomenal. According to Nelson, "Lutheran World Action money together with material aid gathered by Lutheran World Relief after 1945 amounted to over $250 million."[122] In sheer volume, it is estimated that more than a billion pounds of food, clothing, medicine, and other relief goods were distributed by 1965.[123] Refugee resettlement was another major concern. Working hand in hand with the Lutheran World Federation, the Lutheran Resettlement Service brought thousands to North America and helped them establish new lives.[124] In 1953 this work was reconstituted under the Lutheran Refugee Service with both the NLC churches and the Missouri Synod as partners.[125]

The National Lutheran Council, of course, was involved in other activities as well. In 1945 the "Regulations" under which it had operated since 1926 were put into constitutional form. This permitted the greatly expanded activities of the postwar era and also the incorporation of a preamble which Richard Wolf indicates "gave expression to the degree of doctrinal unity discernible among its constituent bodies."[126] Some of these programs included a Commission on Student Service, initially headed by Morris Wee and later by Donald Heiges; a Division of American Missions; expansion of the Division of Welfare to include institutional chaplaincies; a Washington office in the Division of Public Relations; and a Commission on Younger Churches and Orphaned Missions. This commission was headed by Fredrik A. Schiotz, who was destined to become president of the merged American Lutheran Church in 1960.[127]

Beginning in 1942, the leaders of the Council had been pushing for free conferences aimed at advancing Lutheran unity, but these were delayed by the war. Executive Ralph Long persisted in his hope for closer relations. Only a few weeks before his death in February 1948, he sent a message to a meeting of the councilors. As Frederick K. Wentz writes, "It was a restatement of his belief that cooperation should continue and 'must eventually lead to unity of American Lutheranism.' "[128]

In large measure, however, it was the persistence of Augustana in trying to bring about a merger within the Council that resulted in a conference to address the issue. Following an action by its 1948 convention, Augustana's representatives pushed at the November

Paul C. Empie

1948 meeting of the American Lutheran Conference for petition-
ing the National Lutheran Council to call a free conference. Although this did not occur under NLC auspices, a "Committee of
Thirty-four on Lutheran Unity" was formed by the Council bodies
in 1949.[129] A proposal was developed for either a federation or a
merger of the eight member churches. It was submitted in 1950 to
the church bodies for reaction. According to Richard Wolf, "The
results of the poll (Doc. 198) were discouraging for the proponents
of comprehensive merger of the Council bodies, for both organic
union and the intermediate step of federation were rejected. The
immediate future, as we shall see, was with the proponents of limited mergers."[130]

The Lutheran churches in Canada following World War II showed
increasingly a sense of national identity and a desire for closer cooperation among the Canadian units of the binational bodies.[131] As
early as 1944, the Canada Home Missions Conference agreed unanimously "that a Canadian Lutheran Council should be established
after the pattern of the National Lutheran Council."[132] The conference also pointed to a recognized unity of faith that it was hoped
would ultimately lead to one Canadian church. The dream of a
merged church in Canada would not be realized for almost forty
years and then only partially so.[133] The Canadian Lutheran Council
finally came into being in 1955. The council could have come about
as early as 1947 if it had not been for negative votes cast by the
American Lutheran Church and the Missouri Synod.[134]

Lutheran World Federation. Lutherans were "Johnny-come-late-
lies" when it came to forming a world organization, which is strange
in view of their being by far the largest group among Protestants. By
the time the Lutherans got around to it, the Anglicans, Baptists,
Congregationalists, Methodists, and Presbyterians all had their own
world organizations.[135] There had been earlier suggestions, of
course, but the real impetus came in the wake of World War I. The
newly formed NLC sent a commission to Europe in 1919 to oversee
relief and reconstruction work.[136] The commissioners traveled
widely in the war-ravaged areas and established contacts with the
various Lutheran churches there. No one was more persistent in this
work than their chairman, John A. Morehead, who had given up his
position as president of Roanoke College in Virginia to take "to the
uncertain railroads and highways of postwar Europe in an exhausting

and lonely pilgrimage, weaving ties of mutual aid for Lutherans across the face of a continent."[137]

After months of effort, the commissioners met October 6–7, 1919, in Berlin. They were convinced that the newly established relations should form the basis for a worldwide federation of Lutheran churches. On December 18 Morehead and the commissioners were back in the United States to address a meeting of the National Lutheran Council. They explained, as Nelson put it, that "great and irreparable losses to Lutheranism everywhere would be sustained unless solidarity could be given by some international organization."[138] A resolution was passed which set in motion a process that resulted in the first Lutheran World Convention being held in Eisenach, Germany, in August 1923. Churches in twenty-two nations sent 151 delegates, of whom seventeen were Americans.[139]

The delegates were sufficiently moved by a sense of unity to create a permanent organization based upon a six-line doctrinal statement that declared, "The Lutheran World Convention acknowledges the Holy Scriptures of the Old and New Testaments as the only source and infallible norm of all church doctrine and practice, and sees in the Confessions of the Lutheran Church, especially in the Unaltered Augsburg Confession and Luther's Small Catechism, a pure exposition of the Word of God."[140] The Convention was to meet every five years, and John Morehead was chosen chairman of an executive committee which met annually. By 1935 the work had expanded sufficiently that Frederick H. Knubel presented plans for a reorganization, and Hanns Lilje, of Germany, was chosen full-time executive secretary.

Once again war intervened, and a convention planned for 1940 had to be canceled. During World War II, however, the Lutheran World Convention was kept alive largely through the efforts of the American Section chaired by Ralph Long. When the war ended, it was possible for the American Lutherans to reestablish the links with their European sisters and brothers because of the prior role of the LWC.[141] Sylvester C. Michelfelder was "borrowed" from his Toledo congregation to become commissioner of the American Section of the Lutheran World Convention to the World Council of Churches with the promise that he would return within a year. "His title amused him," E. Theodore Bachmann writes, "for in French, commissioner can mean 'messenger' or 'baggage carrier.' On a big scale, he became just that."[142]

In addition to administering the relief program, however, Michelfelder soon became executive secretary of the Lutheran World Convention at a meeting of the executive committee in 1946. He succeeded Lilje, who had resigned because he felt a German could not serve in that capacity in the postwar situation. Michelfelder had urged the executive committee to strengthen the organization for the enormous tasks that lay before it.[143] Work was already underway on a new constitution by a committee headed by Abdel Ross Wentz that would transform the LWC into a federation. Plans were set in motion at the Convention's first postwar meeting in Lund, Sweden, in 1947. Here the Lutheran World Federation was born. Anders Nygren, the noted theologian from Lund University and author of *Agape and Eros,* was elected president, and Michelfelder, executive secretary of the new Federation.[144] All of the bodies in the National Lutheran Council became members. Missouri, however, did not join and has continued that stance, although it has on occasion sent observers to LWF meetings.

World Council of Churches. Two landmark conferences, one on Life and Work at Stockholm in 1925 and the other on Faith and Order at Lausanne in 1927, brought Christian churches from around the globe together in movements that would lead more than two decades later to the formation of the World Council of Churches. When a second Life and Work conference was held at Oxford in 1937 and another on Faith and Order the same year in Edinburgh,[145] work had already been done on integrating the two movements, and there was ready acceptance of a proposal to form a committee that would meet in Utrecht the following year to write a constitution for the new body. Although World War II delayed formation of the World Council until 1948, a small staff was at work in Geneva throughout the period.[146]

American Lutherans proved to have a great influence both in the shape of the WCC and its later history.[147] One of the pivotal questions for Lutherans was the nature of representation in the Council. The view of most Protestant groups was that this should be on a national basis. This would have meant that in the United States, for example, delegates would be chosen by the Federal Council of Churches. Foreseeing this problem, Frederick Knubel asked Abdel Ross Wentz to draft a statement on "Lutherans and the Ecumenical Movement."[148] The statement, which was closely related to the concepts in the ULCA's Washington Declaration, was adopted by the Lutheran World Convention executive committee in 1936. Its key confessional and representative principles have continued to guide Lutherans in ecumenical relations until the present time. In Nelson's judgment, "Representation and participation on the basis of confessions rather than of countries is to recognize that the essential manifestation of a church is its faith rather than its nationality."[149]

It took more than a decade before the Lutheran position was accepted that delegates should represent their churches in World Council of Churches affairs, but this did become part of the constitution. Augustana was the first of the North American Lutheran churches to accept membership in the Council.[150] When the First Assembly convened in Amsterdam in 1948, however, ALC, AELC, ULCA, and UELC were also represented.[151] Suomi joined later. It was not until 1956, however, that the Evangelical Lutheran Church resolved a sharp internal division and voted affirmatively on membership.[152]

There were many American Lutherans who played prominent roles in the WCC, but none held more strategic responsibilities than Franklin Clark Fry. As Erik Modean put it, "For the first six years of the World Council's existence, Dr. Fry served as vice-chairman of its policy-making Central Committee. He was elected chairman of both its Central Committee and its Executive Committee in 1954, was re-elected in 1961 and was to retire from these vital posts at the WCC's Fourth Assembly at Upsala, Sweden."[153] Dr. Fry, however, died only a few months before what would have been his final assembly in this key role.

National Council of Churches of Christ in the USA. Perhaps more than any other ecumenical body, the NCCCUSA has been the point where Lutherans in the United States have taken different ecumenical stances. ULCA's President Fry was one of the chief architects of the NCC and presided at its constituting convention in 1950. Fry's meticulous attention to detail led him to insist on forty-four amendments to the governing documents before he was satisfied. "This was said to have caused one prominent churchwoman to sink into her seat one day after an absence from the sessions and whisper to her neighbor: 'What do the Lutherans want now?' "[154] Whatever the specific change was that the ULCA wanted at that point, Dr. Fry's basic concern was to insure the recognition of the ecumenical and representative principles by the NCCCUSA. Unfortunately, establishing those principles was not enough to reassure all of the Lutheran bodies in the United States. While the other churches that formed the LCA joined the Council, Nelson observes, "The American Lutheran Church and the Missouri Synod found it expedient to remain outside and yet to accept the invitation to be represented in committees and commissions of their own choice."[155]

THE MERGER TAKES SHAPE

The moves and countermoves, the urgent invitations to unity and the polite declinations, as well as factors in cooperative work, all preludes to the mergers that would create The American Lutheran Church and the Lutheran Church in America, were dealt with briefly earlier in this chapter. They have been described in careful detail by noted historians in other volumes.[156] A few points, however, deserve to be underscored.

From the time of its formation, the United Lutheran Church had taken the stance that it favored uniting with all Lutheran bodies in North America. For the most part, other churches were uncomfortable with ULCA aggressiveness in this area as well as with what they felt was laxity in doctrine and practice. As we have seen, however, the Slovak Zion Synod and the Icelandic Synod did unite in time with the ULCA. During these decades, the various bodies themselves were changing, and cooperative efforts in many areas were breaking down some of the walls of suspicion and separation. The stage was set for the next act of the drama in which Augustana was destined to play a pivotal role.

Augustana's overtures had been the moving force in forming the Committee of Thirty-four, and for a while there had been some signs of hope. At the January 1949 meeting of the committee, Henry F. Schuh (later to become president of the old ALC) asked, "What are we waiting for? We are already co-operating here at home and in all parts of the world. Is there some valid reason why we can't work together in foreign missions, home missions, education, pensions, and publications?"[157] Oscar Benson, of Augustana, blamed vested interests for thwarting unity and declared, "Our difficulties are largely psychological."[158] A resolution proposed by Emmanuel Poppen of ALC calling for closer organizational affiliation among the National Lutheran Council churches was adopted unanimously by a written ballot.

While the Committee of Thirty-four was drafting its plan, however, the ELC and UELC had been exploring the possibilities of "a smaller union than that of the National Lutheran Council."[159] These negotiations led to a meeting on September 26, 1949, eleven days prior to a meeting of the Committee of Thirty-four, where representatives of ELC, ALC, and UELC discussed a possible federation of all Lutherans. Nelson describes what happened: "Missouri's traditional stance made this a safe proposal and at the same time gave to what was in reality an empty gesture the appearance of even greater amplitude of concern for unity. Gullixson [ELC] then presented a resolution that urged merger of the three bodies and asked that such a resolution be presented to the conventions of the ELC, ALC, and UELC."[160] On November 25, representatives of these three churches met in Chicago as the Joint Committee on Union, which adopted a series of resolutions proposing a union of ALC, ELC, and UELC "as a step in the unfolding unification of the Lutheran Churches in America."[161] The proposal by the Committee of Thirty-four for either a merger or federation of the National Council churches, therefore, was apparently foredoomed to failure when it was submitted to the member bodies in January 1950. That left the invitation open technically for an American Lutheran Conference merger, but in reality resulted in alignment of those bodies that eventually formed The American Lutheran Church in 1960.[162]

The Augustana Church continued to pursue every avenue for a broader unity. Its representatives sought within the American Lutheran Conference to find a way to avoid having that body become an exclusive merger that would frustrate wider unity for another generation. At its 1950 convention, Augustana named a Committee on Lutheran Unity to study the options. It met with the Joint Union Committee in February 1952, and to the surprise of many in Augustana endorsed that committee's "United Testimony on Faith and Life," which was based on the old Minneapolis Theses of 1925 and affirmed the stance of "exclusive confessionalism."[163] In addition, the Augustana committee met at separate times with representatives of Suomi, AELC, and ULCA to explore the views of those bodies. On the basis of these negotiations, a proposal was made to the 1952 Augustana convention that called both for maintaining friendship with those in the American Lutheran Conference and to ask the Joint Union Committee "to invite the other general bodies of the National Lutheran Council to participate in merger discussions."[164]

As the 1952 convention of Augustana approached, there was vigorous debate in the church's official journal, *The Lutheran Companion*.

S. E. Engstrom, then president of the American Lutheran Conference, wrote articles questioning the proposal on theological, ecumenical, and practical grounds because of its underlying acceptance of the "United Testimony." If merger of all NLC churches could not be achieved, he urged negotiations with the United Lutherans.[165] E. E. Ryden, editor of the journal, on the other hand favored preserving the values that had come through twenty years of membership in the American Lutheran Conference.[166] At the convention itself, the highly respected Conrad Bergendoff attacked the "United Testimony" as contrary to the basic doctrinal position of the Augustana Church and protested that the United Lutheran Church had been left out of the American Lutheran Conference approach to merger.[167] After some temporizing, the convention made clear that it wanted a broad-based merger, not one limited to the members of the American Lutheran Conference.

At a meeting in Minneapolis on November 10, 1955, Augustana presented its terms to the other members of the Conference but was de facto rebuffed by the representatives of those churches involved in the Joint Committee on Union. President Benson replied for Augustana that "we have only one door through which we can go, and we shall do that as graciously as we can."[168] In the words of the editor of *The Lutheran Companion,* "It was a solemn moment, and every one present sensed its significance as the Augustana representatives arose and walked quietly from the conference chamber while the other committee members sat in silence. A chapter in Lutheran unity strivings in American had come to a close."[169]

Despite the failure of Augustana's efforts to open the American Lutheran Conference to wider unity, it had in hand an invitation from the United Lutheran Church delivered by President Fry to join it in an overture to "any and all" bodies which desired to merge.[170] On December 16, 1955, a commission from the two churches met in Chicago and issued a call to all fourteen other Lutheran bodies to send commissioners "to consider such organic union as will give real evidence of our unity in faith."[171] Missouri declined on the basis of doctrinal differences. The Joint Union Committee of ALC, ELC, and UELC replied that in view of its own union commitments it could not participate in such a meeting "whose sole purpose is to consider organic union."[172] While some other bodies chose to ignore the invitation completely, the AELC and Suomi accepted. The door had opened at last for the negotiations that would lead to formation of the Lutheran Church in America.

The Joint Commission on Lutheran Unity

In the words of an eyewitness, "There was an air of subdued excitement on the twelfth day of December, 1956 in the Conrad Hilton Hotel in Chicago, when forty-six representatives of four churches, gathered from many walks of life, met for the purpose of creating a new instrument to be called a church."[173] The means for dealing with the host of decisions that had to be made to bring the Lutheran Church in America into being was the Joint Commission on Lutheran Unity. The composition of the group was a reflection of the times. No one seemed to question that the members were all male, Caucasian, and, for the most part, clergy. In fact, it may surprise us now to note that, apart from the two committees that worked out plans for a women's auxiliary, there were only two women among 172 appointees to various subgroups.

No one in the JCLU appeared to be under the illusion that it was creating a new church. As Johannes Knudsen put it, "For the thoughtful the immediate answer was that we do not create a church in the profoundest sense of the word. The church is created by the spirit of God; we can only accept it and participate in it."[174] The Commission saw its task as the building of a supportive and enabling institution. The representatives did not come to the meeting, however, without a great deal of prior thought and groundwork having been done in their churches. For example, President Fry of the ULCA had prepared a statement on Lutheran unity earlier in 1956 "which was immediately recognized," Nelson notes, "as an unofficial charter for the new church and as a guide to the joint commission."[175]

For those who have followed the story of continual wrangling among Lutherans over doctrinal matters, it is refreshing to know that after hearing a presentation on the doctrinal statements of the four bodies, the JCLU members were in no mood to submit one another to some sort of extraconfessional Lutheran litmus test. They firmly rejected any thought that further confessional documents were needed and adopted the following resolution: "After hearing the reading and interpretation of the doctrinal statements of the four churches here represented, the Commission rejoices to note that we have among us sufficient ground of agreement in the common confession of our faith, as witnessed by the Lutheran confessions, to justify further organic union of our churches, including the formulation of a proposed constitution having in it articles on doctrine and practical matters of organization."[176]

With this spirit prevailing, the Commission wasted no time getting down to business. It had already elected as chairman Malvin H. Lundeen, a parish pastor who later became president of the Augustana Church; Raymond W. Wargelin, president of the Suomi Synod, as vice-chairman; Carl C. Rasmussen (ULCA), professor of systematic theology at Gettysburg Seminary, as secretary; and Johannes Knudsen, former president of the AELC Grand View College and Seminary in Des Moines, as assistant secretary.[177] Initially, three committees were appointed. Functional tasks were assigned to a Committee on Doctrine and Living Tradition and a Committee on Patterns of Organization. The most important group, however, was the Steering Committee, made up of the president and one additional member from each church body.

The work of the theologians on the Committee on Doctrine and Living Tradition laid the groundwork for the article on "Confession of Faith" in the constitution which broke with the usual practice in American Lutheranism of beginning with a statement on biblical authority. The article begins instead by confessing that "Jesus Christ is the Lord of the Church. The Holy Spirit creates and sustains the Church through the Gospel and thereby unites believers with their Lord and with one another in the fellowship of faith."[178] The statement then focuses on the gospel as the revelation of God's sovereign will and saving grace in Jesus Christ and emphasizes that Christ himself is the Word Incarnate. The article next proceeds in order to the Holy Scriptures, the historic ecumenical creeds, the Unaltered Augsburg Confession and Luther's Small Catechism, the symbolical books of the Lutheran church, and closes with an affirmation of the gospel transmitted by the Scriptures and witnessed to by the creeds and confessions as "the true treasure of the Church, the substance of its proclamation, and the basis of its unity and continuity."[179] This carefully nuanced statement is a key to understanding the Lutheran Church in America's stance in many relationships and negotiations throughout its history.[180]

Issues and Answers

Although overall there seemed no doubt in the minds of the commissioners that there would be a merger and that they would fulfill their timetable for a constituting convention in June 1962, the road taken was often tedious and at times, rocky. The JCLU itself met eighteen times, and the subcommittees came together for thousands of person-days. The pattern of late-night sessions left little time for leisure. According to one story, a bellman in an oft-used hotel remarked, "These Lutherans come here with the Ten Commandments in one hand and a ten dollar bill in the other, and they aren't about to break either." The questions to be debated and solutions to be found were too numerous to catalogue. But among all these issues, there were some that loomed particularly large and should be mentioned here.

Lodges. Historian E. Clifford Nelson points out that "Lutheran unity efforts in the 20th century had usually foundered on three or four major problems: the relation of the Word of God to the Scriptures and confessions . . ., 'unionism,' ecumenism, and membership of pastors in lodges."[181] Of these the one that came closest to threatening the LCA merger was the lodge question. Augustana had been adamant against allowing pastors to belong to lodges and felt that ULCA was lax at this point. The United Lutherans had traditionally chosen not to deal with the matter in a legalistic way. Suomi and AELC held views similar to Augustana. The issue finally came to a head on Friday the thirteenth, December 1957. At first, proposals were made for constitutional provisions that would require ministers ordained by the new church to refrain from belonging to such groups "or be willing to demit this ministry."[182]

Following dinner and a prolonged discussion, amendments were made in the original motion that shifted the focus so that "ministers ordained by the new church shall refrain from membership in such organizations or be subject to discipline."[183] At this point, the ULCA delegation requested an opportunity to caucus for ten minutes. After the recess, Dr. Fry presented the following statement: "As a concession in love to the living tradition of our sister churches, the Commission of the U.L.C.A. acquiesces unanimously in the vote just taken."[184] There was great relief that this hurdle had been passed, although there were those persons who wondered later whether the United Lutherans had purposely put themselves in the position of being defeated on this question to demonstrate that they were not trying to dominate the JCLU proceedings. In any event, the LCA Constitution makes provisions about membership of pastors in secret societies in accord with this agreement.[185]

Nature of the Church. Here there was ample opportunity to reexamine the concept of congregational polity prevalent among so much of American Protestantism which held that congregations were the basic form of the church and, in effect, could decide to form a general body and delegate certain responsibilities to it. Within the Commission, however, there was a strong sense that congregational polity was not enough. Taking into account the totality of Article VII of the Augsburg Confession, the Commission recognized not only that the assembly of believers is where the gospel is preached and the sacraments administered but also that there is a historic and universal character to the whole Christian church as well.[186] The final wording in Article IV of the constitution, which proved crucial for the LCA throughout its history and in future dealings with other bodies is as follows:

"Section 2. The Church exists both as an inclusive fellowship and as local congregations gathered for worship and Christian service. Congregations find their fulfillment in the universal community of the Church, and the universal Church exists in and through congregations. This church, therefore, derives its character and powers both from the sanction and representation of its congregations and from its inherent nature as an expression of the broader fellowship of the faithful. In length, it acknowledges itself to be in the historic continuity of the communion of saints; in breadth, it expresses the fellowship of believers and congregations in this our day."[187]

Role of Synods. It was obvious that a church as large as the LCA would need some intermediate judicatories between the congregations and the general body. Augustana had thirteen geographical units called conferences; Suomi, seven conferences; and AELC, eleven districts. The United Lutheran Church had thirty-two synods. Two of these, Slovak Zion and Icelandic, were nongeographical, linguistic bodies. While the other churches looked upon their judicatories as creations of their general bodies, the ULCA was in many respects a federation of synods. Some ULCA synods with long histories and a measure of independence were not ready to yield fully to a central church authority when the 1918 merger occurred. The question for the new church, therefore, was, "What were these intermediate entities to be called and what would be their functions?"

There were two particularly influential papers presented to the Commission that related to this problem. The one by Conrad Ber-

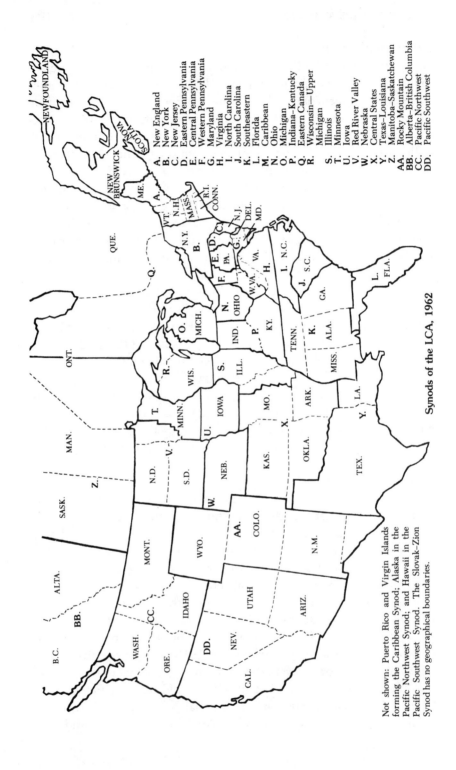

A. New England
B. New York
C. New Jersey
D. Eastern Pennsylvania
E. Central Pennsylvania
F. Western Pennsylvania
G. Maryland
H. Virginia
I. North Carolina
J. South Carolina
K. Southeastern
L. Florida
M. Caribbean
N. Ohio
O. Michigan
P. Indiana–Kentucky
Q. Eastern Canada
R. Wisconsin—Upper Michigan
S. Illinois
T. Minnesota
U. Iowa
V. Red River Valley
W. Nebraska
X. Central States
Y. Texas–Louisiana
Z. Manitoba–Saskatchewan
AA. Rocky Mountain
BB. Alberta–British Columbia
CC. Pacific Northwest
DD. Pacific Southwest

Synods of the LCA, 1962

Not shown: Puerto Rico and Virgin Islands forming the Caribbean Synod; Alaska in the Pacific Northwest Synod; and Hawaii in the Pacific Southwest Synod. The Slovak–Zion Synod has no geographical boundaries.

gendoff was on "The Lutheran Doctrine of the Church," which laid out an overview of the place that the doctrine of the church had held in Lutheran history.[188] The other paper on "Possible Patterns of Organization" was presented by Henry Bagger, president of Philadelphia Seminary. He stated that there were three "extreme emphases" in polity which placed primary authority in either the congregation, the synods, or the central body, and argued for "something more mixed in character." Bagger asserted that "mere federation or a conferential relationship is not enough since merger or organic union is both our directive and our aim."[189]

From all indications there was little sentiment in the JCLU favorable to the United Lutheran pattern of federation that seemed to have outlived its usefulness. As finally adopted, Article VIII of the LCA Constitution made clear that the church-at-large would determine the number and boundaries of synods. Provision was also made for nongeographic synods for those groups with distinctive linguistic or national characteristics that chose this option at the time of formation of the LCA. Only Slovak Zion selected this course.[190]

The constitution also spelled out, "The principal function of synods shall be shepherding of their constituent congregations and ministers, including oversight to conserve unity in the true faith and to guard against any departure therefrom, encouragement to the fuller employment of all resources of spirit and means for the furtherance of the Kingdom of God, guidance in filling vacancies in pastorates, and intervention and mediation at times of strife and division. The synods shall have primary responsibility for the recruiting, preparation and ordination of ministers, for the reception of congregations, and for the discipline of both congregations and ministers, as stated in Articles VI and VII."[191] Other responsibilities of synods, such as those for seminaries, colleges, and social mission agencies, are described later in this chapter.

During the drafting of these articles, it became apparent that the Commission needed a Committee on Constitutions to work out these complex documents. One was formed with Fry as chairman, a role for which he was uniquely equipped. Fry liked to joke about his role. At one meeting of the Commission he repeated a story then making the rounds in the church about his own passing to the other world and knocking on the door of heaven. When Saint Peter asked him what he had been doing on earth, Fry answered, "I have been busy writing constitutions." "Come right in," said Saint Peter, "We need a new one up here." Fry was given the assignment of drafting a new constitution for heaven and soon brought it back for review. As he looked at the document, Peter said, "It looks good, but, Franklin, what's this part about God being only a vice-president?"[192]

Membership in the Church. One of the areas where historic precedent prevailed was in the definition of membership in the church. The constitutions of AELC, Augustana, and Suomi all defined the basic entities of the church as congregations and ministers. This concept had not been spelled out in the United Lutheran constitution, although it had first been developed in the pioneer days of the German Lutherans when "synods" were actually "ministerium" meetings to which voting congregational lay representatives were later added. As Knudsen pointed out, "Not only was the 'synodical' organization practical and justified but it was probably the only manner in which a common effort could be maintained in pioneer times. The precedent having been set, however, it became an indigenous institution. Churches founded as late as the second half of the nineteenth century adopted the traditional American example, and the commonly used name for a church was 'synod.' This is a curious concept of the church, however, which is hard to defend except on historical grounds, and it has no parallel outside of North America."[193] Ministers, therefore, have been voting members of synods from the formation of the LCA, while laity are represented through their congregations.[194]

One important change in polity from that followed by the United Lutheran Church was in the area of ordination. Although synods would still be responsible for ordination, the church-at-large defined standards for acceptance into and continuance in the ministry. Ministers, therefore, were to be ordained as ministers of the whole church in contrast to the ULCA where a pastor transferring from one synod to another had to apply for acceptance into the latter and sometimes had to undergo an examination on his qualifications and credentials as a Lutheran.[195]

Seminaries, Colleges, and Institutions. One of the liveliest debates in the Commission had to do with who would own and control seminaries. Augustana, AELC, and Suomi each had a single seminary that was owned by the church. The ULCA had ten that were owned by synods and sometimes were inadequately supported. Augustana particularly pushed for churchwide ownership and control. The traditional and long-standing loyalties of ULCA synods to their theological schools, particularly in the East, proved too strong. After many sessions it was at last decided that seminaries would be owned by the synods, and each synod would be responsible for support of a single seminary as determined by the church.[196]

The churchwide responsibility for seminary education was lodged with a Board of Theological Education that was charged with drawing up "a master plan of location and possible areas of specialization of theological seminaries."[197] It was agreed that this plan would be readied for the second biennial convention of the church. Meanwhile, a merger was already underway that would locate Augustana, Suomi, Grand View (AELC), and Maywood (ULCA) seminaries on a new campus near the University of Chicago.

Church colleges provided another complicated problem for the JCLU. The Danes and the Finns each had a junior college. Augustana had four senior colleges that were supported by the conferences. ULCA had fourteen four-year colleges and one junior college, each of which was related to synods in a variety of ways. The basic decision was that, with limited exceptions, the relations of the church to colleges were to be "sustained entirely through the synods."[198] As a matter of necessity, the colleges had to be realigned for support as new synodical boundaries were drawn. According to Solberg, "These realignments made serious changes in traditional geographic constituencies of several of the schools and in some cases narrowed their base of financial support as well."[199]

On the churchwide level, a Board of College Education and Church Vocations was created with the authority to set standards, counsel and advise colleges, to grant supplementary financial aid, and to act on detailed arrangements proposed by synods for cooperation in colleges related to other church bodies. In addition, it had the important roles of maintaining and fostering deaconess work, assisting synods in recruiting candidates for the ministry, itself recruiting workers for other church vocations, and operating a unified scholarship fund.[200]

Support of social mission institutions and agencies proved to be another complex issue. Augustana had been deeply involved in such efforts. Although in 1961 its membership was only 7 percent of the Lutheran population, Arden points out that Augustana "owned, operated, and maintained fifteen per cent of the three hundred Lutheran institutions of mercy in the United States, and of the charitable institutions . . . which were properties of individual Lu-

theran bodies, no less than thirty per cent were in the hands of the
Augustana Church."[201] Once again the decision was to lodge relationships to institutions and agencies with the synods, guided and
assisted with limited financial grants for projects by the church's
Board of Social Ministry.[202] In the future, this decision was to become
increasingly important as legal and financial liability for institutions
escalated dramatically.

Pensions and Benefits. Few problems faced by the new church demanded as much patience and technical expertise as developing a
pension and benefits plan. For decades American church bodies had
tried a variety of special appeals and other schemes to cover the
needs of retired pastors and their dependents that were normally
provided by the governments of the European countries from which
the immigrants had come. What made the situation worse in the
United States was that it was not until the 1950s that clergy were
permitted to participate in Social Security.

At the time of merger planning, both Augustana and ULCA had
come to the point where they had "contributory" or "money-pur-
chase" plans for those who had been young enough to participate.[203]
Suomi and AELC did not have funded pension reserves.[204] To com-
pound the problem, twenty-seven different hospitalization and medical plans which varied greatly were operative in the synods of the
merging churches.[205] After careful analysis, the plans adopted called
for a voluntary contributory pension plan for those still employed, a
minimum pension for those who could not benefit fully from this plan
or Social Security, a modest death benefit, and a health plan funded
from the benevolence budget of the church. In addition, a lay pension plan was instituted which made allowance for employer contributions to Social Security that churches were not allowed to make for
ministers under the law.[206] The ongoing necessity for adjusting these
plans to meet new circumstances and requirements resulted in some
three hundred amendments through the years.

Decisions, Decisions, Decisions. Limitations of space do not allow
detailing all of the questions which confronted the JCLU, but a few
deserve mention. For example, the new body's name was a topic on
which everyone could register an opinion. The "Evangelical Lutheran Church in America" was tested in what turned out to be a
prelude to another merger in 1987.[207] "Lutheran Evangelical

Church in America" was proposed until it was shot down as too awkward.[208] Finally, the shorter and simpler name of Lutheran Church in America was chosen.

The status of Canadian synods should be noted. As early as 1958, a special Committee on Canadian Matters presented a report to JCLU acknowledging that continuation as part of a binational church was necessary at that point in history. The report went on to say, however, "We believe the time is rapidly approaching when there should be established an autonomous, indigenous Lutheran Church in Canada."[209] The solution was to create a Canada Section of the church that would endure for almost a quarter century.

Locating headquarters is always a subject for endless discussion among Lutherans. Two locations, New York and Chicago, were seriously considered, which is interesting in light of the decisions in forming the new Evangelical Lutheran Church in America hammered out in 1986. The minutes of JCLU include a map that outlines concentrations of Lutherans in one-hundred-mile bands with each city as a locus.[210] New York won out as the central headquarters, but some churchwide agencies were located in Philadelphia, Minneapolis, and Chicago.

A Te Deum

After three centuries of presence in North America and more than five years of rigorous negotiations, four bodies finally made the formal decisions in 1961 that would form the Lutheran Church in America. Malvin Lundeen, president of Augustana, sounded the note of joy when he sent a telegram on June 13, 1961, to the other church bodies saying, "Join us in a Te Deum. Final merger vote 495 for; 21 against. Majority of 96 percent, 29 percent beyond the required two-thirds." Suomi's convention followed suit on June 28, and AELC voted overwhelmingly for merger on August 17. Because of its polity, the United Lutheran Church had to submit the articles of agreement for consolidation to its synods for ratification. At its meeting in July, the Executive Board of the ULCA heard the good news that its synods had affirmed the plan with only a handful of delegates dissenting.[211]

Following conventions to formalize their final responsibilities as individual churches, delegates of the four bodies convened in Detroit, Michigan, on June 28, 1962, to celebrate an end to the long, sometimes arduous, road to union. No one felt that the heritages of the Danes, Finns, Swedes, Germans, Slovaks, Icelanders, Blacks, Hungarians, Hispanics, Asians, Pacific Islanders, Native Americans, and the host of other ethnic groups who came together that day were being lost. Instead, they sensed the birth of a church enriched by all that these peoples had brought to its forming. But more than that, those persons gifted with prescience sensed that this moment, joyous as it might be, was but one more way station on the path to a greater unity among Lutherans, and, perhaps, with other Christians in the land.

NOTES

1. Robert L. Heilbroner, *The Future as History* (New York: Harper & Brothers, 1960), 31.
2. Ahlstrom, *Religious History*, chaps. 53, 54, 56.
3. Walter Consuelo Langsam, *The World Since 1914* (New York: Macmillan Co., 1948), 77–78.
4. The Missouri Synod and other churches in the Synodical Conference did not belong to the commission but maintained a carefully defined working relationship in matters that required a single Lutheran approach to the military or governmental agencies. See Meuser, "Twentieth Century," 401–2.
5. Nelson, *Lutheranism 1914–1970*, 18–19.
6. Frederick K. Wentz, *Lutherans in Concert* (Minneapolis: Augsburg Publishing House, 1968), 11–13. This book is the most complete and authoritative history of the National Lutheran Council.
7. Nelson, *Lutheranism 1914–1970*, 19. See also F. K. Wentz, *Lutherans in Concert*, 14–17.
8. F. K. Wentz, *Lutherans in Concert*, 18.
9. Meuser, "Twentieth Century," 405.
10. A. R. Wentz, *Basic History*, 305–6.
11. F. K. Wentz, *Lutherans in Concert*, 62. Wentz gives a full description of the overseas program in chap. 3.
12. Nelson, *Lutheranism 1914–1970*, 26.
13. Meuser, "Twentieth Century," 408.
14. *NLC Annual Report, 1919*, 13–14.
15. Nelson, *Lutheranism 1914–1970*, 22.
16. Meuser, "Twentieth Century," 408.
17. Nelson, *Lutheranism 1914–1970*, 23.
18. Wolf, *Documents*, 298.
19. Ibid., 301.
20. Nelson, *Lutheranism 1914–1970*, 23–25.
21. Meuser, "Twentieth Century," 409. For text of the Minneapolis Theses, see Wolf, *Documents*, 340–44.
22. Wolf, *Documents*, 301–12.

23. Nelson, *Lutheranism 1914–1970,* 23.

24. F. K. Wentz, *Lutherans in Concert,* 29–31.

25. *ULCA Minutes, 1920,* 92–101, 449–55.

26. Wolf, *Documents,* 148.

27. Charles M. Jacobs, "The Washington Declaration: an Interpretation," *The Lutheran Church Review,* no. 1 (January 1921):8. Jacobs sets forth his own views about the whole statement and the reasons for its development in this article, pp. 1–21.

28. Wolf, *Documents,* 328.

29. Ahlstrom gives an excellent description of the whole Fundamentalist controversy in *Religious History,* 909–15.

30. Nelson, *Lutheranism 1914–1970,* 27; and Meuser, "Twentieth Century," 463.

31. Meuser, "Twentieth Century," 443.

32. Wolf, *Documents,* 340.

33. Ibid.

34. Ibid., 341.

35. Fred W. Meuser's *The Formation of the American Lutheran Church* (Columbus: Wartburg, 1958) is the most thorough and detailed treatment of the ALC merger of 1930.

36. Wolf, *Documents,* 328–38.

37. Nelson, *Lutheranism 1914–1970,* 29.

38. Wolf, *Documents,* 343–44.

39. Meuser, *Formation,* 249.

40. A. R. Wentz, *Basic History,* 321.

41. Arden, *Augustana,* 280, quoting P. O. Bersell.

42. Nelson, *Lutheranism 1914–1970,* 43–44.

43. Langsam, *World Since 1914,* 695. Interestingly, in the bull market of the mideighties, a hundred million shares was regarded as "a slow trading day." By then, much larger totals were common.

44. Ahlstrom, *Religious History,* 919.

45. Howard Zinn, *The Twentieth Century, a People's History* (New York: Harper & Row, 1984), 89.

46. Arthur M. Schlesinger, Jr., *The Coming of the New Deal* (Boston: Houghton Mifflin, 1958), 2:20–21.

47. Langsam, *World Since 1914,* 457.

48. Ibid., 737.

49. This created an interesting situation for bodies such as the ULCA and Augustana, which had congregations on both sides of the border.

50. Ahlstrom, *Religious History,* 931.

51. The ULCA found it necessary to send an appeal to its congregations to refrain from this "violation of a most sacred trust." See Nelson, *Lutheranism 1914–1970,* 49.

52. Ibid., 50.

53. E. Clifford Nelson, "The New Shape of Lutheranism," in *The Lutherans in North America,* 454–55.

54. A. R. Wentz, *Basic History,* 331.

55. Quoted by Nelson, *Lutheranism 1914–1970*, 45.

56. F. K. Wentz, *Lutherans in Concert*, 86–88.

57. Wolf, *Documents*, 356.

58. Ibid., 356–57.

59. Ibid., 382.

60. Nelson, *Lutheranism 1914–1970*, 94.

61. Ibid., 94–95.

62. Wolf, *Documents*, 378.

63. A. R. Wentz, *Basic History*, 356–57.

64. Nelson gives a detailed analysis of the whole controversy in *Lutheranism 1914–1970*, 97–104.

65. Wolf, *Documents*, 357. Wolf provides key excerpts from the Baltimore Declaration, 357–59.

66. Ibid., 357.

67. Ibid., 358.

68. Ibid., 358–59.

69. Ibid., 394–95.

70. Nelson, "New Shape of Lutheranism," 469–70.

71. Wolf, *Documents*, 379.

72. Nelson, "New Shape of Lutheranism," 470.

73. Herbert C. Alleman, "The Pittsburgh Agreement and Lutheran Unity," *The Lutheran Church Quarterly*, 13 (October 1940): 356–57. It should be noted that Professor Reu had attacked Alleman in absentia at a meeting of the ALC-ULCA commissioners because of his *Old Testament Commentary*, which Reu claimed denied that the Bible was the Word of God. Both Charles M. Jacobs and Henry Offermann, of the ULCA, had come to Alleman's defense on the grounds that he had not written a book on dogmatics but a study of Old Testament literature. See Nelson, *Lutheranism 1914–1970*, 98–99.

74. *ULCA Minutes, 1940*, 262–64.

75. Nelson, *Lutheranism 1914–1970*, 106–8.

76. Ibid., 83–84.

77. Everett Arden gives a description of these developments in *Augustana*, 289–97. Conrad Bergendoff describes the "clean sweep" at Augustana Seminary that occurred in 1930 in an interview for *The Oral History Collection*, LCUSA Archives, 1979, 32. "This was a turning point in our history, and I myself am surprised that we heard so few voices raised against what was going on at the seminary."

78. Langsam, *World Since 1914*, 848.

79. Ibid., 853.

80. Ibid., 858.

81. See F. K. Wentz, *Lutherans in Concert*, 126.

82. Zinn, *A People's History*, 130. The Korean conflict was referred to as a United Nations "police action" rather than a "war."

83. Ahlstrom, *Religious History*, 951.

84. Martin E. Marty, *The New Shape of American Religion* (New York: Harper & Brothers, 1959), 7.

85. Ibid., 10. The phrase is Marty's. See also pp. 31–44.

86. Ahlstrom, *Religious History*, 954.

87. Marty, *New Shape of Religion*, 32.

88. In 1960 Gibson Winter wrote his *Suburban Captivity of the Churches* (New York: Doubleday & Co.) that shook the complacency of many mainline Protestant denominations.

89. The United Lutheran Church serves as an example. As early as 1948, it authorized its Board of Social Missions to address the urban problem (see *ULCA Minutes, 1948*, 300–8). In 1957 the ULCA social mission board published a landmark study edited by Harold C. Letts, *Christian Social Responsibility*, 3 vols. (Philadelphia: Muhlenberg Press, 1957).

90. Ahlstrom, *Religious History*, 962–63.

91. Nelson, *Lutheranism 1914–1970*, 140.

92. Ibid., 140–41.

93. Helen M. Knubel, daughter of the president, provides a candid and helpful account of her father's illness as well as important aspects of his career in *The Oral History Collection*, LCUSA Archives, 1982. According to Miss Knubel, Dr. Knubel had repeatedly expressed his desire to resign the presidency in the belief that no one person should occupy the office so long, but the offer was never accepted. Finally, he became convinced that the only course was for the church to make its own decision when it was ready for a successor. See particularly pp. 33–34 of *The Oral History Collection*.

94. *ULCA Minutes, 1944*, 135. At the same convention, Walton H. Greever was chosen secretary and Henry Beisler, treasurer, to create a new slate of officers for the largest Lutheran body in North America. See G. Elson Ruff, *The Lutheran* 27, no. 5 (November 1, 1944).

95. Robert H. Fischer's collection of vignettes, *Franklin Clark Fry. A Palette for a Portrait* (a supplementary number of *The Lutheran Quarterly*, 24 [1972]) provides a profound insight into the career of Fry as seen by colleagues and a variety of world religious leaders.

96. Mortensen, *Danish Church*, 237.

97. Edward T. Horn III, "Preparation of the Service Book and Hymnal," in *Liturgical Reconnaissance*, ed. Edgar S. Brown, Jr. (Philadelphia: Fortress Press, 1968), 91. This series of papers by persons intimately involved with development of the *Service Book and Hymnal* is an excellent summary of key factors in the project.

98. Ibid., 93. Luther D. Reed's own books, *The Lutheran Liturgy* (Philadelphia: Muhlenberg Press, 1947) and *Worship* (Philadelphia: Muhlenberg Press, 1959) are basic to understanding the traditions and decisions that lay behind development of the *SBH*.

99. William R. Seaman, "The Service Book and Hymnal Since 1958," in *Liturgical Reconnaissance*, ed. Edgar S. Brown, 105–14.

100. *ULCA Minutes, 1942*, 101.

101. *The Christian Growth Series* is described in detail in the *ULCA Minutes, 1944*, 297–98.

102. The writer participated in a thorough staff review of the series in the midfifties prior to a board decision to revise and update the materials.

103. A brief description of the program appears under "Lutheran Church in America," in *The Westminster Dictionary of Christian Education,* ed. Kendig Brubaker Cully (Philadelphia: Westminster Press, 1963), 401–3.

104. It is important not to confuse the American Lutheran Church, which had largely Germanic roots and came into being in 1930, with "The American Lutheran Church" (TALC) that was a new body formed by a merger of the "old ALC" with the ELC (Norwegian) and the UELC (Danish) in 1960.

105. E. Clifford Nelson provides an excellent summary of these developments in *Lutheranism 1914–1970,* 206–9. He points out that when the long-range program was presented to the Joint Union Committee for TALC, "T. F. Gullixson, supported by R. A. Ofstedal and O. G. Malmin, felt that the proposed curriculum would be dominated by the ULCA's 'liberal' view of the Bible." Nelson concludes, "Only the most defensive could fail to see that the same dynamics, present within the National Lutheran Council, had been at work in the long range program for parish education." Other details of the negotiations and the development of the program itself are described by the director of the program, W. Kent Gilbert, in an interview by John Reumann, in *The Oral History Collection,* LCUSA Archives, 1984, 4–19.

106. More specifics about parish education in the LCA appear in chap. 3.

107. Solberg, *Higher Education,* 305.

108. Ibid., 305–6.

109. Ibid., 311–12.

110. Ibid., 308.

111. Ibid., 280–82.

112. Ibid., 316.

113. Arden, *Augustana,* 125–26. S. Hjalmar Swanson gives an account of Augustana world mission work in *Foundation for Tomorrow* (Rock Island: Augustana Book Concern, 1960).

114. Mortensen, *Danish Church,* 162.

115. See Vikner, "LCA World Mission," 160; and A. R. Wentz, *Basic History,* 192.

116. Vikner, "LCA World Mission," 160.

117. Ibid., 157.

118. Nelson, *Lutheranism 1914–1970,* 148–49.

119. Vikner, "LCA World Mission," 163. This statement, with some minor revisions, eventually became the policy of the LCA Board of World Missions.

120. From an interview September 22, 1986, in Chicago with David A. Vikner, who himself had been a missionary in China and later in Japan.

121. The events of this period as well as some of significant impact that Lutheran missionaries had on Japan are described in the 1983 interview with Earl S. Erb, who was the executive of the ULCA Board of Foreign Missions at the time. See *The Oral History Collection,* LCUSA Archives, 1983, 47–50.

122. Nelson, "New Shape of Lutheranism," 487.

123. F. K. Wentz, *Lutherans in Concert,* 129.

124. E. Theodore Bachmann, in *Epic of Faith* (New York: National Lutheran Council, 1952), 42, estimates that 31,000 displaced persons were sponsored by America's Lutherans up until 1950.

125. F. K. Wentz, *Lutherans in Concert,* 160–61. In 1960 the work was expanded to include regular immigrants and became known as the Lutheran Immigration Service. The total effort today is named Lutheran Immigration and Refugee Service.

126. Wolf, *Documents,* 462. See also 463–66.

127. F. K. Wentz, *Lutherans in Concert,* 118–43.

128. Ibid., 117.

129. Arden, *Augustana,* details these steps, pp. 379–83.

130. Wolf, *Documents,* 473.

131. Nelson, "New Shape of Lutheranism," 508.

132. Wolf, *Documents,* 575.

133. When the Evangelical Lutheran Church in Canada came into being May 16, 1985, it included LCA's Canada Section and the Evangelical Lutheran Church of Canada (former ALC) but not the Canadian arm of the Missouri Synod.

134. Wolf describes the various steps taken and documents developed in forming the Canadian Lutheran Council in *Documents,* 574–85.

135. Nelson, *Rise of World Lutheranism,* 84–85. This is a definitive book on the subject.

136. Members of the commission were John A. Morehead (ULCA), Sven G. Youngert (Augustana), Gustav A. Fandrey (Iowa Synod), George Taylor Rygh (Norwegian), and Henry J. Schuh (Ohio Synod).

137. F. K. Wentz, *Lutherans in Concert,* 59.

138. Nelson, *Rise of World Lutheranism,* 95.

139. A. R. Wentz, *Basic History,* 338–39.

140. Wolf, *Documents,* 598.

141. F. K. Wentz, *Lutherans in Concert,* 131.

142. Bachmann, *Epic of Faith,* 19.

143. Nelson, *Rise of World Lutheranism,* 376–80.

144. For an account of the Lund assembly, see Nelson, *Rise of World Lutheranism,* 390–401. The constitution of the LWF is in Wolf, *Documents,* 598–601.

145. Both Augustana and the ULCA were at Edinburgh, but only Augustana was represented at Oxford. See Nelson, "New Shape of Lutheranism," 467. Arden points out in *Augustana,* 305, that "it was at Oxford and Edinburgh, 1937, that the Augustana Church identified itself with the mainstream of the modern ecumenical movement."

146. See William G. Rusch, *Ecumenism—A Movement Toward Church Unity* (Philadelphia: Fortress Press, 1985), 28–29. A fuller account of this history is in W. A. Visser 't Hooft, *The Genesis and Formation of the World Council of Churches* (Geneva: World Council of Churches, 1982).

147. Dorris A. Flesner, *American Lutherans Help Shape the World Council* (Dubuque, Iowa: William C. Brown, 1981), Publication No. 2, Lutheran Historical Conference, is a carefully researched account of this subject.

148. Knubel's letter conveying this request is reproduced by Flesner, ibid., 300–2.

149. Nelson, *Rise of World Lutheranism,* 292.

150. Flesner, *American Lutherans,* 69.

151. A. R. Wentz, *Basic History,* 380.

152. Nelson, "New Shape of Lutheranism," 513.

153. From a release by Erik W. Modean from the Lutheran Council News Bureau, June 7, 1968, quoted in Fischer, *Palette for a Portrait,* 2.

154. Ibid., 3.

155. Nelson, "New Shape of Lutheranism," 536.

156. See particularly Arden, *Augustana,* 379–413; Nelson, *Lutheranism 1914–1970,* 156–82; and Wolf, *Documents,* 466–573.

157. Quoted by Arden, *Augustana,* 382.

158. Ibid.

159. Ibid., 383. Arden pointed out that this was consistent with a resolution adopted by the American Lutheran Conference January 5, 1949, indicating that "while every effort ought to be made to achieve as broad a union of Lutherans as possible, *there ought to be no objection to lesser approaches to unity within the American Lutheran Conference,"* 383–84.

160. Nelson, *Lutheranism 1914–1970,* 177.

161. Arden, *Augustana,* 384.

162. Nelson, *Lutheranism 1914–1970,* 178; and "New Shape of Lutheranism," 505.

163. Arden, *Augustana,* 386. The complete text of the Minneapolis Theses is in Wolf, *Documents,* 340–42.

164. Arden, *Augustana,* 388.

165. Ibid., 358–60.

166. *The Lutheran Companion,* February 27 and March 26, 1952.

167. Arden, *Augustana,* 391–92.

168. Ibid., 395.

169. *The Lutheran Companion,* November 26, 1952.

170. The report of the JCLU to the constituting convention of the LCA indicates that this invitation was presented at a meeting of the Augustana Commission of Ecumenical Relations and the ULCA Special Commission on Relations of American Lutheran Church Bodies in Chicago, March 28, 1955. "As the conference drew to a close the United Lutheran Church representatives presented a proposition which electrified those in attendance." *LCA Minutes, June 28–July 1, 1962,* 39. George Harkins states in an interview for *The Oral History Collection,* LCUSA Archives, 1984, 34–35, that Fry had written the invitation the night before he left for the meeting. "This was done so privately that even his secretary did not know about it. Mrs. Fry typed it out at home."

171. Wolf, *Documents,* 543.

172. Ibid., 544.

173. Johannes Knudsen, *The Formation of the Lutheran Church in America* (Philadelphia: Fortress Press, 1978), 22.

174. Ibid.

175. Nelson, "New Shape of Lutheranism," 506. The full text of this statement is in the *ULCA Minutes, 1956,* 29–38. An abridged version is in Wolf, *Documents,* 546–54.

176. Wolf, *Documents,* 554.

177. *Minutes of the Joint Commission on Lutheran Unity* (December 12, 1956): 15, in the Archives of the Lutheran Church in America, Chicago.

178. *LCA Constitution,* Article II, Section 1.

179. See Appendix A for the text of Article II.

180. Knudsen gives a careful analysis of what lay behind this article and its relationship to other parts of the constitution in *Formation,* 30–38.

181. Nelson, *Lutheranism 1914–1970,* 183.

182. *JCLU Minutes,* 55.

183. *JCLU Minutes,* 57. It should be noted that those clergy who had already been ordained were exempted from this provision.

184. Ibid.

185. *LCA Constitution,* Article VII, Section 4.

186. See Knudsen, *Formation,* 35–36. The text of Article VII of the Augsburg Confession appears in *The Book of Concord,* ed., Theodore G. Tappert (Philadelphia: Fortress Press, 1959), 32.

187. *LCA Constitution,* Article IV, Section 2.

188. Bergendoff's paper is an exhibit for the minutes of the December 12, 1956, meeting of JCLU. An expanded form of his views is in his Knubel-Miller Lectures, *The Doctrine of the Church in American Lutheranism* (Philadelphia: Muhlenberg Press, 1956).

189. Knudsen, *Formation,* 41–42.

190. The Icelandic Synod of ULCA, AELC, and Suomi all chose to preserve something of their unique heritages through the avenue of special interest conferences. The Hungarian Conference of the ULCA was also continued. (See *Minutes of Constituting Convention,* 44, 127–28, 231–32.) In an interview by the writer August 27, 1986, with Raymond Wargelin, former president of Suomi, the latter indicated that the Finns did not favor the "halfway house" of a nongeographical synod but full partnership.

191. *LCA Constitution,* Article VIII, Section 7.

192. Knudsen relates this story in *Formation,* 26.

193. Ibid., 66. See also Tappert, "Church's Infancy," 50, for the origin of the "ministerium" concept and the role of lay representatives at synod meetings during the colonial period.

194. See *LCA Constitution,* Article VI, Section 3, and Article VII, Section 6.

195. The writer had this experience himself when he was ordained by the Central Pennsylvania Synod on the basis of a call to a congregation in New York City. He was informed by the Secretary of the New York Synod, however, that he would have to appear before the synodical examining committee, which was not due to meet for almost a year, because "after all we don't just *automatically* accept ministers ordained in other ULCA synods into *our* synod." The LCA practice is detailed in the *LCA Constitution,* Article VII, and the *Approved Constitution for Synods,* Article three, section III, 3.

196. Knudsen, *Formation,* 67–73.

197. *LCA By-Laws,* Section X, Boards, G, Item 3.

198. Ibid., B, Item 2.

199. Solberg, *Higher Education,* 316.

200. *LCA By-Laws,* Section X, Boards, B, Items 3–7.

201. Arden, *Augustana,* 115.

202. *LCA By-Laws,* Section X, Boards, F, Items 2–3.

203. In the case of the ULCA, this plan had been established in the mid-1940s.

204. Knudsen, *Formation,* 114.

205. A detailed analysis of the situation before and after merger has been prepared for the writer by Kathryn Barrus of the LCA Board of Pensions at the request of L. Edwin Wang, president.

206. These various plans are detailed in the *LCA Minutes, 1962,* 138–64, 167–68, 171–81, 188, 206.

207. Albert Stauderman, later editor of *The Lutheran,* points out that this name was rejected because it was then used for another small body in the United States. See the *Oral History Collection,* LCUSA Archives, 68.

208. Franklin Clark Fry describes the naming of the new church in *The Pastor's Desk Book* (February 1960): 1079–85.

209. This report is contained in the records of the JCLU in the LCA Archives in Chicago.

210. *JCLU Minutes,* December 10, 1959.

211. The votes of the four bodies are recorded in the *ULCA Minutes, 1962,* 335–37.

Chapter **3** | GROWING
TOGETHER

THE DECADE OF THE SIXTIES INTO WHICH THE
Lutheran Church in America was born was as tumultuous as the
fifties had seemed, on the surface at least, to be placid and stable. The
churches that formed the LCA had been preoccupied with merger,
which demanded large investments of time, energy, and money. The
sixties, however, could not be a time for living on the euphoria of
merger. Important as it was for the church to consolidate its new
relationships, the world was changing radically and confronted all
religious bodies with challenges that stretched imagination and resources.

In many ways this was a paradoxical period. Some futurists were
holding out dazzling designs for a bright and affluent tomorrow
where human work would be minimized, leisure would be maximized, and poverty would be virtually eradicated. Others, in sharp
contrast, exhibited a chronic apprehensiveness about the coming
age.[1] The computer revolution was at hand, and the conquest of
space opened exciting frontiers. At the same time, the cold war with
Russia was escalating, and tensions were growing in Southeast Asia.
Unrest and confrontation were common on college campuses. The
bulge in the population profile caused by the Baby Boom had moved
up the age scale so that young people were suddenly the largest
segment in society and were demanding a larger voice. The urban
crisis and racial tensions reached explosive proportions. The assassi-
nations of President John F. Kennedy, Robert Kennedy, and the Rev.
Dr. Martin Luther King, Jr., sent shock waves through the whole
world. Certain of these events and situations deserve more attention
here because they provided the framework within which the church
had to chart its course.

121

THE SPECTER OF WAR

It was once more a time when the United States found itself slipping inexorably toward war. The debacle of the invasion of Cuba in 1961 at the Bay of Pigs by an ill-prepared force made up largely of Cuban refugees with ineffective support from the United States government was a prelude to even graver international crises. The attempt by Russia to install ballistic missiles on Cuban soil in 1962 led President Kennedy to exercise unusual powers in confronting the Soviets. In the words of Arthur M. Schlesinger, Jr., "Alas, Kennedy's action, which should have been celebrated as an exception, was instantly enshrined as a rule. . . . The missile crisis, I believe, was superbly handled, and could not have been handled in any other way. But one of its legacies was the imperial conception of the Presidency that brought the republic so low in Viet Nam."[2]

The United States had had military advisers in South Vietnam for several years, but in 1965 President Lyndon Johnson suddenly "Americanized" the war with North Vietnam by ordering combat troops into the south and bombing of the north without Congress having declared war. "It was a momentous decision—one that brought the United States into a war lasting longer than any other in American history, a war causing more deaths in combat than any except the Civil War and the two World Wars."[3] It was also a war that brought deep polarization within American society and caused severe strains in relations with some of its closest allies. In the end, the whole effort seemed futile, for not long after the United States withdrew its forces in the 1970s, South Vietnam collapsed and Hanoi's troops occupied the country. Tens of thousands of refugees fled the country, and many of them found their way to North America. The war sequence and its aftermath caused serious soul-searching and often division within the religious community while providing new challenges for social action and service.

IMPACT OF TECHNOLOGY

It is difficult to catalog, much less evaluate fully, the technological changes that were impacting society. The public was largely unaware that far-reaching experiments were underway that would open the Pandora's box of genetic engineering. Even in the mid-sixties, the computer seemed like a baffling black box, and most people did not sense the revolutionary changes it would make in communications, industrial production, the ability to cope with vast amounts of information and solve intricate problems in fractions of a second.[4] Nor was it apparent that miniaturization of components would put computer power at the fingertips of virtually everyone in North American society, often without their realizing it.

Americans were caught up in the drama of the multibillion-dollar plan to put an astronaut on the moon and watched fascinated as television pictures were beamed back to earth. But science was also probing deeper into space with radio telescopes, and people began to ask, "In view of the billions of stars and their swirling planets, are we really alone?" For Christians, that posed new questions about the relevance of the gospel to an expanded concept of the universe.

Technology was also changing radically the nature of agriculture, which had always been a backbone of the Canadian and American economies. Production expanded enormously, and fewer workers were needed on the farms.[5] A whole segment of the population was being dislocated, and cherished rural life-styles were being disrupted. Movement of those displaced from the land to urban areas accelerated, but the cities could not handle the influx. Sydney Ahlstrom points out that "problems of bureaucratic organization, political process, crime, medical care, education, sanitation, communication, housing, pollution, and transportation rendered American cities barely capable of sustaining minimum levels of existence and popular acquiescence. This situation had a timetable of its own, and crises were developing even in cities where race conflict was almost nonexistent."[6] Before the end of the decade, some major American cities would literally be in flames and pillaged by looters.

THE BLACK REVOLUTION

The great hopes engendered among the Black population by Lincoln's Emancipation Proclamation had largely been eroded in the decades that followed. The United States fought World War II largely with segregated armed forces. Not until 1954 did the Supreme Court order desegregation of the schools, an order whose implementation was long delayed in many places. By the beginning of the twentieth century, the civil rights movement was gaining force, but by the mid-sixties the patience of Blacks with "gradualism" in eradicating inequalities was stretched dangerously thin. By this time three-fourths of the Black population was living in the decaying cities. Severe strains were being placed on economic status, social values, and family structures. Added to all this was the continuing fact of degrading discrimination.[7]

Although the Black protest movement had a number of significant leaders, none seemed to capture the imagination of all segments of society as did Martin Luther King, Jr. A Baptist minister who had studied for his doctorate at Boston University, King became the first president of the Southern Christian Leadership Conference in 1957. His approach was nonviolent and employed boycotts and marches to great effect. In 1963 he electrified a crowd of a quarter million freedom marchers at the Lincoln Memorial in Washington with his famous speech, "I Have a Dream."[8] But King's nonviolence did not prevail, and riots and torchings erupted repeatedly in the cities, culminating with violent uprisings in Newark and Detroit in the "long, hot summer" of 1967. Finally, Dr. King himself was gunned down on a hotel balcony in Memphis. A sorrowing nation saw new meaning in the lines of the Negro spiritual he had quoted in his dream speech, "Free at last, Free at last, Great God a-mighty, We are free at last." Ironically, the death of the man who stood against violence itself provoked a wave of riots. As a historian reported, "In Washington, D.C., smoke from burning buildings in the black slums billowed over the White House and through the cherry blossoms; on the Capitol steps, machine gunners stood guard. The rioting resulted in the biggest military build-up to deal with a civil disorder in the history of the country."[9]

What emerged as the prevailing slogan in the ensuing years was "Black Power," which often involved confrontational techniques in pressing its demands.[10] The emergence of Black Power was also a challenge to the Negro churches, which had often been accused of retarding the achievement of equality by preserving their own segregated memberships. As church leaders rallied around establishing a new sense of identity for Blacks, they could now claim "that from time immemorial it was religion (organized and unorganized) that had held the Afro-American heritage together and preserved black solidarity."[11] Various persons sought to articulate a connection between Black Power and the Christian faith. One of the best known was James H. Cone, who sought to establish the consistency of Black Power with the gospel of Jesus Christ.[12] The coming years would be fraught with struggle, but the movement toward Black liberation was irrevocable.

THE CHANGING ROLE OF WOMEN

Although it was little understood and sometimes discounted by a male-dominated society, the women's movement for equality in all areas of life gained new momentum in the sixties. The right to vote in national elections in the United States had been given to women in 1920 by passage of the nineteenth amendment to the Constitution. Proportionately, however, women continued to be sadly under-represented at the decision-making levels of government, business, and virtually every other part of society.

World War II was a turning point. Women began to enter the work force in droves, often filling what normally had been regarded as male jobs. By the sixties this trend had accelerated, but women still did not enjoy equal status or equal pay in the workplace. As women's roles changed, however, other changes were also occurring in traditional social patterns. The idealized family of mother, father, and several children was giving way to smaller units, and the phenomenon of the single-parent family was appearing with greater frequency. More and more women attended college, and greater numbers went on to graduate school with the intention of entering law, medicine, business, and, to the amazement of some, the ordained ministry. Women began to ask searching questions about built-in structures of social relations such as language, where male and female were subsumed under generic, masculine terms.

The movement for women's liberation was far more, however, than a series of disconnected changes. As Ahlstrom points out, "late in the sixties the movement took on broader and more truly revolutionary dimensions both by renewing the older (but widely ignored) demands for equality and by posing deeper questions about the moral structure of Western culture. Out of this new perspective for considering male and female values emerged a line of inquiry and action whose implications were at least as profound as that which stemmed from the black revolution."[13]

THE YOUTH CULTURE

When the Baby Boom began following World War II, few people realized that the newly born generation was a time bomb ticking away in society. While generalizations always run the risk of oversimplification, the youth of the fifties had seemed quite conventional.[14] The comfortable assumption that the young people of the sixties would follow past patterns in coming of age, however, was rudely shattered when the Baby Boomers became the largest segment of the population. In the late sixties particularly, the explosion came in a series of actions that demonstrated their desire for political power to match their numbers. "A generation of youth . . . kept out of the labor market, drafted for an unpopular war, and disillusioned with the plastic affluence of a society which had no place for them except in school, registered its frustration in protest against all established authority, whether government, family, or the current code of social mores."[15]

What occurred on college campuses in this period was a microcosm that reflected what was happening among young people throughout society. Initially, the tension had revolved around racial issues, but later it extended to environmental pollution, nuclear testing, the Vietnam War, ROTC, issues of college administration, and questions of a new morality. Berkeley was the site of the first major protest in 1964, but sit-ins, violence, and strikes escalated. A climax came when National Guard troops opened fire on students at Kent State, Ohio, in 1970, killing four and wounding nine others. Richard Solberg notes, "The tragedy at Kent State and its counterpart 10 days later at Jackson State College in Mississippi stunned the campuses and seemed to exercise a sobering influence on the whole country. It also opened the way for soul-searching and for critical review of the responsibility for the disasters of the previous six years."[16]

THE RELIGIOUS MILIEU

The decade was a period when there was a resurgence of cults and a celebration of the "Age of Aquarius." Many simply "opted out" of mainline Christianity and society in general. Some sought expression as flower children or Jesus People; others found meaning in ancient Eastern religions.[17] Protestant churches found themselves challenged to demonstrate that their kind of Christianity was relevant in a radically altered world. Even the venerable Roman Catholic Church was shaken into reexamining its age-old positions on many issues by an elderly cardinal who became Pope John XXIII and who apparently had no intention of serving as a "caretaker pope." He convened the Second Vatican Council (1962–65), which was designed to bring his church fully into the modern world.[18]

It was also a time when some writers began to speak seriously about the "death of God," a concept that had originally been posited by Nietzsche.[19] The popular press had a field day with the shock value of this phrase and dire predictions of the demise of Christianity. What was perhaps closer to the mark was the emphasis upon the secular character of the age. As Langdon Gilkey put it, "It is as if for our age the receiving set for religion had been tuned way down, or in some cases turned quite off. For multitudes of us (and they seem to be most characteristic of our time) no experience of God is either expected or felt, no word from God listened to or heard, and no command from God received or obeyed. . . . Most of us go about our lives quite as though there were no God at all, and until tragedy or something equally forceful strikes us, we do not notice this lack."[20] It was in this kind of spiritual climate that American churches had to reassess their own identity and mission. It was into this setting that the newly formed Lutheran Church in America was launched and had to find its way.

ORGANIZING FOR ACTION

When delegates from each of the four predecessor bodies descended on Cobo Hall, Detroit, in late June of 1962 for the final conventions of their own churches, there was an air of high anticipation mingled with a touch of nostalgia. They knew the gateway would open on uncharted territory to be explored together with newfound sisters and brothers. Yet something of the comfortable surroundings in which they had lived would be left behind, and perhaps their own identities would be lost in the passing. Enok Mortensen put it well in his history of the AELC: "It was like tidying up a room before leaving on a long journey—reluctantly now that the hour of departure had come at last, yet fully determined to go. The mood was reminiscent of Østergaard's immigrant who 'fain would stay and yet must leave.' "[21]

The tidying-up process done, more than seven thousand delegates and visitors converged on the huge arena of Cobo Hall. Shortly after 9:00 A.M. on Thursday, June 28, Malvin H. Lundeen, president of the Augustana Church and chair of the Joint Commission, brought the assembly to its feet and conducted the Order for the Opening of Synods. Swiftly, Lundeen was approved as presiding officer and George F. Harkins as secretary for the convention. A report of approval of the Agreement of Consolidation by each of the merging churches was read by its president, and the long-awaited moment was at hand. The mood was electric as a choir, robed in four colors recalling the traditions of the Danish, Finnish, Swedish, and German churches, presented a speech oratorio that described the coming of the immigrants to the new land. As four quarter candles were brought together to blaze as one, the choir proclaimed:

> It is not the form that brings us together.
> It is not a piece of paper on which we wrote words.
> It is not a common song or a common pledge.
>
> It is the One who led us,
> the One who seeks man,
> the One who became man
> To show us the way.
>
> That we may fall silent,
> submitting
> to what our minds cannot grasp,
> and bowing in reverence
> to the fact that is
> and ever shall be,
> the mystery of God
> who gave his body and blood
> that man might live.[22]

Following the oratorio, the thousands found new fellowship in receiving the body and blood of Christ in the Service of Holy Communion. Forty Communion assistants were needed as the throng made their way to kneel and receive the elements.[23] The long waiting was over. Their unity in the body of Christ was visible. The Lutheran Church in America was a reality.

Getting in Gear

If anyone had assumed that moving a denomination of more than 3,200,000 members along the road to the future was going to be all drama and excitement, that illusion was quickly dispelled in the business sessions that followed. It was here the delegates got down to the nitty-gritty of decision making that makes church conventions such an amazing blend of sharply debated issues and mind-numbing detail. Out of the host of actions, however, some did loom large.

Elections. The election of officers brought no real surprises. Using the ecclesiastical ballot, the convention selected Franklin Clark Fry as president on the second ballot and promptly chose Malvin H.

Lundeen as secretary.[24] When Dr. Lundeen declared Dr. Fry's election and called him to the podium, the new president said solemnly, "This admits only one answer. God helping me, I accept the office. Pray for me and with me for the unity for which this church was founded and let us do it with abandon and devotion."[25] In one sentence, he had set the tone that was to characterize the LCA's quest for wider unity during the next quarter century.

Edmund F. Wagner, a New York banker who had served as treasurer of the United Lutheran Church, was elected treasurer of the new body, and G. Elson Ruff was chosen editor of *The Lutheran,* a position he had held in the ULCA.[26] Ruff later remarked to Fry, who had been a longtime friend, that he could not understand why the constitution provided that the president of the church could serve until age seventy but the editor of *The Lutheran* could not. Fry replied that it was because senility was much more easily detected in editors than in church presidents.

The elections of boards and the Executive Council provided an insight into the place of men and women in the church in those days. Out of 201 possible elective positions, only seventeen went to women. The Court of Adjudication and the Boards of American Missions, Pensions, and Publication had none. Much more attention had gone into insuring in the nomination process that there was a balance of persons from the four church bodies among the nominees than in representation of women and minorities. Members of the seven commissions were not elected by the convention but were appointed later by the Executive Council.

The choice of chief executives for the boards and commissions had provoked some lively debate and ultimately some compromises in the JCLU.[27] The plan was for the JCLU to present to the convention a list of nominees whom the convention would designate "as its choices to be the first chief staff officials of the indicated boards and commissions and place their names before the several electing bodies for election." The slate of eleven clergy and four laymen was approved by the convention without discussion.[28] Executives of Lutheran Church Women and Lutheran Church Men were elected by their own boards without nominations from the church convention.

Major Steps Toward the Future

There were many major decisions made by the first convention, but several deserve special mention because of their long-range implications.

The installation of Franklin Clark Fry as the first president of the Lutheran Church in America by Raymond W. Wargelin, last president of the Suomi Synod

Malvin H. Lundeen, Franklin Clark Fry, and Edmund F. Wagner, first officers of the LCA

G. Elson Ruff, editor of *The Lutheran*

Viola Price, first LCW president

Master Plan for Seminaries. The number and location of theological seminaries had been a hotly debated issue in merger negotiations. The bylaws provided that the Board of Theological Education was to bring recommendations about the church's program "at its discretion." No discretion about timing was given on the first of these, however. The board was instructed "to report to the convention of the church in 1964 on the master plan for theological seminaries."[29] This triggered a report that would still be under discussion and implementation decades later.

Confirmation. In 1960 the ULCA convention had authorized a study of confirmation and had invited the other merging churches to set up a joint commission for the purpose. It was clear when the commission's report was presented to the constituting convention that it represented a consensus of the group but not a unanimous view. The report included proposals that at the time seemed revolutionary, such as admitting children to Communion at age ten and not making confirmation a prerequisite for admission to the Lord's Table.[30] Opposition revolved around not only the specific proposals in the report but also concern that the newly formed LCA should not move unilaterally in this important area without offering to conduct a joint study with the ALC and Missouri. Finally, a motion was adopted:

> That the Joint Commission on Confirmation be discharged with thanks for its provocative study and that this church invite The American Lutheran Church and The Lutheran Church—Missouri Synod to appoint members to a Joint Commission on the Theology and Practice of Confirmation to which the foregoing report shall be transmitted as information and authorize the Executive Council to take all necessary steps to implement such an invitation and study.[31]

By this action, the LCA demonstrated its desire to move in concert where possible with the other major Lutheran bodies in North America.

Toward a New Inter-Lutheran Agency. As anticipated, the convention voted to meet the various technical requirements that would enable the LCA to become a member of the National Lutheran Council, the Canadian Lutheran Council, the National Council of Churches of Christ in the USA, the Lutheran World Federation, and the World Council of Churches.[32] Not until earlier in the week, however, had word come that another major step had been taken to pave the way for inter-Lutheran cooperation. Meeting in Cleveland, the Missouri Synod had voted to join in planning a tripartite agency that would replace the NLC.[33] The LCA convention voted unanimously and enthusiastically to do the same.[34] It remained only for the ALC to concur in October to set the process in motion that would result in forming the Lutheran Council in the USA.

Welfare Agencies. Because of the widely varied patterns of ownership and control of social welfare institutions and agencies in the merging bodies, a crucial document was presented by JCLU that recommended a synodical polity in which the Board of Social Ministry would play an active role on behalf of the whole church. The board was given the immediate responsibility of working out the myriad details of arrangements with the synods.[35] The basic policy was one that would be tested many times in the coming years as government became more and more active in social welfare and as synods found themselves confronted with complex issues and sometimes potentially large financial liability.

Next Stages. The delegates left Detroit excited about the future but scarcely dreaming how much remained to be done. Within a few months, every board, commission, auxiliary, and synod would hold organizing meetings. Nearly 150 officers would be elected; constitutions would be revised and adopted; new corporations would be formed; financial resources would be realigned; and scores of staff chosen—all of this a mere prelude to the church's real business, carrying out its God-given mission in thousands of settings at home and abroad. The remainder of the decade would find the new church tested and tried in many arenas. Here we can describe only a few.

CHURCH AND SOCIETY

The way the Lutheran Church in America sought to interact with and meet the needs of the society in which it functioned could not be separated from the realities of its own composition. Although there were small and significant numbers of Blacks and other groups among its membership, the LCA was overwhelmingly white, and middle-class white at that. Given the origin of the streams of Lutheran immigrants, the LCA at its inception could hardly have been anything else.[36] The consequence for the LCA throughout its history, however, was a continuing struggle with its own identity that was often tinged with guilt as it confronted a rapidly changing society. Clearly, on the basis of its own theological understanding, Philip Hefner states, "The LCA wants to follow the leading of God's Spirit into the world, to be a part of God's actualizing of his gospel of grace."[37] Articulating a course of social action for the church, however, has proved difficult and has often come only after intense debate.

Forging Social Statements

The principal means of making clear the LCA's position on major issues has been through the development of social statements. In the first decade of the church's existence, preparing such statements was the responsibility of the Board of Social Ministry. From the outset this board recognized that any positions taken by the LCA must be developed from a biblical and theological perspective. During the second biennium, however, it drafted a *Theological Statement on Social Ministry* that was to become the foundation of its work.

Largely the work of theologian William Lazareth, the document declares that "the urgent need for the church's social ministry is accentuated by the convergence of two momentous revolutions."[38] The one is rapid social change where "our whole world view is undergoing a radical transformation. As a result the modern world of the last 400 years is dying before our eyes. . . . In its stead the 20th century is painfully giving birth to an awful yet wonderful 'postmodern' world." The second is that the church "has been engaged in repentant self-examination and renewal. . . . In face of the new situation, Christians must reaffirm their commitment to a vital social ministry as an integral part of the church's total mission in the world."[39]

The statement bases the church's social ministry upon its obedience to the Servant Lord. "Christ must be the norm. Christians are called in obedience of faith to minister in and for the world as the servant church of the Servant Lord." In describing the church's role, the document warns against the twin pitfalls of activism and quietism, and it points to the fact that "it is through the continual interaction of the law and the gospel that the triune God rules the two realms of creation and redemption."[40] It goes on to spell out that God is the Lord of both realms, Christians live in both realms, and the two realms of creation and redemption interpenetrate each other. It cautions, however, against either church or state usurping the responsibility of the other. The document concludes by reaffirming the intrinsic character of Christian social ministry as an essential part of the church's total mission.[41] This statement proved to be a seminal document as the church moved to define its stance on specific social issues.

Normally, social statements were brought to the convention by the board for approval, but the Executive Council could act between conventions when delay would "destroy the effectiveness or seriously impair the timeliness of a word which the Lutheran Church in America needs in conscience to speak."[42] During the sixties, the LCA approved eight major policy statements.

Race Relations. An estimated one thousand Lutherans took part in the dramatic march on Washington, August 28, 1963, that underscored the reality of the racial revolution spreading through American society. On July 8, President Fry had addressed a pastoral letter to the church in which he declared, "The position that Christians take on race has spiritual roots. It arises directly out of our view of God and man; and belongs to the essence of our faith. It is accusingly simple and brooks no disagreement. Men, created by God and redeemed by Christ, are equals and are meant to be brothers. No man is a hair's breadth above or below another in God's affection nor can he be in a Christian's regard. Any disabilities on the basis of race within the Christian family are evil. They are an affront to the Lord and a sign of deviation from him. We all agree on this. The time has come to act."[43]

At the 1964 convention in Pittsburgh, the Board of Social Ministry presented what was to become the first social statement approved by the Lutheran Church in America. The statement on race relations was adroitly drafted around the petitions of the Prayer of the Church from the *Service Book and Hymnal* and bluntly declared, "Unless we mean what we say, and live as men who intend to do what we mean, the holy gravity of our prayer itself condemns us."[44]

The statement then calls upon the church, its congregations, synods, agencies, and institutions to avoid discrimination; support social justice in all its business involvements and give critical scrutiny to its own employment practices; acknowledge the imperative of worship, fellowship, and mission without regard to race; bring about understanding at points of racial tension; and work for civil rights legislation at all levels of government. Editors were told that church publications "should present an objective picture of racial diversity and emphasize the Christian's responsibility in the struggle for racial justice."[45] These points addressed real issues in the church. There were congregations that excluded Blacks from membership, and many Lutherans were ambivalent about bringing the church's power to bear in the racial struggle.

The most controversial point in the policy came last. It put the LCA on record in terms of the Christian's responsibility regarding the law of the land and civil disobedience. This part of the statement was hammered out over several convention sessions and is so important as a precedent in the LCA that it deserves quotation in full here.

> Christians are committed to the rule of law as an expression of the moral law of God. Nevertheless, it must be recognized that laws have been and may in the future be enacted, or social customs may exist, which are believed to be in basic conflict with the constitutional law of the land or the moral law of God. In such circumstances, the church, its congregations, synods, agencies, and institutions, including their representatives, as well as individual members, are recognized as free by all lawful means, including participation in peaceful public demonstrations, to urge repeal or invalidation of such laws or to effect change of such customs.
>
> If and when the means of legal recourse have been exhausted or are demonstrably inadequate, Christians may then choose to serve the cause of racial justice by disobeying a law that clearly involves the violation of their obligations as Christians, so long as they are:
> a. willing to accept the penalty for their action;
> b. willing to limit and direct their protest as precisely as possible against a specific grievance or injustice;
> c. willing to carry out their protest in a nonviolent, responsible manner, after earnestly seeking the counsel of fellow Christians and the will of God in prayer.

In all of this, we are guided and supported by the normative teaching of the church in Article XVI of the Augsburg Confession: 'Christians are obliged to be subject to civil authority and obey its commands and laws in all that can be done without sin. But when commands of the civil authority cannot be obeyed without sin, we must obey God rather than men (Acts 5:29).'[46]

Marriage and Family. Sometimes when the church delved deeply into a social concern, it found the issues much more complex than had been anticipated. At the 1964 convention, the Board of Social

Ministry proposed a statement on marriage and family that was intended to serve as guidance to congregations until a fuller study could be prepared for the next convention. The document dealt with such matters as commitment to lifelong fidelity as the "essential characteristic of marriage," responsible planning of parenthood, recognition that divorce may be necessary in the case of a failed marriage, guidance about and restrictions on remarriage, the importance of sex education, the "special problems in mixed marriages" (this seemed to focus on marriages with persons of other faiths), and preparation of pastors to deal with these matters.[47] The statement was adopted with little discussion, but it would not be until 1970 that the Board of Social Ministry would be ready with a more definitive document.

School Prayer and Bible Reading. When the Supreme Court of the United States in 1963 declared unconstitutional the widespread practice of prayer and Bible reading in the public schools, there was a public outcry and a move to pass a constitutional amendment restoring the privilege. Again the march of events had made it necessary for the Executive Council to declare the Lutheran Church in America's stand on the issue. At its June 1963 meeting, the Executive Council issued a three-paragraph statement which said that not much had been lost through the decision and warned, "The more we attempt as Christians or Americans to insist on common denominator religious exercise or instruction in public schools, the greater risk we run of diluting our faith and contributing to a vague religiosity which identifies religion with patriotism and becomes a national folk religion." The statement went on to say that the decision was a watershed which signaled that the United States "is past the place where underlying Christian culture and beliefs are assumed in its life." This event intensified the need for the church to stand alone in society and for a greater depth of conviction for its members.[48]

In its report to the 1964 convention, the Board of Social Ministry included an "interpretive memorandum" that spelled out more fully the church's position. Although it concurred with the Executive Council that not much had been lost, the board acknowledged the legitimacy of having reservations about the Supreme Court's decisions and raised a serious question as to whether the schools could be absolutely neutral in religious matters. It cautioned, "Any education premised on indifference to the religious factors in history, in Ameri-

can life and the life of the individual, is an inadequate education.
Furthermore, the vacuum introduced by the exclusion of religion
opens the door to the cult of secularism."[49] The board went on to
state that the Supreme Court had properly made way for objective
teaching about religion and the Bible but indicated that the church
should not count on the schools too much in dealing with religious
matters. It concluded that a constitutional amendment would not be
wise. The convention had ratified the Executive Council's statement,
but it was clear that the whole issue of school prayer particularly
would arise again and again in American society in the years that
followed.[50]

Church and State. Building upon its theological document briefly
described above, the BSM presented to the 1966 convention in Kansas City a statement on "Church and State: A Lutheran Perspective."
In it the church spells out the way in which church and state should
relate in the settings of the United States and Canada. The key
conclusion was, "We affirm the sacredness of the secular life of God's
people as they worship, witness, and work in God's world. We advocate the institutional separation and functional interaction of church
and state. This position rejects both the absolute separation of church
and state and the domination of either one by the other, while seeking a mutually beneficial relationship in which each institution contributes to the common good by remaining true to its own nature and
task."[51] As one Lutheran theologian put it in the early 1960s, church
and state are not separated by a wall but by a picket fence.[52] The
church and state statement illustrates a technique used by the BSM
to help the constituency gain a deeper understanding of major issues
through a series of study booklets on Christian social responsibility
that were used quite widely.

Capital Punishment. In both the United States and Canada the issue
of the death penalty for crime was hotly debated during the late
fifties and early sixties. The church's social statement of 1966 is unequivocal in urging abolition of capital punishment and in challenging whether the imposition of the death penalty for crime is not a
misuse of the state's God-given powers. It also urges citizens to work
for improvement of the criminal justice system and to attack the
social conditions that breed hostility to society and disrespect for the
law.[53]

Poverty. President Lyndon Johnson had made the "War on Poverty" a keystone of the effort to build a more just society in the United States. As might be expected, the program had strong supporters and vocal critics. While not endorsing all the specifics, the LCA did respond to such initiatives by a statement on "Poverty" that said, "We approve of declarations of public policy in our own countries (U.S.A. and Canada) which seek to eliminate the paradox of poverty in the midst of plenty and further seek to open to everyone opportunities for education and training, for work, and for living in decency and dignity."[54] The document aligned the LCA with the struggle against poverty, which it regarded as in continuity with biblical concern for the poor, and declared that while there was room for disagreement on means, commitment to the struggle itself was not an open question for Christians. Perhaps few at that time realized how long and frustrating that effort would be.

Religious Liberty. Although the Atlanta convention in 1968 was initially preoccupied with the election of a new president and secretary, it did find time to approve three more social statements. One, dealing with "Religious Liberty in the United States," was the further development of a resolution presented two years earlier. Recognizing that the Christian church has not always had an exemplary record on interreligious understanding and prejudice, the document gives a thoughtful analysis of the special dimensions of the question within the whole of American society. It affirms the right of both those who believe in God and those who do not to practice their own convictions without fear of coercion. It also affirms the rights of corporate expression by church and religious organizations as based on civil law and actions. It does not, however, regard religious liberty as an "absolute right," but declares that "nothing less than a serious and immediately threatened violation of other basic rights should warrant restrictions on religious liberty."[55] This statement is an example of the way the BSM brought together experts from a variety of disciplines to draft a policy for the church. In this instance, the group included theologians, a law professor, and a noted sociologist of religion.[56]

Church and Social Welfare. As government expanded its role in social welfare, it seemed necessary for the LCA to define the continuing need for nongovernmental agencies in the field. The statement on "The Church and Social Welfare" indicates the impossibility of churches and voluntary agencies coping by themselves with massive and pervasive social problems. At the same time, it concludes that the church does have tasks of service to perform in obedience to Jesus Christ, its Servant Lord. "The foremost task of the church in social welfare is to proclaim the Word of God in such ways that it makes all of its members alert and responsive to human need at home and abroad and to the many faces of injustice."[57] It calls upon church members to support these works of mercy with time, talents, and substance.

Conscientious Objection. The most controversial statement to come to the Atlanta convention was the one on "Conscientious Objection." The debate was fueled by the increasing unpopularity of the Vietnam War and the flight of some young men to Canada to avoid the draft. Long lines formed at convention microphones, and no less than thirty persons spoke on the question.[58] Although the basic privilege of conscientious objection for religious reasons had long been granted in the United States and was supported by the church, the new statement had two new and important provisions. One was the affirmation that "all conscientious objectors should be accorded equal treatment before the law, whether the basis for their stand is specifically religious or not. It is contrary to biblical teaching (cf. Romans 2:15f) for the church to expect special status for the Christian or religious objector."[59] The second was the section which affirmed the right of selective objection to participation in a particular war. Although the statement was finally adopted by a vote of 426 to 126, feelings were so intense that sixty-four delegates made the unusual request that their negative votes be recorded in the minutes.[60]

Rising to Needs

The LCA, of course, did not limit its response to societal needs to just making pronouncements. Although every one of its agencies had to grapple with social issues in one way or another, the urgency seemed to be felt more keenly in some quarters than in others. Social problems seldom can be isolated discretely. What happens in one area almost always has an impact on others, but it is possible to focus here on two examples of what was happening regarding major concerns.

Race Relations. The 1964 social statement on race relations had far-reaching results in the church, although to many it seemed that the process of implementation was painfully slow. Congregational constitutions were amended to eliminate exclusionary language; mission congregations were informed in no uncertain terms that support would be withheld if there were any discriminatory practices; active support of civil rights legislation grew; a Coordinating Committee on Race Relations chaired by President Fry was formed among church-wide agencies; church institutions opened their doors more widely to minorities; and Lutherans did indeed participate in acts of civil disobedience. Ground was broken barely a month after the convention when Lee H. Wesley, a pastor in Los Angeles, was called by the Board of Parish Education to become Secretary for Youth Work and, as a consequence, the first Black staff member in the history of the LCA or its predecessor bodies.[61]

As the decade wore on, colleges became an arena of change. A survey in 1965 by the Board of College Education and Church Vocations showed that, despite the fact that there were no discriminatory admissions practices, two LCA colleges had no Black students.[62] "Lutheran colleges which made serious efforts at the recruitment of black students were confronted by two hard facts." Solberg notes, "Black youth were most often from poor families and many were academically unprepared for college education. To meet these problems colleges tried a variety of remedial and financial-aid programs assisted in part by federal and state funding."[63] The BCECV also committed funds for scholarships and compensatory education.[64] Progress was slow, but it can be said that by the 1984–85 academic year there were 1,284 Black students at LCA colleges.[65] The largest percentage was reported by Upsala College in New Jersey, where 26.5 percent of the student population was Black.[66]

The wave of riots and destruction that had erupted in American cities became the catalyst in 1968 for a frontal attack by the LCA on racial injustice and the urban crisis.[67] The Atlanta convention had been moved by a series of addresses on the problem, climaxed by a powerful speech by Martin Luther King, Sr., father of the slain civil rights leader. Dr. King declared, "They didn't kill Jesus for eating with sinners; they just criticized Him for it. They didn't kill Him for being a country preacher talking about love. They killed Him when He went into the Temple and began fooling with that power structure."[68] Board after board had reported on the need, and the convention responded by voting a special appeal for $6,500,000 over the next two years to deal with the urban crisis.[69] Although the ACT Appeal, as it was known, did not attain the dollar goal set, the effort did galvanize the church in a way that would change dramatically its priorities in the years that followed.

The Women's Movement. During the first half-dozen years of the LCA's existence, the movement for women's rights was just beginning to inch its way into the church's consciousness. One barometer of the perceived role of women was the number of those elected for positions on the Executive Council and the boards. As late as 1968 only one woman was nominated at the convention for the Executive Council and nine others for boards. At that same convention, however, Laura Klick was recognized as the first person in the church to fulfill the requirements for the new category of certified lay professional.[70]

One important straw in the wind was a proposal in 1966 by a special Commission on the Comprehensive Study of the Doctrine of the Ministry that "this church make a study of the role of women in the ministry of this church and of the advisability of ordaining women into the clergy."[71] In his report to the convention, President Fry had recommended that the inquiry be postponed indefinitely, in part because of its implications for ecumenical dialogues with other church bodies.[72] Debate on the issue was lengthy, but the convention finally approved going ahead with such a study. It would be four years, however, before the question would be resolved.

THE NEW FACES OF MISSION

The sociological and theological ferment of the 1960s, which had occupied the attention of the Board of Social Ministry, led also to a fresh examination of the church's mission both at home and abroad. As one LCA study put it, "Currently there is a nearly exclusive emphasis on the function or mission of the church—an emphasis that is virtually a pre-occupation. The current emphasis is manifested in diverse ways: the World Council of Churches' study of the structure of the missionary congregation, greater church involvement in social issues, virulent criticisms of existing denominational and congregational structures, a vital interest in liturgical renewal.

Lee H. Wesley, first black staff member in the LCA

Dr. Martin Luther King, Sr., addressing delegates at the 1968 Atlanta convention

Current emphasis is on the world or society as the arena for God's activity."[73]

This was the time when certain catch phrases such as "the world sets the church's agenda" and "the church *is* the mission" captured widespread attention. Most Christian churches were struggling with the problem of communicating the gospel in meaningful terms to an increasingly secularized society. Attempting to bridge the popularly perceived chasm between sacred and secular led to radical changes in church priorities and frequent experimentation by mission agencies. The LCA's Boards of American Missions and World Missions were not unaware of these trends, and the way they began to recast their roles was indicative of how the Lutheran Church in America as a whole was redefining its responsibility as God's servant people in and to the world.

American Missions

The pattern that had obtained in home missions in the years preceding merger carried over into the new church. During the shakedown cruise of the first biennium, the Board of American Missions spelled out what it regarded to be its responsibilities and reported these to the 1964 convention. The following points loomed as particularly significant:

First, the board defined its mission as reaching people for Christ through the ministry of congregations. This was to be done in partnership with synods. Not only were new congregations to be started but also those with special problems could seek aid. A "calculated proportion" of pioneer work would be undertaken at economic levels and in geographic areas where there were no Lutheran churches. Ministry by congregations was to be to all people, especially in urban areas.

Second, it defined "a mission congregation" as "one receiving aid in any form from the board." The church building program was geared to "short-term financing" and having congregations in first units by their first anniversaries.

Third, mission congregations would, in situations where the original language of the people was other than English, carry on ministry in the language of the people but at "an early date" provide a service each Sunday and a Sunday school in English. Congregations were expected to participate in the total program of the LCA and contribute its full benevolence quota.[74]

During its first two years the BAM entered 95 new fields, and 138 congregations were organized. The largest number were in areas of rapid growth, and suburban settings continued to receive the major attention.[75] Although the board confidently predicted increased numbers for the future, its own planning division was underscoring the immensity and complexity of the task in a highly mobile, changing society. Pointing to California as an example, the planners declared that it would require starting a new congregation of nine hundred baptized members every twenty days to keep up with the influx of Lutherans. At the same time, the board acknowledged that many missions, started with enthusiasm a short time before in Los Angeles County, were already in trouble and were losing members. It also noted that the nonwhite population of California was already growing more than twice as fast as the white.[76]

During the 1964–66 biennium, expansion was again the emphasis in American Missions. In its report to the church, the BAM declared, "The size of the program can be noted by these statistics:

120 congregations organized during biennium
168 fields entered
1,450 congregations assisted
356 parsonages and sites purchased
$54,000,000 loaned to missions
$23,266,077 placed in escrow in 1965
$2,657 placed in escrow every hour, 24 hours a day, 365 days
2,000 checks written per month
$14,460,733 guaranteed by board
$16,645,091 debt of board January 1, 1966

"All of this is for one purpose—people. It is 'big business,' but big business for our Lord."[77]

By this time, however, basic changes in BAM priorities were beginning to appear. The Division of Church Planning pointed out that because of a lagging economy, many hoped-for suburban developments had been stopped dead in their tracks, with one California community having two thousand houses standing empty. Mission developers were withdrawn from some planned entries and reassigned. The Urban Church Division stressed the needs and demands of sprawling metropolitan areas where it admitted, "No one has as yet discovered the final and complete answers to the problems of the urban church."[78] The board reported briefly on its newly authorized responsibility for work with community organizations. Nearly one-third of its report to the church dealt with "LCA Responsibility to American Indians."

Nevertheless, a crucial turning point for the BAM came in an address to the 1966 convention by Edmund A. Steimle, an LCA professor at New York's Union Seminary. He urged that the BAM consider the way the "outmoded numbers game" of the board's expectations of mission congregations bred *incurvatus in se,* a process of turning in upon themselves rather than dealing with the needs of their own communities. "Yesterday's methods cannot keep up with today's peoples-on-the-go," he declared. "I propose that we need experimentation not only on the fringe, but at the heart of the mission of the Church. *Not* just for the sake of experimentation, but in an attempt to find *structures* that may provide a means for turning the Church outward toward the world rather than inward upon itself."[79]

Almost a year later Donald Houser, the executive secretary, reminded the board again of the Steimle address and said, "It would be nice if our only responsibility was to establish new congregations in growing suburbs. . . . We are not living in that kind of world today. . . . The church demands far more of us. Urbanization, poverty, the racial revolution, leisure-recreation, community organization, the ghettoes and high-rise apartments, new cities, etc., all cry out to us to experiment, to break out of existing molds to find ways and means to reach people and help people where they are."[80]

During the biennium the BAM not only restructured itself, it also shifted its emphasis from the suburbs to the inner city and introduced the policy of "program grants," which was more wide-ranging than salary aid to missions. Only seventy-one new fields were entered, the lowest number since the LCA was formed. During the next two years, the number of new entries dropped to thirty-four. "As stories of effective ministries in new ventures are circulated," the Urban Division reported, "more and more churches are looking to the Board of American Missions for assistance as they realistically face up to the challenges that are everywhere around them."[81] The board's budgets reflected the new emphases, as investment in urban church programs expanded dramatically and grants to community organizations began to command substantial sums.[82] Needless to say, the shifts had both supporters and critics, but one study implied that the full implications of the BAM's decisions for the future of the LCA could not have been known in advance.[83]

World Missions

The changes that were taking shape in world missions were no less sweeping than those on the home front. As the era of independence reached its height among the younger churches, there was often a spectacular increase in membership, although it would be a mistake to assume that there was always a causal relationship. Lutherans in North America were understandably excited and encouraged by what was happening. Following are a few highlights (all figures are in thousands of baptized members):

LUTHERAN CHURCHES IN AFRICA AND ASIA

	1958	1969
Ethiopia and Eritrea	25	97
Tanzania	320	462
Liberia	5	15
Madagascar	219	328
Namibia	202	276
South Africa	427	514
India	662	797
Indonesia	717	1,257
Papua-New Guinea	202	394[84]

Countless thousands of others were being reached with the church's message throughout much of the world by the Radio Voice of the Gospel, a powerful radio station established in Addis Ababa in 1963 by the Lutheran World Federation. The station had a dozen feeder studios in different countries and broadcast in sixteen different languages.[85] RVOG was an amazing technological achievement by the church in the use of media that continued to operate until the Marxists toppled the Haile Selassie government in Ethiopia in 1974.

Not everything that accompanied the move from a state of dependence to independence by the younger churches, however, was an unqualified success, nor were the transitions accomplished without stress.[86] Each church faced a different set of circumstances politically, economically, educationally, and ecumenically on its home turf. Japan, for example, was already a highly industrialized, affluent, and literate society. Tanzania, on the other hand, had only achieved independence from the United Kingdom in 1961 and eschewed dependence on foreign assistance as it moved toward socialism. Ninety-three percent of its population were living marginal existences through agriculture, and illiteracy was high.[87]

The financial resources and indigenous leadership were often not equal to the tasks of autonomy. As a result, there was still substantial dependence upon overseas financial and personnel assistance. "In eight of the nine LCA-related churches self-support plans were adopted, implemented for a period, and then aborted for a variety of reasons. These reasons included local economic depressions; natural catastrophes; difficulties in adjusting foreign initiated structures, staff, and institutions to manageable levels; and the compulsion of affluent overseas churches and agencies to relieve the pressures."[88]

The Board of World Missions did take steps to deal with the problems and move things toward a new stage of relationship. In 1963 it launched an interpretation program that tried to help the LCA membership grow beyond the "sending church mentality" to see the dimensions of responsible mission policy. The keystone was a new periodical, *World Encounter,* that confronted its readers with some of the gritty realities the Christian churches faced in overseas situations. For example, it reported on the first All-Africa Christian Youth Assembly in Nairobi, Kenya, and printed condensations of "speeches not meant for American ears" that predicted that the struggle for social justice on the continent was "going to be fierce and ruthless."[89] Other articles raised such questions as "Are Institutions a Millstone of the Mission Field?"[90] and "What Is an Indigenous Church?" which declared that "American and European Protestants, afraid to let the gospel flower in Asian or African soil, have turned the young churches into tragic ghettoes of Western culture."[91]

The board tried to communicate to the church that not only were fewer missionaries needed but also that the majority of those called for were persons with technical skills in agriculture, medicine, education, and the like, rather than pastors. The average church member, however, clung to the romantic and outmoded notion that all missionaries were somewhere out there converting benighted heathen to Christianity and, of course, Lutheranism.

By 1965 Earl S. Erb, executive secretary, announced that the BWM staff would be engaging in long-range planning with representatives of younger churches to deal with such questions as: "What features of old programs should be increased or dropped? Which institutions should be gradually, or even suddenly, closed? . . . Is the Lutheran Church in America pauperizing, rather than helping, by providing heavy financial aid?"[92] The simultaneous transition from a recognition of the independence of young churches to a further stage that became known as "independence/interdependence" was underway.

Two definitive actions were taken in 1968 that signaled the profound changes that were afoot in world missions. One was the approval by the Atlanta convention of elimination of Article XXI of the constitution, which provided for a category of "Associated Churches" that were permitted two delegates at the LCA conventions.[93] The second was that the BWM staff was to negotiate with appropriate committees of the overseas church step-by-step reductions of operating subsidies while informing them that funds would be available for justified programs on a limited term basis.[94] "Two of the churches affirmed the decision and moved immediately into positive action. Five were apprehensive and had to go through a period of negotiation to accept the challenge. Two were so disturbed by the action they refused to negotiate, forcing BWM to set up, reluctantly, unilateral step-by-step subsidy cut-off schedules."[95]

One other major development occurred when Earl Erb retired as board executive at the end of 1967. Arne Sovik, who had originally been a missionary to China and for twelve years director of the LWF's Department of World Mission, was called as Erb's successor. Since Sovik was an American Lutheran Church pastor, there was speculation for a while that this might lead to a merging of the ALC and LCA boards. Indeed, even broader ties were considered when the boards of ALC, LCA, and LCMS met together on May 11, 1971, and asked a World Mission Study Group to explore the "possibility of the formation of a common Board of World Mission or a common inclusive Board of Missions for the North American Lutheran Churches."[96]

By the end of 1971, LCMS had withdrawn, and the conversations continued between ALC and LCA with an eye not only to cooperation but also to possible joint administration. By January 1972 representatives from ALC and LCA met and forged ahead, and for a time, hopes were high that the strengthening of cooperative efforts could still lead to a joint board.[97] Such proved not to be the case, however, and it seemed almost prophetic that the board said to the 1968 convention, "The report speaks more of continuation than of change, simply perhaps because the Kingdom of Heaven is more like a tree than a daisy."[98]

CONGREGATIONS ON THE FIRING LINE

Casual sniping at congregational life as at best outmoded and at worst irrelevant had turned into a kind of big game hunt by the 1960s, with weapons aimed at the parish from every direction. Books like *The Comfortable Pew* charged the church in general and the congregation in particular with being weak and equivocal, often standing aloof from the real issues of the times.[99] Such attacks on the church were not surprising in view of the climate of the times, but there were also many searching questions asked by committed Christians who were concerned about renewal of congregational life.

At the 1964 convention in Pittsburgh, the Eastern Pennsylvania Synod memorialized the church "to authorize a study of the nature and mission of the congregation." The proposal was approved and a commission of fifteen persons appointed that brought back to the next convention a report that addressed a ringing "Manifesto" challenging every congregation to reexamine its mission. "In this modern mass society and in these changing times," the commission declared, "there is danger that our congregations may have lost touch with the dynamics of our society. If congregations are static and immobile in spiritual life or in outward service to mankind, the church will be irrelevant in this urban-oriented culture and unable to grasp its many and varied opportunities. Each congregation must find the means and methods by which it best fulfills God's call to be his people. . . . The forces with which it must deal are in ferment. This is the natural climate and condition in which the church carries on its work."[100]

The report had made a cogent analysis of "modern man" and the communities in which he lived. It concluded that "the Christian community has its most frequent and most stable expression in the congregation."[101] The congregation, as the place where the gospel is preached and the sacraments administered, was seen as the place where the church that is boundless in time and space becomes visible and concrete. In order that congregations not become obsessed with their own internal life, however, the commission proposed that they test their faithfulness in sixteen areas of their ministry.[102]

After lengthy debate and various amendments, the convention adopted *The Manifesto* and instructed the Executive Council to arrange for study materials based on the report. The president was asked to call upon each congregation to undertake a study and judgment of its life and work. Donald R. Pichaske, editorial director for the Board of Parish Education, was released from his duties for two months to write the mandated study materials. *A Study Book on the Manifesto* was published early in 1967, and thousands were used by church councils and other groups to probe the effectiveness of the ministry of their own congregations.[103] It was the first time that the LCA engaged in such a massive and broad-scale effort to assess an aspect of its work, but it would not be the last. A pattern for future studies had been set. Meanwhile, several different churchwide agencies were busily engaged in trying to support different facets of congregational life, sometimes in ways that seemed to bear little relation to one another.

Worship

Nothing comes closer to the heart of parish life than its worship, and the LCA committed broad powers for guidance, oversight, and approval to the Commission on Worship. The two-man staff and the commission itself reviewed worship materials ranging from children's hymnals to filmstrips, services for special occasions, and a host of items produced by the Board of Publication, such as choir and organ music, settings for introits and graduals, the *Journal of Church Music,* and scholarly books about worship. In addition, the commission produced its own guidance materials on such subjects as vestments, directives for celebration of the liturgy, planning and conduct of funerals, lay assistants at services, and private confession and absolution. These carefully worded statements were often published in *The Ministers Information Service* and were regarded by many pastors as church policy.[104] Although the point could certainly be disputed, it seemed to some that the church was going through a period of increasing liturgical formality and rigidity in worship practices. It remained to be seen how the church might react to the more freewheeling climate and the spirit of experimentation typical of the late sixties and seventies.

Communion Practices Revisited. So often in the life of the church a specific question of limited scope is raised that leads to a much broader answer than expected. A special committee of the Executive Council in 1963 addressed the question of how authorization should be given for administration of Holy Communion at conventions of auxiliaries. What emerged was appointment of a study group to revise the 1960 statement of the ULCA on "The Sacrament of the Altar and Its Implications" that was presented to the 1964 convention for approval.[105]

The new statement on Communion practices was finally adopted by the convention after the customary parliamentary tinkering and efforts to postpone the whole matter.[106] Since people in a highly mobile society were disturbed by the disparity of practices among parishes, the report contended that "a basic uniformity" was desirable. It proposed many practical procedures, such as the use of wafers as a convenient form of the bread, to be placed in the hand rather than the mouth; the use of wine rather than grape juice (special provisions were appropriate for alcoholics); a chalice was preferred for administering the wine, although a pouring chalice with individual glasses was acceptable (paper cups or plastic glasses were out); communicants were to kneel at the altar; continuous Communion was deemed better than "by tables"; and music was appropriate during administration. It was interesting that "a lay person may assist in the distribution by administering the cup, but this privilege must be carefully guarded." The lay person was to be instructed by the pastor and commissioned by the church council on an annual basis and only for service in that congregation.

On the basic question that had precipitated the study in the first place, permission was to be granted by the president of the church for Communion at conventions of auxiliaries or other special occasions. The same provisions applied to seminaries, colleges, and other "established administrative centers" of the church. Synod presidents could authorize Communion services where only their synods were involved.

The statement also gave careful guidance regarding intercommunion on the premises that Lutheran ministry be recognized as a "full ministry"; nothing should imply a unity not already present in other areas of faith and order; the church's doctrine of the Lord's Supper should be set forth "without reservation"; ministers of the LCA should use the rite of the LCA and no mixture of rites should be allowed; authorization must be given to a minister by the synodical or church president; and eucharistic hospitality should be encouraged when certain conditions are met. Interestingly, some issues that would be hotly debated in the LCA within a decade, such as infant Communion, were not mentioned. It seemed evident that no matter how carefully the church nailed down its planks in a certain area, some that went unnoticed would become "unstuck" in time.

Another New Service Book? Early in August 1965 President Fry received a letter from Oliver Harms, president of the Lutheran Church —Missouri Synod, that was described as "potentially historic and warmly appreciated."[107] In it was an invitation, based on an action of the LCMS's Detroit convention, to the LCA and other Lutheran bodies to " 'express the faith which we hold in common through more uniform texts and musical settings both in liturgy and hymnody' by cooperating in the development and publication of a common hymnal." Following discussion of the proposal, the Commission on Worship recommended to the Executive Council that "the LCA express its willingness . . . to accept in principle the invitation" but asked that certain conditions be met about starting with exploratory conversations that would be reported to the churches before work was officially begun.[108] The Executive Council, however, voted in the name of the LCA to "accept with gratitude the invitation" and to assure the LCMS that "the 'joy, willingness, and confidence' with which it extended this invitation are reflected equally in us as we accept it."[109]

By November 1966 the Inter-Lutheran Commission on Worship had been formed with representatives from ALC, LCA, LCMS, the Evangelical Lutheran Church of Canada, and the Slovak Evangelical Lutheran Church.[110] It was clear that the ILCW had ambitious plans including experimenting with new liturgical forms that used contemporary language and music, new hymns, and contemporary versions of existing worship forms in usage in the churches. By its November 1967 meeting, the ILCW voted to invite the Roman Catholic International Committee on English in the Liturgy and the Commission on Worship of the Consultation on Church Union to seek agreement on "common wordings for the Our Father, the Apostles' and Nicene Creeds, and other liturgical formulations, such as the Gloria in Excelsis, Te Deum, etc."[111] In addition, it urged the Lutheran World Federation to call an all-Lutheran conference to study the possibility of developing a common lectionary. These and other proposals to come would keep the ILCW busy into the 1980s. As had been true of every previous project to produce a Lutheran worship book, the road would often be tedious and rocky.

Parish Education

In many ways, the 1960s proved to be a high point for Christian education in the parish, not just for the LCA but also for most other Protestant bodies. A barrage of books and a blizzard of articles appeared covering every aspect of the subject from foundational studies, curriculum theory and research, to highly specific topics such as teaching preschoolers, finger painting, church camps, storytelling, group process, building designs, choral speaking, and a host of others.[112] Many denominations, to say nothing of independent publishers, conceived major curriculum projects in the fifties and launched the published materials in the sixties. Few church members seriously questioned that Christian education, particularly for the young, was one of the basic tasks of the congregation. Sunday schools were inundated by waves of children, and many congregations embarked on costly building programs for educational units.[113] Most of the buildings provided for individual classrooms, a trend that would be reversed in the 1970s when the educational trend was toward "open classrooms."

It was in this period that the Board of Parish Education introduced the most comprehensive curriculum program ever undertaken in Christian education. It was the first time any church body had attempted to coordinate the materials for every course in the curriculum both vertically (from one age level to another) and horizontally (among all educational arms of the parish) to insure sequence and to avoid gaps and duplication of effort in learning. Many religious educators doubted that such a complex job of curriculum planning could be done. Not only Protestant but also Roman Catholic educators studied the results.[114]

The project had been started by the predecessor boards, and by the time of the merger a joint staff was already in place and the transition to the new church virtually a *fait accompli.* Launching the program began with two years of intensive leadership training. In his report to the 1964 convention, President Fry pointed out that more than a quarter million leaders had been trained in skills ranging from the rationale for Christian education to teaching Bible and doctrine. "This plan, plus the efforts that will continue, will go far," he said, "toward filling up what has been the sorriest lack in many, if not most, of our parishes . . . the paucity of trained leadership."[115]

Once leaders had been trained, the educational resources were introduced in 1964 for every school of the parish, retreats, Confirmation classes, the family, and church camps. The reception surprised even the program's designers. "Never before had anything been so promptly and widely accepted by the congregations of the LCA (or its pre-merger churches) as the new curriculum for parish education," reported *The Lutheran.* "Ninety-one percent of the 6,200 LCA congregations are using the new courses of study."[116] The executive of the BPE, however, cautioned that "the ultimate success or failure of the program will not be known until the year 2000, when three-year-olds now learning about God will have become church leaders."[117] That seemed fairly safe, but it fit in with the BPE's own estimate that any curriculum project had a life expectancy of about ten years and that the LCA should already be about the business of planning the next generation of educational materials for the mid-seventies. Others felt, however, that so much time and effort had been put into the current effort that the church could coast for a while. As a result, the BPE budget and staff were reduced in 1967 by about 10 percent.[118] The BPE reported to the 1968 convention the serious results of these cutbacks.[119]

Demographics and the mood of the times, however, began to erode the enthusiasm for parish education. Although the BPE had emphasized new settings for Christian education, Sunday school enrollment was still the barometer of progress or retrogression for parish education. On this scale, the church hit its peak of participation in 1964 with 1,246,846 persons involved. After this, the dwindling numbers of younger children and the shift of adult participation to other types of educational programs began to show up in the statistics, so that Sunday school enrollment dropped below a million by the seventies.[120] The battle to convince the church of the importance of quality Christian education was uphill from that time onward.

Cooperation with other Lutherans had been a characteristic of parish education. Beginning in 1928, those churches that eventually became the ALC, LCA, and LCMS had taken part in what was known as the "Intersynodical Committee of Parish Education."[121] One of its major projects was a new translation of Luther's Catechism. It was a ten-year project that involved some of the leading scholars of the member churches and was finally completed in 1963 with the publication of *The Small Catechism in Contemporary English.*[122]

The LCA had barely been born when an overture came from the Board of Parish Education of TALC to restore the cooperation that had been aborted in 1957 by withdrawal from the Long-Range Program of Parish Education by the group that would form TALC. In February 1963 the ALC board voted "to declare its favorable attitude toward cooperative parish education projects" with the LCA.[123] It was a totally unexpected action, but one that was warmly welcomed by the LCA. Within months a proposal was drafted that pointed out that the common evangelical heritage of the two churches was a sound basis for cooperation, that there had been remarkable parallels in the curricula recently published by the two bodies, and that the stewardship of "time, effort, and money impels us to eliminate the duplication of effort involved in independently producing essentially similar materials for our two churches."[124] The plan was approved by both bodies, and the first project undertaken was a pre-reading hymnal. Other cooperative efforts included joint production of a vacation church school series and the *Augsburg Adult Bible Studies,* a quarterly series based on the international uniform Sunday school texts. The groundwork had been laid for a second attempt at full-scale cooperation in educational ministry that for a while buoyed hopes but eventually ended in disillusionment.

Evangelism

The momentum in membership growth that had been a source of encouragement in the 1950s continued in the first few years after merger, but the pace was obviously beginning to slow. The high point for LCA membership was reached in 1967 when there were 3,288,037 baptized members reported, but by the following year, the number had dropped by more than eight thousand.[125] An even more ominous sign was in the number of communicants, which is often regarded as an indicator of congregational health. From 1967 to 1968, that figure dropped nearly fourteen thousand. Communing membership continued to slide for about five years before inching upward again, but baptized membership drifted steadily downward until the 1980s when there were a few years with slight increases.

A number of factors have been cited for the erosion of membership. People were moving out of the Northeast, where the LCA had its heaviest concentration of congregations, into other parts of the United States and Canada where there often were no LCA churches. The birthrate was on a downward curve, and immigration from Lutheran lands had long ceased to be a significant factor. Fewer new missions were being started in populous suburban areas. The widespread negative attitude toward "institutionalized religion" and the reluctance of pastors to "play the numbers game" were having their toll. Especially distressing was the growing tendency simply to drop people from the roles in the imprecise category of "losses for other reasons." Known familiarly as "roll cleaning," the tendency sometimes betrayed a lack of concern for restoring members who had either "lapsed" or "been mislaid."

The unenviable task of trying to stanch this negative flow belonged to the Commission on Evangelism. In order to try to sensitize the more than six thousand congregations to the need and coach their leaders in the methods of outreach, the commission had a total of three staff at the New York headquarters and five others scattered across the length and breadth of the continent. As was true of most other agencies, the commission had to struggle with budget cuts and dwindling purchasing power in the face of increasing demands.

In spite of its limited resources, the commission did mount a variety of approaches to the problem. The staff conducted hundreds of training events annually for congregational evangelism committees and leaders. Experimental programs were tried in outreach to apartment dwellers, who were becoming more and more inaccessible in American society. Guidance was given to congregations in outreach to minorities, something that many parishes had never even attempted. Preaching missions were organized, and the number of spiritual retreats grew. A Membership Contact and Referral Service was set up to send to congregations the names of LCA members who were known to have moved into their areas.[126] Studies showed, however, that for a referral to be most effective, a contact would need to be made within about six or eight weeks after a person moved to a new neighborhood. "Faith-in-life dialogues" were initiated, and various kinds of guidance materials were produced. Ecumenical evangelism efforts were supported in local communities. There was very little that the commission did not try, but the LCA simply did not seem willing to make evangelism a priority during these years.

Auxiliaries—Then There Was One

At the outset of the LCA, the church had approved creation of three auxiliary organizations: the Luther League for youth, Lutheran Church Men, and Lutheran Church Women. By the end of 1968, only the women's group remained as a churchwide organization.

Lutheran Church Men. The auxiliary had labored under difficulty from the outset because it was expected to "be a new organization rather than the absorption of several groups into a merged group."[127]

By March of 1964 it had 1,460 affiliated units, but it was operating with a deficit approaching $40,000. The cost-conscious church convention responded to a memorial from the Pacific Northwest Synod asking for a study of the possibility of discontinuing the auxiliary by authorizing the Executive Council to study the whole question of men's work.[128]

A special task force was set up which presented a twenty-seven page report to the Executive Council in June 1965. Essentially, the report proposed discontinuing the "national structure" and that synods provide for an association or committee on men's work.[129] After a lengthy discussion, the Council decided to form a larger and more representative committee which reported in January 1966. The committee suggested there were several possible options: phasing out the auxiliary, continuing it as it was, or creating a Commission on Men's Work with an annual budget of about $135,000. The Executive Council recommendation finally adopted by the convention had three parts: (1) to put the emphasis in the future on congregational men's organizations; (2) to discontinue the auxiliary; (3) to give synods the option of having synodical men's groups.[130] The churchwide organization was dead, but some synods, particularly in the south, have continued the work on their own territories until the present time.

Luther League and Youth. The stories of the Luther League and Lutheran Church Men were quite different. In the case of LCM, it was probably a matter of trying to create something new—a binational organization—without acknowledging the limited sectional character of the existing support base. In the case of the Luther League, the base seemed to exist, but a gradual shift in youth work which had begun after World War II suddenly reached tidal wave dimensions in the 1960s. In the mid-forties, Luther Leagues had been dominated by young adults. Franklin Clark Fry commented that when he was chosen president of the ULCA in 1944, the president of that church's Luther League was only two years his junior.[131]

In the 1950s, membership age moved downward toward the high school level with some top Luther League officers being college students. By the time the LCA was formed, the shift was all but complete, although largely unrecognized by adults for what it presaged. Many youth, in the LCA at least, were changing from complacent followers to persons who were ready to challenge institutional authority and demand recognition for their own culture.

In 1964 the Luther League was able to report to the convention that it had 132,919 members from age twelve through twenty-five in 4,205 congregational groups.[132] Thirty synods had synodical units, and many of them assigned staff specifically to this work. Churchwide support came from the staff of the Commission on Youth Activities. The program included publication of topics for League meetings, leadership schools, work camps, caravaning (a program where teams of trained youth spent an average of four days in a congregation to help strengthen the local group), and volunteer church service opportunities. By the end of 1963, the auxiliary had a cash balance of $67,383 and had given $45,000 to the LCA to send to the National Council of Churches Commission on Religion and Race.[133] At the 1964 convention, however, the Commission on Youth Activities reported that it had formed a committee to "articulate the basic philosophy of the church's ministry to youth" as guidance for the future.[134]

In August 1965 an all-LCA Youth Gathering was held in Miami with more than seven thousand persons in attendance. It seemed to be a high point, but in its report to the 1966 LCA convention, the Luther League declared, "If outwardly everything appears to be operating smoothly, inwardly symptoms of ill health are strikingly observable."[135] The report pointed to failure of synodical units to meet their pledges and said that the whole concept of a youth auxiliary was being called into question. It stated that the way the league was structured implied it was a "training ground for junior ecclesiastical officials whose primary task is administration." It went on to say that the example of other Protestant denominations showed that the need for a structured youth auxiliary was past. It asserted that the compartmentalization of youth ministry in the LCA between a commission and an auxiliary showed that youth ministry was not an integral part of the church. "It appears that the primary purpose of youth ministry is aimed at one of two directions: either as creating a patronizing organization whose goal is to keep youth inside the church until they can be given responsibilities or as maintaining a junior church which is not as important as the 'adult' church but which does constitute a pale mirror reflection of it."[136]

At the same convention, the commission asked that its name be changed to "Commission on Youth Ministry" and outlined a new philosophy aimed at recognizing the reality of the youth subculture. It, in effect, asked that youth be made full partners in the church's ministry.[137] Plans were announced for another churchwide youth gathering; but as it turned out, the event scheduled for Detroit had to be canceled because of the racial riots and general unrest that had taken place in that city.

By the 1968 convention, several synodical units had indicated that they were planning to discontinue their organizations. Both the commission and the Luther League executive committee joined forces to ask the convention to amend the bylaws to eliminate the auxiliary and transform the commission into one on "youth ministry" rather than "activities." Although the move was opposed by many in the church who had found that the Luther League had been meaningful in their own lives, the decision was made.[138] As a churchwide organization, the Luther League was ended, even though it was expected that congregations would still have their own youth groups. The LCA had embarked on a new venture in youth ministry that many took with confidence, believing it to be the direction of the future. While some of the same rethinking about youth ministry had gone on in the ALC and LCMS, neither of these churches went the route of eliminating their national youth organizations.[139]

Lutheran Church Women. Although the women's auxiliary also experienced changes, it developed into a strong organization with a powerful influence in the life of the church at every level. All of the groups in the predecessor bodies had originally grown out of women's missionary societies.[140] Although interest in foreign mission work continued to be strong, both the Augustana and ULCA units had dropped the word *missionary* from their names well before merger.[141] The name chosen in the new church, Lutheran Church Women, reflected this same broadened scope of concern for the total work of the church.

Some of the long-standing traditions of the predecessor groups continued, such as the Advent Day of Prayer (dating from 1911 in the General Council), the Week of Prayer for Lent (started by the ULCA women in 1919), use of mission study materials produced by the National Council of Churches and United Church Women, and publication of its own study topics and magazine. The LCW was beginning, however, to work in the areas of social concerns, literacy, welfare reform, mental retardation, migrant workers, unemployment, the elderly, and race relations. Letters to the editor of *Lutheran Women* did reflect resistance by some members to what was considered too much emphasis on "contemporary concerns" and "high-sounding modern intellectualism."[142] The leaders did not back away, however, from confronting the members with those issues that were looming large in church and society.[143]

One issue that did not seem to loom large, at least in the LCW's publications in this period, was that of the rights of women themselves. That would soon change, however, as the concern for women's liberation moved into the foreground in American society.[144] That women were not well represented in the elective positions in the church was painfully clear. In 1968, apart from LCW itself, there were only twenty-seven women chosen among 350 representatives on the Executive Council, boards, commissions, and the like. There were only nine women staff officials (not including LCW) out of 180 positions.[145]

Financial support of the church's work had always been part of the mission of women's organizations. Usually, gifts had been designated for specific causes, but at the LCW's first convention the decision was made that the auxiliary should make "One Gift" to the total work of the LCA. This idea was not accepted easily, but there was a perception that this was what the president of the LCA wanted. Later there was some question about whether the perception had been accurate, but the die was cast.[146] The LCW's goal for its One Gift was $1,500,000 per year for the first triennium, but that proved to be optimistic. The actual gifts ranged from about $1,082,000 to $1,250,000, and that required dipping into reserves.[147] Nevertheless, by the end of 1985 the LCW had "provided almost $22 million in financial support to the work of the LCA."[148]

LCW members, of course, were involved in many types of service activities and not simply in providing financial assistance to the church. One outstanding example has been the Volunteer Reading Aides Program aimed at combating illiteracy in the United States and Canada. Begun in 1967, the program has grown steadily until it has become the third largest volunteer adult literacy project in the United States. It has expanded to include teaching English to refugees and others for whom English is a second language. Many thousands of persons have been helped through the years.[149]

THEOLOGICAL EDUCATION, COLLEGES, AND CHURCH VOCATIONS

Merger negotiations always seem to leave their legacy of unsettled issues to be dealt with in the early years of the new church's life. This was certainly the case with a number of simmering questions bequeathed to the Board of Theological Education (BTE) and the Board of College Education and Church Vocations (BCECV). In some instances, years would pass before matters could be sorted out, and even then not always with the sense of satisfaction that comes with the belief, however illusory it might be, that permanent solutions have been found.

Master Plan for Seminaries

The constituting convention of the LCA instructed the BTE to bring to the 1964 convention the master plan for theological seminaries called for in the bylaws.[150] Executive Secretary Conrad Bergendoff set about a comprehensive study of "The Lutheran Church in America and Theological Education" that was first reported to the board in October 1963. With some modifications, it was printed and distributed about a month later, although the board waited until March 1964 to receive it "as a factual report."[151] It did serve as the basis for the BTE's recommendation of a "master plan" to the convention.

Known popularly as "The Bergendoff Report," the forty-four-page document minced no words in dealing with such subjects as the nature of the ministry, seminary curriculum, the academic level seminary students had shown in college (Bergendoff concluded that 60 percent would not have been admitted to graduate school in other fields), size of faculties (disproportionate to number of students in some cases), per-student costs (much higher than other Lutheran bodies), what might be a reasonable number and location of seminaries (ideally four located in East, South, Midwest, and Far West), and the need to consider joint ventures with other Lutheran bodies.[152] Needless to say, some people's favorite oxen were gored in the process.

A basic source of the problem faced by the LCA was seen as stemming from the varied origins of existing schools. The result was a situation that would not have been created *de novo* in the 1960s. "As often in the case of second marriages," Bergendoff wrote, "children of various parentage find themselves in the same family, so the Lutheran Church in America brought together theological seminaries of other family relationships. Gettysburg reminds us of the General Synod, as does Hamma, and Central of later date. The General Council is represented by Philadelphia and Maywood. Southern recalls the General Synod, South. All of these became children of the United Lutheran Church in America, along with

Northwestern as a younger offspring. And when Grand View, Suomi, and Rock Island joined the newest relationship of parent groups, the number of theological schools was crowding the home. In addition to the USA institutions, Canada provided two undernourished representatives. The situation hardly exemplifies any planned parenthood."[153]

There were many proposals that emerged from the report, but it was evident that priorities included reduction in the number of seminaries, cooperation with ALC where possible, location of seminaries in university settings, development of graduate programs, and the need to train graduates for ministry in other than traditional parish settings. The convention debated the BTE's recommendations for hours and finally took a series of actions that set a sizable agenda for the rest of the life of the LCA.. These included granting the BTE authority to approve cooperative arrangements between LCA and ALC seminaries (preferably in university settings); urging Gettysburg and Philadelphia to work toward unification; requesting Hamma to explore merging with either Chicago or the ALC seminary in Columbus, Ohio; encouraging Northwestern to relocate on the campus of ALC's Luther Seminary in St. Paul, Minnesota; bringing recommendations about the future of Central to the 1966 convention; approving merger of the seminaries in Saskatoon; commending the decision of Maywood, Augustana, Suomi, and Grand View seminaries to merge on a campus adjacent to the University of Chicago; providing for review of the whole master plan in 1970; and studying opportunities given to women for study and contribution in the field of theology.[154]

During this period, there were a number of encouraging developments. The Lutheran School of Theology at Chicago completed the move to its new complex, and Central Seminary eventually joined that merger. Gettysburg and Philadelphia did work out a joint administration with Donald R. Heiges as president of both institutions, but the dream of merging on a campus near the University of Pennsylvania was never realized. Pacific received financial support from ALC and continued to work for a joint school at Berkeley. Southern Seminary in South Carolina and Waterloo in Canada were strengthened.[155] The board also encouraged development of continuing education programs for clergy, established a testing program for candidates for the ministry, and supported faculty and ministers in working for advanced degrees.

Colleges and Church Vocations

The new Board of College Education and Church Vocation was said to be the result of "fission and fusion."[156] The fission occurred for some of the predecessor churches through the separation of seminary and college education. Student work, of course, had long since been turned over to the National Lutheran Council. The new board, however, did bring together the church's relations with colleges and "church vocations," which included deaconess work. The latter had enjoyed the status of a separate board in the ULCA.[157]

The new agency was launched at a time when colleges were experiencing unprecedented growth but were just beginning to become aware of the student unrest that would rock campuses in the late sixties. The BCECV's initial report to the church listed twenty-five institutions on its roster of colleges. There were seventeen four-year colleges. The rest were either two-year schools or institutions where ALC and LCA worked together. Interestingly, the Deaconess School in Baltimore was included in the total.[158] By 1965 the deaconess school would be closed in favor of an educational program at Philadelphia Seminary,[159] and by 1968 Hartwick College in Oneonta, New York, would have severed its church relationship to benefit from state financial aid.[160] By 1968 the junior college at Marion, Virginia, had also disappeared from the list.[161]

Precisely what a Lutheran college was supposed to be and do was the subject of endless debate during the sixties. The variety of relationships with the church were almost as numerous as there were institutions. All but two synods reported some financial support to colleges ranging in 1967 from $2,700 by Central Canada to $424,000 by Minnesota.[162] To try to achieve some clarity, BCECV requested Edgar M. Carlson, president of Gustavus Adolphus College, to study the problem of the church's role in higher education. His report, *Church Sponsored Higher Education and the Lutheran Church in America,* was adopted by the board as the basis for dialogue with the LCA institutions as a way of clarifying the criteria for continued recognition by the LCA.[163]

Church Vocations. Recognizing its mandate to deal with the growing need for professional workers in the church other than ministers, the BCECV tackled the task of defining what such a church occupation was. In *The LCA Plan for Church Occupations* developed in 1967, the board carefully avoided the theological pitfall of limiting Christian vocation to full-time employment by the church while still providing a rationale for certification of lay workers.[164] Together with certain colleges, BCECV developed curricula for training church workers and further professional development for those already in place. Limited financial aid was made available for those wishing to train for church occupations, and a placement service was established so that their skills would not go unused. The LCA Education Fund was created to provide assistance for a wide range of purposes, such as loans to LCA faculty for doctoral studies and "opportunity grants" for minority students with college potential.

Deaconess Work. Part of the unfinished merger task was to try to create one sisterhood within the church. In 1961 the ULCA had made a decision to merge the Deaconess Community centered in Philadelphia, which had been connected with the General Council, with the group from the Baltimore Motherhouse, which had its roots in the General Synod.[165] As noted earlier, the Baltimore center was operated as the training school until 1965, when a graduate program was set up at Philadelphia. The beautifully located Baltimore property was sold and some of the proceeds used to build an addition to the Motherhouse in Gladwyne, an equally attractive location in the Philadelphia suburbs.[166]

These moves left the LCA with two other sisterhoods. One was related to the Immanuel Deaconess Institute, which had operated under the Augustana Church in connection with a multiservice hospital in Omaha, Nebraska.[167] By January 1966, arrangements had been worked out for the Omaha, Baltimore, and Philadelphia sisters to form one community.[168] The remaining group was associated with the Bethphage Mission in Axtell, Nebraska, which is an outstanding institution serving handicapped persons of all ages. The mission is modeled after the famous Bethel institution that pioneered such service in Bielefeld, Germany. Although cordial relations were maintained with the LCA Deaconess Community through the years, the Bethphage group maintained a separate existence.[169] By 1968 the LCA had a total of 198 deaconesses, of whom sixty-three were retired or semiretired. They constituted the largest continuing group of women who had been in full-time service to the church.

COMMUNICATING THE CHURCH'S MESSAGE

There were three prongs to the LCA's strategy in communications: *The Lutheran*, the official church magazine; the Department of Press, Radio and Television; and the Board of Publication. The three were carefully separated from one another organizationally. This had not been the case in the ULCA, at least, where *The Lutheran* had been related to the Board of Publication and where, up until 1954, the "News Bureau" had been set up and funded from the same source. The autonomy of *The Lutheran* and PRT, each of which operated under a separate commission, was calculated to insure that they could exercise "freedom of the press" without seeming to be captive to another board.

The Lutheran

The Lutheran's own views about its lineage seem to have differed at various times. In 1960 G. Elson Ruff, who became the first editor of the LCA magazine, wrote an article proclaiming that *The Lutheran* was now one hundred years old and traced its history to *The Lutheran and Home Journal*, which eventually became the official organ of the General Council in 1896.[170] In 1981 Ruff's successor, Albert P. Stauderman, began an article with the words "The magazine you are now reading is the lineal successor to a periodical begun 150 years ago."[171] He had traced *The Lutheran* to *The Lutheran Observer*, which had grown up in the old General Synod. Whatever its origin, *The Lutheran* had ample precedent for an independent spirit and a line of generally feisty editors. Benjamin Kurtz, editor of the *Observer*, and Charles P. Krauth, of the rival paper, loved to aim salvos not only at what they considered the problems in their own churches but also at one another.[172]

When the LCA's version of *The Lutheran* was issued in January 1963, it was hoped that there would be about 300,000 subscribers. Actually there were 354,000, and the number grew during the first fifteen months to 480,594.[173] Using an "every-home plan" to boost subscriptions, the magazine's circulation reached almost 582,000 by the time of the 1968 church convention.[174]

The policies of *The Lutheran* remained largely unchanged from those enunciated in its first report to the church: recognition that the heterogeneous constituency of the church comprise its clients; willingness to publish "things likely to disconcert some individuals"; avoiding partisanship on controversial subjects but giving opportunity for differing views; supporting the program of the church without becoming a promotional instrument; providing a forum for different opinions and exposing readers to a wide range of information about developments in the Christian world.[175]

Repeated reader surveys showed that subscribers were most likely to turn first to the last page, where the editor's opinion appeared. Next, they were likely to turn to the letters to the editor, where readers recorded their nods of approval or wrote in no uncertain terms about their disagreements with what had appeared in earlier issues. The editorial policy was often intended to provoke discussion of basic issues with the view that this open interchange was a healthy ingredient in the church's life.[176] The result was a journal that soon became the most widely read Protestant church magazine in North America.

Press, Radio and Television

The planners of the LCA recognized that it was necessary in the kind of communications-oriented society into which we were moving to have effective ways of communicating the church's story to the world. The print media were served with a barrage of releases about newsworthy events in the life of the church as well as numerous articles in major secular magazines.[177] The news bureau did not see itself as a public relations arm for the church but as a source of objective information.

The expanding frontier for communications, of course, was in broadcast media. The church had had some experience in radio in "Church World News" and "The Protestant Hour." The former was a fifteen-minute newscast carried on 355 stations in the United States and Canada in 1967. The LCA provided twelve segments of "The Protestant Hour" each year with noted Lutheran preachers and music by college choirs that were heard on 560 stations for a total of 3,360 hours.[178]

Television, however, was becoming a dominant element of American life, and the LCA was faced with how to utilize this pervasive force in a way that reached more than the faithful core of Christians.

Davey and Goliath

The answer was "Davey and Goliath," an animated children's television series that had been launched by the ULCA in 1961 and by 1965
was being aired on 321 stations. Seasonal specials have been added
to the original series, and the program was dubbed in other languages, such as Spanish. This durable program is still being broadcast
in many parts of the world and has been watched by several genera-
tions of children.[179] PRT also launched two television specials aimed
at adults, "The Antkeeper" and "Stalked," which were well received
but did not have the staying power on television of the children's
series.[180]

The Business of Publishing

Publishing had been an integral part of the operations of the Lutheran churches in North America since the middle of the nineteenth century.[181] All of the LCA predecessor bodies except AELC
had operated their own publishing houses and printing plants. Put-

ting the merged operation on a sound financial footing was essential because the LCA expected its Board of Publication not only to function as a business without subsidy but also to pay an annual royalty to the church in partial return for editorial work done by the Board of Parish Education.[182]

Part of the challenge was deciding what to do with three separate printing plants. The Suomi plant was too small to handle the volume of jobs required for the new church, and it was sold in 1963 to the former manager.[183] While the Augustana plant in Rock Island and the ULCA operation in Philadelphia continued, they had suffered a serious blow when it was found that the off-size format chosen for *The Lutheran* could not be handled on presses used for the previous church magazines.[184] As a result, the contract for *The Lutheran* went to a commercial printer.

The large volume and illustrations in color of the material for the new LCA parish education curriculum also made it necessary for the publishing house itself to contract out this work. By 1966 the board had concluded that continuing in the printing business with its huge capital requirements for equipment that quickly became outmoded was impractical. The Rock Island property that had been carried on the books at $1,107,000 was sold in 1967 to Augustana College for $750,000, payable over a ten-year period.[185] The printing operation was also phased out in Philadelphia and the building used as a warehouse until 1971 when it was sold.[186]

The heavy expenses involved in merger and royalties paid to the LCA actually caused the publishing house to operate at a net loss in its first full year.[187] As the new education materials came on stream, the financial tide changed, and in the 1964–65 biennium, the board was able to report net income before royalties of $1,577,000.[188] In its 1968 report to the church, the board indicated that curriculum materials then accounted for more than a third of its income.[189]

The publishing house was also moving aggressively into other areas. Ecclesiastical arts became an increasingly important element as the board went heavily into manufacturing and sale of paraments, vestments, and church furnishings. It also began to expand its network of church supply stores as a principal means of distribution and service to the constituency. By the end of the decade, the Board of Publication had assets of around $10 million and was clearly big business, although it consistently put service to the church rather than money making as its first priority.

GRIM BUDGETS AND THE
QUEST FOR ANSWERS

The high-spirited optimism that had been present when the LCA was formed soon collided with harsh financial realities. Perhaps it was a postmerger syndrome that has afflicted some other denominational families, but the simple fact was that LCA benevolence receipts fell far short of budget projections in the years 1963 through 1965. As early as the 1964 church convention, the Executive Council pointed to disturbing signs: steadily increasing costs estimated at about 3 percent per year; an actual shortfall in 1963 that would have necessitated a 14 percent increase in receipts in 1964 to enable the church to meet commitments; a slowing in the rate of membership growth; and the increasing share of benevolence receipts retained by synods. The Executive Council's aim of "an attainable budget" for the 1965–66 biennium soon proved unattainable.[190]

The Report of the President to the 1966 convention in Kansas City devoted more than four pages to describing the "grim budgets" proposed for the next two years.[191] He wrote of the Finance Committee's budget hearings in March as being "black Tuesday and even blacker Wednesday." New claims being made on already strained resources caused a series of jolts. "An unwelcome but inescapable fresh liability for a wholly church-owned institution inherited by the Florida Synod," he said, "will drain off some funds, in an as yet undetermined amount."[192] Inter-Lutheran work to which the church was strongly committed necessitated a $350,000 increase in 1966 over 1965. "The deduction is inescapable," President Fry declared. "We need increased giving for LCA benevolence and we need it desperately."[193]

The hoped-for increases in giving to churchwide causes did not materialize, however, in the magnitude needed. People were giving, but a greater proportion was being retained to meet needs at the congregational level. Congregational "current expenses" jumped from $84,814,000 in 1963 to $114,097,000 by the end of the decade, an increase of 34.5 percent. By the same token, total "regular benevolence" went from $29,739,000 to $36,390,000 in the same period, an increase of 22 percent. The amount of benevolence funds actually remitted by synods to the LCA treasury, however, increased only 13.9 percent from $19,033,000 to $21,650,000 while the synodical share increased 46.3 percent. In fact, the total dollars received by the church-at-large actually went down from 1968 to 1969. Obviously, a dramatic shift in the way the gifts of members were being divided among congregational, synodical, and churchwide causes was occurring.[194]

Stewardship in the Sixties

The unenviable task of trying to encourage responsible giving patterns had been assigned by the LCA structure to the Commission on Stewardship, which worked in close concert with the Lutheran Laymen's Movement for Stewardship. The same administrative staff served both agencies. The LCA was scarcely underway when the stewardship director, Henry Endress, resigned to become vice-president of Waterloo University. Endress, who was a layman, had directed the stewardship operations of the ULCA and was known as an innovator and an outstanding film producer.[195] He was succeeded by Thorsten A. Gustafson, who had been a stewardship director of Augustana and later president of its New York Conference.[196]

The blending of the efforts of COS and LLM was one that dated from ULCA days. The LLM was an organization of committed laymen throughout the church who gave not only time but also a sizable membership contribution to help underwrite production of stewardship materials and other activities. It also supported the LLM Fund-Raising and Counseling Service, which had been set up to assist congregations, synods, agencies, and institutions to conduct fund-raising campaigns without resorting to commercial groups. It was intended that this would undergird fund-raising with sound stewardship principles.[197] By the end of 1967, the service had a staff of twenty-four and was helping congregations and other agencies to raise over $12 million per year.[198]

The basic stewardship work of the commission had modest resources for its huge task. It had only seven field staff deployed over the length and breadth of the continent and a total budget of around $500,000.[199] Its program included not only production of more than three million items of stewardship materials used each year by congregations but also workshops for stewardship leaders, the Every Member Response Program, regional conferences, family money management workshops, and assistance to new mission congregations.

The LCA Foundation

The longer-term view of Christian stewardship was taken by the LCA Foundation. This agency encouraged members to provide for the church through various avenues, such as bequests, deferred giving, and gift annuities. The beneficiaries of the gifts included not only the LCA and its churchwide agencies but also synods, colleges, social ministry agencies, and congregations. During the sixties, for example, there were two large gifts made to the LCA that were quite different in character. One was the gift of stock then worth more than $1,564,000 that became known as the "Prosser Trust."[200] The other was the gift of a seventeen-acre estate along the Delaware River and an endowment of $500,000 toward its maintenance.[201] The estate was converted to a conference and retreat center known as the Glen Foerd Center for Education and the Arts. It was operated by the LCA until the eighties when it was determined that funds were not available for major capital improvements and the estate reverted according to terms of the gift.[202]

ECUMENICAL RELATIONS

Existing as it did in a pluralistic society, the LCA found a natural avenue for expressing its ecumenical spirit in the conciliar movement. It did not plunge into these relationships, however, without clearly enunciated principles for such participation. In drafting a statement endorsing the *evangelical* and *representative* principles for review by the 1964 convention of the church, the Executive Council drew on a long tradition that went back in the ULCA to 1920 and the Washington Declaration, and in the Augustana Synod to a formal action in 1954.[203] The Executive Council affirmed that these principles, defined as follows, should be the bases for evaluating both inter-Lutheran and interdenominational relationships:

> The *evangelical* principle means that official relationship with interchurch agencies will be established only with such agencies as are composed exclusively of churches which confess Jesus Christ as Divine Lord and Saviour.
> The *representative* principle means that in interchurch associations the official representatives of churches should never be expected to sit on a parity with individuals who represent only themselves or at most organizations which are less than churches.[204]

The Council then spelled out in great detail how these principles should be applied to LCA congregations and ministers. It meant, for example, that the fact the LCA held membership in an organization such as the NCCCUSA at the churchwide level did not necessarily mean that a state or local council affiliated with that body met the same criteria.[205]

As the sixties wore on, the urgency for social action created a need for clarifying the legitimacy of certain types of cooperation that did not quite fit the earlier definitions. In the "Manifesto to Congregations," the LCA had called upon each of them, "to lift its voice in concord and to work in concert with forces for good, cooperating with church and other groups participating in activities that promote justice, relieve misery, and reconcile the estranged."[206] Where were the congregations to draw the line, if at all? In January 1967, the Executive Council adopted an official interpretation that said the evangelical and representative principles need not apply when cooperation "does not take the form of official *interchurch* relations among religious bodies."[207] The door was now opened to working with community action groups, "both voluntary and governmental." Other tests of the principles were to come with changing conditions in the future.

From NLC to LCUSA

As the plans began to unfold for the formation of the ALC and LCA, questions inevitably began to arise about what this might mean for the National Lutheran Council when it would be reduced to two member churches.[208] Paul Empie, executive director of the NLC, sensed that this might be a time for new approaches to the LCMS, not to insure survival of the Council but to look for the possibility of broader Lutheran cooperation.[209] At its 1958 meeting, the NLC voted to request the member bodies to approve an exploratory meeting with other Lutheran churches "to examine present cooperative activities in American Lutheranism and the possibility of extension of such activities."[210] After conferring with the other members of the Synodical Conference, the LCMS at first declined the invitation. But pressures were building within Missouri itself for a more open stance, and the Synodical Conference seemed near dissolution.[211]

Empie renewed the invitation, emphasizing that the NLC churches were as concerned as LCMS about "doctrinal soundness as a basis for all church relationships."[212] The LCMS did respond affirmatively to this overture, and matters moved swiftly so that by 1962 all three churches had approved a resolution to move ahead with drawing up documents as a basis for a new inter-Lutheran agency. By 1964 a constitution was prepared for the new Lutheran Council in the USA and submitted to the churches. Interestingly, the timing was such that ALC acted first in October 1964, Missouri followed at its convention in June 1965, and LCA followed in June 1966.[213] On January 1, 1967, LCUSA became a reality, and a new page had been turned in inter-Lutheran relations.

The major concession that had been made to Missouri was to make theological discussions a basic part of LCUSA's purpose. There were areas of Christian service in which member churches could decide whether to participate or not, but the doctrinal discussions were a given. It was a new direction for those NLC bodies who had not put the emphasis on theological issues in the Council in the past, just as it was a new approach for Missouri to be involved in an organization when doctrinal questions had not been sorted out beforehand to its satisfaction.[214]

There were aspects of the NLC program, however, that now moved outside of the conciliar arrangement. The NLC, for example, had served as the United States national committee for the Lutheran World Federation. Since LCMS was not a part of the LWF, this work had to be done in a bilateral arrangement between ALC and LCA.[215] Comity arrangements on establishing new missions, which had been one of the reasons for forming the NLC in the first place, were no longer under the Council. Cooperative campus ministry also had to be set up separately from LCUSA. It seemed that everyone got a little and everyone gave up a little.

One area of major Lutheran interest that was sometimes in the Council and sometimes out of the Council was that of bilateral dialogs. This way of getting to know one another without being judgmental about the other's convictions became a major avenue for opening up new relations during this period. "Dialog sought convergence; it eschewed compromise or confrontation."[216] Beginning in 1962 with Reformed-Lutheran conversations before LCUSA came into existence, the three churches began a long series of discussions that eventually led the dialog group, at least, to conclude that they saw "no insuperable obstacle to pulpit and altar fellowship" and encouraged discussions "looking forward to intercommunion and fuller recognition of one another's ministries."[217] Obviously, the participants were a bit ahead of any official actions by their churches, but fresh ground had been broken. Soon the Lutherans were deeply involved in discussions with Roman Catholics, Orthodox, Episcopalians, and "an academic colloquium" with the Jews.[218]

In the mid-sixties many Lutherans saw LCUSA as a harbinger of a greater unity that might come among the three Lutheran bodies. "Happily for the Missouri Synod, one of its best known younger churchmen, C. Thomas Spitz, was soon elected to fill the top position as director of the Lutheran Council in the USA."[219] Already, however, a reaction to what was perceived as liberal tendencies was setting in among ultra-right-wing Missouri conservatives. A carefully planned campaign was begun by a group that placed its sympathizers in key board posts and eventually ousted moderate President Oliver Harms and elected J. A. O. Preus to the office in 1969. Ironically, when a few years later a schism occurred in the LCMS that led to formation of the Association of Evangelical Lutheran Churches, Thomas Spitz was one of the leaders of the group that withdrew.[220] As one Lutheran historian put it, "For the first time in American history, crusading fundamentalism has captured and rigorously purged a major Protestant denomination."[221]

Lutheran World Federation

In many ways the North American Lutherans reached new levels of influence in the LWF during the late fifties and sixties. Franklin Clark Fry was elected president of the Federation at its assembly in Minneapolis in 1957. At that assembly action was taken to initiate conversations with the Roman Catholic Church which led to forming the Foundation for Ecumenical Research in 1963. This was followed by the establishment of the Institute for Ecumenical Research in Strasbourg in 1963.[222] Lutherans were active on virtually every commission and committee during the period between assemblies. One sad note was that failing health made it necessary for Carl E. Lundquist, of the Augustana Church, to resign his position as general secretary in 1960. He was succeeded by Kurt Schmidt-Clausen of West Germany, who served until 1965 when he was followed by André Appel of France.[223]

Both the newly formed ALC and LCA had chosen membership in the LWF; and at the Helsinki Assembly in 1963, Fredrik A. Schiotz, ALC's president, was elected to succeed Fry at the helm of LWF.[224] At Helsinki, Oliver Harms, president of LCMS, brought greetings to the assembly.[225] For a while things looked bright for the possibility of Missouri's joining the LWF. "President Harms spoke encouragingly to the 1965 Lutheran Church-Missouri Synod convention, pointing out that the Lutheran World Federation had, at Helsinki, amended its constitution in such a way as to make it easier for a church body like Missouri to be associated."[226] Although the LWF showed an openness that at times almost seemed to treat LCMS as a member, Missouri never took the step to join.

The National Council of Churches

The Lutheran Church in America was alone among the major Lutheran bodies in the United States that chose to become a full mem-

Oliver R. Harms, Franklin Clark Fry, and Fredrik A. Schiotz, presidents of the three Lutheran church bodies which formed the LCUSA

ber of the National Council of Churches of Christ in the USA. The American Lutheran Church, by contrast, elected to play a more selective role. Although it did not belong to the Council itself, the ALC did participate in certain of the NCCCUSA's programs, such as that of the Division of Christian Education. The LCMS also found it expedient not to belong to the Council but to accept participation in limited areas.[227] In the case of Canada, full membership in the Canadian Council of Churches by the LCA's Canada Section did not come until that Council was judged to have adjusted its constitution to recognize the evangelical and representative principles. The first time that delegates of the Canada Section participated as full members at a Canadian Council of Churches assembly was in November 1969.[228]

LCA participation in the NCCCUSA was not always a completely satisfying one to everyone concerned. For example, LCA leaders resisted any pretenses of the Council in these years to assume an ecclesial character. At the 1963 assembly in Philadelphia, President Fry quietly led the LCA delegates out of the hall when the Council sponsored a service of Holy Communion that violated the LCA's principles regarding such administration of the Sacrament by conciliar organizations.[229]

Frequently, LCA members were troubled by what were regarded as unwise proclamations by NCCCUSA on political and economic issues. In every convention from 1964 through 1968, there were memorials by synods to the LCA convention expressing these concerns that the Council seemed to be speaking publicly on behalf of all member churches. "As a response to the concern of the synods, the Executive Council began to develop in 1966 a *modus operandi* for keeping closer surveillance over statements of the NCCCUSA. The Council wanted as much advance information as possible, a chance to debate the issues if timing would allow, and the freedom to advise representatives of the church to the inter-church meetings. The procedure was completed in 1968 (LCAM, 1966, p. 272; 1968, p. 276)."[230]

There were many aspects of the NCCCUSA's programs, of course, that the LCA found valuable and which it could support wholeheartedly, such as its support of the Civil Rights Act and the Voting Rights Act, the Delta Ministry, the Week of Prayer for Christian Unity, World Communion Sunday, agricultural and rural life programs overseas, the promotion of "Living Room Dialogues" with Roman

Catholics, support of tax exemption for churches, and the wide-ranging cooperation of Lutheran World Relief with Church World Service.[231]

One anomaly was that many LCA members assumed that huge amounts of benevolence dollars were going to support the Council. Actually, while the LCA usually fulfilled what was considered a "fair share" of the general budget, it ranked tenth among major denominations in per capita contributions to the Council's total work, far behind such denominations as the United Presbyterian Church, USA; the Reformed Church in America; Church of the Brethren; and the United Church of Christ.[232] Clearly, ecumenical commitment in the NCCCUSA had a price attached to it, but for the LCA the price was not very high.

World Council of Churches

The World Council of Churches was a point in ecumenical work where both the ALC and the LCA stood together. Franklin Clark Fry's leadership as chair of the WCC's powerful Central Committee was pivotal for the exercise of the role of Lutherans as a worldwide confessional family. It is significant that the Lutheran World Federation and the World Council of Churches share the Ecumenical Center in Geneva as headquarters. Before the modern Ecumenical Center was built in the 1960s, the LWF offices were in a gatehouse of the WCC grounds. This proximity in headquarters has enabled both organizations to work closely in the development and support of mutually approved programs.

It should be noted that Lutheran scholars have had a profound influence on Christian thought worldwide through the arena of WCC events. One example will serve to illustrate the point. At the World Council Assembly in New Delhi, India, in 1961, the keynote address by Joseph Sittler stirred theological circles with a concept that was fresh to ecumenical thought. As he wrote later, the address "proposed the thesis that only a Christology capable of administering the cosmic scope of biblical and catholic Christ-testimony would be adequate to the question about Christ and his meaning as it is necessarily put by men of modernity."[233] As Theodore Bachmann put it, "While he turned off some German Lutheran theologians, he drew an amazing response from Asians as he unfolded the theme of unity on its grandest scale."[234] Sittler was far ahead of most other thinkers of that time in seeing the intimate relationship between the doctrine of redemption and creation. "For God's creation of earth cannot be redeemed in any intelligible sense of the word," he declared, "apart from a doctrine of the cosmos which is man's home, his definite place, the theatre of his self-hood under God, in cooperation with his neighbor, and in caring-relationship with nature."[235] That theme would be spun out, examined, and reexamined for years to come.

FEELING THE PULSE; PROBING THE FUTURE

At the beginning of its life, the LCA seemed to have only an elementary grasp of the role that research, planning, and evaluation might play in making its work more efficient and effective. The constitution did give the Executive Council authority to "do long range planning of the work of this church, with emphasis on spiritual life and growth, for approval by the convention," although there was no specific mechanism for carrying out this function.[236]

The constituting convention did, however, adopt a recommendation instructing the Executive Council to devise the best means of providing research facilities needed for its own use in long-range planning and also for the use of other church agencies.[237] A study was made involving church executives and five LCA members with special training in research. It was estimated that a full-fledged research facility would cost as much as $200,000, a sum that did not seem available. The decision was to recommend that the 1964 convention authorize the Executive Council to engage a staff official to assist the secretary primarily in his role as statistician and to consult with other units about research projects.[238] The convention approved, but in April 1965 the Council changed the position to that of an administrative assistant. The secretary, therefore, reported to the 1966 convention that "this means the staff position of assistant to the secretary . . . will not be filled at the present time."[239] Any full-scale research facility for the LCA was effectively on hold.

Decentralization of Research in the LCA

"The first decade of the life of the LCA was marked by complete decentralization of research and evaluation work among a few program agencies."[240] It was also a period of applied research which was geared to particular program needs of the units involved. Because of the primitive state of electronic data storage, only hard copies of reports were generally available, so that there was no real possibility of sophisticated analysis of data between agencies.

Because its predecessors had been involved in the "Long-Range Program" that used extensive research and testing in its development, the Board of Parish Education was off and running with a research department at the outset. The first major project of the department after merger was an extensive postpublication field test of the new parish education curriculum materials. This completed the three-part cycle of research, planning, and evaluation laid out when the LRP was initiated. "Since the BPE department represented the only operating research facility in the LCA and was the first to install a computer, it was increasingly asked to take on projects for other agencies and the officers of the church."[241] By the end of the decade, it was even processing on its computer data from the parochial reports for the secretary, a task that had previously been farmed out to a service bureau. The in-house operation made possible the starting of an ongoing process of analyzing the data for use in the church's program that is still going on in more advanced ways today.[242]

The only other research and evaluation work of an ongoing nature during this decade was by the Department of Church Extension of the Board of American Missions. Using census data and information gathered directly from congregations, the department made highly specialized analyses used in making decisions about location of new congregations; redevelopment, relocation, merger, or closure of existing congregations; and the development of area or regional strategies for mission.[243]

While other churchwide units engaged consultants or outside research groups to gather information or conduct studies, "there was relatively little research conducted or sponsored by agencies other than BPE and BAM."[244] One could speculate that there was a lack of appreciation and, perhaps, even an element of distrust of research in the church at this time.

The Place of Planning

By the very nature of the LCA structure, boards were fairly autonomous, and they set about the task of internal planning following merger in relative isolation from one another and in a variety of ways.[245] "As the church grappled with new problems, the structural distinctions and assignments of responsibility began to break down.

As program initiatives changed to meet new challenges, there was no longer a clear understanding of the distinctive function of each agency, a clear conception of the most effective ways to relate similar functions in different agencies, and a clear sense of direction and priorities for the church as a whole."[246]

A test case regarding interagency planning developed when the executive committee of the BPE reported to the board in January 1965 that it had authorized the executive secretary to form a task group "to begin planning for further curriculum development."[247] The BPE quickly realized that trying to develop an educational program for the next decade required the sort of trend analysis that would be equally important for other agencies. The executive secretary consulted President Fry as to whether this kind of broad-scale study did not properly fall within the scope of the Executive Council's authority for long-range planning.[248]

The question was promptly presented to the Executive Council at its April meeting, and all units were consulted about their interest in a long-range study along the lines proposed by the BPE that might be of mutual benefit. All units gave affirmative responses, although the Board of Pensions and the Board of Theological Education expressed reservations. At its June meeting the Council voted to proceed. In September the president called a meeting of all executives, and it was agreed that there were at least three elements in the BPE design that could be studied on a cooperative basis and could "well serve as a forerunner of the 'long-range planning for the church'" that was the Executive Council's responsibility. These included theological trends, changes in society, and the nature and mission of the church in contemporary society.[249]

Once the basic design was endorsed as a two-year study, the BPE was asked to designate a director for the project, and other agencies were asked to contribute one week of a staff person's time per month if possible. Those agencies not able to free staff time were required either to make a financial contribution toward expenses or volunteer a reduction in 1966 apportionment income. Nine agencies chose to use staff time, and five made financial contributions. Edward W. Uthe was assigned by BPE as director of the study by the co-opted staff of thirteen persons.

The task force interviewed or used as consultants ninety-two experts in such fields as theology, biblical study, sociology, education, communications, and the physical sciences. The findings of the task force were reviewed by seventy church leaders at a consultation at the University of Maryland, and the final report was made to the 1968 church convention in Atlanta.[250] Although later critics benefiting from 20-20 hindsight could criticize the study for having missed some major issues that emerged in the seventies, the effort laid the groundwork for future work by the LCA in planning.[251]

CHANGING OF THE GUARD

There can be no doubt that 1968 marked the end of an era, not only for the LCA but also for world Lutheranism and much of the ecumenical movement. On June 6 Franklin Clark Fry, who had been a dominant figure in each of those arenas, died. Some close associates and his family had been aware that he was desperately ill, but few were prepared for the suddenness of his passing. Aware that the end was near on Memorial Day, Dr. Fry dictated from his hospital bed this addition to his President's Report to the coming convention, *"Ave Atque Vale"*—Hail and Farewell!

On the day of his death, Dr. Fry said to his physician, "Is this the day, Doctor, that I'm going to die?" And the doctor replied, "Oh, we can't tell that, Dr. Fry." Dr. Fry said, "Well, I think it is, and I'd like to have Communion with my wife and children." Later that day, his son Franklin celebrated Communion in the hospital room for just the family. That night Franklin Clark Fry died.[252]

The church was shaken by the news. It was aware that Malvin H. Lundeen would retire as secretary at the convention. It quickly dawned on the delegates that the two principal leaders who had guided the LCA during its first six years would no longer be there to counsel and guide and direct. When the assembly convened, Secretary Lundeen was in the chair and ably led the convention through its complex agenda.

Commenting on the election process, the writers of the convention summary said, "Every clergyman of the LCA under the age of 67 was eligible for election as president; it seemed most of them received votes on the first ballot. Actually, the 654 ballots cast were divided among 63 men!"[253] The direction of the delegates' thinking was soon apparent, for Robert J. Marshall, president of the Illinois Synod, received 236 votes. Next came Samuel E. Kidd, president of the Eastern Pennsylvania Synod, with 37, and George F. Harkins, Fry's assistant, with 35. Marshall was elected on the third ballot with

Robert J. Marshall and George F. Harkins

419 votes, and there was a standing ovation before the chair could even declare him elected.

Marshall, who would turn fifty in a few weeks, was a native of Iowa. A graduate of Chicago Seminary, he served for three years as pastor in Alhambra, California, before accepting a post in the Department of Religion at Muhlenberg College. From there he was called to Chicago Seminary as Professor of Old Testament Interpretation in 1953. At Chicago he soon developed a reputation as a biblical scholar, writer, and lecturer. When the Illinois Synod was formed, he was elected president and became known as an able administrator, an incisive thinker with a thorough understanding of the LCA, and a skilled parliamentarian.

When the first ballot for secretary was cast, George F. Harkins was elected by a clear majority.[254] A native of Philadelphia, he was a graduate of Gettysburg Seminary. While awaiting the time when he was to assume the duties of pastor at a suburban Harrisburg congregation, he spent much of his time in the Harrisburg Public Library reading all of the minutes of the ULCA.[255] Harkins early showed an ability in organization and skill as a writer and speaker. In 1949 he was called to the newly created position of assistant to the president of the ULCA. He served in that capacity until 1960 when he was elected the ULCA's secretary for its final two years. In the LCA he returned to the role of Fry's assistant.

Even before they left Atlanta, it became obvious that the new team of officers had inherited their positions in what would prove to be one of the most turbulent periods in the history of the LCA and in North American society. Racial unrest, war, a general malaise in society, and declining resources in the church were going to test their energy and abilities in the years immediately ahead.

NOTES

1. Forecasting the future became a major interest of "think tanks" and individual scholars. There was a tidal wave of books and articles that explored the possibilities of the future and the impact of change from a wide variety of perspectives. A few examples of such volumes include: Herman Kahn and Anthony J. Wiener, *The Year 2000* (New York: Macmillan Co., 1967); Donald N. Michael, *The Next Generation* (New York: Vantage Press, 1965); Robert L. Heilbroner, *The Future as History* (New York: Harper & Brothers, 1960); Kenneth Boulding, *The Meaning of the Twentieth Century* (New York: Harper & Row, 1964).

2. Arthur M. Schlesinger, Jr., *The Imperial Presidency* (Boston: Houghton Mifflin, 1973), 176.

3. Ibid., 178.

4. At the 1964 convention of the LCA, the Board of Parish Education presented a film, "Questions that Have Never Been Asked," that startled delegates and challenged them to grapple with the implications of such developments as genetic engineering and computer technology for education in church and society. See *Convention Summary* by the Commission of Press, Radio, and Television, 5.

5. "It has been estimated . . . that at the time of the American Revolution 90 per cent of all Americans were engaged in agriculture. Today the estimate is 10 per cent and soon will be half that." Donald R. Pichaske, *The Manifesto* (Philadelphia: Board of Publication of the LCA, 1967), 90.

6. Ahlstrom, *Religious History,* 1091.

7. Ahlstrom details this situation and its impact on Black religion in *Religious History,* 1055–78.

8. See Martin Luther King, Jr., *I Have a Dream* (Los Angeles: John Henry and Mary Louise Dunn Bryant Foundation, 1963).

9. Samuel Eliot Morison, Henry Steele Commager, William E. Leuchten-
burg, *The Growth of the American Republic*, vol. 2, 7th ed. (New York and
Oxford: Oxford University Press, 1980).

10. See Nathan Wright, Jr., *Black Power and Urban Unrest* (New York:
Hawthorne Books, 1967).

11. Ahlstrom, *Religious History*, 1074–75.

12. James H. Cone, *Black Theology and Black Power* (New York: Seabury
Press, 1969).

13. Ahlstrom, *Religious History*, 1084.

14. Merton P. Strommen in *Profiles of Church Youth* (St. Louis: Concordia
Publishing House, 1963) describes a four-year study of 3,000 Lutheran youth,
largely concentrated in the Midwest. He states, "In a day which tends to
romanticize the pathological, it may seem dull to present youth as relatively
obedient, accepting, and moral," (p. 232) but that is the picture that emerges
from this particular survey. Strommen's careful analysis continually cautions,
however, against generalizations that ignore the major findings about individual uniqueness revealed in the study.

15. Solberg, *Higher Education*, 318–19.

16. Ibid., 329–30. Solberg provides a helpful analysis of the issues and
events on campus in the sixties, 318–33.

17. Ahlstrom, *Religious History*, 1037–54.

18. Ibid., 1016–17.

19. The reintroduction of Nietzsche's idea first came in Gabriel
Vahanian's book *The Death of God: The Culture of a Post-Christian Era*
(New York: George Braziller, 1961).

20. Langdon Gilkey, *How the Church Can Minister to the World Without
Losing Itself* (New York: Harper & Row, 1964), 21.

21. Mortensen, *Danish Church*, 273. The quotation is from a poem by
Kristian Østergaard in *Sange fra Praerien* (Copenhagen, 1912), 65.

22. *LCA Minutes, 1962*, 35. The speech oratorio had been written by
Robert E. Huldschiner of the staff of *The Lutheran* and was directed by
Robert E. Bornemann, professor at Philadelphia Seminary.

23. In order to accommodate 175 communicants at a time, there were
three auxiliary Communion tables and long Communion rails arranged in
cruciform. The different arrangements used in later LCA convention Communion services with their many separate stations are clues to changing
liturgical practices.

24. Fry received 733 of 919 votes. Lundeen, who had received 210
votes on the first ballot for president, was elected secretary on the first
ballot for that office by a vote of 750 out of 867 ballots cast. See *LCAM,
1962*, 95, 102–3.

25. Ibid., 95.

26. Ibid., 127.

27. Harkins describes the situation in his oral history interview, *The Oral
History Collection*, LCUSA Archives, 1977, 123–24. Key votes on positions
are recorded in the *JCLU Minutes, March 2, 1962*, 260–61.

28. *LCAM, 1962*, 90–91. The following were named:

Boards

American Missions	Donald L. Houser
College Education and Church Vocation	E. Theodore Bachmann
Parish Education	W. Kent Gilbert
Pensions	L. Edwin Wang
Publication	H. Torrey Walker
Social Ministry	Harold Haas
Theological Education	Conrad Bergendoff
World Missions	Earl S. Erb

Commissions

Architecture	Edward S. Frey
Church Papers	G. Elson Ruff
Evangelism	Reynold N. Johnson
Press, Radio and Television	Charles C. Hushaw
Stewardship	Henry Endress
Worship	Edgar S. Brown, Jr.
Youth Activities	Carl C. Manfred

Lutheran Church Women elected Dorothy Marple as its executive, and Lutheran Church Men selected J. H. Oetgen. The executive for Youth Activities served in the same capacity for the Luther League. President Fry chose as his assistants George F. Harkins, who had been secretary of the ULCA, and Martin E. Carlson, who had been Augustana's executive director of stewardship and finance. Raymond W. Wargelin, president of Suomi, and A. Ejnar Farstrup, AELC president, both had high-level positions as regional secretaries of the Board of American Missions.

29. *LCAM, 1962,* 226.

30. The report had been presented by Edward T. Horn III, who had chaired the commission. Two members who registered dissenting views were Martin Heinecken, the highly respected systematic theology professor at Philadelphia Seminary, and Robert Hetico, who headed Suomi's Board of Parish Education. See *LCAM, 1962,* 131–36.

31. Ibid., 127.

32. Ibid., 232–36.

33. *1962 Convention Summary,* 8.

34. *LCAM, 1962,* 235.

35. Ibid., 237–45.

36. See Philip Hefner, "The Identity and Mission of the Church: Theological Reflections on the Concrete Existence of The Lutheran Church in America," in *The Church Emerging,* ed. John Reumann, (Philadelphia: Fortress Press, 1977), 141–43.

37. Ibid., 147. Hefner calls attention to Article V of the LCA Constitution, Section 1, which declares that the LCA "lives to be an instrument of the Holy Spirit," and seeks to relate the gospel "to human need in every situation."

38. *LCAM, 1966,* 498.

39. Ibid., 498–99.

40. Ibid., 501.

41. Ibid., 502.

42. *LCA Bylaws, 1964,* Section X, F, Board of Social Ministry, Item 6.

43. At its June 28–29 meeting the Executive Council had issued a strongly worded document in which it affirmed the 1952 statement of the ULCA and the 1956 statement of Augustana condemning "the evils of segregation and discrimination, on the basis of race" pending convention action on the matter, and stated flatly "that any segregation and discrimination . . . in the congregations, agencies, and institutions of the church is a violation of God's will." *LCAM, 1964,* 329.

44. Ibid., 663.

45. Ibid., 664–65.

46. Ibid., 665–66. In later printings of this social statement a term such as "fellow" was changed to the gender neutral word "other." The wording quoted here is that of the minutes.

47. Ibid., 494–96, 677.

48. *Executive Council Minutes, June 1963,* 611.

49. The entire memorandum appears in the *LCAM, 1964,* 334–37.

50. Interestingly, the problem never seemed to assume the same dimensions in Canada.

51. *LCAM, 1966,* 531.

52. The writer heard Dr. George W. Forell, of the University of Iowa, use this phrase at a National Council of Churches meeting in St. Louis.

53. *LCAM, 1966,* 531–32, 821–24.

54. Ibid., 534.

55. *LCAM, 1968,* 752.

56. Among those involved were Carl A. Braaten, associate professor of theology at LSTC; Romaine Gardner, professor of philosophy, Wagner College; Charles Y. Glock, professor of sociology, University of California, Berkeley; George W. Forell, head of the Department of Religion, University of Iowa; and Dwight Oberholtzer, a graduate student at Berkeley.

57. *LCAM, 1968,* 770–71.

58. *1968 Convention Summary,* 12.

59. *LCAM, 1968,* 764.

60. Ibid., 762.

61. Pastor Wesley had become the first Black pastor to serve in the Augustana Church when he was ordained in 1957.

62. *LCAM, 1966,* 518.

63. Solberg, *Higher Education,* 326.

64. Two examples of compensatory programs were HARCAP (Harlem College Assistance Project) and ORHAP (Orange Higher Achievement Program) where Black youth were given college preparatory training by competent teachers and students from Wagner and Upsala College in the metropolitan New York area. See *LCAM, 1966,* 518.

65. Solberg, *Higher Education,* 381, n. 33.

66. Ibid., 327.

67. The Kerner Report, issued by a special commission appointed by the United States president after the riots of 1967, had stressed the connection between urban unrest and racial injustice.

68. *1968 Convention Summary*, 10.

69. *LCAM, 1968*, 600, 713–14, 724–26.

70. *1968 Convention Summary*, 6.

71. *LCAM, 1966*, 447.

72. Ibid., 43, 479.

73. *Theology, An Assessment of Current Trends* (Philadelphia: Fortress Press, 1968), 138. This is one of the three volumes which constitute the "Report of the Lutheran Church in America Task Group for Long-Range Planning." Edward W. Uthe served as both director of the study and editor of the report.

74. *LCAM, 1964*, 432–34.

75. *LCAM, 1962*, 436–37.

76. Ibid., 434–36.

77. *LCAM, 1966*, 582.

78. Ibid., 391.

79. *1966 Convention Summary*, 6.

80. *BAM Minutes, June 1967*, 3216.

81. *LCAM, 1968*, 583.

82. Lloyd E. Sheneman gives a thought-provoking analysis of the whole situation in *Decision Making in the Lutheran Church in America: Typology and Tabulation*, 1970, 121–34. In this study commissioned by Robert J. Marshall, new president of the LCA, Sheneman describes what he calls "decision by budget" as a major indicator of priorities.

83. Ibid., 131. In the case of the BAM's decision to embark on community organizational work, Sheneman uses the typology "Decision Unawares," 142–52.

84. James A. Scherer, "Growth Toward Self-hood and Maturity in Africa, Asia, and Australasia," 351.

85. News report in *The Lutheran* 1, no. 6 (March 13, 1963): 26.

86. James A. Scherer, who headed the School of Missions at Maywood Seminary, gives a picture of the kind of agonizing reassessment that was taking place generally in missions in his book *Missionary, Go Home: A Reappraisal of the Christian World Mission* (Englewood Cliffs, N.J.: Prentice Hall, 1964). The phrase "Missionary, Go Home" is attributed to Gandhi.

87. Scherer, "Self-hood and Maturity," 342–43.

88. Vikner, "LCA World Mission," 166–67.

89. Bola Ige, "The Contemporary African Revolution," *World Encounter* 1, no. 2 (December 1963): 11–13. Ige was a Nigerian Anglican lawyer.

90. Panel discussion in issue of *World Encounter* 1, no. 4 (April 1964): 12–16.

91. Article by R. Pierce Beaver, *World Encounter* 2, no. 1 (October 1964): 6.

92. Editorial in *World Encounter* 2, no. 3 (February 1965): 5.

93. *LCAM, 1968*, 772.

94. *BWM Minutes, November 11–13, 1968,* 367.

95. Vikner, "LCA World Mission," 168.

96. *BWM Minutes,* 71-045. The Executive Council at its June 25–26, 1971, meeting gave "hearty approval to participation by the Board of World Missions in the exploration."

97. The whole series of steps is recorded in the *BWM Minutes, December 6–8, 1971,* 241–44, and in the November 1972 Executive Committee report to the board, *Minutes,* 342–44. There is no record, however, that consideration was given to a specific individual as a possible chief executive in the event of a common board.

98. *LCAM, 1968,* 647.

99. Pierre Berton, *The Comfortable Pew* (Philadelphia and New York: J. B. Lippincott, 1965).

100. *LCAM, 1966,* 557.

101. Ibid., 550.

102. Ibid., 556–57.

103. See Donald R. Pichaske, *A Study Book on the Manifesto* (Philadelphia: Board of Publication of the LCA, 1967). William A. Koppe, research director of the BPE, prepared *A Search for Congregational Renewal* as a process guide for parishes engaged in implementing *The Manifesto.*

104. Lists of materials reviewed and produced appeared in each report of the Commission on Worship to the convention. See *LCAM, 1964,* 290–93; and *LCAM, 1968,* 174–76, as examples. *The Ministers Information Service* was a packet of materials sent periodically to pastors to update them on latest developments. It usually included a message from the president that gave his views about current church issues.

105. *ECM, April 1963,* 516–17; *June 1963,* 611; *October 1963,* 616.

106. *LCAM, 1964,* 295–302, 549, 648, 668–76.

107. *LCAM, 1966,* 347–48.

108. Ibid. The commission's action was cautious in asking that the initial conversations consider scope, problems to be faced, and procedures to be used. The Executive Council's action was more positive in tone while still reserving the Council's right of approval of negotiations.

109. *ECM, October 1965,* 504–7.

110. The LCA initially had the following representatives on the ILCW: John W. Arthur, Edgar S. Brown, Jr., L. Crosby Deaton, Edward T. Horn III, Frederick F. Jackisch, Ulrich S. Leupold, Daniel T. Moe, and Krister Stendahl. *LCAM, 1968,* 179–80.

111. Ibid., 181.

112. Kendig Brubaker Cully listed 194 books just on the topic of Christian education itself, most of which were published in the late fifties and early sixties. See *The Westminster Dictionary of Christian Education* (Philadelphia: Westminster Press, 1963). His total bibliography, which was intended to be representative and not exhaustive, runs to nearly thirteen hundred titles.

113. In 1964 the Commission on Church Architecture reported that it had conducted a five-day consultation of religious educators and architects at Purdue University to study the problems in building for educational ministry

(*LCAM, 1964,* 287). During this period the Board of Parish Education had its own staff person to assist congregations with questions about buildings and equipment for their educational programs.

114. The Confraternity of Christian Doctrine of the Roman Catholic Church devoted twenty pages of its education journal to a careful analysis of the LCA's curriculum. James R. Schaefer, "What Catholic Religious Education Can Learn from the 'Long-Range Program of Parish Education' of the Lutheran Church in America," *Living Light* 4, no. 2 (Summer 1967): 57–76.

115. *LCAM, 1964,* 40.

116. Edgar Trexler, "Big Day Comes in Church School," *The Lutheran* 2, no. 23 (November 4, 1963): 13. The Board of Publication reported to the 1966 convention that more than 4,750,000 texts plus "thousands of filmstrips and recordings" had been distributed.

117. Ibid., 11.

118. In explaining the proposed budgets at the 1966 convention, the Executive Council stated, "Since a substantial portion of the new curriculum has been developed, a reduction could be effected here." *LCAM, 1966,* 223. The actual budget cut for 1967 was 10.8 percent, ibid., 227.

119. *LCAM, 1968,* 512.

120. Statistics have been compiled in a special analysis by Robert Strohl, Research Department, Division for Parish Services, 1986.

121. The first reference to this group was in the *ULCA Minutes, 1928,* 411. It has continued until the present time but has expanded its role to cooperation in the whole area of parish life.

122. The translation was issued jointly by the publication houses of the participating churches in 1963 and has gone through many printings since that time. In the 1980s it was revised by the ALC and LCA to include the new texts of the Lord's Prayer and the Apostles' Creed.

123. *LCAM, 1964,* 395.

124. Ibid., 396.

125. All figures quoted in this section and in following chapters are from a special analysis prepared in 1986 for the writer by Robert Strohl, assistant director of the Research Department of the Division for Parish Services.

126. The service relied on referrals from pastors whose members had moved out of the parish and address changes from *The Lutheran,* but these were often out of date by the time they reached the congregations to which they were sent. See *LCAM, 1966,* 176.

127. "Report of Lutheran Church Men" to the 1964 LCA convention, *LCAM, 1964* 600.

128. Ibid., 331, 606.

129. *ECM, June 1965,* 389.

130. *LCAM, 1966,* 391–97, 625–26, 811, 819–21.

131. Nelson, *Lutheranism 1914–1970,* 240, n. 83.

132. *LCAM, 1964,* 404.

133. Ibid., 406–7.

134. Ibid., 323.

135. *LCAM, 1966,* 475.

136. Ibid.

137. Ibid., 192–98.

138. Ibid., 496–98.

139. Nelson, *Lutheranism 1914–1970*, 233–34.

140. Ibid., 231–32.

141. See Lani L. Johnson, *Led by the Spirit*, 22. The ULCA auxiliary had changed its name in 1955, and the Augustana group, in 1958.

142. Ibid., 47.

143. An examination of the pages of *Lutheran Women* from the earliest issues onward shows articles dealing with such topics as "Race: a Gift of Human Diversity," 1, no. 2 (February 1963): 5–7; "Social Change and Christian Obedience," ibid., 18–21; "Social Welfare: Whose Responsibility?" 1, no. 3 (March 1963): 18–20; "I Shared in the March on Washington" and "How to Write to a Congressman," 1, no. 10 (November 1963); "Latch Key Kids Need Our Love," 3, no. 7 (July 1965).

144. Ahlstrom observes that it was in the late sixties that the women's liberation movement "took on broader and more truly revolutionary dimensions . . . by posing deeper questions about the moral structure of the Western culture," *Religious History*, 1084.

145. "Directory of the LCA," printed in *LCAM, 1968*, 832–42.

146. Lani L. Johnson, *Led by the Spirit*, 41–42.

147. *LCAM, 1964*, 556–57; and *1966*, 494–95.

148. Letter from Kathryn E. Kopf, executive director, to the writer, January 29, 1986.

149. "VRA Program," an unpublished document of LCW, 1985.

150. The action appears in the *LCAM, 1962*, 226. The bylaws, Section X, G, Item 3 actually were a bit more generous in indicating that the BTE could bring such recommendations "at its discretion."

151. *LCAM, 1964*, 582.

152. References here are to Conrad Bergendoff, *The Lutheran Church in America and Theological Education* (New York: BTE, 1964).

153. Ibid., 27.

154. *LCAM, 1964*, 588–89, 592–95.

155. *LCAM, 1966*, 638–63.

156. Ibid., 501.

157. The General Synod had given responsibility for deaconess work to a separate board, and the recommendation of that board on June 25, 1918, was that this practice be continued in the ULCA ("Report of the Deaconess Board" to the General Synod Convention, 1918, 115). This precedent was followed in the ULCA.

158. *LCAM, 1964*, 508–10.

159. Frederick S. Weiser, *To Serve the Lord and His People* (Philadelphia: Deaconess Community, LCA, 1984), 28.

160. Solberg, *Higher Education*, 330. Interestingly, Hartwick traced its roots to the original Hartwick Seminary begun in 1797, although it was chartered as a four-year college in 1928.

161. *LCAM, 1968*, 478.

162. Ibid., 479.

163. Edgar M. Carlson, *Church Sponsored Higher Education and the Lutheran Church in America* (New York: LCA, 1967).

164. *LCAM, 1968,* 470–73.

165. *ULCA Minutes, 1962,* 586–90.

166. *LCAM, 1968,* 468–69.

167. There was no official relationship between BCECV and the Omaha Deaconesses, but conversations went on until the decision was reached to merge with the sisters from Baltimore and Philadelphia. One reason for the delay was the complicated process of sorting out the assets of the diaconate from those of the parent corporation that was also involved with the hospital and social service agency. See Weiser, *To Serve the Lord and His People,* 16.

168. Details of the agreement are spelled out in the *BCECV Minutes, July 14–16, 1965,* 94–95.

169. *LCAM, 1968,* 469. The BCECV had taken action in 1967 recognizing the seven members of the Bethphage Sisterhood and encouraged the LCA Deaconess Community to seek cooperative relationships with the group. The *LCA Yearbook, 1986,* 209, still listed one retired deaconess under the heading "Bethphage Sisterhood."

170. G. Elson Ruff, "Church Editors Were Fighting Men," *The Lutheran* (July 6, 1960): 11–15.

171. Albert P. Stauderman, "First Came the 'Observer,'" *The Lutheran* (August 1981): 8–11. Stauderman himself had retired as editor by this time.

172. Ruff, "Church Editors," 12–13, gives examples of Krauth's sharp and witty criticisms. "Krauth replied to the Kurtz assertion that *The Lutheran* was more expensive per square inch than *The Observer* by saying (August 17, 1860) that 'on the supposition that we are not better than it is, we still think it would be good policy to encourage us, on the ground that the less there is of a bad thing, the better.'"

173. "Report of the Commission on Church Papers," *LCAM, 1964,* 147.

174. *1968 Convention Summary,* 3.

175. *LCAM, 1964,* 147.

176. Editor Ruff described this approach more than once to the writer, explaining why this type of journalism was essential for an open-minded Lutheran Church in America. See also Ruff's memo in *Franklin Clark Fry. A Palette for a Portrait,* Robert H. Fischer, ed., 65–66.

177. In its report to the 1968 convention, PRT stated that it had distributed 393 general releases to newspapers and the wire services, in addition to 176 specialized articles and hundreds of pictures for publication. *LCAM, 1968,* 163.

178. Ibid., 164.

179. The most thorough analysis of "Davey and Goliath" has been done by Frank W. Klos in an unpublished doctoral dissertation at Temple University, 1978.

180. *LCAM, 1968,* 164; and *1970,* 151.

181. The General Synod established the Lutheran Publication Society in 1855 as an auxiliary association but recognized it two years later as its board

of publication. The General Council established its board of publication in 1867, which developed the General Council Publication House in 1899. The Augustana Book Concern was formed in 1889 from the Swedish Lutheran Publication Society, which traced its roots to work done by Tufve Hasselquist in 1855. See Suelflow and Nelson, "Frontier," 208–9.

182. *LCA Bylaws*, Section XVIII, Item 3, f.

183. *LCAM, 1964*, 462.

184. "The decision on the format of *The Lutheran* . . . made it impossible to produce the magazine on any of the presses in the Philadelphia or Rock Island plants. In Philadelphia the employees affected did not have long seniority and a reduction in work force was made quickly." Ibid., 462.

185. *LCAM, 1968*, 716.

186. *Minutes of Board of Publication, 1971*, 1510.

187. The net loss before royalties was $44,070. Added to this were royalties of $112,994. *LCAM, 1964*, 468.

188. *LCAM, 1966*, 486.

189. *LCAM, 1968*, 717.

190. *LCAM, 1964*, 178–83.

191. *LCAM, 1966*, 43–47.

192. The reference was to the financial difficulties of the Florida Lutheran Retirement Center in DeLand. The Board of Social Ministry reported to the 1968 convention on a plan to deal with the problem. "Essentially the plan calls for $125,000 a year from the general church for a six-year period . . . ," *LCAM, 1968*, 628–29. The situation was the first test of the possible legal liability of church-owned and church-recognized agencies. The Legal Matters Committee of the Executive Council had issued a lengthy "Memorandum of Law" in 1965, which dealt with the implications of the LCA Constitution, Article VIII, Section 8, e, and the Bylaws, Section X, F, Item 2, which are concerned with social mission institutions and agencies. See *LCAM, 1966*, 355–60.

193. *LCAM, 1966*, 45. The budgets as finally adopted by the convention and a detailed analysis appear in the minutes, pp. 220–21, 806–7.

194. There are, of course, many interesting figures that can be cited. One revealing comparison is that total congregational assets increased during this period from $1.066 billion to $1.446 billion. All figures cited in this section are from the LCA yearbooks and LCA treasurer's reports for the period.

195. Endress had not only pioneered the use of motion pictures for stewardship motivation in the ULCA but also had produced through the NLC the film *Martin Luther* that was shown in first-run theaters throughout the United States and Canada. *Martin Luther* had the distinction of being banned in some cities because of Roman Catholic opposition.

196. Arden, *Augustana*, 339.

197. Although the LLM gave a grant towards costs, those being served paid modest fees to the Fund-Raising and Counseling Service, which operated on a nonprofit basis.

198. The service helped congregations alone to raise some $9,573,000 in 1967. See *LCAM, 1968*, 641.

199. The COS received a church grant of $358,500 in 1967. Most of the balance of its budget came from the LLM. See *LCAM, 1968,* 259.

200. *LCAM, 1970,* 236. As the corpus of the gift by Harrison W. and Myrtle M. Prosser grew, more than $12.4 million was distributed through 1987 and another $7.2 million was distributed soon after the Evangelical Lutheran Church in America came into existence in 1988. See *The Lutheran,* March 16, 1988, 32.

201. A report of the gift by Florence Foerderer Tonner appears in the *LCAM, 1968,* 211–12; and *1970,* 237–38.

202. A careful review of the Glen Foerd situation was presented in a background paper prepared by the Office for Administration and Finance in 1981 in light of possible divestiture. In June 1985, the Judge of the Orphan's Court, Philadelphia, awarded trusteeship to the City of Philadelphia, Fairmount Park Commission. The center contained a collection of prints, rare Bibles, books, and other artwork. Some of these are now "on loan" from the LCA to the Philadelphia Art Museum and certain LCA institutions (*OAF Historical Data 1972–1986,* supplied to the writer by Nancy Oakford, assistant to the OAF executive director, February 6, 1986). The last major convention report on Glen Foerd operations appears in the *LCAM, 1982,* 510–11. An extensive write-up of the history of Glen Foerd from the perspective of those who worked in the program was provided to this writer by Frank and Roseanne Muhly, the last managers of the center.

203. *LCAM, 1964,* 230–31.

204. Ibid., 231.

205. Ibid., 244–49.

206. *LCAM, 1966,* 557.

207. *LCAM, 1968,* 302.

208. F. K. Wentz, *Lutherans in Concert,* 170.

209. Empie made such a suggestion to the NLC representatives at their 1958 meeting, *Agenda,* 71–73.

210. Wolf, *Documents,* 616–17.

211. E. Theodore Bachmann describes the significant developments in Missouri during these years in *The Ecumenical Involvement of the LCA Predecessor Bodies* (New York: DWME, 1983), Appendix, 41–43.

212. Letter of Empie to LCMS President Behnken, February 3, 1959. See Wolf, *Documents,* 618–19.

213. Ibid., 615–16. The constitution without bylaws appears on pages 630–37.

214. F. K. Wentz gives a concise analysis of the give-and-take in these new arrangements in *Lutherans in Concert,* 172–73.

215. "Legally, this organization continued the NLC, so that technically the NLC did not die in 1967, but simply limited itself to its international aspects." Ibid., 173.

216. Nelson, *Lutheranism 1914–1970,* 268.

217. Paul C. Empie and James I. McCord, eds., *Marburg Revisited* (Minneapolis: Augsburg Publishing House, 1966), 191.

218. Nelson, *Lutheranism 1914–1970,* 268–73.

219. Bachmann, *Ecumenical Involvement,* Appendix, 43.

220. Bachmann gives a detailed account of the events within LCMS and the rise of the AELC. Ibid., Appendix, 29–65.

221. Robert H. Fischer, "Lutheranism in North America," in Vilmos Vajta, ed., *Lutheran Church Past and Present* (1977), 306.

222. Professors George Lindbeck of Yale and Warren Quanbeck of Luther Seminary were leaders in this movement. See Nelson, *Lutheranism 1914–1970,* 190, and article on Fry by Kurt Schmidt-Clausen in Fischer, *Palette for a Portrait,* 267.

223. Bachmann, *Ecumenical Involvement,* 131.

224. *Proceedings of the Fourth Assembly,* 418.

225. Ibid., 417.

226. Bachmann, *Ecumenical Involvement,* 46.

227. Nelson, *Lutheranism 1914–1970,* 273.

228. The unfolding history of this relationship can be traced first in the *ECM, January 1963,* 344. Later, the *LCAM* make references in *1964,* 309; *1966,* 696–97; *1968,* 729; *1970,* 454.

229. The writer was a delegate at the Philadelphia Assembly when this action was taken after the NCCCUSA did not recognize LCA's understandings of prior agreements about such services.

230. Robert J. Marshall, *An Evaluation of the Relationship of the Lutheran Church in America with the National Council of Churches of Christ in the USA* (New York: DWME, 1985), 18.

231. Ibid., 16–17.

232. Marshall refers to an LCA study of this question in 1974. Ibid., 28.

233. Joseph Sittler, *Essays on Nature and Grace* (Philadelphia: Fortress Press, 1972), 8.

234. Bachmann, *Ecumenical Involvement,* 128.

235. *The New Delhi Report. The Third Assembly of the World Council of Churches* (New York: Association Press, 1962), 15.

236. *LCA Constitution,* Article XII, Section 3, b.

237. *LCAM, 1964,* 169.

238. Ibid., 102–5.

239. *LCAM, 1966,* 68.

240. Leonard A. Sibley and Stephen Hart, *Research and Evaluation in the Lutheran Church in America* (Philadelphia: Office of the Bishop, 1985), 7. This careful analysis by the staff of the Department of Planning, Research and Evaluation will be a basic source of information for this section.

241. Ibid., 7.

242. Ibid., 8.

243. Ibid., 7.

244. Ibid.

245. The writer is indebted to Leonard A. Sibley's paper *Planning in the Lutheran Church in America,* May 1985, for much of the information in this section.

246. Sibley, *Planning,* 9.

247. *BPE Minutes,* January 1965, 5.

248. Based on the writer's own involvement in the matter.

249. The record of these developments is the *ECM, April 1965*, 266–67; *June 1965*, 368–69; *October 1965*, 451–52; *January 1966*, 554–55; *April 1966*, 662–63; and *LCAM, 1966*, 412–15. See also Sheneman, *Decision Making*, 7–13.

250. *LCAM, 1968*, 397–402. A more detailed report is contained in three volumes edited by Edward W. Uthe: *Theology, An Assessment of Current Trends; Social Change, An Assessment of Current Trends; Significant Issues for the 1970's* (Philadelphia: Fortress Press, 1968).

251. Sibley, *Planning*, 10.

252. *The Oral History Collection*, LCUSA Archives, 1984, 25. Interview with George F. Harkins.

253. *1968 Convention Summary*, 2.

254. *LCAM, 1968*, 464–65.

255. Harkins shared this fact with the writer in an interview in August 1986.

Chapter 4 | OLD PROBLEMS AND NEW STRATEGIES

DECADES ARE OUR FAVORITE WAY OF ENCAP-
sulating history, although they seldom do justice to the continuity of
events. We need to hinge our history more realistically upon refer-
ents that correspond to the particular subject with which we are
concerned. In the case of the Lutheran Church in America, the years
1968 through 1972 represented a far-reaching change in the way in
which the church was organized and understood its mission.

The four years that bridged the end of the sixties and the beginning of the seventies were wracked by problems that seemed to grow
ever deeper and more intractable. There was a pervasive feeling that
society was moving ineluctably from crisis to crisis without much
hope on the horizon. It was also a time that often prompted new
initiatives for dealing with problems while people clung tenaciously
to timeworn patterns even when they obviously no longer met the
needs. It is possible to cite only a few examples here.

THE TURMOIL IN ASIA

The United States, which had become deeply involved in Vietnam
during the Kennedy years and had seen the war escalate under the
Johnson administration, elected Richard M. Nixon president in 1968
on the promise of achieving "peace with honor." Instead, the nation
became mired more deeply in a war that was becoming increasingly
unpopular at home and was costing the support of allies abroad. The
concept of "Vietnamization" was intended to extricate the United
States and its forces by vastly increasing aid and training for South
Vietnamese troops (ARVN) while stepping up the air war against the
North's supply lines and bases in Cambodia. In the words of historian
Barbara Tuchman, "Considering that arming, training and indoc-

197

trinating under American auspices had been pursued for fifteen years without spectacular results, the expectation that these would now enable ARVN successfully to take over the war could qualify as wooden-headedness."[1]

Protests against the war mounted in the United States. More than a quarter million demonstrators massed on Vietnam Moratorium Day in Washington in November 1969. In hope of counteracting anti-war sentiment, the president announced that 150,000 American troops would be brought home in 1970, but then fanned the flames by ordering an invasion of Cambodia in April of that year. On May 4 the nation was aghast when National Guard troops opened fire on student anti-war demonstrators at Kent State University, Ohio, killing four and wounding nine. Ten days later there was a counterpart tragedy at Jackson State College in Mississippi.[2]

In 1971 the ARVN invaded Laos with American air support in an action similar to the invasion of Cambodia. Casualties for the South Vietnamese were high, and anti-American sentiment grew as many began to conclude that the high cost of Vietnamization was to enable Americans to leave. Morale of American forces fell as the war dragged into 1972 and became the longest in American history.[3] In the midst of all this, elections loomed in the United States, and an event occurred that would ultimately result in Nixon's downfall. Minions of the Committee to Re-elect the President broke into the offices of the Democratic National Committee in the Watergate office building and were caught red-handed.

In spite of this, it became apparent that Nixon would be reelected. Pressure was put on both South and North Vietnam to effect a peace settlement. "Signed in Paris on 27 January 1973, the treaty left the situation on paper no different from the insecure settlement in Geneva nineteen years before. To the physical reality had since been added more than a half million deaths in North and South, hundreds of thousands of wounded and destitute, burned and crippled children, landless peasants, a ravaged land deforested and pitted with bomb craters and a people torn by mutual hatred. . . . In the aftermath, as everyone knows, Hanoi overcame Saigon within two years."[4]

The southeastern sector was not the only part of Asia that was in turmoil. The People's Republic of China was in the throes of the Great Proletarian Cultural Revolution that had begun in 1966 and lasted a decade. Students took to the streets, and education came to a virtual standstill. Ironically, the Red Guards, as the youth were called, had been recruited by Chairman Mao Zedong himself as the ideological shock troops for his efforts at cultural change. Many of the traditions of the country were repudiated; political leaders were openly humiliated and forced to do menial labor; the economy staggered and violence erupted repeatedly. More constructive reform, however, would have to wait until the ascent to power of Deng Xiaoping and the ousting of Mao's Gang of Four in 1976.

In the midst of all the grim events in Asia, however, there were some hopeful signals on the international scene. In 1972 President Nixon visited China with the intention of restoring relations that had been interrupted more than twenty years before. Shortly thereafter he received a cordial welcome from Soviet Premier Leonid Brezhnev, who seemed eager to effect detente with the United States. "Like the new relations with China, the Soviet-American detente yielded few specific returns. The two nations reached some agreement of regulating their nuclear weapons. . . . Many of the old antagonisms proved to be very much alive. Nevertheless, beginning in 1972, long-standing fears of nuclear war eased."[5]

THE CONTINUING RACIAL CRISIS

The racial unrest that had seethed through North American society in the preceding years gained momentum and took some new directions during this period. In 1969 the churches were rocked by the issuance of a "Black Manifesto" by the National Black Economic Development Conference that was addressed to the "White Christian Churches and Synagogues in the U.S.A. and All Other Racist Institutions."[6]

Headed by James Forman, who had been executive of the Student Nonviolent Coordinating Committee,[7] the conference demanded $500 million in reparations to atone for the discrimination, persecution, and suffering endured by Blacks since the days of slavery. Followers of Forman interrupted church services in many places to push their demands and even threatened to occupy denominational headquarters.

The General Board of the NCCCUSA listened to a presentation by Forman at its May 1–2 meeting and urged "that the communions give serious study to the Manifesto, expecting that each communion will act on the matter in its own way."[8] While recognizing that the

Black Economic Development Conference was a new agency among others directed towards achievement of economic justice for deprived peoples, the General Board rejected the theology of the Manifesto at its September meeting and called for raising a half million dollars to combat racial injustice. These funds were to be expended through the Interreligious Foundation for Community Organization and the National Committee of Black Churchmen.[9]

Although major attention focused on the Black revolution, other racial and ethnic groups were also beginning to make themselves heard. The increasing protests and demonstrations of the Native Americans were an example. Although President Nixon had sent a special message on Indian affairs to Congress on July 8, 1970, it was only a statement of intent that required further concrete action by the government. "It did not, by itself, bring about self-determination or any of the measures it proposed. It created no new conditions on the reservations, and it did not halt abruptly the paternalism of the Bureau of Indian Affairs."[10]

Even as the administration readied its legislative program, Indians moved on their own to express grievances in many ways. A Bureau of Indian Affairs building was occupied in Colorado; South Dakota Sioux and others camped atop the monument at Mount Rushmore to dramatize their anger; 250 Chippewa, some in war paint, laid claim to land along Lake Superior; the Pit River Tribe in Northern California struggled for return of 3,368,000 acres of land that a commission had decided in 1956 had been taken from them illegally.[11] It would not be long before the churches also would be confronted by major Indian demands.

THE WOMEN'S MOVEMENT

The Women's Liberation Movement, which had been taken all too lightly at first by most males in North America, suddenly exploded into a worldwide phenomenon.[12] Women were working in a wide variety of ways to break the power of institutionalized sexism from Asia to Africa to Latin America.

In the United States, organizations such as NOW grew from relatively small beginnings in the mid-sixties to powerful political forces in the seventies. One of the major triumphs for women came when the Equal Rights Amendment received the necessary two-thirds vote in Congress in 1972 to allow it to be submitted to the states for ratification. Ironically, the vote had come almost fifty years after the amendment was first introduced.[13] Initially, twenty-eight states ratified ERA, but a strong counteroffensive was launched in 1973 that eventually stymied approval.

The struggle was waged on other fronts, however, and was not solely dependent on ERA. "Many people first became aware of the women's liberation movement in September 1968. The Radical Women's protest of the Miss America Contest was the first feminist activity to get front-page coverage."[14] Unequal wages between men and women became a major issue. Although the Equal Pay Act of 1963 and Title VII of the Civil Rights Act of 1964 were intended to rectify the problem, women in the 1970s wore badges that read "59 cents" to underscore the continuing discrepancy in wages.[15] The right of women to have abortions soon became a volatile issue that would result in many legal challenges. The insidious effect of masculine-oriented language in shaping male and female images began to surface with a study of elementary school textbooks in New Jersey. The results of the study were published under the title *Dick and Jane as Victims.*[16] Understandably, organized religion came in for criticism as a force that rationalized and legitimized patriarchal practices elsewhere in society.[17]

ECOLOGY AND ECONOMY

If the 1960s were the time North Americans "discovered" ecology, the seventies were the years when environmental concerns began to take on a new urgency. Having lived in an incredibly productive and fertile quarter of the globe, North Americans had assumed that this was a world without limits. The fact that there was a global interdependence linked to available resources of food, fuel, and other necessities of life seemed to be dawning upon them in a new way. The correlation between reckless wartime spending and developing shortages in many areas put a severe strain on the world's economic system. To avoid a run on the dollar by other countries, the United States decided to end the exchange of dollars for gold in 1971 and made an abortive attempt at domestic wage-price controls.[18]

The winter of 1971–72 was a terrible disaster for Eastern Europeans, with one-third of the critical Russian winter wheat crop destroyed. Belatedly, a deal was struck with the United States for massive purchases of grain. The result was that even the breadbaskets of the United States and Canada were strained and world prices soared.[19] It was the beginning of a grim lesson that would be reinforced time and again in the decade ahead. What happened in one part of the world inevitably influenced all other areas.

In 1972 the Club of Rome issued a report that dealt with the "limits of growth," a concept that was anathema to Americans, who had a view of the future that was based on unrestrained expansion.[20] Even though this particular report was seen by undeveloped nations as a threat to their own growth, the point had been made that the planet can support only a given level of human consumption. Misuse of resources and consequent pollution that threatened air, water, and earth suddenly became a concern for activist groups. The profligate way in which humanity had failed in its stewardship of the planet earth was beginning to come home, at least to those who gave a thought to the future.

THE RELIGIOUS SCENE

The years under discussion continued to be a strange mixture of secularizing trends and religious reaction. It was a time when much of the institutional vitality of the major denominations was waning, but Pentecostalism was on the rise, and a new movement among the young known as the "Jesus People" began to emerge. Even though it raised theological questions for many thoughtful Christians, the rock opera *Jesus Christ Superstar* was first a hugely successful record album and then a Broadway hit.[21] The older generation, of course, could not assume that these evidences of religious interest among the young presaged a resurgence in accepting traditional church structures and beliefs.

It became a time when the church was forced to reexamine its goals and indeed its own identity.[22] Among Lutherans there was considerable soul-searching about such questions as: "Within the spectrum of American Christianity, did Lutheranism have a viable future as a separate confessional church? In the face of the so-called great issues of the last third of the twentieth century, was there anything unique and, therefore, worthy of preservation about Lutheranism?"[23] Once raised, such questions could not be dismissed lightly and would be debated repeatedly by Lutherans for the next decade or more. President Marshall had recognized the problem early and devoted a large part of his first convention report in 1970 to a discussion of Lutheran confessional identity in light of the LCA's ecumenical commitment and "self-conscious involvement in a complex world."[24]

CHURCH AND SOCIETY

During the years from 1968 through 1972, the LCA continued its two-pronged approach to social issues. On the one hand, it engaged in the study process that resulted in social statements. On the other hand, it pursued an activist course in dealing with some of the most pressing problems in society.

Social Statements

Although the Board of Social Ministry was studying a variety of issues,[25] it produced four major statements that were endorsed by the church convention.

Sex, Marriage, and Family. When the Pittsburgh convention in 1964 adopted an interim statement on marriage and family, it was confidently expected that a fuller document would be ready in another biennium. As things turned out, the Commission on Marriage formed in 1966 labored for four more years before issuing a proposed social statement on "Sex, Marriage, and Family." The BSM commented in its report to the convention, "Perhaps no other study has posed such major problems for a commission."[26] Matters certainly became no easier at the convention where delegates debated long before approving the document with numerous amendments.

The statement was in many ways a departure from the church's earlier views. It affirmed sexuality as "a gift of God for the expression of love and the generation of life" but declared firmly that nothing in the statement was to be interpreted to mean that the church "either condones or approves premarital or extra-marital sexual intercourse."[27] Marriage itself was defined as "a covenant of fidelity— a dynamic, life-long commitment of one man and one woman in a personal and sexual union."

Some persons reacted with concern to such sentences as: "A marital union can be legally valid yet not be a covenant of fidelity, just as it can be a covenant of fidelity and not a legal contract." Such sentences, however, need be taken in context since the statement declared, "The existence of a true covenant of fidelity outside marriage as a legal contract is extremely hard to identify." Although asserting that marriage is a primary setting in which Christians "live out their calling from the Lord," it also made clear that marriage is not to be exalted over the choice to be single. The family is described as the basic community in which God intended personhood to be developed and as the base from which its members can move out into society.

The study acknowledged that there were issues where guidance was necessary for ethical decision making. For example, it discussed the question of homosexual behavior. It indicated that "scientific research has not been able to provide conclusive evidence regarding the causes of homosexuality. Nevertheless, homosexuality is viewed biblically as a departure from the heterosexual structure of God's creation." Acknowledging that homosexuals are frequently objects of prejudice and discrimination in law, it went on to say, "It is essential to see such persons as entitled to understanding and justice in church and community." The brief paragraph included obviously could not answer all of the church's questions about homosexuality, and the issue was destined to be studied and restudied in the years ahead.

The report also dealt with the matter of divorce. Although stressing the importance of the church's supporting persons in times of marital difficulty, the statement said that "there may be situations in which securing a divorce is more responsible than staying together."

The document stated unequivocally that "marriage between persons without reference to racial and ethnic differences and background is a witness to the oneness of humanity under the one God."

In the matter of birth control, it stated that use of medically approved contraceptive methods within a covenant of fidelity depends on the motivations of the users. Such decisions need to be made responsibly in the light of certain criteria.

Abortion was another complex problem dealt with in the document. The key issue, it said, was the status of the unborn fetus since it is the organic beginning of human life. "On the basis of the evangelical ethic, a woman or couple may decide responsibly to seek an abortion. Earnest consideration should be given to the life and total health of the mother, her responsibilities to others in her family, the stage of development of the fetus, the economic and psychological stability of the home, the laws of the land, and the consequences for society as a whole." The abortion question would continue, however, to be a recurring one for both church and society.

World Community. In preparation for this document, the BSM published four background papers—"Armament or Disarmament," "International Law and Institutions," "International Development," and "World Community: Challenge and Opportunity"—as part of the series *Justice, Peace, and Freedom.* The statement itself focused on ethical imperatives for an interdependent age. In the light of the threats of nuclear holocaust and environmental pollution, it warned that "people are beginning to sense that if they do not soon devise some means of living together they will surely perish together."[28] It declared that the concern for human survival and community "flows from the very heart of the Christian faith." Civil authority was viewed in the classic way "as a sign of God's loving activity of advancing human justice and well-being and of preserving humanity from its tendency to violence and self-destruction."

The statement saw the United Nations as the chief example of transnational structures of law and authority for settling disputes. It urged that the agencies for economic and social development be given increased support, particularly by the wealthy nations. It viewed the Universal Declaration of Human Rights as a hopeful sign of movement toward global civil order.

The concept of the international public domain was regarded as essential in light of depletion of natural resources and pollution. The nations needed to recognize that it was no longer possible to regard the use or abuse of their own resources as their exclusive concern. Protection by law of the oceans, polar regions, and outer space was an essential first step.

The threat of war required a rethinking of national security which "can no longer be defined in terms of either nuclear superiority or even nuclear stalemate." Unilateral initiatives by the United States were encouraged as a way of providing a climate for arms limitations. At the root of the threat of armed violence, the statement held, is injustice as well as the frustration and despair of oppressed peoples. The Christian community had a role to play in mobilizing support for massive assistance to developing nations. "Underlying all this is the fundamental premise that, as a corporate entity within a given nation, a church body has the God-given responsibility of generating support for national policies which contribute to the building of a world community."

Criminal Justice. The BSM study of the criminal justice system in the United States and Canada was carried out at a time when prison riots were frequently in the headlines.[29] It was also a time when the general public was frightened by the rapid increase in violent crimes, and law-abiding citizens were angrily demanding a restoration of law and order in society. At its 1972 convention in Dallas, the LCA adopted a social statement with the tongue-twisting title "In Pursuit of Justice and Dignity: Society, the Offender, and Systems of Correction."[30]

The statement openly questioned "warehousing" offenders as an effective way of dealing with criminal behavior. It pointed out that "jails and prisons have too often become schools of alienation and violence." Two popular notions with which the statement took issue were that incarceration of offenders necessarily made society safer and that "solitude and deprivation are in some sense 'redemptive.' " The young, poor, and minorities, it said, bore the brunt of society's ire toward the lawless.

From a theological perspective, distinctions between persons as "law-abiding" or "criminal" are relative, provisional, and subject to divine judgment. "The human condition of radical estrangement from God manifests itself in the constant tendency on the part of societies to absolutize these provisional distinctions." The statement pointed out that Jesus Christ was defined by the society of his own day as a political/religious criminal. Particularly troublesome is the tendency of social institutions whose task it is to socialize offenders to view themselves as "agents of 'redemption.' " The Lutheran social ethic has traditionally stressed that the roles of social/political institutions are maintaining civil peace and achieving justice.

The document listed eleven different policy goals which included such things as revising criminal codes by removing certain kinds of behavior from the category of crime; encouraging the participation of those serving sentences in the governing of their own affairs; treating the young and first offenders separately from the general offender population; and urging the replacement of local jails with competently staffed facilities suited to the communities they serve. The church was seen as having a variety of responsibilities, such as creating a community climate; establishing through its social agencies programs for offenders, ex-offenders, and their families; being willing to employ ex-offenders; helping the general public understand the special problems faced by personnel in correctional institutions; and working for the abolition of capital punishment.

The Human Crisis in Ecology. Although concern about the environment had become widespread in North America, the drafters of this proposal felt that the term *ecology* itself was sufficiently unfamiliar to most persons that they supplied a dictionary definition as a footnote. Affirming that "God so orders creation that everything in it is related to everything else," the statement saw the crisis in ecology as a violation of the very systems God creates.[31] Unrestrained growth, pollution bred by a "throwaway" life-style, depletion of natural resources, population pressures, and social injustice were all seen as inherent parts of the total problem.

"The underlying cause of the ecological crisis," the statement declared, "is not natural forces but human arrogance and rebellion against God, what the Christian faith calls sin." The church was viewed as having a crucial role to play in developing new value systems in a society where the "good life" is too often described in materialistic terms. The actions called for included reaffirmation of the biblical doctrine of creation; development of life-styles sensitive to the needs of both the human and nonhuman worlds; questioning the validity of the philosophy of material growth; challenging the assumption that technology can solve the crisis; concern about social costs of industrial and governmental actions; the church's own witness and encouragement of public action. What may have escaped many who endorsed the statement, however, was that implementing these concerns could not be done through simplistic actions. The very concept of ecological interrelatedness cautioned against facile solutions to incredibly complex problems.

Investment Criteria. The tip of another iceberg began to emerge at the 1972 convention. The BSM presented a document on *Social Criteria for Investments* with the intent that it would be studied during the next biennium.[32] It attempted to illustrate the divergence in views regarding the church's own investments in light of concerns about war, the environment, and racial injustice at home and abroad. A beginning was made in setting forth some criteria to guide investment policy as well as strategies that could be employed. It recognized selling a stock as one way of dealing with a moral issue, but the paper suggested that there were often more effective strategies, such as shareholder actions. Once the problem of investment and divestment had been raised, however, the issue would continue to be hotly debated throughout the life of the LCA.

Social Action

During these years the LCA was propelled more and more into aggressive and direct involvement with the social problems besetting society. It was not a direction welcomed by some church members. In his report to the 1970 convention, President Marshall sketched the historical background of the shift from immigrant days and the days during the depression, when congregations had engaged in philanthropic work either privately or through cooperative agencies, to the situation of the seventies where government supplemented a vast public welfare program with grants through private agencies in a pluralistic system.[33] Although the ways of providing service had changed through the years, he said, "These were changes in the form of activity, but in principle, the church was unchanged in its willingness to adapt to meet human need."[34] It was certainly not a time for either the quietism that had been typical of many Lutherans in the past or business as usual.

The Racial/Urban Crisis. The 1968 convention had been a watershed in many ways, but two actions had been decisive in determining the ways in which the LCA responded to the social crisis. One had been the decision, after prolonged debate, to authorize the ACT Appeal to provide funds to meet the urban crisis. This enabled churchwide agencies that had been hamstrung by austere budgets to deal with the problem in fresh ways. The second action, which had passed with minimal debate, was one authorizing the Priority Program for Justice and Social Change that was aimed at white racism. ACT became a source of funds for the Priority Program, but that was not its sole purpose.

Almost before ACT and the Priority Program could get under way, James Forman tried to make a media event out of delivering the Black Manifesto to the LCA headquarters in New York on May 6, 1969. Some reporters had expected that he would nail the Manifesto to the door of 231 Madison Avenue in the spirit of Luther and his Ninety-five Theses. It would have been difficult since the door was glass and wrought iron. Instead, Forman gave the paper to President Marshall who said it would be studied, and studied carefully it was.

The BSM convened a consultation of eleven Black and six white church members to give advice to the Coordinating Committee on Race Relations as to how the LCA should respond. Recommendations went to the Executive Council through BSM, which declared the political philosophy of the Black Manifesto to be "unacceptable" and declined to pursue discussion of the concept of "reparations." Instead, it endorsed the coordinating committee's recommendations that "the Lutheran Church in America, its synods, congregations and people, creatively use its economic power which will contribute to justice and social change."[35] This included reexamining budgets, examining investment policies and practices, and doing business with firms that followed fair employment practices.

Under the Priority Program, the BSM set out to combat white racism. Lee H. Wesley, a Black pastor serving on the staff of the Board of Parish Education, was called by BSM to direct the effort. A new process was devised for use in congregations where whites were confronted in graphic ways with their own racism as well as the way in which racism was ingrained in institutional forms.[36] By 1972 the BSM was able to report that more than a thousand congregations in twenty-six synods had participated.[37] A similar program was used with the Executive Council and churchwide agencies. Predictably, many persons reacted strongly to the program and the idea that they were racists, but the shock tactics did seem to result in soul-searching and change in attitudes. The program also brought to the fore hundreds of minority members of the LCA who provided leadership; and, as a by-product, the program stimulated congregations to begin many local programs ranging from day-care centers to police-community relationships.[38]

By the end of 1969, the ACT program had generated more than $2,879,000 in new money after expenses. The first $2,000,000 was allocated to urban crisis programs through the following units:

BAM	$1,000,000
BCECV	225,000
BPE	150,000
BSM	500,000
BTE	100,000
COE	25,000

Although the church had been plunged into ACT suddenly, certain criteria for projects were set: projects must be wanted by the people served; projects should strengthen congregations for mission among the underprivileged; grants should generate funds from other sources where possible; projects should stimulate self-help; projects should produce learnings that can be shared with others; where possible, projects should have an ecumenical dimension.[39]

Part of the strategy was to invite requests for grants through synodical committees that were supposed to prioritize them. Unfortunately, the volume of requests far outran available funds.[40] In addition, grants that were originally intended as "seed money" resulted in long-term expectations that had an impact on the whole LCA budget.[41] Excellent results were achieved in many instances, however, such as grants to congregations in changing communities, initiation of the Lay Associate Program, migrant ministries, day-care centers, college opportunity grants for minority students, interracial camping programs, urban leadership training, special curriculum materials for inner-city parishes, nonprofit housing, minority economic development, urban church seminary internships, and scholarships for Black seminary students.

Hopes were running high among many that the LCA was making a frontal attack on many problems, but the question was raised early about whether the work could continue. The Committee of Executives overseeing the program recommended in September 1969 that the appeal be continued through 1970. Instead, the Executive Council voted that the LCA set as its goal in 1970 the achievement of 110 percent of apportionment with the idea of providing funds for ACT-type projects. In addition, the ACT account was to be kept open for designated gifts.[42] The results were little short of disastrous. Benevolence showed only a 1.09 percent increase in 1970 and actually dropped by more than $128,000 in 1971.[43]

At the 1970 convention in Minneapolis, the LCA was challenged from another quarter in the racial crisis. Representatives of the American Indian Movement (AIM) addressed the convention and demanded that all further construction of churches be stopped until "all social injustices which have been committed against the Indians have been corrected."[44] The church responded at a later session by taking an action that supported formation of an office for Indian Ministry in the LCUSA and expressed the determination of the LCA to move toward meeting the challenges placed before the delegates by Indian Americans.[45] LCUSA did set up such a related agency, and Eugene Crawford, an Indian American, became the director.

Ethnic groups were also raising their voices as different segments of society began to press their claims. At the 1972 convention in Dallas, the National Lutheran Hispanic Caucus presented *A Hispanic Lutheran Declaration* which set forth in firm but not abrasive language the needs of "Hispano-Americans" for recognition of their cultural differences, equal opportunity and services, trained personnel, literature in the Spanish language, adequate church buildings,

Representatives of the American Indian Movement address the 1970 convention

Eugene Crawford

education to sensitize all peoples to the needs of Hispanics, and immediate establishment of the caucus to implement many of the concerns. The convention took an action welcoming the work of the caucus and referring the declaration to LCUSA for implementation. It also asked that an LCA staff member be assigned to follow and expedite matters in the meantime.[46] The statement was a signal that Hispanics were rapidly becoming one of the largest of the "minorities" in the United States.

The Role of Women. The year 1970 was a pivotal one for women in the LCA. Several attempts had been made by the church to complete a comprehensive study of the doctrine of ministry without much success. In 1968 the convention authorized the president to appoint a new commission of fifteen persons to prepare a new study and to include in its mandate a study of the role of women in the ministry. The report brought to the 1970 convention in Minneapolis created a stir for several reasons that will be examined later, but significant here was the proposal to enable the ordination of women.

The commission had buttressed its recommendation with a lengthy position paper on *The Role of Women in the Life of the Church.* Calling attention to the revolution occurring in society, the report declared, "It is already too late for the church to exercise its genius for the role of pioneer, but not too late for the church to provide creative responses to a volatile situation it inadvertently helped to create, does not fully comprehend, and is now trying rather frantically to investigate. . . . The point has now been reached where a responsible church has no choice but to participate in the movement toward a greater freedom of thought and action for women."[47] It rejected the stereotyped roles for women that the secular community had recognized no longer held true, but where the religious community, "including the women in it," seemed blind to the problem and lagged behind in many obvious ways.[48]

The position paper acknowledged the lively interest in the subject of the role of professional women in the church but said reliable information on the subject simply was not available. Although the first survey on the subject had been conducted by the Federal Council of Churches in 1921, it was still not possible by 1969 "for a dogged researcher to come up with a reliable estimate of even the professionally educated women who are engaged in the work of the church."[49]

Turning specifically to ordination, which it regarded as "the most controversial and most threatening of all problems," the study group said that the crux of the matter was justice. It stated that "traditionally the church has gone along with society in treating women as inferior human beings and stunting their ability to exploit their gifts to the fullest. To be barred from ordination perpetuates this tradition."[50] In examining the biblical and theological considerations, the study concurred in the report to the 1968 convention that "there were no hard and fast biblical or theological reasons for denying ordination to women."[51] It also discounted the argument that for the LCA to ordain women would create serious problems in ecumenical circles.

The position taken by the commission in its basic report was simply, "Both men and women are eligible for call and ordination."[52] The basic recommendation required only changing the governing bylaw of the church that specified that "a minister of this church shall be a man" to "a minister of this church shall be a person."[53] Despite a feeble attempt to defer action, it was obvious that the convention was in no mood for delay, and the amendment was approved by a "resounding voice vote."[54] The ease with which the change was made inevitably made some wonder why the church had dragged its feet so long. The Board of Publication, of course, was not inclined to delay. Ever ready to serve a potential market, it immediately put on display clergy vestments that had been prepared well in advance for women.

The fact that the convention voted so willingly for the ordination of women at the end should not obscure the careful groundwork that had been laid in many areas. The LCW had done its own in-depth study on the role of women in the church; and its board, after a retreat that involved considerable soul-searching, issued a formal statement on March 12, 1970, supporting the proposal brought to the LCA convention.[55] On the inter-Lutheran front, the Division of Theological Studies of LCUSA had made a two-year study of the subject that was reported to the presidents of the member churches in February 1970.[56] The World Council of Churches had also produced a study document a half dozen years earlier.[57]

One thing that surprised many people was that Lutheran women had been going through the process of obtaining Bachelor of Divinity degrees at seminaries decades before the doors of ordination were open to them. "Apparently Gettysburg Seminary granted B.D.'s to women in the early part of the twentieth century. One of them was the preceptress of Susquehanna University before 1918. . . . In 1960 there were 50 women in the LCA who had graduated from seminary but were not ordained."[58]

One of those who had been waiting in the wings was Elizabeth Platz. She was approved for ordination by the Maryland Synod on October 24 and was ordained November 22, 1970. As was true of many women candidates for the ministry, Beth Platz did not view her ordination as a social statement but as a fulfillment of her call to the ministry of Word and Sacrament. In an interview she said, "I'm not much of a women's lib type. I'm not being ordained to prove a point—that I'm as good as any man."[59] Within five years twenty-three more women had been ordained, and some seventy-five were in seminary preparing for the ministry.[60] The door long closed had indeed been opened.

MOVING IN MISSIONS

In retrospect, it is possible to raise questions about any course of action the church took in a given situation, but it is difficult to rekindle the sense of urgency that pressed upon those who were charged with seeking solutions to new and often intractable problems. Both of the major mission boards of the LCA during these years were in the midst of changing dramatically the focus of their work from what it had been at the time of merger. In large measure their decisions were responses to the turmoil swirling through society at home and abroad.

American Missions

The shifting of priorities by the Board of American Missions from establishing new congregations to other kinds of ministries that had begun in earnest in 1967 now reached major proportions. In describing the 1968–69 biennium, the BAM declared, "Dollars which previously went to mission developers now went to provide personnel for congregations in areas of change, chiefly ghettos, but also in fast-growing missions needing staff and program money to survive."[61] The decline in the number of congregations organized each year during the church's first decade bears mute testimony to this continuing trend. In the first biennium there had been 138 congregations organized. In the 1970–71 biennium there were thirty-three with only twelve of those formed in 1971.[62] Ironically, it appears that the availability of ACT monies may have accelerated the process in the long run.

Initially, the BAM had regarded those congregations it assisted as "mission congregations." In this period, the term was changed to "program grant congregations," which seemed to imply that BAM would be prepared to give help to any congregation having a demonstrable need for assistance in ministry and not just to those traditionally thought of as "missions."[63] A wide variety of ministries were underwritten. Ethnic work was underway among Indians in Montana, Arizona, and Ontario; among French-speaking people in Quebec City and Montreal; and among Finns in Los Angeles and Vancouver, British Columbia.[64] Leisure ministries, apartment ministries, work among the aging, inner city Christian day schools for the disadvantaged,[65] and special ministries in new towns all came within the scope of program grants. All told, 788 congregations received some financial support in 1968.

As funds became tighter, BAM outlined a detailed procedure for terminating support to congregations not considered viable and urged synods to put proceeds from disbanded congregations in the Restricted Loan Fund of the board for use within the synod.[66] Although the board continued to purchase anticipatory sites for future work, the sale of what were regarded as "excess" parsonages, land, and church buildings became an increasingly important source of money for the Church Property loan fund.[67]

In order to meet what it perceived as a special need for a new type of lay worker in inner city congregations, the BAM initiated the Lay Associate Program. Most of the new personnel were Black or Hispanic and came from the communities where they served. The first training session held at Philadelphia Seminary in 1969 was explosive at times, and the newly formed group sent a list of recommendations to the BAM, which transmitted them to the Executive Council. The proposals were concerned with such things as overcoming what was perceived as the separation between pulpit and pew, people and pastors, and church officials and congregations. Some proposals that were aimed at improving the education of pastors tended to value ecumenicity over traditional theological standards. The Executive Council affirmed the fact that the units of the church responsible for pertinent parts of the church's life were committed to the principles underlying most of the points made. While supporting the ecumenical intent, however, the Council indicated that pastors did need to have a thorough understanding of the church's confessions.[68]

In spite of some initial problems, the Lay Associate Program did add a sizable cadre of workers from minority groups. Many of them steadily upgraded their skills through education, and some chose to attend seminary and enter the ordained ministry. Much of the credit for the program's successes belongs to BAM's staff member for program personnel, Massie L. Kennard. A Black pastor, Kennard had been brought on staff specifically, although not exclusively, to work on the problem of recruiting and equipping persons for minority ministries.[69]

The BAM, of course, did not confine its efforts to intra-LCA activities. On the interchurch scene, it engaged in joint efforts with other Lutheran mission boards through the Division for Mission Services of LCUSA in an effort to avoid competition and carry on joint planning. DMS also became the avenue through which BAM participated in the Joint Strategy and Action Committee (JSAC), an instrument for cooperation among interdenominational mission boards.[70] Interestingly, involvement with JSAC tended to reduce BAM participation in the Division of Christian Life and Mission of the NCCCUSA.[71] BAM also took part in the Commission on Religion in Appalachia (CORA) to find ways of strengthening work in that economically depressed region. In addition, BAM continued grants to community organizations, often using the conduit of the Interreligious Foundation for Community Organization (IFCO). On the whole, its activities were wide-ranging, and at times its resources of personnel and funds were stretched thin. All in all, BAM had become quite a different animal in the years since merger, a change that was applauded in many parts of the LCA and sharply criticized in others.

World Missions

"Maybe the population bomb strikes home better if we realize that every morning when we awake and have breakfast, there are 230,000 more people to feed, and 230,000 more souls about whom we need to show concern than there were at breakfast time the morning before."[72] With these words, Arvin W. Hahn, a member of the Board of World Missions, sought to drive home to the 1970 LCA convention that the exploding world population confronted the church with a "possibly impossible mission" in the remainder of the twentieth century. Dramatic as that statement was, it simply underscored the fact that BWM was wrestling with a whole range of problems that would keep altering the equation in world mission.

One indication of the new flexibility in BWM's approach to rapid changes overseas was the decision to amend the LCA Bylaws by striking the list of fourteen designated mission fields and making it possible for either the convention or the Executive Council to approve termination of major programs or authorize work in new geographical areas.[73] It was one more step in recognizing that BWM was involved in a new ball game that required prompt action to engage in mission in a fluid international scene. At times the involvements were long-range; at others, consciously of short duration.

An example of the kind of opportunity for new work that arose came when the Lutheran World Federation expressed the judgment that the "emergency" role that it had played in Indonesia for twenty years should be brought to a close and mission efforts in the area should be carried on by member churches. In response, the BWM offered to be of assistance to those churches in Indonesia that were being helped by the LWF. By 1970 agreements had been forged for BWM to work with the Batak churches, initially in Northern Sumatra.[74] The involvement in this work came at a strategic time to assist a younger church through a period of phenomenal growth.[75] The LCA soon had a dozen missionaries at work there, something that was made possible by the freeing of funds and personnel that had been needed previously for churches now moving toward self-support.

One of the designated fields that had moved rapidly to assume responsibility for its own affairs was the Japan Evangelical Lutheran Church. By October 1971 a master plan had been developed that described in great detail the steps to be taken toward self-support and self-government. "As a child under his parents' care must some day stand on his own feet, we, the JELC, take the 1970's as a time of growth and metamorphosis," the report said. "We know it is not an easy task and we do not deny that in spite of some past history we are still a church in a pioneering state."[76] The goal of self-support by the end of 1974 was undertaken without lessening the JELC's emphasis on "pioneer evangelism." An indication of how seriously the people took this step was a decision of five members in one congregation to mortgage their own homes to provide funds to buy land for a day nursery the church wanted to build.[77]

Other changes were occurring in the way the BWM carried on its work. The number of missionaries sent from North America continued to decline from 520 at the beginning of 1968 to 378 at the start of 1972.[78] The number of missionary pastors during this period peaked at 106 in 1968 and dropped to 89 by the beginning of 1972. The largest decrease, however, was in teachers, who numbered 102 at the start of 1968 and only 43 four years later. At the same time, experiments were being tried with short-term personnel, including young people who served in a manner analogous to the Peace Corps.[79]

Another change related to personnel was the decision to close the School of Missions at the Lutheran School of Theology at Chicago in 1969 and to replace it with a joint Lutheran Missionary Orientation Program with ALC and LCMS. The training sessions of the new program were held in the summer and were followed by continuing orientation on the field.[80] Plans were also explored by the ALC, LCA, and LCMS boards to establish a World Church Institute, "a center for missiological research which would undertake to stimulate and carry on a 'massive attack on the problems which face the church in its missionary obedience,' and to anticipate the 'probable need for radical change in the thought patterns of the whole missionary movement.' "[81] This grand vision, however, was never realized.

A budding new concept called "Mission on Six Continents" emerged in 1972 that further underscored the fact that North American churches needed to see themselves as part of a global mission enterprise and that they had much to learn from churches in other parts of the world. The question of exploring such an approach was raised with the LCA Executive Council by Paul Empie, general secretary of the USA National Committee of LWF. The responsibility of investigating the possibilities was given to the executives of BSM, BAM, and BWM.[82] In time a program would develop that brought representatives from churches abroad to challenge the thinking of LCA leaders in sessions that broke down many long-cherished beliefs about North America's role in the whole mission enterprise.

As the planning process with indigenous churches went on, the BWM developed program budgeting to the point where 332 activities were clustered around 66 different types of projects in various parts of the world. These were grouped in seven types of ministries, and significant trends were identified in each of them:

First, in parish ministry the trend was toward developing leadership according to indigenous cultural patterns. This often meant identifying recognized spiritual leaders among the laity who were trained to preach and administer the sacraments under the supervision of trained pastors.[83]

Second, the trend in health ministry was away from the direct curing of diseases to an emphasis on community health programs and preventive medicine.

Third, as more and more nations assumed responsibility for primary and secondary education, the church's role shifted to what has been thought of as "parish education" or "educational ministry" in the United States and Canada.

Fourth, extensive use of mass media grew in the former mission churches, and, as was the case in Taiwan, this meant cooperating with ALC and LCMS in television and radio outreach.

Fifth, as many Third World countries proceeded with "nation-building," the churches engaged more in community organization and were often sent back to the drawing boards for program development.

Sixth, it became apparent in many of the societies that there were "thrown-away people," the unwanted and unloved who were in desperate need of ministry. These included the blind, deaf, handicapped, and the political refugees who seemed to surface everywhere.

Seventh, the BWM was patiently working with indigenous churches in helping them to assume responsibility for their own central administration by tailoring it to the real needs of the area rather than duplicating the systems in North American churches.

Getting the members of the LCA to understand why these changes were occurring required a major interpretation effort. Seminars were conducted on the territory of younger churches for key people, such as synodical presidents. "Missionaries-in-residence" programs were set up to enable personnel on furlough to help the people in a synod to obtain an in-depth understanding of what mission in the seventies really meant. A barrage of study materials and articles on every facet of what was happening was launched at home. In spite of all this, many persons in the pew clung to the ideas with which they had grown up and with which they felt comfortable.

CONGREGATIONS ON THE THRESHOLD
OF THE SEVENTIES

In many ways it seemed that as the church entered the 1970s congregations were reaching the nadir of the negativism that had been characteristic of the previous decade. One study showed that among LCA pastors and laity alike the overwhelming concern was poor morale and diminishing membership.[84] Of nine major categories studied, the report showed that the problems of the congregation itself were uppermost in their hierarchy of concerns.[85]

At the same time, there were other general factors in the picture that were having a profound influence on parish life. One was the LCA's growing interest in working cooperatively with its other major Lutheran partners in congregational programming and policy making whenever possible. Another was the trend towards seeing parish life as a whole rather than as split up among discrete functions. Two broad-scale examples of these tendencies were a study of confirmation and an experiment in parish life development. Of course, there were many more changes in practice afoot, but cooperation and a holistic view of parish life were interwoven in one way or another in almost all of them.

Confirmation and First Communion

When the LCA constituting convention issued an invitation to the ALC and LCMS to join in a study of confirmation and first Communion, it took a while until the other churches could act, but both accepted. On September 22, 1964, President Fry convened the first meeting of the fifteen-member Commission on the Theology and Practice of Confirmation in Chicago.[86] The topic with which the commission was dealing had been a recurrent theological issue since Reformation times, but it had become the subject of renewed study in many parts of the world during the previous two decades.[87]

The question of what confirmation was and how it related to the sacraments and the church's life was obviously not just a matter of academic curiosity. In almost every instance, confirmation practices tended to reflect in some way the culture within which the church existed. Since World War II and the establishment of a Communist government in East Germany, for example, confirmation had become a political issue with serious implications for both confirmand and family. The government had set up its own youth dedication ceremony that was in direct competition with confirmation, and this became a time for a clear-cut decision between primary loyalty to church or state. In some African countries, Lutherans saw confirmation as an alternative to the rites of passage practiced by pagan religions.

Perhaps the study that attracted the most attention was by the LWF Commission on Education, which investigated the question between 1957 and 1963 and held a world seminar on the theme at Loccum, Germany, in 1961.[88] The study had opened up quite deliberately the possibility of first Communion prior to confirmation but did not take a definitive stance, partly in recognition of the different societal settings in which Lutheran churches operated. Although informed by the LWF's work, the member churches continued to proceed at their own pace in deciding upon their own practices. It was not until much later, for example, that some of the Scandinavian and German churches took the step of admitting children to Holy Communion prior to confirmation. Usually this was done during the early school years.[89]

In North America, the Joint Commission on the Theology and Practice of Confirmation effort followed the usual bent of studying the subject from a dozen angles, and a clutch of erudite background papers were prepared by experts in different fields.[90] After two years of work, however, the commission decided on a novel approach. Instead of inflicting its own views about confirmation on the constituency without consultation, the commission felt it would be helpful to know what North American Lutherans actually thought about the subject before presuming to tell them what they should think. The result was an extensive survey in the member churches on *Current Concepts and Practices of Confirmation in Lutheran Churches.*[91] The survey showed that both pastors and lay persons held one or a combination of six views about confirmation:

1. A renewing of one's baptismal covenant
2. A personal confession of faith confessed by one's sponsors at Baptism
3. A public affirmation of one's faith
4. The making of a lifelong commitment to Christ
5. A taking of increased responsibilities as a member of the church
6. A necessary prerequisite for receiving Holy Communion

Other results showed that the average time for the confirmation rite was Grade 8.4. Most respondents were willing to consider first Communion at an earlier age but still believed the confirmation rite should come first. This did not jibe, however, with the view that confirmation should come later than Grade 8. There seemed to be some confusion in all this as to whether confirmation was the rite or the catechetical process that usually led up to the rite and admission to the Sacrament.

What the survey showed most clearly was that there was a hodgepodge of concepts and practices, many of which were held with a tenacity born of a particular tradition. Although the commission completed its initial report by the end of 1967, it decided that before putting the proposals in final form, there should be a churchwide study program to help church members deal with some of the same issues with which the commission itself had been wrestling. The job of conducting the study program was assigned to the Boards of Parish Education of the three churches, and Frank W. Klos, the commission's recorder, was chosen as writer of the study book.[92] The commission was amazed at the intense interest in the process. More than 192,000 copies of the book were sold, and reports were sent in by study groups involving 86,000 persons in over 24 percent of the congregations of the three churches.[93] The commission also received more than 250 letters and some lengthy position papers sent in by interested persons and groups.

A further surprise was that the persons who had taken part now strongly favored the commission's recommendations on such points as confirmation's role in the young person's identification with the adult Christian community; and the need for a program of instruction, a testimony of faith in Christ, and a public rite. The preferred time for a confirmation rite was Grade 10. A bit over half of the responses favored admission to the Lord's Supper before confirmation, which was up sharply from the 12.8 percent of laity and 38.1 per cent of pastors who took that position in 1966. The preferred time for first Communion was Grade 5, and the people urged by an 83.3 percent majority that the ages for both first Communion and confirmation be uniform among the churches. All of this evidence was dismissed by critics of the process as "so much bureaucratic brainwashing of the people."

The report that the commission presented to the three church body presidents in March 1970 took seriously the reactions to its first draft but did not change the basic thrust of disassociating any confirmation rite from admission to first Communion. After describing the process used in developing the report, the commission sketched the historical background of confirmation and described the theological issues involved. It then proposed this definition, "Confirmation is a pastoral and educational ministry of the church which helps the baptized child through Word and Sacrament to identify more deeply with the Christian community and participate more fully in its mission."[94] The definition was based on several important points:

First, Holy Baptism is the means of grace by which God lays claim on the sinner. It is wholly God's doing and is in no way contingent upon any human promise or act. In Baptism God gives himself fully to the baptized person without reservation. To imply that confirmation somehow "completes" or "supplements" Baptism is theologically indefensible.[95]

Second, while Baptism is the initiating sacrament, Holy Communion is the sustaining sacrament. "Both give forgiveness of sins, life, and salvation. . . . The distinction is one of emphasis. The relationship is not exclusive or supplementary but collateral."[96]

Third, membership in the church is bestowed through Baptism and not through some later experience such as confirmation.[97] When a person is not baptized as an infant, pastoral judgment determines how much prior instruction is desirable. In the case of youth and adults, Baptism is still the sacrament whereby one enters the new relationship with God and his church. Confirmation in addition to Baptism is not necessary or appropriate.

Fourth, the church provides learning experiences before children first receive the Lord's Supper in order that participation may be meaningful. "To receive Holy Communion without understanding would be to perform a meaningless act . . . to each Communion there applies the apostle Paul's insistence on self-examination."[98]

Fifth, confirmation is essentially a *process* of pastoral and educational ministry. Its purpose is to enable the baptized child to identify more fully with the Christian community and its mission. Catechetical instruction is an important phase in this process. "Participation in Holy Communion is thought of here as a part of confirmation ministry, a means of strengthening, rather than a goal toward which the entire confirmation process points."[99] Confirmation, therefore, is not a single event, although completion of the process may be celebrated by a rite. In this case, the language of the rite should be meaningful to the age level.[100]

Sixth, the usual time for admission to first Communion would come at about Grade 5, and completion of the confirmation process about Grade 10. Even so, completion of confirmation is not an end to educational ministry but part of a lifelong catechumenate.[101]

When the commission's report and recommendations were brought to the 1970 LCA convention, there was some opposition.[102] One source was the Commission on Youth Ministry, which wanted the recommendations of the report rejected and confirmation essentially eliminated as a church practice. Another effort was to allow Communion to be given to any baptized person "regardless of age," which would have opened the way to communing infants. The convention did not accept this proposal but authorized a study of the issue for report to the 1972 convention.[103] The LCA had found itself an issue to which it could return again and again for another decade.

When the dust had cleared, the confirmation commission's recommendation was accepted that the report be adopted by the LCA "as a guide for its confirmation ministry to children and youth." At its convention a few months later, the ALC also approved the report with the addition that a rite for confirmation be considered "normative."[104] The ALC and LCA BPEs set to work on common materials for preparation for first Communion and the final year of catechetical instruction. The ILCW assumed responsibility for preparing a confirmation rite. When the LCMS held its convention in 1971, the Synod was divided about the commission's report and simply recommended that congregations study their confirmation and Communion practices.[105]

Parish Life and Ministry Development

As the seventies unfolded, there seemed to be a growing understanding that every aspect of a congregation's life interacted not only with every other aspect of the parish itself but also with its community and the church-at-large. *The Manifesto for the Congregation* had proved a challenge, but the church had not changed as hoped. "To many students of the situation, it became evident that merely producing documents does not change organizations."[106] It seemed apparent that the church could learn from research that had been going on in organizational change and leadership development. Early in 1969 the newly formed Standing Committee on Parish Life of the LCA Cabinet initiated an experiment in what was first known as Parish Life Development to see whether such insights could be adapted for the church's use.[107] The pilot, which took place in twenty-four congregations in Central Pennsylvania and Maryland, was encouraging, and it was decided to go churchwide with PLD on a gradual basis.

Conceived as a team effort involving both churchwide and synodical staff, the PLD project was more intensive than anything the church had tried to that point. It was built around two kinds of events. One type was pastor-lay institutes where teams of at least three persons from a congregation met for twenty hours of training in analysis of a congregation's needs, statement of mission, development of strategies for change, identification of resources, and implementation of plans. The second was a series of church council workshops on decision making, problem solving, goal setting, communication, and constructive use of conflict. Although early reports of parish renewal were encouraging, one basic concern about PLD was whether the high level of time investment by staff and congregational leaders would be a barrier to widespread use of the technique.

Meanwhile, a second development occurred that led to a redesigning of PLD. The Boards of Parish Education of ALC and LCA, together with the other agencies in the two churches involved with congregational life, had joined forces in developing a strategy for educational ministry. The two BPEs had begun in the traditional way of developing general and age-level objectives for Christian education, but it soon became apparent that the many other agencies also were preparing educational programs for the parish.[108] The "educational ministry" concept was an effort to coordinate these efforts to avoid duplication and make things simpler at the parish level, a need about which congregations were becoming increasingly vocal.

As work on EM progressed, it became apparent that many of the same factors were present that were crucial in PLD. Congregations were becoming more and more aware of their own unique situations and needs for ministry so that there was a tendency to reject uniformity in prepackaged programs from the church-at-large. In 1971 a breakthrough was achieved in developing an imaginative way to help congregations customize programs in the various functional areas of their ministry to fit their own unique characteristics.[109] The plan depended on helping congregations use resource banks that included media, a network of trained volunteers, information on training events, and innovative program ideas. It was also possible to have the churchwide agency provide a tailor-made design for a parish based on the congregation's own program priorities, an idea that was probably too avant-garde at a time when people were unfamiliar with and quite suspicious of computers.

As the developments in PLD and Educational Ministry converged, it was recognized that the same strategy might work for both. The ALC and LCA congregational life agencies agreed to test this hypothesis through a two-year pilot program in 175 parishes in seventeen centers spread across the United States and Canada.[110] In order to avoid confusion with the earlier PLD effort, the new program was called Parish Life and Ministry Development (PLMD). The experiment had the strong backing of both LCA President Marshall and ALC President Knutson, who had called the executives together in New York late in 1971 to explore the possibilities.[111] The decision to proceed cooperatively was made following a communication from Knutson to Marshall conveying a request from the ALC Coordinating Committee on Congregational Life to appoint a group to develop the joint strategy.[112]

Two things intervened, however, that changed the picture. One was the untimely death of President Kent Knutson; the other was a restructuring in ALC that brought into being a new board and division with responsibility for all aspects of congregational life. Although the reactions from the PLMD pilot test were quite positive, the newly formed Division for Life and Mission in the Congregation of the ALC decided not to continue with the program. The LCA did continue, however, and PLMD became an umbrella strategy of the LCA's Division for Parish Services for interrelating the different functions of the congregation.

The Changing Styles of Worship

As the church moved from the sixties into the seventies, its ways of worship were not exempt from the influences of the times. "Events throughout Christendom, notably the liturgical reforms arising out of Vatican II, conspired to create an uneasiness, if not a dissatisfaction, with much of the liturgical forms and hymnody then in use," wrote Edgar S. Brown, Jr., director of the LCA Commission on Worship. "Language was considered to be archaic, music often ill-suited to contemporary taste, and ceremonies more redolent of medieval days than the complicated society of the 1960's."[113]

It was in this climate for change that the Inter-Lutheran Commission on Worship set about its work on a new worship book for North American Lutherans.[114] But the way would not be easy. When the LCA's own Commission on Worship reported to the 1972 convention, it said, "Though there are signs that a new consensus is beginning to emerge, attitudes toward worship have been polarized: at one extreme are those who want to discard or at least remodel traditional forms; at the other are those who resist all change."[115]

In order to test the waters, therefore, the ILCW chose to prepare a series of paperbound booklets called *Contemporary Worship* that were consciously intended to be temporary and experimental.[116]

The first was a collection of twenty-one hymns followed by a new eucharistic rite with four settings, one of which was a folk music setting complete with guitar chords to acknowledge the emphasis on informality and intimacy then current in some parts of the church. There was also a marriage service, and a set of Services of the Word.[117] The feedback from these publications provided the ILCW with valuable information as it shaped the new hymnal and worship book.

Meanwhile, other work of ecumenical significance was proceeding. A three-year lectionary was being developed by ILCW with a target date of January 1973 for completion of the manuscript and introduction in 1974. The plan called for changing the liturgical calendar to extend the Epiphany season until Ash Wednesday, thereby eliminating those names for Sundays that people referred to as "the 'gesimas," and renumbering the Sundays in the nonfestival half of the year to "after Pentecost" instead of "after (the festival of) Trinity."[118]

The lectionary itself was developed with two principles in mind. One was the use of a thematic principle during the festival seasons. The Gospel was the principal reading, with other readings related to it. The second principle was that during the nonfestival part of the church year there generally would be a semicontinuous reading from the Gospel with an Old Testament lesson selected to relate to it. The Epistle lessons on these Sundays would also be semicontinuous but with no necessary relation to the Gospel for the day.[119] Essentially the same lectionary is used by the Episcopal Church, the Presbyterian churches, the Roman Catholic Church, and other Lutheran churches.

Another major area of ecumenical effort was in the careful scholarly work that went into preparing common English texts for certain liturgical materials, such as the Lord's Prayer and historic Creeds, that are used throughout Christendom.[120] The North American work group was known as the Consultation on Common Texts, and on the world scene the committee became the International Consultation on English Texts. The texts were first published in 1970 as *Prayers We Have in Common.*[121] The ICET texts, as they were called, are now used in Roman Catholic liturgies, the *Book of Common Prayer* of the Episcopal Church, and the *Lutheran Book of Worship.*[122]

An indication of the cooperative spirit in Lutheran worship circles during this period was the decision in 1971 to hold a continent-wide conference on worship sponsored by the ALC, LCA, LCMS, and the Lutheran Society for Worship, Music and the Arts.[123] It was hoped that the event planned for June 1973 in Minneapolis might draw 1,200 to 1,500 participants. Actually, this projection underestimated the growing interest in worship among Lutherans, for approximately two thousand attended the conference.[124] It was a clue to the resurgence of interest that would be true of the decade to come.

Educational Ministry

The planning and experimentation that went on in an effort to develop a joint ALC/LCA program in educational ministry formed the dominant element in the picture during these years. It produced substantive work in articulating a philosophy of Christian education that was geared both to new developments in the field and also to the changing character of the times.[125] It also resulted in producing a wide range of educational materials, joint efforts in basic research,[126] and cooperative fieldwork. The two Boards of Parish Education even went to the point of beginning to phase their personnel into a joint staff for field and editorial work with administrative centers in Minneapolis and Philadelphia.[127] At that time many of the educational leaders were confident that a merger of ALC and LCA was just a matter of time, a hope that would require another fifteen years to become reality.

Cooperation in some programs involved not only ALC but also LCMS. Proposals were developed in a group with the tongue-twisting name Coordinating Committee on Cooperative Parish Education Projects, which was given the acronym "Triple-C Pep."[128] Some of the projects undertaken included *Welcome to the Lord's Table,* a course to prepare children for first Communion; *Community, Communication, Communion,* a program for the final year of confirmation instruction; *Rejoice with Us,* an adult membership course; *Men of Color, Men of Faith,* a study of racial issues; and a series of regional conferences for congregational directors of Christian education. The BPE also took part in the work of the Division of Christian Education NCCCUSA, where one important project was the production of a curriculum for the trainable mentally retarded.

Basic changes were occurring, however, in the way parish education was carried on in the church. The drop in birthrate had brought a 12 percent reduction in the number of preschoolers by 1971, and the smaller numbers of children were beginning to affect the elementary school years.[129] After increasing slightly to 1,018,815 in 1969, Sunday school enrollment dropped by almost 150,000 by 1972.[130] The shift was due not only to demographics but also to a wider range of options for Christian education offered to adults and youth that siphoned off some of the participation from the traditional Sunday morning class. One study showed that 60 percent of the congregations reported an increase in participation by adults in some form of parish education between the years 1968–70.[131]

The reduction in funds and professional personnel for parish education, however, was a serious problem. The BPE reported that in the five years between 1966 and 1971, the financial resources available to the board had decreased by 25 percent. In addition, the combined synodical and churchwide staff responsible for parish education work had dwindled from sixty-seven to thirty-eight.[132] It was clear that LCA priorities had shifted away from congregational nurture to other areas of concern. One unanticipated effect of these changes was the impact it would have in time on the Board of Publication. During the eight years from 1963 to 1971, sales of parish education materials had amounted to $27,659,544—a figure that in today's terms would probably be in excess of sixty million dollars.[133] In the future the overall sale of educational materials would begin to decline.

Call for Evangelism

The downward drift in baptized membership that began in the late sixties continued so that in the period from 1968 through 1972 the loss in the LCA was almost 124,000. Confirmed membership inched slowly upward after a low point in 1972; and communing membership, no doubt spurred by the admission of children, began moving higher by 1973.[134] The nagging concern about membership decline persisted. In April 1970 the Executive Council approved a Commission on Evangelism proposal to designate 1973 as a "Year for Evangelism," and the convention followed suit.[135]

As planning for the evangelism year proceeded, the LCA effort was linked with "Key '73," a cooperative thrust by some 130 denominations and para-ecclesiastical groups.[136] It soon became evident that conservative evangelicals were having a strong influence on Key '73. Many within the LCA worried that "person-to-person" evangelism would become synonymous with proselytizing, and Jewish groups became apprehensive that Key '73 was aimed at their conversion. At the same time, the social ministry forces in the LCA became concerned that the highly personalistic approach to witnessing would divert the church's attention from the pressing social issues of the seventies.[137] Special materials were provided to congregations to implement the strategy, but the whole Key '73 program had been attacked so widely in the media that it met with only "restrained enthusiasm" in the LCA.

New Roles for Youth

The large numbers of youth in the population were having an impact not only on society in general but also the church. With no youth auxiliary to absorb their energies, they focused their attention on the mainstream of LCA life. In 1970 the first Youth Convo was held in connection with the Minneapolis convention, and adults were suddenly confronted with young people as a political force. Some two hundred youth from all parts of the United States and Canada descended on Minneapolis not only to learn how a convention worked but also to find ways of influencing decisions.

Delegates were buttonholed by young people pressing for certain actions. Women delegates were invited to a special luncheon and urged to join forces with youth to make sure synods elected more delegates from both groups to the next convention in Dallas.[138] Convo representatives made well-prepared presentations at forums and hearings. They were given permission to distribute a statement to delegates describing the youths' position on the confirmation study. "Early in the convention it became obvious that their influence was inaugurating as well as supporting action. For instance, a recommendation was originated by a New York youth delegate urging the development of educational programs . . . dealing with people involved in various life-styles, such as communes, the drug culture and others."[139]

Youth involvement expanded at the 1972 convention. This time 256 young people came to Dallas two days early and spent ten full days making themselves heard. A coffeehouse called the "Common Cup" was set up outside the convention floor as a place to talk with delegates. Lists were distributed to delegates of nominees for the Executive Council and management committees who would be "acceptable to youth," the first time that this kind of electioneering had occurred at a convention. It did set a pattern, however, that would be used by other special interest groups in the future.

In order to provide expanding opportunities for young people in the LCA, the Commission on Youth Ministry had launched or continued a wide variety of programs. These included work camps, synodical youth leadership events, training and deployment of 127 youth consultation teams, a Professional Youth Workers Conference, the Youth Ministry Subscription Service that provided latest resources to congregational leaders, information on youth movements ranging from free-lance Lutheran groups to Jesus People, draft counseling for minority youth, support of Black Youth Unlimited, teaching by youth staff at seminaries and adult leadership events.[140] One innovative program that would continue through the life of the LCA was the Youth Staffer Program. Beginning in 1971, young people were trained to give a year of volunteer service as Youth Staffers in synods and later with churchwide agencies.[141]

One major disappointment came for the Commission on Youth Ministry in 1969. A YOUTHEXPO was planned to attract young people to a churchwide gathering at Cobo Hall in Detroit. As urban unrest swept the area, however, hundreds of registrations were canceled, and the CYM reluctantly called off the event.[142] It proved to be the last attempt at an LCA youth gathering until 1981. As an alternative, however, the CYM joined with its counterparts in the ALC and LCMS to sponsor an All Lutheran Youth Conference in August 1973, when more than twenty thousand youth and adults flocked to the Astrodome in Houston for repentance, reflection, celebration, proclamation, witness, and service.[143] The success led to projecting another event for 1976 in New Orleans.[144]

AN ACTIVE ROLE FOR
LUTHERAN CHURCH WOMEN

As the LCW moved into the seventies, the auxiliary assumed a forward-looking and sometimes aggressive stance. The LCW often became an initiator on social issues. For example, as early as 1970, the organization made an offer to the Executive Council to help underwrite expenses for a consultation on investment criteria.[145] In June of 1972, Board of Social Ministry Executive Carl Thomas stated, "Thanks largely to the initiation by the LCW of the consultation on investments, we are happy to finally report that the BSM has approved a set of Social Criteria for Investments."[146]

Long before the LCA began its World Hunger Appeal in 1974,

Alice Marshall, wife of the LCA president, contributes to the Fast Fund for World Hunger sponsored by the Youth Convo at the Minneapolis convention

Vietnam War protest at the 1972 Youth Convo, LCA Convention

LCW representatives responded to a call from the National Council of Negro Women Incorporated to join with more than eighty-five other national organizations in a program to combat hunger. Local LCW members were mobilized in twenty workshops throughout the church and forwarded recommendations to the 1969 White House Conference on Food, Nutrition, and Health.[147] On the civil rights front, the LCW Board of Directors adopted a policy that ruled out holding its meetings or conventions in facilities that did not practice equal employment opportunity in all categories.[148]

LCW study materials in these years reflected concern about social issues such as North American Indian concerns, the generation gap, drugs, church-state conflicts, and human rights.[149] The auxiliary was also becoming more outspoken on the question of women's rights. The editor of *Lutheran Women,* LaVonne Althouse, wrote an editorial "On Liberation" in 1970 that declared, "Christian women can come to see the movement for woman's full liberation—full acceptance of the right to develop her gifts and her humanity as God created her—in the light of the gospel. When they do, they can begin to see why it is necessary to affirm their own liberation in order to enable men—all men—to secure *their* liberation."[150] A year later the magazine ran a series of three major articles on feminism, including one by Shirley Chisholm, Black United States representative to Congress, entitled *Women Must Rebel.*[151]

The auxiliary was experiencing setbacks in two areas, however. First, as more and more women entered the work force, fewer young women were becoming involved in LCW; and for the first time, membership declined in 1968, a trend that resulted in a decrease of 27 percent by 1977.[152] Second, there was a serious decline in offerings, which by 1971 fell 21 percent from a postmerger high in 1964.[153] Part of the problem seemed to be that the "One Gift" idea adopted at merger never really stirred the imagination of women the way the daily Thankoffering had in the past. When the Thankoffering and special gifts were reinstituted, funding stabilized, but many women missed the fact that there was no clear connection to devotional life. "As a daily act of prayer and giving Thankoffering before 1962 was a disciplined, almost ritualistic process—a regular offering of one's worldly goods."[154] It would take a while for the idea to be accepted that time spent on social concerns and other endeavors was as important in the church's mission as financial contributions.

FACING NEW REALITIES IN
HIGHER EDUCATION

As the church rethought its concepts of ordained ministry and the ministry of the whole people of God, it faced some stubborn realities. Strategies that seemed theoretically sound and defensible always had to contend with entrenched loyalties, institutional lethargy, and the ever-present specter of rising cost. As a result, each biennium brought reassessment of decisions that had once seemed securely in place.

The "Master Plan" Revisited

When the LCA approved the Board of Theological Education's Master Plan for seminaries in 1964, it was intended that there be a review of progress toward the goals in 1970. By 1967, however, the BTE itself was beginning to question how realistic some of those earlier decisions had been in view of the "swift currents of massive problems," such as financing of moves.[155] When its review of the Master Plan was presented to the 1970 convention, therefore, the BTE expressed concern that certain seminary consolidations had not taken place but also showed flexibility about what could now be envisioned.[156]

The situation involving Gettysburg and Philadelphia Seminaries has become almost a classic example of how difficult it is for the church convention to act on a particular proposal and then assume that everything will fall simply into place.[157] While the whole story cannot be recounted here, it was obvious that factors other than institutional loyalties were crucial to a viable solution. People were stunned to discover how much it would cost to relocate the two seminaries in a university setting at Philadelphia. Originally, it had been estimated this could be done for $7,000,000; but by 1970 that figure had ballooned to $25,000,000, which would have precluded adequate funding for programs.[158] The two schools had experimented with a joint administration for six years, but that did not seem to be a final answer. A new concept was developed of locating Lutheran "houses of studies" near urban universities instead of attempting complete relocation. The price was attractive, and Gettysburg undertook such an experiment in Washington. Meanwhile, some were rethinking whether Gettysburg's location in itself might have certain values for the church. "In an age of excessive urbanization," BTE reported, "the advantage of Gettysburg must be utilized."[159]

Not all of the issues, of course, were confined to possible mergers. Some seminaries were striving to update their curriculum offerings to become more relevant to the current scene. Perhaps the best example of far-reaching experimentation was at Hamma Divinity School, where church historian Frederick K. Wentz agreed to accept the presidency knowing there were already those who wanted either to close the school or have it merge with another. As William Kinnison pointed out, "A seminary scheduled for consolidation or closure was ideally suited for experimentation. Its survival was no longer the issue. . . . The need for new directions in theological education, on the other hand, was so urgent and necessary that such a role for Hamma would be a great contribution to the national church."[160] Wentz had a perspective on the place of laity and clergy as part of the whole people of God that sought to respect the ministry of both. He sought to have students equipped in interpersonal relations, group dynamics, sociology, and social ethics, as well as the traditional theological disciplines.[161] Unfortunately, as opposition mounted, both time and the shortage of funds conspired to frustrate the experiment. Eventually, after Wentz accepted a position of leadership in a theological consortium in Chicago, Hamma merged with the ALC seminary in Ohio to form Trinity Lutheran Seminary.

An additional new element in the picture was the authorization by the American Association of Theological Schools of a new type of graduate program leading to a Doctor of Ministry degree. As the whole matter was studied and restudied, a report was made to the 1972 convention proposing establishing a Council for Theological Education in the Northeast involving both Gettysburg and Philadelphia as well as the supporting synods. The purpose was to coordinate planning for a range of concerns, including developing the D.Min. program and working cooperatively with other Lutheran bodies in theological education.[162] The decision was to move in this way for the foreseeable future, but no one seriously believed that questions would never arise again about Lutheran theological education in the region.

Other important developments were taking place, of course, that went beyond location of seminaries. In 1971 the theological boards of ALC and LCA met together and agreed to work jointly in a variety of areas, such as supervised internship, educational standards, continuing education, career guidance, and assistance to pastors in continuing education. A mutual concern was the number of Lutheran students attending non-Lutheran schools and how they were to be equipped to serve in the Lutheran ministry.[163]

The College Crunch

The upheavals and unrest that had wracked colleges in the late sixties gave way to what the president of Yale called an "eerie tranquillity" during the first two academic years of the seventies.[164] While the general public may have breathed a sigh of relief that calm seemed to have been restored, college administrators knew that they were facing a different crisis spelled *money.* In 1971 the Association of American Colleges released a study of five hundred institutions entitled *The Red on the Black,* which pointed out that most private colleges in the red were getting redder, while those in the black were growing grayer.[165] Lutheran schools proved to be no exception to the pervasive problem.[166]

One of the unavoidable questions was whether the church was prepared to step into the breach and provide additional funding. By 1970 LCA synods were pouring almost $3,150,000 annually into their various institutions, which was equivalent to over 15 percent of the benevolence provided to the church-at-large.[167] No one doubted that there was a need, but in January 1970 the Executive Council reluctantly responded to a BCECV recommendation for increased funding by stating, "Until the church has developed a better means than is presently available of establishing program priorities within an increasingly restricted income, the Executive Council is not in a position to endorse either the maintenance or increase of present levels of support as recommended by BCECV."[168] This did not mean that the LCA was abandoning college education, but that it was trying to come to grips with the problem within the context of the church's total mission.

Meanwhile, there were forces at work that would cause the LCA to lose its connection with two of its institutions of higher education. Hartwick College, which traced its Lutheran heritage back to 1797, decided in 1968 that in order to enable its students to become eligible for grants from the state of New York, it would have to disassociate itself from its two supporting synods. The second case was Waterloo University in Ontario, Canada, which had grown dramatically in the sixties to the point where it had a student body of over four thousand. Changing policies of funding with regard to church colleges, however, made it necessary in 1973 for the Eastern Canada Synod to accept an arrangement whereby the government would reimburse the synod for its investment and make Waterloo a federated college of the neighboring provincial institution, Wilfrid Laurier University.[169]

In the United States the relationship between church colleges and the state was being tested in the courts, and in 1971 the Supreme Court issued a landmark decision that clarified the kind of support that would be an infringement of the First Amendment regarding the establishment of religion. The Court held that federal and state grants for such purposes as construction, institutional aid, and student aid were legal as long as they had a secular purpose and did not cause excessive government entanglement with religion.[170] The significance of the legitimizing of these government programs for church-related colleges during these years of financial stress is almost impossible to overestimate.

During this period the BCECV was struggling with the question of how the LCA could best relate to the colleges that had been associated with its predecessor bodies for many decades. Two important steps were taken. One was a policy statement developed by the Council on the Mission of LCA Colleges and Universities that proposed the church establish "covenant relationships" with its institutions which took into account the widely varied situations and possibilities that existed.[171] The board reported to the 1972 convention that it had already forged eleven of these covenants and expected the remainder to be completed by the end of that year.[172] The second major step was the development of a statement on *Public Policy and Church-Related Higher Education,* which sought to spell out the importance of the kind of church and state relationships that were possible in this area while respecting the unique roles and integrity of each.[173]

Diaconate or Diaconates?

During the first ten years of the LCA's existence, there were repeated changes in the church's strategy regarding deaconess work in an effort to strengthen the movement. Membership in the community had declined steadily from 209 in 1964 to 177 in 1972.[174] Efforts at recruitment continued, but retirements, deaths, and resignations outpaced the number of new deaconesses consecrated.

There were several important developments around the turn of the decade. One was the decision reached in 1969 to allow deaconesses to marry and continue on the active role.[175] It was expected, however, that they continue in full-time service in the office. A second decision dealt with education of students for the diaconate. After the closing of the Baltimore school, arrangements had been made for students to take part in a graduate program at Philadelphia Seminary, but this agreement was terminated in 1970.[176] Following this step, an experiment was undertaken at Muhlenberg College to provide a baccalaureate level program with the study concentrated during two or three summer sessions.[177] The efforts to find a viable method of deaconess education, however, would continue.

Perhaps of most far-reaching significance had been the proposal of the Commission on the Comprehensive Study of the Doctrine of the Ministry that a study be made of "the form and function of the ministry of deacons."[178] Implicit in this recommendation was the possibility of a male diaconate, a form of service that had long existed in some European Lutheran churches. The Executive Council sought the advice of the BTE, which proposed that there be an experiment with an expanded diaconate during the 1972–74 biennium to test the feasibility of a diaconic community for men and the possible inclusion of "the professional full-time lay workers of the church and persons involved in special ministries through congregations and para-congregational groups."[179] The experiments proceeded, but a final resolution of the question of an expanded diaconate would not come until 1978.[180]

COMMUNICATING IN THE SEVENTIES

Congregations were becoming increasingly restive about the barrage of promotional materials that descended on them from the various churchwide agencies. Pastors particularly believed that they were being swamped with mailings from the church-at-large, even when some of the items that littered their desks had come from other sources. As early as 1966, a delegate had proposed a study to determine whether increased interagency coordination might provide more efficient and low-cost production of printed materials.[181] The president appointed a committee, at the suggestion of the Cabinet, to examine all promotional material to assess the amount of duplication, quantity, quality, audiences addressed, and usage made by those for whom it was intended.[182] The task was enormous, but a report was promised by January 1969.[183]

What the study revealed was that there were more than a hundred specialized audiences to whom printed materials were addressed. Many of these audiences depended on what was sent to them as a source of necessary information and help. Nevertheless, the committee proposed that a task force design "the development of a coherent, cohesive, multi-media, multi-level flow of communications to audiences both within and without the Lutheran Church in America," which was a new and major assignment.[184] Since the LCA had undertaken a total study of Function and Structure in 1970, it was deemed best to establish an interim plan of coordinating communications to pastors and congregations that included an eight-page news sheet for congregational leaders dealing with programmatic aids, a brief newsletter from the president to pastors and a limited number of key leaders, a quarterly sample packet of churchwide agency items to congregations, and an annual listing of available resources. Responsibility for the interim system was assigned to the Task Force on Communications that had conducted the study.[185] The basic system, with modifications, came to be the pattern for the rest of the life of the LCA.

The Lutheran

In a period of "shake-outs" in the magazine business, when mass market publications such as the venerable *Saturday Evening Post* had disappeared, *The Lutheran* continued to thrive. When G. Elson Ruff had become editor of its ULCA forerunner in 1945, *The Lutheran* had a circulation of 30,000. By January 1970 the figure had peaked at 591,830, which placed it second among church periodicals in North America. By 1972 circulation slipped by about 41,000, but this was a time when many church magazines, hit by rapidly increasing postal rates, were forced to discontinue publication completely.[186]

Even when he was elected editor at the Minneapolis convention in 1970, it was obvious that Ruff's health was failing, and in November 1971 Albert Stauderman, who had been on the staff since 1951, was named Acting Editor. Ruff was given a leave of absence until his death not long thereafter. When the 1972 convention elected Stauderman to head the magazine, he became only its second editor in twenty-eight years.[187] Stauderman did continue *The Lutheran's* tradition of unbiased reporting and the kind of no-holds-barred editorials that had been a trademark of the magazine.

Press, Radio and Television

As the Commission on Press, Radio and Television rounded out its first decade, it harked back in its report to the relatively brief history that public relations had had in the Lutheran church. As late as 1919, Augustana's *The Lutheran Companion* had "warned against news publicity for the church and advised just 'tell the people that you have the Gospel.' "[188] The need to communicate with the public during World War I had begun to break down that reluctance among Lutherans, and by 1921 the National Lutheran Council had undertaken this responsibility. It was not until 1954, however, that the ULCA had established a separate department for Press, Radio and Television.

By the seventies PRT was not only issuing news releases but also conducting regional workshops on communications for synods and congregations. The Lutheran Series on the Protestant Hour provided more than 6,400 hours of air time for LCA preachers each biennium.[189] In 1970 ALC and LCA agreed to combine their weekly radio newscasts in a version of Church World News that was heard on 484 stations.[190]

The children's program "Davey and Goliath" continued to be the crown jewel of PRT's television projects. According to Nielsen reports, the program was reaching a potential of 1,723,000 children a week, which of course did not include audiences in South America, the Far East, Australia, New Zealand, and Europe.[191] In addition, closed circuit television was carrying the program into Roman Catholic parochial schools in six major metropolitan areas. A departure from the television precedent was set when PRT agreed to allow the Boards of Parish Education and Publication to use the "Davey and Goliath" characters in a film to help introduce children to first Communion.[192] All in all, Davey and his friends seemed to age as gracefully as Little Orphan Annie through the years.

NEW WAYS OF DEALING WITH FINANCE

By 1970 the basic trend in giving had reached crisis proportions in the LCA. The fact that the problem was common to most church bodies was certainly no source of comfort. From 1964 through 1969, giving to religious institutions in the United States had declined from 49 percent of total philanthropy to less than 46 percent, and there did not seem to be any end in sight.[193] As for the LCA, it had experienced very modest increases in regular giving to apportionment through 1968, but 1969 saw an actual decrease of $34,372. By itself that figure did not mean much, but the fact was that inflation had eroded the purchasing power of benevolence dollars by $1,950,000 in five years. Clearly, something had to be done to reverse the decline.[194] The LCA's approach involved three steps: a new channel for giving, the linking of planning with budgeting, and consultation with synods about mutual commitments.

Designated Advance Giving

From the time of merger, the LCA had followed the practice of providing within its total budget proposal to conventions a line called "Emergency and Advance."[195] The total benevolence needs were then apportioned among synods according to a formula that gave equal weighting to the number of active confirmed members and congregational current expenses.[196] The usefulness of the apportionment concept was debated frequently, and most synods found that the goals set before them were unachievable.[197] As for Emergency and Advance, only once had there been anything to distribute to churchwide agencies, and that was a miniscule $20,945 in 1968.[198]

In April 1969 a fiscal consultation was held following the meeting of the Conference of Synodical Presidents "to explore with synods the possibility of some cooperative planning; probe the nature of our fiscal problems and their possible solutions; [and] seek to determine whether or not more effective program relationships can be developed."[199] Among the findings were a call for better communication with the constituency about mission and purpose leading to establishment of commitment (this was to include more effective fund-raising) and providing ways that individuals and congregations could sense greater participation in the program decision-making process.

What emerged was an Executive Council proposal to the 1970 Minneapolis convention that was a complete change in the Emergency and Advance concept so that specific items could be described as projects to be funded as money was received. The term to be used was "Designated Advance." Individuals could contribute directly to those purposes they felt were high-level concerns. Congregations also could designate funds for specific programs, provided they were already remitting 100 percent or more of their apportionment.[200]

The proposal provoked vigorous debate. Opposition came largely from those who felt allowing congregations to designate gifts would simply draw funds away from "regular" benevolence and not generate additional giving.[201] Actually, the idea of congregations' designating gifts was not as radical as it seemed. The BWM received about $535,000 and the BAM $77,000 in direct contributions from congregations and individuals in 1969.[202] When the convention voted, however, 374 delegates were favorable to the Designated Advance plan and 259 against. Since the necessary bylaw changes would have required a two-thirds majority, the motion was defeated. As delegates had more time to digest the implications of this decision, a motion was made later in the convention for reconsideration, and this time the proposed bylaw changes were adopted.[203]

A special Designated Advance Gifts office was set up in the Stewardship Department, and in the first year of operation $156,000 was received.[204] By 1973 the figure passed the half-million dollar mark and became an increasingly significant part of the budget thereafter.[205] It would be difficult to assess all of the factors involved, but the fact is that by 1972, apportioned benevolence receipts had begun an upward trend.

Program Planning and Budgeting

When the study of *Significant Issues for the Seventies* had been completed, the Executive Council referred the report to the various churchwide agencies for study and asked the Cabinet of Executives to propose the next steps in total program planning for the LCA to address the needs of the decade. In April 1969 the Cabinet proposed a second Task Group on Long-Range Planning to state, collect, and analyze the many short- and long-term goals of the LCA and its agencies. The task force's efforts were "to rationalize and deal with what appeared as thorny problems—uncoordinated programs, duplication of effort, lack of agreed-upon churchwide priorities, resistance to change, decision by politics, incremental budgeting procedures, and 'fire-fighting' today's issues rather than anticipating through long-range planning."[206]

The task force did find a genuine desire on the part of the agencies to bring planning into some rational form that would coordinate what was going on in different places. A stumbling block was the "line object" form of budgeting used in the church, which made it extremely difficult to relate costs to specific projects. For example, a budget line for salaries was little help in understanding how personnel were to spend their time and on what specific projects.[207] At the time, many organizations and government were using a process known as PPBS (Planning, Programming and Budgeting System) that gave promise of drawing seemingly unrelated programs into a coherent whole. The Cabinet was trained in the process at a week-long seminar at the University of Michigan in the summer of 1970. There they learned the technique for "management by objectives" and began to apply the concept to planning in their own agencies.

Meanwhile, the task force developed a "Program Structure" for the LCA that began with a statement of the church's mission and went through the steps of "functions, aims, programs, and projects."[208] The "mission" was stated as follows:

> It is the purpose of the Lutheran Church in America
> to engage as many persons
> as will share its confession of faith
> in a fellowship of worship, learning, witness and service
> that the Word of God in Jesus Christ
> may become effective in their lives
> together and individually
> including relationships
> with other Christian fellowships and
> with social institutions
> at home and throughout the world.

The six functional areas under which all programs were gathered were "Communicating the Gospel, Helping Persons Mature as Christians, Fostering Responsible Action as Christians in the World, Contributing to Ecumenical and Interfaith Relationships, Developing and Supporting Personnel, and Developing and Supporting Organizations."[209]

By the time of the 1972 convention in Dallas, the budgets of the various churchwide agencies as well as the grants to inter-Lutheran and ecumenical groups had been fitted into the structure. It began to be possible to discern exactly what a particular part of the budget was to accomplish and to provide a basis for evaluating whether and how well it had been done.[210] Synods also were encouraged to use the system. During the years that followed, the plan would be refined and simplified, but the basic concept of PPBS continued throughout the life of the LCA.

Consulting with Synods on Commitments

The frustration that many synods had experienced in trying to fulfill an apportionment objective was that the goal always seemed to retreat as they approached it. This was one factor creating pressure for change in the system. The other was a growing sense of partnership between the synods and the church-at-large. As one who had been a synod president himself, Robert Marshall was well aware of the problems and was searching for a viable solution. During his first two years as president of the LCA, he became convinced that an open consultation process with synods would encourage cooperative planning and realistic assessment of potential.[211]

A change was made in the bylaws at the Dallas convention so that in lieu of a fixed apportionment figure, representatives from the church-at-large and the synods could arrive at an agreed-upon synodical commitment that met three criteria.[212] First, synodical support would be at a level no less than 1971 actual results and 1972 experience to date. Second, 1971 experience was to be used as a base plus a growth factor. Third, it would be possible to maintain the same percentage of division of funds between synod and churchwide causes as had been true in 1971, regardless of current synodical receipts. This last was an escape hatch for synods that feared their benevolence receipts might decline or those which genuinely expected an increase but were unsure of the amount.[213] Synods, in turn, were expected to use the same consultation process with congregations in order to set realistic commitments at that level. Implementing the procedures resulted in some lively encounters until mutual trust was achieved.[214]

ECUMENICAL RELATIONS

Along with everything else in which it was involved, the LCA found the inter-Lutheran and wider ecumenical scene in a state of rapid flux. The same kinds of demands that confronted the church internally because of changes in society were being experienced by interchurch organizations. To add to the tension, the LCA, as a confessional body, was continually faced with the question of its own identity and priorities in an increasingly ecumenical age.[215] The accepted interpretation of the Preamble, Confession of Faith, and the Article on Objects and Powers in the constitution was that the desire for Lutheran union held precedence over involvement in ecumenical activities.[216] Developments at the turn of the decade certainly gave high visibility to relations with other Lutherans.

Relating to Other Lutherans
in North America

As we have already seen, cooperative work with the ALC was going on in almost every area—worship, evangelism, youth ministry, education, social ministry, and publications, to name obvious examples. The declaration by the ALC of pulpit and altar fellowship with the LCA was received with the kind of enthusiasm that comes after long years of waiting.[217] As President Schiotz of ALC put it in a letter indicating that the vote had been overwhelming to ratify the declaration, "This vote, in which all our congregations are represented, is an eloquent testimony to the deep desires of our people. With you, I thank God that the fellowship which we have practiced for many years on a *de facto* basis is now officially authorized by The American Lutheran Church."[218]

When Kent S. Knutson was elected president of the ALC on Fredrik Schiotz's retirement in 1970, there was every reason to expect that the warming trend with LCA would continue. ALC had issued an invitation to both LCA and LCMS to consider statements on unity and development of common organizational structures. Missouri chose to be only an observer, but LCA agreed to full participation in an inter-Lutheran committee. At the Dallas convention of the LCA, President Knutson was asked about the possible relationship between LCA restructuring proposals and possible Lutheran merger. He replied that he did not believe the LCA proposals would be any hindrance to either cooperation or possible merger plans, but was very candid in saying that "the ALC has not at this time made a judgment that it will merge with the LCA without Missouri being involved."[219] Nonetheless, hopes for a merger in the near future reached a high point in LCA circles.[220] On March 12, 1973, a shock wave went through Lutheranism at the news that Dr. Knutson had died at the threshold of his career and at a kairotic moment in relations between his church and the LCA. He was succeeded by David W. Preus, who had served as the ALC vice president and was pastor of a large congregation in Minneapolis.[221]

The Canadian Scene. The trend toward Lutheran unity seemed even further advanced in Canada than in the United States. The Evangelical Lutheran Church of Canada, which had its roots in TALC, voted at its first convention in June 1968 to declare pulpit and altar fellowship with the LCA.[222] The ELCC had also instructed its representatives on the Joint Commission on Inter-Lutheran Relationships to initiate merger negotiations with the LCA Canada Section, The Lutheran Church-Canada, and the Canadian Section of the Synod of Evangelical Lutheran Churches. These steps led Otto A. Olson, president of the Canada Section, to report to the 1970 LCA convention that merger in Canada was "likely to come before consolidation in the USA."[223] That prediction would come true but not for another fourteen years.

Lutheran Council in the USA

LCUSA had gotten off to a running start when it was formed in 1967 and was able to report to the LCA convention in 1970 that "inter-Lutheran cooperation today is certainly far more extensive than that envisioned at the formation of the Lutheran Council."[224] The existence of LCUSA, it said, had given impetus to local and regional inter-Lutheran work. At that time a survey had shown there were forty-six local or regional councils of Lutherans, with another forty in process of formation. Every LCUSA division was engaged in innovative work.

By 1971, however, a cloud appeared on the horizon. On September 13, LCMS President Jacob A. O. Preus wrote to President Marshall that the Missouri convention had voted that there should be an independent and objective study of LCUSA "to evaluate the need for the various divisions, departments, commissions, and officers; their efficiency and effectiveness; their procedures and policies; their planning and programming; their fiscal posture and budgeting; their services; and any other relevant matters."[225] On the basis of such a report, the Missouri Board of Directors had been authorized to determine in which programs the Synod would participate and to which it would allocate funds. The LCMS had set out on a path toward selective participation in the Council.

One area of LCUSA's work where Missouri continued to participate with the other member bodies was that of bilateral dialogues. As was pointed out in the previous chapter, this was the "age of dialogues." Although these discussions with the Reformed, Episcopalians, and other denominations often required many years, their importance for the ALC and LCA in interchurch relationships would become increasingly apparent in the future.

Lutheran World Federation

Finding an appropriate site for the Fifth Assembly of LWF in 1970 proved to be a major problem. Originally it had been scheduled for Weimar in East Germany, but permission was suddenly withdrawn by the Communist government. Next, Pôrto Alegre, Brazil, was chosen, but concern about repressive government actions in that country led to a major defection in delegates, largely from the Scandinavian churches. Only weeks before the assembly was to convene, the location was moved again to Évian-les-Bains, France, just a short distance from the LWF headquarters in Geneva. When he spoke to the LCA convention in Minneapolis, ALC President Schiotz, who was also president of LWF, said, "I regret that we could not meet in Brazil, but we could not meet with half an assembly."[226]

Relocating the assembly proved a masterful job in logistics. But the convention was not without its tensions. Youth, who were delegates for the first time, made their voices heard in debate and campaigned for election of members to the Executive Committee who were younger and not identified with church hierarchies. Women delegates succeeded in winning a commitment that for the first time a woman would be chosen for a LWF staff position. The delegates challenged the churches to sensitize their members to social responsibility and racial issues, and to foster ecumenical commitment, including declaring pulpit and altar fellowship with other churches in the LWF family.[227]

In tune with the times, the LWF had gone through a process of restructuring that was approved at the Évian meeting. The major changes included reducing the number of commissions to three: Church Cooperation, World Service, and Studies. The last of these combined the work that had previously been done by the Commissions on Theology, Education, Worship, Evangelism, and Stewardship in such a way that it maximized studies and reduced drastically the consultative services previously provided to Third World churches.[228] The change in name of the Commission on World Mission to Church Cooperation provoked heated debate at the assembly. It seemed to many that the LWF was abandoning the whole mission thrust that had been a major part of its work in the past. Others argued that the change in name was necessary to make it possible for Eastern European churches to participate fully in LWF at a time when the word *mission* created problems with their Socialist governments.[229] The fallout from Évian would result in an experimental and unsettled period for the LWF and the national committees of the member churches.[230]

National Council of Churches

The currents of the late sixties and early seventies created stress within the NCCCUSA that threatened at times to destroy the Council itself. A climax was reached at the 1969 Assembly in Detroit when demonstrations frequently interrupted proceedings. At one point red paint, symbolizing blood, was thrown on the officers by a draft resister when the delegates refused to hold his draft card in trust.[231] As Robert Marshall put it, "On one side there was resentment against such confrontation; on the other there was equal anger about long-standing injustice and the violence of war. The tension led to a time of retrenchment and reorganization for the churches and the Council."[232]

The Council went through a series of efforts at setting goals and restructuring. Some decisions seem strange in retrospect. During the triennium following 1969, the program board of the Division of Christian Unity was not activated, although ecumenism had always been a high priority of the NCCCUSA.[233] Expansive new programs were voted, although the staff that were supposed to implement them had been cut in half. Some of the changes, however, were a positive response to the mood of the time. The Executive Committee was increased from twenty-seven to thirty-two to provide five places for young people. Greater emphasis was placed on participation by women and minorities.[234]

Tensions between the Council and the churches grew as the NCCCUSA issued a barrage of statements on almost every social issue of the moment. Restructuring also raised a pivotal problem about the ecumenical and representative principles for the LCA. The Executive Council responded on behalf of the LCA to a series of proposed constitutional changes in the NCCCUSA in 1972. It objected strongly to a proposal that would dilute the trinitarian formulation in the preamble to the constitution of the NCCCUSA and would have opened membership to religious groups that did not confess "Jesus Christ as Divine Lord and Savior."[235] It also was opposed to the suggestion that the Governing Board could grant voting membership to persons with special expertise who were not appointed by member churches but might represent certain kinds of special interest groups in society. This would have diluted the "churchly character" of the Council and would have given decision-making power impacting the member communions to persons who had no accountability to them.[236] The debate and rethinking about the Council's nature and priorities would continue well into the eighties.

World Council of Churches

The death of Franklin Clark Fry, chairman of the powerful Central Committee, marked the end of an era for the World Council of Churches. But Robert Marshall soon became recognized in ecumenical circles as a gifted leader and held a series of important positions in the WCC. By the time of the Fourth Assembly in Uppsala, Sweden, in 1968, membership in the WCC had grown to 228 church bodies, with some 350 million members in more than eighty countries.[237] The Council continued to grow in this sense, with new member churches being added at almost every meeting of the Central Committee, but the WCC was at the same time undergoing some of the same stresses as the churches themselves.[238] Profound social changes, particularly in Third World countries, often prompted the WCC to issue statements and take actions that distressed more conservative elements of the member churches. It was not unusual for LCA leaders to be called upon to interpret and defend the WCC to their own constituency.

RESHAPING THE CHURCH'S FUNCTION
AND STRUCTURE

Organizations, large and small, change shape and direction over the years. Sometimes the process is slow and incremental; at other times it is sudden and dramatic. But change they do. In this respect, the LCA was certainly no exception. During its first decade, two new synods were born. Two auxiliaries had disappeared. Priorities had shifted in the face of traumatic events in society. Hundreds of congregations were started, others had disbanded, and some had merged. New relations were forged with sister churches overseas. Programs were begun in hope and discontinued in disappointment.

In no sense was the LCA a rigid and static organization. But these and a hundred other redirections tended to be corporate in nature and could be charted and evaluated.

Much more difficult to assess in the life of the church was the human factor in the equation. There was a completely new trio of officers in the church-at-large.[239] There were twenty-one new synodical presidents who had not been in their strategic positions in the first biennium.[240] Only three of the eight LCA boards had had the same executive throughout the period. Only one commission's leadership was unchanged.[241] Hundreds of different persons had served as decision-makers on boards, commissions, and task forces, and as representatives to inter-Lutheran and ecumenical agencies. Thousands of pastors had changed parishes, and the number of those who served in various volunteer roles is simply incalculable. Congregations were changing in age-level composition, religious backgrounds, and the social and political views of their constituencies. Each change, for better or worse, made a difference, and the cumulative effect staggers the imagination. The LCA, in every sense of the term, was a living, dynamic organism that had essential continuity with its origin but had also altered its outlines and texture by the end of its first decade.

The Decision to Redesign the Structure

As evolutionary change occurs in an organization, new developments often seem to spring up in topsy-turvy fashion, and people become impatient with processes that had once served well but now are seen as impediments to progress. When that happens, pressure builds for taking a fresh look at the whole instead of seeking piecemeal solutions. That point was reached in 1970 for the LCA, and a few of the factors that brought matters to a head deserve mention here.

The LCA had been designed originally so that there would be organizational parallels among the structures of churchwide agencies, synods, and congregations. What had been logically conceived developed points of friction in practice. Several synods were already experimenting with new structures that were discontinuous with those of the church-at-large. Many congregations simply did not use the complex system of committees that demanded more leaders than they had. Their imaginations about mission in their own community had been stirred by *The Manifesto*. Both synods and congregations were impatient with the deluge of redundant programs pouring from seventeen different churchwide offices that did not appear to be cooperating with one another.[242] The task forces on long-range planning had brought to light many of these problems in ways that demanded attention.

The impetus for a study of function and structure came first from the Cabinet, which had been struggling with the implications of long-range planning.[243] Initially, President Marshall had not favored dealing with the situation in this wholesale way; but after more than a year in office and having tested the mood firsthand throughout the church, he came to the conclusion that a fresh look was needed.[244] The proposal that finally went to the convention called for appointment of a fifteen-person Commission on Function and Structure that was to bring its report to the Dallas meeting in 1972.[245] It is significant that the Commission was to put the question of "function" prior to "structure" in its work. Considering the magnitude of the proposal, it provoked surprisingly little discussion at the convention, but the process set in motion would generate torrents of debate throughout the church during the next two years. The implication was that people were ready for a change but would not agree on exactly what should be done.

How the Study Was Done

No time was wasted in getting things moving because there simply was not time to spare. Members of the Commission were chosen immediately after the convention by the Executive Council, and the group held its first meeting September 24–26 in New York.[246] William H. Ziehl, an executive at the United Nations, was named chairperson of the Commission, and Dorothy J. Marple, executive secretary of Lutheran Church Women, was co-opted to serve two-thirds time as staff coordinator.[247] The officers of the church chose to attend Commission meetings only upon request in order not to influence the proceedings unduly.

To appreciate the awesome task the Commission faced, it is important to keep in mind the climate within which it had to do its work. The social upheavals of the late sixties had not yet subsided. Resistance to authority and suspicion of "the system" were commonplace. Special interest groups, youth, minorities, and women were all lifting their voices in society and church. In retrospect, some scholars see it as a time of theological anarchy when "almost anything that any-

William Ziehl, chairperson, and Dorothy Marple, coordinator for Commission on Function and Structure

one wished to say might be called 'theology.' "[248] Faced with decline in numbers and influence, churches struggled with their own identity. It was a paradoxical time when change was demanded and simultaneously resisted.

The Commission quickly established five principles for its work: First, the persons most deeply concerned should be involved in shaping the study, which meant women, men, clergy, lay, youth, minorities, members of boards and commissions, staff of churchwide agencies and synods, and personnel from institutions of the church.[249] Second, persons with special knowledge and expertise would be consulted. Third, the Commission would arrive at its decision by consensus rather than vote whenever possible. Fourth, the study would be regarded not as a single event but as an ongoing process. Fifth, every effort would be made to be informed about similar studies in other church bodies.[250]

There were several stages in the process itself. The first dealt with identification of issues. Instead of simply using its own judgment in the matter, the Commission convened sixteen regional panels throughout the United States and Canada involving 269 persons selected by the synods. These representatives spent a twenty-four-hour period discussing, listing, and refining those issues they felt were most important to address in the study. In addition, each synodical president was interviewed at length to determine his views. When all this mass of data was analyzed, ninety-four issues emerged, which brought the comment, "How could Lutherans fail to come up with Ninety-five Theses?" The issues were grouped in nine major categories: the congregation; congregational life; voluntary leadership; professional leadership; interchurch relationships; social responsibility; districts, synods, and churchwide agencies; communications; apportionment, budget and finance.[251]

When the issues were identified, a questionnaire was sent to a random sample of one thousand congregations, plus persons such as the Executive Council, boards, commissions, the Canada Section Executive Committee, synodical presidents and staff, seminary and college presidents, and staff of churchwide agencies and social ministry agencies.[252] The questionnaire produced an avalanche of more than 5,690 replies. The issues that ranked highest in concern were poor morale and diminishing membership, the meaning and application of the gospel in a pluralistic world, the meaning and development of Christian community in society today, the place of the Bible in educational programs, and the pastor's task in the church today. The lowest ranked issues dealt with the number of seminaries, synodical standing committees vs. ad hoc committees, national headquarters location, and a separate Lutheran Church in Canada.[253] In addition to the survey results, the Commission was provided with reports of several basic LCA studies as it grappled with issue analysis.[254]

The second major stage of the study involved analyzing the issues themselves and searching for solutions. The Commission set up seven task forces dealing with congregations; personnel; social responsibility; communications; interchurch relations; churchwide agencies, synods, and districts; and finance.[255] In addition, Commission members discussed the issues with the Executive Council, the Conference of Synodical Presidents, the Coordinating Committee on Race Relations, and the Cabinet. Churchwide agencies were invited to prepare papers and make an oral presentation to the Commission on those issues related to their areas of responsibility.

The third step was to prepare a preliminary draft of the Commission's report for review in the church.[256] A second round of regional panels was held, and a questionnaire was sent to church councils in a second sample of a thousand congregations. Review sessions were held by the Executive Council, boards, commissions, the auxiliary, and a variety of self-constituted groups throughout the church. Hundreds of letters were received from individuals, and some groups even submitted position papers.[257]

The concluding stage in the whole process was a revision of the Commission's report in final form for submission to the 1972 Dallas convention. A closer look, however, at the reactions to the first draft, the nature of the revisions, the convention decisions, and the issues deferred until 1974 is in order.

The Preliminary Plan

The first report of the Commission was prefaced with a summary that attempted to set forth in a half dozen pages the major points in the proposal. Since no précis can do justice to the nuances of any study, it seemed that this summary served more as a target for critics to zero in on than as a helpful device for assisting the reader. In any event, this device was eliminated from the final version.

The body of the report was divided into two sections. One dealt with a very brief statement on theological perspectives that was criticized because it seemed to have little correlation to any organizational principles that governed the proposals that followed. People felt that there was too much emphasis upon the church as a mechanism or legal entity rather than an expression of the church in terms of people working together in an organic relationship to fulfill a God-given mission.[258]

The second section on "Proposals" began with a chapter on *Congregations* that met with general approval. It suggested as a definition:

> A congregation is an identifiable group of Christian believers in which the gospel is taught and the sacraments administered, which has a continuing corporate existence recognized by the Lutheran Church in America, and which assists its members to cultivate, express, and witness to their Christian faith.[259]

The major emphasis was on the congregational function of caring, which the respondents wanted sharpened to make the traditional roles of the congregation in terms of worship, learning, witness, service, and support more visible. The chapter also stressed congregational goal setting, member commitment to goals, and a structure based on working groups built around functions rather than committees.

The next chapter on *Synods* understandably provoked mixed reactions. It was proposed that Articles VI and VII of the approved constitution for synods be amended to combine the synodical functions and the long list of other synodical duties and powers into five functions:

1. Care of congregations
2. Counseling and enabling of full-time professional workers
3. Development and supervision of special congregational and institutional ministries
4. Advancement of continent-wide and worldwide work of the church
5. Administration of the synod

The respondents wanted "social action" specifically mentioned in the third and a sixth function added that would make clear the synod's participation in amending the LCA Constitution.[260]

Greater emphasis on cooperative planning between the synod and churchwide agencies as well as between synods and congregations was affirmed. There was a high level of agreement on allowing synods more freedom in determining their own structures. Two trial balloons that were shot down promptly were one permitting the

LCA president to nominate candidates for synodical presidents and the second to make secretaries and treasurers appointees of executive boards.[261]

The third chapter on *Churchwide Agencies* that proposed consolidating the large number of boards and commissions into four divisions and three offices was strongly affirmed with a number of specific refinements suggested. Although there was general agreement on having fewer agencies, some persons also worried whether the scope of some units was too broad.

The organizational concept behind the realignment was that of "constituencies served." The four divisions were to relate to congregations, synods, professional leaders, and other church bodies (including overseas missions). The offices were to support the divisions and the work of the officers of the church. The basic structure set forth below is essentially what was used throughout most of the remaining life of the LCA. It provided for the following:

A *Division for Parish Services* was to combine the functions of the Board of Parish Education and the Commissions on Worship, Youth Ministry, Evangelism, Stewardship (except resource development), and Architecture, along with the congregational aspects of the Board of Social Ministry.[262]

A *Division for Mission in North American Society* (later shortened to Division for Mission in North America) was to provide "a meeting point for churchwide and synodical experiences and perceptions [to] develop churchwide strategy as well as assist with the special needs and opportunities in each synod."[263] This meant bringing together much of the work of the Boards of American Missions, Social Ministry, and the church college dimension of BCECV. DMNA had primary responsibility for the consultation process with synods, which became increasingly important in the life of the LCA.[264]

A *Division for Ministry* (later called Division for Professional Leadership) was to combine responsibilities of the Board of Theological Education with deaconess work, and would oversee the recruitment and development of professional leaders and the Personnel Support Service (then lodged in the Office of the Secretary). The most controversial part of this section had to do with whether seminaries should be supported by synods or the church-at-large, an issue that had been hotly debated at the time of merger.[265] The change in name of the division had less to do with affirming the ministry of the laity than it did with the potential confusion with the ordained ministry.

A *Division for World Mission and Ecumenical Cooperation* (later changed to Division for World Mission and Ecumenism) was to bring together overseas mission work, now seen as interchurch in nature, with relationships to the Lutheran World Federation, Lutheran World Relief, Canadian World Relief, World Council of Churches, and certain other ecumenical agencies. Left unclear was how this unit would relate to the president as the chief ecumenical officer of the church. For the most part the concept of this division was supported, but questions were raised as to whether a separate ecumenical office was needed, an issue that would persist into the eighties.[266]

An *Office for Administration and Finance* was to take over the separate treasuries of the boards; administer the funds of the Board of American Missions; be responsible for budget planning and control, the central computer installation, office services in New York, financial resource development, personnel administration, and legal services; and relate to the Board of Pensions and the Lutheran Laymen's Movement. This kind of centralization of church operations was supported, although some respondents commented that these aspects of the work were outside the scope of their knowledge.[267]

An *Office for Research and Planning* was to be a new operation that would coordinate the research, planning, and evaluation work of other agencies and provide support in these areas when an agency did not have the necessary capabilities. In the Commission there had been vigorous debate about whether this should be a separate unit or should be part of the Office for Administration and Finance. Interestingly, the ORP as created did not control the data processing facility, and its planning function seemed to overlap that of OAF when it came to budgeting. The survey indicated that people were not opposed to such an office but did not really understand what it was to do.[268]

An *Office for Communications* was to be created to deal with the plethora of internal communications efforts of the LCA as well as to strengthen its work in external media. The tension within the Commission itself had been between those who wanted one group of "professionals" to do the communications job *for* all other agencies and those who saw a problem in the interpretation "secondhand" of work with which the OC staff would not be directly involved. *The Lutheran* was to be related to this office, although maintaining its functional independence as was the case with the Board of Publication. The core of the operation, therefore, became the oversight of Press, Radio and Television plus a coordinating role in other publication and communication efforts. The reaction of parish pastors seemed to be, "We're for anything that reduces mailings to our desks."[269]

The final chapter of the report dealt with the *Church Convention, Governing Council, and Officers.* Here the Commission's proposals ran into a buzzsaw. What respondents perceived was that the real locus of authority would be in the Office of the President and a Governing Council of ninety-nine persons that would meet twice a year. An Executive Committee would meet bimonthly to transact interim business, thereby concentrating power further. Both the secretary and treasurer would be appointed by the president. The secretary was reduced to little more than a recorder, and the treasurer seemed to be a part of OAF. The convention would meet every four years instead of biennially and would not have the kind of legislative role that had been the case previously.

Those reacting to the proposal saw the danger of the church becoming highly centralized in the hands of a few while diminishing the roles of synods and congregations. The concern about centralization and a mechanical, impersonal structure similar to the world of business occasioned the most negative comments about the report and posed a real threat to the adoption of any revision submitted to the convention.[270]

Revising the Plan

Confronted with the broad spectrum of reactions to its first draft, the Commission set to work on a revision. Changes of real substance were made in the final report that went to the Dallas convention. The most significant changes included the following:

First, a new chapter was written that described both the theological and organizational premises upon which the proposals were based. It used the biblical image of the church as the body of Christ as clue to the interrelationship and interdependence of all the parts. It did not assume that organizational patterns flowed automatically from the church's theology but insisted they must be consistent with it. "Thinking of the church in organic terms, however, frees the people of God to develop new ways of action and styles of life together in order to become more authentically the active serving body of Christ for their times," it declared. "It frees them to utilize insights from other than the church's own experience in order to improve and make the church's structures more effective."[271]

The Commission viewed the structure that it was proposing, therefore, as a "system" in the organic rather than the mechanical sense. "We speak of the human body as a 'system,' " it said, "and indeed it is a marvelously intricate and interdependent organic system. It is important to keep this meaning in mind when the commission refers to the church body as a system."[272] The Commission then highlighted as valid eight basic organizational concepts that included such things as continual involvement of the membership in decision making through consultation, the need for clear lines of legislative and administrative responsibility, greater representation of certain groups (women, youth, and minorities), purposeful interdependency of all parts while preserving freedom of initiative, encouraging responsible involvement in ecumenical relationships, and providing for research, planning, and evaluation as a way of ongoing change as new needs arose.

Second, the most sweeping changes were made in the chapter that dealt with churchwide structures and the church convention. In the revision, the Commission sought to provide a continuity in the legislative process that it felt did not exist in the current structure.[273] The key was a legislative convention that was to be the highest legislative authority in the church and its chief policy-making body. The convention was to have 250 delegates including the presidents of the church and each synod. The convention would meet annually, and the other delegates would be elected for three-year terms that would be staggered to provide continuity. The convention was to elect an executive committee from among its own members to provide further continuity. The executive committee would serve as the board of trustees and transact business ad interim. Since any change in the makeup and powers of the LCA convention and Executive Council would have required amendments to the constitution, the Commission's strategy was to provide for a first reading of such amendments at Dallas and to ask synods to study and discuss them at their 1973 conventions. Decisions were to be deferred until the 1974 convention in Baltimore.

The description of the role of the president was expanded to emphasize the pastoral nature of the office without diminishing its administrative responsibility. The positions of secretary and treasurer were restored to the status of elective offices, but the secretary was still largely a recorder and the treasurer was on the staff of OAF and responsible to that agency's chief executive.

The description of the Conference of Synodical Presidents was revised to make its importance in the whole process more visible.

The committees that oversaw the work of the churchwide agencies were renamed "management committees" and given much greater authority.[274] Consulting committees were to be established to provide for wider involvement of persons with special expertise and interests in the whole process. The Canada Section, which had been overlooked in this part of the first draft, was affirmed as important and properly described in existing church documents. The auxiliary, Lutheran Church Women, strangely absent from this chapter originally, was included in the revised draft, and it was clear that the executive was to be part of the president's Cabinet. Staff teams were described as a way of coordinating work of an ongoing nature among churchwide agencies. Special provisions were made for youth staffers in churchwide agencies. Throughout this section, as well as the document as a whole, there was frequent reference to providing for better representation of youth, women, and minorities at every level.

Finally, the report sharpened in many ways the chapters dealing with the four divisions and three offices to make their responsibilities more clear, but relatively few changes were made in the substance of these sections.

Decision Time in Dallas

As the convention approached, it became necessary to prepare for the two possibilities that the delegates could either adopt or reject the proposed restructuring. This meant that the Nominating Committee had to provide two entirely different slates of candidates for boards or management committees. In addition, two completely different fiscal proposals for 1973 and 1974 had to be drafted along the lines of the new program budget. The whole process was called "the great game of what if?"

It was understood that if the Commission's report were adopted, a joint meeting of management committees would be held in September and staff would be needed to care for large volumes of preparatory work following the convention. President Marshall, therefore, arranged for those persons whom he had decided to nominate as executive directors to meet in New York on June 22. Since the names of these potential nominees would not be known until the

Executive Council met the morning after the convention, the individuals selected walked into a small meeting room at the Williams Club not knowing who else would be present.[275] Beginning at ground zero, they were to plan how a transition could take place. The group wondered whether it was somehow prophetic of storms to come that they met while the strongest hurricane in years swept up the East Coast toward New York.

It had also become increasingly apparent that the synodical presidents would play a key role at Dallas in determining whether or not restructuring would become a reality. On the morning before the opening session of the convention, therefore, President Marshall called a special meeting of the Conference of Synodical Presidents. In that meeting, lingering questions about the report were dealt with, and plans were laid as to how to process the report through the possible maze of parliamentary procedures that could bog down consideration of the report. It was decided to provide for general discussion by having the convention constitute itself as a "committee of the whole" with Secretary Harkins in the chair—a plan that worked very well and enabled the president to speak on questions as necessary.

The tension was palpable when the convention began its work. Since the Commission's report could be adopted by a simple majority, Robert Marshall suggested that the bylaw changes be dealt with first on the ground that they required a two-thirds vote.[276] After a few attempts were made to refer the report for further study by synods, it became obvious that the delegates wanted to be about the business of debating and refining the proposals. Significant amendments made from the floor included strengthening the policy-making role of management committees; providing for annual performance review of executive directors by the president; and changing the proposed name of the "Division for Interchurch Cooperation and World Mission" to "World Mission and Ecumenism."[277] Finally, the crucial vote was taken adopting an amendment to the constitution to eliminate Articles XIII and XIV dealing with boards and commissions that had been approved for a first reading two years before.[278] This meant in effect that the Report on Function and Structure had been approved, and the way was cleared for the numerous bylaw changes that implemented the new structure. As one delegate put it, "Now all that remains is the small detail of making it work!"

Bishops and Theological Affirmations

Function and structure were not the only concerns on the minds of delegates at Dallas, as has already been indicated, but two additional actions deserve mention here. The first was the report of a special Committee to Study the Office of Bishop that was an outgrowth of the report on Doctrine of the Ministry in 1970. Essentially, the committee proposed that the title "bishop" be used for synodical presidents and "bishop" or "bishop of the church" for the president of the LCA.[279] When these proposals were put in the form of amendments to the constitution by the Executive Council, however, the title for the president of the church was changed to "presiding bishop."[280] Although a sizable majority of delegates voted in favor, the number fell short of the two-thirds required, "showing that the LCA was not ready for 'bishops.' "[281] Actually, the church would change its mind in a few more years.

Of more immediate significance was a proposal from President Marshall that the LCA undertake a study of theological affirmations during the 1972–74 biennium.[282] The recommendation was approved without dissent and thereby set the stage for the next convention in Baltimore.

NOTES

1. Barbara W. Tuchman, *The March of Folly, From Troy to Vietnam* (New York: Alfred A. Knopf, 1984), 360.

2. Solberg, *Higher Education,* 329.

3. Tuchman, *Folly,* 368–69. Gabriel Kolko describes the demoralization of American troops, the widespread use of drugs, the racial conflict within the armed forces, and the actual refusal of servicemen to carry out combat missions as planned. See *Anatomy of a War* (New York: Pantheon Books, 1985), 363–66.

4. Tuchman, *Folly,* 373.

5. Bernard Bailyn, David Brion Davis, David Herbert Donald, John L. Thomas, Robert H. Wiebe, Gordon S. Wood, *The Great Republic* (Boston: Little, Brown & Co., 1977), 1253.

6. *LCAM, 1970,* 280. The NBEDC met in Detroit on April 26, 1969, under the sponsorship of the Interreligious Foundation for Community Organization (IFCO), which was composed of twenty-three local community groups and national religious agencies. See *Facts on File* (New York: Facts on File, May 15–21, 1969), 309.

7. Ahlstrom, *Religious History,* 1074.

8. *LCAM, 1970,* 281.

9. Ibid., 281–82.

10. Alvin M. Josephy, Jr., *Red Power, The American Indians' Fight for Freedom* (New York: American Heritage Press, 1971), 223.

11. Ibid., 243–44.

12. Lynne B. Iglitzin and Ruth Ross, eds., document the scope of the movement in some twenty different societies in *Women in the World* (Santa Barbara, Calif., and Oxford, England: ABC-Clio, 1986).

13. Marjorie Lansing, "The Gender Gap in American Politics," in *Women in the World*, ed. Lynne B. Iglitzin and Ruth Ross, 166.

14. Barbara Sinclair Deckard, *The Women's Movement* (New York: Harper & Row, 1979), 352.

15. Lansing, "Gender Gap," 168.

16. Deckard, *Women's Movement*, 401.

17. Iglitzin and Ross, *Women in the World*, xv. An analysis of the problem is made in Carol Andreas, *Sex and Caste in America* (Englewood Cliffs, N.J.: Prentice-Hall, 1971).

18. Bailyn et al., *Great Republic*, 1254–58.

19. Lee A. Snook, "Ecology and Ecclesiology, An American View," in *The Church Emerging*, ed. John Reumann (Philadelphia: Fortress Press, 1977), 40.

20. Donella H. Meadows et al., *The Limits of Growth* (Washington: Potomac Association Press, 1972).

21. The music and lyrics of *Jesus Christ Superstar* were by Andrew Lloyd Webber and Tim Rice, two young Englishmen. The recording appeared in 1969 and the stage production in 1971.

22. John Reumann explores the ecclesiological significance of this identity crisis in "Identifying the Church in a Time of Change" in *The Church Emerging*, 1–27.

23. Nelson, "New Shape of Lutheranism," 515.

24. *LCAM, 1970*, 30. The "Report of the President" appears in its entirety in the minutes, pp. 28–42.

25. The BSM had the practice of issuing the result of certain studies that were not intended to establish new church policies. As examples during this biennium the board published "Drug Use and Abuse," "Replacement Therapy," "Violence and Nonviolence," "The Church and the Relief Client," "The Church and World Hunger," and "The Crisis in Public Welfare."

26. *LCAM, 1970*, 478.

27. All quotations are from the statement as finally adopted, *LCAM, 1970*, 655–58. The document has been issued in several editions through the years by the Board of Social Ministry and the Division for Mission in North America.

28. All quotations from the statement appear in the draft adopted by the convention, *LCAM, 1970*, 562–65.

29. *LCAM, 1972*, 577–78.

30. All references are to the *LCAM, 1972*, 581–85. The fact that this proposal and the statement on ecology were given lengthy review in hear-

ings before being brought to the convention floor speeded up the adoption process in the plenary sessions.

31. All quotations in this section are from the statement as adopted, *LCAM, 1972,* 611–15.

32. Ibid., 590–97.

33. *LCAM, 1970,* 33.

34. Ibid., 35.

35. *ECM, October 1969,* 493. The complete background is in the *ECM,* 490–93.

36. *LCAM, 1970,* 476.

37. *LCAM, 1972,* 477.

38. Ibid., 575–76.

39. *LCAM, 1970,* 227–34.

40. The BSM, for example, had requests totaling almost $2,685,000 and all told received $763,000 through the appeal (*LCAM, 1970,* 276). The result often was disappointment and frustration from applicants.

41. Sheneman made an analysis of what happened as a result of the "seed money" strategy used by BAM, BCECV, and BSM in his study *Decision Making,* 153–59.

42. *LCAM, 1970,* 224–26. It should be noted that the 1968 convention had defeated a proposal to extend the terminal year of the ACT Appeal from 1969 to 1970 but also had made the Appeal an extrabudgetary item (*LCAM, 1968,* 725–26).

43. *LCAM, 1972,* 66–67.

44. *LCAM, 1970,* 591.

45. Ibid., 645–47. The agency was named the National Indian Lutheran Board, and was one of the operations known as "related agencies" to LCUSA.

46. *LCAM, 1972,* 635–37. A separate "Manifesto of Ministry to Hispanic Peoples" that had been prepared by a group attending a 1971 course on orientation to Hispanic ministries held in Chicago was read into the minutes by the president of the Illinois Synod (p. 573).

47. *LCAM, 1970,* 441.

48. Ibid., 444.

49. Ibid., 445.

50. Ibid., 450.

51. Ibid., 442.

52. Ibid., 432.

53. The LCA bylaw in question was Section II, Item 1, which had read, "A minister of this church shall be a man whose soundness of faith, etc."

54. Ibid., 539.

55. Lani L. Johnson, *Led by the Spirit,* 69. The text of the statement appeared in *Lutheran Women* 8, no. 6 (June 1970): 32.

56. The results of the study were published by LCUSA in 1970 under the title *The Ordination of Women.*

57. World Council of Churches, *Concerning the Ordination of Women* (Geneva: WCC, 1964).

58. Marjorie Garhart, *Women in the Ordained Ministry* (Philadelphia: DPL, 1976). Garhart herself had graduated from Yale Divinity School in the mid-1940s and was ordained in 1976.

59. *The Lutheran* 8, no. 22 (November 18, 1970): 26.

60. Garhart, *Women in Ordained Ministry*, vi.

61. *LCAM, 1970,* 601.

62. *LCAM, 1972,* 567.

63. *LCAM, 1970,* 602.

64. Ibid., 607.

65. The establishing of such schools by congregations or groups of congregations raised many questions that were studied by the BPE at the request of the Executive Council. These included such concerns as meeting educational standards, providing leadership, insuring that the schools were not racially discriminatory and that long-term funding seemed realistic. The schools in some instances had been started because of the woeful condition of inner-city public education and the special needs of linguistic groups. See *LCAM, 1970,* 120–21.

66. Ibid., 602–3. The BAM had made a strong case with the Executive Council at its January 1970 meeting that the board was in the best position to handle the proceeds from disbanded congregations because of its experience in strategy studies, in dealing with property, and for a variety of other reasons. The Council concurred with the plan (*ECM, January 1970,* 601–2).

67. *LCAM, 1972,* 569.

68. *ECM, October 1969,* 484–85.

69. Originally, the position was called "Secretary for Urban Personnel" (*LCAM, 1968,* 582). Sheneman traces the events that led to setting up the Lay Associates Program in a case study titled "Decision by Incursion" in *Decision Making,* 135–42. The question with which he deals is whether BAM was the unit within the LCA structure that should have been involved in recruiting and training persons for this type of work in the church. This was particularly the case with regard to assertions made by BAM that more lay workers were needed because of a decline in the number of ministers becoming available in the church (*BAMM, December 1968,* 4410). Sheneman points out that LCA seminaries alone were "producing more graduates than the church finds easy to place—partly because of BAM's own deemphasis on establishing new congregations." See *Decision Making,* 138.

70. The steps taken to gain clearances to work in this way with JSAC are detailed in the report of the Executive Council to the 1972 convention (*LCAM,* 315–16, 320, 327).

71. *LCAM, 1972,* 571.

72. From a speech to the 1970 convention by Arvin W. Hahn, the president of Bethany College and a member of the BWM, reported in the convention summary, p. 7.

73. The amendment was to *LCA Bylaws,* Section X, H, Items 3, 5, and 6, which were consolidated in a new, more flexible Item 3. See *ECM, June 1970,* 915; and *LCAM, 1970,* 131, 632.

74. *LCAM, 1970,* 130–31, 627.

75. *LCAM, 1972,* 643, 47.

76. *Master Plan of the JELC,* 1, a document distributed to BWM, October 25, 1973.

77. *LCAM, 1970,* 641.

78. *LCAM, 1972,* 647. Statistics at this time included both missionaries and spouses.

79. Ibid., 648.

80. *LCAM, 1970,* 623. Background for this decision is given briefly in the *LCAM, 1966,* 725; *1968,* 648.

81. Nelson, "New Shape of Lutheranism," 517.

82. *ECM, February 1972,* 585–86; and *June 1972,* 789–90.

83. All of these trends are described in the BWM report to the LCA convention, *LCAM, 1972,* 645–48.

84. *Survey of Issues for Function and Structure,* LCA Commission on Function and Structure, 1971, p. 12. This survey was done at the outset of the Function and Structure study and involved 5,960 responses in an attempt to identify and rank the issues of greatest concern to church members that needed to be dealt with by the commission. There were a total of ninety-four issues raised that ranked from 4.22 (highest) to 1.65 (lowest) on a scale of 5 to 0. Statistical data and analyses are described in Appendix A through Appendix D.

85. Ibid., 6–40. When responses were grouped in categories, social responsibility and questions related to finances tied for second place in importance.

86. *LCAM, 1964,* 100, and *ECM, October 1964,* 15. The LCA members of the commission were Francis Gamelin, a psychologist and executive secretary of BCECV; W. Kent Gilbert, executive of the BPE; Martin Heinecken, systematic theologian; Edward T. Horn III, parish pastor and expert on liturgics; Robert J. Marshall, biblical scholar and president of the Illinois Synod. When Marshall was elected president of the LCA in 1968, he appointed as his successor Frank W. Klos, an editor for BPE who had been serving as staff recorder for the commission.

87. In 1954 the Intersynodical Committee on Parish Education had held a seminar of several days on the subject at Racine, Wisconsin. One of the papers presented was by Paul Lindberg, professor of Christian education at Augustana Seminary. He proposed that children be admitted to Communion in the elementary school years and confirmed toward the end of high school (the writer was present at the seminar and checked the details with Lindberg in an interview in November 1986). Lutheran historian Robert H. Fischer wrote about the variety of views and practices in "Confirmation Outside the Anglican Tradition," *Confirmation,* ed. Kendig Brubaker Cully (Greenwich: Seabury Press, 1962).

88. See *Commission on Education Report, 1957–63, Document 16,* submitted to the Fourth Assembly of LWF in Helsinki. One of the major preparatory conferences was at Hofgeismar, Germany. The lectures were edited by Kurt Frör and published as *Confirmatio: Forschungen zur Geschichte und Praxis der Konfirmation* (Munich: Ev. Pressverband fur Bayern, 1959).

89. The writer was present as the LCA representative in 1977 when the Synod of the United Evangelical Lutheran Church of Germany (VELKD) approved admission to Communion at around age seven.

90. The several volumes of background papers and carefully detailed minutes of the commission are in the LCA Archives in Chicago.

91. The survey was conducted by use of a questionnaire that was sent to 2,152 lay leaders, 538 parish pastors, and 291 nonparish pastors. The response was 81 percent from pastors and 52 percent from lay persons. The summary of the survey, *Current Concepts and Practices of Confirmation in Lutheran Churches* (Philadelphia: LCA Board of Parish Education, 1966) is in the LCA Archives in Chicago. The analysis of data was done by the research department of the LCA BPE.

92. The study book *Confirmation and First Communion* was a 214-page volume that included a pre-study and a post-study questionnaire. It was accompanied by a leader's guide that described the five-session study and response process. The books were published jointly by the publishing houses of the three churches in 1968. A third volume, *Confirmation and Education*, ed. W. Kent Gilbert (Philadelphia: Fortress Press, 1969), was prepared under the auspices of the ALC and LCA BPEs as the first in a series of "Yearbooks in Christian Education." This was a collection of scholarly essays by noted theologians, educators, sociologists, and psychologists. The volume was targeted for pastors and professional educators.

93. See *The Report of the Joint Commission on the Theology and Practice of Confirmation* (Minneapolis, St. Louis, Philadelphia: Augsburg Publishing House, Concordia Publishing House, Board of Publication, LCA, 1970), 4–5. The full analysis of the data is in *A Report of the Study of Confirmation and First Communion by Lutheran Churches* (Philadelphia: LCA Board of Parish Education, 1969).

94. *Commission Report*, 21. The text of the section dealing with definition, which is the heart of the report, is printed in Appendix B.

95. Ibid., 14.

96. Ibid., 15.

97. Ibid., 17–18.

98. Ibid., 16.

99. Ibid., 25.

100. Ibid., 30–31.

101. Ibid., 26–29, 32.

102. In order to trace the relevant material, it is necessary to refer to the *LCAM, 1970*, 567–91, 613–14, 649–50.

103. A small study commission was appointed for this purpose and brought a report to the 1972 convention that urged that the practice of communing persons regardless of age not be approved. Action, however, was deferred until 1974. In the course of its study, the commission had studied not only the practices among Lutheran churches but also those of other Christian bodies, such as the Orthodox. See *LCAM, 1972*, 193–204, 734–35.

104. After adopting a recommendation similar to that approved by the LCA, the ALC convention passed a further resolution underscoring that part

of the commission's report that spoke of a variety of rites to mark stages of growth in the Christian life. It encouraged congregations to continue periods of intensive cathetical instruction as part of their confirmation ministry to children and youth; and "that after instruction, it be considered normative that an opportunity be given, in a confirmation rite, for youth to confess as their own the Christian faith and to assume greater responsibility for ministry and mission." See *ALCM, 1970,* 633–34.

105. Nelson, "New Shape of Lutheranism," 519.

106. *LCAM, 1970,* 136.

107. Ibid., 135–38. The standing committee had been set up by the LCA president to include the chief executives of BPE, BSM, COE, COS, CW, CYM, and LCW with a representative from the President's Office (*ECM, January 1969,* 224). Plans for the experiment were first reviewed with the Conference of Synodical Presidents and were then approved by the Executive Council in January 1970 (*ECM,* 651–54).

108. Detailed work that had been done by staff and then reviewed in ALC-LCA consultations resulted in the following basic documents to 1971: *A Central Objective for Educational Ministry in the Parish: ALC and LCA, Age-Level Objectives for Educational Ministry in the Parish: ALC and LCA,* and *Age-Level Program Proposals for Educational Ministry in the Parish: ALC and LCA.*

109. This plan was described in step-by-step detail in *Strategy for Developing Educational Ministry in the Parish, ALC/LCA,* a document copyrighted in the names of both churches.

110. Detailed reports on the PLMD pilot test and an analysis of the findings are in Arvid E. Anderson, "The Pilot Test of Parish Life and Ministry Development," and Judith McWilliams, "Reflections on the PLMD Pilot Test," in *The Shaping of the Parish for the Future,* ed. W. Kent Gilbert (Philadelphia: Parish Life Press, 1975).

111. The writer was a participant in this meeting, which was held at a motel near the LaGuardia Airport. It was clear in the discussion that the presidents favored both closer coordination in the sphere of congregational life in their own churches and as close cooperation between the two churches in this area as possible. The writer has checked the accuracy of this perception with C. Richard Evenson, who chaired the ALC coordinating committee at that time.

112. *LCAM, 1972,* 346–47.

113. Preface to *Liturgical Reconnaissance* (Philadelphia: Fortress Press, 1968), ed. Edgar S. Brown, Jr., vii–viii.

114. The establishment of ILCW is described in Chapter 3 of the present volume. The original representatives from LCA on ILCW were L. Crosby Deaton (chair), John W. Arthur, Edward T. Horn III, Frederick F. Jackisch, Ulrich S. Leupold, Daniel T. Moe, Krister Stendahl and Edgar S. Brown, Jr. In 1971 Brown left his position as director of the LCA Commission on Worship and was succeeded by Eugene L. Brand. Brand, who was professor of theology and worship at the Evangelical Lutheran Seminary in Columbus, had served from the beginning as an ALC member of

ILCW. Later, when ILCW was granted a full-time executive to complete work on the *Lutheran Book of Worship*, Brand was chosen for that position.

115. *LCAM, 1972*, 149.

116. *LCAM, 1970*, 160–61. The Executive Council had given the Commission on Worship the authority to approve such experimental materials "for provisional use in the LCA" (*ECM, October 1968*, 66–67).

117. *LCAM, 1972*, 150. All told, the *Contemporary Worship Series* included eleven volumes; see Philip H. Pfatteicher and Carlos R. Messerli, *Manual on the Liturgy* (Minneapolis: Augsburg Publishing House, 1979), 5–6. Some of the volumes sold very widely. By 1976, the Eucharistic Service, for example, had sold more than 360,000 copies, plus about 125,000 of the four individual settings (*LCAM, 1976*, 534–35).

118. *LCAM, 1972*, 351.

119. The semicontinuous Gospel readings generally were from Matthew in Series A, Mark in Series B, and Luke in Series C. Readings from the Gospel of John were employed in the festival half of all three years, with a semicontinuous reading for the tenth to the fourteenth Sundays after Pentecost in Series B. See the "Introduction" to *The Lessons* (Minneapolis and Philadelphia: Augsburg Publishing House and Board of Publication, LCA), 4–5, for further descriptions of the principles used.

120. *LCAM, 1972*, 151, 154.

121. The publisher was Fortress Press of the LCA.

122. Pfatteicher and Messerli, *Manual on Liturgy*, 8.

123. *LCAM, 1972*, 350–51.

124. *LCAM, 1974*, 593.

125. The best description of these concepts is in a series of fifteen scholarly essays in a volume edited by C. Richard Evenson, *Foundations for Educational Ministry* (Philadelphia: Fortress Press, 1971), vol. 3, "Yearbooks in Christian Education."

126. The major research effort was the Lutheran Longitudinal Study in which more than ten thousand persons cooperated to discover new insights about the way children and youth learn to participate in the Christian church. It tested many of the premises, such as *The Age Level Objectives of Christian Education*, upon which the LCA had been developing educational programs. The results are described in William A. Koppe, *How Persons Grow in Christian Community* (Philadelphia: Fortress Press, 1973), vol. 4, "Yearbooks in Christian Education."

127. *LCAM, 1970*, 321–23, describes in detail the implementing actions to permit this level of cooperation. The minutes indicate that the plan was intended to enable the BPEs not only to work together but also to work with the two Boards of Publication. The ALC went an extra step to facilitate EM when it amended its constitution to move editorial responsibility for parish education materials from the Board of Publication to the Board of Parish Education. See *ALCM, 1970*, 633. This was essentially the arrangement that had existed all along in the LCA (*LCA Bylaws*, Section X, C, Item 4). The plan of cooperation called for most editorial work on children's materials to

be done in Minneapolis, and that for youth and adult materials, in Philadelphia.

128. *LCAM, 1970,* 324; and *ECM, February 1971,* 245–46.

129. See chart on *LCAM, 1972,* 639.

130. Strohl, "LCA Statistical Study," 1986.

131. *LCAM, 1970,* 640. Big gains were scored in such areas as new-member classes, leadership education, retreats and conferences, and short-term courses.

132. *LCAM, 1972,* 551.

133. Ibid., 552. The current figure is predicated on the increase in cost of living during the intervening years.

134. Strohl, "LCA Statistical Study," 1986.

135. *LCAM, 1970,* 556; and *ECM, April 1970,* 797–98.

136. *1972 Convention Summary,* 6–7, describes the launching of the thrust in a special order with Franklin Drewes Fry as the keynote speaker.

137. *LCAM, 1972,* 136–39. The COE sought to dispel some of these concerns, and the 1972 convention adopted guidelines to insure that the effort would be carried out with full recognition of "other significant activities in the church." See *LCAM,* 561.

138. There were sixteen delegates at Minneapolis who were classified as youth, the youngest being Toby Paulson, age fourteen, from Lamont, California. See *The Lutheran,* 8, no. 15 (August 5, 1970): 27.

139. *1970 Convention Summary,* 7.

140. *LCAM, 1972,* 156–60.

141. Youth Staffers usually received their expenses plus a small monthly stipend for pocket money. Each year twenty or more young people served in this way, which provided a reservoir of several hundred workers in the church. Many of the staffers found their way into the ordained ministry or other professional service in the LCA.

142. *CYMM, June 1969,* 1–5.

143. *LCAM, 1972,* 160–61; and *LCAM, 1974,* 593.

144. *ECM, July 1974,* 685.

145. *LCAM, 1970,* 419.

146. Lani L. Johnson, *Led by the Spirit,* 74.

147. *LCAM, 1970,* 418–19.

148. Ibid., 419–20.

149. The LCW had worked out an arrangement with the BPE to provide editorial services for program materials that were designed and written for the most part by women.

150. *Lutheran Women,* 8, no. 7 (July–August, 1970): 26.

151. Chisholm's article appeared in the issue of *Lutheran Women* for June 1971, 6–7. Other articles in the same issue were "Let's Take God's Gifts Seriously" by Rachel Conrad Wahlberg (pp. 3–5) and "The New Feminism, Yes and No" by Allan and Betty Hoaglund.

152. Based on a study by Emily Hattery, Secretary for Congregational Organizations, reported in Lani L. Johnson, *Led by the Spirit,* 79.

153. Lani L. Johnson, *Led by the Spirit,* 75.

154. Ibid., 78.

155. The BTE discussion revolved around four points: financing the moves that had already been directed for seminaries, uncertainty about what the LCA would declare to be the "proper ministry of the church," developments providing for theological education in colleges, and studies of the clustering ecumenically of seminaries. See *BTEM, October 1967*, 45–46.

156. *LCAM, 1970*, 524–34. BTE pointed out the delicate balance in LCA constitutional provisions between churchwide responsibility for theological education and synodical ownership of seminaries.

157. Sheneman analyzes the factors that affected the implementation of the Master Plan in *Decision Making*, 82–99. He does not deal just with the situation in the Northeast but also with that of all the seminaries. He calls his case study on how decisions take effect in voluntary organizations "decision by unfinished negotiation." He summarizes the category in this way: "Recognizing that decision-making bodies do not have effective control over those affected by the decisions, indeed that the network of controls may actually work at cross purposes with explicit decision-making, the church regularly engages in negotiations so that there can be accommodation of goals among the various interested groups" (pp. 82–83).

158. *LCAM, 1970*, 529.

159. Ibid., 532.

160. William A. Kinnison, *An American Seminary: A History of Hamma School of Theology* (Columbus, Ohio: Ohio Synod LCA, 1980), 198. Kinnison's book is an excellent summary not only of this ill-fated experiment but also the whole history of Hamma and the various political forces at work in determining its viability.

161. Wentz himself emphasized that he was not trying to downgrade theology or biblical disciplines. "I'll admit," Wentz confessed, "that as a professor of church history, I am somewhat threatened by what I have been saying as president, simply because it will be quite a challenge to teach church history that way." Ibid., 200.

162. The proposal, which was adopted by the convention, had been the result of a study by a Commission of Eighteen charged with finding a viable way of proceeding in theological education in the Northeast. See *LCAM, 1972*, 710–17. See also chap. 5, n. 26.

163. By 1970 the BTE was pointing out that there was a problem in setting standards for the ministry if, as the convention had determined in setting new criteria in 1968 (*LCAM, 1968*, 774), there was to be no specific requirement that such students spend a year in a Lutheran seminary before being accepted for ordination (*LCAM, 1970*, 532). Sheneman concludes in his study that the BTE had de facto lost its authority to require the same standards for graduates from non-Lutheran seminaries as were required of graduates from the church's own schools (see *Decision Making*, 99–106).

164. The quotation is cited by Solberg in *Higher Education*, 335, as he sets the stage for the new problems colleges faced in the seventies.

165. The study by William Jellema is cited by the BCECV in its report to the 1972 convention (*LCAM*, 601).

166. A study made by Francis Gamelin, the former executive of the BCECV, showed that in 1970 sixteen of the twenty-eight Lutheran colleges surveyed were running a deficit. Costs of operating Lutheran schools had more than doubled in the sixties while enrollments were increasing by 54 percent. See Solberg, *Higher Education*, 335–36.

167. *LCAM, 1972*, 67, 608.

168. *ECM, January 1970*, 964.

169. Solberg traces the complicated series of decisions involving both Hartwick and Waterloo in *Higher Education*, 330–31. In the latter case, the Eastern Canada Synod received a settlement of $3,100,000 and retained control of Waterloo Seminary, which had been part of the university complex.

170. The Supreme Court decision was in the case of *Tilton vs. Richardson*, which had to do with the right of certain Catholic colleges to receive construction grants under the Higher Education Facilities Act. See *LCAM, 1972*, 604; and Solberg, *Higher Education*, 338.

171. *LCAM, 1970*, 465–66. The policy involved setting forth the mission of the church-related college, a strategy for implementing and financing that mission, and a covenant stating the mutual roles of the church and the college (*BCECVM, July 1968*, 8). Oddly, the board did not submit the policy to the Executive Council or convention for approval (see Sheneman, *Decision Making*, 53).

172. *LCAM, 1972*, 601.

173. Ibid., 602–5.

174. Ibid., 606–7. At the beginning of 1972 there were ninety-one active deaconesses, eighty retired, and six who were awaiting a call, on leave, or ill.

175. A mail vote by the BCECV, which never debated the policy change, approved the proposal of the Deaconess Community to allow married deaconesses to serve in their office "as long as, in the opinion of the Sisters Council, they are available for full-time service" (*DCBM, October 1969*, 7; and *BCECV-ECM, June 1969*, 2).

176. Apparently, cost was one factor in this decision since the Deaconess Board had been subsidizing the program with an annual grant of $25,000. See *DCBM, January 1968*, 3; and *June 1970*, 4.

177. *DCBM, January 1972*, 4.

178. *LCAM, 1970*, 440–41.

179. *LCAM, 1972*, 600. The Executive Council had discussed the question of a study at four meetings during the biennium and had approved the experimental steps in February 1972 (*ECM*, 524–25).

180. Frederick Weiser points out that the deaconesses serving on the task force making the study went on record early as being in favor of admitting men to the diaconate. See *To Serve the Lord and His People*, 37.

181. *LCAM, 1966*, 627, 742–43.

182. *Cabinet Minutes, March 21, 1967.*

183. *LCAM, 1968*, 383–84.

184. The Cabinet voted at its April 1969 meeting to recommend this course of action, and the Executive Council concurred. By the time of the 1970 convention, this work was still in process (*LCAM, 1970*, 131–32).

185. *LCAM, 1972*, 110–13. The products of this effort included *The Congregation* (a newspaper dealing with program information for congregational leaders), *Dear Partners* (a newsletter from the president), and *Aids in Mission* (the packet of materials that came to be known as "AIM").

186. Ibid., 133–35.

187. Ibid., 689.

188. Ibid., 144.

189. *LCAM, 1970*, 151.

190. *LCAM, 1972*, 142. Portions of the newscasts were carried in Spanish on stations in Puerto Rico.

191. Ibid., 143–44.

192. *LCAM, 1972*, 143–44; and *ECM, October 1970*, 65.

193. *LCAM, 1970*, 191–92.

194. Ibid., 193.

195. The *LCA Bylaws*, Section XVIII, Item 3c, required that this be done.

196. *LCA Bylaws*, Section XVIII, Item 3.

197. The only synod that consistently met or exceeded its apportionment was South Carolina. In 1972 Rocky Mountain became the second synod to do so. The information about synodical benevolence records during the preceding year was published each year in one of the issues of *The Lutheran*, usually in February.

198. *LCAM, 1970*, 248. The amount was so small that it was decided it would cost more to bring together an allocation commission to distribute it than it was worth.

199. *LCAM, 1970*, 234–35.

200. *LCAM, 1970*, 248–51, provides the rationale and details of the plan. In 1969 it was reported that 34.6 percent of the congregations had contributed 100 percent or more of benevolence, which was down from 42.3 percent in 1967 when a special "New Life Offering" was included (ibid., 153).

201. See *1970 Convention Summary*, 5.

202. *LCAM, 1970*, 692, 752. The BWM had for years had a program where gifts could be made specifically for missionary support, and many congregations took genuine satisfaction in being related to a particular missionary abroad. The board reported that $325,000 had been designated in this way in 1969 (ibid., 631).

203. Ibid., 427, 464, 556.

204. *LCAM, 1972*, 66.

205. *LCAM, 1974*, 704.

206. Sibley, *Planning*, 11.

207. The system that the LCA developed established "person-day costs" for each staff position (which varied among agencies) and a projection of the number of days required for each project. Since much churchwide agency work tends to be staff intensive, this gave a helpful basis for estimating

project costs. Staff were required to account for their time, and these reports were an important part of evaluating whether a project was on target or over budget. Sibley describes this process which became an accepted part of LCA budgeting (*Planning*, 12–13).

208. The complete process is described by Sibley, who chaired the task force (ibid., 11–14).

209. *LCAM, 1972*, 209–19.

210. The budgets presented at Dallas had to be arranged both according to the existing agency structure as well as how they would appear if the church chose to realign agencies according to the proposals of the Commission on Function and Structure.

211. Marshall described his thinking on this subject and its relation to restructuring of the church in an interview conducted by the writer at the LCA headquarters in New York, October 23, 1986.

212. The changes to the LCA Bylaws in Section XVIII, Items 3d and e, provided as an exception that a synod's responsibility could be adjusted through mutual agreement in a consultation.

213. *LCAM, 1972*, 361–62, 725. See also *1972 Convention Summary*, 12.

214. The writer was a member of many consultation teams through the years, but the initial round following the Dallas decision was exceptionally challenging.

215. George A. Lindbeck, an LCA professor at Yale Divinity School, raised some of the issues in "Ecumenism: Foundations, Principles, Policies," one of the chapters in *Major Issues for the Lutheran Church in America*, an unpublished and undated resource book supplied to the Commission on Function and Structure as a follow-up to *Significant Issues for the Seventies*. The book consisted of a dozen essays by leading authorities in fields such as theology, sociology, political developments, life sciences, and human sexuality. Lindbeck, in effect, was questioning whether the church needed to rethink its traditional stance of placing inter-Lutheran concerns above ecumenical action. He also raised the possibility that at times the LCA might need to support non-Lutheran work that is not ecumenical in order to advance the total cause of Jesus Christ in the world (pp. 154–75).

216. President Marshall described this progression in the LCA Constitution in a carefully nuanced part of his first report to the church in Minneapolis (*LCAM, 1970*, 30–31).

217. Nelson, "New Shape of Lutheranism," 530. At the same time, ALC had made the same declaration regarding Missouri.

218. *ECM, October 1969*, 436–37. The ALC had acted in its churchwide convention in October 1968, but the decision had to be ratified by the eighteen districts. This was done by a 92.1 percent majority.

219. *1972 Convention Summary*, 4–5.

220. President Marshall had pointed out in his own report to the Dallas convention that there were basic differences in polity between ALC and LCA. However, he concluded that the proposals of the Commission on Function and Structure would not harm inter-Lutheran relations but would facilitate them (*LCAM, 1972*, 34–35).

221. Nelson, "New Shape of Lutheranism," 537.

222. The announcement was sent to the LCA by President K. Holfeld of the ELCC. The complete resolution included an acknowledgment not only of the many forms of cooperation already underway but also of the fact that the LCA convention in 1966 had declared, during the time that the ELCC was still a part of ALC, that the LCA would welcome pulpit and altar fellowship (*LCAM, 1970*, 334–35).

223. *1970 Convention Summary*, 6.

224. *LCAM, 1970*, 550.

225. *ECM, October 1971*, 474–75.

226. *1970 Convention Summary*, 10.

227. The LCA Executive Council made such a declaration on behalf of the church in accordance with Article II, Section 5 of the LCA Constitution (*ECM, February 1971*, 220–34). A full report of the assembly and the LCA responses to actions appears in the *LCAM 1972*, 294–307.

228. John Reumann describes the changes in the makeup of the Commission on Studies and the methodology of its work during the period following Évian in "Identifying the Church," *The Church Emerging*, 8–14.

229. The assembly resolution on "Lutheran World Federation's Role in World Missions" appears in the *LCAM, 1972*, 300–1.

230. The report of the USA National Committee of LWF to the 1972 LCA convention is a helpful analysis of the implications of the Fifth Assembly's decisions for the churches in the United States. See *LCAM, 1972*, 659–64.

231. *LCAM, 1970*, 276. Television crews were present to record the demonstrations; and at one point, a reporter urged the dissidents to restage part of the action because the cameraman had missed it. The writer was a delegate to the assembly and witnessed the events.

232. Robert J. Marshall, *Evaluation of Relationship of LCA with NCCCUSA* (New York: DWME, 1985), 17.

233. *LCAM, 1970*, 284.

234. The first woman president of NCCCUSA, Cynthia Wedel, was elected in 1969, and the first woman general secretary, Claire Randall, in 1973. Minority staff members grew in number from 8.3 to 17 percent in three years, and the number of women on staff increased from 16.7 to 23 percent. The first Black president, W. Sterling Cary, was elected in 1972. See Nathan VanderWerth, *The Times Were Very Full* (New York: NCCCUSA, 1975), 86; and *LCAM, 1974*, 293–98.

235. *LCAM, 1972*, 284–88. The minutes give the full text of the Executive Council's detailed response to all proposed changes.

236. Robert Marshall describes the pros and cons of having persons on NCCCUSA decision-making bodies who are not chosen by the churches in *Evaluation of Relationship of LCA with NCCCUSA*, 23–24.

237. *LCAM, 1970*, 264–65.

238. At the 1970 LCA convention, Eugene Smith, executive of the USA Conference of the WCC, described the problems the Council was confronting, not the least of which was whether the WCC was an organization of *churches* (*Convention Summary*, 6). At Dallas in 1972, H. Ober Hess, an

LCA member of the Central Committee, interpreted the work of the WCC but spoke of "his concern for the lessening of the use of the representative principle, since there are now a number of 'floating' or 'free-lance' delegates who do not represent member churches" (*Convention Summary*, 9).

239. The officers and their terms are listed in Appendix C.

240. Synodical presidents/bishops are listed in Appendix D.

241. BCECV had three different executives; Publication, two; BTE, two; BSM, two; BWM, three; Church Papers, two; COE, two; PRT, two; COS, three; CW, two; CYA, two. A complete roster of the LCA executives through the years appears in Appendix E.

242. Actually, the only way in which boards could enter into cooperative arrangements with one another that were not spelled out in the constitution was by seeking approval first from the Executive Council.

243. The Cabinet was not of one mind about the need for a study. Although the Cabinet had requested of the Executive Council in October 1969 that an outline be developed for a study, the proposal drafted by an ad hoc committee of its own members appointed by the president was debated for more than five hours at a meeting in April 1970 before it was transmitted to the officers and the Executive Council. See *ECM, October 1969*, 497; *January 1970*, 662, 726–32; *April 1970*, 769–74; *June 1970*, 938–39.

244. The writer confirmed this in an interview with Robert Marshall in which the former president described the factors that led him to this point of view.

245. *LCAM, 1970*, 402–5, describes the rationale, basic methodology, timetable, and budget. The convention actions are on pp. 45–52. Several synodical memorials were also referred to the Commission by the convention.

246. Members of the Commission were Myrl E. Alexander, Thyra Fischer, Wesley J. Fuerst, Melvin Hammerberg, Melvin E. Hansen, Roger Peterson, Robert S. Romeis, Arthur L. Ruths, Kenneth H. Sauer, G. Frederick Schott III, William N. Smith, Victor Ursaki, Royall Yount, Franklin N. Zimmerman, and W. H. Ziehl, chairperson. The balance in the Commission was interesting. There were eight lay persons (one of whom was Black) and seven clergy. There were two synodical presidents, four parish pastors, one seminary professor, a criminologist, two businessmen, an educator, a synodical staff member, a state senator, a homemaker, and the deputy comptroller of the United Nations.

247. A five-person committee was named from the Cabinet of Executives to arrange for the necessary staff services required for carrying out Commission assignments. The chairperson of the group was W. Kent Gilbert, who was permitted to attend Commission meetings in order to understand what was needed from staff.

248. From a review by Gordon K. Kaufman quoted by Reumann in *The Church Emerging*, 2.

249. The Commission even made an effort to solicit views from those not directly involved in the church, particularly to learn what it could about reasons for their disaffection. The five principles listed appear in *Report of the Commission on Function and Structure* (New York: LCA, 1972), 11.

250. This was particularly important with regard to the ALC, which had begun a study in 1966 that resulted in a restructuring of that body in many ways similar to the new structure for LCA. In *Toward Greater Effectiveness in Mission,* a preliminary report on a proposal for new structures in the ALC national offices, President Kent S. Knutson cited the importance of these steps for relationships between the two churches. "It appears," he wrote, "that this present proposal will bring us several steps closer to a common structure in the national offices." See his report issued March 15, 1972, under the above title.

251. The results were summarized in a document, *Report of 1970 Regional Panel Meetings and Synod President Interviews* (New York: Commission on Function and Structure, 1971), which was circulated only to those directly involved. The major task of analysis of this and later data-gathering efforts was done by the Research Department of BPE. The same panels (with some additions to provide a better representation of youth, minorities, and women) were convened again in October 1971 to review the preliminary report of the Commission. All reports and documentation relating to the Commission on Function and Structure are in the LCA Archives in Chicago.

252. The analysis was produced in a document of almost two hundred pages, *Survey of Issues for Function and Structure* (Philadelphia: BPE, LCA, 1971). The volume contains not only a rank-ordering of responses on a 0-5 scale but also extensive cross-tabulations by such categories as various age-groups, parish pastors, lay persons, and various geographical regions. As might be expected, the largest variations in ranking of the importance of issues tended to come among age-groups. Generally, the differences among geographical regions were not dramatic.

253. Ibid., Appendix A, 4, 17. The low ranking regarding a separate church in Canada was probably, but not entirely, the result of the smaller number of Canadians than persons from the United States in the sample.

254. These reports included *Major Issues for the Lutheran Church in America* (which was the analysis referred to earlier that was prepared by a panel of specialists as a follow-up to *Significant Issues for the Seventies); Decision Making in the Lutheran Church in America* (the study by Lloyd Sheneman); *Financial Trends in Churchwide Agencies and Synods; Personnel Trends in Churchwide Agencies and Synods;* and *Consultation on the Role of Institutions in the Corporate Life of the Lutheran Church in America.* It was clear that the Commission wanted as much in the way of background studies and objective information as it could obtain.

255. The task forces averaged seven members and were made up of persons with some special knowledge of the area under discussion. One member of the Commission related to each group, and a staff member acted as recorder. The complete list of task force members appears in *Report of CFS,* 86–87.

256. See *Preliminary Report of the Commission on Function and Structure* (Philadelphia: Board of Publication, 1971).

257. All of this material was analyzed in *Survey of Responses to the Preliminary Report of the Commission on Function and Structure* (Philadelphia: Board of Parish Education, 1972).

258. *Preliminary Report,* 17–18; *Survey of Responses,* 65.

259. *Preliminary Report,* 25.

260. *Preliminary Report,* 33; *Report of CFS,* 26.

261. *Survey of Responses,* 16–20.

262. *Preliminary Report,* 39–42; *Survey of Responses,* 29–33.

263. *Preliminary Report,* 46.

264. *Preliminary Report,* 46–49; *Survey of Responses,* 40–45.

265. *Preliminary Report,* 43–45; *Survey of Responses,* 33–40.

266. *Preliminary Report,* 50–55; *Survey of Responses,* 45–48.

267. *Preliminary Report,* 55–60; *Survey of Responses,* 48–52. The financial operations of the Board of Publication were not included because it functioned as a business, and the Board of Pensions retained its corporate status because of fiduciary factors. BAM remained a corporate shell, largely to handle such things as the Church Property Fund and Mission Development Certificates. The other boards ceased to be incorporated, partly because it was believed this gave them too much autonomy.

268. *Preliminary Report,* 60–63; *Survey of Responses,* 51–52.

269. *Preliminary Report,* 63–65; *Survey of Responses,* 52–54.

270. *Preliminary Report,* 66–69; *Survey of Responses,* 54–63, 65.

271. *Report of the Commission on Function and Structure* (New York: LCA, 1972), 15–16. The final report also appears in the *LCAM, 1970,* 463–541.

272. *Report of CFS,* 16.

273. The section dealing with churchwide functions and structures appears in *Report of CFS,* 32–43.

274. The name "management committee" proved to be a source of confusion later because it implied more of a responsibility for administration than a policy-making role.

275. President Marshall himself was not present. The nominees were as follows: DMNA, Kenneth C. Senft; DPL, Louis T. Almen; DPS, W. Kent Gilbert; DWME (not known at that time); OAF, Martin E. Carlson; OC (not known at that time); ORP, John V. Lindholm. Together with Secretary Harkins, this group would become the Staff Executive Team that met monthly with the president primarily for coordination of agency planning and budgeting. At the Executive Council meeting in Dallas, Robert W. Stackel was named to head DWME, but the executive for communications, Howard Sandum, was not chosen until much later. Ralph Eckard, an assistant to the president, headed communications in the interim.

276. *1972 Convention Summary,* 5.

277. Ibid., 11–12. The name for the unit that became DWME had been changed from the time of the first draft to that proposed in the Commission's final report.

278. *LCAM, 1972,* 621.

279. Ibid., 182–88.

280. Ibid., 357–59.

281. *1972 Convention Summary,* 11.

282. *LCAM, 1972,* 36, 728–29.

Chapter 5 | CHALLENGES, VICTORIES, AND CHANGES

THE PERIOD FROM 1973 THROUGH 1978 WAS A strange mixture of highs and lows both for society and church. The world seemed to lurch from one crisis to another in a way that led most people to live in constant anxiety about what new trauma the next day would bring. Even when events gave reason for an upsurge of hope, the mood was usually short-lived and succeeded by a dip into despair. The situations in world affairs, the United States political scene, and the economy serve as examples.

THE WORLD SCENE

So much attention had been focused on Vietnam by the United States that many believed bringing the war there to an end would lead to peace and stability. That dream was shattered in several ways. One was the sudden eruption of hostilities in the Middle East when Egypt and Syria launched a coordinated attack on Israel on Yom Kippur, the holiest day of the Jewish calendar, October 6, 1973. As the Israeli forces were forced back on both fronts with massive losses of materiel, the United States answered an urgent plea from Prime Minister Golda Meir by airlifting to Israel more than two billion dollars in arms. The Israelis counterattacked and, by the time a cease-fire was declared October 24, had advanced within range of Damascus and had surged across the Suez Canal to isolate a large part of the Egyptian army.[1]

The struggle provoked major power saber rattling when Egyptian President Anwar Sadat appealed to the Soviets for help. Secretary Brezhnev urged that both United States and Soviet troops be sent into the Middle East to restore order and warned that otherwise the USSR might act alone. President Nixon countered by putting United States forces on Condition 3 alert and declared that the United States would not accept any unilateral action. "The Kremlin understood perfectly, and the crisis dissipated on the night of October 25 when the Security Council adopted a resolution for a U.N. emergency force" made up of troops from countries not represented on the Council.[2] While an uneasy peace was restored, the struggle took a new turn that was to have ominous consequences over the long term.

Oil now became a weapon as OPEC, led by the Arab states, slashed production, imposed a boycott, and within less than a year had quadrupled prices. The economic results were devastating. While Americans lined up for hours at gasoline stations and worried whether they were going to be able to heat their homes, developing nations were plunged deeper into debt, and inflation grew worldwide. "The Arab producers . . . in one bold stroke altered the flow of international finance."[3] Money flowed from West to East, and it became increasingly clear that determined smaller countries could find various ways of holding the Western powers hostage when they so desired.

War, of course, was hardly a thing of the past. While there seemed to be a nuclear standoff for the time being between the superpowers, there were more than thirty conventional wars in the seventies.[4] After North Vietnam again invaded the South and crushed Saigon in April 1975, it seemed to be a signal for Communist elites to seize power all over Indochina. Perhaps the bloodiest struggle came in Cambodia, where one estimate placed the death toll by executions, battle, displacement, and disease at 1,200,000, or one-fifth of the population.[5] The situation was almost as desperate in Laos.

Africa was also a continent wracked by war. The feudal regime of Haile Selassie was ousted in Ethiopia with the new government exterminating thousands and waging war on neighbors. Nigeria had its civil war.[6] Tanzania sent troops against Idi Amin and his repressive government in Uganda. Cuba dispatched a large expeditionary force to Angola to support the Popular Movement for Liberation in a way that set a pattern for "war by proxy" in Africa.[7] The Gadafy government in Libya exported terrorism and revolution. The people of Namibia struggled for independence from the racist white regime in South Africa. Eritrea, Somalia, Chad, Cameroon, Ghana—the list of trouble spots went on and on so that peace seemed the exception in Africa.[8]

POLITICAL TURMOIL IN THE
UNITED STATES

Although many administrations in the two-hundred-year history of the United States had their share of scandals, there had never been anything to equal the political debacle in the first two years of Richard Nixon's second term. The first blow came when the United States Attorney for Maryland launched an investigation into allegations that Vice-President Spiro Agnew had accepted bribes while he was governor of that state. Faced with possible imprisonment, Agnew pleaded *nolo contendere* on October 10, 1973, to a charge of filing a fraudulent tax return and was fined and placed on probation for three years by the federal court. Agnew resigned and the Justice Department dropped further prosecution, although "it released an extensive account of Agnew's malefactions which, it stated, continued during the period when he was 'only a heartbeat away' from becoming President of the United States."[9] It was the first time that a U.S. official had been forced out of such a high office. On the basis of the Twenty-fifth Amendment, Nixon named the Republican Minority Leader of the House of Representatives, Gerald R. Ford, as Vice-President. Ford's reputation for honesty was welcomed by a public that had been stung by the chicanery in the administration.

The Agnew scandal was only the beginning, however, as attention swung to the story behind the Watergate break-in at the Democratic National Committee's headquarters in June 1972. Nixon had denied knowledge of both the burglary and the subsequent cover-up. When it became known that tapes of conversations existed that might prove the president's involvement, Nixon first claimed "executive privilege," but was ordered by the Supreme Court in a unanimous decision to surrender the tapes. As the sordid story unwound, the House Judiciary Committee voted three bills of impeachment. Faced with the probability that the House would approve the bills, Nixon, on August 9, became the first president in United States history to resign the office.[10] During the whole affair, public cynicism about all Washington politics ran deep and was reflected in opinion polls. "When a majority first expressed the belief that Nixon was lying about Watergate, four out of five also judged him no more corrupt than his predecessors."[11]

Gerald Ford succeeded to the presidency and showed an unaffected style that was a "perfect contrast to Nixon's."[12] On September

8 he granted Nixon a full pardon. Although the action precipitated strong protests, "Ford said he believed history would prove his decision correct."[13] He apparently believed that Nixon had suffered enough from his disgrace and that the nation had best put the whole sorry mess behind it and focus on the future. The national spirit was certainly at a low ebb, and although there was a brief upward surge at the time of the Bicentennial of the signing of the Declaration of Independence in 1976, more stormy times lay ahead.

Ford's rather stodgy administration gave the Democrats a great opportunity to regain the White House in 1976. When James Earl Carter, Jr., was nominated, he held a 33 percent lead over Ford in the polls, but by the election a series of mishaps almost resulted in a Republican victory. In fact, a difference of only a few thousand votes in Ohio and Hawaii would have thrown the electoral college majority to Ford.

The fact that Carter avowed that he was "a born-again Christian" created some concern at home and abroad because no one could be sure how this would influence policy. As it turned out, "Carter altered the policies of his predecessors only moderately."[14] He did make reducing American dependency on foreign oil a goal and established a Department of Energy. He also fulfilled a campaign promise to pardon Vietnam draft evaders, promoted major changes in civil service laws, and persuaded Congress to extend the period for ratification of the Equal Rights Amendment. Blacks were appointed to key government positions, but there was little improvement in dealing with urban decay and unemployment among Black youth. The country staggered under the combined impact of spiraling inflation, a weakening dollar, and high unemployment.[15]

Carter adopted the role of champion of human rights in world affairs that did help to hasten the downfall of some despotic regimes, such as that of the Shah of Iran, but the question remained as to whether the Khomeini-led Islamic Republic that followed was even worse.[16] Carter was successful in effecting the Camp David Accord that brought a settlement between Egypt and Israel. A dramatic symbol of the accord came when Egyptian President Sadat stepped aground at the Jerusalem Airport in November 1977 and thus became the first Egyptian head of state to set foot on Israeli soil since the founding of the country in 1948.[17] An equally significant moment came in December 1978 when Carter went on television to announce that the United States and the People's Republic of China had agreed to mutual recognition, which led to a greater normalizing of relations.[18] Although many conservatives were angered, a White House press officer said, "The idea of our not having relations with nearly a billion people is just ridiculous." Most people seemed to agree.

INFLATION, DEMOGRAPHICS, AND ALL THAT

The OPEC upward pressure on oil prices, domestic tensions in many countries, dislocation of people because of wars, and a host of factors combined to make the late seventies one of the most unsettled periods economically since the Great Depression. The Dow Jones Industrial Average, a widely watched barometer, closed above the 1,000 mark for the first time in history on November 14, 1972, but by January 1973 began a nosedive that reached a low of 577 in December 1974.[19] For the person on the street, however, what was more pertinent was the increase in inflation and unemployment that had become worldwide problems.

By the end of the decade, a new word, *stagflation,* was coined in the United States to describe "spiraling prices accompanied by a stagnant economy and severe unemployment."[20] The double-digit increases in the consumer price indexes and interest rates in the United States and Canada, of course, paled in comparison to triple-digit figures in countries such as Israel and Argentina. The United States, which had long prided itself on having the world's highest living standard, found itself eclipsed by no fewer than six Northern European countries.[21] Meanwhile, Japan was rising as a new economic power in the Far East. Most people were amazed when a country that had been devastated in World War II had total exports of over a billion dollars in 1962.[22] By 1975, however, the United States had a trade deficit with Japan of 2.8 billion dollars, a figure that would escalate to 58.6 billion in a little over a decade.[23]

Industrial workers particularly began to discover that their jobs were being lost to competition overseas. "Labor took hard knocks in the 1970s. Union membership as a proportion of total non-agricultural labor force declined—from 33.2 percent in 1955 to 25 percent in 1970 to 21 percent in 1980."[24] At the same time, the labor force was becoming unbalanced for two other reasons. First, the products of the postwar baby boom were coming onto the job market at the same time that the birthrate had dropped below the replacement level.[25] Second, the United States continued to be a haven for immigrants, many of whom lacked skills.[26] As usual, women, minorities, and youth bore the brunt of unemployment, but this time Vietnam veterans were an additional group experiencing discrimination. The farm and the oil patch were bright spots in the employment and economic picture, but that situation was destined to change in the eighties.

What impact did all this have on the churches? A great deal! As the energy crisis hit, congregations were faced with not only increased costs for fuel but also the need to remodel old, inefficient church buildings. As incomes declined, jobs disappeared, and costs spiraled, many parishes found it necessary to keep more funds at home and commit less to benevolence. At the same time, synods and the church-at-large were faced with the same cost increases and proportionately less income. A particularly grim problem for American missions resulted from the fact that much of the money for the Church Property Fund, which when borrowed was tied to the double-digit prime interest rate charged by banks, had been lent to congregations at minimal rates.

THAT SECOND HORSEMAN OF
THE APOCALYPSE

Famine had stalked humanity throughout history, but the sheer immensity of the problem in the 1970s was staggering. In spite of the temporary relief given by the "Green Revolution" of the 1960s, world food stocks in 1974 dropped to a precarious level. Only a thirty-three-day supply of food stood between humanity and mass starvation.[27] Hard hit were the sub-Saharan region of Africa, where more than 100,000 persons died in a prolonged drought, and India, where 929,000 starved to death in the three states of Bihar, Orissa, and Uttar Pradesh. The United Nations World Food Conference in 1974 estimated that 460 million persons were undernourished, a condition which inevitably brought birth defects and disease. As usual, the heaviest burden was borne by the poor, the old, and the very young. The Western world, with its relief agencies and churches, struggled to help in what seemed a losing battle that would drag on into the eighties with devastating results.

THE RELIGIOUS CLIMATE

It is difficult to characterize the place of religion in the seventies without running the risk of caricature. At the same time, it is apparent that certain forces were on the rise. A newly militant Islamic fundamentalism was on the march in Africa and the Middle-East. There was even the ominous reality that sects that designated themselves "Christian" or "Muslim" raised private armies to advance their causes in Lebanon. In Latin America, Liberation Theology was often linked to neo-Marxist political concepts.[28]

As youth in North America became disillusioned about traditional Christianity, there was an upsurge of interest in Eastern religions, and cults were often accused of using duress and brainwashing to win converts.

More pervasive was what Robert N. Bellah had called "civil religion," a controversial concept that he himself indicated grew to mean many things beyond anything he had meant by the term.[29] It did reflect a tendency to link quasi-religion and a kind of "liturgical significance" to patriotic practices. It was not confined to any one religious group and frequently was accepted by even those who did not regard themselves as part of a religious group. Interestingly, as fundamentalist Christian groups prospered in the United States, they were frequently linked to the patriotic fervor that grew out of a certain type of "civil religion." For the most part, mainline Protestant churches continued to experience declines in membership and support.

THE LCA FACES THE PROBLEM

As was true of many churches at the time, the Lutheran Church in America was wrestling with its own identity in a period of profound social change and widespread erosion of confidence in the relevance of traditional Christianity to the world in which people had to live. Like most mainline denominations, the LCA had gone through a lengthy process of restructuring in the quest for greater efficiency and effectiveness in fulfilling its mission.

Now, President Marshall urged at the 1972 convention that it was time for the church to "search and study and agree upon key affirmations of faith. They should be affirmations stated in such a manner as can motivate us to Christian life and work significant for our time.

We need to say clearly, for our own understanding and for our witness to the world, who we are as Christians, what is our church's reason for being, what the power is that moves us, and where it directs us."[30]

Studying Theological Affirmations

The study of theological affirmations mandated by the LCA's Dallas convention had two important consequences. Not only did it help bring into perspective the church's theological position for the future; it also brought to a high level of visibility two men who were to play an important role in the unfolding of that future. Not long after the 1972 action, a consulting committee of fifteen persons was chosen to oversee the study, and William H. Lazareth, dean of the Philadelphia Seminary and a systematician, was appointed to direct the work. The committee itself was chaired by James R. Crumley, Jr., pastor of Ascension Lutheran Church in Savannah, Georgia.[31]

The objectives of the study were ambitious in seeking to develop for the convention key affirmations:

1. To motivate Christians meaningfully to relate their faith to the crucial issues of life;
2. To reinterpret the distinctive heritage and calling of the LCA among other Christian churches in serving God's mission in and to the contemporary world; and
3. To serve a fundamental role in a mode of operation where theological evaluations (a) influence planning and decision making in the congregations, synods, and churchwide agencies of the LCA and (b) contribute to the shaping and restructuring of society at large.[32]

The process used to initiate the study was an interesting one. One hundred congregations were sent an audiocassette with the request that the pastor lead a recorded discussion with a representative group of lay persons in which they would express concerns and questions about their faith. The results often showed the depth of the faith of these lay persons, but also revealed their confusion in trying to relate their beliefs to the uncertain world of the seventies. The many hours of recordings were analyzed by researchers who supplied the information to the committee as a basis for their work.[33] The director visited all of the LCA's seminaries to consult the faculties, met for a full day with the Conference of Synodical Presidents, and spoke to more than fifteen thousand people at meetings of twenty-one synods and sixteen churchwide agencies and organizations as the study unfolded.

Case Study Method

In order to help people come to grips with the issues that had been identified in a meaningful way, a three-session discussion guide entitled *Exploration in Faith* was sent to each congregation with the request that reactions be registered on a questionnaire. The discussions were to deal with six case studies based on actual experiences of persons in the original one hundred congregations. The case studies had been correlated with the articles of the Apostles' Creed and appropriate parts of Luther's Small and Large Catechisms. Some 38,000 people participated, and more than ten thousand questionnaires were returned from over a thousand congregations. The data gathered also included diary reports from many participants, more tape recordings of discussions, and thousands of prayer petitions written on a special Sunday bulletin.

Careful analysis of the data showed that while many divergent theological views were held, they were "generally within the evangelical norms of the Holy Scriptures and the Lutheran Confessions."[34] The greatest difficulty that people seemed to have was how to relate their Sunday faith and their Monday world. As Lazareth wrote in the report, "We sometimes see Christ in the heavens on Sunday, but we don't know how to recognize him in a brother or sister on Monday. We need help in moving from the heavens above to the earth below. We begin to think that the church is a Sunday kingdom of God, and the world is some other kind of kingdom. Sunday and the church are sacred; Monday and the world are secular. We need to move from worship to service. . . . Lutherans are well versed in the Second Article of the Creed, that Jesus saves, but they are confused about the First Article, that God creates, and about the Third Article, that the Spirit sanctifies. Many bumper stickers say, 'Jesus saves,' but none says, 'God creates.' "[35]

Affirmation in Baptism

The key concept that emerged from the study was that the unifying theme for the LCA should be affirmation of our life together in Baptism. It concluded that "too many believe that the baptismal sacrament is solely a rite rather than the introduction to the sacramental life. They see the sacrament as a moment of magic rather than as a beginning of the daily dying and living of the Christian life. Baptism holds many implications for life in the world that aren't coming through. It has an ethical commitment we need to recover. . . . It tells the church who it is and what its vocation is. It unifies the personal, communal, and universal aspects of the church. By studying and affirming their baptismal faith and life, LCA members could express partnership in Christ and obedience to the work of God in the world."[36]

The consulting committee, therefore, proposed *An Order for Affirming Our Life Together in Baptism* that would serve the three-fold purpose of congregational worship, education in the congregation, and planning for congregations, synods, and church-wide agencies.[37] The consulting committee's proposals were adopted by the Baltimore convention of the LCA with minor amendments and additions.[38] The order itself was used in the closing worship of the convention, with delegates and visitors alike joining in the affirmation.

CHALLENGES AND CHANGES
IN LEADERSHIP

For the first time in LCA history and in that of some of the predecessor bodies, a pastor announced on May 1, 1974, that he would campaign openly for the presidency of the church. On April 18, Wallace E. Fisher, pastor of the Lutheran Church of the Holy Trinity, Lancaster, Pennsylvania, wrote to President Marshall informing him of his intention to release a formal statement of candidacy and platform. Fisher also invited Marshall to discuss this platform at synodical conventions and other meetings throughout the church.[39]

In his reply, Marshall informed the candidate, "As in former instances, so now, I will not seek election, but will accept it only if it occurs by the will of others, registered by vote at the convention."[40] The president went on to explain that he would be willing to meet with Fisher in "a personal conference" but that his own participation in the five synodical conventions he planned to attend would be "restricted to the role of the official representative of the church. . . . I will not champion a personal platform."

Fisher, who was well known as a preacher, lecturer, and writer, strongly questioned "the LCA President's managerial style of leadership" and said, "The President's Report is in effect a corporation

Wallace E. Fisher addressing the 1974 convention

report to the stockholders."[41] He stressed the need for a "pastoral-priestly-prophetic-enabler style of ministry" and promised to administer the LCA as a continental *congregation.* "Over the last two decades," he said, "the LCA has become an aggregation of vested interests increasingly isolated from congregations. Depersonalizing administration fosters this."[42]

The campaign generated lively discussion throughout the church and resulted in some changes in convention procedures. In response to a memorial from the Wisconsin-Upper Michigan Synod, the LCA convention adopted a motion that in the event of there being no election on the first ballot for president, candidates receiving more than 5 percent of the votes be granted an opportunity to address the convention before a second ballot.[43] Later that afternoon, the report of the Committee on the Conduct of Elections indicated that Marshall had received 339 votes and Fisher 168 on the first ballot. The remaining 121 votes were scattered among thirty-one other persons.[44] Since it would require three-fourths of the votes cast for a first-ballot election, it was declared that the next vote would be taken the following morning.

The LCUSA News Bureau reported that Dr. Fisher, in his presentation to the convention, "dealt with no specific issues as he called upon delegates to consider the importance of 'experience of the ministry of Word and Sacrament where the church meets the world —in the local parish.' "[45] He stressed that the church must face up to crises in today's world, such as war, pollution, waste of resources, and the danger that the nature of life itself might be changed. Dr. Marshall said the number one issue facing the church was the confessional issue of the church's own identity, which had led to the church-wide study of theological affirmations. He also laid emphasis upon the LCA's ecumenical responsibilities.[46]

The delegates immediately voted, and about two hours later the Committee on the Conduct of Elections reported that Marshall had received 534 votes and Fisher 107, with 446 required for election.[47] Following a standing ovation by the delegates, President Marshall said, "I am grateful for the applause and for those who voted for me. I want to assure those who did not cast their votes for me of my great respect for them and their place in the church, and the place for differences of opinion in the church. And above all, I wish to express my commitment to working with all the people of the church—those who agree, and those who disagree; those who change my mind, and those who are gracious enough to let me change theirs on occasion —simply because we are all committed to having God change our selves."[48]

Electing the Other Officers

Although L. Milton Woods was reelected treasurer on the first ballot by an overwhelming majority, the selection of a secretary was another matter.[49] Two factors entered into the latter election. One factor was the decision of George Harkins, who had served six years as secretary, to resign and accept the position of general secretary of the Lutheran Council.[50] The other was a proposal in the Report of the Committee for the Study of the Convention and Other Organizational Matters (promptly labeled "TCFTSOTCAOOM goes Boom!") that the secretary could be either clergy or lay and could serve either full- or part-time. "If these changes were adopted," the committee said, "the office could be more similar to that of the treasurer than to the office of the president."[51] Delegates were concerned that the position they had regarded as the second highest office in the church be reduced to something akin to clerical help and voted that the secretary continue to be full-time but did open the way for the possibility of a lay person to serve in the future.[52] The 1974 convention, however, did make its choice on the basis of the secretary's being ordained.

Once the ground rules had been established about the nature of the office, the ecclesiastical balloting for secretary began, with eighty-nine persons nominated on the first round.[53] Both of the persons who had been so prominent in the Theological Affirmations Study, William H. Lazareth and James R. Crumley, Jr., received substantial numbers of votes. Lazareth led with 103 votes, and Crumley trailed in third place with forty-nine. It is unlikely that either of them had any thought of being elected secretary on coming to Baltimore.[54] Nevertheless, the process went on with Dr. Lazareth receiving 282 votes on the third ballot, exactly one hundred more than Dr. Crumley. At that point, Dr. Howard Weeg, a well-known pastor in the Pacific Southwest Synod who had received 146 votes, withdrew his name. On the fourth ballot, a complete reversal took place, and Crumley was elected with 333 votes, just eleven more than the majority needed. Lazareth's total was 287. Few, if any, realized it, but the stage had been set for a rematch in another election four years later.[55]

Rejecting Changes in the Convention

One of the trial balloons that was sent aloft by the Commission on Function and Structure in 1972 was shot down decisively at Baltimore. The CFS had suggested the possibility of changing the size and frequency of conventions with an eye to continuity and more effective decision making. It asked that a special committee be appointed to study this and other organizational matters during the ensuing biennium.

The twelve-person committee selected (TCFTSOTCAOOM) set up a process for discussing and gaining reactions at the 1973 synodical conventions to four possible types of conventions. These included (1) an annual convention of 250, (2) an annual convention of 350, (3) an annual 250-delegate convention with a convocation of 700 every four years, (4) the existing pattern of biennial conventions of 700. The fact that only 4,873 of the 14,000 attending the synodical meetings responded to the questions probably showed that many had greeted the proposals with a stifled yawn. Those who did respond were

James R. Crumley, Robert J. Marshall, L. Milton Woods, elected officers in 1974

William H. Lazareth

widely split in their reactions.[56] What the committee proposed at Baltimore was an annual 300-delegate convention meeting in October. All of the enabling motions were defeated, and the process remained as it had been established when the LCA was formed in 1962.[57] LCA delegates apparently had had it with structural changes for a while.

What About Synodical Presidents?

As early as the Dallas convention in 1972, it was becoming apparent that the influence of synodical presidents was growing, but it was during the following biennium that the Conference of Synodical Presidents made a bid for an expanded role in the LCA decision-making process. At its November 1973 meeting, the Conference adopted a resolution asking for the appointment of a consulting committee to develop a brief for redefinition of its role in decisions, such as those relating to congregations and ministers; priorities, goals, and budgets; ecumenical and inter-Lutheran relations; social and moral issues; the interface between synods and churchwide agencies. The intention was that appropriate amendments would be introduced at the Baltimore convention.[58]

The proposed amendment that came to the Executive Council from the committee in April 1974 was far-ranging and would have added an item "b" to Article VIII, Section 13, of the LCA Constitution reading:

b. It shall be within the powers of the conference to:
  1) Develop the agenda for its meetings, which shall include:
    a) Scholarly theological presentations for discussion.
    b) Means for nurturing spiritual and professional growth.
    c) Opportunities for the presidents to counsel together about their work.
    d) Dialogue with the president of the church and the chief executive officers of the churchwide agencies or their appointees.
    e) Briefing on new materials and programs.
    f) Other program elements to enable fulfillment of the powers of the conference.
  2) Review present priorities and consider long-range policies, goals, and strategies in order to give advice and make recommendations to the Executive Council.

3) Review proposals from churchwide agencies and the Executive Council and provide advice on:
   a) Policies and programs affecting congregations, ministers, and synods.
   b) Statements on social and theological issues.
   c) Program budgets of the church and synodical commitments to it.
4) Indicate the needs of synods to the Executive Council.
5) Agree on the method for cooperation in recommending ministers for call outside the territory of the synod in which they are located.[59]

The Executive Council was concerned that the amendment would not only set formal procedures in concrete in a restrictive way but also delay such matters as development of budgets and spending authorizations in an untimely manner. The Executive Council, therefore, suggested that the list under "b" be commended to the Conference as guidelines.[60]

When the whole matter was presented to the 1974 convention, it was recommended that a joint committee from the Executive Council and the Conference study the question before final action on an amendment would be taken in 1976. At that point, a delegate proposed that the pending amendment be regarded as a "rule of procedure" during the next biennium, and this was adopted.[61] As a result, the Conference began to function with the broadened scope of responsibilities before it.

The process did prove cumbersome, especially when the synodical presidents were presented with the mountains of material that went into developing the detailed program budgets of churchwide agencies. By its March 1976 meeting, the Conference concluded that a constitutional amendment was not needed and that slightly scaled down rules of procedures would suffice. It requested that the Executive Council report this to the convention, and the proposed constitutional amendment died a quiet death in Boston.[62] The fact remained, however, that the role of the Conference of Synodical Presidents had been greatly strengthened from what had been envisioned at the formation of the LCA.

CHURCH AND SOCIETY

Although the LCA continued to work at articulating its position on social issues, there actually were no new statements adopted between 1972 and 1978. The newly formed Division for Mission in North America, however, did establish a major department on church and society, which included a Center for Ethics and Society.[63] Responding to the Commission on Function and Structure concern about the involvement/noninvolvement of the constituency in the development of earlier social statements, DMNA set as one of its first tasks reexamining the whole purpose of these documents and developing a process to remedy the situation.[64] Although seeking participation and feedback from the LCA membership sometimes meant a more time-consuming procedure, the result tended to be a greater understanding of the issues and acceptance when social statements were brought to the convention.

Meanwhile, DMNA built upon the foundation of earlier statements to undertake implementation/action programs dealing with the human crisis in ecology, amnesty and reconciliation, reform of the criminal justice system, and world community. It also tackled emerging or continuing issues, such as legal recourse by victims of crime, drug abuse, health care insurance, social criteria for investments, and the problem of domestic and world hunger.[65] Special consulting committees were established to address concerns related to women, minority group interests, the aging, and observance of the bicentenary of the United States. These groups tended to focus the church's attention on major issues and bring concrete action proposals for convention decision.

One major new social statement, "Human Rights, Doing Justice in God's World," was adopted by the 1978 convention in Chicago.[66] In some respects, the statement drew together insights from earlier documents, such as those on ecology and world community, but went beyond them in addressing the global human rights issue. Although acknowledging the reasons for hope that recent advances would reduce the scourges of starvation, ill health, and poverty, it underscored such problems as widespread oppression, the growing culture of fear, racism, sexism, discrimination against the handicapped, abridging of the right to practice one's religion, and the use of torture, imprisonment, and terror. It called the church to a confession about belief in the Creator's intention for creation but also our fallen state and our vocation in Christ.[67]

The statement drew a distinction between human rights and the legal entitlements and protections that flow from them. "Human rights," it declared, "are *moral* assertions of what justice demands in particular historical situations. Civil, political, and economic rights

are *legal* guarantees that have been established by governments."[68]
God calls us to serve in this ongoing struggle both as individual
Christians and also corporately as the church. "When temporal authority performs its legitimate function of securing human rights, we
can thankfully support it (Rom. 13:1–7; 1 Peter 2:13f); when it does
not, we can just as freely work for its reform or replacement and, if
need be, disobey or resist it (Rev. 13), accepting the consequences of
such action."[69]

The document then went on to cite specific human rights that
need to be protected including the following: to worship or not to
worship, free expression through verbal or nonverbal communication, protection from efforts to control the mind or debase the person, personal identity, familial rights of parents and children, the
entitlement of older adults to continue as full participants in society,
basic necessities and healthful existence, human sexuality as a gift of
love and generation of life not to be debased, equal access to the
opportunities and resources of society, and many others.

The convention then adopted a series of ten detailed resolutions
based on the statement that dealt with (1) employment, income,
housing, health care, education, and nutrition, (2) institutionalized
populations, (3) refugees, (4) undocumented aliens, (5) children, (6)
torture, (7) political oppression, (8) economic rule, (9) voluntary action, and (10) equality of men and women.[70] The resolutions were,
in effect, a set of guidelines for the church's social action agenda.

What Is a Minority?

The restructuring of the LCA provided new ways of dealing with the
needs of racial and ethnic groups through the creation of a Consulting Committee on Minority Group Interests and an interagency staff
team that were related to DMNA. Although there could be little
disagreement about the size and seriousness of the problems in society, proceeding in a way that would be most helpful to the persons
involved sometimes proved difficult and frustrating for the church.
Well-intentioned efforts often provoked annoyance and even anger
among the so-called minorities themselves. Nomenclature, for example, was regarded in itself a reflection of white racism and insen-
sitivity.

The consulting committee of fifteen was representative of the
Black, Hispanic, Asian, Native American, and Caucasian communities, which was more inclusive than the Coordinating Committee on

Race Relations had been. In connection with the tenth anniversary of the adoption of the LCA's social statement on "Race Relations," the CCMGI presented a resolution to the 1974 convention that questioned the assumptions of accomplishment over the past decade and asked for two major actions. One was a "qualitative as well as quantitative inventory regarding the status of minority persons in the church."[71]

For several years the LCA had not been gathering statistics about minority membership because of the widespread practice of trying to play down racial and ethnic differences as in themselves being discriminatory.[72] When the LCA tried to obtain information from congregations for the inventory, there was strong resistance in many quarters. In some cases, objection was to the term *minority* itself as being inaccurate in a world where Caucasians were really the minority, and indeed this was obviously the case in places such as the Virgin Islands, where there were LCA congregations but relatively few whites.[73] The term "Black" became an issue in some instances, and the category "Oriental" that was originally chosen was challenged by Southeast Asians. Others simply objected to any "nose counting" of this kind on the basis of Paul's injunction in Galatians 3:28. For a while these objections made the CCMGI's efforts more difficult, but as definitions were clarified, more accurate information began to be gathered.

The second proposal was that a task force be created to develop plans and goals for the period until 1984 and report these to the 1976 convention.[74] The CCMGI, in cooperation with others, did arrange for the desired inventory and based its 1976 report on it.[75] On the basis of the categories defined, it was concluded that there were 29,104 persons in the LCA who could be numbered among "minorities."[76] The CCMGI report was highly critical and said that on the basis of the voluminous material presented, "if the LCA is going to give more serious attention to combating institutional racism then it would appear that structural and procedural options other than those presently in existence need to be explored."[77] What it proposed was a department in DMNA, directed by a minority person, that would have the necessary budget and staff time to monitor LCA progress in this area and, in effect, to help establish the necessary goals and criteria. While DMNA did not establish a separate department, it created a position of Director of Minority Concerns attached to the executive office of the division. Massie L. Kennard was selected for this post.[78] With this staff support, the CCMGI was ready with detailed plans at the 1978 convention.

The *Goals and Plans for Minority Ministry, 1978–1984,* as the report was titled, was both comprehensive and challenging. The overall goal was that during this period, "The LCA shall continue to become more inclusive in membership while continuing and expanding its emphasis on justice in society."[79] The report called upon all segments of the church to examine their racism and devise strategies for its elimination so that the LCA might exhibit an understanding of what it means to be the church in a diverse culture.

It set specific numerical goals to be achieved by 1984, such as establishing at least forty congregations in areas with more than 50 percent minority group persons; increasing the number of minority pastors to one hundred, one-third of whom would be serving predominantly white congregations; enlisting sixty minority persons for executive or professional staff positions in CWAs, synods, agencies, and institutions; increasing the number of minority delegates at LCA conventions to at least fifty; appointing at least 5 percent of all members on consulting committees from among minorities; and nominating at least 10 percent minority persons for elective positions. The most debated goal of this kind was one that the LCA set as its aim—an annual growth of 15,000 minority members until the LCA membership reflected the percentage of minority persons in the total population. In defending these goals, the chairperson of CCMGI stressed that the numbers were just that—"goals, not quotas," a term that was to become increasingly controversial in other contexts during the remaining life of the LCA.[80] The report, of course, addressed many concerns other than numbers and provided the church with goals and suggested plans in a wide variety of important areas.[81]

Women in Church and Society

Authorized by the 1972 convention and appointed soon thereafter by President Marshall, the twelve-person Consulting Committee on Women in Church and Society wasted no time in getting to work on an ambitious agenda to give greater recognition and power to women in the church. By the end of the biennium, it had drafted an impressive report to the Baltimore convention that provided for the first time some hard data on the place of women in the church.[82] It had launched surveys of congregations, synods, and CWAs that gave significant insights as to where women were included and excluded from leadership responsibilities. For example, while 55.9 percent of the confirmed membership of the church were women, those on the roll of "active confirmed" outnumbered men by 56.7 to 43.3 percent.[83]

Each biennium new figures were gathered in order to monitor participation by women in roles of leadership. In most instances there was a significant increase over the years, much of which can be attributed to the efforts of the consulting committee and LCW, which usually saw their work as mutually supportive.[84] From 1972 to 1978, women lay delegates to the LCA convention increased from 28.7 to 42 percent, although men still predominated because of the much smaller number of ordained women.[85] The numbers were less favorable at synodical conventions. The committee found that "the representation of women is disproportionately low on church councils and disproportionately high among Sunday Church School and Vacation Church School teachers."[86]

Male dominance in churchwide staff positions was a serious problem, with only twenty out of 169 professional level places held by women in 1978, and eleven of those were in the Division for Parish Services.[87] One small breakthrough had occurred in 1974 when Margaret Krych became the first ordained woman staff person, but by the end of the decade, there still was only one.[88] Of particular importance in giving visibility to the role of women was the selection of Dorothy J. Marple as assistant to the president of the LCA in 1975.[89] The most dramatic overall increase in numbers came in 1980 when many high-level support staff positions were reclassified as professional staff, resulting in the number of women staff jumping to forty-nine, or 22.8 percent of the total.[90]

Looking at Language. There were issues other than numbers, however, that concerned the consulting committee. One was masculine-oriented language in the official documents and worship materials of the church. The 1974 convention had instructed that there be a study of this issue, which was carried out under the aegis of the Executive Council. The Council did have the constitution and bylaws revised to eliminate gender-related language and reported the results to the 1976 convention in Boston as editorial changes.[91]

The questions of theological and liturgical language were more complex. The Executive Council referred the immediate issue regarding approved worship materials to the Division for Parish Services.[92] On the more comprehensive issue, the Council commissioned preparatory work by a theologian and used a study by DMNA on *Theological Issues Related to Men and Women in the Body of Christ* in developing an initial statement on liturgical and theological language. The resulting document, which was transmitted to the convention, indicated that language inevitably reflects the culture in which it is written. Acknowledging the patriarchal character of the society in which the Bible was written, it said, "We need therefore carefully to differentiate between the essential truth being expressed and the culturally conditioned linguistic expression in which it is wrapped."[93] The report went on to point out that a new sensitivity about masculine terms to express generic concepts was emerging. It said that a beginning needed to be made in three areas:

1. "A correction of androcentric imagery by a comprehensive assessment of biblical terminology." Although it said the exact nuances of one language cannot be captured in the syntax of another, it indicated that masculine terms no longer were suitable to refer to all humanity and using them perpetuated unjust stereotypes.

2. "A new look at the gender characteristics of God." Asserting that God is neither masculine or feminine is important, but the limitations of English make references to God difficult. Use of both masculine and feminine metaphors are appropriate. It cautioned, however, that "one symbol which can never be completely eliminated is the designation of God as 'father' by Jesus." It did suggest that historical descriptions of the Trinity need interpretation for greater clarity today.

3. "A re-emphasis of the positive elements of inclusiveness and equality." The way in which we use language, it said, is an indication of our commitment to full human community in church and world.[94]

Although the Executive Council had laid out an agenda for future study, the language question would occur again and again in the life of the LCA, often generating heated controversy.

The Equal Rights Amendment. The Consulting Committee on Women in Church and Society, along with many others in the LCA, was solidly behind ratification of the ERA. The 1972 convention had, in fact, gone on record in favor of the amendment.[95] One point at which the whole matter came to prominence was in the selection of Chicago as the site of the 1978 convention. It was not known at the time that Illinois would be one of the states that would vote against ratification, but when this did happen, there was vigorous objection to holding an LCA convention in that state.[96] In order to register their opposition, 144 delegates asked that their names be recorded in the minutes as objecting to holding the meeting in a state that had rejected ERA.[97] By 1980 a policy was set that committed the LCA to holding its conventions only in states that had ratified ERA.[98]

The Cause of the Aging

One of the special groups that was beginning to receive belated attention in the LCA was the aging. In October 1973 the church held its first Convo on Aging that brought together two hundred persons to stress a positive concept of the aging process and to foster a more constructive attitude toward older people in society.[99] The Convo's proposals resulted in forming a Consulting Committee on Aging that brought its first report to the Boston convention.[100] The work of the committee resulted in a barrage of materials intended to sensitize the church to the issues, including a study book, *A Theological Basis for Ministry to and with Older Adults;* a multimedia packet, *A Ministry with Older Persons;* a handbook for parishes, *Aging Persons in the Community of Faith;* and a host of articles in church periodicals.

By 1978 DMNA was prepared with a social statement on "Aging and the Older Adult."[101] The statement was critical of the unnecessary restrictions placed on the elderly by society and the negative image often conveyed in the media. After laying a theological groundwork that emphasized the Christian view of aging as one in which God gave reason for hope and joy at every stage of life, the statement set forth an agenda for action. It stressed that many older persons continue to learn, are open to new ideas, enjoy a variety of interpersonal relationships, and can engage in constructive activity. The document then called upon families, congregations, synods, social service agencies, colleges, and seminaries to work for the dignity of the elderly and to give them the opportunity to use their experience and skills in service. It addition, it recognized that there are special needs of many older persons that must be understood and met at all of these levels. It called on the church to reexamine its own policies regarding retirement of pastors and other workers and bring the results of this reconsideration back to the 1980 convention. It also defined a series of public policy goals that the church should advocate to assure justice for the elderly.

New Recognition for the Laity

Although the laity had always been a source of strength for Lutheranism in North America, the seventies were a period when a new awareness of the meaning of "the whole people of God" began to emerge. As a follow-up to the Dallas convention, the Division for Parish Services reported on a study of lay ministry at the congregational level in 1974.[102] The research showed that, although many lay people were eager for involvement in the congregation's life, they felt that there was insufficient recognition of their potential and inadequate attention to recruiting, development, and support of lay leadership. Lay members often felt excluded from major decision-making roles in the church. They saw the importance of the church's mission in and to the world but felt ill equipped for their role. The findings were consistent with those in the Theological Affirmations study; therefore, DPS proposed building upon that base and coordinating all churchwide agency efforts through an interagency staff team.

The Baltimore convention had also asked the Division for Mission in North America to address the issue of the ministry of the laity in its Faith and Life Institutes.[103] In March 1976 an institute was held in Chicago on "The Concerns of the Laity for Their Ministry in the World" that proved to be a watershed event. Those attending the institute issued a statement that included a "Credo and Commitment" and a "Call for Action."[104] The credo began with the sentences "We believe that as lay people within the church, we are called upon to be priests in our ministry in the world. We believe that as Christians with a vocation, we are called to live our total lives in service to God and all people." The call to action challenged the church, its institutions, and its clergy to affirm and increase the support and equipping of the laity for this ministry. It also called upon other lay members of the church to acknowledge their daily ministry in the world and to seek training to enable them in it.

The statement was translated into action at the Baltimore convention when a resolution was adopted that affirmed the report from the institute, commended it to the church at all levels, and asked the Executive Council to assign responsibility to provide for a two-year experimental period and staff support to encourage lay ministry in the world.[105] The result was birth of a movement known as "Laos in Ministry" that was to become increasingly influential in the life of the LCA. The Executive Council authorized funding of $45,000 for the biennium and asked DMNA to provide staff services "until such time as the structural and organizational status of Laos in Ministry is determined."[106]

There were several organizational options for Laos that were explored, such as becoming a "free movement," being assigned as a new program element to DPS, becoming one segment of a new "department on laity" in an existing agency, becoming a new auxiliary, or becoming a voluntary fellowship within the church similar to the Lutheran Laymen's Movement for Stewardship. The Steering Committee of what was now called "LAOS"[107] reported to the Executive Council that the group considered itself a fellowship whose membership consisted of those on its mailing list. It envisioned a minimal organizational structure, consisting of a steering committee, and suggested that the group be related to the LCA through DMNA.[108] LAOS issued a quarterly newsletter called *Monday's Ministers* that went to more than three thousand persons. In order to acquaint seminarians with the problems faced by Christians in the secular work place, week-long programs were conducted in several LCA seminaries. A special study course, *Monday's Ministries*, was developed by DPS for adults.[109] LAOS in Ministry was on its way as a new type of entity in the church's life.

HAUNTED BY THE SPECTER OF HUNGER

Delegates came to the Baltimore convention in 1974 minds filled with pictures of starving people that appeared on television and in the press almost daily. The scourge of famine in a score of countries and the grim statistics were so real that synod after synod sent memorials urging the church to act to relieve the suffering of millions on a scale not known since the days following World War II.[110] The convention did endorse a statement from Lutheran World Relief, *Toward the Development of a United States Food Policy,* that called for massive government intervention to alleviate the crisis and augment the efforts of voluntary organizations.[111]

The delegates, however, were not content to call only governments to account. They also wanted the church itself to take direct action. The Executive Council had proposed that the existing Love

Compels Action Appeal be extended, including both synodical and churchwide projects of the type funded in the past, with an additional avenue provided for giving directly towards alleviating the hunger crisis.[112] A substitute motion was proposed that would have set a specific goal of $9,000,000 for the 1974–76 biennium to be used for direct relief, developing programs to meet endemic needs, sensitization of the constituency to the problem, and advocacy with government. This motion was defeated, however, and the convention voted for the "open-ended appeal" concept.[113]

Following the convention, President Marshall and the Executive Council moved quickly to implement the appeal. A task force was created, objectives were set, and Robert W. Stackel, who had been the executive director of DWME, was named to spearhead the effort.[114] The response was enthusiastic. By April 15, 1976, allocations of $5,819,620 had been made, with the vast bulk of the funds going to direct relief and programs to meet endemic needs through the USA National Committee of LWF, Canadian Lutheran World Relief, DWME, and DMNA. So popular and successful was the appeal that it was extended repeatedly throughout the life of the LCA, with nearly $65,000,000 having been raised and literally millions of suffering persons helped throughout the world by mid-1987.[115] LCA's efforts were paralleled by a vigorous world hunger program in ALC.

Not everything, of course, went flawlessly with the World Hunger Appeal. People at the grass roots, for example, had difficulty sometimes in understanding that long-term development programs were often more beneficial than direct distribution of food to the hungry. Nor was it easy to communicate that advocacy with governmental agencies in support of programs that brought to bear resources far in excess of anything that private agencies could muster was a legitimate church function.[116] Nevertheless, the World Hunger effort not only achieved remarkable direct results both overseas and at home but also changed dramatically the priorities of some churchwide agencies through the years.[117]

FINDING NEW STRENGTH
FOR MISSION

During the mid-seventies severe strains were beginning to show in the LCA's mission enterprises both at home and overseas. Not only was the turbulent world scene a cause but also the very tight financial situation brought about by the twin problems of inflation and shifting patterns of church income. The World Hunger Appeal did provide answers to some problems, but there was a backlog of needs in American missions, world missions, and evangelism that could not be met through the usual means. A root cause of the situation, of course, was the fact that the basic benevolence giving to the church-at-large had lagged from the very beginning of the LCA.[118]

Convention delegates at Baltimore recognized the problem, particularly as it impacted home and world mission work, and they approved a churchwide appeal for these purposes contingent upon a feasibility study and action at the next convention in Boston.[119] The Executive Council recommended that the president appoint a consulting committee to develop the case for the appeal and later authorized employment of a professional fund-raising company to conduct the feasibility study.[120] After an extensive process involving interviews and questionnaires, the consultants concluded that LCA members favored an appeal, although they did not all agree on the methods to be used. The firm proposed that "a very challenging goal would be $25,000,000."[121] By the time of the 1976 convention, the Executive Council was prepared to recommend that the LCA proceed with a minimum goal of $25,000,000 and that Community Counseling Service be engaged to provide the professional help required.[122] A new element beyond home and foreign missions, however, had entered the picture as an objective for the appeal. The LCA was about to enter a joint program of Evangelical Outreach with the ALC, so the Executive Council proposed that the first $25,000,000 in expendable funds be allocated among world missions, mission in North America, and Evangelical Outreach/Media Evangelism in the ratio of 12:12:1.[123]

During a one-hour session at Boston, when the convention met as a "committee of the whole," it became apparent that there were strong elements in the church who were more concerned with lifting the general level of stewardship than in engaging in a special fund drive. The final decision was to proceed with the appeal, now called Strength for Mission, but to use $1,000,000 of the receipts to strengthen the ongoing stewardship responsibilities of members so that the LCA could achieve a $50,000,000 budget by 1980. That seemed a quantum leap at that time, but the motion was adopted. The die was cast.[124]

Although there was some concern that Strength for Mission and the general stewardship effort, known as Intensified Christian Giving, would interfere with one another, such was not the case. David R. Gerberding, a parish pastor, was chosen to direct SFM and began his duties October 1.[125] The whole campaign was a whirlwind affair that involved both a major gifts phase as well as a stage for pledging in the congregations. Literally thousands of people became involved, and it was estimated that more than a million hours of volunteer service were devoted to the cause. By the time for a Service of Thanksgiving at the 1978 convention in Chicago, the director was able to report total pledges to that point of $35,387,411.[126] Many members seemed not only gratified but also a bit surprised at just how much financial strength the LCA had when it chose to flex its muscles.

WORLD MISSION AND ECUMENISM

The impact of the new structure creating a Division for World Mission and Ecumenism began to be felt almost immediately in the way the LCA was able to integrate its work in social ministry overseas with that of inter-Lutheran and interchurch agencies. Most of the LCA's efforts in such areas as social justice, economic self-help, community development, and family life were carried out through LWF World Service, Lutheran World Relief, and WCC World Service. "Prior to 1972 there was little coordination of the LCA's overseas operation through the Board of World Missions and the international interchurch agencies. Bringing together all the overseas relationships into one division—the DWME—was a major step in the direction of integration."[127] This placed DWME in a position not only to participate in the decision-making process but also to monitor the work of the interchurch agencies.

As the DWME sought to define its role during the first biennium of the new structure, it became clear that the division's major focus would be on the global scene outside of North America. The "Statement of Purpose" adopted in 1973 by the management committee, in fact, incorporated the phrase "outside North America" in all but one of six major roles that it envisioned for the division.[128] The emphasis was placed on the interrelationship of proclamation, service, and ecumenism which were seen as mutually supportive and advancing together. What this entailed was developing a holistic design of the "global task of the LCA . . . relating world proclamation, world development, and world relief activities."[129]

The DWME was clearly aware that one of the major objectives in Function and Structure had been to coordinate more fully the activities of the various churchwide agencies within the LCA itself. The division, therefore, presented to the Executive Council in April 1974 a detailed list of how it proposed to work with the other CWAs. Although relationship between the former Board of World Missions and boards such as American Missions and Parish Education had always been cordial in the past, the newly stated principles laid the groundwork for much closer cooperative effort in the future.[130] One symbol of the way in which world mission became a common concern of more than a single agency was the series of churchwide Global Mission Events begun in 1976. These events, which were held annually throughout the life of the LCA, reached thousands of people and underscored dramatically the interdependent relationships of the global mission enterprise.[131]

The DWME also proposed developing principles and guidelines to govern the church's ecumenical, interfaith, and secular relations for submission to the LCA convention for approval.[132] This proved to be a task that would occupy the division's attention in a variety of stages over the next decade.

Although the dream of fully cooperative work in missions overseas by all North American Lutherans was never realized, the ALC and LCA did achieve a close partnership in many areas of the globe. By the Boston convention in 1976, DWME was able to report that the two churches had found ways to coordinate their efforts with those of indigenous churches in Japan, Taiwan, Hong Kong, Tanzania, and Ethiopia.[133] The withdrawal of LCMS from any further negotiations toward a common Lutheran mission agency, Missouri's decision not to support LCUSA overseas projects, and the restructuring of the LWF-USA National Committee, all seemed to bring the ALC and LCA agencies closer and closer together.[134]

Changing Conditions; Changing Strategies

The rapid political and social changes in country after country in the seventies meant that DWME was in a continual process of reassessing its way of carrying out the global mission enterprise. Ethiopia serves as a prime example of how the church can not only survive social upheaval but even grow in the midst of adversity. Late in 1974 Haile Selassie, the feudal monarch of Ethiopia, who had the title "Lion of Judah and Elect of God," was overthrown by a Marxist revolution.

The ancient Coptic Church lost its privileged position. Lands were appropriated, banks and major industries nationalized, young people forced to take part in a "cultural revolution," and a long-lasting civil war waged between the central government and the northern province of Eritrea, which was trying to resist forced assimilation.[135] The LWF's key facility and transmitter for the Radio Voice of the Gospel near Addis Ababa was seized, and the broadcasts of the Christian message to dozens of nations ceased.

Although the Lutheran Evangelical Church Mekane Yesus welcomed some of the social reforms, it too suffered from the repressive tactics and reign of terror unleashed by the government. Its lay president, Emmanuel Abraham, was imprisoned, and the church lost contact with many of its congregations. Adopting a position of self-reliance, however, the ECMY continued a courageous witness and by 1978 was estimated to have 330,000 members—more than thirteen times its number in a little over two decades.[136]

The People's Republic of China was another area in which the Christian church was undergoing dramatic change. Prior to the Cultural Revolution (1966–76), the traditional denominational groups were superseded by the Christian Patriotic Three Self Movement, and many places of worship were reduced and consolidated under pressure from the government's Religious Affairs Bureau.[137] This was widely interpreted as the beginning of a postdenominational era.

As David Vikner points out, "During the turbulent Cultural Revolution, 1966–1976, the Christian churches, along with their religious compatriots and other units of Chinese society, went through a period of internal disruption. All church services were banned. Church properties were expropriated and used for a variety of purposes, such as living quarters, factories, school classrooms, public meeting halls and warehouses. Under the pressures of communist doctrinal purity, intense indoctrination and overt anti-religious activities, even family home worship was difficult."[138]

When the Cultural Revolution failed, a more pragmatic group of leaders took over in the People's Republic. Deng Xiaoping, the primary leader, began to move China in the direction of a more modern and open society. By 1979 the Religious Affairs Bureau was revitalized and gave support to restoring the properties of religious groups and their right to worship. Although the days of the foreign mission enterprise in China were long since gone, Western observers were surprised at the vitality of the Christian community that emerged following the period of repression. In addition to the fact that some two thousand church buildings were reopened within five years, there were an estimated fifty thousand Christian house gatherings all over the country.[139] It was not the familiar church of the past, however, but a new manifestation with much to learn about its new role and much to teach the more traditional churches in the West.

Although in some situations such as China the LCA could only watch and pray and wait, there were other arenas in which missionaries were compelled by the gospel to shift their roles from guests to activists.[140] It became necessary for DWME to issue a set of guidelines to be followed in "oppressive situations." This carefully worded statement underscored the DWME's recognition of the integrity of the churches that found themselves in oppressive situations, and offered to support their struggle for justice in ways they felt appropriate. It recognized that individual missioners in fulfilling their assignments might encounter physical danger, arrest, imprisonment, and deportation. The interests of the host church were to be protected, and the individual missioner would be supported to the limits of the DWME's capacity. It was a time when missioners were confronted with the stark realism of decisions that could prove dangerous.[141]

Mission on Six Continents

The "Mission on Six Continents" concept that had been born in the early seventies began to bear fruit in sometimes surprising ways. Generally speaking, the intent was to drive home that all churches of the world should be not only giving but also receiving churches. This meant ideally that Christians in parts of the world other than Europe and North America would be serving as missionaries in countries such as the United States, and even that financial grants would flow to the affluent West. At first this hope was beyond the resources of the younger churches, but later in the decade the picture began to change.[142]

One of the first evidences of this wider vision of mission was the decision of the Japan Evangelical Lutheran Church to join in a ministry to Japanese immigrants to São Paulo, Brazil.[143] By 1978, however, DWME was able to report that Lutheran churches in East Asia were expressing concern for the spiritual care of their people who had immigrated to Canada and the United States. The Chinese Rhenish Church in Hong Kong subsidized a Chinese-language congregation in Toronto. The Japanese church dispatched pastors to serve in

Florida and California.[144] It was but the beginning of a concrete expression of "global mission."

Meanwhile, the LCA's own sense of mission responsibility was changing. The steady decline in the number of persons sent overseas was slowed and then reversed. In Argentina, where only one American missionary remained in 1976, two additional persons were sent in the next biennium, and the church there was asking for more. Overall, the number of missionaries grew from 151 to 158 from 1976 to 1977. "In the recruiting year, September 1, 1976, through August 31, 1977, the largest number of missioner assignments were filled for any one year, since the LCA was established. Thirty-five missioners accepted calls in that period."[145] Somewhere, somehow a tide had turned.

MISSION IN NORTH AMERICA

As has been described earlier, the newly formed Division for Mission in North America was deeply involved in many areas, such as minority concerns, women's rights, development of studies on social issues, and the domestic side of the hunger crisis. There were, however, other major dimensions to its work, since it had consolidated many of the responsibilities of the Boards of American Missions, Colleges and Church Vocations, and Social Ministry, as well as the complex planning process with synods. It may be helpful to highlight certain developments during this period when DMNA's influence in the church gradually expanded.

North American Missions

One popular measure of effectiveness in home mission work was traditionally the number of new congregations established in a given year. From this standpoint, the 1970s were a disappointment to many persons. From a low of eleven in 1971, the number edged upward to twenty-five in 1974, only to drift downward to nineteen two years later, and then, assisted by SFM funds, to rebound to twenty-seven by the decade's end.[146] It wasn't that there was a lack of opportunities. New communities sprang up in scores of places, and an estimated eight million people poured into the Sunbelt states during one five-year period.[147] In addition, waves of immigrants, largely Asian and Hispanic, surged into both Canada and the United States.

The fluctuations in the numbers of new congregations, however, had their roots in a complex set of circumstances that included the LCA's own priorities, other new types of ministries, escalating costs, and the shortage of funds. As building costs and interest rates skyrocketed, it became less and less possible to finance the facilities needed for a new congregation to carry on its ministry. As *The Lutheran* pointed out in an article in 1973, there had been a precipitous drop in new buildings from a high of 146 in 1967 to 19 five years later.[148] The trend was clear. Finally, the state of the Church Property Fund, through which buildings were financed for mission congregations, was such that the Board of American Missions was forced to declare a moratorium on all building in the latter part of 1974.[149] Strength for Mission and sales of Mission Development Certificates would provide some relief, but the church property problem would linger throughout the life of the LCA and lead eventually to another major fund appeal.[150]

Synodical Planning

One of the key strategies that the LCA had adopted at its convention in 1972 was that of fiscal consultations between synods and churchwide agencies which were to be followed in turn by synodical-congregational consultations. The representatives of the church-at-large and the synods often worked intentionally in a "fishbowl" environment under the watchful eyes of a large number of observers from every agency and interest in the synod. Part of the hope was to develop a climate of trust and "to get everything out on the table" where mutual problems could be addressed in the hope of arriving at an equitable sharing of resources and an evaluation of needs to be met.[151]

Although not all synods were willing to take part at first, at least twenty-five had been involved in the consultation process by the end of 1974.[152] By that time, sixteen synods had followed through on the second phase of holding similar consultations with their congregations. What was at stake in all of this was finding a viable approach to budgeting and funding that was different from the ironclad apportionment system of former years. The process soon grew beyond the matter of financial commitments, however, and extended to all programmatic commitments between synods and the church-at-large. The key instrument was the "Synod Mission Profile" that was intended to be a description of all of the current and projected ministries on the territory of a given synod. It was conceived of as a way to allocate personnel and monetary resources of both the synod and the CWAs to the ministry in that place in the most effective way. The results varied, but the needs for assistance expressed by synods frequently outstripped the LCA's ability to respond. In one respect, this became a graphic demonstration of the necessity for all synods and the church-at-large to struggle together in a never-ending process where available resources would never match the demonstrated needs.[153]

Gradually, the synodical planning process developed other parameters. One was a technique known as the "audit," where a synod voluntarily would ask for a specially trained churchwide team to spend time on the territory examining every facet of its work, providing a lengthy written analysis of its program, and recommending areas for change and improvement.[154] An even broader approach to strategy development was the use of regional planning consultations established under the Division of Mission Services of LCUSA. These inter-Lutheran consultations that went beyond the interests of one church body involved "mission and ministry endeavor; church development and adjustment of ministries, social ministry, campus and educational ministry, ethnic and special ministries. Therefore, the emphasis has shifted from only American missions planning to a more comprehensive approach to planning within regions."[155]

By 1978 DMNA could report that the LCA was participating in twenty-one such consultations through LCUSA and through the Canada Section in similar efforts with other Lutheran bodies in that country.[156] A further evidence of planning came in the form of coalitions which made it possible for congregations in a particular area to pool their resources in order to carry out more effective ministries, particularly in highly specialized fields that could not be done by a congregation alone. By 1976 fourteen areas had been identified for this kind of cooperation, and by 1978 an additional twenty-two ministries of a more limited scope than coalitions were being supported.[157]

A New Rationale for Church Colleges

Restructuring of the LCA in 1972 had a profound effect on what had once been the sphere of the Board of College Education and Church Vocations. Only a few years before when budgets were adopted for the 1967–68 biennium, BCECV was the third largest beneficiary among the program boards, ranking behind only BAM and BWM.[158]

In the restructuring, church vocations and deaconess work were spun off to the new Division for Professional Leadership, and college education became a relatively minor department in DMNA.[159] "A major task of the DMNA through the Department of Higher Education during the 70s was the effort to interpret college education as a critical ministry of the church in a new age."[160] A new organization had been formed to deal with such concerns as fundraising, student recruitment, and church relations. Known as the Council of LCA Colleges, it was made up of the presidents of the institutions.[161] The Council and DMNA together undertook two major studies. One was designed as a churchwide survey of the images and expectation of church colleges that were current in the LCA. The second developed a statement on the basis of partnership between church and college.

The first study, which involved a professional research agency, analyzed the responses of more than seven thousand persons from various segments of the constituency. In 1976 a progress report was made to the LCA convention, although the full interpretation of the data was published later.[162] The study was wide-ranging in the questions it raised, but the progress report revealed few surprises. For example, the constituency showed that a large majority felt the church college was an instrument for the church's fulfilling its mission in society; about 22 percent sensed a growing separation between church and college; but only 7 percent believed that the church should withdraw from supporting colleges.[163]

The definitive policy document presented to the Boston convention was *A Statement of the Lutheran Church in America: The Basis for Partnership Between Church and College.*[164] "Based on Luther's doctrine of the orders of creation and preservation, the statement affirmed the integrity of the educational task of the college as a God-ordained ministry carried out in close partnership with the church. While cherishing this relationship and celebrating the common concerns of college and church for God's people and for God's world, the statement drew a distinction between the primary functions of the church as the mediator of the means of grace and the college as an educational institution."[165] The statement was used along with the survey data as the basis of regional conferences involving representatives of synods and their related colleges.

Support of National Lutheran Campus Ministry continued to be a major concern for the LCA and its synods. This was an area in which

DMNA worked closely with its ALC counterpart through the Division of Campus Ministry and Educational Services of LCUSA. In 1974, for example, a measure of the importance attached to this work was the fact that the DMNA and synods together contributed more that $1,624,000 to the cooperative ministry in 125 different college and university settings.[166]

Lutheran Social Service System

In seeking an effective way to coordinate consultation and evaluation work in the social service areas, DMNA and ALC's Division for Service and Mission concluded that it would be cumbersome to assign the direct responsibility to LCUSA. It was deemed better to set up a common agency that would be directly responsible to the divisions/ boards applying standards and providing resources. The result was the Lutheran Social Services System, which would be governed by a Policy Committee appointed by the executives of the sponsoring units.[167] At the outset, it was not clear whether Missouri's Board of Social Ministry and World Relief would be able to participate, but this problem was later solved. LS\3, as it came to be called, proved to be an effective instrument for DMNA in dealing with the 118 social service agencies and institutions related to LCA synods on questions that were often extremely complex and technical in nature.[168]

COORDINATING CONGREGATIONAL
SERVICES

When the Division for Parish Services began operation in September of 1972, it already had a full agenda of projects undertaken by the predecessor agencies in almost every functional area of congregational life plus a variety of special assignments arising from the Dallas convention. When the management committee met for the first time, it was almost swamped by a deluge of documents that made the members keenly aware of the scope of their responsibilities. A detailed *Plan of Operation* that included procedures and descriptions for all sixty-four authorized staff positions for the division was adopted; staff appointments were approved; basic documents for educational ministry and PLMD were accepted; and plans for the "Key '73" evangelism effort, the 1973 All-Lutheran Youth Gathering in Houston, a common congregational data system with ALC, and a progress report on ILCW's work were reviewed.

It was a busy few days as the committee struggled to find its own role and sort out what constituted policy and administrative decisions. The next several years would involve the management committee in a plethora of sticky decisions that led one member to say, "In parish life you have 7,000 pastors, 6,100 congregations, and 3 million members looking over your shoulder, and *every one* is an expert in the field!"

The shape of congregational operations was determined to some extent after restructuring by a study of the functions of a congregation with an eye to possible revision of the Approved Constitution for Congregations.[169] The DPS conducted the study ordered by the Dallas convention and found that in many instances some of the prescribed committees rarely functioned, and there was a general sense of frustration about trying to keep the machinery working.[170] Experimentation was carried out by selected congregations and synods under the guidance of the DPS Research Department to see whether a more functional approach that would recognize the holistic nature of congregational life would be advisable. On the basis of information gathered, the Executive Council proposed to the 1976 convention a series of amendments to the ACC that would permit greater flexibility of organization around the five basic functions of worship, witness, learning, service, and support.[171]

The congregation itself was defined as "a worshiping, learning, witnessing, and serving community of baptized persons among whom the Word is proclaimed and the Sacraments are celebrated according to the Gospel, and whose corporate existence is recognized by the Lutheran Church in America."[172] The revised constitution also provided that the congregation should adopt a statement of mission, which would be inserted in the bylaws and revised periodically in response to God's call in the midst of the changing conditions of society.[173]

The DPS's major strategy for assisting congregations in developing mission statements and finding appropriate ways to focus their resources for action was Parish Life and Ministry Development. Conceived of as a way to help congregations, synods, and the church-at-large to work together in a partnership for ministry, the process involved analyzing the parish's situation and potential, developing objectives and priorities, deciding upon plans, carrying out the plans, and evaluating the results.[174] PLMD was consistent with the LCA's emphasis on planning and coordination in those years.[175] Since it required substantial time investment by their leaders, many

congregations chose not to become involved, but those who did often found that it was a source of parish renewal.[176]

The "Greening" of Worship

Almost two and one-half centuries had passed from the time that Henry Melchior Muhlenberg and his colleagues prepared the first "American" liturgy that was adopted by the inaugural convention of the Pennsylvania Ministerium until the *Lutheran Book of Worship* became a reality in 1978. The dream had always been to have a common liturgy and hymnal for all Lutherans in North America, and although that hope came close to realization in the *LBW,* it fell short at the last moment when the Lutheran Church-Missouri Synod did not adopt the book even though its publishing house shared the copyright.[177] LCMS did publish its own book, *Lutheran Worship,* in

1982. It contained a substantial amount of material that was identical to the *LBW*.[178]

Developing a liturgy and hymnal is always a long and tedious process that is likely to be fraught with controversy, and the ten thick volumes of minutes of the ILCW and its subcommittees are mute testimony that preparing the *LBW* was no exception. Not only did these groups commit thousands of hours of work to the project, but the official review groups of the churches also spent many days wading through the mountains of survey reports, drafts, and revisions to make their own proposals. A few highlights from the LCA perspective must suffice here.

After producing its experimental *Contemporary Worship* series, the ILCW settled down to the task of preparing a single "pew edition" plus editions for the minister and the accompanist for liturgy and hymns.[179] Naturally, rumors are rife during any such process. For example, many believed that the ILCW would omit their most-beloved hymns and, therefore, wanted all of those in the existing hymnals included. Even if it had been desirable, this would have been impossible because the book would have been too large to fit in church pew racks. The DPS Management Committee proposed a survey of all LCA congregations to find out which hymns in the *Service Book and Hymnal* had actually been used in the previous three years. Response came from 3,169 congregations and revealed that while many familiar hymns in the *SBH* were used regularly by virtually every congregation, there were some that were used seldom or not all.[180] Congregations also asked that certain hymns not in *SBH* be added, such as "How Great Thou Art" and "Amazing Grace," both of which were eventually included. What some people did not realize was that where possible there would be changes in text to deal with such concerns as sexist language, and familiar hymns would appear with new harmonizations or tunes different from the ones to which they had been accustomed.

By the time of the Boston convention in 1976, the LCA had already gone through an extensive review process involving the Consulting Committee on Worship, the DPS Management Committee, articles in *The Lutheran Quarterly* developed at a symposium of scholars,[181] LCA seminary faculties (although only two took time to respond), and a pilot test of liturgical materials by a sample of LCA congregations.[182] What the DPS Management Committee recommended at Boston was approval by the convention of the list of hymns and tunes plus granting the Executive Council authority to approve the final version of the liturgical portion upon recommendation by the management committee. If such approval was not given, the matter was to come back to the 1978 convention. Publication was also contingent on approval or acceptance by church bodies constituting a majority of Lutherans in North America.[183]

When the recommendations came to the convention floor, there was a surprise motion to delete from the LCA Bylaws that section which gave to the Division for Parish Services the responsibility to "approve liturgical and hymnological materials which constitute the official or authorized worship books of the church, and other such materials which are to bear the imprint of this church or a churchwide agency."[184] The result would have been to throw back upon the convention approval not only of the *LBW* but also a host of other worship materials produced by the church. Since this was a bylaw amendment, it would have required a two-thirds majority, which meant 417 votes in favor. The amendment failed by only twenty-eight votes. In all probability, a motion to require final approval of the *LBW* by the 1978 convention would have passed since it would have required a simple majority.

The compromise that finally emerged was to approve the liturgical portion of the book "in principle" and authorize the Executive Council "to provide for a thorough review of theology and whatever testing is deemed necessary, these, as may be feasible, to be done on an inter-Lutheran basis with other church bodies involved in the ILCW Project or through LCUSA; then, after review by the Consulting Committee on Worship and by the DPS Management Committee, and upon recommendation of the DPS Management Committee to take action on the final version of the liturgical portion of the new book by mid-1977, or failing that, to request the division to submit the matter to the 1978 LCA Convention for action."[185] A motion was also adopted to seek the counsel and advice of the Conference of Synodical Presidents.

The process of review was thorough and time-consuming but paid off in numerous revisions of the liturgical materials.[186] It was gratifying that the ALC joined wholeheartedly in the effort. Colloquiums were held on the liturgical texts at the nine LCA seminaries with affirmative reactions at key points. The materials were sent to all LCA pastors and one thousand lay leaders for reaction. A sample of 115 congregations was provided with test materials as they would appear in a finished publication with rubrics actually printed in red (something which seemed to delight the people who learned the real meaning of *rubric*).

When the results of the testing and review were shared with the Conference of Synodical Presidents at their July 1977 meeting, an effort to postpone decision until the 1978 convention was defeated (25 to 6) and the recommendation of the DPS Management Committee to proceed was affirmed (27 to 1).[187] The Executive Council voted at its September 1977 meeting to approve the pew edition, the other related materials already having been approved by the DPS Management Committee.[188]

In a very real sense the manuscript approved was a careful blending of preservation and change. "The framers of the *Lutheran Book of Worship* had as an unwritten guiding principle the view that the book must be no less rich than its predecessors."[189] There is a clear linkage to the Lutheran worship tradition in the liturgy, but there is also an ecumenical awareness evident. The language of the liturgy is not only modernized but also moves "away from philosophical concepts and toward evocative images."[190] New emphasis is given to the Psalter, and there are significant changes in the Christian year to focus on the Resurrection. The musical settings for the Holy Communion are arranged for singing in harmony, and the newly added Hymn of Praise, "This is the feast of victory for our God," has become widely popular. Church members are continually surprised by the almost infinite variety of worship possibilities that are included.[191]

The hymnal portion represents a striving to preserve many of the treasured hymns of various ethnic and racial traditions as well as to introduce fresh, new material. In the process, the hymn text committee screened more than 2,300 texts before arriving at the final group of 537 hymns and 21 canticles.[192]

Finally, after twelve years, the *Lutheran Book of Worship* was on its way, and a first printing of 1,200,000 copies began to roll off the presses in summer 1978. Leather-bound copies were presented at the Chicago convention to President Marshall and Secretary Crumley.[193] And the color? Since Missouri's book was blue and the *SBH* was red, the *LBW* was green. A massive program of introduction was undertaken by DPS and its counterparts in ALC and ELCC, with 750 events strategically spread over the United States and Canada. As one writer put it, the "greening" of Lutheran worship in North America had begun!

Educational Ministry

Great hopes had been generated in the close cooperation that had developed between the Boards of Parish Education of ALC and LCA from the mid-sixties until the early seventies. Detailed plans had been drawn for a common Educational Ministry Program to be launched in 1975. When restructuring occurred in the LCA in 1972 and the ALC in 1973, the newly formed Division for Life and Mission in the Congregation of the ALC felt it appropriate to reassess these earlier commitments. Both DPS and the LCA Board of Publication understood that the Augsburg Publishing House and the DLMC Board were requesting a delay in introduction of the new program until 1976.

Although there were clear signals that some change was in the offing, the DPS Management Committee was dismayed to learn at its May 1974 meeting that the ALC Boards were withdrawing not only from joint work in PLMD but also Educational Ministry.[194] The LCA committee was also distressed to learn that the ALC had decided to go ahead with preparing and introducing in 1975 special Sunday school curriculum resources for small/rural congregations as well as "broad spectrum curriculum resources" that were to be "biblical, flexible in usage, closely graded, and containing a variety of media and teaching approaches" that would begin to appear in 1976.[195] The ALC Boards did ask Church Council approval to cooperate with their LCA counterparts in the future on a "project-by-project" basis.[196]

The DPS Executive Committee adopted a resolution that made clear that the LCA was in no sense withdrawing from cooperation and would welcome a return to the original agreements. It did, however, convey its disappointment regarding ALC's intent to terminate participation in PLMD before the pilot test was completed, and its regret that the decisions made by predecessor ALC agencies about educational ministry had been reversed. It stated that "anything which diminishes cooperation between the parish-serving agencies of our churches is a serious step backward at this point in Lutheran history in North America."[197] The committee went on to point out that it was understood that many of the plans now projected by ALC to be done unilaterally, such as the materials for small/rural congregations, were already a part of the EM design scheduled for implementation in 1976. In many other respects, such as the desire "for biblical and confessional visibility in resources," the committee said the LCA shared the same concerns.[198]

With its basic LCA Parish Education Curriculum already a dozen years old, the DPS had no choice but to complete the resources for the Educational Ministry Program and introduce them in 1976.[199] The program not only provided a way to customize curriculum recommendations to local specifications; it also provided two clearly defined tracks that emphasized biblical and life-centered approaches to learning. The Educational Ministry concept did gather a strong following in the LCA, but there can be little doubt that a concerted effort by both churches would have provided a richer range of resources and produced a more effective overall effort.

Although some of the traditional parish education agencies, such as the Sunday and vacation church schools, continued to decline in enrollment, other types of learning opportunities were growing by leaps and bounds. Outdoor ministries serve as one example. At one time, this ministry had been thought of solely as camping, but it had long since become a year-round program. By 1976, nearly 150,000 people a year were being served in programs of this kind at camps and conference centers across the United States and Canada.[200]

Witness and Evangelical Outreach

When the interchurch evangelism campaign Key '73 announced its theme as "Calling the Continent to Christ," some Jewish leaders were outraged, and prominent Rabbi Marc Tannenbaum declared that it implied "second-class citizenship for Jews."[201] By September, however, *The Lutheran* Editor Albert Stauderman quoted another rabbi as saying his concerns had disappeared when he found that Key '73 hadn't even caught fire among Christians. Stauderman's conclusion was that the whole effort had "been greeted with more yawns than cheers."[202]

Although 4,800 LCA congregations reported some involvement in Key '73, the campaign failed to stir the imaginations of most LCA members. Perhaps the most lingering feeling that resulted was a deep uneasiness about the fact that this central function of witnessing to the gospel was not being fulfilled in most parishes.[203] While there was a slight increase in confirmed and communing membership beginning in 1973, the downward drift in baptized membership continued.[204] Although total accessions hovered around the 100,000 level, an alarming trend toward "roll cleaning" had set in among many congregations by 1975, when over 107,000 baptized members were dropped from the rolls for a variety of "other" reasons. Particularly disturbing was the fact that three-fourths of LCA congregations

received an average of only four unchurched persons into membership each year.[205]

The concern about evangelism was not confined to the LCA. In
September 1975 President Marshall received an invitation from the
ALC for the two churches to join in a joint emphasis on "Evangelical
Outreach" in 1977. On October 7 Presidents Preus and Marshall met
with staff of DPS and DLMC in Chicago to explore the possibilities.
It was agreed to have a task force of three staff from DLMC, two from
DPS, and one from LCW to prepare a proposal for submission to
LCA's Executive Council and ALC's Church Council.[206] The task
group's report pointed out that the two church constitutions were
remarkably similar in their emphases on evangelism and that the
program agencies had many plans underway that could be carried
out jointly or shared for mutual benefit. Both the Executive Council
and the ALC Church Council gave approval to the 1977 emphasis,
although the LCA viewed Evangelical Outreach as an ongoing
rather than a one-year effort.[207] Fortunately, the Strength for Mission
Appeal made funds available in the LCA for a multiyear emphasis.
DPS was given primary responsibility in the LCA in cooperation
with DPL, OC, and LCW.

The four major goals of EO in the LCA were to help congregations
(1) renew their understanding and commitment to the bold witness
of the gospel through study and action; (2) seek out the unchurched
regardless of race, creed, color, condition, or age; (3) seek out and
restore the inactive members; and (4) integrate new and restored
members that they may know they are called by their Baptism to
celebrate the gift of grace and to share in the discipleship of the
Christian community by caring for God's world and ministering to
the human community.[208] Careful theological groundwork was laid
in a book, *Evangelical Outreach Foundations,* that was written by
the executive director of DPL and was used also by ALC.[209] Through
the partnership among the churchwide agencies, districts, and synods of ALC, an impressive array of new and creative programs were
launched. Some of the most innovative of the LCA approaches included the following:

Pastor Evangelists. Rather than relying solely on staff, DPS decided
to ask active parish pastors with proven track records in evangelism
to help design the program and devote up to a month a year in
conducting various kinds of events throughout the United States and
Canada. Heading this cadre of twelve to fifteen well-known leaders

was a Pastor Director who convened their planning sessions and guided their efforts. The first person to serve in this role of director was Ronald J. Lavin of Davenport, Iowa.[210] The Pastor Evangelists received no honorarium from the LCA, but their congregations were reimbursed for their time. They included men, women, Blacks, and persons with primary language other than English.

Word and Witness. In 1975 DPS and DPL forged a partnership to develop a program of intensive Bible study coupled with a laboratory experience in personal witnessing to the gospel that proved to be one of the most effective outreach efforts the LCA had ever tried.[211] When the Boston convention endorsed EO as a joint effort with ALC, a pilot test in Word and Witness was already underway with two dozen pastors who spent two weeks of intensive training at Southern Seminary. One of the dramatic moments of that training came when the pastors were asked to make "cold" (uninvited) calls on the homes of people where they were expected to witness to their own faith. Many confessed it was one of the most unsettling experiences of their ministry, and it drove home to them the problem that lay people faced in talking about their faith in daily life. Their coaches in the intensive biblical study and the techniques of witnessing were a team of biblical scholars, a seminary professor in personal counseling and communication, plus churchwide staff.[212]

When the EO emphasis came in 1977, Word and Witness was introduced to 465 professional leaders in seventeen twelve-day seminars on campuses throughout the church. Some of the church's outstanding biblical scholars and specialists in personal communications staffed the events.[213] Within a year more than five thousand church members had been involved in a fifty-four-week effort that made them staunch advocates of Word and Witness. Within ten years more than two thousand congregations and fifty thousand people would go through the process. Many congregations reported that it revolutionized their approach to evangelism.[214] In time the program would spread worldwide, with courses offered in Spanish, German, Swedish, and Finnish, as well as in English in some southeastern Asian situations.[215]

Conserving Members. Long before formation of the LCA, Augustana and ULCA in particular struggled with the problem of an increasingly mobile population and the difficulty of keeping track of members who moved to new places. About the only way the churches had of making referrals to other Lutheran congregations in the communities where people had relocated was to depend on pastors to report when members of their own parish moved. Although by the seventies it was estimated conservatively that over fifty thousand LCA families relocated each year, referrals from former parishes were only a fraction of that number.[216] Names were often forwarded too late to do any good, even though studies showed that when congregations made a contact within six months after a family moved into the community, the response was positive.

New hope of keeping tabs on moving members came in 1971 when *The Lutheran* made its address change lists available, but the process was still cumbersome because the work had to be done by hand.[217] After restructuring in 1972, DPS inherited the task but had to send the lists to synodical offices where there was often no one available to forward the referrals to appropriate congregations. When the LCA installed its first central computer in 1972, a unified mailing list was created by the Department of Information Services that provided address changes for all LCA publications to DPS. It was not until 1979, however, that a way was developed with the synods to automate referrals directly to congregations on the basis of zip code designations provided for each parish by the synods.[218] No system, of course, could do more than provide information unless the appropriate persons chose to act upon it.

Stewardship and Christian Giving

The 1970s proved a turning point in giving for the LCA. From a low point in 1971, when regular apportionment receipts by the church-at-large declined 1.3 percent from the prior year, the picture shifted to the plus side until the increase from 1977 to 1978 was 5.09 percent. This was in addition to the large receipts for Strength for Mission; $2,112,000 for the World Hunger Program; and Designated Advance Giving, which was running around $1,500,000 a year.[219] Double-digit inflation, however, was lurking around the corner and would pose further threats to the LCA's fiscal program.

In 1976 the Executive Council had authorized development of plans for a program of intensified Christian giving that was to be based on a biblical and theological statement describing the context within which members support the church.[220] DPS was asked to set up a special consulting group to develop the statement on "Stewardship and Christian Giving," which was then studied and commented upon by congregations.[221] After numerous revisions, the final statement was adopted by the Executive Council in 1980. It stressed the biblical basis for Christian giving as a response to God's gifts of creation, his own Son, and a renewed community nurtured by the Holy Spirit. The document stated that "commitment in giving is the external evidence of internal priorities" and spoke candidly of money as "an extension of ourselves; in a sense it is a symbol of life itself."[222] The characteristics of our Christian giving should be that it is done gratefully, faithfully, regularly, proportionately, responsibly, joyfully, and expectantly. Running through the statement was a tone that was not tied to legalistic interpretations but reflected the freedom of the gospel.

Sparked by a variety of new efforts, such as the Every Member Response Growth Program that provided intensive direct staff assistance to individual congregations with potential for increasing their giving, the Intensified Christian Giving Program produced some surprising results. In time whole synods began to take up the cause of intensifying their stewardship efforts, and gradually a new coordinated program emerged that brought together the various channels for giving in the LCA that had for so long functioned almost independent of one another.

Congregational Social Ministry

One of the most difficult tasks facing the DPS was creating an awareness among many congregations of the meaning and urgency of the service function of their ministry. It was easy enough for them to see social ministry at work in agencies beyond the parish itself, but identifying the range of local needs and developing strategies to meet them were another matter.

One problem in many cases was the lack of a support system that linked the church-at-large through synods to the congregations. It took time to develop a network of social ministry resource teams and to identify and recruit volunteers who could and would contribute the necessary skills for dealing with the needs of exceptional persons, the aging, family ministries, and minority group concerns, as well as persons who could work with the special situations of urban or town and country parishes.[223] The special efforts that the LCA put into dealing with the urban crisis, racism, social justice issues, world and domestic hunger, all helped to make members of congregations aware of the breadth and depth of those particular problems.

Cooperative efforts with DMNA and DPL and often with other Lutheran church bodies and ecumenical agencies were especially important. It was clear that the needs were so massive that unilateral action was seldom a responsible solution. DPS's special contributions usually came in such areas as action research to test new programs, sensitizing the constituency to needs, providing educational and "how-to" resources, sponsoring training events and conferences that brought specialists together to address problems, and building the networks of human resources available to the local parish.

Youth Ministry

Among the many facets of youth ministry, the two that loomed large in these years were the Youth Staffer Program and the two all-Lutheran youth events. Youth staffers served in synods, churchwide agencies, and clusters of congregations to develop a holistic approach to youth work. In 1974–75, for example, there were thirty-two young people serving either full- or part-time in these roles. All told there have been through the years hundreds of youth staffers, including Blacks, Hispanics, and Asians; and many of them have gone on to careers of full-time work in the church.

The 1973 All-Lutheran Youth Gathering was an outgrowth of a meeting of the ALC, LCA, and LCMS youth directors to plan some way for young people to be a part of the Key '73 evangelism emphasis.[224] More than twenty thousand youth and adult leaders descended on the Astrodome in Houston, Texas, for what was the first time in history that an intersynodical Lutheran gathering of this size was held in North America. The participants engaged in worship, Bible study, mass events with prominent speakers, and visits to exhibits of various program agencies.[225] One sign of the times was that more than ten thousand young people spent time in the exhibit sponsored by the church colleges. There were problems, of course, but many were solved through a twenty-four-hour crisis hotline called "Switchboard Friend" that handled some three thousand calls ranging from simple requests for information to real cries for help on such things as drug counseling.

The Astrodome event was judged successful enough that the three churches agreed to hold another in 1976 at the Superdome in New Orleans. The response was beyond expectations and overwhelmed the available hotel facilities. More than twenty-six thousand persons from all over the United States and Canada swarmed into the city, only to find that one hotel that had planned to house a large number was unfinished. When the first major meeting began, the air conditioning in the Superdome was not working properly. Participants sweltered, but perspiration didn't dampen the spirits of the youth. They sang, worshiped, cheered, studied the baptismal theme via closed circuit television in their hotel rooms, explored the sights, and were publicly commended for their decorum. It seemed, however, that the event had exceeded the optimum size for achieving the kind of goals that had been planned. The three churches decided to go their own ways in the future, and the next all-LCA event was destined to be held in 1981.[226]

Research, Studies, and Planning

DPS built upon the former BPE Research Department to develop quickly an operation that tied research, evaluation, studies, and planning closely together. One study that was already underway in 1973 dealt with the way people in the LCA viewed and used the Bible.[227] A second that was mandated by the 1972 convention provided guidance to congregations about the burgeoning charismatic movement. The report made to the 1974 convention, *The Charismatic Movement of the Lutheran Church in America,* stressed a pastoral perspective. In addition to providing historical and theological background about the modern phenomenon involving the Roman Catholic and mainline Protestant churches, the report suggested a series of guidelines for the LCA itself in dealing with the movement.[228]

DPS also laid great emphasis on systematic evaluation of programs in all functional areas as an aid to strategic planning. In 1976 the division reported to the convention its goals for the period 1976 to 1980, which became a starting point for cooperative planning with other churchwide agencies and assisting in an ambitious project of the Executive Council to lay out ten-year goals for the whole LCA.[229] The continual reassessment and revisions of such objectives became an ongoing task of the DPS, with responsibility eventually lodged in the Office of the Executive Director.

From PEP to "Pickle"

From 1928 onward the parish education agencies of most North American Lutheran bodies had found ways to meet together and plan common projects that ranged from a contemporary translation of Luther's Small Catechism to consultations on confirmation.[230] As was mentioned in an earlier chapter, the formation of the ALC and the LCA had led to the creation of a new cooperative organization with Missouri, the Coordinating Committee on Cooperative Parish Education Projects, which was nicknamed "Triple-C-PEP." As each of the churches adopted structures that brought all aspects of congregational life into similar divisions, it seemed wise to find a way to do cooperative planning of all parish life projects in an interrelated way. The result was the Coordinating Committee on Cooperative Projects in Congregational Life, which was shortened to CCCPCL or "Kick-a-pickle."[231] The committee had subgroups relating each functional area of the parish, and the CCCPCL itself had a related committee involving the three publishing houses to work out common projects in that area. The list of projects undertaken through the years by way of these mechanisms had been long and impressive.

LUTHERAN CHURCH WOMEN IN
AN ERA OF CHANGE

The seventies were certainly a time for opening new doors for women in both church and society. The ordaining of women, the increase in the number of women elected to governing boards and agencies, and the creation of a special Consulting Committee on Women in Church and Society were among the evidences of significant change in the LCA. Few would have questioned, however, that there were still miles to go before women gained the kind of recognition and opportunities they fully deserved.

Two actions in 1974, however, were clues to the fact that, although women were being accepted more and more into what had once been distinctly "male preserves," there was still a felt need among women for structures within which they could "get together and discuss things from their own perspective." It was that year when the Lutheran Laymen's Movement for Stewardship asked the church convention to change the bylaws on its membership from "laymen" to "lay persons."[232] It had taken a mere sixty-seven years to make that shift, and it would be a few years more before the LLM became the Lutheran *Laity* Movement. It seems that Lutherans are not inclined to rush wildly into the future.

The contrasting action came at the triennial convention of LCW in August of the same year when "a resolution encouraging men's involvement in LCW programs was quickly rejected. Lutheran Church Women was for *women.*"[233] The chairperson of the Long-Range Planning Team explained, "There are innate differences in the way we structure our social life and our study life. . . . Women can help men step into a better understanding of what quality of life is all about."[234] This point of view was quite understandable in the light of the particular needs of women at the time, and it seems to have been an important factor in the formation of a women's organization in the Evangelical Lutheran Church in America.

Lifting Up Social Concerns

One of the areas of increasing emphasis for LCW during these years was that of social concerns. Priority areas for study and action that appeared repeatedly were children's rights, aging, hunger, literacy, race relations, ecology, criminal justice, and welfare reform. The LCW provided a wide range of resources in these areas, and there was no hesitancy in grappling with issues such as *Women and Alcoholism, Medical Issues of the Seventies, Aging Is Everybody's Business, Making a Global Difference, Women Offenders,* and *Caring for*

Marti Lane, director of LCW literacy program

the World. And the topics were by no means confined to concerns in the United States, since the organization's catalog always included resources available through the Canada Section, such as studies on *Poverty and Youth, Health Care for All Canadians, Adequate Housing for All Canadians,* and *Greater International Responsibility.* Social issues, however, were always matched with a regular series of biblical topics plus a variety of devotional materials that did nourish the spiritual life of the members.

As might be expected of any large organization, there were often debates at triennial conventions as to just how far LCW should go in support of certain issues. For example, there was a resolution introduced at the 1974 convention to give prayer support to the first eleven women ordained by the Episcopal Church and to support efforts "to remove all barriers of sex discrimination within the body of Christ." For a variety of reasons, the motion was narrowly defeated. The writer of the official LCW history observed, "It was perhaps another year or two before a majority of LCW members could concur with the legitimacy of women's claims to all priestly and professional roles in equality with men."[235] As the same writer points out, however, a survey of readers of *Lutheran Women* a year later showed broad support for the Equal Rights Amendment.

The Ecumenical Dimension

Lutheran Church Women was always interested in the wider expressions of the Christian church and consistently recommended the study materials produced by the National Council of Churches. These frequently dealt with in-depth studies of mission opportunities in the Third World as well as topics on the forefront of thinking in North America. The LCW also cooperated closely with Church Women United and the Women's Inter-Church Council of Canada. Particularly important in the Lutheran context was participation in the Lutheran Women's Cooperating Committee, which included American Lutheran Church Women and the Lutheran Women's Missionary League.[236]

Seminars were developed by LCW to give women firsthand experiences in Latin America, India, Africa, Hong Kong, Japan, and other parts of Asia. Participants came back to spread the word about the worldwide concerns of Christian women. The concept of a "global sisterhood" began to come alive through ecumenical dialogues, prayer, and action.[237]

Kathryn Kopf

When LCW executive Dorothy Marple was appointed assistant to President Marshall, the choice of her successor was in itself a demonstration of the international vision of LCW. Dr. Kathryn Kopf had received her doctorate in educational psychology from the University of Iowa. A Canadian by birth, she held the position of chair of the Department of Family and Consumer Studies at the University of Guelph, Ontario, when she was chosen executive of LCW. She brought with her not only a binational background but a firm grounding in the educational, social, and ecumenical areas that had become so important in the life of the organization.

THE ENIGMA OF THE
PROFESSIONAL LEADER

From the time that the Division for Professional Leadership was formed, there were those who found the term less than satisfactory. What made a leader a "professional"? Was it employment, and if so, did that mean full-time or part-time? Was it educational level or skills? Was a trained psychologist who gave time freely to the church not a "professional leader"? Or was someone who was employed full-time in a less-skilled position the "real professional"? There seemed to be little question about whether the ordained clergy fitted that category—unless that implied that a lay person who was engaged in a "Christian vocation" was any less a professional. Even though definitions were drawn with almost legalistic precision, these seldom were truly satisfactory to everyone. The whole LCA, along with the Division for Professional Leadership, struggled with the question. Even in the 1980s the LCA refought the battle in new and different forms as it strove to engage in a more inclusive Lutheran merger. During the seventies, the DPL sought to define more precisely the meaning of the traditional ministry of Word and Sacrament while trying to clarify the criteria for lay professionals, preserve the traditional deaconess movement, explore the possibilities for a male diaconate, and still give proper recognition to the hosts of lay volunteers upon whom the church depended daily.

The division understood its mandate from the church as having three dimensions: (1) developing and maintaining a comprehensive personnel system to serve professional and paraprofessional leaders through synodical structures; (2) representing the church's concern for and collective action regarding theological education; (3) serving as the agency through which the church relates to the deaconess community.[238] By 1977 DPL had streamlined its own operations from five departments to two major units—Theological Education and Leadership Support—with other functions such as diaconal ministry and research and planning being related to the Office of the Executive Director.[239] It was a clue to where the program emphases of DPL would be in the future.

Theological Education

During the 1960s many writers were predicting a crisis among the clergy in North America that would be reflected in the diminished status of the ministry and a decline in seminary enrollments. Although Lutheran ministers were certainly not exempt from many of the conflicts about role that plagued their counterparts in other denominations, the forecast continuing drop in the number of seminary students simply did not happen in the LCA. In fact, a more pressing concern was that the increase in seminary enrollments implied a surplus of clergy by 1980.[240] DPL had given the church an early warning about the potential oversupply of ministers in a study of *Trends and Needs* reported to the Baltimore convention in 1974.[241]

At the same time, inflation and a variety of other factors conspired to increase the cost of theological education in the LCA by an average of 10.24 percent annually during the LCA's first decade, and the combined operation in most years showed a current operating deficit. At its spring 1974 meeting, the DPL Management Committee reported that there was a financial crisis in funding seminaries, and Executive Director Louis Almen declared, "Within a decade it could overwhelm us."[242]

As DPL probed more deeply into the questions of seminary financing and the numbers of clergy, the LCA raised anew the issues of the quality of theological education and the number and location of seminaries. With the assistance of the Consulting Committee on Theological Education and the cooperation of the seminaries themselves in self-evaluations, the division made a lengthy report and a series of ten recommendations to the 1976 convention in Boston.[243] Basically, the DPL reaffirmed earlier convention decisions that called for three major LCA centers for theological education in the Northeast; Columbia, South Carolina; and Chicago. A cooperative approach with the ALC was to be used in Minnesota, Ohio, and California. The future of the two Canadian seminaries was being pursued together with the Canada Section. In order to strengthen the financial situation, DPL asked the LCA to put a high priority on seminary support by urging each synod to provide adequately for the seminary it supported, by increasing funding available on a churchwide basis beyond regular benevolence sources, and by encouraging seminaries to seek gifts from private sources to increase their endowments.

By the next convention, DPL was able to report that some major strides had been made.[244] Most dramatic was the decision of Hamma School of Theology in Springfield, Ohio, to merge with the ALC seminary in Columbus in a new institution to be known as Trinity Lutheran Seminary, which began operation in September 1978. "Maximal functional unification" of Luther (ALC) and Northwestern (LCA) had been achieved in St. Paul, Minnesota, where the institutions were adjacent on a common campus, libraries were merged, a common curriculum adopted, and a single administration in place for both institutions. A third cooperative arrangement was made at

Pacific Seminary in Berkeley, California, where ALC now elected one-third of the board of directors and had about as many students as those from LCA. A joint venture had been worked out with the Evangelical Lutheran Church of Canada at Saskatoon with a special emphasis on preparing students for multilingual ministries.

Meanwhile, other significant changes were underway in theological education. For one thing, the mix of seminary undergraduates was changing. In the 1975–76 school year, there were 903 male and 113 female Master of Divinity (M.Div.) candidates. By the end of the decade, the balance had shifted to 728 men and 232 women.[245] DPL was not oblivious to the fact that the change from an all-male clergy would demand adjustments in actions and attitudes as more and more women entered the ranks of the ordained. A major study of what was occurring and might be anticipated in the future was conducted in 1975 by Marjorie Garhart, herself a seminary graduate who had had to wait almost thirty years for ordination. The report, *Women in the Ordained Ministry*, identified the kind of obstacles women were already experiencing in seminary and in the parish, and proposed a series of practical recommendations to the church to ease the transition to the future.[246]

At the same time the number of students working for lay professional degrees was steadily increasing.[247] Another phenomenon was the upswing in older students who were entering seminary to prepare for a "second career" as professional church workers. Nothing quite like it had been experienced before, but these students made a significant impact on the whole seminary environment as well as the dynamics of placing graduates in positions within the church.

At the outset of its existence, DPL had set a goal of at least one hundred clergy or lay professional ethnic minority persons in various church positions by the end of the decade. As a result of aggressive recruitment and scholarship programs by DPL, DMNA, and the seminaries themselves, this initial goal was achieved but was superseded by the "Goals and Plans for Minority Ministry" adopted by the 1978 convention.[248] The enrollment of "minority" students was also moving slowly upward. In the 1976–77 academic year there were only twelve Black and two Hispanic students reported, but by 1979–80 the figures were twenty Blacks, six Hispanics, two Asians, and two Native Americans.[249] Although all of this clearly represented an advance, it still was a far cry from the hope for a truly inclusive ministry.

Leadership Support

In addition to theological education, the second major area that demanded DPL's attention in the seventies was the researching and developing of a variety of ways to support the many types of professional leaders upon which the church had come to depend.

Understanding Lay Ministry. Although a full study of the relationship between the ministry of the laity and that of the ordained would carry into the next decade, DPL did attempt to deal in the midseventies with the specific questions of recognition and support for lay workers in the church. A Consulting Committee on Lay Ministry was formed in 1975 to deal with such issues, and a progress report was submitted to the Boston convention of the church.[250] It defined "lay professionals" as unordained members of the LCA who have suitable training and skills to function on the staff of a church or church-related organization; have registered with and are accountable to the synod according to certain standards; are employed at least twenty hours a week in a congregation, synod, churchwide agency, or other recognized church setting; and have agreed to function through a written contract with the employing organization.

The committee proposed that there be two categories of such workers: "recognized" and "certified," the difference being chiefly the educational and training standards to meet the criteria for certification by the synod. The report also laid out plans for the process of recognition and certification, and asked for a variety of types of support for these workers from the synods and churchwide agencies. Much of this proved practical and useful, but the underlying theological issue of the nature of the "ministry of the laity" would be debated well into the future.

Growth in Ministry. Beginning in 1973 the LCA and LCMS joined in a three-phase process to identify the needs and undergird the work of the professional leaders in the two churches. A sample of four hundred congregations was involved in gathering data about the effectiveness of pastors and their satisfaction with their work. Not only were the clergy themselves involved in the study but also their spouses and the lay leaders of their congregations. The complex process of testing and analysis yielded "six basic [pastoral] roles: priest and preacher; personal and spiritual development; enabler;

teacher and visitor; community and social involvement; and office administrator."[251]

The research brought to light a number of surprising insights. Interestingly, many pastors had not previously thought of their work in terms of major roles but as a series of many different activities that were not necessarily interrelated. They did, however, sense the significance of the roles for their own planning. Generally, the pastors rated their own performance much lower than did their spouses and the lay members of the parish. Originally, the researchers had expected just the opposite, that the lay persons would rate the pastors lower than the pastors rated themselves. "The major contribution of Growth in Ministry research in understanding the struggle between pastors and laity," the researchers declared, "is the finding that those pastors who believe they are supervised also believe they receive more support from their local support group. . . . It is possible that, where role conflict is intense, the pastor does not accept the supervisory role of his official church council and the unofficial supervisory feedback from his key leaders."[252]

On the basis of the detailed research, the next step was to devise a pilot test of workshops that would assist pastors, spouses, and selected lay leaders to share in growth experiences. By 1978, four kinds of workshops had been developed and some 1,500 persons were involved in the previous biennium. The "Model A Workshop" helped people to develop greater self-insight and to set goals for professional and personal growth. Additional workshops were introduced on "Spiritual Growth," "Pastor as Teacher," and "Shared Ministry." Three additional types of events were developed later on "Growth in Marriage," "Support System," and "Pre-Retirement."[253]

Other Support Services. DPL, of course, did not depend only on Growth in Ministry as a way of supporting professional leaders. It had inherited the Personnel Support Service at the time of restructuring. This computerized system was designed to make available biographical information on all clergy and as many lay professionals as possible in order that searches could be initiated by authorized persons, such as synodical presidents, in the process of matching people to positions and opportunities for service.[254] Although conceptually an excellent idea, the system proved difficult to maintain and administer, especially in light of the inherent suspicion that many people had about computer files as tools of an impending "Big Brother" era.[255]

Continuing education was a major concern of DPL with a wide variety of opportunities offered by seminaries, including the newly minted Doctor of Ministry (D.Min.) program. By the end of the decade, 289 church professionals were involved in studies including advanced master (beyond M.Div.), D.Min., and academic doctoral programs.[256] On the other side of the picture, DPL also carried responsibility for the vital LCA Evaluation and Treatment Program that had been set up in 1969 by the Executive Council and was located at Trinity Lutheran Hospital in Kansas City, Missouri.[257]

Expand the Diaconate?

Although deaconesses had been a recognized part of the life of the LCA and its predecessors for nearly a century, the idea of an expanded diaconate that would include men came sharply into focus in the 1970s. Efforts to experiment with the concept of deacons had arisen in Michigan, New York, Pennsylvania, and New Jersey. An organization known as the "Order of St. Stephen, Deacon" was even incorporated in Baltimore, Maryland.[258] The Deaconess Community had gone on record as favoring the admission of men to the diaconate.[259] In fact, one male candidate had been recruited for the Associates in Diaconal Service Program, in which a person contributed a year of service with only maintenance support and no salary.[260]

In 1975 DPL had formed a Task Force on the Form and Function of the Ministry of Deacons, whose report and recommendations were made to the 1976 convention.[261] The report, which essentially would have recognized the function of deacons and set up certain criteria for deacons and further evaluation of the program, was not acted upon by the convention because of time constraints. Instead, it was received as a study document for the coming biennium with a decision to be made in 1978.

When the question was brought back to the Chicago convention, the DPL had done considerable additional work on the report and proposed that the next biennium be used as a time for careful experimentation with a final report scheduled for 1980.[262] After having wrestled, sometimes halfheartedly, with the issue for eight years, the LCA spent additional time amending the proposal at the 1978 convention and then ironically voted the whole matter down. A male diaconate for the foreseeable future was in limbo.

Although the Deaconess Community itself struggled to strengthen its ranks and maintain the broad range of service the movement had given through the years, their numbers dwindled until by 1978 there were only 71 active members out of a total of 153.[263] Concern about operating deficits of $100,000 in 1975 and $174,000 the following year, plus the mounting obligation the LCA had to maintain deaconesses on the cooperative plan during retirement, prompted the Deaconess Community Board to ask DPL to initiate a study of the future of the movement and report to the Chicago convention.[264]

The report reviewed the history of the movement, provided detailed information about trends and financial implications for the future, and explored a series of options. It closed with a series of affirmations of DPL's commitment to the work of all professional leaders and a recognition of the special circumstances involved with the diaconate. In addition, it proposed a series of LCA Bylaw amendments that restructured the relationship of the community to DPL and gave the division additional responsibility for long-range planning, standards, and asset management. The convention action insured the lifelong care of those admitted to the cooperative plan prior to July 1, 1978.[265] In effect, the continuation of the deaconess movement was assured, but the way in which it related to DPL had

Sister Margaret Tsan and Sister Miriam Shirey

been changed substantially so that the Community took full responsibility for its own internal affairs.

COORDINATING COMMUNICATIONS

Creation of the Office for Communications was a major step toward bringing some order out of the chaos of signals in various media that emanated from the churchwide agencies, synods, and other entities of the Lutheran Church in America. It was impossible, of course, for an office of the church-at-large to have a monitoring role to try to insure that pastors and lay members of the church were not inundated by the flood of printed material, filmstrips, audiotapes, advertising, motion pictures, and video programs that flowed from every agency at every level that wanted to tell its story, even when the long-suffering constituency did not want to see or hear the product. No one was ever able to track accurately, much less evaluate, just how much these thousands of parts of the church invested in their surfeit of efforts to get their message "across to the people who really needed it." Seldom was there a very clear idea about who these intended audiences were and whether they wanted this intervention in their lives or not.

What the OC *was* created to do was to help the church-at-large to get its act together and give counsel to synods, congregations, institutions, and agencies on how to do their own communicating more effectively. It was an enormous task when every part of the church insisted on its own freedom and resisted most efforts at help as being at best intrusion and at worst an attempt at censorship. The office was able to make inroads chiefly in the way the churchwide expressions of the LCA did their jobs. It was able to a lesser extent to make an impact upon congregations, synods, and institutions.

After all, OC had identified 105 separate audiences to which the LCA as a whole was trying to address its messages. OC also was beginning to recognize that each audience in turn became a second-stage communicator. "This concept recognizes the audience itself as a system with its own dynamics, so any communication input produces unlimited repeats and applications," the office declared in explaining why the LCA needed to develop a coordinated communications strategy of its own.[266] It sought to accomplish this through a staff team on communications; the Department of Press, Radio and

Television; and *The Lutheran.* It also related, in a less direct way, to the Board of Publication.

Press, Radio and Television

The Department of Press, Radio and Television was given a laundry list of responsibilities in the bylaws that dealt primarily with telling the LCA's story to the general public through the mass media. One way of "getting out the news" was through a barrage of between three and four hundred general and special releases to the press each year. These appeared in newspapers and magazines with circulation numbering in the millions. Each convention, with its pressroom where reporters from major publications and wire services were helped to obtain information and reach key church personalities, was a microcosm of the way PRT worked directly with the media. Through the years, cooperating directly with radio and television reporters in such settings became an increasingly important and technically complex part of the job.

PRT also generated broadcast media programs of its own. Together with the ALC, it produced and distributed Church World News, an interfaith newscast that was aired weekly over more than four hundred radio stations. Through cooperation with the Episcopal Church, the program was produced for Spanish language stations. The Lutheran Series on the Protestant Hour also brought outstanding preaching and religious music to a vast radio audience.

Producing television programs became increasingly costly. The LCA did generate programs, but none compared in staying power to the "Davey and Goliath" series. The episodes of this popular children's program not only were repeated year after year in the United States and Canada but also were eventually broadcast in seven different languages worldwide.[267] "When Netherlands television began carrying the series in 1972, all continents but Antarctica had been logged."[268]

The advent of cable television and videotaping provided new opportunities for local parishes or groups of congregations to participate in a television ministry. PRT assisted in experiments, provided training events for synodical communication chairpersons, and prepared special media kits that could be adapted to local situations.[269] As was true of every part of OC, PRT had to stay abreast of opportunities afforded the church by emerging technologies, as well as use the tried and proven methods of the past.

The Lutheran

At the time that the United States was celebrating the bicentennial of its Declaration of Independence, *The Lutheran* marked in the same month the 115th anniversary of its own first publication and the 145th anniversary of its other progenitor, *The Lutheran Observer.* Editor Albert Stauderman wrote in his report to the Boston convention that the magazine had the same editorial policy enunciated by its first editor more than a century earlier—that *The Lutheran* would "aim at presenting the facts and reasonings necessary to the formulation of just views on the momentous questions which now occupy the church. . . . It will be perfectly independent, never indeed neutral, except where honesty demands a suspension of judgment, but always impartial."[270]

Of course, a lot of things, including the "momentous questions," had changed over the years. Amazingly, however, the subscription rate established in 1963 of $1.50 a year under the every home plan was less than the $2.00 per year charged in 1860. With some trepidation, the decision was made in 1975 that the only way left to fight inflation and skyrocketing postal rates was to move gradually up to the $2.00 charged 115 years before.[271]

The management had already made some moves that had reduced costs dramatically. For example, the eccentric size of 6⅜ inches by 9⅛ that had been selected in 1963 was changed to a standard 8½-by-11-inch format at a saving of $4,000 an issue, with the additional advantage of being able to accept color advertising.[272] Since the magazine used forty-four tons of paper in a single issue, reducing the weight and type of paper also lowered costs significantly. Further saving came from the development of the unified mailing list that was computerized and used *The Lutheran* subscribers as the base point for maintaining the addresses for all church periodicals. One intractable problem was the quadrupling of postal rates in a few years.

Normally, all these changes would have hurt a magazine's circulation, but this did not occur with *The Lutheran*. Its circulation actually increased from a low of 529,823 in 1973 to 580,042 in 1978, even though the membership of the church was declining in the same period. This gave *The Lutheran* by far the largest circulation among religious periodicals in the United States and placed it in the top one hundred of all publications in the country.[273]

Numbers in themselves would have meant little if the magazine had not served a valuable purpose for internal LCA communications. Although many illustrations could be given, perhaps the most telling example of the power of *The Lutheran* to interpret the church's story came when the World Hunger Appeal was introduced in 1974. For the first few months, the magazine was almost the only churchwide contact for interpreting the program. The director of the appeal gave *The Lutheran* much of the credit for the way receipts jumped from about $4,400 to over $64,000 in December.[274] After that the hunger appeal was off and running.

After more than a quarter century on the staff and over six years as editor, Albert Stauderman retired from that position in 1978. For the first time, the church launched an open search process to find a successor. Fifty-two applications were received by the management committee of the Office of Communications, which had the bylaw responsibility to nominate an editor to the convention. After the applications were reviewed and the top candidates interviewed, the committee nominated Edgar R. Trexler, who had served as associate editor. He was elected at the 1978 convention by a vote of 579–25 and became only the third person to hold the position in thirty-three years.[275]

TRENDS IN PUBLISHING

Although the Board of Publication was not affected as much as the program units of the church, the restructuring of the LCA in Dallas did make some significant changes. For example, the board had previously been responsible for the printing, sale of advertising, obtaining of subscriptions, and distribution of *The Lutheran.* In November 1972 the editor informed the board that *The Lutheran* would take over on January 1, 1973, personnel administration for circulation, advertising, and subscription fulfillment, and the payroll operation would be handled by OAF.[276] This in effect left the publishing house only with responsibility for accounting work for the magazine, which was a far cry from ULCA days when it was the publisher of *The Lutheran* in the full sense of the term. Restructuring also required the Board of Publication to report on its own finances to OAF. Both the executive directors of OAF and OC, or their appointees, had seat and voice at meetings of the board. By 1976 the publishing house was required to discontinue its own computer operations and have this work performed by the central computer in OAF's Department of Information Services.[277]

There were other trends, however, that ultimately would become more significant in the church's publishing programs. For one thing, Fortress Press, after years of patient development, was becoming one of the most highly regarded publishers of scholarly works and religious books for the laity. As *America,* the Jesuit weekly, put it in its November 22, 1975, issue, "Fortress Press is rapidly emerging as the leading publisher of theological books, both scholarly and popular, in North America."[278] At one time Fortress was known primarily as a publisher of translations of European works, but the balance had changed "partly through the cultivation of American authors and partly because of a change in the tide of scholarship."[279]

The publishing house was more than a source of books, however. It also produced such important resources as devotional booklets with a circulation of more than a half million, a weekly church bulletin service (700,000), the weekly insert of prayers and other liturgical material called *Celebrate* (490,000), *The Journal of Church Music,* and selected anthems. Under the logo of "Lutheran Church Press," it published and marketed the curriculum and other congregational life resources prepared by the Division for Parish Services. Cooperating with the other Lutheran publishers, the board played a major role in publishing and distributing the *Lutheran Book of Worship.*

During these years, ecclesiastical arts became an increasingly important part of the Board of Publication's strategy. It not only produced and marketed vestments and paraments but also combed the world for religious art objects. It had its own facilities for assisting congregations in designing their chancels and furnishings. It sold not only church furniture but also Communion vessels, altar appointments, and virtually everything needed for congregational worship.

When certain churchwide agencies were moved to Philadelphia in 1973, the publishing house was bursting at the seams. The board decided in 1973 to complete the west wing of the Muhlenberg Building that had never been extended above the ground floor. The move added 28,000 square feet to make room for additional office space, a new board room, and the largest religious supply store in the United States. At about the same time, the board decided to change the name of its fleet of outlets from "Lutheran Church Supply Stores" to "Fortress Church Supply Stores." It was a signal that the LCA agency was placing greater emphasis on the interdenominational market.[280]

TRYING TO RELATE
RESEARCH AND PLANNING

The Office for Research and Planning was the only agency created *de novo* by the Commission on Function and Structure. It did not bring together existing elements, as was the case with other agencies, but sought to fill a recognized gap by devising a completely new structure and operating system. It is not surprising, therefore, that ORP went through several metamorphoses before being absorbed into the Office of the Bishop in 1980, less than eight years after its formation.[281]

The original intention had been to develop a close interrelationship among research, planning, and evaluation. At the same time, it was recognized that, desirable as coordination was, churchwide agencies that were the end-users of research and the ones who had to implement plans needed to be directly involved in decisions about their own areas of responsibility. To complicate matters more, ORP pointed out in its 1976 report that there were "varied understandings and expectations related to the role of management committees, the Conference of Synodical Presidents, the Staff Executive Team, and the Executive Council in churchwide agency planning."[282] This was a polite way of saying that there was often confusion and sometimes outright conflict about where the authority of one group ended and that of another began. What became obvious was that no one part of the structure could simply dictate a comprehensive long-range strategy and expect others to make it happen. The resulting overall plan for the LCA, therefore, tended to be more a conflation of the goals and priorities of different decision-making groups than a completely unified strategy.[283]

The Early Emphasis on Budgeting

Although a program budget and program structure had been adopted by the Dallas convention at the time of restructuring, it was a far different matter to make the new system work in practice. "It was an abstract beginning that caused churchwide agency staff, the Executive Council and synods in the consultation process to experience what it was like to be handed a new and unfamiliar tool and asked to produce an equally unfamiliar but high quality product."[284] For this reason, the whole planning function during the 1973–74 biennium really came to the bottom line in fiscal planning and budgeting. A tip-off was that the first interagency Staff Team on Planning was made up largely of budget control officers. Not surprisingly, "Budget development, not planning, led the whole procedure."[285] In other words, the cart kept getting in front of the horse.

Still there were some breakthroughs as the LCA began to stretch its vision towards the future. ORP itself had been reorganized in 1974 with new leadership and a rebuilding of the staff to emphasize skills in statistical analysis and program evaluation.[286] Five-year goals were developed by the CWAs and brought together by a new Staff Team on Planning that provided the first comprehensive view of churchwide agency plans. The result was immediate identification of some areas of overlap and a need for articulating common assumptions about future developments in church and society.[287]

The Emerging Importance of Research

Many church leaders, it seemed, had little appreciation of the scope and various types of research that could serve the LCA. To some it was simply gathering raw statistics; to others, burrowing in archives or sending out questionnaires. Such techniques as action research, trend studies, sophisticated sampling methods, correlations, opinion surveys, and testing—to mention a few—had been used by individual churchwide agencies but seldom by the LCA in any coordinated way. No one really knew exactly what research had already been done and where the unexplored areas were. In late 1974 ORP began to address this problem by making an inventory of all known research conducted by CWAs since the beginning of the Lutheran Church in America. The resulting LCA *Index of Studies* showed that various agencies had already completed approximately three hundred studies, some of which were duplicative or no longer useful. The plan was to update this index every six months.[288]

As ORP surveyed the research scene and developed its own staff capabilities, the office became involved in cooperative projects with other LCA units and undertook some significant studies on its own. It is possible here to describe only a few of these efforts.

The Congregational Data System

Like archivists, researchers are frequently horrified at the way valuable information is lost or intentionally destroyed. It seems to be a never-ending contest between a kind of selective "pack rat" mentality and the "spring housecleaning" mind-set. A case in point is what happened in the collection of data about the congregations of the LCA.

It is no secret that parish pastors do not eagerly anticipate filling out the annual parochial report that provides basic information about such things as membership and finances. When the LCA was formed, therefore, it was decided to keep the amount of this data requested each year to a bare minimum. Prior to 1968, the information was put on punch cards by an outside service bureau and prepared as statistical reports to synods and the LCA convention and as copy for the *LCA Yearbook.* After the information was assembled, the punch cards were destroyed because of the amount of storage space that would have been required. In 1968 the Board of Parish Education was asked by the Secretary to process the data on its small computer largely because it was the only machine available. Beginning at that point, all of the reports were stored on computer tape and preserved.[289] This opened the way to further analyses and studies that could not be done before.

The next major step was a decision by ALC and LCA to begin developing a common congregational data system in 1972, a decision that was to have far-reaching implications in the future. The basic building block, *Form A,* was patterned closely on the ALC statistical report and contained much more information than LCA parishes had been accustomed to gathering. *Form B* had nonstatistical information, such as mailing address, pastor's name, languages used, and a mailing list for key congregational leaders.[290] *Form C* dealt with congregational program and planning. Only items for which there was a demonstrated use were included, and the congregation was invited to submit any open-ended comments that it wished.

When the new system was introduced in 1974, the reactions ranged from appreciation to outright anger at the amount of information requested.[291] Some of the forms were spiced with ancient Arabic curses invoked against the perpetrators of this scourge. At least they made interesting reading. As the forms were perfected and pastors actually began to receive feedback from their questions and trend analyses for their own congregations, the uproar subsided, although the appointed time for submitting the forms was greeted with about the same enthusiasm that went with filing one's income tax return. The tremendous value to synods and the church-at-large became apparent, however, when ORP submitted a report, *A First Look, LCA Trends, 1963–74,* that showed the insights that could be gleaned from an integrated system.[292]

Listening to the People

One of the perplexing problems all churches face is knowing what their members consider the most pressing issues and their attitudes toward future priorities. Beginning in mid-1974, ORP initiated a Delphi study that obtained from some two hundred key leaders in the LCA their opinions of major issues confronting the church. The responses were correlated and reduced to thirty-two concerns. The top five included (1) world hunger; (2) seminary education and pastoral competence; (3) the congregation as a community for mutual support, care, and growth; (4) the gap between church experience, including preaching and teaching, and everyday life; and (5) racial justice.[293]

Partly as an outcome of this effort, ORP designed with the help of professional consultants a plan that was to provide a pipeline through which information and opinions could flow between a scientifically selected sample of members and the LCA. Known as "The Lutheran Listening Post," the process involved a panel of seven hundred pastors and two thousand lay people who were asked to provide information about their background, views, attitudes, and perceptions on a wide range of subjects crucial to the life and ministry of the church.[294] The first panel was asked to respond to seven questionnaires during 1977–78 that produced a gold mine of data as to how the people at the grass roots were thinking.[295]

One of the most important of the LLP studies was one which dealt with "Religious Beliefs and Experiences" of LCA members. It is treated in depth in a book, *Views from the Pews,* which not only interprets the results of the survey but also includes commentary by a number of scholars.[296] Although the findings cannot be summarized here, the evidence indicates that formal religious beliefs among LCA members were much more important in their daily lives than other, more generalized studies of the sociology of religion had assumed. "Church members may not wear their beliefs on their sleeves, but this is no indication that their beliefs are unimportant."[297]

Congregational Nurture

One example of cooperation between ORP and other CWAs in research was in the study conducted with DPS to identify the major characteristics of congregational nurture. An intensive study was made of the experiences of persons in nine carefully selected congre-

gations to discover what it was in congregational life that had nurtured their faith. The findings and interpretation were published in
a volume called *Congregations as Nurturing Communities.*[298] One
significant conclusion was that in many cases belonging to the Christian community preceded belief.[299] It also posits the interesting view
"that the most effective translation of the gospel may occur in the
medium of behavior and experience, through interactions that are
not primarily linguistic."[300]

BRINGING TOGETHER
ADMINISTRATION AND FINANCE

The Office for Administration and Finance was created by the Commission on Function and Structure as a way to bring together as
many as possible of the basic financial and administrative functions
that had been scattered previously among many different churchwide agencies.[301] The key concept that lay behind the quest for
greater efficiency was the centralization of as many services as possible. In most instances this worked very well, but at times OAF itself
admitted that some operations could be handled better if dispersed.
For example, the attempt to centralize all word processing for the
agencies in New York never fulfilled the original expectations and
was modified.[302] This particular plan was never extended to the
Philadelphia offices, nor was centralized purchasing of all equipment
and supplies because of the widely divergent needs of the agencies
located there and the complexity of dealing with local suppliers.

OAF began operations in a rather modest way with just five departments: Accounting Services, Asset Management, Information
Services, Personnel Services, and Resource Development. An indication of the limited size of the initial staff was the fact that the director
of personnel also had to double as director of resource development.
By 1978 the situation was eased with the office having increased its
personnel sufficiently to handle the work assigned.[303] By that time,
of course, OAF had begun to provide several additional services,
such as records management and a casualty and liability insurance
program for congregations and other eligible entities.[304]

The OAF's broad mandate created a huge task of integrating so
many responsibilities, particularly at a time when the whole financial
picture was clouded by mounting inflationary pressures in both the
United States and Canada. Although the increase in regular benevo-

lence receipts topped 5 percent for the first time in 1978, by 1979 inflation was raging at a 13.2 percent rate in the United States. Budget development and fine-tuning of expenditures were a continual exercise in teamwork involving OAF, ORP, the Office of the President, and the Staff Executive Team. The necessity of fiscal surgery that chopped back churchwide programs was always painful, not only for the CWAs but also for the constituency who had difficulty in understanding why the services on which they depended were being reduced. The problem of raising the funds became a joint effort of the Department of Resource Development, DPS, and DMNA.[305]

Managing the assets of the LCA was a major operation in itself. This included handling both the long- and short-term investments of the church to maximize return; purchase and sale of real estate involved in the mission development program of DMNA as well as in some cases providing similar services to synods and other agencies; managing the Church Property Fund for the Board of American Missions which involved hundreds of loans to congregations, mortgage placement, necessary borrowings, and the sale of Mission Development Certificates; maintaining the Common Investing Fund; and managing the church's endowments.[306]

Accounting services for an entity the size and as diverse as the LCA involved maintaining complex records required not only for the smooth operation of churchwide agencies but also for government agencies. The church wanted to know precisely how every dollar was spent and exactly how personnel time was invested in various projects.[307] Personnel services were another growing function of OAF as the LCA sought to deal equitably with its employees. This department was responsible for employee benefits, personnel records needed by both the church and government, career development counseling, posting job openings, pre-retirement seminars, regular physical examinations, performance evaluations, and salary administration.[308] OAF was clearly becoming a major factor in the whole LCA operation.

PERSISTENT PENSION PROBLEMS

Although restructuring provided that the Board of Pensions report through the Office for Administration and Finance and that the executive of that office have seat and voice on the board, the basic functions of administering pensions and health benefit programs for church employees were not radically changed.[309] The fiduciary responsibility of the board on behalf of its participants gave it considerable autonomy. The tensions arose most frequently over how much of the benevolence funds of the church should be invested in maintaining the various benefit plans. Inflation was playing havoc with the small minimum pensions provided those who had retired early in the LCA's life, and escalating medical costs were placing additional demands on the church's budget. Although the whole picture is much too involved and technical to describe here, certain basic points should be made.

Ministerial Pensions

At the outset in the LCA, certain facts had to be acknowledged in cobbling together a pension plan. First, ministers in the United States were not eligible to participate in Social Security until 1956. Second, contributory pension plans in the merging churches were relatively new so that many clergy had not been able to participate very long and would have received miniscule pensions at retirement. For these reasons among others, a minimum pension of $1,500 was assured in 1963 and had been increased to $3,450 by 1977 for those on the "closed roll," that is, prior to the Social Security option. Their widows were supposed to live on $900 per year in 1963 and $2,124 in 1977.[310] These figures implied at best a poverty level of existence.

In 1978 the Executive Council upped these amounts by $30 a month for retired ministers or $18 for widows. Synods and LCA conventions agonized about the problem, but given the level of benevolence giving, not much more could be done. Most clergy who had been able to enter Social Security and had more years of service under the contributory pension plan, of course, were better off. But even some of these fell within the minimum pension category. During these difficult times, the pension board worked continually for ways to alleviate the most distressing cases and to better the whole situation.

The Lay Pension Problem

The situation with lay employees of the church at all levels was different and frequently worse than that of ministers. Since lay persons had been part of the Social Security system from the beginning, church employers had been obliged to provide for them as employees just as would have been the case with any corporation.[311] As a partial offset, the church pension plan provided that the employing agency could deduct 2 percent of the normal employer's 8 percent contribution. The employee contribution to the pension plan was set at 2 percent, instead of the 4 percent required of ministers, as an offset against their Social Security tax.[312] As a result, what accrued in the pension account of a lay person was less than what would have been the case with a minister receiving the same salary. Beginning in 1974, the church began a series of steps to redress this imbalance to insure that the lay benefit plan would be equal to the clergy plan.[313]

Paying for Health Benefits

When the LCA came into existence, the predecessor bodies were involved with over twenty different health benefit plans. At first, the claims against the Ministerial Health Benefit Plan for the more than twenty thousand persons covered were a modest $758,000 and did not exceed premiums.[314] By the end of 1976, however, the costs of the MHBP that came from benevolence had escalated by nearly 220 percent.[315] With the beginning of 1979, a concept called "dynamic cost-sharing" became effective, which essentially was a deductible paid by the insured up to a certain limit. The health plan for lay employees did not have the same direct impact on the churchwide budget since employers paid the premiums for employee coverage, and the contract was handled through a commercial insurance company.

THE ROCKY ROAD OF
LUTHERAN COOPERATION

"The promise of Lutheran unity that seemed so bright ten years ago has not been fulfilled," Robert Marshall declared in an interview with the editor of *The Lutheran* in 1978.[316] In his report to the LCA convention the same year, he said that in spite of many accomplishments, "the road of cooperation is a rocky one. There continue to be fears that LC-MS will withdraw from LCUSA, despite assurances to the contrary. . . . If cooperation is undependable and even disruptive," he warned, "the LCA needs to take care lest it make stronger commitments than others and pays too great a price."[317] Although the LCA had never really backed away from its constitutional stance

on Lutheran unity, there had been enough disturbing events in the
mid-seventies to give anyone reason for concern.

The Paths of ALC and LCA

At the risk of oversimplification, it seems fair to say that ALC and
LCA were on converging paths but approaching the question of
relationships from different directions and, perhaps, with a different
ultimate goal in mind. LCA kept pressing for organic unity and was
willing to engage in individual cooperative projects and common
structures along the way. ALC preferred to "develop as rapidly as
possible common organizational structures that will lend themselves
most easily to joint activity."[318] Meanwhile, LCMS wanted to go in
the direction of discussions of such questions as pulpit and altar fellowship, cooperative activities but not organic union. Consultations
between ALC and LCA on common structures, with LCMS representatives as observers, were attempted between 1972 and 1974
without success.[319]

What emerged in 1974 was a recommendation at Baltimore that
the LCA "Standing Committee on Approaches to Lutheran Unity be
directed to consult with representatives of The American Lutheran
Church with respect to such organic unity."[320] ALC in return proposed a small advisory committee to the presidents as a forum "to
discuss joint ALC-LCA interests in future Lutheran Church relations
and possible future structures for Lutherans in the United States."[321]
One staff person from each church was assigned to consult and draw
up an agenda for a Consulting Committee on Church Cooperation
that would hold three meetings prior to the Boston convention in
1976.[322]

The committee reported at Boston that the two churches were in
substantial agreement on theological matters and the mission of the
church, although LCA did place more emphasis on "cooperative
activities beyond the Lutheran family."[323] Although there were
some differences in emphases in the geographical regions encompassed in the churches, these were not regarded as significant issues.
Some differences in basic polity were identified, and the committee
proposed to the convention that studies be made to resolve these and
evaluate possible structures. These resolutions were passed, but an
additional motion was adopted directing the committee "to pursue
the negotiations with the ALC with the goal of organic unity."[324]

By the time of the 1978 LCA convention in Chicago there had

been a number of developments that changed the chemistry. The studies had shown that there were differences between ALC and LCA positions on the Holy Scriptures and the definition of the church that warranted further discussion.[325] While the committee found common viewpoints on many important questions, such as ordination, standards for the ordained ministry and the source of call, as well as a host of practical matters, there were still differences to be resolved on the size of legislative assemblies, selection of representatives, assignment of program and support responsibilities, number and responsibility of church offices, the number of geographical divisions, and the manner in which financial support is secured. The committee wanted to explore further structural options, including retention of existing structures with emphasis on cooperation, development of merged regional entities, and creation of a single church body. Into this mix, however, was introduced a new element, the Association of Evangelical Lutheran Churches and its "Call for Lutheran Union."[326]

From "Exile" to ELIM to AELC to ???

For a long time a moderate movement had been afoot in the Lutheran Church-Missouri Synod that was reflected in the views of a number of outstanding scholars who questioned the traditional and exclusive theological conservatism of the Synod.[327] Much of the controversy focused on Concordia Seminary in St. Louis, and when Jacob A. O. Preus was elected president in 1969 by a well-organized conservative group, an investigation of "liberalism" at the seminary was soon set in motion.[328] By the 1973 convention in New Orleans, forty-five of the fifty faculty members, including President John H. Tietjen, were under attack by the conservatives. The stage was set for what was called "the Second Battle of New Orleans."[329] An attempt to oppose Preus with a moderate candidate failed, and Preus was re-elected on the first ballot.

The Concordia Seminary Board proceeded with its investigation that led to Tietjen's ouster as president of the school early in 1974. On February 19 almost the entire faculty and some four hundred of the six hundred students solemnly walked out of the seminary. "From the Luther Tower, the carillon pealed 'A Mighty Fortress' as the procession, in solemn determination, moved through the Walther Arch and past the black-draped statue of Martin Luther. Pausing for Scripture reading, prayers, and the singing of the Doxology, the pilgrim band watched as make-shift wooden doors were placed across the archway. On the doors was the one-word summary of a self-imposed condition, 'Exiled.' "[330] The Concordia Seminary in Exile, which became known as "Christ Seminary-Seminex," was given temporary haven at Jesuit St. Louis Seminary and Eden Theological Seminary until rented quarters could be found. Sympathizers organized themselves as Evangelical Lutherans in Mission (ELIM) to support Seminex.[331]

ELIM also found its supporters among the ranks of the LCA, and the following year the delegates at the Baltimore convention a- dopted "A Statement of Concern" and invited a spokesperson for ELIM to address the assembly.[332] No efforts at reconciliation could heal the breach in Missouri, however, and the final blow fell when the time came for Seminex graduates to be ordained and other stu- dents assigned as vicars. Four district presidents proceeded to ordain graduates and place the interns. In April 1974, the four presidents were officially removed from office.[333] In despair, the adherents to ELIM finally organized a new church body, the Association of Evan- gelical Lutheran Churches, in December 1976. William H. Kohn, a former LCMS mission executive, was elected the first president. Some 200 congregations and about 280 pastors joined the Association at the outset.

The AELC wasted no time in expressing its ecumenical commit- ment. In March 1977 it was received into membership in the Lu- theran Council in the USA.[334] In June the AELC became a member of the Lutheran World Federation, a step the LCMS had repeatedly refused to take.[335] Through one of its seminary professors, it was also a participant in the Faith and Order Commission of the World Coun- cil of Churches.[336] Within a year after its formation, the AELC had issued its "Call for Lutheran Union," which made abundantly clear that the Association's ultimate aim was to join with other Lutherans in the formation of a new church body in the United States. It had cast its lot on the side of "organic union."

Balancing Two Proposals

When the LCA convention met in Chicago, it had before it not only the recommendations of the ALC/LCA Committee on Church Co- operation but also the approach from AELC. The Standing Commit- tee on Approaches to Unity concluded that it was possible to respond affirmatively on both points, although it recognized that the Committee on Church Cooperation regarded union as only one of three options, while the AELC proposal called "for a singular commitment to union and a consultation to agree on the process for fulfilling that commitment."[337] What the convention voted, therefore, essentially was to adopt the recommendations of the CCC and at the same time accept AELC's invitation to a consultation in the fall of 1979 to establish an implementation process. The LCA president was authorized to join with the other church presidents to arrange the consultation.[338] Even though there were two distinct approaches to deal with in the coming biennium, a process had been set in motion that would lead eventually to the formation of the Evangelical Lutheran Church in America.

Almost unnoticed by many delegates was the fact that the LCA's Canadian synods were moving slowly but surely toward their own merger with the Evangelical Lutheran Church of Canada. The target date reported by the Canada Section at Chicago was 1980, but that proved a bit too optimistic.[339] S. Theodore Jacobson, president of the ELCC, told delegates that "inter-Lutheran relationships are at a low ebb because of an impasse regarding the interpretation of the Scriptures and the ordination of women. But," he concluded, "those two groups interested would be conferring to effect a union soon."[340]

Keeping Cooperation in Gear

While all of this maneuvering was going on in searching for a path to Lutheran unity, it should be borne in mind that the LCA and ALC were engaged in a long series of joint programs and studies. Some of these took place within the context of LCUSA or Lutheran World Ministries.[341] Others were done bilaterally, such as the development of cooperative programs at key theological seminaries, which required the LCA to amend its constitution to permit churchwide financial support for a seminary where there is common ownership with another church body.[342]

A major step was taken in formulating a joint Statement of Communion Practices for the two churches. Initially introduced to the LCA at its 1976 convention, the statement was adopted provisionally as a working document that was to be studied and revised during the following biennium in light of lengthy debate and suggestions on the convention floor.[343] One of the major developments in the statement as finally adopted in 1978 provided greater freedom for clergy to minister in the company of clergy of other churches, especially

where interconfessional dialogues provided the theological basis.[344]
In the section that dealt with admission to the Sacrament of Holy
Communion, one sentence appeared that generated intense reaction
in some circles. After citing a number of criteria for admission, the
statement declared flatly, "Thus infant communion is precluded."
Although the practice was almost nonexistent in the LCA, proponents of infant Communion were incensed. Others were troubled
that an authoritarian sentence like this could be used as though it
settled the question finally. Since infant Communion was a worldwide issue, the debate was destined to continue.

THE CRISIS IN ECUMENISM

In the mid-seventies historian Martin Marty wrote, "The ecumenical
movement is in a coma. Some would say it is dead. Born in its modern
form in 1910, it came to maturity in 1948 when the World Council
of Churches was formed. The Second Vatican Council was its most
surprising expression. Senility and disease followed."[345] Although
writing the obituary of ecumenism at that point would have been
premature, there can be little doubt that much that went on in these
circles had little interest for the person in the pew unless some social
statement or other pronouncement rubbed the raw end of a nerve.
For most church members, the whole ecumenical engagement was
a high-level game that pursued esoteric questions about which they
understood little and usually cared less.

Nevertheless, the stakes were high, and the LCA was subtly changing the rules by which it played the game. The "evangelical and
representative principles" by which the LCA had conducted ecumenical relations from the outset were coming under fresh scrutiny.
On inter-Lutheran relations, it held firmly to maximum cooperation
and a commitment to unity where church bodies shared the same
confessional witness. With regard to interchurch agencies, the LCA
came to grips with the changing tenor of the times and modified its
stance to say, "This church, for proper accountability, considers it
crucial that the decisive power in the privilege of the ballot in interchurch agencies rest with the official representatives of the member
churches."[346]

When this question came to the convention floor in Baltimore, the
president "said that he would interpret the phrase 'decisive power'
to mean that at least ¾ of the governing body would be official

representatives of churches or church agencies."[347] The convention adopted the new position with little discussion, but the fact was that the strict guidelines of former years had been relaxed.[348] Previously, the church had stated its principle largely in terms of "with whom may we *not* be in official relations." The 1974 statement was more in terms of "with whom *should* we be in official relations."

Interconfessional dialogue was another area in which the LCA was becoming more extensively involved through both Lutheran World Ministries and LCUSA. The Executive Council, therefore, asked DWME to recommend a policy that would indicate (1) the purpose of participation, (2) the role of LCA representatives, and (3) the status of reports and recommendations issuing from the conversations. The document that was approved by the Executive Council in April 1976 was titled "Guidelines for Participation in Interconfessional Dialogue."[349] The lengthy statement made clear that while representatives are "free to speak creatively, as theologians of the church, especially when facing new issues. . . . They are not, however, to be regarded as 'negotiators,' bishops, or 'canon lawyers' concluding agreements, the authority for which rests in the Executive Council of Convention." Recognizing that there was a widespread feeling that the "dialogue results are never implemented," DWME was to report and make recommendations to the Executive Council to implement results important to the life of the church and LCA ecumenical plans and expectations. It was clear that the dialogue teams were not free-floating entities and that there was a specific route to be followed in having proposals acted upon by the church.

More and more as dialogue teams, the NCCCUSA, and the World Council of Churches addressed ecumenical issues, the LCA evolved careful processes for responding to all of the proposals that emerged from such groups. To do so was the only responsible course for the church to avoid confusion and even conflict with its own historic positions. A case in point was the way that the LCA responded to the WCC Commission on Faith and Order's study *One Baptism, One Eucharist, and a Mutually Recognized Ministry.* The Fifth Assembly of WCC, which had met in Nairobi in 1975, had referred to the member churches for reaction Faith and Order Paper No. 73 which, in a sense, was an outgrowth of nearly a half century of discussion stretching back to the first Faith and Order Conference at Lausanne in 1927.[350]

The LCA's response was a lengthy paper, thoroughly documented from the Lutheran Confessions and church policy actions.[351] The document contained fifty-six separate points that indicated both the particular parts of Paper No. 73 that the LCA could affirm and those where it had reservations or disagreed. For example, the response went into great detail about the question of ministry, reflecting the discussion that had been going on in the LCA itself concerning the ministry of the whole people of God and the particular role of the ordained ministry. The LCA would return to intense discussion of a revised version of Paper No. 73 in the development of which one of its own ministers, William H. Lazareth, would play a key role as Director of the Secretariat on Faith and Order of the World Council.

ENDING THE "MARSHALL YEARS"

If the church was stricken by grief at the news of the death of Franklin Clark Fry in 1968, it was stunned by the announcement on March 31, 1978, that Robert J. Marshall would not accept another term as president. Not even his closest associates were privy to the decision, but the president had determined that the time had come to accept a call to serve the church in another role. When his term ended on October 31, he would become Director of the Office of Mission, Service, and Development of Lutheran World Ministries.

There were several reasons for his decision. First, many of the major goals he had set, such as completion of the *Lutheran Book of Worship*, the Strength for Mission Appeal, restructuring of the LCA, the study of Theological Affirmations, the adoption of the statement on the Theology and Practice of Confirmation, a heightened emphasis on racial and social justice, the World Hunger Appeal, the Intensified Christian Giving Program, and Evangelical Outreach were either achieved or safely launched. Second, he knew that if a decision were reached to move ahead on a merger of Lutheran church bodies, he would feel constrained to continue in office until that was accomplished. And a distant third in his own thinking was a reluctant recognition that his own health and strength would not be equal forever to the rigorous demands that he himself placed upon them in fulfilling the presidency.[352]

Once people adjusted to the initial shock of the announcement, speculation began as to who would fill the office. One name mentioned frequently was that of H. George Anderson, president of Southern Seminary, but he had repeatedly disclaimed any wish to be elected. By the time the convention began in Chicago on a steamy July 12, the rumor mill was every bit as hot as the weather.

Choosing a New President

Before balloting could even begin, an effort was made to suspend the bylaws governing the election to change some of the procedures, but this was defeated.[353] When the results of the first ballot were announced, H. George Anderson had a commanding lead with 244 votes, followed by William H. Lazareth, 48; Kenneth H. Sauer, 38; Herbert W. Chilstrom, 37; James R. Crumley, Jr., 29; Howard J. McCarney, 27; Reuben T. Swanson, 25; Paul E. Erickson, 22; Philip L. Wahlberg, Jr., 18; Franklin D. Fry, 15; Edward K. Perry, 15. The remaining votes were scattered among fifty-nine other candidates.[354]

Dr. Anderson asked for the privilege of the floor and in a brief but moving statement said, "In the light of God-given responsibilities which I feel are still vital for me, I am moved to say that, as far as faithfulness to that responsibility is concerned, I would not be available for the position and would ask that those members here would consider other candidates. And if anyone is disappointed or disapproving of this, please forgive me."[355] Dr. Sauer, president of the Ohio Synod,[356] and Dr. McCarney, president of the Central Pennsylvania Synod, also asked not to be considered. For a few moments, it looked as though there would be mass declinations, but that did not occur.

Faced with a new situation, the convention reconsidered its earlier action about suspending the bylaws and voted approval of a process that would gradually narrow the field and would provide after the third ballot that the top four persons would speak for five minutes each before another vote was taken. On the second ballot, Herbert Chilstrom received 136 votes; William Lazareth, 107; George Anderson, 92; James Crumley, 87; and Reuben Swanson, 62.[357] On the third ballot, the four leaders were William Lazareth, 169; Herbert Chilstrom, 157; Reuben Swanson, 124; James Crumley, 103.[358] Each addressed the convention briefly, and the fourth ballot was taken. The results were Lazareth, 214; Chilstrom, 160; Crumley, 158; Swanson, 139.[359] After the field was narrowed to three, a dramatic change took place, and the new totals were Lazareth, 261; Crumley, 210; Chilstrom, 200.[360]

The sixth and final ballot was a replay of the voting for secretary

Reuben T. Swanson

in Baltimore. James R. Crumley suddenly surged to the fore and was elected over William H. Lazareth by the narrow margin of 337 to 330.[361] In his remarks to the convention before the fourth ballot, Dr. Crumley had said, "You may find this hard to believe, but I have not sought and am not now seeking the presidency of the LCA. I still view myself primarily as a parish pastor. I serve the Church, and it's the Church's place to tell me where to serve." Apparently, this struck the right note with the delegates. When he was elected, the new president said simply, "There is only one possible answer for me: I accept the office. I do so with fear and trembling."[362]

Selecting a Secretary and More

The vacancy in the office of secretary created by James R. Crumley's election as president precipitated another round of balloting. For the first time in LCA history, it was possible to vote for a lay person for this office, and theoretically more than two million active LCA members were eligible. On the first ballot, ninety persons received votes. Heading the list was Dorothy J. Marple, assistant to Dr. Marshall, with 99 votes; Reuben T. Swanson, president of the Nebraska Synod, with 76; and James E. Gunther, a Black parish pastor from New York, was third with 46 votes.[363]

On the third ballot, however, Dr. Swanson won handily, with 350 votes to Dorothy Marple's 119 and James Gunther's 95.[364] Together with L. Milton Woods, who had been reelected treasurer overwhelmingly on the first ballot for that office, the LCA now had a new trio of officers. It was a team that would lead the LCA to some momentous decisions about Lutheran unity four years later at Louisville. But an interesting sidelight was the fact that the four top contenders for the presidency—Crumley, Lazareth, Chilstrom, and Swanson—would be back on the ballot for bishop when a new church was formed in 1987.

NOTES

1. Paul Johnson, *Modern Times, the World of the Twenties to Eighties* (New York: Harper & Row, 1983), 668.
2. Julius W. Pratt, Vincent P. De Santis, Joseph M. Siracusa, *A History of United States Foreign Policy*, 4th ed. (Englewood Cliffs, N.J.: Prentice-Hall, 1980), 499.
3. Bailyn et al., *Great Republic*, 1258–59.
4. Paul Johnson, *Modern Times*, 687.
5. Ibid., 654–57.
6. During the attempted secession of Biafra from Nigeria, it is estimated that when food supplies were cut off from Biafra some two million people died of starvation and related diseases between 1968 and 1970. Cited in a review by Colin Campbell of Dan Jacobs, *The Brutality of Nations* (New York: Alfred A. Knopf, 1987) in *The New York Times Book Review* (March 29, 1987): 15.
7. This was not the first time, however, that Cuban troops had been sent abroad. They had been dispatched to Syria in 1973. See Constantine C. Menges, "Detente's Dark History," *Wall Street Journal* (January 9, 1987): 20.
8. Pratt et al., *U.S. Foreign Policy*, 520; Johnson, *Modern Times*, 538–43.
9. Morison et al., *Growth of American Republic*, 800.
10. The whole sequence of events is described in Morison et al., *Growth of American Republic*, 799–803. The text of Nixon's letter of resignation delivered to Secretary of State Henry Kissinger appears in Carolyn Mathiasen, ed., *Congressional Quarterly Almanac* (Washington: Congressional Quarterly Almanac Inc., 1974), 902.
11. Bailyn et al., *Great Republic*, 1265.
12. Ibid.
13. *1974 CQ Almanac*, 904.
14. Morison et al., *Growth of American Republic*, 804.
15. Ibid., 805.
16. Paul Johnson describes factors that contributed to the Shah's downfall and the ensuing executions and political upheaval in *Modern Times*, 704–8.
17. Pratt et al., *U.S. Foreign Policy*, 531–32.
18. Ibid., 806.

19. *Time* (January 19, 1987):50. By contrast, the Dow began a dizzying climb from a low of 776.92 on August 12, 1982, to break the 2,000 level on January 9, 1987, and was closing in on 2,400 by late March 1987 when this chapter was written.

20. *1980 CQ Almanac*, 271. In the first quarter of 1980, the increase in the Consumer Price Index in the United States reached a peak rate of 18.2 percent, and the prime rate—the rate of interest charged by banks to their best customers—hit 22.5 percent later in the year.

21. See *America in Perspective*, Oxford Analytica, David R. Young, director (Boston: Houghton Mifflin, 1986), 57.

22. *Forbes* (April 6, 1987):199.

23. *New York Times* (March 8, 1987):Section E2.

24. *America in Perspective*, 144.

25. Ibid., 18–19.

26. "The US, with 5 percent of the world's population, takes about 50 percent of its international migrants, not counting refugees. . . . The majority of legal immigrants (77 percent by the end of the 1970s) were born in Third World countries. . . . Fifty-three percent are female, 26 percent are under sixteen, and 60 percent have no occupation" (ibid., 20–21).

27. The statistics here are cited in Paul Abrecht, ed., *Faith Science and the Future* (Geneva, Switzerland: World Council of Churches, 1978), 125–32. The Green Revolution was a remarkable effort to expand production in food-deficient countries by the use of new high-yielding types of grain and heavy fertilization. Some countries, such as Mexico and the Philippines, actually became exporters of grain for a while but returned to a deficit position in a few years, partly because of the high cost of fertilizers.

28. See Gustavo Gutierrez, *A Theology of Liberation* (Maryknoll, N.Y.: Orbis, 1973) as an example of a strong voice for the liberation movement.

29. Bellah originally used the term in an article, "Civil Religion in America," *Daedalus* 96 (Winter 1967). A reprint of a chapter that describes his later reflections, "Religion and the Legitimation of the American Republic," in *Varieties of Civil Religion*, ed. Robert N. Bellah and Phillip E. Hammond (New York: Harper & Row, 1980), appears in *The Church and Civil Religion* (New York: Lutheran World Ministries, 1986).

30. *LCAM, 1972*, 36.

31. Other members were Charles Y. Glock, Berkeley, CA, professor of sociology, University of California; Gertrude Gobbel, Gettysburg, PA, professor of psychology, Gettysburg College; LaVern K. Grosc, York, PA, pastor, Christ Lutheran Church; Gerald K. Johnson, Chicago, IL, president, Illinois Synod; Claudine Lee Martin, Chicago, IL, professor of psychology, Malcom X University; Raymond M. Lukes, Santa Ana, CA, engineer, Physics Group; Daniel F. Martensen, Springfield, OH, professor, Hamma School of Theology; Richard Weis, Wappingers Falls, NY, manager of operations, Advanced Systems, IBM; Robert A. West, Denver, CO, pastor, St. Paul's Lutheran Church. See *LCAM, 1974*, 396.

32. Ibid., 397.

33. Information about the study appears not only in the LCA minutes but also in William H. Lazareth and Raymond Tiemeyer, *In, Not Of, Living Our*

Baptism in the World, participant's book (Philadelphia: Lutheran Church Press, 1974). See especially pp. 75–77.

34. Ibid., 87.

35. *LCAM, 1974*, 408–9. In addition to the participant's book, Lazareth and Tiemeyer prepared a leader's guide for *In, Not Of,* which contained a fuller commentary on the commission's study report itself (Philadelphia: Lutheran Church Press, 1974).

36. *LCAM, 1974*, 415–16.

37. The order approved by the 1974 convention was a forerunner of the rite for Affirmation of Baptism that appears in the *Lutheran Book of Worship*, 198–201.

38. *LCAM, 1974*, 419–22.

39. Fisher's letter and the document "An Invitation to Dialogue and Decision," which was mailed to all pastors on the clerical roll and lay delegates to the convention May 1, are in the LCA Archives.

40. LCA News Bureau release, May 10, 1974.

41. On June 17, Fisher had mailed a second pamphlet of questions and answers to all convention delegates in which he detailed his own extensive experience as pastor of Trinity Church "recognized as one of the leading renewal congregations in Protestant America," lecturer/teacher at seminaries, member of boards and committees, leader of more than 140 convocations and retreats for pastors and lay people in various denominational settings, and author of seven books. He also detailed specifics about such matters as structural operations in the LCA.

42. "Invitation to Dialogue," 2.

43. *LCAM, 1974*, 37.

44. Ibid., 391. In the excitement, some interesting facts went almost unnoticed. Two persons whose names would figure prominently in the election of president in 1978 received votes. They were H. George Anderson and William Lazareth, with fifteen and seven votes respectively. Also, for the first time a woman, Elizabeth Platz, received votes for president.

45. LCUSA News Bureau release 74-49, July 9, 1974, p. 3.

46. Ibid.

47. *LCAM, 1974*, 419–20.

48. *1974 Convention Summary*, 3–4.

49. *LCAM, 1974*, 395. Woods, a vice-president of the Mobil Oil Corporation, had been elected treasurer by the Executive Council to fill the unexpired term of Carl Anderson, who died in 1972.

50. C. Thomas Spitz, an LCMS pastor, had resigned as general secretary of LCUSA on December 4, 1973 (see *LCAM, 1974*, 267). Dr. Harkins had been elected unanimously to the position by a mail ballot on May 6, 1970. He assumed his new duties on October 1.

51. *LCAM, 1974*, 494.

52. The wording of the necessary change in the *LCA Constitution*, Article XII, Section 7, that allowed for the secretary to be either lay or clergy was adopted in 1976 (see *LCAM, 1974*, 579; and *1976*, 331).

53. The series of ballots for secretary is recorded in the *LCAM, 1974*, 511–12, 559, 578, 582, 648.

54. Both Lazareth and Crumley made this clear to the writer at the time.

55. Crumley, who was 49 at the time, was a native of Bluff City, Tennessee. He had served as pastor in Oak Ridge and Savannah. He had written for the LCA BPE and was chosen to chair the Committee on Theological Affirmations.

56. *LCAM, 1974,* 479–88.

57. Ibid., 496–98. A few of the recommendations of the committee were adopted, such as one asking synods to effect ways of increasing the number of youth, minorities, and women in their delegations (p. 499).

58. Ibid., 233–34.

59. Ibid., 318–19.

60. *ECM, April 1974,* 656–57.

61. *LCAM, 1974,* 720–21.

62. *LCAM, 1976,* 228–30, 432.

63. *LCAM, 1974,* 429, 436, 900.

64. The document describing this approach was called "Social Statements: Their Purpose and Development."

65. *LCAM, 1974,* 433–37.

66. A second statement dealing with "Aging and the Older Adult" was also adopted in 1978 and will be discussed later in this chapter.

67. *LCAM, 1978,* 353–67, gives the final text of the statement as amended and adopted.

68. Ibid., 355.

69. Ibid., 357.

70. Ibid., 361–62.

71. *LCAM, 1974,* 459.

72. In the United States, for example, it was against the law to require persons to state their race or religion on employment applications. In public schools these questions were not supposed to appear on permanent record forms of pupils, although under the Civil Rights Act of 1964, school districts were expected to provide numerical information about racial categories.

73. The question of the appropriateness of the term *minority* was brought to the attention of the Executive Council in 1975, but the advice of the CCMGI was that "the term 'minority group' should not be changed at this time." See *ECM, February 1975,* 138; and *April 1975,* 568–69.

74. *LCAM, 1974,* 459.

75. The study *An Inventory of the Lutheran Church in America: Race Relations* was presented to the convention and is in the LCA Archives. The CCMGI also had before it two other documents: *LCA Budgets in Relation to Minority Group Interests* and *LCA Minutes Regarding Minority Group Interests,* also in the Archives.

76. The figures were compiled by the DPS Research Department on the basis of congregational reports. James Kenneth Echols concludes that in 1976 there were 18,971 Blacks on the LCA membership roles. See "Inclusiveness and Catholicity," *Partners* (April/May, 1984):15. These figures correspond to the DPS breakdown.

77. *LCAM, 1976,* 480.

78. *LCAM, 1978,* 394. The person selected for the position was Massie L. Kennard, a Black minister, who was on the DMNA staff and had served as chairperson of the Staff Team on MGI from 1975.

79. Ibid., 251–61, includes the complete statement and the actions taken.

80. Carver Portlock, the chairperson, explained that although the term *quota* had never appeared in the document, "the language has been changed so that even the fear of the suggestion might be removed." See *1978 Convention Summary,* 11–12.

81. There were eight goals in all, with a total of twenty-three subordinate aims and scores of specific plans for working toward them.

82. *LCAM, 1974,* 451–58.

83. There was an interesting statistical difference between Canadian and United States percentages of women members. The figures for confirmed were as follows: Canada, 53.3; U.S., 56.2; active confirmed: Canada, 54.1; U.S., 56.8. The difference was even more marked in church council membership, where only 13 percent were women in Canada as compared with 18.3 percent in the United States.

84. When the question was raised at the 1974 convention about the relationship between Lutheran Church Women and the committee, Dorothy Marple, executive of LCW, stated that the two were not in competition. See *Convention Summary,* 5.

85. Figures here are from the consulting committee's report, *LCAM, 1978,* 394–402.

86. Women members of church councils had increased from 18.1 percent of the total to 26.7 between 1973 and 1977, but traditional arenas of female participation, such as Sunday school leaders, actually increased to almost three-fourths of the total number in that time. Unfortunately, women teachers tended to be concentrated at the lower age levels.

87. *LCAM, 1978,* 399.

88. Dr. Krych served as a children's editor in DPS until she was called to the Philadelphia Seminary to teach Christian education. The Rev. S. Anita Stauffer also joined the staff of DPS as worship editor in 1978, but Margaret Krych had left by that time and was succeeded by Dr. Miriam Johnson, a lay educator. Even by 1982, the consulting committee reported no increase in the number of ordained women on staff (*LCAM, 1982,* 388). In 1986, DPS added a second ordained woman, the Rev. Ivis LaRiviere-Mestre, as editor of Spanish language resources. She had served part-time in that role from 1984 while also serving in a parish. In 1985 the Rev. Mary Forell-Davis, who had served a parish in New Jersey, joined the staff of DMNA as director of the Urban Ministry Section.

89. Dr. Marple, who had served as executive of LCW and staff coordinator for the Commission on Function and Structure, was succeeded by Dr. Kathryn E. Kopf, a Canadian, to head the women's auxiliary. See *1976 Convention Summary,* 8; and *LCAM, 1976,* 693.

90. *LCAM, 1980,* 388.

91. *LCAM, 1976,* 300–1 and Exhibit A. The Committee on Legal Matters had advised the Executive Council that the normal process of amendment

of the constitution, which would have taken until 1978, was not necessary
since the changes were editorial "perfections."

92. The DPS Management Committee requested the ILCW to undertake
a study of gender-related language in the proposed *LBW*. The ILCW appointed a language review committee that included two LCA women, the
Rev. LaVonne Althouse and Marilyn Waniek. The review group made a
series of proposals for changes in hymns and liturgical texts. It even succeeded in having the word *men* eliminated from the ICET text of the Nicene
Creed that had previously read ". . . who for us men and our salvation . . ." The management committee endorsed these proposals and reported them to the Executive Council; it also committed the division to be
guided by the convention action in the preparation of its own materials for
worship. See *DPSM, September 25–27, 1975*; and *LCAM, 1976*, 314–15.

93. *LCAM, 1976*, 316.

94. The full text of the report is in the *LCAM, 1976*, 316–19.

95. *LCAM, 1972*, 671.

96. There had been efforts by DMNA and the consulting committee to
have a policy adopted that would require that churchwide meetings be held
only in states that had approved ERA. The exceptions would have been for
meetings involving synods whose own territories were in such states. The
Executive Council chose to reaffirm support of ERA and urged DMNA to
work with synods for its passage. See *ECM, February 1978*, 448; and *April
1978*, 571.

97. *LCAM, 1978*, 15–16.

98. *LCAM, 1980*, 130. The motion did provide for the possibility that the
time limit for ratification would expire without approval, which was actually
the case.

99. *LCAM, 1974*, 437.

100. *LCAM, 1976*, 473–76.

101. *LCAM, 1978*, 192–97, 322–23.

102. *LCAM, 1974*, 625–47.

103. Ibid., 421.

104. *LCAM, 1976*, 454.

105. Ibid., 368–69, 438.

106. *LCAM, 1978*, 649, 778–81. The Staff Team on Ministry of the Laity
was given the coordinating role among CWAs, but the staffing and budget
administration were under DMNA.

107. In the course of its early development, the group decided to capitalize LAOS in Ministry as its name. In the New Testament, *Laos* normally
refers to the whole people of God.

108. *LCAM, 1980*, 735–36.

109. Ibid., 351–52.

110. *LCAM, 1974*, 65–67, 465, 739.

111. Ibid., 466–69, 739–43. The statement underscored the dangers inherent in the world's dwindling food supply and urged a series of government
actions including committing 10 percent of the nation's grain available for
export to assist the hungry, developing an international network of food

reserves, supporting UNICEF and the World Food Program, encouraging citizens to avoid wasteful use of food, establishing safeguards against dangerous fluctuations in commodity prices, working closely with charitable organizations, and sponsoring research in increased food production. Although addressed to the United States government, the statement was also intended to serve as the church's policy in Canada.

112. Ibid., 699–700.

113. Ibid., 700, 725–26. The delegates also voted for several additional motions, including one that would enlist youth in the effort and set up a world hunger task force.

114. Extensive reports and discussions are recorded in the minutes of the Executive Council at every meeting throughout the biennium as the LCA leaders wrestled with the complex questions of how to administer most responsibly the influx of funds.

115. Up-to-date information was supplied to the writer in a telephone interview with Vernon Cronmiller and confirmed in a letter on May 21, 1987. Pastor Cronmiller succeeded Robert Stackel when the latter retired as director in 1980.

116. *LCAM, 1976,* 120–22. DPS received $325,000 for programs to sensitize and educate the constituency about the crisis, and $475,000 was allocated to DMNA in support of governmental programs.

117. Extensive reports and actions regarding world hunger appear in the minutes of every biennial convention beginning in 1976. In 1976, for example, sixteen synods sent memorials asking that the appeal be extended (*LCAM,* 421). A consulting committee was appointed from the constituency to monitor the program and evaluate results.

118. Although income from apportionment had climbed from 19.03 million dollars in 1963 to about 22.47 million in a decade, inflation was already taking its toll. And despite the fact that the amount allocated to churchwide agencies in 1975 *from all sources of income* had increased to a little over 24 million dollars, *the actual purchasing power* had slipped to slightly more than 16 million. See *LCAM, 1974,* 704–5; *LCAM, 1976,* 76; *Confessing Christ Today* (DPS, 1981), 4–5. Meanwhile, the proportion of total funds needed for such mandated expenses as the health benefits plan, minimum pensions, and interest on borrowings spiraled upward.

119. *LCAM, 1974,* 725.

120. President Marshall appointed a consulting committee of seven who proposed the firm of Marts and Lundy, Inc., to do the study. See *ECM, October 1974,* 52; *February 1975,* 130–31; *June 1975,* 219–21.

121. *LCAM, 1976,* 145. The entire report appears on pp. 136–48.

122. Ibid., 148–50. CCS had previously conducted a very successful appeal for the American Lutheran Church.

123. Ibid., 150.

124. Ibid., 407, 420.

125. *LCAM, 1978,* 588.

126. Ibid., 138. The complete report to the 1978 convention and the text of the Service of Thanksgiving appear on pp. 119–40. A special resolution

honoring the work of Pastor Gerberding, who had suffered a heart attack from overwork during the campaign, is on p. 797. Arthur O. F. Bauer, who had substituted as director during Gerberding's illness, was also honored.

127. Vikner, "LCA World Mission," 188.

128. The four-page statement was adopted by the DWME Management Committee at its meeting, November 8–10, 1973. The one statement of purpose that did not specifically use the phrase "outside North America" was one which dealt with participation in efforts of Christians to work together both in supporting one another's efforts to fulfill the church's mission and relating to agencies of other faiths and of secular good will.

129. *DWME/MC Minutes, November 8–10, 1973,* 3.

130. *ECM, April 1974,* 650–52.

131. *LCAM, 1976,* 615. So well received were the events that two were needed in 1977 and six were projected for 1979–82 (*LCAM, 1978,* 471).

132. Ibid., 4. Attention to the full range of inter-Lutheran and interchurch relationships will be dealt with later in this chapter.

133. The position paper prepared for the management committee on January 11, 1974, that was titled simply "Tanzania" is illustrative of the careful planning that DWME put into developing joint work with ALC. Together with a staff paper, "ALC/LCA Africa Committee," dated January 1977, it sets forth the way in which the two churches intended to carry out their ministry with the Evangelical Lutheran Church in Tanzania (see documentation from DWME minutes).

134. *LCAM, 1976,* 615–16. See also 258–59.

135. Scherer, "Self-Hood and Maturity," 341.

136. *LCAM, 1978,* 464–65. See also Scherer, "Self-Hood and Maturity," 341–42, 351. As early as August 1976, LCA Executive Director Vikner and Emmanuel Abraham, President of ECMY, forged a six-page "Agreement of Cooperation" to guide the relationships of the two churches in the volatile situation. In September 1978 a document was drafted at a meeting in Oslo establishing a "Committee on Mutual Christian Responsibility" that became the avenue through which all mission agencies functioned in their partnership with the Ethiopian church. The Terms of Reference were approved by the DWME Management Committee, September 1978.

137. David L. Vikner, *The Church in the People's Republic of China* (Unpublished manuscript, 1984), 2. In Beijing, for example, Protestant places of worship were reduced from 20 to 4, and in Shanghai from 200 to 26.

138. Ibid.

139. Ibid., 3.

140. This point was made clear to the writer in the interview with DWME staff referred to earlier.

141. *Guidelines in Regard to Oppressive Situations, DWME/MC Minutes, March 11–14, 1978,* 67; *DWME/CD Minutes, June 13,* 171.

142. David L. Vikner, "The Era of Interdependence," *Missiology: An International Review* (October 1974):13–14.

143. *LCAM, 1974,* 351.

144. *LCAM, 1978,* 465.

145. Ibid., 465, 472.

146. *LCAM, 1980,* 357.

147. *LCAM, 1978,* 379. The years involved were 1970 through 1975.

148. *The Lutheran* (November 23, 1973):18.

149. *LCAM, 1976,* 449. It must be remembered that the BAM was the shell corporation through which DMNA and OAF worked to handle the Church Property Fund.

150. It should be noted that the Aid Association for Lutherans and the Lutheran Brotherhood were major sources of loans to congregations during this decade. In addition, they provided grants and interest rebates in some instances to help ease the church building crisis. See *LCAM, 1978,* 385.

151. The writer himself was often a member of churchwide consultation teams that met in these face-to-face exchanges. At times the climate was tense as the needs of synods and the LCA as a whole were measured against one another and an agreement hammered out that could be approved by the consultation, the synodical executive board, and eventually the LCA Executive Council. Although exchanges, at times, could be sharp, the consultations over the years developed a sense of partnership and reality about both synodical and churchwide budgeting. One feature that frequently resulted in facing problems frankly was the inclusion of the president of another synod on the churchwide team. This brought a kind of "peer pressure" that would not have been the case if the team had been only CWA "bureaucrats" vs. the synodical representatives.

152. *LCAM, 1974,* 452. Results of the 1973 consultations appear on pp. 123–24. In some instances it was necessary for a synod to amend its constitution to make the negotiations possible. See *LCAM, 1974,* 229–32.

153. *LCAM, 1976,* 447–48. As the consultations proceeded, they became more sophisticated, and the instruments used were honed to accomplish the job more effectively. The help of the DPS was enlisted in devising the processes used by synods with congregations at that stage.

154. Ibid., 446.

155. *ECM, January 1973,* 119–120; *May 1973,* 208; *January-February 1974,* 399–401; *April 1974,* 534–35. The primary responsibility in this area was assigned to DMNA.

156. *LCAM, 1978,* 370.

157. *LCAM, 1976,* 451–52; *1978,* 353.

158. *LCAM, 1966,* 223, 227.

159. See Solberg, *Higher Education,* 342. Dr. Solberg was himself director of the department.

160. Ibid., 342.

161. *LCAM, 1974,* 446–47.

162. *LCAM, 1976,* 466–72. There were three publications over the next few years that dealt with the data: Merton P. Strommen, *Research Report to the Joint Commission of the Division for Mission in North America and the Council of LCA Colleges on a Survey of Images and Expectations of LCA Colleges* (Minneapolis: Youth Research Center, 1976); Charles R. Bruning, *Relationships Between Church-Related Colleges and Their Constituencies*

(New York: LCA, 1975); Richard W. Solberg and Merton P. Strommen, *How Church-Related Are Church-Related Colleges?* (Philadelphia: Board of Publication, LCA, 1980).

163. *LCAM, 1976,* 470.

164. Ibid., 460–66. In a related action, the convention asked the Executive Council to take steps to recommend to synods and appropriate agencies that terminology other than "covenant" be used to describe the church and related institutions (*LCAM, 1976,* 408). This was a departure from the term that had been used in developing the "covenant" agreements between colleges and the LCA in the past.

165. Solberg, *Higher Education,* 342.

166. *LCAM, 1976,* 459, 710–11.

167. Arrangements were made initially for the Division of Mission and Ministry of LCUSA to provide administrative and other services (ibid., 262–63).

168. *LCAM, 1978,* 387–88.

169. The Approved Constitution for Congregations as adopted by the 1962 convention provided for a rather rigid internal structure of committees that often proved cumbersome to maintain, particularly for small congregations. The ACC, as adopted, appears in the *LCAM, 1962,* 208–219.

170. *LCAM, 1974,* 617–18. The complete study report appears on pp. 614–25.

171. The least understood of these terms was *support.* For many persons this conveyed the idea of financial support. While this was certainly a major factor, the concept was also intended to include regular evaluation of the total life of the congregation and the recruiting, equipping, and support of members for their ministry.

172. *LCAM, 1976,* 238. See *ACC,* Article III, Section 1. The full text of the Executive Council report is on pp. 236–47.

173. Ibid., 239, Article II, Section 3. This provision not only fulfilled the intent of the Commission on Function and Structure but also carried out the thrust of the earlier Manifesto for the congregation from the Report of the Commission on the Nature and Mission of the Congregation (*LCAM, 1966,* 539–58).

174. The congregation was supplied with a packet of material including information about itself and a step-by-step series of booklets to guide the leaders through the process. These included *Discovering What This Approach Is All About, The Theology Behind Our Ministry, Exploring God's Call and Our Response, Developing Our Statement of Mission, Discovering Our Hopes, Taking Our Ministry into Our Neighborhood* (Philadelphia: DPS, 1975). There were also report sheets to be sent to DPS where customized program and resource recommendations were prepared for that particular congregation. Assistance by trained consultants was also available.

175. A basic book prepared by the LCA on parish development was W. Kent Gilbert, ed., *The Shaping of the Parish for the Future* (Philadelphia: Parish Life Press, 1975). It included chapters by such writers as Arvid E. Anderson, H. George Anderson, Robert N. Bacher, Robert D. Benne, Har-

vey L. Huntley, Sr., William E. Lesher, Luther E. Lindberg, Robert J. Marshall, Judith L. McWilliams, Edward K. Perry, Donald R. Pichaske, Harvey L. Prinz, Robert F. Sims, S. Anita Stauffer, Raymond Tiemeyer, and Wilson E. Touhsaent. The book was intended principally for pastors and other professional church leaders.

176. Judith McWilliams Dickhart carried out a study of *Parish Development: A Summary of Key Learnings* (Philadelphia: 1986) for the Coordinating Committee for Cooperative Projects in Congregational Life (CCCPCL) that assessed the parish planning processes used in ALC, LCA, ELCC, and LCMS. She estimates that between 25 and 40 percent of the congregations in these bodies were involved in one or another parish development process. In LCA about 10 percent went through the complete PLMD procedure, while many other congregations engaged in more limited efforts. See p. 9 of report.

177. A seven-member Special Hymnal Review Committee established by the LCMS 1977 convention reported at a meeting December 9–10 a basic proposal that Missouri publish its own "revised edition" of the *LBW* that would correct what were deemed to be theological errors and inadequacies in the hymn selection (news release from LCMS Department of Public Relations, December 12, 1977). The chairman of the committee said that it would "give Lutherans a choice in the use of a hymnal—not only our own people but those in the American Lutheran Church and the Lutheran Church in America who had expressed misgivings with the *LBW.*" Detailed "Procedures for Copyright Administration" reported by the publishers to the Executive Committee of ILCW explained that Augsburg and the LCA Board of Publication would publish the complete body of materials. Concordia had the right to publish any or all of the materials compiled under ILCW. See *ILCW-XC-M, November 27, 1978, Exhibit C.*

178. The final report of the Review Committee (*Report and Recommendations of the Special Hymnal Review Committee,* St. Louis: The Lutheran Church-Missouri Synod, undated publication) contained the sentence "At the close of the December meeting the committee unanimously resolved to recommend to the congregations of Synod that the *LBW* be accepted with modifications. Here is a summary of those modifications:" [approximately 40 pages of detailed material followed]. A lengthy article about the committee's work and recommendations appeared in the official LCMS journal, *Lutheran Witness,* in May 1978. The article made clear that the *LBW* would be made available to congregations for study through the Concordia Publishing House.

179. The pew edition ultimately was 960 pages long with 565 hymns and canticles (plus four "national songs"), three settings for Holy Communion, Morning Prayer, Evening Prayer, Compline, Responsive Prayers, The Litany, Corporate and Individual orders for Confession and Forgiveness, Holy Baptism, Affirmation of Baptism, Marriage, Burial of the Dead, The Psalms, Propers for Daily Prayer, Psalms for Daily Prayer, a Daily Lectionary, Petitions, Intercessions and Thanksgivings, plus a wealth of other material. The *Ministers Edition* came in two sizes: one was in large size and print for

liturgical use; the other was a smaller desk edition. Both contained detailed instructions and rubrics plus other material not included in the pew edition that would be needed by the minister. The *Accompaniment Edition Liturgy* was for the musician using either a piano or organ. There was also an *Organist Edition Hymns.* All of these were considered the corpus of the whole *LBW.*

180. *LCAM, 1976,* 530–31. The top ten in rank order were "Holy, holy, holy," "A mighty fortress," "The Church's one foundation," "Joy to the world," Beautiful Saviour," "Jesus Christ is risen today," "Come, thou almighty King," Praise to the Lord," "My faith looks up to thee," and "I know that my Redeemer lives." Both ALC and LCMS conducted similar surveys, and the vast majority of frequently used hymns, plus some excellent hymns that had not been in the previous books, such as "Lift high the cross," were included in the final selection.

181. The three-day symposium was arranged by ILCW with the cooperation of the Department of Theological Studies, LCUSA. The articles appeared in *The Lutheran Quarterly,* May 1974.

182. *LCAM, 1976,* 528–31.

183. Ibid., 531.

184. Ibid., 422–23. The bylaw in question was Section X, B, 3, j.

185. Ibid., 424–25.

186. *LCAM, 1978,* 405. Following its April 1977 meeting, the DPS Management Committee made 124 specific proposals about the book. Of these, the ILCW accepted 77 recommendations for change and 21 affirmations. It must be remembered that the other partner churches were also making proposals which had to be taken into consideration in arriving at a solution.

187. Ibid., 712–13. The whole process including the reactions of the ALC, ELCC, and LCMS appears on pp. 710–15.

188. *ECM, September 1977,* 249–55.

189. Pfatteicher and Messerli, *Manual on the Liturgy,* 16.

190. Ibid., 18. The writers point to the change from the earlier language of the Brief Order for Public Confession from "we poor sinners confess unto thee that we are sinful and unclean" to "we confess that we are in bondage to sin and cannot free ourselves" as an example. They indicate, "One can picture what it is to be in bondage, and one can feel slavery and its chains. Studies of Black history have made painfully vivid the agony of bondage and the hopelessness of slavery."

191. Supplemental publications such as *Celebrate* and *Living Liturgy* add to the rich variety of content and practice.

192. "The numerical total in the hymnal comes to 569 because (a) the opening 21 are a collection of canticles and (b) hymn texts with more than one tune are separately numbered." See R. Harold Terry, "Lutheran Hymnody in North America," in Marilyn Kay Stulken, *Hymnal Companion to the Lutheran Book of Worship* (Philadelphia: Fortress Press, 1981), 113. Stulken's volume contains a helpful collection of essays about the hymnic traditions represented in the *LBW* as well as individual commentaries on each of the hymns and tunes.

193. *1978 Convention Summary,* 6. All sorts of rumors had been rampant about how expensive the new book would be. "Guesstimates" ran from $12.00 to $15.00. Actually, the *LBW* pew edition was offered to congregations on an introductory basis for $7.50 a copy. When a congregation ordered the book in quantity, it received the *Ministers Edition* for the altar without charge. All ordained ministers in the LCA received a complimentary copy of the pew edition.

194. The joint resolutions were included in *Documents Regarding Augsburg Publishing House and Division for Life and Mission in the Congregation of the American Lutheran Church,* dated March 15, 1974. These materials were shared with the LCA and are included in photocopy form as *Exhibit A* to the *DPS-MCM, May 1974.*

195. See *Exhibit A,* 12–13.

196. Ibid., 16–17.

197. *DPS-ECM, May 10, 1974,* 31. The entire subject is dealt with on pp. 27–33.

198. Nothing was said specifically about the very practical problem faced by DPS in that it had developed its editorial staff to emphasize youth and adult materials according to the original plans for cooperation and now faced a shortage of children's editors in proceeding on its own to fulfill its commitments to the LCA constituency regarding the EM program.

199. *LCAM, 1976,* 501–4; *LCAM, 1978,* 413–16. Two of the basic tools used to introduce the EM concept and help congregations plan their programs were a manual on *Planning Educational Ministry in the Parish* (Philadelphia: Parish Life Press, 1976); and W. Kent Gilbert, *What Is Educational Ministry?* (Philadelphia: Parish Life Press, 1976).

200. *LCAM, 1976,* 415–16.

201. *The Lutheran* (February 7, 1973):28.

202. Editorial in *The Lutheran,* September 19, 1973.

203. *LCAM, 1974,* 595. See also Carl Uehling, "Did Key '73 Work?" *The Lutheran* (January 23, 1974):14.

204. Statistics supplied by Robert Strohl, Department of Research and Studies, DPS, show that baptized membership dropped from 3,155,907 in 1972 to 3,122,331 in 1974. Confirmed membership grew during the same years from 2,248,681 to 2,259,249 in the same period, and communing membership from 1,659,943 to 1,692,151. Part of these shifts can be accounted for by shifts in the population age-groups and the increase in communing of children.

205. The figure comes from an evangelism survey made by the DPS in 1974, although four out of five congregations had witness as one of their highest-ranking priorities. See *LCAM, 1976,* 498.

206. *LCAM, 1976,* 499–500. See also pp. 247–50. It should be noted that the American Lutheran Church Women were related to the Division for Life and Mission in the Congregation. This accounts for the slightly different makeup of the LCA work group.

207. See *ECM, November 1975,* 324–26; *February 1976,* 459–63; *April 1976,* 594–97.

208. *LCAM, 1978,* 407.

209. Louis T. Almen, *Evangelical Outreach Foundations* (Philadelphia: Parish Life Press, 1977). There were many other media resources produced by the two churches including a new adult study course for new or restored members, *Being in the Body of Christ.*

210. Dr. Lavin gave approximately two months per year to the position through 1978. Other pastor directors included Robert L. Hock, Winter Park, FL; James R. Stephenson, Hickory, NC; Jerry L. Schmalenberger, Des Moines, IA; James M. Capers, Savannah, GA.

211. What made development of Word and Witness possible was an anonymous gift of $50,000 by a New Jersey layman who did not believe the LCA was doing enough to match the zeal of conservative evangelicals in bringing the biblical message of God's grace to not only the unchurched but also the LCA's own members. DPS was in the process of designing a plan of intensive Bible study, and DPL was aware of experiments at Southern Seminary in ways of helping people to articulate their own faith to others in everyday situations. The unsolicited gift was the catalyst that brought these two concepts together long before the Evangelical Outreach emphasis had been proposed.

212. Basic to the effort was a course in Bible study designed by Professors John Reumann and Foster McCurley of Philadelphia Seminary to bring the whole message of the Scriptures into focus around the concept of witness to the gospel. The laboratory experiences in witnessing were planned by Professor Austin F. Shell of Southern Seminary. Through the pilot test, the materials and processes were refined and made ready for introduction in 1977, a year ahead of schedule.

213. The biblical scholars included such persons as President Robert Marshall, Reumann, McCurley, and Krister Stendahl, dean of the Harvard Divinity School.

214. The basic books in the program were *Word and Witness: Understanding the Bible I and II* (Philadelphia: DPS, 1977) by Reumann and McCurley, plus two volumes on *Telling the Good News* by Shell and John Kerr. Congregations that enrolled in the program generally sent their pastor for training, and he or she organized a study group on returning from the initial seminar. In midyear the leaders were called back together for a two- or three-day "booster shot" to help them overcome any problems they had encountered. The $750 cost of the program included the full expense of a leader attending the training events, a set of leader's materials, ten sets of participant's materials, and a basic library for biblical study in the congregation. Scholarships administered by a special committee convened by DPL were made available by DPS and through a generous grant from the Aid Association for Lutherans for those congregations which otherwise could not afford to participate. This obviously was not a commercial venture and would not have been possible without subsidies for the congregations most in need of the service.

215. The Spanish translation was *Palabra y Testimonio: Entendiendo La Biblia 1 and 2* (Philadelphia: DPS, 1983). The Church of Sweden produced

Dialog Ord som föenar (Discussing the Word Together). The Lutheran Church in Finland version is *Sanasta Eläma"* (Life from the Word, 1984), and The United Evangelical Lutheran Church in Germany produced *Wort und Antwort* (Word and Answer).

216. The system in ULCA had originally been for pastors to mail a form to the Office of the Secretary, which forwarded the names and addresses to congregations in the new communities. Later this work was taken over by the Commission on Evangelism in the LCA. Often the information was sent to the New York offices long after the members had moved, if at all, with the result that there were frequent complaints that information arrived much too late to be helpful. This work was taken over after restructuring by DPS, but in 1975, for example, only 4,602 such referrals came directly from congregations (see *LCAM, 1976,* 499).

217. Report of COE, *LCAM, 1972,* 138. The COE hoped to process over 70,000 address changes per year.

218. *LCAM, 1980,* 413–14. Although the system never worked perfectly, two further advances were made later. It became technically possible to inform the persons themselves where the nearest Lutheran church was when they moved. Agreements were also reached that made it possible to refer names of LCA members to other Lutheran church bodies when there was no LCA parish within a reasonable distance of the new address.

219. Report of the Treasurer, *LCAM, 1980,* 101. The World Hunger Appeal and Designated Advance Giving were carried out under the Office for Administration and Finance.

220. President Marshall had submitted to the Executive Council a collateral paper on the subject which led to the proposal. See *ECM, February 1976,* 403; *April 1976,* 603–4.

221. The twelve-person group was chaired by Reuben T. Swanson, the president of the Nebraska Synod. LaVern K. Grosc, a theologian and pastor from York, PA, was the writer. The study guide *Stewardship and Christian Giving, a Biblical and Theological Perspective* (Philadelphia: DPS, 1977) was prepared by Ralph R. Hellerich and contained the full text of Dr. Grosc's draft of the statement.

222. The quotations are from the 1980 version of the statement, pp. 3 and 4. The document also emphasized that our response involves the giving of ourselves through service in the world in pursuit of justice and in a wide variety of other ways, our stewardship of the gospel as ambassadors of the King, and our giving in and through the Christian community.

223. An examination of the DPS reports to the LCA conventions is helpful in understanding how this aspect of congregational ministry expanded and included new areas during the seventies. See *LCAM, 1974,* 595–96; *1976,* 504–7; *1978,* 416–18; *1980,* 415–18.

224. *DPS-ECM, May, 1974,* 10. A full report and evaluation of the Houston event appears on pp. 9–22.

225. By prior agreement there was no mass celebration of the Eucharist.

226. *LCAM, 1978,* 420; *1980,* 415. One of the difficulties, apart from finding facilities that would handle the burgeoning number of participants,

was the fact that the gatherings had to include the triennial convention of the ALC Luther League, which caused the youth from other bodies to feel somewhat separated at that point. The other problem resulted from the substantial deficit incurred by having to cope with the housing dislocations at the last moment.

227. *LCAM, 1974,* 597–98, provides a brief report on the study. The actual detailed research report was made to the DPS Management Committee in 1973. It revealed the dichotomy between the importance attached to the Scriptures by youth and older members. The overriding concern of all, however, was the question, What does the Bible have to say to us today? Although people realized that the Bible seemed to have less and less importance in society generally, they felt it was basic for the LCA. Most rejected a literalistic interpretation of the Scriptures. "The evangelical emphasis of the Bible carrying the message of God's love in Christ [was] by far the most common view." This attitude about literalism and the Bible was confirmed in a later study made as part of the LCA "Lutheran Listening Post" series of surveys initiated by the Office for Research and Planning. See Robert Wuthnow, "Basic Patterns," in *Views from the Pews,* ed. Roger A. Johnson (Philadelphia: Fortress Press, 1983), 21.

228. *LCAM, 1974,* 600–13. There were fourteen of these guidelines, including pointing out that where the charismatic experience is authentic (bears good fruits) there is no reason to assume that a person cannot be both a charismatic and an LCA member in good standing; defining the borderline between charismatic renewal and Pentecostalism; helping charismatics in the church to understand the legitimacy of the Christian experience of other members that differs from their own; resisting any effort to substitute charismatic experience for proclamation of the Word, the sacraments, or the Christian fellowship; a series of specific suggestions to pastors in counseling charismatics and dealing with tensions which sometimes arise within congregations over their presence; suggestions to seminaries to provide programs of continuing education to pastors about the movement; and proposals for additional studies by theologians. DPS not only made the report itself available to pastors but also prepared several study items for congregational use, such as Hartland H. Gifford, ed., *The Charismatic Movement, A Special Study for Adults and Youth* (Philadelphia: Lutheran Church Press, 1973).

229. *LCAM, 1976,* 516–19.

230. This account is based in part on an unpublished paper, "History of CCCPCL," prepared by C. Richard Evenson in 1985 and based largely on the minutes of the ULCA and the LCA.

231. *LCAM, 1978,* 751.

232. *LCAM, 1974,* 529–30, 599. The bylaw involved was Section XI, A, Item 3b.

233. Lani L. Johnson, *Led by the Spirit,* 92.

234. Ibid.

235. Ibid., 89.

236. *LCAM, 1974,* 660.

237. Lani L. Johnson, *Led by the Spirit,* 88–89, 92–93.

238. *LCAM, 1978*, 437.

239. Ibid., 438.

240. *LCAM, 1976*, 569. Enrollments in LCA seminaries hit a low of 916 in 1973 but had rebounded to 1,125 by 1977. In addition, there were seventy-eight students studying at non-LCA institutions (*LCAM, 1978*, 457).

241. *LCAM, 1974*, 562.

242. The problem was described in an LCA News Bureau release dated April 22, 1974. The management committee made a preliminary report about the problem to the convention in 1974 and promised a complete study and recommendations by 1976 (*LCAM, 1974*, 562–63, 574–76).

243. *LCAM, 1976*, 571–73, 578–80, 592–605. The convention actions on the recommendations are on pp. 413–15.

244. *LCAM, 1978*, 441–44, detail the various mergers and other steps taken.

245. Statistics are based on *LCAM, 1978*, 445; and *1980*, 433.

246. See Garhart, *Women in Ordained Ministry*. The eleven recommendations (pp. 45–46) covered a wide range of matters, including reexamining seminary curriculum, workshops for faculty and students to deal positively with the presence of women students, support systems for female clergy, ways of preparing congregations for accepting women pastors, investigation of what had happened in other denominations that experienced a high dropout rate among women clergy. In its 1978 convention report, DPL described the responses to the Garhart report and indicated it had convened a consultation to work out specific steps to be taken to support and assist women clergy during the coming biennium (*LCAM, 1978*, 448–49).

247. In the school years 1978–79 and 1979–80, the number of those working for lay professional degrees jumped from 39 to 55.

248. *LCAM, 1978*, 258. There actually were 106 pastors from minority groups by the end of 1979, but the number of lay professionals in this category is more difficult to determine (*LCAM, 1980*, 380). Some of the special efforts made in theological education are described in DPL convention reports for *1978*, 449–50; and *1980*, 436.

249. *LCAM, 1980*, 435.

250. *LCAM, 1976*, 586–92.

251. Marvin Johnson, Harold Lohr, Joseph Wagner, William Barge, *Growth in Ministry* (Philadelphia: DPL, 1975), 151. This report not only provides detailed statistical tables and analysis but also interprets highlights of the findings.

252. Ibid., 158.

253. *LCAM, 1978*, 438–39.

254. DPL's reports to the church describe the many efforts to make the system more usable and acceptable in the church. See *LCAM, 1974*, 570; *1976*, 576; *1978*, 576.

255. When the LCA introduced its first centralized computer facility under OAF, Leonard Sibley, director of the operation, likened the concern about the "demonic powers" in new technology to the controversy that raged around a Brooklyn Sunday school teacher in the 1890s "because she

dared to introduce 'an instrument of the devil' . . . a blackboard." See article in *The Lutheran* (May 16, 1973):18–21.

256. *LCAM, 1980,* 433. The Doctor of Ministry degree was not intended as preparation for teaching or research. It provided an opportunity for clergy to intensify skill development in their pastoral ministry.

257. *LCAM, 1978,* 439. DPL's share of the cost of this program during the 1977–78 biennium amounted to almost $50,000.

258. *LCAM, 1976,* 582.

259. Weiser, *To Serve the Lord and His People,* 37.

260. *LCAM, 1974,* 570. Frederick S. Weiser describes the origin of this program that has attracted approximately 350 participants since it was begun in the ULCA in 1957 in *To Serve the Lord and His People,* 29.

261. *LCAM, 1976,* 582–86.

262. *LCAM, 1978,* 161–74.

263. Ibid., 448. Those not active were classified as "retired," "semi-retired," or on "Leave of Absence."

264. Ibid. The full report is on pp. 293–310 and is followed by the convention actions.

265. The amended Bylaw X, C, Item 6, read, "The division shall conduct longrange planning and establish policy and standards for deaconess work in this church. It shall enter into arrangements with the Deaconess Community of the Lutheran Church in America for recruitment, education, setting apart of approved candidates, supervision of the services of deaconesses, and for developing guidelines for their temporal support. It shall assure the lifelong care of those admitted to the cooperative plan prior to July 1, 1978."

266. *LCAM, 1974,* 667.

267. *LCAM, 1978,* 632. In the 1976–77 biennium, Davey and his friends learned to speak Icelandic and Japanese in addition to the earlier use of English, Spanish, Portuguese, Dutch, and Cantonese. Most of the programs had been produced in the sixties, but thirteen regular episodes and two specials were produced in the seventies.

268. *LCAM, 1974,* 668.

269. One such media kit was developed together with ALC as part of the Evangelical Outreach emphasis. It helped congregations in an area band together to utilize all available media as avenues for evangelism (*LCAM, 1978,* 531–32).

270. *LCAM, 1976,* 655. The original *The Lutheran* was merged with the *Lutheran Observer* when the ULCA was formed in 1918. *Augustana,* the first magazine of the Augustana Synod, was combined with *The Lutheran* at the time of the LCA merger. Stauderman stated that more than 40 other publications were part of *The Lutheran*'s heritage.

271. Ibid., 656–57.

272. *LCAM, 1974,* 671–2. The size was shaved by a fraction of an inch later, *LCAM, 1976,* 656.

273. *LCAM, 1978,* 535.

274. *LCAM, 1976,* 657.

275. *LCAM, 1978,* 216, 530–31.

276. *BPubM, 1972,* 1670. The LCA Bylaws originally assigned these responsibilities to the Board of Publication (*Bylaws,* Section XI, C, Item 5). New provisions were adopted at the Dallas convention in 1972. See present *Bylaws,* Section XI, B, Item 4d.

277. See *ECM, October 1974,* 30–31; *February 1975,* 117–20; *June 1975,* 193–94; *November 1975,* 285.

278. *LCAM, 1976,* 661. A similar kind of statement from the *Christian Century* was quoted in the minutes.

279. *LCAM, 1974,* 674.

280. *LCAM, 1976,* 675–76.

281. *LCAM, 1980,* 106–8, 266.

282. *LCAM, 1976,* 667.

283. Sibley and Hart describe something of the problem in *Research and Evaluation in the LCA* (Philadelphia: Department of Planning, Research and Evaluation, Office of the Bishop, 1985), 10–11. See also Report of ORP, *LCAM, 1978,* 544–46.

284. *LCAM, 1974,* 424.

285. Sibley, *Planning,* 17. Sibley indicates that this situation continued through much of the life of ORP in spite of various efforts to reverse the process. No doubt, the dual pressure of limited available funds and the rate of inflation made this almost inevitable.

286. In the spring of 1974, John Lindholm, the first executive of ORP, resigned to begin his own consulting firm, and Albert Haversat was named to fill the vacancy.

287. *LCAM, 1978,* 544. The intention was that by the spring of 1979, the Executive Council and the Conference of Synodical Presidents would have before them projections of programs through 1986.

288. *LCAM, 1976,* 667. The index was provided to every churchwide agency, LCUSA, ALC, LCMS, and the NCCCUSA. Copies were made available at cost to synods and seminaries. A related effort was the development of a catalog of other research agencies that could be tapped by the LCA for information in a variety of fields.

289. See Sibley and Hart, *Research and Evaluation,* 14–17, which describes the basic problem and the way in which a cooperative data system was developed with the ALC. When the LCA established its central computer department in 1973, the congregational report forms (as the parochial report was renamed) were gathered and edited by DPS and processed on the central computer. Because of time and expense, only the 1971 tapes were ever converted to the format for the central computer.

290. This mailing list became the basic list of persons to whom *The Congregation* was mailed free of charge. A printout was returned to the congregation each year for updating.

291. *LCAM, 1976,* 513.

292. Ibid., 678–92. The report addressed such questions as the following: "Where have all the members gone?" "If receipts are up, how come it hurts so much?" and the problem of "roll cleaning." It supplied detailed analyses

of membership trends, financial receipts, inflation impact, and the redistribution of income among congregations, synods, and CWAs.

293. Sibley, *Planning,* 17. See also *LCAM, 1976,* 668.

294. Sibley and Hart summarize the process in *Research and Evaluation,* 18–21.

295. The seven subjects were Evangelical Outreach, March 1977; Religious Behavior and Attitudes, June 1977; Aging and Retirement, October 1977; World Hunger, Ministry of the Laity, and "Because of You" (a series of *Lutheran* ads about the effect of benevolence), May 1978; Options About the Future, September 1978; Evaluation of the Listening Post, October 1978; Religious Beliefs and Experience, April 1979. These reports are in the LCA Archives in Chicago and are rich in information about the thinking and practices of LCA members. They reveal some unexpected insights.

296. Roger A. Johnson, ed., *Views from the Pews.* The contributors included Jerald Brauer, Charles Y. Glock, Timothy Lull, Lyman Lundeen, Krister Stendahl, Mary Cahill Weber, Robert Wuthnow, and Johnson himself.

297. Robert Wuthnow, "Basic Patterns," in *Views from the Pews,* ed. Roger A. Johnson, 31. Wuthnow concludes that laity and clergy are in basic agreement with each other and among themselves on such tenets as Jesus' being fully divine and fully human, the purpose of the crucifixion in providing forgiveness of sins, the existence of God, God's love for sinful humanity, God's granting new life to individuals, and the truth of the beliefs expressed in the Apostles' Creed. One salient point on which lay and clergy differed was in the fact that sizable numbers of lay persons "leaned more toward a concept of faith that emphasized 'trying to do what is right' rather than viewing faith simply as trusting in God's grace." Interestingly, the study purposely used the wording of a Gallup poll item about the way people regarded the Bible, which led Gallup to conclude that 47% of Lutherans in North America believe the Bible should be taken literally, word-for-word. This did not fit the LCA members, however. "Only one in six laypersons and less than 2% of clergy gave the literalist response. The overwhelming majority of both laity and clergy said they regard the Bible as the inspired word of God, but not to be taken literally, word-for-word" (p. 21).

298. Roger A. Johnson, *Congregations as Nurturing Communities* (Philadelphia: DPS, 1979).

299. Ibid., 82. The study makes much of the concept of "bondedness" in a caring community. "To be religious," Johnson says, "is to tend to that which claims and binds us, that which holds us together, the source of our shared life with others. It is to acknowledge or confess the bondedness of our human condition, both our ties with other people and our inseparable ties with the Lord and giver of life" (p. 29).

300. Ibid., 82. Johnson admits that this is at odds with "most modern theologies, from neoorthodoxy of the 1920s through the recent wave of secular theology, [that] presuppose translating the gospel from one set of concepts to another, all within the limits of the medium of language."

301. See *Report of the Commission on Function and Structure* (New York: LCA, 1972), 63–66. In describing the existing situation, the Commission

stated, "The present organization of the Lutheran Church in America gives rise to eleven separate and virtually autonomous churchwide operations in the area of administration and finance. . . . This fragmentation results in separate balance sheets, individual regulation of cash flow with the possibility of unrealistically high cash reserves, separate payrolls, and overlapping representation to agencies of government" (p. 63). It went on to contend that this resulted in duplication of effort, inability to use assets and credit efficiently, and the possibility of inadequate services in some areas.

302. *LCAM, 1978,* 476.

303. Ibid., 484. Both the personnel and resource development operations now had full-time directors. Departments for financial services and administrative services had been added. There were at that point thirty-two staff and a total of some ninety employees engaged in the various financial and administrative work services handled by OAF.

304. The insurance service was provided through a broker. "The purpose was to provide competitive rates to everyone and at the same time assure that no congregation could be denied insurance because it was a high risk unit" (from *OAF, Historical Data 1972–86,* a document provided in January 1986 to the writer). This service was of particular importance to congregations located in what were considered by insurance companies as "high risk areas."

305. Resource development focused on Designated Advance Giving, Love Compels Action/World Hunger, LLM (including its extensive fundraising and counseling service) and the LCA Foundation. It also was responsible for contacts with fraternal insurance companies and other sources of external grants. DPS carried primary responsibility for the stewardship program in congregations. LLM cooperated in this with an annual grant to DPS to help underwrite the cost of free stewardship materials for congregations. DMNA carried the primary responsibility for the consultation process with synods where agreements were reached on synodical commitments to the churchwide budget.

306. One glimpse into the size of this operation is the fact that at the end of 1977, the assets of the BAM alone were $65,861,000. BAM was the corporate shell maintained after restructuring to deal primarily with the Church Property Fund.

307. In 1977 alone the Department of Accounting Services issued 38,000 checks and provided detailed reports to all CWAs on fiscal matters every month (*LCAM, 1978,* 475). Time investment reports of employees were a great help to CWAs in the efficient management of their operations. The DAS also provided accounting services for several synods.

308. In 1978 the church recognized that its salary scales were badly outmoded so that employees were falling farther and farther behind the rate of inflation. The LCA engaged a nationally known consulting firm and developed an entirely new system that gave greater assurance of internal equity among agencies and brought the church's compensation plan closer to that of other "nonprofit" organizations (*LCAM, 1980,* 599–603). The plan also included a performance appraisal system that provided review of employee performance before any increases in compensation were granted. Although

financial constraints prevented making up all of the ground lost by church-wide personnel in compensation through the years, the new plan was a major step in the right direction.

309. A comparison of the pertinent *LCA Bylaws* in 1970, Section X, D, with the 1974 version, Section XII, A illustrates the similarity.

310. *LCAM, 1978,* 501, Table III. The figures differed in Canada because of that country's different social security system.

311. This meant that the employer paid an amount equal to the deduction made from the employee's salary. Ministers were classified as "self-employed" and, therefore, paid the higher rate for that category as would have been the case with a self-employed physician or a lawyer.

312. In reality, most congregations, synods, and agencies reimbursed both ministers and lay persons for whatever their share of the tax was, although these sums, of course, were in themselves taxable. It was, in effect, an addition to salary. Churchwide agencies, however, were not permitted to make this sort of "reimbursement."

313. *LCAM, 1974,* 213–18; *1976,* 107–8. In addition to what appears in convention minutes, summaries of the problems and steps taken in pension and health benefit plans have been provided to the writer by the Office of the President of the Board of Pensions as of January 16, 1986.

314. The medical and hospitalization costs for ministers were paid from the Board of Pension's share of the LCA budget. Premiums for dependent coverage were the minister's responsibility, although most congregations and synods paid these premiums. Churchwide agencies never paid for dependent coverage.

315. *LCAM, 1978,* 520. A more detailed analysis of the problem and the Executive Council's reaction appear on pp. 651–53.

316. Albert P. Stauderman, "The Robert Marshall Years," *The Lutheran* (July 1978):9.

317. *LCAM, 1978,* 42.

318. *LCAM, 1974,* 558. This quotation from ALC's response to a 1972 invitation to a Consultation on Lutheran Unity that would have included Missouri as well as LCA appears in the "Report of the Standing Committee on Approaches to Unity" to the LCA convention in Baltimore. The LCA had responded, "The goal of Lutheran unity is that the oneness of those who are committed to the fulfillment of the will of God shall be evidenced by their oneness of understanding, activity and structure." It went on to express the hope that the consultation would "initiate the process needed for the churches to move forward to achieve the goal."

319. Ibid., 558; see also 280–82.

320. *LCAM, 1974,* 747–48.

321. *LCAM, 1976,* 269.

322. The two persons were Albert E. Anderson, manager of the Augsburg Publishing House, and Martin E. Carlson, assistant to Dr. Marshall (ibid., 270). The LCA representatives on the committee itself, in addition to the president, were H. George Anderson, Robert Brorby, Martin Carlson, Raymond Hedberg, and Howard J. McCarney.

323. References here are to the committee's report and recommendations in *LCAM, 1976,* 383–85.

324. Ibid., 385. The committee's recommendation was that other Lutheran churches in the United States and Canada "which join us in expression of our confessional unity" be welcomed to join in these studies. During the next biennium the Evangelical Lutheran Church of Canada and the LCA Canada Section were represented at the committee's meetings.

325. *LCAM, 1976,* 205–8, records the committee's report and the LCA actions. The sticking point on Scripture involved the ALC's use of the term *inerrant.* The definition of the church posed a problem in that the LCA described the church as made up of "congregations and ordained ministers," while ALC referred to a "union of congregations." A special study by theologians concluded that "the difference between the two churches reflected the divergent historical and cultural situations of the two churches rather than significant theological variations."

326. The text of this call for union is included in the report of the Standing Committee on Approaches to Unity in the *LCAM, 1976,* 201–3. How the LCA dealt with this call will follow a description of the origin and purposes of the AELC.

327. A few of the names that come to mind include Arthur Carl Piepkorn, Martin E. Marty, Martin L. Kretzmann, Jaroslav Pelikan, and John H. Tietjen, although the list of those who were at the forefront of Missouri scholarship would be long.

328. One firsthand and personal description of the course of events appears in Frederick S. Danker, *No Room in the Brotherhood: The Preus-Otten Purge of Missouri* (St. Louis: Clayton, 1977).

329. Nelson, "New Shape of Lutheranism," 531. Nelson provides a careful analysis of the tensions between the conservatives and the liberals that led to the painful schism which followed (pp. 528–35).

330. Bachmann, *Ecumenical Involvement,* Appendix p. 60.

331. Nelson, "New Shape of Lutheranism," 534, n. 76.

332. *1974 Convention Summary* contains the carefully worded statement that prayed for healing in Missouri and recognized that "at the heart of the struggle is the authority of the Word of God." Affirming the LCA's own Confession of Faith, it expressed regret over "all official efforts to legislate adherence to additional documents that fence God's Word and fracture God's people." (See p. 8.)

333. Bachmann, *Ecumenical Involvement,* 64.

334. *LCAM, 1978,* 561. President Marshall indicated in his report to the Chicago convention that LCMS had objected to AELC's being admitted to LCUSA (see p. 41). AELC also joined in the National Lutheran Campus Ministry program where Missouri was not a participant.

335. Ibid., 576. This immediately made AELC a member of Lutheran World Ministries, which is the USA National Committee for LWF. It had also become a supporter of Lutheran World Relief.

336. Bachmann, *Ecumenical Involvement,* 65.

337. *LCAM, 1978,* 203.

338. Ibid., 204, 208.

339. Ibid., 556.

340. *1978 Convention Summary,* 11.

341. Detailed reports of the work of these common agencies appear in the LCA minutes for each biennium. It is impossible to describe all of these activities here.

342. *LCAM, 1978,* 238. Previously, ownership and support of seminaries were confined to the synods of the LCA.

343. *LCAM, 1976,* 386–90, contains the first draft of the statement, and the action appears on p. 412.

344. *LCAM, 1978,* 41, an observation in the president's report. The text of the committee's report appears on pp. 209–14. The final version of the Recommendations for Practice as adopted appear on pp. 332–36.

345. Martin E. Marty, "Ecumenism: the End of an Affair," *The Lutheran* (February 6, 1974):10.

346. *LCAM, 1974,* 309. This action was related in part to an earlier proposal of the NCCCUSA that 15% of the Governing Board could be named by the board itself in order to provide greater balance of minorities, women, and persons representing special concerns or having special expertise. In response to the urging of church bodies, such as the LCA, the actual amendment was modified so that persons nominated in this way required "(a) that all such additional persons must be communicants of member communions or of non-member communions eligible for membership and (b) that an additional member that belongs to an eligible non-member communion is to be approved by a member communion after consultation with the proposed additional member's communion." See *LCAM, 1974,* 296.

347. *1974 Convention Summary,* 12. Robert Marshall later gave a fuller interpretation of how this provision applied to the NCCCUSA in *An Evaluation of the Relationship of the Lutheran Church in America with the National Council of Churches of Christ in the USA* (New York: DWME, 1985), 13–14. He concluded, "In relation to the NCCCUSA, the LCA has experienced some change in how it might adapt its [representative] principle to fulfill the expectations of the Council. The church has been more successful than not in having its expectations met by the Council."

348. *LCAM, 1974,* 459.

349. *LCAM, 1976,* 282–86. The minutes also include updates on the Episcopal; Methodist, Conservative-Evangelical, Pentecostal; and Roman Catholic dialogues (pp. 286–87).

350. What had prompted the development of Paper No. 73 was the mandate to Faith and Order in the WCC Bylaws "to proclaim the oneness of the Church of Jesus Christ and to call the churches to the goal of visible unity in one faith and one eucharistic fellowship, expressed in worship and common life in Christ, in order that the world might believe." The varying views of the churches on baptism, eucharist, and ministry had always been sticking points in achieving this goal.

351. *LCAM, 1978,* 754–62.

352. Dr. Marshall described the situation in retrospect in an interview by the writer on October 23, 1986, in New York. On the matter of health,

President Marshall had suffered for many years from severe asthma attacks, one of which had hospitalized him only a short time prior to his decision.

353. *LCAM, 1978*, 98. The bylaw in question was Section VI, Item 3b. The motion to suspend failed by a narrow margin because it would have required a two-thirds majority.

354. Ibid., 100–1.

355. *1978 Convention Summary*, 4. In an interview by the writer on August 27, 1986, Dr. Anderson said that he had struggled long with the question of allowing his name to be considered but simply was convinced that he was not called to serve in that position. What not even he knew at the time of the convention was that his wife would be diagnosed a few weeks later as having a terminal illness. If Dr. Anderson had been elected president, the responsibilities to the office and to his family would have been virtually unbearable for anyone in the situation.

356. Perhaps it was prescience on Dr. Sauer's part, but he was stricken shortly before the conclusion of the convention and was rushed to the hospital for heart bypass surgery.

357. *LCAM, 1978*, 111–12.

358. Ibid., 146–47.

359. Ibid., 158.

360. Ibid., 160.

361. Ibid., 175.

362. *1978 Convention Summary*, 5.

363. *LCAM, 1978*, 198. The balloting was unique in that twelve women received votes, and it was the first time that a Black had run as high as third. The LCA obviously was beginning to take note of women and minorities.

364. Ibid., 246.

Chapter 6 | REACHING OUT TO OTHERS

ALTHOUGH THE LUTHERAN CHURCH IN America had been committed to Lutheran unity from its formation, the period between 1978 and 1982 proved decisive in bringing the whole question to a point where the AELC, ALC, and LCA were at last ready to move toward forming a new church body. In his response at the service in Riverside Church, New York, where he was installed as president, James R. Crumley, Jr., set the tone when he stated that pursuit of Lutheran unity must be a high and immediate priority for the church in these years.[1] In many ways, these four years would prove to be a time of reaching out to others in the Christian family. But it would also be a time when world events would place severe strains on all churches as they sought to carry out their mission in an atmosphere of international turmoil, economic distress, and societal tension. This chapter can provide only a glimpse of the setting within which the church had to set a course and carry on its ministry; but a glimpse, at least, is necessary.

THE WORLD SCENE

As the decade of the seventies came to an end and the eighties began, new trouble spots erupted around the world at an alarming rate. The Middle East was particularly turbulent. After the Shah of Iran had been driven out and the fundamentalist Islamic government of the Ayatollah Khomeini seized power, relations worsened with Arab neighbors and Western nations alike. Matters came to a head between Iran and the United States when the Shah was allowed to enter a New York hospital for cancer treatment in October 1979. Militant Iranians seized the United States embassy in Tehran and took sixty-six persons hostage on November 4.[2]

Moves and countermoves by the two countries as the United States sought release of the hostages only escalated the tension. After almost four months, the United States launched an abortive rescue mission by a commando team that ended with equipment failures and an accident in which eight Americans were killed. Finally, after 444 days the release of the last of the hostages was achieved on January 20, 1981. Ironically, it was the day that Carter's successor, Ronald Reagan, was inaugurated president of the United States. As though to underscore the instability of the region, however, a bitter war had erupted between Iran and Iraq that was still continuing seven years later.

Taking advantage of the situation in Iran, Russia invaded Afghanistan on December 27, 1979, allegedly at the request of the puppet Marxist government. The incursion evoked a storm of criticism by many countries but little concrete action.[3] On January 4 President Carter threatened that if the troops were not removed, the United States would impose a grain embargo, suspend sale of high technology equipment to Russia, curtail fishing rights in American waters, and delay opening new consular facilities. In what seemed to many critics a bizarre addition to the list of diplomatic pressures, President Carter stated that the United States might go so far as to boycott the 1980 Olympic Games to be held in Moscow.[4]

Three weeks later in his State of the Union message, Carter declared, "An attempt by any outside force to gain control of the Persian Gulf region will be regarded as an assault on the vital interests of the United States of America and such an assault will be repelled by any means necessary, including military force."[5] The United States was now on record as being willing to use military force to protect the vital flow of oil from the Persian Gulf region. One problem was that it did not seem to have forces adequate to back up its position.[6]

The United States had already begun in 1979 to rebuild its military strength that had been allowed to deteriorate after Vietnam. The MX nuclear missile program was approved, additional warships and planes were authorized, and in 1980, for the first time in thirteen years, Congress actually voted a military budget that went beyond the amount requested by a president.[7] Congress even approved Carter's plan for a renewal of draft registration in July 1980 after a lapse of five years, in spite of strong public opposition.[8] Another casualty of the times was the SALT II nuclear arms treaty that had been negotiated with Russia but was never approved by the Senate.

There were numerous other trouble spots around the globe. Central America was in turmoil. In 1979 a revolution in Nicaragua ousted the repressive Somoza government, and Carter reluctantly decided to support the leftist guerrillas who had staged the coup.[9] The picture changed, however, when El Salvador also became unstable as extreme rightist and leftist groups opposed a centrist government.[10]

There seemed to be no letup in political tensions worldwide. The oppressive tactics of right-wing governments that the United States supported in South Korea and the Philippines became an increasing embarrassment. Unrest among workers in Poland not only resulted in recognition of the first independent labor union in the Soviet bloc but also alarmed Russia enough that it massed troops on the Polish border. South Africa's relentless policy of apartheid resulted in increasing protests and violence. More and more, United States companies were urged to stop doing business with the repressive white regime. Even Great Britain and Argentina managed to get into a bloody conflict over the tiny Falkland Islands that were claimed by both nations. Everywhere one looked it seemed there was another war, another coup, another act of terrorism or repression.

THE NORTH AMERICAN SCENE

Significant changes were occurring in both Canada and the United States during these years that affected their economies, political structures, human rights, and the environment. The cost of living, interest rates, and unemployment soared.[11] The agricultural sector in the United States was particularly hard hit by the embargo on grain shipments to Russia, prolonged drought conditions, and higher interest rates.[12] More and more family farms began to fail.

Although the tight energy situation abated somewhat as North Sea oil production increased and conservation measures took effect, the hopes that had been pinned on nuclear energy were blasted when a major accident occurred at the Three Mile Island plant near Harrisburg, Pennsylvania, on March 28, 1979.[13] The disaster resulted in a rash of cancellations of orders for nuclear plants and long delays with vastly increased costs for others. From all indications the hope that nuclear energy would become the primary alternate source was doomed. The "Catch-22" was that concern was growing about pollution from burning fossil fuels and the resulting threat of acid rain. And acid rain was an increasingly sensitive issue in Canada, where many believed dying forests and lakes were victims of pollutants floating across the border from American industries.

Changing Political Patterns

Disheartened by humiliation in foreign affairs and suffering from a chaotic economy at home, American voters turned their backs on Jimmy Carter in the 1980 elections and gave a landslide victory to Ronald Reagan, a former actor and governor of California.[14] It was also the first time in twenty-eight years that the Republican Party had won control of the Senate. Reagan had captured the imagination of many voters with his persuasive speaking style and his promises of "getting the government off the people's backs," cutting taxes, and restoring American prestige abroad. In reality, his election was one more step in a march toward conservatism. Once in office, Reagan took a tough stance towards Communism, switched United States support to the *contras* in Nicaragua, slashed taxes, and expanded the defense budget at the expense of social programs and an unbalanced budget.[15] Reagan did fulfill a number of campaign promises, such as naming the first woman justice to the Supreme Court. The Equal Rights Amendment, however, died in the state legislatures.[16]

Although the situation was quite different, Canada also faced a crucial election in 1980. The provinces in Canada for many years have had more independence from the national government than has been true of the states in the United States. Even so, a serious threat to the unity of the country was mounted by Premier René Lévesque of Quebec. Lévesque sought to have that French-speaking province maintain only a "sovereignty association" with the rest of Canada. Prime Minister Pierre Trudeau, himself from Quebec, campaigned against the separatist move, and the proposal was defeated by a margin of three to two in the provincial election. Hard bargaining lay ahead, however, as the nation drafted a new constitution to balance more adequately the roles of the federal and provincial governments.[17]

New Refugees and Old Problems

Emma Lazarus's poem inscribed on the base of the Statue of Liberty in New York harbor has always seemed to exceed America's ability to accept the "tired, the poor . . . [the] huddled masses yearning to breathe free." What is more, each time the United States has tried to open its doors to refugees, it seems to flounder into new problems. It was so again in 1980. In March, Congress approved the Refugee Reform Act that broadened earlier requirements to focus on whether a person was fleeing because of racial or religious discrimination, or membership in a particular social or political group. It also nearly tripled the number of persons the country would accept.

"Not long after the ink had dried from President Carter's signature, the new act was given a baptism of fire" as tens of thousands of Cubans flooded into the country.[18] The influx was called "Castro's revenge" because it appeared to be the Cuban leader's retaliation for America's recruiting Cuba's elite in the early sixties.[19] It was estimated that within a few months the "boatlift" brought 117,000 Cubans mostly to the Miami area, and the government struggled to deal with them.[20] The question was not good intentions but the problem of how to provide for so many in so short a time.[21]

Only a few months after the influx of refugees began, the Miami area was rocked on May 18 by the worst race riot since the 1967 debacle in Detroit. If anyone had been lulled into believing that Black outrage at discrimination had passed with the sixties, the bloodbath of 1980 when fourteen died and four hundred were injured quickly changed their minds. Tension had been building within the Black community for months after a series of incidents were climaxed by the acquittal of white police accused of having beaten to death a Black insurance official after a high-speed chase.[22] The three-day rampage that resulted was different from earlier riots. "I've never seen anything like it," a Black psychologist at Florida International University is quoted as saying. "In the 1960s people got hurt because they got in the way. But in this riot, people have set out to kill white people."[23] By the time some semblance of order was restored, however, the majority of those who died were Blacks. It is clear that Black indignation persists over what is seen as a "double standard of justice."[24]

In another case of obvious racial injustice, Japanese Americans had been waiting for thirty-eight years for the United States to recognize the fact that 120,000 of their number had been interned in concentration camps during World War II. In February 1942 the government had responded to war hysteria by summarily detaining not only the Japanese but some natives from the Aleutian Islands. At no other time in United States history had masses of people been imprisoned simply because of their ethnic origins.[25] "The impact of the mass internment on the Japanese Americans was devastating. The financial impact alone was massive. There were forced, hasty sales of homes, furniture, and other belongings before being shipped off to internment. Businesses built over a lifetime of hard work had to be liquidated in a few weeks. The financial losses to Japanese Americans were estimated by the government itself at about $400,000,000—at 1942 price levels."[26] Finally, Congress created a commission in 1980 to study what should be done about the long-standing injustice.[27]

THE RELIGIOUS CLIMATE

"Events have taken religious studies by surprise," declared the journal *Daedalus* in 1982 in commenting on the way that the resurgent role of religious and quasi-religious groups in world affairs had shown how shortsighted those observers were who had been prepared to write religion off as no longer relevant.[28] No one could doubt the potency of such movements as Islamic fundamentalism in the Middle East, but the significance of the increase of religious involvement in the United States was less clear. It has been widely accepted as a truism that as a nation became more modernized, religious affiliation would decline. In this case, however, "the United States stubbornly bucks the trend: *it is both the most modernized nation in the world and the most religious of the modern nations."*[29] The question, of course, is not simply one of statistics but what they mean.

Some scholars, such as George A. Lindbeck, see a widespread "individualistic religious consumerism in which people shop freely among the available religious options for what is personally most congenial or fulfilling. The growth of a large floating clientele in American society places the churches under heavy pressure to minimize their historic characteristics and accommodate to the prevailing fads and fashions of the right or left in order to appeal to as large a number of customers as possible."[30] What is likely to result is a weakening of denominational loyalties when divisive issues, such as the stance on a particular social question, are at stake. The strain is even greater for ecumenical organizations that normally do not enjoy strong commitment from rank and file church members.

What happens when church leaders do stick to their guns in the face of growing diversity of opinion within their own constituencies is illustrated by the Roman Catholic Church. In October of 1979, Pope John Paul II became only the second pope to visit the United States and the first to be received at the White House.[31] An exceedingly popular pontiff, John Paul II was greeted by enthusiastic crowds everywhere he went. More than a million persons jammed a parkway in Philadelphia for an outdoor mass.[32] But the pope's strong stands against abortion, birth control, ordination of women as priests,

Paul L. Brndjar, the first Slovak-Zion Synod bishop, and later, Church and Society executive

and other issues evoked protests by laity, nuns, and priests at many points. Although most observers had long been aware that the Roman Church was not a monolithic structure, it was becoming evident that the deeply felt differences in views would in time test severely the loyalty of many members.

Within this kind of religious climate and against the backdrop of a turbulent world, the Lutheran Church in America was moving during this period toward crucial decisions on Lutheran unity, ecumenical commitment, social issues, congregational life, global mission, and a host of other pressing concerns. All the while it probed its own theological identity and its own servanthood.

CHURCH AND SOCIETY

There were times during the late seventies and early eighties when the Lutheran Church in America seemed to be trying to address every major social problem that emerged in an explosive world.

These were not issues that were thrust upon an unwilling constituency from "the top down." More often than not the church-at-large was struggling to keep pace with the demands that welled up from the grass roots. The number of memorials from synodical conventions that bombarded LCA conventions was one indicator. In 1980 synods forwarded 148 memorials to Seattle, and in 1982 ninety-eight were considered at Louisville. In the majority of cases at both conventions, these requests for action dealt in some way with a social concern. At Louisville, for example, there were twenty-one memorials relating to the complex issues that surrounded peace, war, and nuclear weapons. The convention action set in motion certain interim steps plus a request that a full social statement be brought back in 1984.[33]

Add to these the matters addressed to the LCA from inter-Lutheran and ecumenical agencies, and the number of requests for study or action became almost overwhelming. The LCA responded not only with basic studies and social statements but also with new ways of listening to people,[34] social action, and a detailed monitoring of its own performance in certain crucial areas.

Social Statements

What was beginning to become more and more apparent as the church sought to forge new social statements was that they became part of the fabric of interwoven policies that had been adopted through the years. This does not mean that the LCA was simply replicating what had gone before but was building upon earlier positions and pulling together pertinent views within a new context and with new implications.

Economic Justice. The document that came to the 1980 convention, "Economic Justice, Stewardship of Creation in Human Community," had been mandated two years earlier and had grown out of the LCA's experience in trying to deal with the world hunger crisis.[35] In preparing the way, an initial draft of the statement had been distributed in the congregational resource packet AIM.[36] The later draft "had been extensively revised (some would say 'toned down') prior to its presentation to the Convention."[37] Nevertheless, after wrangling over the wording at several sessions, the delegates adopted the final version almost without dissent.[38]

The statement firmly grounds economic justice upon the biblical view that the earth is the Lord's and that humanity bears the responsibility to care for creation and share its benefits in community. The way in which a society carries out production and distribution reflects both its values and its power structures. Although no economic system is permanent, the same basic issues of work, fairness, exploitation, discrimination, environmental protection, and the like are present in all. The document describes justice itself as "distributive love" and cautions against "pitting . . . benevolence against justice and the confusion of justice with righteousness." Work is seen as a "God-given means by which human creatures exercise dominion" and perpetuate and enhance the quality of life. For the Christian, baptismal vocation in God's kingdom is not to be equated with economic occupations in the world.

In applying its theological insights to economic questions, the document underscores the importance of values in society but warns against absolutizing a particular ideology. Government is seen as the means which God intends for insuring justice in a sinful world. When basic human rights are violated by governments and all other means of recourse are exhausted, civil disobedience or, as a last resort, rebellion may be justifiable.

The statement avoids equating equity or fairness with economic equality but points out that "private property is not an absolute human right but is always conditioned by the will of God and the needs of the community." Carefully nuanced interpretations are given for basic questions about accessibility to redress under the law, substantive entitlements, accountability, efficiency, and planning. The statement concludes with an affirmation that the economy cannot be separated from the whole of human life. The reshaping of the economic institutions and relations is a fundamental moral task for Christians. "Economy, rightly understood, is the God-given stewardship of life."

Death and Dying. The second major social issue that the LCA tackled in this period dealt with the questions that have arisen because of advances in medical technology that make it possible to prolong life even when that does not seem to be in the best interests of the patient. The problem was made very real for delegates to the Louisville convention in 1982 by a number of celebrated cases where courts were wrestling with both the rights of patients and their families and the responsibilities of the medical profession. At issue were such things as "mercy killings," prolonging artificially lives of persons experiencing intense suffering, and the question of when "to pull the plug" on life support systems of comatose persons where there is no hope of recovery.

The statement that was adopted by the LCA convention was the work of a panel of medical experts, theologians, pastors, and lay persons.[39] The document followed the usual pattern of beginning with a section that placed the question in theological perspective. Under the heading "Death as Natural," it stated that "both living and dying are part of the dynamic processes of the created order, which biblical faith affirms as being good." At the same time, it declared that death can be tragic, but that there are times when death can be either "friend" or "enemy."[40] The statement clearly affirms the hope of the resurrection of the body and eternal life given through Christ's victory over death.

The document lays down certain ethical principles that can be useful in the widely varying circumstances that may be faced. These include recognizing life as a gift of God to be received with thanksgiving; the integrity of the created processes that include both life and death; that both living and dying should take place within a caring community; respect for an individual's preferences; truthfulness and faithfulness in these relationships; and that hope and meaning are possible even in times of adversity and suffering.

The statement deals with the question of withdrawing or withholding treatment in certain instances, for example: (1) the situation of the irreversibly dying person, where trying to maintain vital signs in the face of imminent death "is inconsistent with a Christian ethic that mandates respect for dying, as well as for living"; (2) where there is the tension of deciding on burdensome treatments that pit quantity of life against quality; (3) where there is the danger of presuming that chronically ill persons "should be allowed to die because their lives are judged to be not worth living or . . . as burdensome or useless to society."

The statement illustrates the complexity of some pressing questions, such as the right of the patient to refuse treatment and the use of pain-killing drugs when to do so may shorten the life span. In each case, it seeks to indicate the limitations within which these judgments must be made. On the question of "active euthanasia" or "mercy killing," it takes a firm stand that deliberately destroying life created in God's image "is contrary to Christian conscience."

Throughout, the document stresses the supporting care that is needed by the dying from both the medical community and the family. The church also has a role to play, especially through the ministry of Word and Sacrament. The document concludes with an acknowledgment of the need for forgiveness when wrong decisions are made as well as the reason for thanksgiving for God's mercy and continuing love.

Breadth and Depth of Minority Concerns

The adoption of *Goals and Plans for Minority Ministry* by the 1978 convention provided the Consulting Committee on Minority Group Interests with a yardstick for evaluating movement toward these goals. In both of the succeeding conventions the CCMGI presented detailed reports that were a blend of encouragement and disappointment.[41] For example, the goal of one hundred minority persons on the role of ordained clergy had already been passed by 1980, and by the end of 1981 the total had reached 125.[42] There was also sustained growth in the number of minority persons reported as baptized members, but the total fell far short of the hoped-for addition of fifteen thousand per year.[43] The gains were occurring, however, at a time when the total baptized membership of the LCA was declining slightly. The CCMGI reports do show clearly that significant efforts were being made to advance in almost all categories; but to many persons, the gains were painfully slow. Some of the changes, however, were more important in terms of direction than numbers.

American Indians. For more than a decade, most of the grants made by the DMNA at the request of the National Indian Lutheran Board were to fund various kinds of community development projects. By 1982, however, the focus was broadening to include approaches to Word and Sacrament ministries among American Indians. At the same time, the LCA backed the NILB strongly in the struggle for recognition of American Indian sovereignty and treaty rights.[44]

Asians. For the first time, in September 1978 the LCA brought together representatives from among those of Asian ancestry to seek a better understanding of the needs of these North Americans and to plan more effective ministries among them. This conference and similar ones in subsequent years led to work within the Japanese, Chinese, Korean, Vietnamese, and Pacific Islander communities.[45]

The development of bilingual educational and worship materials for some of the groups was begun, but this proved to be a painstaking and time-consuming process. In the area of advocacy, the LCA supported formation of a presidential commission to study the wartime relocation and internment of civilians during World War II.[46]

Association of Black Lutherans. As a follow-up to a meeting of Black pastors in 1977, the Division for Professional Leadership, in cooperation with DMNA, called a major conference of Black Lutherans in Detroit, October 20–22, 1978. The group articulated a number of urgent concerns but emphasized the need for an organization to speak for Blacks in the LCA. The following year, more than three hundred persons gathered in Philadelphia to form the Association of Black Lutherans. One of its unique characteristics was that the ABL welcomed participation by persons who were not Black. In succeeding years, it formed a powerful caucus not only to bring pressure upon the LCA to address the concerns of Blacks but also to encourage the maximum involvement of Blacks themselves in the life of the church.[47] Out of its 1981 conference in Fort Worth, Texas, came a strong determination to work for divestment of church funds in companies doing business in South Africa.[48]

Hispanic Conference. During these years the several groups that were represented in the Hispanic Conference worked together to define the necessary steps for the LCA to minister to this rapidly expanding segment of North American society. As a result of their efforts, DPL began to investigate the possibility of a center for theological education connected to a seminary in Puerto Rico; DMNA stepped up the establishing of congregations for Spanish-speaking persons; development of new worship materials in Spanish was begun; greater attention was given to the plight of undocumented aliens; and pressure was brought to bear on churchwide agencies to employ Hispanics on their staffs. The wide cultural diversity among Hispanic groups presented both problems and opportunities in implementing plans.[49]

Women in the Eighties

Like travelers trying to board a train that is already leaving the station, almost every group—ecumenical and otherwise—seemed to be trying to catch up with the women's movement. Many consulta-

Native American job counseling

Association of Black Lutherans, 1981 conference

tions tended to begin at square one in their deliberations and assumed that little or nothing had been done by the church to meet the legitimate concerns of women. Meanwhile, ongoing groups such as the Consulting Committee on Women in Church and Society and Lutheran Church Women built systematically on prior developments and proceeded to nudge the LCA towards more advanced goals.

In 1979 LCUSA forwarded a long list of recommendations from a Consultation on Women: Work and Vocation to all four member churches on the steps that they should take to deal with the concerns of women.[50] Among other things, the proposals included creating a new staff position in LCUSA, calling a major national assembly, and establishing another consulting committee. The Executive Council asked DMNA to study the recommendations and report back its findings. DMNA supported the idea of an assembly and a committee, provided LCUSA covered the costs from its own budget. It also called upon LCUSA "to make every effort to fill executive staff positions with women as these positions become vacant" but did not endorse the idea of expanding Council staff.[51] The Executive Council asked DMNA to respond on behalf of the LCA, which it did by reviewing the steps already taken within the LCA and pointing out where the locus of responsibility was within the church's structure to address the issues.[52] It seemed that the LCA was eager to get on with the task but did not favor the bureaucratic solution of adding personnel and more meetings on the assumption that all Lutheran bodies were at the same point in their own development.[53]

In many ways, the decade of the seventies had been a turning point for the LCA with regard to women. In 1980 the church marked the tenth anniversary of the ordination of women with a Conference of Ordained Women at Rochester, Minnesota. The conference not only celebrated the strides that had been made but outlined some of the problems yet to be solved, such as the placement of ordained women and the difficulties in transition to a second call. The LCA, however, had come from "ground zero" to the point in 1980 where there were 123 ordained women. By the end of 1981, this number had increased to 208. In addition, 344 (or 26.7 percent) of the 1,338 students enrolled in Master of Divinity programs were women.[54]

Women were making other advances in the LCA. From the time that the Consulting Committee on Women in Church and Society had been formed in 1972, the number of women lay delegates to the

LCA convention had climbed from 28.7 percent to 49.1 percent, although only 5 percent of the clergy delegates were female. The number of women serving in key positions, such as on synodical executive boards, had jumped from 9.9 percent to 21.2 percent. Gains were also being made in churchwide staff positions and appointive roles on consulting committees. But the CCWCS warned in its report to the 1982 convention that "we find that the large early gains of the 1970s have given way to a much slower growth toward proportionate representation. During this biennium we moved from a pattern of across the board increases to a situation of small gains and small losses with little actual progress toward our goals."[55]

In addition to the question of representation, the CCWCS was also pressing the church on other issues, such as the study of domestic violence, advocacy of the Equal Rights Amendment, personnel practices, inclusive language, and monitoring the way in which women were portrayed in church publications. A *Workbook for Equality and Justice for Women* was prepared for use in synods.[56] It was clear that much had been accomplished, but the CCWCS was not resting on its laurels.

Rethinking World Hunger

For the first six years of the World Hunger Appeal, the LCA made its decisions about continuing the effort biennium by biennium. This procedure posed a number of problems. For one thing, agencies that were supposed to administer the funds had to maintain sufficient reserves to guarantee completion of projects once commitments were made. Another problem was that the tentative status of the appeal made it difficult to create an ongoing network of persons who would be world hunger advocates within the synods. Finally, the synods themselves inundated the Seattle convention in 1980 with twenty-one memorials on world hunger, almost all of which urged continuing the appeal for ten years and referred to the eighties as a "decade of decision."[57]

When the matter came to the convention floor for a vote, there was no question that extension would be voted overwhelmingly, although at the time delegates did not realize they were authorizing an appeal that would have a life span two years greater than the LCA itself. Equally important was the conscious decision to change the objectives of the appeal in order to recognize that hunger was a long-term problem throughout the world, a problem that required addressing "root causes" rather than a "bandaid" approach.[58] The revised objectives adopted were—

To help alleviate the problem of hunger at home and abroad, the Lutheran Church in America, through its world hunger appeal, will—

1. Provide immediate relief of hunger.
2. Assist people in the struggle to deal with endemic need through long-range development.
3. Educate the church to understand and confront the causes of hunger.
4. Advocate social and economic justice as it relates to hunger, including support and advocacy for governmental programs.

Apparently, the approach struck the right note in the church, for from 1980 through 1982, members responded with an outpouring of gifts that topped $15,067,000.[59] The bulk of the funds were channeled through Lutheran World Ministries and Canadian Lutheran World Relief, although somewhat larger amounts than previously were directed through DWME.[60] By linking hands with Lutherans elsewhere on the globe, the LCA was able to deal with needs that far exceeded its own capacity. For example, the World Service arm of LWF poured over $3,200,000 into Bangladesh in 1982 alone to tackle the endemic problem of hunger that ravaged this impoverished country. Some twelve hundred Bangladeshi were employed at about $200 a year, and 250 volunteers were recruited to work in villages to help with water management, agriculture, community health, and a host of other projects necessary to cope with the basic hunger problem.[61]

The increasing domestic hunger crisis and advocacy with governmental agencies were handled by DMNA through synods and its network of related agencies.[62] DPS was responsible for education of the constituency to understand that the very real hunger in the world was usually traceable to "root causes" that ran deep within the structures of society and needed to be confronted if there was to be any hope of long-term solutions.[63] All in all, the World Hunger Appeal had captured the imagination of LCA members and gave them an opportunity to put their declarations on economic justice to the test.

The Troubled Road to Divestment

As early as its second convention, the Lutheran Church in America declared in its social statement on "Race Relations" that "the church, together with its congregations, synods, agencies and institutions, should support its concern for racial justice in all its business involvements."[64] Probably no one at that time foresaw all of the ramifications of this forthright statement. But by 1965 the New England Synod had memorialized the LCA convention to provide for scrutiny of the church's investments to determine whether the corporations involved were making constructive contributions to solving the problems of racial injustice at home and abroad, "particularly in the Union of South Africa."[65] From this beginning, the LCA set out on a long and troubled path that reached a crucial point at the Louisville convention in 1982. Even then there were many loose ends of indecision.

After trying several approaches, the 1972 convention adopted a document, *Social Criteria for Investments,* that had been developed by the Board of Social Ministry.[66] Even then, the question of racism at home and abroad was almost overshadowed by the church's preoccupation with investment in "war industries" during the Vietnam conflict and by the fact that it had just adopted a social statement on ecology. It did, however, refer briefly to exploitation of people in South Africa and Latin America, "where the church's investments offer it an opportunity, but not its only opportunity, to influence the economic policy and practice of such corporations in the direction of justice."[67] The strategies outlined included gaining adequate information, advocacy with decision makers, public hearings and petitions, stockholder proposals and proxy votes, litigation (only on a highly selective basis), special purpose investments, and selective investments. In the last of these, it is noted that "more effective witness to a church's concern about a corporation's practices can be achieved by one or more of the strategies referred to above than by selling a stock."[68]

For the balance of the decade, the LCA's basic strategy was to use such leverage as it had with banks and the corporations in which the Board of Pensions had investments to bring pressure against making loans to South Africa and to urge companies doing business there to guarantee equal pay and treatment for their own employees.[69] This was consistent with what were known as the "Sullivan Principles,"

a code of fair-employment practices that had been developed by the
Rev. Leon Sullivan, a Baptist minister in Philadelphia who had been
an early advocate of improving the lot of minorities through education and industrial development. Most U.S. companies had subscribed over the course of time to the Sullivan Principles or had
withdrawn from South Africa.[70]

Several factors combined to lead the LCA into a new course of
action. General repugnance at the intransigence of the South African
government in maintaining apartheid and its continued repression
of the people of Namibia where there was a large concentration of
Black Lutherans provoked a storm of protest from Lutherans
throughout the world. In 1977 the Lutheran World Federation Assembly, meeting in Tanzania, adopted a statement which read: "We
especially appeal to our white member churches in southern Africa
that the situation in southern Africa constitutes *a* [sic] *status confessionis.* This means that, on the basis of faith and in order to manifest
the unity of the church, churches would publicly and unequivocally
reject the existing apartheid system."[71] In response to eighteen
memorials, the 1980 LCA convention voted "to affirm the action of
the Lutheran World Federation and express unequivocal rejection of
apartheid and all other forms of racial discrimination in our own
society as well as in other nations."[72] It also asked the Executive
Council to revise its procedures to make divestment an option but
rejected by only sixteen votes a proposal to make divestment manda-
tory.[73]

By the Louisville convention two years later, the tide turned.
Eleven memorials dealt with Namibia, apartheid, and divestment.
The delegates struggled with the issues for several sessions, testing
numerous amendments and often debating in tones fraught with
emotion. Delegates were unanimously opposed to the evil of apartheid. The question was whether the best strategy for exerting pressure on South Africa was through divestment. Some felt this was
simply walking away from the problem. Others believed it was the
only ethical action the church could take.

Finally, the delegates voted "to recognize diverstment as an option effective in publicly expressing solidarity with the people opposed to apartheid in Namibia and South Africa but not always
advisable as it may minimize or eliminate opportunity for the
church's dialogue and presence with boards of corporations engaged
in business in South Africa."[74] The convention went a step further,

however, and instructed the Executive Council to direct OAF "to exercise the option of divestment of securities of corporations which have direct involvements in South Africa and the withdrawal of funds from banks which make loans to the government or para-statal agencies in South Africa."

Once the decision had been made, L. Milton Woods, who had been elected earlier to his third term as treasurer by a vote of 633 out of 654 ballots cast, asked for the privilege of the floor. Quietly, he tendered his resignation and said,

"The convention has just made a clear witness of love and solidarity with all those who suffer oppression under the apartheid regime in South Africa. I want to say to you in the clearest possible terms that I share that feeling of solidarity and love with you.

"The convention has also decided that it should underscore its witness by directing a separation of this church from those corporations holding interest in South Africa. You should know, if you do not already, that I am one of the chief decision makers in one such corporation. By way of explanation and not in the nature of argument, I would merely say that it has seemed to me that the cause of freedom and the claim which the Gospel makes on me would best be served—during the little while we are passing through—by the efforts we as a corporation have made to enrich the lives of our black employees by giving them wages equal to white workers in similar

Robert F. Blanck, named to succeed L. Milton Woods as treasurer

jobs; by educating them to qualify for better jobs; and now, in some few cases, by having them supervise white workers. Let me be the first to acknowledge that this program is not enough or soon enough for the Black population, oppressed as it has been for some centuries. . . .

"All of this is (as I say) by way of explanation and not to harangue you, for I know the reasons which have led you to a different conclusion are as firmly grounded in your faith and your consciences as the things I have just said are grounded in mine. . . .

"You can, I think, clearly see that in the circumstances my continuance as one of your officers is inconsistent with the clear witness you want to make, and I want to support you in that effort. Accordingly, I am delivering to the secretary my resignation which is effective at this moment without further action on the part of this assembly. . . .

"And so it is done. I speak to you in love and without any feeling of anger or rancor. . . . I leave you in peace. God bless you one and all."[75]

The convention received the news in shocked silence. Sorrowfully and with deep emotion, Bishop Crumley accepted the resignation, saying, "He is a man of deep convictions, a profound faith, and a sensitive conscience. I have the highest regard and love for Milton Woods."[76] And so it was done, but it would not be the last time that the LCA would need to grapple with the difficult problem of how to deal responsibly with South Africa.

TAKING A HARD LOOK AT
WORLD MISSION

Emphasizing the pervasive influence of change has become so commonplace in recent years that most people are tempted to dismiss any reference to the reality as an overworked cliché. But the late seventies and early eighties presented the LCA's world mission enterprise with a shifting landscape for its work that has seldom been more chaotic and yet, in some ways, more rich in opportunities. In the midst of this situation, DWME was determined to take a long, hard look at not only the nature of global mission but also just how well the division itself was carrying on its operations. The reasons are certainly understandable.

Although Christians could take some satisfaction that the church existed in every country on earth, it was sobering to realize that three-fourths of the world's population had either not heard or not responded to the gospel—and that imbalance was growing every day. Despite advances in agriculture, a fourth of the world's people went to bed hungry. Endemic diseases were cutting short the lives of millions. "Systems of political, economic, and religious injustice condemned countless numbers of persons to fear, misery, and hopelessness on all six continents."[77]

As a result of its strategy of urging former mission churches toward "self-reliance" and responding itself to requests on a project basis, DWME was involved by 1982 in more than thirty different countries. Strength for Mission funds had come at a critical time when the value of the dollar was plunging overseas and new opportunities were emerging. Some of the most stable situations of the past, such as Liberia, were rocked by coups or civil wars. Ethiopia's Evangelical Church Mekane Yesus remained a miracle of faithfulness, growing in spite of severe repression by the Marxist government. Its headquarters was seized, two hundred churches were closed, General Secretary Guidina Tumsa was abducted, and many other church leaders detained.[78] Tanzania, which had suffered through a war with neighboring Uganda, was in terrible economic condition, but the Lutheran church there was growing in the face of inflation and a shortage of pastors.[79]

Similar growth was occurring in places like Indonesia, Malaysia, Singapore, Hong Kong, and parts of Latin America. When the LCA's historic mission work in Guyana came to an end in 1981, DWME began assistance to the Lutheran church in neighboring Surinam.[80] The roll call of countries where the DWME was involved either directly or through cooperative agencies was impressive.[81] A series of major consultations were held to develop strategies for the Central Andean region, the Southern Cone of South America, and the Middle East.[82]

The changed political climate in the People's Republic of China presented the most dramatic and intriguing development of the late seventies. During the Cultural Revolution (1966–76) only one Protestant church had remained open in China and that was in Beijing.[83] When primary leader Deng Xiaoping led the nation in a new direction, the Religious Affairs Bureau was revitalized and helped restore religious properties. Within five years, two thousand churches were reopened in all major cities, and it is estimated that there were over fifty thousand house gatherings throughout the country.[84] For the first time in decades, contact was made by Western churches with the amazingly vital Christian community in that vast country. But the LCA had to recognize that China was no longer a mission field. The Christian community there was a postdenominational phenomenon that provided the world "with a model of how the Christian community lives out its life in a secular socialistic setting."[85]

Meanwhile, Europe and North America were having to come to terms more fully with the fact that other parts of the world were beginning to view them as "mission fields."[86] Through the combined efforts of DWME and DMNA, pastors from Asia and Latin America were placed in areas of the United States and Canada where they ministered principally to persons whose primary language was other than English.[87] DWME, on the other hand, had twenty-seven missionaries serving in a variety of ways in places such as Stockholm, Helsinki, Brussels, The Hague, Amsterdam, England, Germany, and Switzerland.

As though all this activity were not enough, the Division for World Mission and Ecumenism set itself in the final years of Executive Director David Vikner's tenure to reexamine both foci of its mandate. Through major study processes, it developed statements on both "global mission" and "ecumenism" that would set the direction in these areas for the remainder of the LCA's existence. The *Call to Global Mission* and *Ecumenism, a Lutheran Commitment* do not reflect a view that these two areas should be treated in isolation from one another but DWME's conviction that they are closely interrelated.

Call to Global Mission

Since the end of World War II, David Vikner has pointed out, LCA world mission thinking had been developing along two channels that now seemed to be converging. "The first is the recognition that the mission of the church involves the verbal proclamation of the Gospel, the serving of human need, and social action—confronting injustices of all sorts wherever they exist. Secondly, in seeking to respond to the human need in the world, service agencies began with relief, added development, and now social action."[88] In its *Call to Global Mission,* DWME dealt in a major way with this convergence. At the Seattle convention, it had signaled the full scope of its intentions when it reported that the division was concerned with "the vocation of

DWME for the remainder of the 20th century."[89] Although the division realized that DWME itself was not likely to exist for the balance of the century, it knew that the church's global mission would.

As background for understanding its statement both before and after it was adopted, the division called upon a dozen experts in various fields to write papers on the issues with which the church needed to grapple in taking a position. Reflecting the ecumenical stance of DWME, these writers included not only LCA members but also an ALC executive, the head of the WCC Commission on World Mission and Evangelism, and the executive director of the Board for World Ministries of the United Church of Christ.[90]

Although the *Call to Global Mission* describes the radically changed world in which the church must witness, it declares that "the mission of the church . . . remains in its most profound sense the same: to express the good news of the kingdom of God in Jesus Christ to the whole world and to the end of time. . . . Mission is the answer to the question of what the community of the endtime is to do in the meantime."[91] What loom as different in the eighties, however, are the frontiers for mission. "In an earlier period, the frontiers were largely geographical. In the future they may more often be functional and situational."

These seven nongeographical frontiers of the future are evangelism, the poor and the oppressed, peace making, the intellectual and scientific fields, unity for mission, relation to people of other faiths, and the crisis of institutions. As though to allay a growing concern that mission agencies had been focusing so much effort on development and social action, the statement calls evangelism "the continuing frontier" and affirms that "evangelism has been and still is the central task of the church." At the same time, it balances this affirmation by showing the ways in which the church's proclamation and witness must come to grips with the reality and urgency of the other six frontiers.

In approving the *Call to Global Mission,* the convention delegates made two significant changes in the accompanying recommendations. First, it deleted the specific reference to DWME in the first resolution, "That this church affirm *(the Division for World Mission and Ecumenism in)* its efforts to extend the ministry of the gospel to all the world and to relate that gospel to human needs in every situation in a manner that is appropriate to the context of the last decades of the twentieth century."[92] In this way, it claimed the new approach to global mission as a responsibility for the LCA as a whole. In a further action, the delegates voted to "give high priority to the Evangelical Outreach Program as a means of implementing this church's commitment to thinking globally and acting locally, as an expression of the working document in the section 'Evangelism: The Continuing Frontier. . . .' "[93] In this way, the church tied the global enterprise directly to the fact it had made evangelism a high priority on the homefront.

Looking at DWME from Outside the LCA

As though to underscore its conviction that the LCA could not be content to look only at what it was doing in world mission through its own eyes, the DWME took the unprecedented step of asking the Lutheran World Federation's Department of Church Cooperation to provide for an evaluation of its work.[94] The LWF department appointed a five-person team including four Lutherans from overseas and one Methodist specialist in missiology, who spent up to two weeks in the study.[95] In addition to reviewing background documents before beginning the process, the team spent many hours interviewing DWME staff, executives of CWAs, and others. A lengthy report was sent to DWME in September 1982 for its response and action.[96]

The evaluation commended DWME as an "extremely well-organized agency within a church that has assumed its full place in the mainstream of American Protestantism," and commended its strongly ecumenical commitment, its orientation towards the future, and its determination to innovate.[97] At the same time, the evaluation was frank in criticizing such matters as the danger inherent in area secretaries becoming the final decision makers on funding and assignment, the dearth of women in leadership positions, the potential ambiguity in the roles of other CWAs in global mission (e.g., possible overlapping of DWME and DMNA actions regarding the South African crisis), the lack of participation of congregations in world missions, and the lack of input from overseas churches in decision making. It acknowledged the difficulty faced in the Third World by North Americans who, rightly or wrongly, are thought of as representing a superpower. The team also spent considerable time "trying to analyze what the factors were in DWME policy or practice that created tension in the international church scene."

The team finally drew the conclusion that the basic question for the DWME could be crystallized in "the choice between . . . the *'center-of-the-world mentality'* and the *'plug-in* practice.' "[98] The first of these is related to such things as the very competence of DWME's staff, its global view vs. sometimes parochial outlooks in other parts of the world, leadership in world organizations, being on the cutting edge of Protestantism in the world's leading nation, and its financial power. To counteract this problem, the team suggested that DWME either ask others—related churches or organizations— to work out certain programs or that it open its own consultations to others and develop programs with international agencies from the earliest stages of programming.[99] DWME showed a remarkable lack of defensiveness in the whole process and took the findings as serious input for its own future work.

PROGRESS IN ECUMENISM

If the ecumenical movement seemed to some to be in the doldrums in the 1970s, it was certainly alive and vigorous in the eighties. Signs of the times were the establishment of a separate department on ecumenical relations in DWME, the adoption of a major policy state-ment on *Ecumenism: A Lutheran Commitment* by the LCA, the drafting of a historic document by the WCC on *Baptism, Eucharist and Ministry,* progress in bilateral dialogues, and the forging of an agreement on interim sharing of the Eucharist by Lutherans and Episcopalians.

From the time of restructuring in 1972, there had been various unsuccessful efforts to separate the ecumenical role of DWME from the task of world missions and place it in a separate churchwide agency.[100] It was not until 1978, however, that the DWME was given authority to create its first full-time staff position of director of ecu-menical relations, a post that was filled by William G. Rusch.[101] The decision to establish this position was consistent with President Crumley's concern about the ecumenical stance of the LCA. In 1982 a second step was taken, and a Department of Ecumenical Relations was formed within the division and an assistant director added to the staff. Meanwhile, there were prolonged efforts to sort out the respec-tive roles of the new staff, the president (then bishop), the Executive Council, as well as the executive director and the management com-mittee of DWME.

The Statement on Ecumenism

The decision of DWME to develop a statement on ecumenism for the
church reached a critical point at a consultation held at Jacksonville
Beach, Florida, February 22–27, 1981, that included not only persons
from the LCA but also a dozen leaders from national and international ecumenical agencies.[102] It was during this conference that a
breakthrough was reached in interpreting that part of the LCA Constitution which deals with unity of the church.[103] This article had
normally been interpreted to mean that the LCA was to seek Lutheran unity first and *then* to move on to closer ties with other
Christian bodies. What seems obvious now was the conclusion the
consultation reached that both of these efforts could proceed simultaneously.[104]

This view, LCA leaders maintained, was consistent with the Augsburg Confession, whose 450th anniversary Lutherans had celebrated
only a year earlier. The *Confessio Augustana* saw Lutheranism as a
reform movement within the church catholic.[105] As William
Lazareth puts it, "The confessors at Augsburg never intended to
write a 'Protestant' Magna Charta, to say nothing of a 'Teutonic'
Declaration of Independence."[106] In another context, George A.
Lindbeck declared, "If Lutheranism is thought of as a reforming
movement rather than as a church, there is no reason why Lutheran
unity should be a prior condition for unity with non-Lutherans."[107]

Following the Jacksonville conference, a small group met to determine follow-up procedures.[108] It was agreed to appoint a steering
committee that would hammer out the draft of *Ecumenism: A Lutheran Commitment* that was adopted by the Louisville convention
in 1982.[109] As William G. Rusch states, "Much in the document had
been implicit in the Lutheran Church in America and its predecessor
bodies, but now this church was making explicit its views of, and
commitment to, ecumenism."[110]

Following a brief preface, the statement includes six major sections. The first sets forth the "Scriptural, Confessional and Constitutional Foundations" for the statement. The Scriptures are seen not
only as calling "us to oneness in Christ" (Gal. 2:5, 14) but also as
picturing "realistically human inclinations against unity and fellowship, especially the tendency to build and retain dividing walls of
hostility" (Eph. 2:14). The Lutheran Confessions are described as
concerned with evangelical reform, "which contrary to intention,

resulted in divisions within the western church. . . . The question is no longer that of preserving an existing church unity, but that of reestablishing a communion which has been broken. Yet Article VII of the Augsburg Confession continues to be ecumenically liberating because of the insistence that agreement in the Gospel suffices for Christian unity." From the standpoint of the LCA Constitution, the statement concludes that there is no reason why striving for the unification of all Lutherans, fostering Christian unity, participating in ecumenical activities with other churches that confess the Trinity, and entering into relation with other Lutheran bodies and with other evangelical churches for furtherance of the gospel cannot go on simultaneously.[111]

The second major point dealt with the church's "Evangelical, Catholic, and Ecumenical Stance" in which it states that the LCA is "pledged to affirm its kinship and to demonstrate its unity with all those who are evangelical and catholic in the Church. Therefore, this church does not commit itself only to Pan-Lutheranism. . . . Rather it is bold to reach out in several directions simultaneously." The third section described the LCA's ecumenical involvements since 1962.[112] The fourth section lists fourteen different insights to be borne in mind as the LCA pursues its ecumenical role.[113] The fifth was a conclusion that uses the biblical image of the grain of wheat falling into the earth and dying (John 12:24) as a metaphor of what may have to happen to ecclesial structures if greater unity is to grow. The final section listed six commitments that the LCA made to continue and further the high priority of its ecumenical vision.

In adopting the statement at this time, the LCA was making clear that its commitment to ecumenism would be an important ingredient in planning for a new Lutheran church body in the future.[114] Obviously, the LCA was in no mood to retreat from the stance that had been taken in predecessor bodies as early as 1920 in applying an understanding of the ecumenical character of the Lutheran Confessions not only to relations with other Lutherans but also to relations with other Christian churches.[115]

The Episcopalians and Eucharistic Hospitality

For decades Lutherans had been participating in bilateral dialogues with other churches under the auspices of LCUSA. In 1980, however, the completion of a second series of conversations with the Episcopalians produced a report that brought to fruition thirteen years of effort.[116] The document reviewed the history of the discussions and included joint statements on justification, the gospel, the Eucharist, and scriptural authority. The report made a series of recommendations asking, among other things, that the churches recognize one another as true churches, work out a way for interim sharing of the Eucharist, provide for joint worship according to guidelines, and encourage congregational covenants. It also proposed that there be a third dialogue series dealing with ministry.

The Commission on Ecumenical Relations of the Episcopal Church unanimously approved the general direction of the dialogue report and called for a study process aimed at making specific recommendations to that church's convention in September 1982. Episcopal Presiding Bishop John M. Allin shared the commission's actions with Bishop Crumley in the hope that the Lutheran churches would undertake a similar process. ALC, LCA, and AELC all developed their own study processes and kept one another informed of progress. With a degree of speed that is seldom seen in interchurch relations, an agreement was reached that the ALC, AELC, LCA, and the Episcopal Church would all present similar recommendations to their conventions in September.

The recommendations, which were adopted by the LCA convention without a dissenting vote, (a) recognized the Episcopal Church as a church in which the gospel is preached and taught; (b) encouraged development of common Christian life throughout the respective churches by such means as mutual prayer, support, and covenantal agreements (at both parish and judicatory levels); common study of the Scriptures and the histories and theological traditions of each church; joint programs of religious education, evangelism, social action, and theological discussion; joint use of physical facilities; (c) affirmed that the basic teachings of each respective church are consonant with the gospel and sufficiently compatible with the teaching of this church (in this case, LCA) to establish interim sharing of the Eucharist according to certain guidelines; (d) authorized a third dialogue series to discuss any remaining questions before establishing full communion (*communio in sacris* /altar and pulpit fellowship).[117]

A historic step had been taken that was welcomed by the members of the participating churches and was celebrated in an impressive eucharistic service in the National Cathedral at Washington in which the bishops of all three Lutheran churches participated. Initially, the actions that had been taken caused some rumblings throughout the Lutheran and Anglican communions elsewhere in the world. In 1986, however, Robert A. K. Runcie, the Archbishop of Canterbury, visited the LCA convention in Milwaukee and received the Holy Communion from Bishop Crumley. The Archbishop, in turn, gave the elements to Bishop Crumley. It was a "tangible symbol," Runcie said, of the interim eucharistic fellowship existing between Lutherans and Episcopalians in this country.[118]

Baptism, Eucharist, and Ministry

On a world scale, Christians of many traditions had been addressing the basic issues surrounding Holy Baptism, the Eucharist, and Ministry for a half century within the theological forum of the World Council of Churches Commission on Faith and Order. After scores of consultations and hundreds of papers and through uncounted hours of discussion by thousands of persons, the commission reached a milestone in ecumenical cooperation when more than a hundred theologians met in Lima, Peru, January 2–16, 1982.[119] At that meeting the Commission on Faith and Order submitted to the churches a slim document of only fifty pages, *Baptism, Eucharist and Ministry*, that distilled insights from fifty-five years of work on this subject.[120] Much of the credit for bringing the effort through the final stages to this historic point was due Lutheran theologian William H. Lazareth, who served as director of the Secretariat on Faith and Order at that time.

The three sections of the volume deal with major areas of theological convergence on the themes plus commentaries that indicate where historical differences have been overcome or where there are still areas of disagreement. In the preface, readers are cautioned, "In the course of critical evaluation the primary purpose of this ecumenical text must be kept in mind. Readers should not expect to find a complete theological treatment of baptism, eucharist and ministry. That would be neither appropriate nor desirable here. The agreed text purposely concentrates on those aspects of the theme that have been directly or indirectly related to the problems of mutual recognition leading to unity."[121]

What the commission asked specifically was the widest possible study by all churches at all levels with detailed official replies that could be analyzed for their ecumenical implications and reported to a future World Conference on Faith and Order.[122] BEM, as it came to be known, created an almost unprecedented wave of interest throughout the Christian world. Along with other churches, the LCA engaged in a thoroughgoing process of review and response, which is described in Chapter 7 of this book.

MISSION IN NORTH AMERICA

The Division for Mission in North America had from its inception maintained a global view and ecumenical perspective. It had teamed its efforts with DWME in such activities as the Mission on Six Continents program and the popular global mission events. It spoke out on a wide range of international issues relative to Namibia, South Africa, and United States involvement in Central America. It related to LCUSA and such agencies as the Lutheran Resources Commission, Lutheran Social Service Systems, Lutheran Educational Conferences in North America, National Lutheran Campus Ministry, Lutheran Domestic Disaster Response Board, National Indian Lutheran Board, and the Lutheran Housing Commission. On an interchurch basis, it was involved with numerous agencies, such as the Commission on Religion in Appalachia, the Alabama Rural Council, Joint Strategy and Action Committee, several units of the NCCCUSA, and the World Council of Churches.[123]

In addition to developing the social statements and social issue studies discussed earlier, it was the lead churchwide agency for the Consulting Committee on Minority Group Interests, Consulting Committee on Women in Church and Society, and LAOS in Ministry. The DMNA Management Committee's minutes and the division's reports to the LCA convention present an almost overwhelming array of activities. At times it seemed difficult to discern where DMNA's understanding of its responsibilities ended and those of other churchwide agencies began. In spite of this complexity, however, there was remarkably little evidence of overlapping or friction among the agencies.

Entering New Fields

Beginning new congregations as a way of furthering mission had always been a high priority in the minds of LCA members. In planning for the period from 1978 through 1982, DMNA had projected a goal of developing 150 new congregations in locations selected to provide a balance between those with potential for quick growth and others in strategic areas where growth might be slower.[124] Actually, DMNA was able to exceed this number by one, and twenty of them were located in minority communities.[125]

During this period, however, significant changes were taking place in population patterns of the United States and Canada. People were beginning to move out of metropolitan areas into "more livable" environments. Many of the places where they located were in areas where the Lutherans did not have a strong presence. Florida, Texas, and the western United States as well as Vancouver and Toronto in Canada were becoming gateways for immigrants from Asia, Latin America, and Europe. One indication of how this vast influx of people had placed demands on the churches was the fact that the Lutheran Immigration and Refugee Service in 1980 had resettled its 100,000th refugee since World War II.[126]

The LCA struggled to deal with these shifting tides, but there were problems. Inflation at the turn of the decade had taken its toll. Interest rates had shot upward, and the cost of land and church construction had risen alarmingly.[127] Despite infusions of cash from Strength for Mission and generous grants from insurance companies, many new congregations were in a holding pattern and forced to use makeshift arrangements for services.[128] Both DMNA and OAF were deeply concerned about the problem, and it was agreed that the bishop would call for a "special order" at the Executive Council meeting in March 1982 to confront the situation. A special committee met in February to explore many different options, which included creating an Endowment Fund and borrowing SFM monies interest free, but there was agreement not to have a capital funds appeal. The Executive Council agreed with these basic moves.[129]

Finally, the outlook had become so bleak by the time of the Louisville convention that five synodical bishops introduced a resolution calling for a feasibility study for a capital funds appeal.[130] When the matter was brought to the floor in the waning hours of the convention, an attempt to broaden the purpose of an appeal was given short shrift, and debate was closed abruptly with almost no opportunity for discussion. The recommendation for the feasibility study was adopted and the Executive Council instructed to bring back a proposal in 1984.[131]

Supporting Congregations

Just starting congregations and helping them to build the necessary facilities, of course, were only part of the picture. The LCA was also faced with finding ways to support congregations as new demands were placed upon them for ministry. In many cases financial assistance was required to deal with a crisis or to meet a new opportunity. But often such help was intended to be a temporary measure. For example, in the 1980–81 biennium alone, sixty-two metropolitan congregations became self-supporting. Of these, however, forty had been receiving aid for from five to twenty years.[132]

Although sometimes it was necessary to grapple with the intractable problems presented by blighted areas like the South Bronx, metropolitan work was by no means limited to the hard core of the inner city. More and more suburban churches, particularly those in the first ring around a city, required guidance and help in meeting changing situations. Conferences were held to train pastors and lay leaders in dealing with emerging problems and possibilities. Sometimes the solution lay in additional staff or the use of volunteers who had been equipped with necessary skills.[133] In other cases the Resource Mobilization Network was used to provide on-site consultations with congregations or related community groups to develop programs and find funding to provide services for the elderly, youth, day care, nutritional, and health services.[134]

Town and country ministry was another arena that demanded attention. With fully one-third of LCA congregations located outside of metropolitan areas and many of them small, the parishes frequently needed financial support and guidance as they dealt with such situations as threats to the family farm or a sudden influx of people moving into the community from the city.[135] No matter what the setting for mission in North America, it seemed there was seldom a place in which congregations were not faced with the need to adapt their ministries and often on an overnight basis.

Higher Education

The colleges and universities related to the LCA were facing the same basic problems that beset all institutions of higher learning in the United States and Canada. On the one hand, there was the relentless rise of costs and the upward spiral of tuition. On the other hand, there was the diminishing number of students who were reaching college age. In fact, it was estimated that between the end of the seventies and the beginning of the nineties, the number of young people reaching the age of eighteen annually would decline about 26 percent, or about a million potential students per year.[136]

To make matters worse, the percentage of Blacks enrolled in college had peaked, and the high cost was squeezing those from less affluent families out of the private schools market.[137] Some of the slack was being taken up by students from other minority groups or those from overseas. At the graduate school level, the number of foreign students enrolled in the United States and Canadian institutions was increasing steadily.[138] One of the most lucrative exports was becoming education and knowledge.

As was true of many institutions of higher learning, the eighteen LCA institutions not only welcomed foreign students but also granted substantial financial assistance to those from the United States and Canada who needed such help. In 1978–79 grants-in-aid at LCA schools were estimated to be $42,516,000.[139] By the 1980–81 academic year, that sum had swelled to $67,257,000, and 77 percent of the students were receiving grants of some type.[140] Support from the LCA, of course, came principally from the synods, and although there had been a slight upturn in this area, the total projected for 1982 was only a fraction of this amount, or about $2,762,000.[141] A large part of the funds needed by the colleges was coming from government sources, foundations, corporations, endowments, and individual givers. This was understandable since the combined grants-in-aid provided by the LCA institutions exceeded the total budget of the church-at-large.

The colleges, however, still saw their church relationship as a distinct asset and an important characteristic of their program. DMNA's Department of Higher Education provided valuable help in evaluation and interpretation of the role of the church-related college. During the 1980–81 biennium six hundred trustees, faculty members, students, alumni, parents, and pastors attended a series of conferences to study the *Survey of Images and Expectations of LCA Colleges* and *The Basis for Partnership Between Church and College*.[142] Following these events, an interpretive book was published and distributed to pastors and other key leaders.[143] The LCA was in no mood to abandon its long history of interest in higher education.

MINISTRY, MINISTERS, AND BISHOPS

If there is one prerogative that the LCA has guarded jealously through the years, it has been the right to change its mind. Certainly this has been true as it dealt with some of the ramifications of the concept of "the whole people of God," the specific nature of the ordained ministry, and the frequently recurring debate over whether to use the term *bishop* for the chief pastor of a synod or the church-at-large. This whole complex of concerns came under scrutiny once more at the Seattle convention in 1980. The decisions at that point revealed a sense of both their implications for relations with other Lutheran churches and their wider ecumenical significance.

A New Study of Ministry

In 1970 the LCA convention had received a major report of *The Commission on the Comprehensive Study of the Doctrine of the Ministry*.[144] When the Division for Professional Leadership was formed in 1972, it was given the responsibility to conduct an "ongoing study of ministry and report regularly to this church on the ministry of the laity in the world and in the church and the role of the ordained ministry."[145] As a result of that process, DPL brought to the 1980 convention a report that viewed ministry from the perspective of the decade following the earlier document.[146] It began with the church's growing awareness of the ministry of the whole people of God and moved on to reexamine the ordained ministry. Factors that precipitated a fresh look at the situation included a concern for inclusiveness not only of minorities but also of women, the inability of some congregations to afford full-time pastors, and the ecumenically sensitive question of reordination of clergy coming from other churches.

Although a full-scale study on the ministry of the laity was to be completed by the 1984 convention, the report at Seattle emphasized that "ministry is God's Word in action through the whole people of God." All believers are stewards of the gospel and the community of ministers who are the priesthood of believers. Since every Christian is called to minister to his or her neighbor in the world, "the word *ministry* is not reserved for the work of ordained ministers." What distinguishes ministry, in this sense, from other human tasks is the way in which the Word is manifest in the distinctive elements of reconciliation, priesthood, proclamation and teaching, witness, service, daily work, justice, and oversight.

Specific attention was given to the last of these elements, "oversight," in a brief paragraph where both lay persons and those in the Office of Word and Sacrament were seen as having responsibilities for overseeing the life and work of the church. At this point the document introduces a short citation emphasizing the fact that the Reformers had retained the functions and title of bishop but reserved to the whole people the right to choose their own bishops.[147] Although those who wrote this document had not been consulted specifically, they could hardly have been unaware that the decision on whether to use the title "bishop" in the LCA would also be made at Seattle.

After dealing with the traditional Marks of the Church, the study goes on to describe in some detail the ministry of the laity in the world as a background for understanding the distinctive character of the ministry of Word and Sacrament. Drawing upon the Augsburg Confession, the statement explains that God "instituted the office of this ministry, that is, provided the gospel and the sacraments" in order that persons may obtain faith in the saving grace of God for Christ's sake.[148] The study goes on to explain that this office is the one indispensable form of ministry. "The functions lodged in this office, moreover, take precedence over all ecclesiastical structures, titles, rites, and liturgies."[149] While this "ministry of the Word stands over churches and, when necessary, even against churches and the world," it is filled only by persons called by the whole people of God.

After describing the expectations of the ordained ministry and the relationship between it and the ministries of lay persons, the document goes on to apply these understandings to some specific questions. These include providing pastoral ministry on a part-time basis in congregations, and ministry in special situations, such as synodical and churchwide agencies, colleges, seminaries, social service agencies, institutions, ecumenical organizations, chaplaincies, nontraditional settings, graduate study, and extended service. It deals with other issues, such as growth in office, personal problems, misgivings about leaving office, and the reception of those previously ordained by other Christian churches.

The management committee of DPL had forwarded its recommendations on various of these matters to the convention through the Executive Council. Two particularly crucial points had to deal with calls to part-time service in a congregation and the reception of ordained clergy from other denominations. On the first of these, the convention voted to add a new item to Section II of the LCA Bylaws that would permit a minister to serve under call to part-time service in a congregation.[150] This was a major change for the LCA, which acknowledged that such "dual ministries" were sometimes necessary because of financial constraints in the congregation or a variety of situations, such as family responsibilities on the part of the pastor.[151] The new concept was widely accepted, and within a few years, nearly two hundred pastors were serving in this way.

With regard to reception of ministers of other denominations into the ordained ministry of the LCA, however, an attempt to amend the constitution and bylaws to pave the way for reception by affirmation in the same manner as pastors from other Lutheran church bodies was defeated.[152] The only route, therefore, that remained for a minister from another denomination to be admitted to the role of ordained clergy in the LCA was ordination.

By 1984, however, the Executive Council concluded that a new amendment should be introduced because of the ecumenical commitment of the church. The amendment, which was adopted in 1986, provided that ordained ministers could be received from other denominations that "teach, believe and confess the Apostles', the Nicene, and the Athanasian creeds."[153] The rationale for this action was the recognition that ordination was into the church catholic but is particularized in a specific manifestation of the church and never in the abstract. The procedures to be followed by synods were spelled out in the bylaws and other documents.

From Presidents to Bishops

Among North American Lutherans, rejection of the use of the title "bishop" for their church leaders had roots that ran far back in history to the deep dissatisfaction that many of the immigrants had toward the European state churches from which they had come. When the Joint Commission on Lutheran Unity was planning the LCA, it continued this tradition by deciding overwhelmingly to call the chief officer of the church-at-large and its synods simply "president." This did not end the matter, however, for the Conference of Synodical Presidents asked that analysis of the theological implications of the office be presented at its 1965 meeting. The paper, prepared by Robert Marshall who was at that time president of the

Illinois Synod, gave an evenhanded treatment of the biblical and confessional background of the office of bishop and the present-day similarities to the responsibilities of a synodical president.[154]

The question surfaced again in 1970 when the Commission on the Comprehensive Study of the Doctrine of the Ministry proposed that the church "look with favor on changing the title of Synod President to Bishop, and that the Executive Council be instructed to take the necessary steps toward the adoption of the title and to define the duties of the office."[155] At the request of the Executive Council, the president appointed a Committee to Study the Office of Bishop.[156]

In its report, the committee stated that the question had not emerged simply because it had seemed "to be a good idea to say something about it." It was central to the nature of the document on the ordained ministry that the individual minister was in need of pastoral oversight just as is the case with those to whom he or she ministers.[157] The committee gave a detailed analysis of the reasons for considering at this time the use of the ecclesiastical title of bishop for this role of "chief pastor," including the more widespread use in Lutheran circles and the significance it would have in ecumenical relations.[158] It stressed, however, that the title should not be construed in the LCA as deriving from authority granted through the historic episcopacy. It did not imply granting additional power to a synodical president or lifelong tenure in the office. Although the original assignment did not include the question, the committee suggested that the president of the LCA be called "presiding bishop."

When the necessary amendments to the constitution were presented to the Dallas convention in 1972 for first reading, however, they failed by fifty votes of achieving the necessary two-thirds majority.[159] An effort to reintroduce the idea of bishops at the 1974 convention failed by the even larger margin of ninety-three votes. As the editors of the *Convention Summary* reported, "Once again, our presidents are *still* presidents!"[160]

By 1978, however, the Michigan Synod memorialized the church to address the question once more, partly because the title of bishop had already been adopted by the American Lutheran Church with which the LCA was seeking to merge.[161] In response to a resolution introduced by the requisite number of delegates, the Executive Council held a late-night session on Sunday, July 16, and brought to the convention a series of amendments for first reading to effect the proposed changes.[162] President Marshall was asked by the Council to draft the explanatory introduction to the resolution. This time the motion was adopted.

In the interim prior to the Seattle convention, the Executive Council asked the Division for Professional Leadership to have a background paper prepared that would detail the whole history of the discussion including the pros and cons of the question.[163] DPL asked John Reumann of the Philadelphia Seminary to prepare the paper, which was shared with the convention delegates.[164] After a thorough and scholarly presentation, Dr. Reumann concluded by saying, "In the anniversary year of 1530–1980, the question may well be not 'Why?' but 'Why not?'" Although some delegates voiced the fear that the change in title would imply some superior power for bishops, the amendments finally passed with a margin of thirty-seven votes.

In a personal word to the convention, the freshly titled *Bishop* Crumley reassured the delegates that the action in no way changed "the function or tenure of the chief executive officer of the church and the synods."[165] In retrospect, however, the change did become more than a difference in name. It opened many ecumenical doors for the synodical bishops as well as for Dr. Crumley himself. On the other side of the coin, it is possible to see that there was a gradual change in the authority and status accorded to bishops within the LCA.[166]

PROVIDING AND SUPPORTING PROFESSIONAL LEADERS

Like a person plagued for life with a name not of his own choosing, the Division for Professional Leadership chafed under the use of "professional" in its title. The division believed this term was coming more and more to be confused with secular professionalism. DPL was concerned that the idea of *service* to the church might be lost in the pursuit of self-interest and personal gain. In its 1980 report to the church, the division devoted several paragraphs to this issue and indicated that it planned to study the whole matter before the 1982 convention.[167] During this period of time the prospects of a merger for Lutherans had become a reality, however, and DPL decided not to ask for a change of name. Instead it decided to request certain bylaw amendments emphasizing its role in providing services for both "ordained ministers and persons in lay professional service."[168]

Trends in Theological Education

There were several trends occurring in the seminary scene that were signs of fundamental changes in the church. One was the upswing in enrollment of women for the Master of Divinity degree in proportion to men. In 1978 there were 192 women and 788 men enrolled in LCA seminaries. By 1981 that number had changed to 245 and 645 respectively, but equally significant was the decline in the total number of candidates from 980 to 890.[169] At the same time, those engaged in lay professional degree programs increased in just one academic year from 39 to 59.[170] The number of minority candidates preparing for the ordained ministry, however, fluctuated from 38 in 1979–80 to 23 in 1980–81 and back up to 33 by 1981–82.[171] At the same time, the age of M. Div. candidates in the LCA secretary's register was trending steadily upward. In 1973, only 12 percent of the seminary graduates were over 30, but by 1982, that number had increased to 41.7 percent of the total. This indicated that more and more persons were choosing the ministry as a second career which, in turn, had implications both for preparation and service.[172] One sobering fact of these inflation years was that seminary graduates were facing their first calls with a much higher debt load for their education.[173] An encouraging sign was that there was a sharp upturn in the number of persons taking advanced degrees in LCA seminaries, although the number of those preparing for "academic doctorates" was declining.[174]

It was not simply the composition of the seminary population that was important; it was the way in which the theological schools themselves were consolidating their efforts to meet new conditions. For example, the withdrawal of the Missouri Synod from the planned formation of a merged church in Canada placed additional financial strain on the inter-Lutheran seminary at Saskatoon.[175] In the United States there were also important developments. By 1982 the jointly owned ALC-LCA Trinity Seminary in Columbus, Ohio, was engaged in a building program. A substantial commitment to Pacific Seminary was made by the ALC from its appeal for funds for theological education.[176] A full corporate merger occurred at Luther-Northwestern in July 1982 so that the school ceased to be "plural and hyphenated." DPL completed a major study of *Lutheran Theological Education in the Northeastern United States* that laid the groundwork for closer cooperation between Gettysburg and Philadelphia Seminaries, although the plan did allow the two schools to continue their individual corporate existences.[177]

One of the most important developments in inter-Lutheran cooperation came when a decision was reached among the AELC, ALC, and LCA for the deployment of students and faculty of Christ Seminary-Seminex in 1983 to the campuses of the Lutheran School of Theology at Chicago, Pacific Seminary, and the American Lutheran Church's Wartburg Seminary House of Studies in Austin, Texas.[178] This did not mean the end of Seminex, which had been created in 1974 out of the efforts of students and faculty of Concordia Seminary in St. Louis to resist the purge of so-called "liberals" during the Jacob Preus presidency of the Missouri Synod.[179] The school continued to act as an autonomous institution, and the LCA theological education enterprise was strengthened at the same time by the addition of fourteen experienced faculty members and seventy students.

Supporting the Leaders

DPL's efforts to support professional leaders in their careers were expanding during these years. Continuing education became increasingly important with PLACE funds being included in the official call form for pastors.[180] An agreement was reached in 1979 with ALC's Division for Theological Education and Ministry to publish a joint statement outlining the resources for continuing education and how they are commonly available in the two churches.[181] The Growth in Ministry program, which had been built on an extensive research effort in the 1970s to find ways of assisting pastors and their spouses to meet the changing demands of ministry, had involved over four thousand persons from ALC, LCMS, and LCA in scores of workshops.[182] Many of the participants had been attracted to the program by a book, *Growth in Ministry,* that not only interpreted the original research in popular form but also described the potential for more effective ministry in the future.[183]

One of the problems that faced more and more ministers was the limited number of opportunities available for a call to a new situation. In order to help clergy address this situation, DPL in cooperation with about two-thirds of the synods had conducted Mobility Conferences since the program was introduced in 1975. By the early eighties, however, the division began to pilot an "Options" program that faced candidly the fact that pastors might want to leave the ordained ministry for other employment.[184] It was a recognition that for years clergy had labored under the feeling that there was some stigma attached to leaving the ranks of the ordained and that both they and their spouses needed to explore the possibilities in a supportive situation.

At the turn of the decade, the Deaconess Community began to function with the greater degree of self-determination approved by the 1978 convention. Finances were once more on a solid footing, and the decision to use the Deaconess Center at Gladwyne, Pennsylvania, as the principal residence for retired members of the Community proved to be a wise one.[185] In 1982 the Associates in Diaconal Service program marked its twenty-fifth anniversary. More than three hundred men and women had participated in this year-long program of voluntary service, and about one-third of them continued for a second year. In 1981, a married couple served in the program for the first time.

A new tool for professional leaders, *LCA Partners*, was launched in 1979. Such a magazine had been proposed at the formation of the LCA by the JCLU Committee on Publications, but the idea remained in limbo for almost two decades. When DPL was formed in 1972, exploration of the idea was renewed, but budgetary constraints always stood in the way. Even though an arrangement had been worked out with DPS to provide editorial services for the publication, the DPL Management Committee itself ranked the project low in priority for funding and shelved the proposal.[186] The project was again revived in 1977, and the journal eventually appeared in 1979 with an editor employed by DPL. The magazine was distributed free to professional leaders and contained the traditional "Dear Partners" letter of the LCA bishop, as well as a wide array of articles dealing with biblical and theological issues, career development, and other matters of special significance to its readership.

"THE DECADE OF THE CONGREGATION"

"If the opinions of key leaders are a reliable guide," declared the LCA Office for Research and Planning, "the 1980s should be the decade of the congregation."[187] After the turbulence of the sixties and the malaise of the seventies when many persons were challenging the viability of the congregation, the mood began to change as the church moved into the eighties. That is not to say there were not serious problems, but there were also encouraging signs of parish renewal, an upsurge of interest in religion among young people, a greater involvement in social concerns, increased participation in adult education, slight gains in membership, and an upswing in giving. Whether these positive trends could be sustained was the question mark hovering on the horizon. Almost every aspect of congregational life was in ferment.

The Unfinished Agenda for Worship

In terms of sheer numbers, the introduction of the *Lutheran Book of Worship* had been an amazing phenomenon. An estimated seventy thousand pastors and lay persons took part in the inter-Lutheran cluster training events. Over fifteen thousand choir members were involved in the celebration of Holy Communion in these events.[188] The LCA Board of Publication reported that by the end of 1979 it had sold more than 1,032,000 copies of the "green book."[189] That, of course, did not mean everyone was happy with the product. Some of the hymn settings were roundly criticized, and the Division for Parish Services promised that a supplement would be produced for singing selected hymns in harmony.[190] The liturgical portions of the book proved to be the most popular, and within three years approximately 85 percent of the LCA congregations were using the *LBW*.[191]

The demise of the Inter-Lutheran Commission on Worship, which had been formed primarily to develop the *LBW*, left the Lutheran church bodies with a full agenda of additional needs.[192] These included work on a book of occasional services and rites for ordination and installation. In anticipation of the overall needs in the worship area, DPS and the cognate agencies of other churches working together in the Coordinating Committee on Cooperative Projects in Congregational Life established a Worship Resources and Events Committee to plan and carry out joint projects.[193] Many of these activities involved the Missouri Synod, but others, such as the *Occasional Services* book, did not.

Developing a book of occasional services is a time-consuming and difficult process that the small dimensions of the product belie. Occasional services are used primarily by pastors in a wide range of special occasions such as reception of Lutherans by transfer or dedication of a church, and specific situations such as commendation of the dying. In this sense, the events differ from the more general congregational services such as Holy Communion. The inter-Lutheran effort to produce such a book extended the preliminary work of ILCW and involved a special task force from the AELC, ALC, LCA, and ELCC.[194]

It seems that everyone wants to be involved in preparation of such a volume, and there is likely to be disagreement on what should be included. In the case of *Occasional Services, A Companion to Lutheran Book of Worship*, both the Executive Council and the Conference of Bishops wanted the opportunity to review and comment on the work in process.[195] The resulting book was quite different from the one that accompanied the *Service Book and Hymnal* and included some completely new items, such as the Installation of a Lay Professional Leader, Commissioning of a Lay Professional Leader, Service of the Word for Healing, Installation of a Bishop, Enrollment of Candidates for Baptism, Affirmation of the Vocation of Christians in the World, Closing of a Congregation, and others that reflected changes in the church during two decades. In some instances, special rites were included because they were relevant for one of the church bodies. For example, the LCA required an order for Setting Apart of a Deaconess, while AELC requested a rite for Induction of a Christian Day School Teacher.[196] Considerable attention was also given to using more contemporary and inclusive language throughout the book.

Additional Needs. The introduction of a new worship book for the church always brings with it the need for supplementary resources, and the *LBW* was certainly no exception to this rule. A Braille edition of the pew edition was prepared for the blind and a large-type version for the visually impaired.[197] A sign-language guide to liturgical portions of the book for ministry with the deaf was developed and in some cases required devising entirely new signs for the terms.[198] It was followed by a videotape on *Signing Hymns,* since it was difficult to portray in static diagrams the flowing motions involved in leading singing.[199] In order to adapt the *LBW* to the Spanish language, a separate edition, *Liturgia Luterana,* was prepared in cooperation with the ALC. The book included musical settings in a Spanish style and attempted to accommodate the different linguistic idioms that were characteristic of the various Hispanic groups in North America.[200]

Infant Communion. As was pointed out in Chapter 5, the adoption of a joint ALC-LCA Statement on Communion Practices in 1978

Pastor Larry W. Bost signing for the hearing impaired

raised the ire of those who favored communing infants because it included the words "thus infant communion is precluded." Dr. Crumley received part of his own initiation into the presidency of the LCA when he was obliged to rule against this practice at Gettysburg Seminary.[201] Although statistical reports indicated that only a handful of congregations communed very young children, six synodical memorials were presented to the 1980 convention asking for either a new study or a change in policy.[202] The Committee on Memorials traced the history of the issue, which had been debated in two of the LCA predecessor bodies, and recommended that the synods be informed that the 1978 convention had specifically allowed the "preclusion" phrase to stand. After several attempts to substitute other actions, the Seattle convention rejected all of them, and the policy was not changed.[203]

Inclusive Language Lectionary. In June 1978 the Division of Education and Mission of the NCCCUSA, which holds the copyright to the Revised Standard Version of the Bible, appointed a task force to study issues in translation that might arise out of changing social contexts. Recognizing that the RSV itself would not be undergoing substantial change in the next several years, the task force proposed in June 1980 that the DEM appoint a group to prepare translations of "those central portions of Scripture most often used in public worship" that would be sensitive to suggestions growing out of a concern for racism, sexism, classism, scientism, and anti-Semitism.[204] The DEM's decision to move ahead with such a project set off a chain reaction that would have repercussions not only among Christian churches but society in general for years to come.

Prior to the fall DPS Management Committee meeting, Bishop Crumley called a consultation of ten persons to review the DEM proposal to the churches and offer advice on the matter.[205] The consultants affirmed the desirability of LCA participation in the experiment, indicated "that it is not appropriate for the LCA to endorse any lectionary especially prior to its actual completion," suggested the product might be useful to scholars who select texts for LCA worship resources, and agreed that Bishop Crumley should suggest a person to serve on the translation committee. The management committee took a cautious approach, indicating there was merit in the experiment and that the LCA should be involved. It urged articulation of the principles to be used and reaffirmed "the LCA practice of not adopting an 'authorized' translation for liturgical use." It voted to share its minute with the LCA representatives to the DEM Unit Committee.[206] As the project proceeded, there were many reports and rumors of what was being done to eliminate sexist language from the translation, but the DPS Management Committee would not see the results until October 1983.

Rethinking Educational Ministry

As the LCA turned its attention to the emerging needs of the eighties, DPS began to take a fresh look at educational ministry in the parish. There were many in the church who wanted to ride on the momentum that had come from introducing the Educational Ministry Program in the mid-seventies, but the division knew that the setting within which education took place was continually shifting, and past attempts at maintaining a status quo had almost ended in disaster.[207] As one study put it, "Educational Ministry is a continually developing process. It is in constant motion. It never really stops and starts over again but is constantly on the move."[208]

Taking its cue from this blending of change and continuity, DPS engaged in extensive research that included evaluating its current strategy and materials, assessing the changes in the parish, the shifting age-level balance,[209] the societal setting, and the expressed needs and expectations of educational leaders.[210] On this last point, for example, research showed that leaders tended to be slightly older and better educated than in the past, but they felt strongly that they needed better training for their role, especially in understanding and teaching the Bible.[211] It also became apparent that the desire to customize educational programs locally from a wide range of resources that characterized the independent spirit of the seventies was no longer a dominant concern. Instead, most parishes were looking for a more structured approach to education with fewer options.

One feature of the Educational Ministry strategy was that new modules could be plugged into the total range of curriculum resources as needed without redoing everything from scratch.[212] This meant that DPS could concentrate on developing a new series of leadership education texts, a new catechetical program, and a new Sunday church school series.[213] The Sunday school series was intended to replace the closely graded materials in the old LCA Parish Education Curriculum that were still being used in some parishes.[214] Interestingly, development of the new Sunday school series benefited from the fact that 1980 marked the two hundredth anniversary of the Sunday school, which was widely celebrated among Protestant churches.[215]

Devising a New Stewardship Development Program

The relentless upward pressure of inflation resulted in some drastic measures to deal with the needs of the LCA, particularly when Strength for Mission funds were exhausted. Regular benevolence from congregations grew from an increase of 4.10 percent in 1979 to 5.60 percent in 1980 to 6.70 percent in 1981. During the same period, Designated Advance Giving had grown from $1,496,000 to almost $2,011,000, and the World Hunger Appeal receipts had swelled from $3,231,000 to $5,360,000. Such levels of giving were unequaled in LCA history, but the needs still outstripped the resources.[216]

To make matters worse, synodical bishops and congregations were becoming irritated at what seemed to be an uncoordinated barrage of requests for funds. Pledges for Strength for Mission were still being paid; both congregations and individuals were being asked for DAGs; Mission Development Certificates were being pushed; an experiment in "potential" giving by DMNA in three synods seemed to be competing with the stewardship emphases staged by DPS in twenty-six synods where benevolence increased by as much as 20 percent in a single year.[217] One bishop protested that a new staff person for a type of fund-raising had been located on the territory of his synod without prior consultation.

Underlying the whole situation was a problem that went deeper than mere organizational overlapping. It was a conflict in philosophy between what came to be labeled as the "fund-raising approach" and the "stewardship education mentality." Although it is an oversimplification to describe the approaches in this way, the former stressed asking people to give to specific causes, while the second concentrated on giving freely to the total work of the church. The advocates of both approaches sincerely believed that the motivation for giving was the grateful response of the individual Christian for all of God's gracious gifts.

In November 1979 the Executive Council set in motion a series of steps aimed at resolving the complex of problems through a stewardship development program for the period from 1982 to 1988.[218] A lengthy process was used that involved the Council itself, the Conference of Bishops, the Cabinet of Executives, several specially convened groups, and the management committees of DMNA, DPS, and OAF.[219] In the discussions it became clear that the Executive Council leaned toward possible restructuring either to create a whole new agency or appoint a churchwide director with authority to enforce coordination among different agencies.[220] The Conference of Bishops, on the other hand, emphasized the stewardship approach for building up the life of the church instead of fund-raising and contended that changing the structure was putting the emphasis in the wrong place.[221]

In view of the lack of consensus in the various consultations, Bishop Crumley presented his own plan to the Executive Council in April 1981.[222] He stated that "stewardship, not fund-raising, is the crucial and primary matter. Such stewardship is motivated not by programs to be supported, but out of a glad and generous spirit in response to God's gracious gifts." He did not favor restructuring or lodging a programmatic function in the Office of the Bishop instead of the divisions. The need for coordination would be met by a coordinating committee headed by the bishop and involving the executives of DMNA, DPS, and OAF. The Division for Parish Services would "be the 'lead' agency, since the primary responsibility for both stewardship and approach to congregations is lodged in that agency by bylaw mandate." DPS was to provide a staff person to relate to the coordinating committee. This person would have responsibility for coordinating the entire range of stewardship and fund-raising efforts.[223] DPS was also asked to reorganize its Consulting Committee on Stewardship to bring all elements of the program within its purview. The bishop also promised a study to improve the effectiveness of CWA/ synodical consultations. Although not everyone was happy with the solution, the LCA seemed launched on a track that would result in greater cooperation and a more satisfactory overall response.[224]

Youth Ministry on the Move

Highlight of the youth program during this period was the first churchwide gathering of young people attempted by the LCA on its own in sixteen years. The two previous events in Houston and New Orleans had been inter-Lutheran, but the massive logistical problems at the second of these contributed to the decision by ALC, LCA, and LCMS to have their next gatherings separately.[225]

The LCA event occurred in July 1981 at Purdue University in West Lafayette, Indiana. DPS had purposely opted for a university setting because of the type of facilities available and the fact that it was easier to develop a community spirit when the participants were not scattered among different hotels. Over 4,500 participants descended on the university from all fifty states, Puerto Rico, the Virgin Islands, and Japan. They came by air, bus, train, bicycle, and motorcades, often camping along the way or sleeping in church basements. The theme was "Joy for You and Me," and the biblical focus was on Paul's Epistle to the Philippians.

The young people responded enthusiastically to speakers, engaged in Bible study, worshiped, enjoyed entertainment, managed to eat their meals in three twenty-five-minute shifts, gave over $10,000 to relieve world hunger, took part in 134 workshops, and received the Sacrament at a closing Communion service. One moving moment came when the youth listened to Kathryn Koob, a former hostage of the Iranians. She told how she had sent a Christmas message to her young nieces and nephews by singing "Away in the Manger" on a television broadcast while she was still in captivity. As she sang the words again, many of the young people joined in spontaneously while tears streamed down their faces. In counterpoint, they erupted in joyous song the next evening under the leadership of Black jazz

William H. Lazareth in conversation at the 1981 LCA Youth Gathering

Eddie Bonnemere at the 1981 Youth Gathering at Purdue

Kathryn Koob,
former U.S.
hostage in Iran

musician and teacher Eddie Bonnemere. Finally, they ended the week exhausted but happy.

Although Purdue was the "big one," youth also met in regional gatherings that brought additional thousands to events in locations across the continent.[226] UN/Washington seminars were held to help youth address hunger and global justice issues and become informed leaders in their home synods. Perhaps in part because of the burgeoning opportunities for young people to get together with others beyond their own congregation, interest began to revive in having a youth organization. Having inherited the fact that the Luther League had been eliminated in the days before the division even existed, the DPS Management Committee took the position that it would support any synodical group that wanted to organize but would not force the decision from above. By 1980 one synod had formed such a group, and thirteen others had met with DPS staff to consider the possibilities.[227] There can be no question that after the anti-institutional spirit of the later sixties and early seventies, youth ministry was bubbling with fresh interest.

Outreach and Inreach

Although the change was small, baptized membership had shown signs of stabilizing during the period of 1979 to 1982 at close to 3,050,000. Baptisms of both children and adults had increased, but the relentless process of congregations pruning their rolls proceeded at a pace that approached a half million in five years.[228] As one writer put it, "Where have all the members gone?" The answer, in many cases, was that they were still there. More encouraging were the figures for communing membership and church attendance which edged up by about 28,000 and 29,000 in that same period. The losses in membership tended to be in the ten northeastern synods, while the other twenty-three synods had a net gain.[229]

Although such hard numbers cannot be converted into a barometer of the spiritual life of the church as a whole or of individual members, they were studied closely by those responsible for Evangelical Outreach. To them each "digit" lost was translatable into a real, live, flesh-and-blood human being—a child of God. For this reason and not the "numbers game," the LCA pursued its Evangelical Outreach Program with the full force of Pastor Evangelists, Word and Witness, Church Growth Seminars, Preaching from Commitment, New Models Labs, Membership Conservation, Catechetical Programs for New Members, and a host of experimental efforts. Every indication was that a great many committed persons were taking this business of communicating the gospel very seriously.

Congregational Social Ministry

"Outreach and Inreach" meant more than evangelism for the congregations of the LCA. It also meant taking an aggressive role in social ministry. For DPS this ministry took many forms. It included special programs for smaller membership congregations, the Senior Staffer Program for work with the aging, work with special persons during "The International Year of the Disabled Person," consultations on *The Congregation and Goals and Plans for Minority Ministry,* single parent workshops, world hunger and global justice events, building a network of social ministry resource people, urban ministry conferences, and a steady flow of educational resources in all available media. For many congregations social concerns were high on their action agendas.[230]

MARKING A CENTURY OF WOMEN'S WORK

During the triennium that bridged the turn of the decade, Lutheran Church Women celebrated a century of organized women's work in the LCA and its predecessor churches. To mark this event the auxiliary published a history of the movement and set to work on charting its goals for the eighties.[231] In developing a new program structure that looked toward 1990, the LCW consciously involved not only its Board of Directors but also leaders of synodical units and hundreds of women in congregational organizations. The plan, which was adopted at the 1980 convention in Atlanta, focused on six functional areas: Spiritual Growth, Mission Education, Personal Growth and Relationships, Justice and Outreach, Ecumenical Relationships, and Organization Support and Renewal.[232]

Probing beneath the surface of the LCW's goals and plans, it is possible to see a blending of the traditional qualities that characterized women's work in the church through the years with a fresh sense of contemporary issues. For example, mission education and mission support were the roots from which the auxiliary had sprung, but the description of the mission function for the 1980s shows the dramatic change from earlier days. It stresses mission both in a pluralistic society at home and a global setting where the churches of Asia, Africa, and Latin America are taking expanded roles. Relationships with worldwide organizations, such as LWF and the WCC that did not even exist until the late 1940s, are explored. An appreciation of the riches of other cultures is fostered. It is a different kind of world and a different kind of mission work that the LCW is describing in its outlook.

"Spiritual growth" also sounds traditional until one looks at the dimensions of the function that include searching for one's own identity, understanding other religious belief systems, dealing with charismatic movements, understanding Scripture and how to witness, reexamining the relationship of faith and change.

"Personal growth and relationships" digs into questions of career change, equal pay for equal work, people vs. machines, strengthening family life, divorce and remarriage, unwanted children, and dependent older family members.

"Justice and outreach" means both reflection and action about the struggle of women and minorities for equal opportunity, food shortages, environmental pollution, impact of technological change, unequal distribution of power and world resources.

"Ecumenical relationships" translate into women raising questions about their role in decision making in the church, and relating to other Christian women and their concerns around the world.

"Organization support and renewal" includes developing skills in

systematic planning, recruiting members, training leaders, understanding stewardship and giving.

Although LCW continued to be a strong but somewhat decreasing
source of financial support for the LCA budget, the auxiliary was also
involved in providing scholarships for mature women and grants for
the development of human resources.[233] The human resources
grants went to a variety of agencies which dealt with such concerns
as emergency shelter and counseling for abused women and children, nutrition education, deaf children, latch-key children, Asian
refugee children, bilingual child care, crisis intervention for the family, child therapy in cases of domestic violence, reading programs for
psychiatric patients, adult day care, skill training for young mothers,
support of rape victims, alcohol and drug problems, and ministry to
women prisoners.[234] Meanwhile, LCW was deeply involved in its
own action programs. Perhaps the best known was its literacy work
with English-speaking adults, but it was also engaged in helping to
teach English as a second language to the Asian refugees who flooded
into the United States and Canada.[235]

RELOCATING RESEARCH AND PLANNING

"It's the first time in the history of the Church that an active, supposedly permanent committee has recommended its own demise,"
declared Charles Y. Glock, chairperson of the management committee of the Office for Research and Planning, in proposing the elimination of ORP and transfer of its responsibilities to the Office of the
Bishop.[236] Although the delegates to the 1980 convention may not
have sensed the full implications, the recommendation was a major
shift in the whole decision-making process of the LCA. Not only was
it aimed at resolving some confusion in responsibilities of ORP, OAF,
and the Executive Council, but it also strengthened the Office of the
Bishop and gave to one of the bishop's assistants authority to act
virtually as the bishop's deputy in dealing with churchwide agencies
on crucial matters.[237]

The change had not been made lightly. It was a reflection of a long
process of trying to integrate the role of an entirely new agency into
the LCA decision-making process after restructuring in 1972. Prior
to that time the church had had no central office charged with research and planning. The research that was being done was largely
carried out by the Boards of Parish Education and American Mis-

sions. Before making its recommendations, both the management committee and the Executive Council had gone through a lengthy process of identifying problems and exploring options.[238]

Coordinating research among those divisions that had such capabilities went reasonably well during the life of ORP, although the office's small staff limited the amount of research it could carry out on its own. When consolidation with the Office of the Bishop occurred in the early 1980s, however, the LCA's total research effort had already begun to erode because of budget limitations and the prospect of a new church being formed. At this point, the new research operation in the Office of the Bishop began to become more active not only in consultation with CWAs on their own studies but also in conducting research for them.[239]

Planning was another matter. It was in this area, along with the concomitant function of budgeting, that there was the greatest overlapping of responsibilities among ORP, OAF, and the Executive Council. President Marshall had depended on ORP and the Staff Team on Planning for laying much of the groundwork for the Program Planning and Budgeting System, although most of the give and take in budgeting took place in the Staff Executive Team.[240] Although the Executive Council was responsible for recommending fiscal proposals to the convention and approving spending authorizations, it also struggled with its constitutional mandate to "do long-range planning of the work of this church."[241]

During the biennium following his election, President Crumley had proposed that the functions of ORP be lodged on an experimental basis in his office and that the executive director of ORP act as an assistant to the president and that the management committee serve as a consulting committee.[242] The arrangement seemed to work well, and the ORP Management Committee proposed to the Executive Council that the necessary changes in the bylaws be effected at the 1980 convention to make "research, planning and evaluation" a permanent part of the president's (bishop's) office.[243]

When James R. Crumley became president, he was concerned that planning should have a churchwide scope and not be simply an aggregate of CWA plans. In fact, his first report as president in 1980 focused on goals for the coming decade in broad strokes and became in itself a planning tool for the church.[244] Dr. Crumley's report listed six emphases: Theological Foundations for LCA Identity, The Ecumenical Nature of the Church in a Global Context, Congregational

Life, The Ministry of All Believers, Justice and Human Dignity—
Everywhere, Our Future as a Church Body. In the planning process
that followed, nine "strategy areas" emerged for special attention in
funding.[245] Neither the bishop's emphases nor the nine strategy
areas corresponded directly with the LCA program structure, although it was possible to correlate them. A major shift in priorities
was underway, and the implications of the new approach became
even clearer in the 1983–84 biennium.[246]

The introduction of "evaluation" into the title of the new unit in
the Office of the Bishop emphasized a function that had received
only passing attention on a churchwide basis in previous years.[247]
The new bylaw provisions, however, described this responsibility in
terms of aiding the convention, the Executive Council, and churchwide agencies in determining major policy and program decisions.[248]
The office did cooperate with agencies that were already involved in
major evaluation efforts and assisted others in doing so.[249] Stressing
evaluation became a powerful tool for the Office of the Bishop in
analyzing the effectiveness of programs and organizational structures.

KEYS TO COMMUNICATION

As was true of every other aspect of the church's work, those entrusted with the cluster of responsibilities in the Office for Communications had to deal with the exigencies of costs and competition. This
was true whether the LCA was seeking to tell its story through
external media or internally to its own members, whether it involved
news releases with the life span of a few days or books intended to
last for a decade.

Early in the eighties, the Office for Communications itself reorganized to deal more effectively with new realities. The Department of
Press, Radio and Television that had existed from the beginning of
the LCA was divided into a Department of News and Information
Services and a Department of Telecommunications. The change was
more than cosmetic; it was an effort to provide more specialized
leadership in areas where new technologies burst on the scene almost overnight.[250] Nowhere was this more apparent than in the electronic media where the Lutherans found themselves competing for
air time with television evangelists and heavily funded commercial
broadcasting.

Proven programs, such as the twelve annual Lutheran segments of "The Protestant Hour," continued to reach vast audiences with a biblically and theologically responsible message.[251] In cooperation with the ALC, a series of thirteen radio programs was produced in Spanish for that rapidly increasing audience. Cable television was also an especially promising field because local outlets were eager for "public service material." In response, OC not only provided guidance for local church groups in effective use of the media but also a series on "Lutherans in Person" that featured interviews with such noted personalities as historian Roland Bainton and theologian Joseph Sittler.[252] As a part of Evangelical Outreach, the office produced a series of television spot announcements called "Welcome . . . The Doors Are Open." Some were addressed to specific audiences, such as single parents and minorities. The spots that were produced in both English and Spanish appeared in all fifty major television markets.

Perhaps the most widely heralded television project was the film *The Joy of Bach* that was produced as a cooperative effort by Lutheran Film Associates.[253] With the help of a corporate grant, the film was premiered on three hundred stations of the Public Broadcasting Network during the 1979 Christmas season.[254] The program was also widely seen during the two hundredth anniversary of the birth of Johann Sebastian Bach in 1985.

The Lutheran

Although *The Lutheran* was bombarded by cost increases, it maintained its position as the most widely read denominational publication in North America.[255] In fact, on January 21, 1981, circulation of the magazine topped the 600,000 mark for the first time in its 120-year (or was it 150-year?) history.[256] A series of cost increases buffeted all periodicals, particularly those of nonprofit agencies, in the late seventies and early eighties. One of the problems was that the cost of paper was increasing as much as 14 percent per year.[257] Even worse was a change in postal rates that shot upward from about $11,000 in 1978 to $51,000 per issue in 1982. By the computerizing and presorting of labels, the staff was able to reduce that figure to $37,000, but it was still triple the amount four years earlier.[258] These factors caused a slight increase in subscription rates.

Cooperation among *The Lutheran,* ALC's *Lutheran Standard,* and AELC's *foreword* was growing steadily. Not only did they share feature articles, but in the ALC and LCA publications there were also series on the Ten Commandments and the five hundredth anniversary of Martin Luther's birth. There was no missing the fact that in its coverage of the Committee on Lutheran Unity and other matters *The Lutheran* was an outspoken booster of Lutheran unity. In this sense the editor, Edgar Trexler, followed in the tradition of many Lutheran editors of the past who prodded church leaders toward greater cooperation, at least, among the American churches.[259]

Board of Publication

Throughout its history, the Board of Publication had never considered its prime reason for existence to be a "profit center" but a source for providing the kinds of books and other resources that the pastors and congregations of the church needed to fulfill an effective ministry. No one had embodied that concept of the servant role of the church's publishing house more than Frank G. Rhody, who retired at the end of the 1979 after a fifty-two-year career that began as a stock boy and ended as general manager.[260]

The publishing house, of course, was not in business to lose money for the church. In fact, during the 1978–79 and 1980–81 biennia, it paid the LCA treasury $711,000 in royalties and contributed $88,000 to the costs of the LCA Communications System.[261] During this same period, the board retired the debt from the final addition to the Muhlenberg Building, opened several new stores as a convenience to the constituency, and maintained a steady flow of the high-level publications that made it one of the most respected religious presses in North America.[262]

TWO PATHS TO UNITY

During the early 1980s the Lutheran Church in America was walking on two paths toward Lutheran unity. One was the process of negotiations with the AELC and the ALC in the United States. The other was the patient effort that the Canada Section had been pursuing to effect one church in Canada ever since the LCA was born. Indeed, the Canadian representatives had made quite clear in the Joint Commission on Lutheran Unity in designing the LCA that their goal ultimately was a unified Lutheran Church in Canada. The LCA officially was committed to supporting that goal, although there were those with a less nationalistic vision in both countries who dreamed that someday there would be one church that encompassed all Lutherans in both nations. As it turned out, the Ca-

nadian synods accomplished their objective a few years before the
Lutherans in the United States could get their act together along
similar lines.

Canada's Reluctant Compromise

The Canadians had hoped for decades that there would be one Lutheran church within their borders. For a while, it seemed that this
hope would become a reality. "This optimism failed to take into
consideration the Canadian fallout from the explosion that rocked
the Missouri Synod in the years between 1969 and 1975."[263] Since
1966 the Canadians had been working through their Joint Commission on Inter-Lutheran Relationships to bridge the doctrinal barriers
historically separating them.[264] In 1970 the groups that had their
roots in ALC, LCA, and Missouri declared that a "consensus sufficient
for fellowship exists."[265] This led the Evangelical Lutheran Church
of Canada (ALC in origin) to invite the LCA Canada Section and the
Lutheran Church-Canada (Missouri related) to work for organic
merger. The Canada Section accepted with enthusiasm, but the LCC
hesitated.

Nevertheless, in the spring of 1977, the commission proposed that
the new Canadian church accept the ordination of women and had
long since affirmed a statement on Scripture that skirted the issue of
inerrancy.[266] Unfortunately, the bitterly contested convention of
LCMS in Dallas that year rejected ordination of women and rejected
completely any view of the Scriptures other than inerrancy. Not only
was this the final blow to any hope of Lutheran unity in the United
States but also to any possibility of a three-way merger in Canada.
What remained was the potential of an ELCC and LCA Canada
Section merger.

At the LCA convention in Seattle, S. Theodore Jacobsen, president
of the Evangelical Lutheran Church of Canada, stated with confidence that their target date for merger was January 1, 1985, a deadline that this time had real meaning. At the same time, he warned
the LCA delegates that they would face some of the same knotty
problems in their negotiations in the United States that the Canadians had struggled with for so long. His statement proved to be almost
a prophecy, for those "south of the border" would indeed wrangle
about regionalism, distribution of power, and other issues much as
their Canadian brothers and sisters had done.[267]

The Painstaking Path to Decision in the United States

From the outset of the deliberations in the Committee on Church Cooperation, it was apparent that ALC and LCA leaders had quite different goals in mind. President Robert Marshall stated at the first meeting in May 1975 that the constitutional mandate of the LCA committed it to "strive for the unification of all Lutherans within its boundaries in one church."[268] President David Preus made clear, however, that the ALC was more concerned with cooperation than with organic union. He explained that the ALC position was based on three factors: the concern for mission rather than structural union, the desire to include the Missouri Synod, and the fact that ALC had recently spent much time and energy on restructuring its national offices and wanted to go forward with mission.[269]

At its April 14–16, 1978, meeting, the AELC adopted its "Call for Lutheran Union" that urged all North American bodies to join in an organic union. The AELC saw its own existence as a temporary one with the wider goal of unity in mind. Both David Preus and Robert Marshall brought greetings to the convention. President Preus once again stressed that organizational matters had "absorbed enormous quantities of time, energy and resources in the last generation" and that they were not the major challenge for congregations.[270] Dr. Marshall, in turn, called a commitment to Lutheran union "part of the identity of the Lutheran Church in America."

The 1978 LCA convention in Chicago had before it both a proposal from the ALC/LCA Committee on Church Cooperation to continue its work to evaluate structural options and AELC's "Call for Lutheran Union."[271] The LCA's own Standing Committee on Approaches to Unity recommended that the convention respond to both proposals affirmatively, which it did overwhelmingly.[272] This included an invitation to AELC to participate in future discussions.

The situation was more complicated when the ALC convention met in the fall. As E. Clifford Nelson writes, "President Preus in a surprise move and for reasons best known to himself invited AELC to become a nongeographic district of the ALC. Fortunately, he soon recognized that this gesture was an ill-founded response to a serious invitation from the AELC, whose President Kohn politely acknowledged Preus's invitation but intimated that it would be declined. In this situation, Preus quickly shifted to the proposal in the 1978 report of the ALC/LCA Committee on Church Cooperation."[273] The net result of these actions was that AELC agreed to become a member of a new group involving the three churches that would be called the "Committee on Lutheran Unity."[274]

As the new committee pursued its discussions, it evolved a proposal to bring to the 1980 church conventions a plan that would provide for a study of four organizational options by the members of the three churches prior to judicatory conventions in the spring of 1981. The intention was that districts/synods would discuss the same material and then conduct a poll to see which option was favored. Basically, the four options were (1) to continue functioning as three bodies with increased efforts in cooperation; (2) to form one church having responsibility in international and some national functions with ALC, AELC, and LCA as "non-geographic entities, each retaining most of its present polity and structure, responsibility and authority"; (3) to form one church body with certain international and national functions with several large "geographic entities," each having its own polity, structure, and autonomy for specific functions in its area; (4) to form one church that would delegate specific responsibility and authority to such geographic entities as it established, with the geographic units having program and other responsibilities in their areas.[275]

When the LCA assembled for its convention in Seattle in 1980, both the ALC and AELC presidents brought greetings. Dr. Preus said once more that there are "even more pressing concerns before us than organizational ones—maintaining strong congregations and vital mission outreach."[276] Dr. Kohn declared, "If you are at all interested in the cause of Lutheran union for the sake of mission, then you must know instinctively that the next two years are exceptionally crucial."[277] When the time came to act, the delegates voted unanimously for the Committee on Lutheran Unity's proposed study and response process, together with the proposal that recommendations for decision about proceeding on a possible merger be brought to the 1982 conventions of the three churches.[278]

Feeling the Pulse and Testing the Options

The debate within the constituency began almost as soon as the 1980 conventions were completed and the Committee on Lutheran Unity issued its study booklet and survey instrument. Many of the church journals carried on a running account of how the discussion was proceeding and some of the issues.[279] David Preus continued to express his strong reservations about organic union in the pages of *The Lutheran Standard*. For example, in the November 25, 1980, issue, he wrote, "I do not believe that organizational merger of only three Lutheran bodies should be a priority for the 1980s," and laid out five other mission causes that he considered more urgent.[280] Another strong voice was that of Albert E. Anderson, executive of the Augsburg Publishing House, who predicted that "a protracted struggle will ensue if three present national churches are dismantled piece by piece in order to build a single church out of the same pieces."[281] Of course, there were writers who took the opposite view, such as E. Clifford Nelson, who challenged "the implication . . . that union is an enemy of evangelism, mission, and education."[282]

In the LCA it seemed clear that there was only a small minority who did not favor a merger. Considerable discussion, however, revolved around the four options themselves, which did not seem to exhaust the possibilities. For example, the "One Church" option included the idea of five to eight regional entities that would have considerable authority over smaller geographical entities similar to the LCA's synods.[283] To some this raised the specter of "regional churches," although the power of the regions in Option 4 was much less than was true of Option 3.[284]

When all the discussion was over, 18,504 delegates to the district/ synod conventions cast their ballots. "The percentage of delegates who favored uniting the ALC, AELC, and LCA was: ALC–64 percent; AELC–96 percent; LCA–87 percent."[285] In the responses from individuals and study groups, the affirmative votes were slightly lower, but even in the ALC they ran around 62 percent.[286] Where the differences were more apparent was in the various options. For some the biggest surprise was that the AELC came out strongly (64 percent) in favor of Option 3, while only 31.7 percent of ALC and 26 percent of LCA considered this a possibility. Where the confusion emerges in these figures is that the choice of options was not mutually exclusive; and when it came to Option 4, the totals were ALC–52 percent in favor; AELC–58.8 percent; LCA–70 percent. The responses from all types of participants in the process included the possibility of writing in comments, which resulted in the Committee on Lutheran Unity being deluged with specific suggestions.[287] What remained in preparation for the 1982 conventions was the task of devising a series of recommendations that could be voted up or down if the process were to proceed.

Decision Time 1982

Once the clear intent of the constituency was known, the Committee on Lutheran Unity set about the complex task of bringing the necessary resolutions to simultaneous meetings of the three bodies for decision on September 8, 1982. The questions to be dealt with involved not only the commitment to proceed but also the number and composition of a group to plan a new church, a timetable, and a relationship to the merger process already under way in Canada. The matter of a schedule was settled without great difficulty; and assuming agreement to proceed, the proposal was to have a constituting convention in 1987 and begin full operation of the new body January 1, 1988.[288] As ecclesiastical mergers go, this posed a tight time schedule.

The size and makeup of a Commission for a New Lutheran Church was a much more difficult matter. The three churches were all committed to having a planning group that would be truly representative of the various groups that formed the constituency. This introduced a factor that had not been involved in the formation of merger commissions in the past. The proposal that was finally developed seemed to some to pit numerical representation against other criteria, such as clergy-lay, male-female, ethnic background, and geographical factors. In order to accommodate as many of the concerns as possible, it was proposed that the commission be composed of seventy persons—thirty-one from ALC, thirty-one from LCA, and eight from AELC.[289] It was agreed that each church should "make its selection according to its own practices and procedures, giving consideration to adequate representation of clergy and laity, male and female persons, racial and ethnic groups, age groups, geographical areas, and various fields of experience and responsibility."[290]

The suggestions of the Committee on Lutheran Unity to the decision-making groups of the churches were more explicit. These criteria included the following: at least one-half of the members should be lay persons; at least one-half of the clergy should be parish pastors; at least 40 percent of all members should be women and at least 40 percent men; at least one-sixth should be persons from ethnic/racial minority groups and at least one-sixth from the white majority; each of four minority groups—Afro-American, Hispanic American, Asian

American, Native American—should be represented by at least two persons.[291]

In the case of the LCA, it fell to the lot of the Executive Council to devise a way of meeting these criteria. The Council appointed a nominating committee from among its own members who brought back to its June 1982 meeting a complex chart as to how the various goals could be met and a list of possible nominees. By dint of intricate balloting, the Executive Council arrived at a slate of double the number of nominees to be presented to the convention based on the following slots: two female parish pastors, two female nonparish clergy, four male parish clergy, two male nonparish clergy, nine female lay persons, and six male lay persons.[292] In addition, the bishop and secretary of the church, plus a lay person to serve as commission chairperson were nominated.[293] Four slots were provided for nominations from the convention floor.

When the LCA delegates converged on Louisville, Kentucky, there was an air of hope and expectancy. In a way, the order of things seemed to be backward. First, the delegates chose the persons who were to represent the LCA on the Commission for a New Lutheran Church—if the three church bodies decided to proceed. Discussion about nominees was lively, and fifty-three persons were nominated for the four at-large positions. The four elected were William H. Lazareth, former President Robert J. Marshall, John H. P. Reumann, and Herbert W. Chilstrom.[294] After four ballots the entire delegation had been selected, and the delegates waited for the big moment of the "go or no go" decision.[295]

Finally, on the afternoon of September 8, the three conventions meeting in Louisville (LCA), San Diego (ALC), and Cleveland (AELC) were linked by an elaborate telephone hookup. As delegates and visitors held their breaths the results were announced: ALC—897 yes, 87 no; AELC—136 yes, 0 no; LCA—669 yes, 11 no. "The exulting applause, it was said, could be heard from city to city even without the electronic amplification."[296] When the roar died down, Martin E. Marty, a member of the AELC on the faculty at the University of Chicago Divinity School, presided over a teleconference with the three bishops. He introduced the session with these remarks:

"Lutherans have been on this continent for a third of a millennium, a sixth of the Christian era. We do not know what was the most dramatic event in that long period. We do know that, so far as their life together is concerned, Lutherans have not had a day that can be more decisive. . . . Today's actions do not bring in the Kingdom of God. They do not do much toward realizing the unity of the *Una Sancta.* They do not even take care of all of the problems in the family of Lutherans in America. But they offer promise.

"We do not organize for the sake of 'five million'-sized bigness. . . . We do not move toward union in order to homogenize. . . . We come together instead for the single reason that it belongs to the *intrinsic* nature of the church under the Holy Spirit for us to be pulled together in the body of Christ and its still separate families. To stay where we are? That is stagnation. To regress? That is death-dealing. Intrinsically we regard it to be better to see our . . . suspicions replaced by new signals of hope and trust and love."[297]

With those words ringing in their ears, 5,200,000 Lutherans took the first long step toward realizing their unity.

NOTES

1. In an interview by the writer on June 25, 1987, in Philadelphia, Bishop Crumley indicated that he did not regard this as a new initiative on his part but that steps already taken by the Committee on Lutheran Unity showed that the time was ripe to move toward a decision on merger.

2. *1980 CQ Almanac,* 352–53. These pages in the volume which deals primarily with 1980 government actions also provide a chronology of events in the whole 444-day crisis from November 4, 1979, until the last of the hostages were released on January 20, 1981. Thirteen of the hostages had been released within a month of the original seizure of the embassy.

3. *Facts on File, 1979,* 973.

4. *Facts on File, 1980,* 1.

5. *1980 CQ Almanac,* 30E.

6. The United States negotiated agreements to establish bases in Oman, Somalia, and Kenya, which seemed at first blush to strengthen its position but did provoke difficulties with Kenya and Ethiopia, where there were tensions with Somalia. The United States also reversed its course in terms of Pakistan, which had been refused military aid a year before because it was reported to be developing an atomic bomb. "After weeks of hesitation, Carter offered Pakistan $400 million in aid to be spread over two years. But Pakistan's President Mohammed Zia ul-Haq rejected that offer as 'peanuts,' and the issue died." See *1980 CQ Almanac,* 310.

7. *1980 CQ Almanac,* 37–38. The United States budget for defense actually increased from $134 billion in 1980 to $252.7 billion by 1985. See *America in Perspective,* Oxford Analytica (Boston: Houghton Mifflin, 1986), 292.

8. *1980 CQ Almanac,* 40, has the text of Carter's proclamation. The plan exempted women but required males eighteen and older to register even though no call-up was planned. Aliens were also expected to register.

9. "In September 1979, the Carter Administration asked Congress to provide economic aid to the Sandinista Government, saying its initial orientation seemed to be 'moderate and pluralistic, and not Marxist or Cuban.' Just before President Carter left office in 1981, the United States suspended such aid, asserting that the Sandinistas had supplied arms to left-wing guerrillas in El Salvador." See "The Week in Review," *The New York Times* (July 19, 1987):1.

10. A popular Roman Catholic archbishop was assassinated in March 1980, and four missionaries were murdered in December in acts that underscored the weakness of government control.

11. For example, unemployment in the United States climbed in 1982 to 10.8%, the highest rate since the days of World War II. The consumer price index in the first three months of 1979 surged an unprecedented 18.2%. See *1980 CQ Almanac,* 271, and *1982 CQ Almanac,* 27.

12. The grain embargo was particularly galling because countries such as Argentina and Australia simply increased production to capture the market from U.S. farmers. When the Reagan administration lifted the embargo in 1981, Russia bought American grain only when other sources were exhausted. See *1980 CQ Almanac,* 93; and *1981 CQ Almanac,* 533.

13. The Nuclear Regulatory Commission warned two days later of the possibility of a core meltdown, and pregnant women and preschool children were told to evacuate an area within five miles of the plant. See *Facts on File, March 28, 1979,* 241–46.

14. Reagan led Carter by 43,901,000 to 35,484,000 in the popular vote and 489 to 49 in the electoral college. John B. Anderson, who ran as an independent, received 5,719,000 votes, many of which were probably drawn from Democratic voters, but even these votes would not have swung the election in Carter's favor.

15. The massive changes in the directions of social welfare were estimated to have resulted in the following: 675,000 households lost their benefits-in-aid for dependent children; 1.1 million were dropped from the food stamp program; Medicaid recipients lost the freedom to choose their own doctors; fewer federally subsidized housing units were available; 900,000 job-training positions were cut; a half million children were dropped from the free school lunch program; some 1.5 million workers lost extended unemployment benefits. See *1981 CQ Almanac,* 461.

16. The first woman to be confirmed as a Supreme Court Justice was Sandra Day O'Connor, a former Arizona legislator and appeals court judge. She replaced Potter Stewart, who tended to be moderate to conservative in his decisions. O'Connor had an outstanding academic record at Stanford University, both in the undergraduate program and the law school. Although she was considered by many liberals to be more conservative than they would have wished, she was confirmed by the Senate by a 99–0 vote. See *1981 CQ Almanac,* 409.

17. *Time* (June 2, 1980):49.

18. *1980 CQ Almanac,* 372.

19. Robert Sherrill, "Can Miami Save Itself?" *The New York Times Magazine* (July 19, 1987):22.

20. *1980 CQ Almanac,* 372. "The Immigration and Naturalization Service estimates that at least 750,000 Cubans have settled here in the past 20 years. . . . It might even be as high as 1 million." See "Open Heart, Open Arms," *Time* (May 19, 1980):17. All in all, the United States received 234,200 documented refugees from all sources in the 1980 fiscal year. The government's problems were heightened when it became known that Castro was also using the occasion as an opportunity to export some convicted felons (ibid., 15–16).

21. Probably as a result of the tide of immigration in the United States, during the first half of the eighties U.S. population increased by 5.3%. By contrast, "Canada's overall rate of growth fell to 4.2% between 1981 and 1986 from 9.7% two decades earlier, primarily because of low immigration and very low growth in rural areas." From an article in *The Wall Street Journal* (July 22, 1987), prepared by the staff of *American Demographics.* For many years Canada has had a liberal refugee law that permits anyone claiming refugee status to live in the country until all appeals have been exhausted. This long-standing policy was being reconsidered by the Canadian government in 1987 because of incidents involving Tamils from Sri Lanka and Sikhs from India who had come ashore in Nova Scotia. See *Time* (July 27, 1987):47.

22. "Fire and Fury in Miami," *Time* (June 2, 1980):14. See also Harry A. Ploski and James Williams, eds., *The Negro Almanac, a Reference Work on the Afro-American,* 4th ed. (New York: John Wiley & Sons, 1983), 84.

23. Ibid., 11.

24. In commenting on the extent to which the explosive situation was a result of the rapidly changing racial and ethnic mix in the area, *Time* reported, "There is no doubt, though, that blacks, who now comprise only 15% of Dade County's 1.5 million residents, feel that they are 'third-class citizens' behind the still dominant non-Latin whites at 48%, and the Hispanics, at about 37%." Ibid., 13.

25. Deborah Gesensway and Mindy Roseman, *Beyond Words, Images from American Concentration Camps* (Ithaca, N.Y.: Cornell University Press, 1987) is a volume illustrated by American Japanese artists who were internees. It reflects graphically the experiences in the camps.

26. Thomas Sowell, *Ethnic America* (New York: Basic Books, 1981), 172. Ironically, thousands of Japanese-Americans fought in World War II, and "their 442nd Regimental Combat Unit emerged the most decorated unit in World War II, or in American history." Ibid., 174.

27. *1980 CQ Almanac,* 380.

28. The quotation from the Winter 1982 issue of *Daedalus* appears in *America in Perspective,* 114.

29. Ibid., 115. *America in Perspective* cites Gallup Poll Ltd. statistics to show that 57% of the population in the United States claimed in 1981 to belong to churches or religious organizations, and 95% said they believed in God. This compares, for example, to figures of 10% (church members) and 72% (belief in God) for Norway; 9% and 52% for Sweden; and 4% and 58% for Denmark. See pp. 121–24.

30. George A. Lindbeck, "The Divided Church," in *Background Papers to Call to Global Mission* (New York: DWME, 1982), 318.

31. Paul VI in 1975 was the only other pope to do so, and his visit was for only fourteen hours.

32. *Time* magazine devoted twenty-four pages of its October 15, 1979, issue to the pope's visit. It included not only vignettes of the pope's warm reception, but also indications of the protests that he encountered in many places. Capsule comments by such varied personalities as radical Jesuit Daniel Berrigan, evangelist Billy Graham, Lutheran historian Martin Marty, Catholic theologian Daniel Maguire, and National Council of Churches executive Claire Randall illustrated something of the wide range of reactions to the man and his views.

33. When the influx of memorials was received, DMNA provided basic information to the Committee on Memorials. This included a collateral paper on the subject which appears in the *LCAM, 1982*, 185–88. In addition to instructing preparation of a social statement for presentation to Toronto and a number of requests of the bishop and CWAs, the convention took the rather unusual course of adopting a sense motion declaring support for "a multilateral, verifiable freeze of the testing, production, stockpiling, and deployment of nuclear weapons and delivery systems as a step toward the eventual elimination of nuclear weapons and to work actively to achieve such a goal." Ibid., 204. The convention had not often adopted such sense motions prior to the development of a social statement. The full text of the convention resolution on "War and Peace in a Nuclear Age" is on pp. 309–11.

34. The LCA had been following for some years the practice of seeking reactions in advance to drafts of social statements. Beginning in 1979, however, DMNA instituted what were known as "Listening to People Conferences," where concerned persons were brought together to discuss an issue such as "The Family Farm" or "Water: Whose Right?" The findings from these groups were then distributed more widely as information or the basis for discussion.

35. *LCAM, 1978*, 362. The action had dealt with the exploitation and consumption of the world's resources and committed the church to "an intensive study of international economic relations and to the consideration of a major policy statement on that subject in 1980."

36. The document made conscious use of several earlier LCA social statements: *Race Relations* (1964), *Poverty* (1966), *Church and State: A Lutheran Perspective* (1966), *World Community* (1970), *The Human Crisis in Ecology* (1972), *Human Rights* (1978), *Aging and the Older Adult* (1978). See Richard J. Niebanck, *Economic Justice, An Evangelical Imperative* (New York: DMNA, 1980), 8–9. This book in the "Christian Social Responsibility Series" was prepared both as a preliminary and a follow-up study piece.

37. *1980 Convention Summary*, 10.

38. *LCAM, 1980*, 304–5. The final text appears on pp. 305–13, and any references here are to that version.

39. *LCAM, 1982*, 258–64, gives the text of the statement. A fuller treatment of the subject is given in Daniel E. Lee, *Death and Dying, Ethical Choices in a Caring Community* (New York: DMNA, 1983), a volume in the "Christian Social Responsibility Series."

40. Although the term "death as friend" was used in the 1982 text to refer to the fact that those suffering may regard death as a merciful deliverance, the 1984 convention took the unusual step of responding to a memorial from the Virginia Synod by directing "that all references in the Death and Dying Statement that call death '(a) friend' be changed to 'merciful' " (*LCAM, 1984,* 40, 225). Part of the rationale was that the term seemed to contradict Paul's statement in 1 Corinthians 15:26 that the last enemy to be defeated is death.

41. *LCAM, 1980,* 373–83; *1982,* 393–406.

42. *LCAM, 1982,* 404, provides the following numbers: Asian, 29; Black, 49; Hispanic, 42; American Indian, 5. There were also 20 minority students enrolled for the 1981–82 academic year in LCA seminaries and an additional three in non-LCA schools.

43. The following data are from *Reflections on 1981 Form A Statistics,* prepared by Robert Strohl:

	1978	*1981*	*Increase*	*% Increase*
American Indian	1,711	1,847	136	7.9%
Asian	4,999	7,120	2,121	42.4%
Black	21,885	29,134	7,249	33.1%
Hispanic	6,290	9,945	3,655	58.1%

Some of the larger percentage increases are believed to be due in part to more accurate reporting.

44. *LCAM, 1982,* 349–50. At various times, the terms "Native American" or "American Indian" were the preferred designations for this part of society.

45. These efforts included such efforts as ministering to the influx of Asian students in North American colleges, development of training programs for Asian persons, seeking to establish an Ethnic Studies Center at Pacific Lutheran University, developing organizational models for Asian ministries, and recognition of the different approach to stewardship necessary. See *LCAM, 1980,* 340–41; and *1982,* 348–49.

46. *LCAM, 1980,* 324; and *1982,* 360. In this effort DMNA worked through the Office of Governmental Affairs of LCUSA.

47. *LCAM, 1980,* 338–40.

48. *LCAM, 1982,* 349.

49. *LCAM, 1980,* 340; and *1982,* 349.

50. *LCAM, 1980,* 707–9.

51. *LCAM, 1982,* 800.

52. Ibid., 801–3. For example, DPL was requested to evaluate a recommendation that urged Lutheran seminaries to introduce a course focused on the theological study of baptismal vocation and relating to men, women, vocation, and work. DPL's response was, "Since the Study of 'Women and Men in the Mission of the Church' by the Division of Theological Studies of LCUSA has not yet been completed, there is no substantive basis on which to evaluate the merit of recommendation 8." Ibid., 803.

53. DMNA had reported to the 1982 convention that its own "Study on Women and Men in Society" had had to be delayed because of lack of staff and funds. An interim report was given, but a final report was to be brought to the next convention. See *LCAM, 1982,* 359.

54. Ibid., 392.

55. Ibid.

56. Ibid., 385–87.

57. These memorials came from both 1979 and 1980 synodical conventions (see *LCAM, 1980,* 59–61, 97–99). The similarity among many of the memorials is an example of a growing pattern for concerned persons to communicate with one another so that the same issue was raised repeatedly and garnered support in a large number of synods. The same kind of pattern was emerging on questions such as apartheid in South Africa, nuclear weapons, Lutheran unity, and certain health benefit provisions.

58. *LCAM, 1980,* 201.

59. The totals are based on figures provided to the writer in a letter from Vernon N. Cronmiller, dated May 21, 1987. In 1980, Cronmiller, a Canadian pastor, had succeeded Robert Stackel when he retired as director after the highly successful launching of the appeal.

60. The way of handling funds overseas was somewhat complex. Most of the U.S. monies went from LWM through Lutheran World Relief to Lutheran World Federation projects. In other instances, DWME or the WCC might be used because of overseas contacts or channels to the infrastructure in a particular country. In other words, the most efficient and effective ways of accomplishing the goals were the ones employed.

61. See *To Bangladesh with Love* (New York: LCA, 1982), one of a series of brief publications by the World Hunger Appeal office to interpret the work being done in dozens of countries.

62. DMNA projects related to direct relief included sponsoring of food cooperatives, agricultural and community development in Appalachia, migrant ministries, meals on wheels, and assistance to the Kenora Indian Ministry in Central Canada. Funds also went into supporting and advocating for governmental programs to deal with crisis situations. See *LCAM, 1980,* 648.

63. These efforts included study materials, audiovisuals, special supplements in *The Congregation,* training events for synodical world hunger leaders, devotional materials, and work/seminars for youth. Ibid.

64. *LCAM, 1964,* 665.

65. *LCAM, 1966,* 55–56. The memorial was referred to the Executive Council for forwarding to the Coordinating Committee on Race Relations (p. 615).

66. *LCAM, 1972,* 590–97.

67. Ibid., 591.

68. Ibid., 595.

69. In May 1973 the Executive Council made provision for DMNA to represent the LCA's interests in carrying out the investment criteria. The DMNA was empowered to vote shares held by such agencies as the Common

Investing Fund and the Board of Pensions after the action was reviewed by the Executive Council or the officers (*ECM, May 1973*, 230–31).

70. After ten years of effort, many of the corporations involved had made significant progress in advancing Blacks to management positions, providing education, and granting equal salary and benefits. But the basic problem of the South African government's policy of apartheid was unaffected and, if anything, had become more oppressive. On June 3, 1987, the Rev. Mr. Sullivan, in effect, abandoned the earlier approach and called for a mass corporate exodus and sanctions against the nation. See *The Wall Street Journal* (June 4, 1987):2.

71. *LCAM, 1980*, 246. This use of the technical term *status confessionis* was the subject of debate that went on in LCA and LWF circles for several years. The LWF issued a study book on the subject in 1983 (see *LCAM, 1982*, 319–20) and prepared a special report, *The Debate on Status Confessionis*, for the Budapest Assembly of the Federation in 1984 (*LCAM, 1984*, 647).

72. Ibid., 248.

73. *1980 Convention Summary*, 10–11.

74. *LCAM, 1982*, 303.

75. Ibid., 304–5. Dr. Woods held the position of vice-president of Mobil Oil, one of the world's largest corporations which has retained an operation in South Africa and has continued to work for the improvement of the lot of Blacks. Following the convention, the Executive Council elected Robert F. Blanck, a lawyer from Philadelphia, to fill the unexpired term as treasurer. He continued to do so throughout the remaining years of the LCA's existence.

76. *1982 Convention Summary*, 11.

77. Vikner, "LCA World Mission," 177.

78. Tumsa was seized in August 1979 (*LCAM, 1980*, 460). Lutheran churches in Europe and North America had sent in millions of dollars worth of food and medical supplies to help fight hunger and disease among the people. But these efforts only seemed to heighten the government claim that Christianity was an "imported foreign religion" (*LCAM, 1982*, 495).

79. *LCAM, 1982*, 494.

80. Ibid., 499–500.

81. These included Namibia, Japan, Fiji, Haiti, Trinidad, Costa Rica, Nicaragua, Peru, Chile, Argentina, Uruguay, India, Burma, Nepal, Thailand, Egypt, Paraguay, the Philippines, Zaire, Ghana, Zambia, Botswana, Zimbabwe, Angola, Kenya, Taiwan, Jerusalem, and others. See Report of DWME in *LCAM, 1980*, 455–69; *1982*, 493–504.

82. Detailed reports of these consultations were produced by DWME: *Central Andean Consultation*, March 1982; *Objectives and Strategy in the Southern Cone of South America*, March 1982; *Mission in the Middle East*, March 1981. Although not regional in nature, consultations were brought together also to develop basic position papers for DWME on *Preparation for Ministry* (March 1981) and a *Policy Concerning Development* (March 1980).

83. The information here is based on an unpublished paper by David L. Vikner, *The Church in the People's Republic of China*, April 30, 1984. Dr. Vikner, former executive of DWME, was born in China and served there as

a missionary prior to the Communist takeover in 1949. He has visited China numerous times since the new openness began in 1979, and is, perhaps, the LCA's leading authority on the Christian church in that country.

84. "The prestigious Nanjing Theological Seminary was reopened in 1980. ... The 1983–84 student body numbers 116 students, of whom 45 are women and 71 men." Ibid., 6. Since 1981, some 300,000 Bibles have been printed and distributed in China. New translations of the Scriptures are being done. The monthly magazine *Tian Feng* (Heavenly Wind) has been revived. A hymnal called *Hymns of Praise* and *The Catechism of the Chinese Christian People* have been published.

85. Ibid., 10.

86. As Orlando E. Costas puts it, "The USA qualifies as a 'mission field' because many of its people are alienated from God and neighbor. In spite of the millions who profess to be Christians by virtue of baptism, church membership or conventionality, an overwhelming number of North Americans have not really heard the gospel. . . . To see the relevance of the USA as 'a mission field' today is not just missiologically urgent for North Americans. It is just as crucial for Third World Christians." From "The USA: A Mission Field for Third World Christians," *Review and Expositor* (Spring 1977):183–84.

87. *LCAM, 1980,* 457. For example, Yutaka Toda, a pastor of the Japan Evangelical Lutheran Church, developed a Japanese language ministry in Garden Grove, California (*1982,* 497).

88. David L. Vikner, *The New International Economic Order from the Standpoint of a Christian Mission Agency,* unpublished paper.

89. *LCAM, 1980,* 457. DWME indicated that the statement would be based on papers dealing with such diverse subjects as mission from the point of view of recent biblical research and Lutheran theology; an elaboration of world views growing out of development in scientific, philosophical, and theological thinking; and projection of the global political, economic, social, and religious situations in which the division would be active in the coming decades.

90. The *Background Papers to the Document—Call to Global Mission* (New York: DWME, 1982) is a volume of 372 pages that deals with such subjects as biblical and theological perspectives on mission, the challenge of contemporary world views, the world mission enterprise of the LCA and its predecessors, three scenarios of the final decades of the century, the form of mission, the poor and oppressed, the divided church, other world religions, scientific and intellectual advancements, the crisis of institutions. The writers included James A. Bergquist, Gordon John Schultz, David Vikner, William A. Kinnison, Katherine Mancke Kidd, Wilfried Kraegel, Emilio Castro, David M. Stowe, George A. Lindbeck, Paul V. Martinson, Philip Hefner, and Ross L. Paulson.

91. *LCAM, 1982,* 116–17. DWME consistently refers to the statement as "a working document." The full text as it appears in the *LCAM, 1982,* 115–126, has been reprinted by the division in a separate publication, *Call to Global Mission* (New York: DWME, 1983).

92. *LCAM, 1982,* 202.

93. Ibid., 203.

94. Ibid., 506.

95. The team members were Horst Becker, director of the mission department of the Lutheran Church in Bavaria; Risto Lehtonen, director the LWF department; Gunnar Lislerud, a bishop of the Church of Norway; Soritus A. N. Nababan, director of the Council of Churches of Indonesia; and Tracey K. Jones, a professor at Drew University and former executive of the Methodist Board of Global Missions.

96. Both the report itself and DWME's reaction to the critique are included in *Report of the Lutheran World Federation Team Evaluating the Division for World Mission and Ecumenism* (New York: DWME, 1983).

97. Ibid., 5–6.

98. Ibid., 17.

99. Ibid., 18–19.

100. At the Dallas convention, when the report of the Commission on Function and Structure was being debated, a proposal was made to create a separate "Office of Ecumenism," but this was defeated (*LCAM, 1972,* 619). As late as 1982, a lengthy recommendation was made that would have amended the *LCA Bylaws,* Section X, D, to spin off the DWME's responsibility to a new division (*LCAM, 1982,* 288–89). The proposal was referred to the Executive Council, which decided that this move would not help the seeming overlapping roles of the bishop, DWME, and the Council itself. Furthermore, the Executive Council found this an inauspicious time to make such a change in view of the probability of a new church being formed by 1988. It chose instead to have DWME and the bishop work out details of accountability for the director of ecumenical relations when that person provided staff services for the bishop. The director, however, remained on the staff of DWME. See *LCAM, 1984,* 900–2. William G. Rusch, who served as director, reviews the history of the placement of ecumenism in the different LCA structures through the years in *Ecumenism, A Movement Toward Church Unity* (Philadelphia: Fortress, 1985), 101–2. He seems to have favored lodgment of the staff role directly in the Office of the Bishop.

101. *LCAM, 1982,* 469, 602. Although the Executive Council approved the post in December 1978, it was not filled until the following July. William G. Rusch, who was appointed to the position, had served as director of Fortress Press and previously as assistant director of the Department of Theological Studies of LCUSA.

102. *LCAM, 1982,* 491. The decision to call a consultation and develop a statement grew out of the DWME's highly developed planning process.

103. Article V on Objects and Powers affirms that "this church lives to be the instrument of the Holy Spirit in obedience to the commission of its Lord, and specifically

a. To proclaim the Gospel through Word and Sacraments, to relate that Gospel to human need in every situation, and to extend the ministry of the Gospel to all the world.

b. To gather into fellowship those who respond in faith to the call of the Gospel and to nurture them in the faith through that fellowship.

c. To affirm its unity in the true faith and to give outward expression to that unity.

d. To safeguard the pure preaching of the Word of God and the right administration of the Sacraments by all its ordained ministers and in all its congregations in conformity with its Confession of Faith.

e. To strive for the unification of all Lutherans within its boundaries in one church and to take constructive measures leading thereto when such action will extend the mission of Christ's reconciling love.

f. To foster Christian unity and to serve humanity by participating in ecumenical Christian activities, contributing its witness and work and cooperating with other churches which confess God the Father, Son and Holy Spirit.

g. To develop relationships with communities of other faiths for dialogue and common action.

h. To lift its voice in concord and to work in concert with forces for good, cooperating with church and other groups participating in activities that promote justice, relieve misery, and reconcile the estranged."

It should be noted that Article V was amended in 1974 and 1976 by:

1. Revision of item "e" by adding "when such action will extend the mission of Christ's reconciling love."
2. Revision of "f" by changing "To participate" to "To foster Christian unity and to serve humanity by participating" . . .
3. Addition of items "g" and "h."

See *LCAM, 1974*, 39, 315, 505, and *LCAM, 1976*, 812.

104. From an interview with David L. Vikner by the writer, who was himself a participant in the conference.

105. See William H. Lazareth, "Evangelical Catholicity: Lutheran Identity in an Ecumenical Age," in *The New Church Debate*, ed. Carl E. Braaten (Philadelphia: Fortress Press, 1983), 15–38. Specifically, Lazareth notes, "In 1980, Lutheran Christians throughout the world engaged in celebrating the 450th anniversary of the Augsburg Confession. For the first time, they had the benefit of viewing themselves and their chief confessional document in the light of the recent ecumenical developments outlined above. . . . The common finding: Lutheran Christians, despite their ecclesiastical identification as Protestants, nevertheless define their ecclesiological identity as 'evangelical catholics'; that is, as a confessing and confessional communion within the church catholic." Ibid., 26.

106. Ibid., 30.

107. George A. Lindbeck, "The Divided Church," in *Background Papers to Call to Global Mission*, 320.

108. According to John Mangum, who chaired that meeting, Bishop Crumley urged the development of a statement setting forth the LCA's stance on ecumenism that could be a dowry for the new church (from an interview with Dr. Mangum by the writer August 4, 1987).

109. The members of the steering committee were H. George Anderson, Franklin D. Fry, George A. Lindbeck, John H. P. Reumann, William G. Rusch, and as ex officio members, David Vikner and Bishop Crumley. See

DWME-MCM, March 17–20, 1982, 40. The convention actions and text of the document appear in the *LCAM, 1982,* 278–87. The statement was later printed in book form by the Board of Publication. This version includes not only the text in English but also French and German translations. A leather-bound copy was presented by Bishop Crumley to Pope John Paul II during an audience at the Vatican.

110. Rusch, *Ecumenism,* 102. This volume gives a clear and succinct summary of the statement, pp. 102–6.

111. Referring to the Jacksonville consultation, the statement says, "The participants agreed that broader Christian unity may be sought even while hoping for Lutheran unification. Fulfillment of the latter is not a condition for taking steps toward the former." The specific parts of the constitution quoted in this connection are Article V, Section 1, e, f, and Section 2, m.

112. These included the WCC (special reference is made here to the Faith and Order Commission's completion of the document on *Baptism, Eucharist and Ministry*), interdependent ties with overseas churches, NCCCUSA, LWF, LCUSA, Lutheran Council in Canada, involvement in bilateral dialogues, and local ecumenism.

113. Rusch, in *Ecumenism,* 104–5, refers to the most important as:

"The centrality of the gospel, affirmed in the Lutheran Confessions, allows for considerable variety in many aspects of ecclesial life and organization, doctrinal expression, and ethical assertions.

Ecumenism embodies all those churches which confess the triune God.

Progress in one area of ecumenism must not be seen as competitive with advancement in another.

The vision of unity shared by the WCC is affirmed for the present stage of ecumenical development.

The Lutheran Confessions are a liberating ecumenical resource.

Where there is agreement in the gospel, forms of eucharistic hospitality may take place.

Bilateral and multilateral dialogues are encouraged.

God may always have surprises for his people that are beyond human comprehension."

114. Bishop David Preus had written to Bishop Crumley asking that the LCA not move unilaterally in adopting a statement on ecumenism. The DWME Management Committee, however, decided that presentation of the document to the convention for decision ought not be delayed. See *DWME-MCM, March 17–20, 1987,* 42.

115. As has been indicated in earlier chapters of this book, E. Clifford Nelson describes the development of the two differing views of "ecumenical confessionalism" and "exclusive confessionalism" that have divided North American Lutherans for decades in *Lutheranism 1914–1970,* 19–27. The ULCA position had been set forth initially by President Frederick Knubel in a paper on the "Essentials of the Catholic Spirit" and been adopted by that church in 1920 as "The Washington Declaration." E. Theodore Bachmann gives a thorough interpretation of the Washington Declaration itself and its subsequent influence in *Ecumenical Involvement,* 26–35. The inclusive

confessional view strongly influenced the tenor of the LCA Constitution as adopted in 1962.

116. In 1967 the General Convention of the Episcopal Church, U.S.A., had extended an invitation to Lutherans in the United States to take part in dialogue. ALC, LCA, and LCMS all accepted, and the first series was sponsored by the Joint Commission on Ecumenical Relations of the Episcopal Church and the Division of Theological Studies of LCUSA. A progress report was issued in 1972, and the second document was published as *Lutheran-Episcopal Dialogue: Report and Recommendations* (Cincinnati: Forward Movement, 1981). The AELC joined the second series of conversations in 1976. Meanwhile, Lutheran-Anglican dialogues had been going on at the world level as a result of an invitation from LWF in 1963. William Rusch describes the sequence of studies and their results in *Ecumenism*, 76–80.

117. The full text of the recommendations appears in the *LCAM, 1982*, 182. The Episcopal House of Bishops had already approved similar recommendations by a vote of 165–0, which paved the way for that church's convention action (see p. 266). Both the AELC and ALC conventions, which were meeting simultaneously with LCA, also adopted similar recommendations (see p. 277).

118. *1986 Convention Summary*, 6.

119. *LCAM, 1982*, 492. Actually, the whole group present, including guests, liaison officers, and observers, numbered more than three hundred.

120. *Baptism, Eucharist and Ministry*, Faith and Order Paper No. 111 (Geneva: WCC, 1982). A summary of the steps that led up to the issuing of the document are detailed in the preface. Work on the questions involved here, of course, did not constitute the whole of Faith and Order's efforts through the years.

121. Ibid., 4.

122. Ibid., 5, sets forth the four basic questions being asked:

The extent to which your church can recognize in this text the faith of the Church through the ages;

The consequences your church can draw from this text for its relations and dialogues with other churches, particularly with those churches which also recognize the text as an expression of the apostolic faith;

The guidance your church can take from this text for its worship, educational, ethical, and spiritual life and witness;

The suggestions your church can make for the ongoing work of Faith and Order as it relates the material of this text on Baptism, Eucharist and Ministry to its long-range research project "Towards the Common Expression of the Apostolic Faith Today."

123. *LCAM, 1980*, 337, 363; *1982*, 350, 365.

124. *LCAM, 1980*, 362–63.

125. *LCAM, 1984*, 425. While it is natural to think of such congregations as being in predominantly Black, Hispanic, Chinese-speaking, or Southeast Asian communities, there were exceptions. For example, in Thunder Bay, Ontario, an existing congregation, St. Mark's, began a Finnish language

ministry among the 25,000 persons of Finnish heritage who had settled in the area (*LCAM, 1982,* 366).

126. An arm of LCUSA, LIRS had originally been set up to handle refugees from Europe following World War II. Its "cases" in the seventies and eighties, however, tended to come more from Southeast Asia, Cuba, Haiti, and Central America. The 100,000th person welcomed was Kao Lor, a Laotian. See Report of LCUSA in *LCAM, 1982,* 598–99.

127. DMNA reported that by the end of 1981 the cost of building had climbed to $43.67 per square foot, more than double the previous decade. The average cost of a church site had gone from $20,000 to $100,000, and a parsonage from $40,000 to $81,000. See *LCAM, 1982,* 360. During the 1980–81 biennium, the prime rate went as high as 21.5% in the United States and 19% in Canada. LCA borrowings were usually a percentage point above prime.

128. Between 1976 and 1981, Lutheran Brotherhood had provided over $5 million in Church Extension Program Subsidies and Interest Subsidies (ibid., 364).

129. *LCAM, 1982,* 714–20. The plan also stressed Mission Development Certificates, a convention offering, designating a Sunday for a churchwide offering, issuing bonds, and disposal of excess property owned by BAM. After confusion about a date for designating a Sunday for a churchwide offering, it was attempted and results were negligible. The endowment fund was established, and the loan of SFM funds was accomplished. The whole panoply of moves had a certain air of desperation that was understandable under the circumstances.

130. Ibid., 169.

131. Ibid., 334–35.

132. Ibid., 366.

133. For example, DMNA had recruited twenty-five volunteers who were willing to live at a subsistence level and help inner city congregations with work in their neighborhoods. These people received only room, board, and a small stipend (ibid., 370).

134. *LCAM, 1980,* 367.

135. Ibid., 364–66.

136. Ibid., 368–69.

137. According to a report of the American Council of Education, Black enrollment in colleges peaked at 9.4% of all college students. By 1984, that percentage had slipped to 8.8%, even though the number of Black high school students was increasing. At the same time, the enrollment of Asians and Hispanics was steadily moving upward. See Meg Dooley, "Bridging the Access Gap," *Columbia* (New York: Columbia University, June 1987), 27.

138. One of the greatest surges in numbers of foreign students came in doctoral programs for engineering, mathematics/computer sciences, and physical sciences. In engineering, for example, the number of foreign students among newly minted Ph.D.s in engineering rose from around 30% to over 50% between 1971 and 1981. Source: National Science Foundation, reported in "American Laboratories, Foreign Brains," *New York Times Week in Review* (July 19, 1987):8.

139. *LCAM, 1980,* 369.

140. *LCAM, 1982,* 380.

141. Ibid. See tables on pp. 382–83.

142. *LCAM, 1982,* 378–79.

143. The volume was Richard W. Solberg and Merton P. Strommen, *How Church-Related Are Church-Related Colleges?* (Philadelphia: Board of Publication, LCA, 1980).

144. *LCAM, 1970,* 428–51, 648–49. A related matter dealt with amending "Standards for Acceptance into and Continuance in the Ministry of the Lutheran Church in America," 781–83.

145. *LCA Bylaws,* Section X, C, 2.

146. *LCAM, 1980,* 139–58. The study, which was done by the Consulting Committee on Theological Education, had actually been begun in the 1976–78 biennium (ibid., 441–4). The committee was chaired by Franklin Sherman, a professor at the Lutheran School of Theology in Chicago.

147. "The Wittenberg reformers recognized the need for maintaining continuity and order among congregations and the institutions of the church. They therefore retained the functions and title of bishops. At the same time, they held that the universal priesthood possessed authority to choose and approve persons publicly to teach, preach and proclaim the Word; baptize; administer the eucharist; proclaim forgiveness and discipline members; pray for others; be examples of Christ-like love; and judge doctrines and spiritual forces. Thus, as with the other elements of ministry, the supervision of the church involves both lay and ordained persons." Ibid., 143.

148. In a footnote, the study points out that traditionally Lutherans have referred to the Ministry of Word and Sacrament as an "office." The Reformers used the German word *Amt* (office) in contrast to *Stand* (status of rank). All Christians have the same status but are called to different offices (ibid., 144).

149. Ibid., 145. The rite of ordination, for example, does not establish the office, but the office gives cause for the rite.

150. The present reading of the pertinent item (now listed in the *LCA Bylaws,* Section 2 as Item 13) is, "A minister may, with the approval of the bishop and the executive board of the synod, serve under call to part-time service in a congregation or parish for a specific term of years. The term shall normally be for no more than four years and each renewal shall require approval by the bishop and executive board of the synod."

151. After consultation with the Conference of Bishops, DPL adopted a set of *Guidelines for Calls to Part-time Service* (Philadelphia: DPL, 1980) that spelled out procedures to be used in such cases and emphasized that "such calls are to be extended for the strengthening of the ministry of the Church rather than in response to the wishes of individual ordained ministers." To enable a responsible ministry to the congregation, it was urged that 20–25 hours per week be spent in this way. DPL cited an extensive study by John Y. Elliott, *Our Pastor Has an Outside Job* (Valley Forge, Pa.: Judson Press, 1980), to support this criterion.

152. *LCAM, 1980,* 192–93, 197. An attempt to have the action reconsidered failed by only one vote (for, 405; against, 204; needed, 406).

153. *LCAM, 1984,* 308–9; and *1986,* 254. The amendment inserted a new Section 3 into Article VII of the constitution that read, "Synods may receive, through procedure defined in the Bylaws and other official documents, ordained clergy from churches which believe, teach and confess the Apostles', the Nicene and the Athanasian creeds." It is interesting that the Executive Council originally had postponed consideration of such an amendment indefinitely *(ECM, March 1984,* 605), but then changed its thinking in light of the expectation that such a proposal would come to the Toronto convention from the delegates *(June 1984,* 691). It judged that this was more than an indiscriminate acceptance of ministries of any group that claimed to be a church and was "presumably more than merely acknowledging the creeds."

154. President Fry wrote that Dr. Marshall's paper was "so straight on target in terms of LCA polity" that he would devote his own report on "The State of the Church" in the *Ministers Information Service* for October and November 1965 to publishing large sections of the document.

155. *LCAM, 1970,* 440, 649.

156. The committee, chaired by theologian Edgar M. Carlson, drew heavily on the earlier study done by Dr. Marshall. In the course of their deliberations, they consulted the Conference of Synodical Presidents, which concurred with the final report *(LCAM, 1972,* 188).

157. The full text of the committee's report and the actions of the Executive Council appear in the *LCAM, 1972,* 183–88.

158. The Lutheran World Federation Department of Theology, for example, had done a comprehensive study of the subject that had recently been published in English as *Episcopacy in the Lutheran Church* (Philadelphia: Fortress Press, 1970).

159. *LCAM, 1972,* 734.

160. *1974 Convention Summary,* 7–8.

161. *LCAM, 1978,* 60–61.

162. Ibid., 311–14. See also *ECM, July 16, 1978,* 642–44. The original proposal had suggested using "presiding bishop" for the president of the LCA, but the Executive Council recommended that this be stricken from the wording, apparently to avoid any implication that the LCA was establishing a hierarchical system.

163. *ECM, November 1979,* 313.

164. *LCAM, 1980,* 686–96.

165. Ibid., 258.

166. Dr. Crumley indicated to the writer in an interview on June 25, 1987, that he himself has observed this phenomenon. His own concern at the time of the Seattle convention had to do not with the use of "bishop" per se but whether the church really was clear as to what it meant by the title.

167. *LCAM, 1980,* 443.

168. *LCAM, 1982,* 291, 444, 771. The amendments were to the *Bylaws,* Section X, C, Items 1, 2, 3. The change also committed the division to "give special attention to equalizing opportunities in professional leadership for ethnic minority group persons, youth and women."

169. Ibid., 434.

170. *LCAM, 1980,* 433. The year was 1978–79 to 1979–80.
171. From *Today's Professional Leadership* (Philadelphia: DPL, 1985), 3.
172. Ibid., 5.
173. Ibid., 8.
174. *LCAM, 1980,* 433. The actual numbers reported by academic year in 1980 were as follows:

Year	Advanced Masters	Academic Doctorate	D.Min.
1978–79	89	15	116
1979–80	102	11	176

Although exact numbers are not quoted, DPL reported more women were preparing for teaching positions in seminaries where the proportion of female faculty members had been woefully low.

175. Ibid., 434. DPL was committed to supplying additional support to the Saskatoon school during this crisis. The same problem did not exist at Waterloo Seminary in Eastern Canada because that institution was related only to the LCA.

176. *LCAM, 1982,* 434. ALC had indicated that it would provide $1,250,000 in appeal funds to Pacific where there were many ALC students, although the school was still owned by LCA synods in the area.

177. Ibid., 455–64, 275. It should be noted that in this same period DPL completed major studies on *Internship* and *Financing of Theological Education* (ibid., 465–88). Both of these reports urged stronger support for these aspects of seminary education. One of the grim facts in the financial study was that there had been a fundamental shift between 1974–75 and 1979–80 in the source of funding seminary programs. As costs rose, synodical support dropped from 53% to 32% of the total, endowment income sank from 14% to 12%, while fees to students rose from 15% to 19% of total expenses. The major source used to plug the gap came from "other sources," which included such things as grants and direct gifts (pp. 480–81).

178. Lloyd E. Sheneman gives the story of these moves in "Christ Seminary-Seminex Deployment and LCA Theological Education," *Partners* (December, 1983):34–38.

179. A firsthand account of the tragic split within LCMS and the formation of Christ Seminary in Exile is told in Frederick W. Danker, *No Room in the Brotherhood* (St. Louis: Clayton Publishing House, 1977). E. Clifford Nelson provides a briefer but carefully documented treatment of the conflict in Missouri and the movement that created Seminex in "New Shape of Lutheranism," 528–35, and "Supplement to the Revised Edition," 559–60, in *Lutherans in North America* (Philadelphia: Fortress Press, 1980).

180. *LCAM, 1982,* 438. PLACE was the acronym for "Professional Leaders' Aid to Continuing Education."

181. Ibid., 439.

182. Ibid., 438–39. Although the other two church bodies did take part in the project, the majority of participants came from the LCA.

183. Thomas E. Kadel, ed., *Growth in Ministry* (Philadelphia: Fortress Press, 1980) dealt with such subjects as "The Postwar Pastorate," "Roles in Pastoring," "Shared Ministry," "Why Conflicts?" "A Different Look at Pastoral Counseling," and "Forgotten Members: The Pastor's Family."

184. See *LCAM, 1980,* 440. By 1983 the program had become a joint AELC, ALC, LCA effort (*1984,* 497). A description of the program is provided in the brochure *Options, the Choice Is Yours.* Interestingly, many of the participants decided after taking part in the workshop that their future calling was still in the ordained ministry even though Options was originally envisioned as an "outplacement service."

185. *LCAM, 1982,* 441–43. A small number of retired deaconesses still remained at the center in Omaha that had originally been operated by the Augustana Lutheran Church.

186. See *DPLM, September/October 1975,* 25–26. The various steps taken through the years are described in a paper by Harold Lohr of the DPL staff that was presented to the LCA Staff Executive Team in August, 1977 ("Proposal for Leader's Publication," pp. 1–2).

187. The statement is made in *Futures Report: the LCA and the Issues of the Eighties,* a study conducted by the Staff Team on Planning under the leadership of ORP. The document had drawn together demographic data, projections by independent research organizations, information from the Lutheran Listening Post, and a survey of key leaders on 63 target issues for the LCA in the eighties. Eleven of the most highly ranked items were issues related to the congregation. See *LCAM, 1980,* 405.

188. *LCAM, 1980,* 418.

189. Ibid., 532.

190. With other worship projects having higher priority, producing the alternate settings did prove more difficult than anticipated. *Selected Hymns for Singing in Harmony* (Philadelphia: Board of Publication, LCA, 1985) was finally published in a paperback edition that also included some familiar tunes that had not been used in the *LBW.*

191. *LCAM, 1982,* 425. This compares with the fact that the *Service Book and Hymnal* achieved a maximum usage of about 90% during its life span. Use of the *LBW* continued to grow during the remainder of the LCA's existence.

192. The ILCW office was closed on July 1, 1978, and the ILCW itself was declared dissolved as of January 1, 1979. This was thirteen years after the LCMS had issued its original invitation to other Lutheran churches to join in developing a common hymnal and worship book. In response, representatives of six Lutheran bodies met at an Inter-Lutheran Consultation on Worship in Chicago and recommended at a session on February 11, 1966, formation of the ILCW. See *Liturgical Reconnaissance,* vii–viii, 134–35.

193. *ECM, December 1–4, 1978,* 133–34. In dealing with the DPS Management Committee's proposal, the Executive Council concluded that procedures for cooperation in worship on the part of DPS did not require the Council's approval. It did urge, however, that AELC be given an opportunity to participate in all inter-Lutheran projects in which the division en-

gaged. This created an interesting situation for Missouri. The WREC itself was later called the Joint Committee on Worship.

194. The LCA representatives were Bishop Herbert Chilstrom of the Minnesota Synod, the Rev. Janice Jensen, the Rev. Philip Pfatteicher, the Rev. Elizabeth Platz, Virginia Trendel, and the Rev. Ralph Van Loon. The chairperson of the task force was Professor Mark Bangert of the AELC.

195. *LCAM, 1980*, 715–16. Final approval for the LCA, of course, had to be given by the DPS Management Committee.

196. See *Occasional Services* (Minneapolis, Philadelphia: Augsburg Publishing House, Board of Publication, LCA, 1982). The book was copyrighted in the names of the four church bodies. An examination of the prayers in the book shows concern about current problems that were not dealt with in the same way earlier, such as addiction, divorce, stillbirth or death shortly after birth, anxiety, and boredom. There was also provision in the Rite for Commendation of the Dying for prayer "when a life-support system is withdrawn" (p. 106) that indicated the way in which the church was seeking to minister to persons in situations that were quite different from traditional settings.

197. *LCAM, 1982*, 532.

198. Ibid., 418, 425.

199. The videotape was an inter-Lutheran project. The tape itself was placed in LCA synodical A-V libraries. See *LCAM, 1984*, 482.

200. Ibid. This was a complex venture since there are variations in words and phrases used by Mexicans, Cubans, Puerto Ricans, Central Americans, and other groups that have Spanish as their common language. Following extensive review and testing, the book was completed in 1983 under the title *Liturgia Luterana* (Minneapolis, Philadelphia: Augsburg Publishing House and Board of Publication, LCA, 1983).

201. The *LCA Constitution*, Article XII, Section 4, gives the bishop responsibility to see "that the enactments of this church are carried out." The Communion Practices Statement itself gives the bishop of the church the responsibility to authorize celebration of Holy Communion in established centers of the church, such as seminaries, to which more than one synod are related.

202. An excellent review of the issues involved in the controversy is in an article by H. George Anderson, "Infant Communion and the LCA," *LCA Partners* (December 1979):14–16, 22. He concludes, "Perhaps the best way forward at the present time is for discussions to continue where interest is high but for the practice to remain within the limits set by the LCA in all its statements since 1964. If a change is to be considered, it should represent the mature mind and informed decision of the church."

203. *LCAM, 1980*, 124–25. See also *1980 Convention Summary*, 8.

204. An analysis of the various steps taken by the DEM, NCCCUSA, and the involvement of the LCA in the lectionary project is described in *NCC Lectionary Project: A Brief History*, which was a collateral paper prepared for the management committee of DPS for its October 1981 meeting. An

even more detailed report of the earlier stages of the NCC proposal appears in the *DPS-MCM, October 30–November 1, 1980,* A44–51.

205. *Report of the Consultation on the NCCCUSA Proposal for Lectionary Translation,* October 29, 1980, submitted to the DPS Management Committee. The group included biblical scholars Krister Stendahl, John Reumann, and Foster McCurley, as well as LCA representatives to the DEM Unit Committee.

206. The DPS Management Committee resolutions were adopted November 1, 1980, and were reported in a PRT news release, November 6. The NCC committee decided on November 24–25 to proceed with the project. Bishop Crumley proposed the name of Dr. Victor Gold, professor of Old Testament at Pacific Lutheran Seminary, to serve on the translation group. The NCC promptly asked Dr. Gold to serve as chairperson of the task force.

207. When its LCA Parish Education Curriculum was virtually complete in 1966, the Board of Parish Education had wanted to begin designing a new program for the seventies on the ground that curriculum materials normally had a life expectancy of ten years. Its budget and staff were cut back severely in 1966, however, with the result that more than twelve years intervened before new resources could be introduced. Meanwhile, congregations had begun to turn to other sources for their educational materials.

208. *Educational Ministry Design: Basic Viewpoints* (Philadelphia: DPS, 1980), 3.

209. A dramatic example of the shift in participation in Sunday church school was that even though the number of children enrolled was dwindling due to demographic factors, the number of adults was steadily increasing. In 1972, there were 149,953 adults enrolled in Sunday school, but by 1980, that number had grown to 163,190. See *LCAM, 1980,* 417.

210. In addition to the leadership study mentioned below, the studies included *An Evaluation of Educational Ministry Resources* (1981) and *Educational Ministry Design: The Research* (1981).

211. A complete report of this research is in *Educational Ministry Leader Study* (Philadelphia: DPS, 1979).

212. See *Strategy for Developing Educational Ministry in the Parish, ALC/LCA,* 1971.

213. The new leadership texts were known as "LEAD Books" and included such titles as *We Believe and Teach, How to Teach God's Story, Understanding and Teaching the Bible, Teaching Worship, The Joy of Teaching Christ,* and *Nurturing Faith.* The new catechetical series was called "Catechetics for Today" and was published in 1980 and 1981. It was accompanied by a leadership manual, *Implementing Confirmation Ministry.* For the first time, videotapes were prepared for training catechists.

214. The new Sunday school materials would be known as the "Living Faith Series" and were scheduled for use beginning in the fall of 1984.

215. The AELC, ALC, LCA, ELCC, and LCMS joined in a major consultation marking the anniversary in October 1980 near Madison, Wisconsin. Excerpts from the presentations were published as *The Sunday School: It Has Made a Difference—It Can Make a Difference* (Minneapolis: Augsburg

Publishing House, 1982). It reviews the history of the Sunday school among Lutherans in North America and includes pertinent research on and directions of the movement in the eighties.

216. *LCAM, 1982,* 98. OAF directed the DAG program and the World Hunger Appeal. Details about the success of these efforts are provided in OAF's convention reports for 1980 (pp. 480–83) and 1982 (pp. 518–21).

217. Ibid., 413–14.

218. *ECM, November 1979,* 374–75. DPS was given responsibility for working out the plan.

219. *LCAM, 1982,* 765–71, describes the whole process followed in hammering out the proposal.

220. Ibid., 768. Bishop Crumley brought together a group of six members of the Council who were attending the DWME Consultation on Evangelism in February 1981 to review developments. The group reinforced the issues raised at the previous Council meeting and focused on the need for "fundraising" and a "strong leader with 'authority' to coordinate."

221. Ibid., 768. The bishops also expressed a need to review the whole CWA/synodical consultation process with a view to improving partnership. They were also concerned that all stewardship and fund-raising (e.g., DAG, LCAF) should be coordinated through the synods.

222. *ECM, April 9–11, 1981,* 176–80.

223. The person chosen for this role was the Rev. Paul Johns, who had coordinated a highly successful stewardship emphasis in the Illinois Synod.

224. Other elements of the churchwide program that had been approved earlier by the Executive Council included focusing on major gifts of $5,000 or more as a source of funds for Level III of the LCA budget, which had never been funded in the past. A number of synods built a major gifts phase into their special stewardship emphases with excellent results. The strategy also recruited a group of "Stewardship Key Leaders," who were lay persons and pastors with proven skills in the stewardship area. They were in some ways similar to Pastor Evangelists and gave an average of two weeks per year of their time to conduct various types of stewardship events throughout the church.

225. Because a major hotel facility was not completed in time for the New Orleans gathering, there was serious overcrowding and the whole event ran a deficit. There was the additional complication that the gathering also had to serve as the regular convention of ALC's youth organization, in which LCA and LCMS youth were not involved.

226. *LCAM, 1982,* 412.

227. *LCAM, 1980,* 415.

228. The total number of baptized members dropped from the rolls "for other reasons" from 1978 through 1982 was 487,843, according to figures supplied from the congregational report forms by the Research and Studies Department of DPS. Robert Strohl, who was in charge of this record keeping, estimated that as many as 40% of these persons eventually were restored to the rolls. The overall statistics, however, gave a picture of church membership that tended to be a conservative, if not negative, estimate.

229. In 1982 the ten northeastern synods lost 15,794 baptized members while the rest had a 5,091 aggregate gain (from *Reflections on 1982 Form A Statistics,* prepared for synodical bishops and statisticians by Robert Strohl). See also C. Richard Evenson and Robert Strohl, "Trends in LCA Membership," *LCA Partners* (December 1979):10–12.

230. *LCAM, 1980,* 415–18; *1982,* 423–25.

231. Lani L. Johnson, *Led by the Spirit.* The volume points out that although there were individual congregational female missionary societies in existence as early as 1820, the broader organized work is usually traced to the formation of the General Synod's Woman's Missionary Society in 1879. Mrs. J. W. H. Stuckenberg of Springfield, Ohio, was elected the first president (see pp. 6–8).

232. The Program Planning Structure is provided in detail in *Lutheran Women* (October 1980):14–20.

233. *LCAM, 1982,* 573. The LCW's gift to the LCA in 1980 was $903,700, and in 1981 was $858,425. Inflation, of course, was affecting the costs of its own program.

234. Details of these grants are provided in the *LCW Executive Committee Minutes*: May 15–16, 1978, p. 17; May 23–25, 1979, pp. 16–17; May 15–17, 1980, p. 17; March 25–28, 1981, pp. 14–16; March 11–14, 1982, pp. 42–44.

235. *LCAM, 1980,* 548, indicates that LCW had developed *The Emergency English Kit* for the refugee situation. In the literacy work with English-speaking adults, LCW had prepared a *Handbook for Volunteer Reading Aides* and a film, *Words to the Wise* (*LCAM, 1982,* 574).

236. *1980 Convention Summary,* 6.

237. See Sibley, *Planning,* 28.

238. The *Executive Council Minutes,* as early as the meetings of November 1975, p. 316; December 1976, p. 120; April 1977, pp. 182–84, indicate that the relationship between ORP and the Council was under discussion. At one point during the last few months of Dr. Marshall's tenure as president, there had been consideration of the possibility of merging ORP and OAF because of the relationship between budgeting and planning. The Executive Council decided to defer this decision, however, to allow the new president to express his views (see *LCAM, 1980,* 106).

239. Sibley and Hart, *Research and Evaluation,* 12. The writers observe, "It is not clear whether this shift has come as a result of the greater authority of the bishop's office, closer working relationships among the individuals involved in OB/PRE and the churchwide agencies, or fiscal restraints wherein agencies had to place greater reliance on the research and evaluation services of OB/PRE. It was probably a mixture of all three."

240. See Sibley, *Planning,* 17–18. He points out that Dr. Marshall often took responsibility for fiscal recommendations when the Cabinet of Executives [sic] was unable to reach consensus (p. 28).

241. *LCA Constitution,* Article XI, Section 3, b.

242. *LCAM, 1980,* 106–8.

243. Ibid., 543–44.

244. Ibid., 24–35, is the text of the president's report. A summary of meetings of the Executive Council beginning in February 1979 on p. 739

indicates that the Council had worked closely with the president to make his report to the convention the basis for future planning. The Committee on the President's Report presented a series of resolutions to the convention in Seattle that set this planning procedure in motion for the ensuing biennium (see pp. 330–34). The way in which this new planning process began to impact the priorities of the LCA is spelled out in the *LCAM, 1982*, 839–42.

245. Ibid., 840. The nine strategy areas were Outreach, Theological Education, Capital Financing for Congregations, New Lutheran Church, Stewardship, Ecumenism, Christian Education, Advocacy for Justice and Peace, and Ministry of the Laity in the World. These categories in effect lifted up certain parts of the bishop's broad aims for special attention. How this procedure impacted the fiscal proposals for 1983–84 is described in the Executive Council's report to the 1982 convention (ibid., 219–20, and Exhibit E, 241).

246. The term used in the next biennium was "intentional planning," which seemed to imply to some that the planning that had gone on before was "unintentional." Leonard Sibley comments on the role of the Staff Team on Planning in all of this by saying, "Although it was not the intention of the Staff Team on Planning to develop a new program structure, this is, in essence, what happened. The intentional planning 'categories' of projects provide a unified framework of churchwide priorities for churchwide agency program and fiscal planning. These categories create a 'hierarchy' of churchwide agency programs" (*Planning*, 21).

247. Ibid., 41–42.

248. See *LCA Bylaws*, Section VII, Item 3.

249. Sibley and Hart describe in detail the five-year cycle of evaluating major program areas carried out by DPS as an example of work already in progress, *Research and Evaluation*, 26–27.

250. *LCAM, 1982*, 552.

251. Ibid., 556. These broadcasts were carried on 452 radio stations in the United States and Canada plus 800 stations worldwide related to the Armed Forces Network and the British Forces Network. Audiocassettes of these programs were distributed to Lutheran homes for the aging and hospitals through Lutheran Social Services.

252. Ibid., 557. Although Bainton was not a Lutheran, he was the author of the best biography of Luther and heavily in demand as a speaker to Lutheran audiences.

253. *LCAM, 1980*, 575. Lutheran Film Associates is a cooperative agency related to LCUSA that has produced a long list of films beginning in the 1950s. Excerpts of the film were used in the "Augustana Jubilee" celebration at the Seattle convention that marked the 450th anniversary of the Augsburg Confession (*1980 Convention Summary*, 5).

254. LCA's share of producing the film came from OC's share of Strength for Mission. The same source was used for the TV spot series and a variety of other projects.

255. *1980 Convention Summary*, 7.

256. Although it began publication as *The Lutheran* on July 6, 1860, the magazine actually followed a small periodical called *The Lutheran Home Journal* that had had a shaky existence for five years. In 1861 *The Lutheran*

merged with *The Missionary* that had been published by William Passavant since 1848. See G. Elson Ruff, "Church Editors Were Fighting Men," *The Lutheran* (July 6, 1960) 11–15. Albert P. Stauderman, who was Ruff's successor as editor, traced *The Lutheran's* history to *The Lutheran Observer* which began publication in 1831. See "First Came The Observer," *The Lutheran* (August 1981):8–11. This history has been described in earlier chapters.

257. *LCAM, 1980,* 530.

258. *LCAM, 1982,* 559–60.

259. See Nelson, *Lutherans in North America,* which points out the role of the National Lutheran Editors' Association in urging steps that led to formation of the National Lutheran Council, greater cooperation during World War II, and the establishing of LCUSA (pp. 404, 479, 499). See also F. K. Wentz, *Lutherans in Concert,* 12, 15.

260. Amazingly, Rhody's career had spanned nearly half of the entire life of the board, which traced its origin to the Lutheran Publication Society of the General Synod in 1855.

261. The $22,000 per year grant to the Communications System helped to defray the cost of *The Congregation* and *AIM,* which were provided without cost to church leaders by DPS.

262. See *LCAM, 1980,* 532–38; *1982,* 562–69.

263. Nelson, *Lutherans in North America,* 564.

264. In fact, informal conversations had been going on among the three bodies that had their origins in ALC, LCMS, and LCA for a decade before the commission was formed.

265. This statement was made in a document, *Affirmation and Appeal.*

266. Ibid., 564.

267. *1980 Convention Summary,* 3–4. The LCA Canada Section reports to the 1980 and 1982 LCA conventions confirmed the progress that was being made in Canada toward one church, but emphasized the desire to maintain close ties with any new church body in the United States (see *LCAM, 1980,* 559–62; *1982,* 584–86).

268. *LCA Constitution,* Article V, Section 1, e. This was LCA's historic stance of seeking commitment to unity first and working out the process for accomplishing the goal once that commitment was assured.

269. See Nelson's analysis of the initial meeting of the committee in *Lutherans in North America,* 562.

270. *Lutheran Standard* (May 2, 1978):16.

271. The Committee on Church Cooperation had suggested three options for exploration: retention of present structures with the emphasis on cooperation, development of merged regional entities related in a broader organization, and creation of a single church body. See *LCAM, 1978,* 207. The AELC "Call for Lutheran Unity" was actually closer to the goal of organic union that the LCA itself favored.

272. Ibid., 204, 208. See also *1978 Convention Summary,* 11.

273. Nelson, *Lutherans in North America,* 562.

274. The proposal to change the name had come from ALC's Church Council and was agreed to by the LCA Executive Council, *ECM, September*

14–16, 1978, 47. The new committee had seven members each from ALC and LCA, two from AELC, and two observers from the ELCC.

275. The specific options and a résumé of the assumptions about each are spelled out in the booklet *Lutheran Unity, Material for Study, Discussion, and Response,* issued in 1980 by the three churches, pp. 15–27.

276. *1980 Convention Summary,* 4.

277. Ibid., 6. The editors of the convention summary noted that "Dr. Kohn's strong endorsement of union was warmly received by the LCA delegates, who four times interrupted his ten-minute address with applause."

278. *LCAM, 1980,* 200.

279. For example, the influential theological journal *Dialog* devoted its Spring 1981 issue to a series of articles on the subject, including William H. Kohn, "Merger Is the Answer!"; Herbert W. Chilstrom, "Lutheran Unity in America"; Edgar R. Trexler, "Lutheran Unity: Behind the Scenes."

280. In "From the President," *The Lutheran Standard* (November 25, 1980):29. Dr. Preus was consistent in his contention that so much effort had been spent on reorganizing and restructuring that it was "most fruitful" to use these structures, "gladly putting together resources and programs where it proves useful to do so." Other "From the President" messages appeared in the March 20, 1981 issue, pp. 26–27, and June 26, 1981, p. 29. In the June 25, 1981 edition, he indicated that although he had stated his own views, he was pledged to "carry out with enthusiasm the will of the church as determined through this process and through the actions of the 1982 ALC General Convention," p. 29.

281. In "I Think," *The Lutheran Standard* (March 20, 1981):14, Dr. Anderson listed no less than thirty-six polity and structural issues that would need to be addressed in any merger and wondered whether congregations really wanted "to endure and to finance another national church reorganization."

282. In "I Think," *The Lutheran Standard* (February 6, 1981): 14.

283. *Lutheran Unity,* 26–27.

284. Ibid., 22–24.

285. *Lutheran Unity, A Summary Report of the District/Synod Opinion Poll and the Responses by Study Groups and Individuals* (September 1981):1.

286. Ibid., 3.

287. These grouped themselves in such categories as the nature of the church, organizational concerns, institutions of the church, focus on mission, and support of an option that would combine aspects of 3 and 4. See ibid., 2–4.

288. The full report of the Committee on Lutheran Unity appears in the *LCAM, 1982,* 208–16. The plan was to have the 1984 conventions discuss, review, and respond to a statement of theological understandings, ecclesial principles, and a narrative description of the "shape of the new church." The 1986 conventions were to discuss, review, and respond to articles of incorporation, the constitution, and bylaws; take action to terminate the function of

the three separate bodies December 31, 1987; and commit their mission and resources to the new body.

289. The writer has based the description here on official minutes, news releases, and material provided in interviews with Bishop James Crumley, Secretary Reuben Swanson, and staff liaison person Dorothy Marple.

290. *LCAM, 1982,* 212.

291. See *ECM, March 11–13, 1982,* 449–51.

292. See *ECM, June 17–19, 1982,* 694–700.

293. The person chosen by mutual agreement of the churches to chair the commission was William A. Kinnison, president of Wittenberg University. It had also been agreed that Arnold Mickelson, who was general secretary of the ALC, would be the staff person for the commission.

294. *LCAM, 1982,* 266. Two of these persons, Dr. Lazareth and Dr. Chilstrom, would figure prominently in 1987 in the selection of a bishop for the new church.

295. Ibid., 306. The complete delegation included the following. Clergy: H. George Anderson, Herbert W. Chilstrom, James R. Crumley, Jr., Franklin D. Fry, Callon W. Holloway, Jr., Lydia D. R. Kalb, Paul D. Kennedy, William H. Lazareth, Barbara K. Lundblad, Robert J. Marshall, Howard J. McCarney, June E. Nilssen, John H. P. Reumann, Reuben T. Swanson, Robert A. West. Lay: Elizabeth A. Bettenhausen, Robert P. Brorby, Kay Conrad, William E. Diehl, William S. Ellis, Judith Finn, Dorothy K. Jacobs, Carl M. Johnson, William A. Kinnison, Mary Y. Matsumoto, Barbara F. Nelson, Josefina Nieves Lebrón, Mary Olson, James J. Raun, Paul N. Schultz, Amalie R. Shannon.

296. *1982 Convention Summary,* 7.

297. *The Lutheran Standard* (October 1, 1982):32.

Chapter 7 | TO THE PRESENT AND INTO THE FUTURE

ONE MIGHT HAVE ASSUMED THE JUBILATION
that greeted the decision to move forward in planning a new church
would have supplied momentum and generated enthusiasm for the
ongoing work of the existing church bodies, but such was not always
the case. The very use of the term *new church* sometimes created
the impression that the Commission for a New Lutheran Church
should proceed as though there were no heritage to be preserved
and it had been mandated to ignore the present programs and concerns of the three churches for fear that they might contaminate a
pristine kind of creativity. The Committee on Lutheran Unity, for
example, had passed on to the commission nine papers on subjects
that it considered important, but the CNLC did not discuss them
although they were made available to the members.[1] The CNLC
itself reported after its first meeting September 27–29, 1982, "The
group was enthusiastic about and committed to its task, ready to
begin the process of envisioning a new church rather than merging
three existing ones."[2]

The Lutheran Church in America, however, was not inclined to
stand on one foot for five years. It operated with the conviction that
the LCA's mission must go forward, and it was hoped that this process would converge at some point with that of planning for the new
church. In this chapter, we will review briefly the societal setting
within which the church functioned, the major work of the LCA
during this period, and even more briefly the steps taken by the
CNLC as the Evangelical Lutheran Church in America was brought
into being. The last of these is properly the subject for a history that
someone with firsthand knowledge of the commission's work may
write in the future.

THE BEWILDERING WORLD OF
THE MID-EIGHTIES

The world scene in the years from 1982 through 1987 was one that shifted in kaleidoscopic fashion so rapidly that it was difficult to focus on one pattern before another took its place. The perspective of another decade may give coherence to what was happening, but at this point, it is only possible to provide a few examples of the kinds of situations in which the Lutheran Church in America tried to pursue simultaneously its twin goals of merger and mission. The incompleteness of the picture in itself may convey something of the uncertainty of the times as people wondered what they could really count on and what really mattered most.

War and Violence

The litany of war, coups, insurrections, and the aftermath of suffering that went with them seemed endless. Lebanon, Libya, Chad, Angola, Iran, Iraq, Afghanistan, Sri Lanka, Nicaragua, Cambodia, Northern Ireland, Ethiopia, the Philippines, South Korea, Chile, South Africa, Sudan, Haiti—the list of troubled areas could go on and on. The United States seemed to have a peculiar capacity for becoming involved in bizarre ways. It invaded tiny Grenada to thwart a Communist takeover, launched an air strike against Libya in retaliation for its terrorist tactics, dispatched Marines to Lebanon and then withdrew them after severe losses, and committed itself to keeping open the sea lanes of the Persian Gulf by naval escorts of reflagged Kuwaiti tankers. Perhaps the strangest of all was the covert sale of arms to Iran and use of proceeds to aid Nicaraguan contras in a way that threatened the Reagan administration.

Terrorism became a continual weapon in an effort to destabilize entire societies, or a symbol of revenge. Great Britain, France, Germany, Spain, Israel, Greece, Italy, and others became targets of bombings. Hostage taking of Westerners was once more prevalent in trouble spots like Beirut. Hijackings of aircraft took place in alarming numbers, and even a passenger liner was seized in the Mediterranean. Travel became precarious in many parts of the globe and was banned completely in others.

The Soviet Union, headed by a new and younger leader, and the United States struggled to achieve some kind of nuclear nonproliferation agreement. By the time of this writing, there was promise of eliminating short- and medium-range missiles, but both superpowers seemed to be working on strategic defense weapons. The "nuclear club" kept growing, however, as nations such as Brazil announced the ability to produce enriched uranium, and Pakistan was angered by United States efforts to tie aid to a commitment not to build an atomic bomb. The Soviets were busily expanding their successful space station while the U.S. space program reeled from the technological and psychological impact of the explosion that destroyed the space shuttle Challenger in 1986.

The Staggering Economy

The United States entered the eighties in the grip of double-digit inflation. Largely because the Federal Reserve Board tightened the monetary reins but partly due to a world oil glut that sharply reduced energy prices, the rate of inflation had dropped to 1.1 percent in 1986.[3] There were problems, however. Unemployment surged to 10.7 percent by the end of 1982 and then slowly slid toward 6 percent by mid-1987. But unemployment among Blacks remained stubbornly high at 12.4 percent, with nearly 30 percent of Black teenagers out of work.[4] Unfortunately, many of the unemployed either lacked the skills needed for available jobs or simply did not live in areas where "help wanted" signs abounded.[5]

The United States seemed to be riding a long period of economic growth after 1982 by mortgaging its future. The federal budget topped a trillion dollars, and the deficit soared above two hundred billion dollars per year. In the hope of stemming a trade deficit that was blamed on overvaluation of the dollar against other major currencies, the U.S. Treasury sought the help of trading partners in early 1985 to lower the dollar's exchange rate. It succeeded all too well, and by mid-1987 the dollar had plunged against the West German mark, British pound, and Japanese yen.[6] The move had not been much immediate help to the trade deficit, however, which reached a figure of over 15.7 billion dollars in the month of June 1987 alone. Meanwhile, the money supply was allowed to expand alarmingly at a 15.3 percent annual rate in 1987.[7] Worries about climbing inflation again started to beset the economy. The stock market bobbed up and down like a cork and topped the 2,700 mark on the Dow Jones Industrial Average for the first time in history on August 17, 1987.[8]

The United States was not the only nation concerned by such problems. Many Third World countries, such as Argentina, Brazil,

Mexico, Peru, and Nigeria, staggered under foreign debt burdens far too great for their fragile economies.[9] Even Communist North Korea went into technical default on its obligations. The impact on the world financial system was disturbing. Some banks and thrift institutions failed, and only the intervention of central banks and government agencies kept others afloat.[10]

Finally, on October 19, 1987, what appeared to be the worst stock market crash in history occurred. The Dow Jones Industrial Average plummeted an astonishing 508 points, or 22.6 percent of its value, on that Monday. The "market meltdown," as some termed it, far eclipsed the 12.8 percent drop of October 28, 1929, and set off a panic on worldwide stock markets, such as Tokyo, Hong Kong, London, and Frankfurt.[11] While headlines in the twenties crash trumpeted the enormous volume of 16 million shares changing hands, computerized trading on October 19, 1987, set a new record of 604.3 million shares. The financial market gyrations continued and left those who still remembered the collapse of 1929 and the Great Depression debating whether history might repeat itself.[12]

The Widening Hunger Gap

One consequence of the slowing in the economic growth of industrial nations was an increase in the poverty of developing nations and with it the number of hungry people in the world. The United Nations World Food Council at its meeting in Beijing in June 1987 declared that the extent of hunger and malnutrition in the developing world was growing at an alarming rate. By 1985 it estimated there were 512 million hungry people and that the number was growing by eight million a year.[13]

Although much attention had been focused on the problem in drought-stricken areas of Africa, a UNICEF study indicated that "in the last two years, more children have died in India and Pakistan than in all the 46 nations of Africa together. In 1986 more children died in Bangladesh than in Ethiopia, more in Mexico than in the Sudan, more in Indonesia than in all eight drought-stricken countries in the Sahel."[14] It was not a case of less individual suffering in Africa; it was the density of the population in the other countries that raised the sheer number of deaths.

Ironically, the problem was taking place at the same time that the world was awash in basic food supplies. Countries like the United States were cutting back production, and mountains of butter, cheese, and grain were in storage.[15] What conspired against the hungry was their inability to buy food when it was available and the inadequacy of the infrastructure in their countries to handle distribution, even when free foodstuffs were supplied by more affluent nations. While churches and public agencies struggled to bring some relief to the most distressed areas, they could only scratch the surface of the endemic problem. Nor was the difficulty confined to the Third World. Even the United States, wealthy as it was, could not seem to find a permanent solution to its hungry and its homeless street people. The gap between those with plenty and the poor seemed to grow steadily worse.[16]

Rethinking the Racial Revolution

Twenty years had passed since the long, hot summer of 1967 when Newark, Detroit, and a hundred other cities erupted in the worst racial riots in the nation's history that left death and burned-out buildings in their wake. At the time, there were promises aplenty of massive programs to solve the problems of the urban ghettoes, but in 1987 four million Black Americans were still trapped there, often in conditions far worse than they were in the sixties. "Why," asked one major periodical, "has the American ghetto become a self-perpetuating nightmare of fatherless children, welfare dependency, crime, gangs, drugs and despair?"[17] Facile answers to such rhetorical questions may have salved individual consciences, but they did little to come to grips with the real misery of people.

While not negating the historic role of white racism in the whole situation, Black leaders were themselves probing more deeply and looking at the problem in new ways.[18] The new emphasis was upon basic values such as education, high expectations, and hard work as Black communities looked more to their own resources rather than the "good" white people or government for aid.[19] "The Black community itself must assume responsibility for dealing with the problems of our communities," declared John E. Jacobs, president of the Urban League, in an address to the convention of N.A.A.C.P. in July 1987. "That doesn't let government off the hook, for only government policies can create the jobs and training and social support programs that enable us to survive and swim in the economic mainstream."[20]

In response, Benjamin L. Hooks, executive director of N.A.A.C.P., stated, "We know that Black America must do much of this work itself, for it is our future we must save. We call upon the more fortunate segments of Black America to enlist or re-enlist in this fight. If we are not prepared to work for our salvation, our race will be doomed."[21]

The question of ethnic or racial inequality, of course, was not confined to Blacks alone. Hispanics, Asians, and the flood of other persons who came to the United States and Canada in search of a better life had to deal with their own particular problems. Even those who were in North America first, the Native Americans, continued to struggle for the preservation of their own culture and the surmounting of formidable social handicaps. Hundreds of thousands were still tied to reservations where unemployment was unbelievably high.[22] Government proposals to create economic enterprise zones on the reservations were suspect as another example of potential exploitation by whites.[23]

Higher education served as another barometer of ethnic access to the mainstream of American life. Although 17 percent, or 2,063,000, students in two- and four-year colleges in the United States in 1984 were from minority groups, the balance was slowly changing. Black enrollment had peaked at 9.4 percent of the total in 1976 but declined to 8.8 percent in 1984, while the percentage of Hispanic and Asian students was steadily increasing.[24] "Since 1980, Asian enrollment in two- and four-year institutions has increased by 33.6 percent and Hispanic enrollment has increased by 12.1 percent."[25] For whatever reasons, the racial and ethnic mix and the opportunities for advancement seemed to be shifting in the eighties.

New "Firsts" for Women

Although the Equal Rights Amendment had not been ratified by the required number of state legislatures, women in the United States were achieving some important advances in their long struggle for equality. In 1984, for the first time in the nation's history a major political party selected a woman as its candidate for vice-president. Even though Geraldine Ferraro and her presidential running mate, Walter Mondale, were defeated in the election, it was evident that new ground had been broken and women would be serious candidates for top positions in the future. The slow pace of American political progress in this respect, however, must have seemed strange to observers in countries such as Great Britain, where Margaret Thatcher had proved to be an unusually strong prime minister.

Major decisions by the Supreme Court also gave new recognition to women's rights. In one ruling in January 1987, the court held by a 6-3 majority that a state can provide special job protection for workers temporarily disabled by pregnancy.[26] The decision had far-reaching significance, since some 65 percent of women of childbearing age are in the work force; and it is estimated that 90 percent of them have had or will have children during their careers.[27] Women, however, were not unanimous as to whether the decision would be to their benefit in the long run.[28]

A second landmark decision was made by the Supreme Court a few months later when it upheld an affirmative action decision in a Santa Clara County, California, transportation agency. The agency in 1980 had no women in the 238 skilled positions among its employees. The case had involved a decision to promote a woman from a road crew to a desk job as a dispatcher, even though a male applicant had seniority and a slightly higher score on a qualification examination. The court's action was hailed by advocates of affirmative action and deplored by opponents, but it had underscored the validity of such voluntary affirmative action programs.[29] The fact was, however, that a dismaying disparity still existed generally in such areas as salary, where women's wages averaged only sixty-eight cents for every dollar earned by men.[30]

The Bubbling Cauldron of Religion

The religious climate within which the new Lutheran church was taking shape was as turbulent as any since the sixties. Most dramatic was the rising power of militant Islamic fundamentalism. When Iran fell under the control of the Ayatollah Ruholla Khomeini, it not only brought to the surface a basic conflict between the strict Shi'ite and the more moderate Sunni form of Islam, but also unleashed on the world a virulent kind of religious crusade that it had not known for centuries. Western society, which had taken Islam a bit lightly in recent years, was awakening belatedly to the numerical strength and zeal of the followers of the Prophet who not only dominated the Middle East, but counted large numbers in places as far-flung as Indonesia, Pakistan, Nigeria, and the Soviet Union.[31]

The new fervor touched every Islamic nation, brought riots to the sacred city of Mecca in Saudi Arabia, and incited fresh tensions in a dozen countries. In the words of one journalist, "As a result, leaders of every Islamic country but Iran, and especially those in the Middle East and North Africa, are more vulnerable than ever. . . . At a time when Marxism is so debilitated it is being shored up by capitalism, when Christianity lacks much of the missionary fire that once drove it, when Maoism is all but entombed with its founder and when democracy sounds a muted appeal to much of the world, Islamic fundamentalism stands out as the movement on the march."[32] Whether one agrees with this assessment or not, Islamic fundamentalism has rocked the political scene in a fashion not caused by any religion in recent times.[33]

On the Home Front. The prospects for mainline Christianity in North America were almost as muddled. Cults were once again on the rise. Conservative evangelicals were fighting what they regarded as "secular humanism" being taught in the public schools.[34] Television evangelists had large and lucrative followings. The scandals involving some of their number not only had an impact on the ministry of other television preachers but also spilled over to cause questioning among those tangentially related to the major church bodies. The press had a field day in reporting on the funds garnered by the television evangelists and the kinds of uses that were made of the receipts.[35]

One highly important indicator of religious attitudes was the second visit that Pope John Paul II made to the United States in September 1987. Although he still drew huge crowds almost everywhere he went, the open questioning of rigid Roman Catholic doctrines was much more prevalent than it had been on his previous visit in 1979. Various polls revealed that many Catholics believed they could be faithful church members and still disagree with the pope on such matters as birth control, abortion, allowing priests to marry, ordination of women, and the right of divorced persons to remarry.[36] What is more, the church that the pope encountered in the United States was characterized not only by articulate and questioning laity but also by an increasingly different ethnic balance. It was estimated that two out of every five Catholics were now Hispanic, and by the turn of the century, Hispanics would make up half of the membership.[37] Some saw this influx of Hispanics into the United States as having the potential for a new lease on life for Roman Catholicism.

CHURCH AND SOCIETY

During its last five years of existence, the interest of the LCA in social concerns did not abate, but the church did find itself subject to intense pressure from various groups with special interests or special needs. Although DMNA prepared only one social statement during this period, it was engaged in other types of studies that resulted in guidelines or background information on major issues for the church.

Peace and Politics

The sixteenth and last social statement of the LCA was one on "Peace and Politics." It had been mandated by the 1982 convention but was built upon several other statements adopted by the church through the years.[38] Obviously, the LCA and its predecessor bodies had not been silent on the complex issue of peace, but the world tensions of the eighties dictated a fresh look at the problem.

Interestingly, the path that the LCA followed in forging this final statement was anything but peaceful. The preliminary draft of the statement, prepared by a special study commission, was discussed by thousands of persons in congregational study groups that often reported sharp debate.[39] There were also hundreds of responses from individuals who registered strong and even acrimonious comments. When the delegates arrived at Toronto, they were prepared to offer dozens of amendments to the revised draft before finally adopting the document by an overwhelming majority.[40] Thirty-five delegates felt strongly enough about the issue, however, that they asked that their negative votes be entered in the minutes.

The resulting document began by explaining that the occasion which made the statement necessary was the proliferation of nuclear weapons not only by the United States and the Soviet Union but also by other nations. It pointed out that the potential for these weapons to fall into the hands of unstable regimes or terrorist groups was a threat to the whole human family. A groundwork of "Theological Affirmations" was laid that emphasized that "God created and still preserves the world for peace with God and with itself." Peace with God, however, is a gift that is not of this world, which the world can neither give nor take away. "Yet those to whom it is given are sent into the world (John 20:21; Matt. 28:19–20), not removed from it (John 17:5)." Sin is seen as the root of war and estrangement among peoples. The Creator, however, is present in the political work of peace. The church's proclamation of the Word of God makes clear that all are sinners and that no nation enjoys a special righteousness. "Our theology of the cross of Christ forbids illusions regarding the possibility of establishing permanent peace and a perfect society in this age."

The statement then moves on to judgments and tasks. It rejects nuclear war as contrary to God's gracious will for the creation. It regards as both imprudent and dangerous the nuclear arms race and the illusion that a nation can isolate itself behind walls of military might. It condemns the use of resources needed for economic growth and political justice at home and abroad in order to continue and escalate the arms race.

Where the statement becomes most controversial is in its discussion of the concept of nuclear arms as a deterrent to nuclear war itself. "For deterrence to succeed in preventing the catastrophe of nuclear war, there must be a credible threat to use nuclear weapons in retaliation for aggression. It is the conviction of this statement that such actual use of nuclear weapons would, even in retaliation, constitute mass murder. What it would be wrong actually to do, it is also wrong to intend or threaten. Yet insofar as aggression (one's own as well as the other's) is restrained by the possession of nuclear weapons (which includes the threat to use them in retaliation), nuclear deterrence remains at the present time as the lesser of evils. Yet evil it is and remains."

The document goes on to call for arms control agreements that are "substantial, equitable, verifiable, and progressive." It urges that peacekeeping must be seen within the context of peacebuilding, which is a political task that refers to a wide range of positive measures. For Christians, peacemaking is the love of enemies and reconciliation of the estranged. While Christians claim no superior knowledge and "no zone of purity for themselves," they bring to the common task of peace "the love of enemies that is their gift in Christ." The statement is followed by eleven enabling resolutions (some of which have as many as seven subpoints) that set a detailed course of study, action, and cooperation with other communions and persons who respond to the call to work for peace. The statement itself had generated so much debate that DMNA staff promptly issued a commentary to explicate further the rationale and intent of the document.[41]

Study of Homosexuality

One of the most controversial sets of issues that confronted the LCA in these years related to homosexuality. The questions were not new. In fact, there had been numerous memorials from synods through the years asking for a variety of studies dealing with homosexuality.[42] There were two things, however, that brought matters to a head in

1982. One was a memorial from the New Jersey Synod asking for guidance, consistent with the church's earlier statement on "Sex, Marriage, and Family" (1970), that would "challenge, support and assist congregations in ministry to and with homosexual persons."[43] The second was a question that had arisen in the Minnesota Synod regarding ordination of persons who live in homosexual relationships.[44]

Since both of these questions came ultimately to the Executive Council for decision, that body explored a number of options and amended its course of action several times. An inquiry as to whether the ALC and AELC with whom the LCA was now engaged in planning for a new church would be interested in a joint study showed that ALC was not, and that although AELC initially looked with some favor on the possibility, it later indicated informally that it did not wish to pursue the matter.[45] DMNA indicated that it was prepared to undertake a general study of homosexuality but that to do so would require an investment of some $153,000, including staff time.[46] The Executive Council Committee on Budget and Finance did not favor this expenditure, since it would use 76 percent of the remaining funds in the LCA Undesignated Fund at a time when the church had presented to the Conference of Synodical Bishops the crisis in meeting the regular budget needs of the LCA.[47] After considerable debate, the Executive Council voted to ask the DMNA to proceed with a study that would be both "comprehensive" and "participatory."[48]

The study undertaken by DMNA was interdisciplinary and did not intend to present a new social statement to the convention.[49] An advisory committee with a wide background of competencies was used, and four regional conferences were held where opportunity was provided to listen to the views of gay and lesbian persons. The resulting report submitted by the DMNA Management Committee to the Executive Council was massive and covered such topics as the theological grounding; human sexuality; biological basis and psychological perspectives; ethical considerations; pastoral strategies; an annotated bibliography; and a series of background papers ranging from an analysis of Old Testament and New Testament passages often cited as dealing with homosexuality to the relatively new problem of AIDS.[50]

The Executive Council received the report and commended it for use "as a means of encouraging dialogue and assisting in shaping informed ministries." All in all, the Executive Council adopted fifteen actions that included forwarding the report to the presiding bishops of ALC and AELC as well as the Transition Team for a new Lutheran church with the request that it be considered by the new Conference of Bishops and a convocation of theologians under the aegis of the Division for Ministry.[51] While the final report was not intended to give answers, it provided a well-informed and sensitive analysis of an extremely complex set of concerns.[52]

Celebrating Inclusiveness and Diversity

When the delegates gathered in Toronto for the twelfth biennial convention in 1984, it was a time to mark 250 years of inclusive ministry by the Lutheran church in the Virgin Islands and the twentieth anniversary of the LCA's pivotal social statement on "Race Relations." It was not only a vastly different world for racial and ethnic groups from the eighteenth century but also a changed climate from the sixties. The spark that ignited the sixties was the Black revolution, as this segment of society struggled for civil rights and for justice within the church. As Massie Kennard, director of the Office for Minority Concerns, told the delegates, "We have indeed progressed, both as a nation and a church, over the past twenty years. But we are nowhere near the end of the trail."[53]

As the church looked back on what had and had not been accomplished since the 1978 convention adopted *Goals and Plans for Minority Ministry,* it was clear that Dr. Kennard's remarks were telling and accurate. The time frame for the original goals had been from 1978 through 1984. The final report presented at Toronto, along with a more detailed accounting of the previous biennium, showed that some of the original objectives had been reached or surpassed but that there were other areas where the LCA had fallen far short of expectations.[54]

The next step the church was challenged to take was to adopt a document *Inclusiveness and Diversity: Gifts of God* that included a series of declarations and commitments covering the remaining years of the LCA's life.[55] Although the statement stressed the continuing sin of racism in the church, it began on a different note, "As a gift of God and by the power of the Holy Spirit, the church includes persons from every race, culture, national origin, and economic class." It viewed this diversity as a source of strength that enriches us. "We are called not to diminish our differences but to share them lovingly with one another."

All members, whatever their background, were called upon to implement not only the law but also the spirit of the declaration. It then spelled out the intentions of the LCA in eight important areas with thirteen specific goals.[56] Although some of the goals would stretch the church's willingness and capacity to perform, only one met with serious resistance on the convention floor. This was a commitment that all churchwide agencies and the Executive Council would include in their goals the intention to appoint at least 20 percent American/Canadian Indian, Asian, Black, and·Hispanic persons on each committee and in each representative appointment made. Efforts to amend what some termed "quotas" were defeated, and the whole document was approved.[57] In adopting *Inclusiveness and Diversity: Gifts of God,* the LCA had not diluted its commitments but had set them within a new and more positive context for the future.[58]

The LCA, of course, did not limit itself to setting goals and monitoring its own performance in racial and ethnic matters. It continued the struggle against apartheid in South Africa and for justice in Namibia through shareholder actions in dozens of corporations and by developing a churchwide network of agencies working for corporate social responsibility.[59] The effort to gain reparations for the thousands of Japanese Americans interned during World War II was pursued through every avenue.[60] The struggle continued to support the treaty rights of American Indians, and grants to assist directly such needs as hunger, health, and rehabilitation programs among Native Americans were made annually through the National Indian Lutheran Board.[61] LCUSA's Department of Immigration and Refugee Services carried on resettlement programs that cared for thousands of persons, 75 percent of whom flooded into the United States from Indochina during the previous decade.[62]

Women in Church and Society

More and more in the final years of the LCA's existence there was a close working relationship between the Consulting Committee on Women in Church and Society and the Consulting Committee on Minority Group Interests. So often it seemed that women in minority groups were the ones who suffered most from poverty and related problems. During 1983 and 1984, DMNA held two Listening to

People conferences dealing with "Women, Work, and the Feminiza-
tion of Poverty" and "Women in Appalachia: Image and Reality,"
which dealt with such needs as those of single parents, women working outside of the home, lack of recognition for women who work
without pay inside the home, health and welfare of women without
adequate financial support, and the special problems of women in
the Appalachian region.[63]

During the last two biennia of the LCA, the CCWCS focused its
attention on five basic areas: women in the new church, women
employed in the church, women and work, women and public policy, and domestic violence.[64] In these areas, the committee worked
closely with the Office for Government Affairs in Washington, Lutheran Church Women, and the newly formed Public Policy Network. The CCWCS delved more deeply into basic research of
subjects such as domestic violence and was instrumental in the development of a publication on battered women.[65] As the formation of
the new Lutheran church approached, it was apparent that the role
and concerns of women had changed dramatically in the quarter
century since the beginning of the LCA in 1962.

ONE IN MISSION

The action of the 1982 convention calling for a feasibility study for
a capital funds appeal that it was hoped could be undertaken jointly
with ALC and AELC resulted in a complex set of negotiations before
a final decision could be reached. There already were several other
proposals and factors in the mix that needed to be explored. The ALC
Church Council had taken an action in May 1982 inviting the other
two bodies to undertake a joint appeal for college and university
endowments.[66] The LCA seminary presidents and deans early in
1982 had asked the DPL Management Committee to propose to the
convention a churchwide appeal for theological education. Bishop
Herbert W. Chilstrom of the Minnesota Synod had written to Bishop
Crumley regarding an appeal for higher education, particularly for
aid to students. Many LCA synods, having deferred their own causes
for the Strength for Mission Appeal, were either engaged in or had
scheduled these programs on their own territories.

Finally, agreement was reached with the ALC and AELC that a
joint feasibility study be commissioned through a professional counseling service to test possible purposes for an appeal, some of which

would be common to all three churches while others might be undertaken by one or two.[67] Other questions were to be studied, including
possible dollar goals, whether the appeal could be done jointly, and
the time frame. Approximately five thousand members of the three
churches were asked to respond. After reviewing the findings, the
LCA committee members concluded that "there is a sufficient commitment to and understanding of the mission needs of the church to
support a nation-wide appeal in the Lutheran Church in America
prior to the formation of a new church."[68] The LCA respondents
indicated by an 82 percent figure that they were in favor of including
the Church Property Fund as a goal; 81 percent favored inclusion of
a theological education fund; fewer wanted a transition fund; and a
higher education endowment fund ranked lowest.[69]

The recommendation that was presented by the Executive Council to the Toronto convention proposed essentially that there be a
joint campaign with the ALC and AELC. The LCA goal was to be
$60 million broken down as follows: $30 million for Church Extension (acquisition of property and assisting congregations in constructing facilities); $20 million for Theological Education, three-fourths of
which was to go to seminaries for endowment and one-fourth for an
endowment fund for internships and student aid; $6 million as a
"birth gift" to begin the ministry of the new church; and $4 million
to be given to the church-related colleges for endowment of scholarships.[70]

Debate on the proposal stretched over three sessions and involved
a long series of motions that left the final form of the recommendation quite different from the original. After having been assured by
Kenneth Senft, executive of DMNA, that "church extension" really
referred to "what is normally included in the church property fund,"
some of the misgivings were erased.[71] Others about timing, conflict
with synodical appeals, and the problem of setting a precedent of the
church-at-large funding synodical institutions persisted.[72] Finally, by
a vote of 412 to 189, the One in Mission Appeal was approved. The
major changes involved dividing the appeal into two levels. Level I
provided for an allocation of $30 million for church extension and $6
million for the new church's "birth gift." Level II was intended to
"be designated as endowment for theological education and higher
education and that level II receipts of the appeal be received and
administered regionally by the synod(s) supporting their respective
colleges and seminaries."[73] The design of the appeal, which in many

cases included timing, was to be worked out with the synods and approved by the Executive Council. Other implementing clauses included going it alone if the other two churches did not vote for a joint effort.[74]

The whole process proved intricate, but the LLM Fund Raising Service was chosen as the prime contractor for the appeal, and the Rev. Richard Peterman, who had a long track record in resource development with OAF and its predecessor, was appointed director.[75] A major gifts program was launched before the congregational and individual pledging phase. Although it was very successful, it did eliminate the major gifts program of the regular benevolence effort that had generated over $1 million in its first full year of operation.[76] By July 1987 the churchwide goal of $36 million in pledges had been reached, and when additional gifts for synodical causes were added the total had passed $51 million.[77] It seemed that the new church would have its "birth gift," the property fund a much needed infusion, and both seminaries and higher education some additional resources.

MISSION IN NORTH AMERICA

During the final five years of the LCA's life, DMNA[78] had set a goal of developing from 120–200 new congregations, including 16–30 in minority communities and 16–30 in slow growth/pioneer areas.[79] The dilemma faced by the church was that it would have been easier to show rapid progress by going only into fast-growing areas to develop new congregations, but to do so would have been a contradiction of the LCA's own commitment to inclusiveness. As DMNA explained repeatedly, it was more expensive to be faithful to the concept that the gospel was for all than to make numbers the only criterion.[80]

Recognizing that there was a potential for entering sixty new fields per year and that a merged church was in the offing, LCA began in 1983 to share with ALC opportunities for new ministries in communities that it had already investigated.[81] By 1985 DMNA and DSMA, its ALC counterpart, were working jointly on choosing places for congregational development to insure that there was no overlapping and that the combined efforts of the two churches were used most effectively.[82] In addition, ALC pastor/developers originally attended LCA training events, but by 1984 this had become a joint project. By

1986 almost forty area strategies were under study or had been implemented. Frequently, these resulted in coalitions where AELC, LCA, and ALC congregations and social ministry agencies and institutions worked cooperatively on ministry.[83]

An encouraging sign in the mid-eighties was that more and more congregations that had been receiving program support were becoming self-supporting. Between 1979 and 1985, for example, there were 227, or 41 percent, fewer metropolitan/suburban congregations that needed such assistance. It still required about a million dollars a year, however, to support ministries such as those in areas with high unemployment, congregations serving military installations, and places where opportunities outstripped the parish's capacity to respond.[84]

The situation was also changing in the town and country arena, where some congregations were located in economically depressed agricultural areas while others were experiencing an influx of retirees who altered the makeup of the community. During 1984–85 almost 150 congregations in such areas needed assistance from DMNA, but thirty-two had become self-reliant. Urban ministries continued to be a high priority for the LCA, as had been the case for over twenty years, but this scene was changing also. There was an increasing need for persons who could work in multicultural and multilingual situations. The process of reentry of the affluent into some inner cities often resulted in economic dislocation and even homelessness for the previous residents. These were just a few of the wide range of demands placed on congregations that required some $1,350,000 in support from DMNA each year to carry on effective ministry.[85]

New Tests for the Colleges

Demographic trends in the United States were creating an increasing problem for LCA's colleges. Population analyses showed that between 1978 and 1992 there would be a 28 percent decrease in the number of eighteen-year-olds. During the decade from 1974 through 1984, the enrollment at LCA institutions had climbed steadily upward, with the exception of two academic years.[86] By 1985–86, however, there was a drop of 2.8 percent, with the most ominous sign being a 6.1 percent decline in the numbers of freshmen.[87] One encouraging sign, however, was that during the period from 1977–78 through 1984–85 the number of persons of color and primary language other than English had increased from 5 percent to 7.9 percent.

LCA colleges and universities were no exception to the general rule that education was expensive at private institutions of higher education. The costs of tuition, room, and board at the church's college averaged $8,845 in 1985–86. Some 77 percent of the students, however, were receiving aid in financing their education. In fact, the LCA institutions made available approximately $85 million in such assistance during 1984–85. Of that amount, $28 million came from the colleges themselves.[88] Synodical support of colleges, after bottoming out in 1979 at $2.4 million, was expected to top $3 million. In addition, DMNA granted around $210,000 in various kinds of direct support for college programs. The biggest investment by the church-at-large, however, was in support of National Lutheran Campus Ministry's extensive work with Lutheran students at non-Lutheran schools, which was budgeted at $1,027,000 in 1986.[89] There was no question that the LCA throughout its life had taken higher education seriously and had carried on a Lutheran tradition that began with the founding of Gettysburg College in 1832.

FORGING A FUTURE FOR
WORLD MISSION

Nearly a century and a half has passed since the Central Missionary Society of the Pennsylvania Ministerium decided in 1841 that it was time for North American Lutherans to begin sending their own missionaries to other lands. Celebrated as the pioneer work of John Christian Frederick Heyer was in India, however, it had signaled a change from the more "ecumenical efforts" in which Lutherans had engaged earlier in the nineteenth century.[90] By the beginning of the 1980s, the world mission enterprise of the Lutheran Church in America had come almost full circle to the position that "DWME should not seek to plant the Lutheran church in new areas of the world."[91] The view was that instead of starting new Lutheran churches, the LCA should cooperate with Christian groups already operating in an area. "The principle, however, was modified by the management committee at its meeting, November 8–10, 1983. . . . The action was: 'That whereas interchurch cooperation is to be encouraged in all areas, the DWME recognizes that whether it should be inter-Lutheran or interconfessional or both will be conditioned by specific situations.' "[92]

Rather than veering away from an ecumenical stance, the DWME was actually being consistent with its statements in *A Call to Global Mission* and *Ecumenism: A Lutheran Commitment*.[93] In some instances, DWME discovered through experience that the best way of proceeding was to work in support of other churches or ecumenical agencies as it had in such places as Egypt, Ghana, and Trinidad. In Peru, however, it discovered, after a period of unsuccessful efforts to work cooperatively with an existing Lutheran congregation of European origin, that the most responsible course was for the LCA to begin a new, and in a sense pioneer, mission on its own.[94] Proceeding on this case-by-case basis acknowledged the reality that "in some situations, the LCA can become a catalyst for a more holistic witness. In others, however, the existing churches may be so rigid in their positions that cooperation would require the LCA to suppress essential facets of its witness. In still others, the situation may be so murky both theologically and in practice that the Lutheran understanding of the gospel needs to be proclaimed with special clarity."[95]

Exploring the Evangelism Frontier

When DWME proposed its *Call to Global Mission* in 1982, it set forth seven nongeographic frontiers that should guide the mission thrust of the future. The first of these was evangelism, and the division gave priority to an in-depth exploration of this term that had been so widely used and yet provoked so much disagreement among Christians. To address the problem, DWME brought together nearly eighty persons from all over the world in a major consultation at Jacksonville Beach, Florida, late in 1983.[96] In addition to dealing with mission and evangelism in theological perspective, the conference divided into work groups that related evangelism to the other frontiers that had been described in the *Call to Global Mission*.[97]

Although the consultation concluded that the church's mission in the world was unthinkable without evangelistic outreach, evangelism was more specific and limited than the total mission. A working definition developed was, "Evangelism is the specific activity of making Christ known by word and deed, especially to those who do not know him, so that all people may have an opportunity to believe in him, to confess him as Lord and Savior, to become his disciples in the fellowship of the church, and to serve him in God's total mission in the world. . . . As mission is the *esse* of the church, so evangelism is the heartbeat of that mission—it expresses what the church considers central in its life."[98] It was hoped that this basic effort would not only result in the development of strategies for the DWME's own work but also provide a global view for those of other churchwide agencies engaged in evangelism.[99] The follow-up steps by DWME were significant and even provided a legacy for the ELCA's Division for Global Mission.[100]

Winding Up Instead of Down

During the final five years of the LCA, the division worked more and more closely with its counterparts in the ALC and AELC in a mutual concern to transmit to the new church as strong and coherent a world mission enterprise as possible. Although proceeding in a teamwork relationship with the other two bodies as well as ecumenical agencies, DWME continued to carry out its own responsibilities in a way that dealt with the shifting, often turbulent, conditions in the areas where it supported mission. It is impossible to provide an exhaustive description here of all that DWME was doing, but a few highlights may give a sense of what was happening.

For eight years the number of "missionary units" had remained fairly stable at around 150 positions.[101] During the final two years, however, that number declined slightly. One reason was that five positions were transferred to the new Evangelical Lutheran Church in Canada.[102] Nevertheless, DWME estimated that it would enter the ELCA with 140 positions, or about 235 overseas missionaries.[103] New ground was broken during the 1983–84 biennium when the first two ordained women missionaries in the history of the LCA and its predecessors were sent overseas. The Rev. Margaret Kreller, a Canadian, was sent to Ecuador and the Rev. Leesa Jacobson, an American, to Uruguay.[104]

Africa continued to be the most fertile field for growth, with the expectation that it would have the largest Christian population of any continent by the end of the century. This amazing story unfolded despite wars, economic chaos in some countries, severe persecution, and widespread hunger and disease. Ethiopia was a prime example of continued growth of the church despite government seizure of property, imprisonment of leaders, and the terrible effects of mass starvation. Millions of dollars of LCA world hunger funds were poured into Ethiopia and other parts of Africa through Lutheran World Relief and LWF.[105] The struggle for independence for Namibia went on with strong support from the LCA and other Lutheran churches around the world.[106] Special efforts went into assisting the development of women, who traditionally have borne the heaviest burdens in Third World countries. For example, DWME has worked together with the Coptic Orthodox Church in Egypt on such development projects.[107]

Other areas of the globe had their own mélange of problems and opportunities. Missionary work in highly prosperous Japan that had been going on since 1892 was under review.[108] New opportunities were arising in the rapidly growing church in China to develop its leadership. A new strategy for Middle East ministry was developed jointly with ALC and AELC to stress reconciliation, witness, service, ecumenism, and relations with people of other faiths in that tension-filled environment.[109] Reassessment was also going on in India, where the church was girding for a new era of self-reliance and service as God's people in the world.[110] The relatively recent phenomenon of the LCA's having a sizable contingent of missionaries in Europe took on new significance not only in ministering to English-speaking people living there but also in dealing with the special needs of the "guest workers" from places like Turkey, who were often virtual outcasts in society.[111] Almost anywhere one looked on the globe, the task of mission was going on unabated, sometimes with a new face and in directions unimagined a decade or so ago.

Will There Be a "Stage Four"?

The history of missions has been described as evolving through three phases that are various combinations of dependence, independence, and interdependence.[112] As DWME worked through the implementation of a *Call to Global Mission,* it seemed that the church might be on the threshold of a new stage. In October 1986 the executive director of DWME, Gerald E. Currens, wrote a seminal paper called *Empowerment for Change: A Strategy for Mission.*[113] As Currens put it, "The elimination of dependence and the recognition of interdependence was, for DWME, *the* issue of the 1970's. This shaped much of what we did as a mission agency. Self-reliance and interdependence provided DWME with a powerful organizing principle, a strategy for engaging in mission."[114]

When the LCA adopted the *Call to Global Mission,* it began to leave behind the spatial imagery of the past and move across new societal frontiers. Whereas the interdependence phase has been somewhat institutional or church-to-church in nature, the shape of the future may well be more oriented to people enabling people to form and implement the goals that they envision as being most appropriate to their own situations. According to this view, "Christians that engage in mission are agents of change. . . . The goal of mission is change that has meaning and direction precisely because it takes place as a response to God's intent for and activity within a world God wills to be changed."[115]

As the division stated in its report to the 1986 convention, "In responding to God's will for his creation it is increasingly obvious that DWME, as the mission arm of the LCA, is committed to purposeful change."[116] Whether the strategy of empowerment of people in working for change is the foreshadowing of a "stage four" in global mission remains to be seen. One thing, however, is obvious. World mission has never been static even when it seemed to be most deeply mired in traditional patterns. World mission will continue to evolve, and at some point there will be a "stage four" and after that . . . ?

ECUMENISM, THE MOVING GLACIER

"The ecumenical movement is a glacier. It moves slowly, but it does move," declared Bishop Herbert W. Chilstrom, newly elected head of the Evangelical Lutheran Church in America, following a meeting of twenty-six Protestant and Orthodox church leaders with Pope John Paul II during the pontiff's visit to the United States and Canada in September 1987.[117] The whole picture of what has happened in this sometimes ponderous development among Christian churches in the twentieth century has resulted in a flood of literature so vast and so complex that it almost defies cataloging, much less detailed analysis.[118]

For North American Lutherans, the ecumenical movement has taken on new significance since World War II. The record is studded with the names of a host of leaders, such as Franklin Clark Fry, Robert J. Marshall, Fredrik A. Schiotz, James R. Crumley, and David W. Preus, who have played prominent roles in the story. By the 1980s the quest for Christian unity, however, seemed to be entering a phase that included not only high-level theological discussions but also a type of personal diplomacy among church leaders and a greater involvement of the whole people of God in local ecumenism.

The Path of Studies and Response

In adopting its statement on ecumenism, the Lutheran Church in America had committed itself to receiving and acting promptly on two types of reports and recommendations: first, those from ecumenical organizations in which it held membership that would affect its external relationships; and second, documents from national and international dialogues.[119] Although the LCA was engaged through various agencies in a large number of such studies in the mid-eighties, there were three that commanded special attention: *Baptism, Eucharist and Ministry;* the Lutheran-Roman Catholic Dialogue; and the Lutheran-Reformed Dialogue.[120] During this period, "reception" was a term that began to take on new and broader significance.

Baptism, Eucharist and Ministry. It is difficult to think of any ecumenically conceived document in the twentieth century that has received more widespread study and reaction than the WCC's "Faith and Order Paper No. 111," *Baptism, Eucharist and Ministry.* From the time of the paper's original publication in 1982, those who spoke for the Commission on Faith and Order said, "It is our intention to compare all the official replies received, to publish the results, and to analyze the ecumenical implications for the churches at a future World Conference on Faith and Order."[121] The outcome of this process is awaited as a clue to the degree of convergence in views that has already occurred and the direction that may be taken in the future.

Responses to the questions raised by BEM have come not only from Protestant and Orthodox churches but also the Roman Catholic Church. In addressing an ecumenical conference in Columbia, South Carolina, the day following Pope John Paul II's visit, Johannes Cardinal Willebrands, head of the Vatican's Secretariat for Promoting Christian Unity, indicated that the reply that had just been sent to the Commission on Faith and Order was the first time that the Vatican had responded officially to this kind of WCC document.[122] The cardinal said, "We made an effort to affirm as much of the text as we could, to criticize it when we saw problems, and to raise critical issues that we believe Faith and Order must pursue if progress is to be made." Those problem areas dealt with such matters as "the Church as 'sacrament,' the apostolic tradition, and church authority." It was observed that "behind those words lurk some of the thorniest ecumenical questions."[123]

For the Lutheran Church in America also it was the first time that it had been asked to respond officially at the highest level to an ecumenical document.[124] A careful process was developed to obtain reactions from selected congregations, seminary faculties, the Conference of Bishops, appropriate churchwide agencies, certain college faculty members, and other individuals.[125] "Reception," however, was another matter since that could take years to permeate the faith and life of the church in a meaningful way.[126] The response proposed to the 1984 convention was amended in several significant ways and then approved for forwarding to Faith and Order. Congregations were encouraged to work with the document with ecumenical partners as the process of reception continued.

The final form of the response began with a historical introduction that made specific note of the ecumenical nature of the Lutheran Confessions and particularly the catholic and evangelical character of the Augsburg Confession.[127] It then moved on to affirm BEM as a witness to the Apostolic Faith but stated that there is more to the Tradition than is included in the document. It asked for a strengthening of BEM in terms of four motifs [italics and style are those of the text]:

1. *A stronger articulation of the Word of God and what this means for an understanding of baptism, eucharist and ministry.*

2. *A clearer expression of the dynamic of sin and grace and what this means for baptism, eucharist and ministry.*

3. *The priority of a certain period of history as normative for the faith.* This motif indicated that while Lutherans affirm their sixteenth century confessions, they place primary emphasis on the Gospel as witnessed to in Scripture. The concept of *ecclesia semper reformanda est* should be maintained.

4. *A wider perspective on ministry.* This motif was the most extensive and found BEM lacking at such points as the following: stressing adequately the role of the universal priesthood of all baptized in proclamation of the Gospel; the pastoral sense of the ordained ministry; the importance of the ordination of women; the way in which the interrelatedness of ordained and lay members is expressed. It also makes clear that there is no consensus among Lutherans on questions relating to varying patterns of the *episcopé.*

The response then goes on to answer in great detail the four questions that had been raised to the churches about *Baptism, Eucharist and Ministry* by the Commission on Faith and Order.

Lutheran-Roman Catholic Dialogues. Although it was the seventh in a series of reports that spanned twenty years, *The Common Statement on Justification by Faith* was first of the Lutheran-Roman Catholic Dialogue reports to which the LCA made an official response.[128] Once more a careful study process was set up by the LCA that distinguished between the technical terms "response" and "reception."[129] Although the number of reactions received was rather limited, a report was drafted and sent to the 1986 convention by the Executive Council.[130] After several amendments, the convention adopted the recommendations but also instructed the Executive Council to prepare a memorandum which would identify issues that should be explored in future dialogues. This memorandum was to be sent to the Transition Team for the new church.[131]

The response itself began with a brief description of the background for the common statement and called particular attention to paragraph 4, which dealt with an agreement by the participants on a christological affirmation but indicated that this did not "necessarily involve full agreement between Catholics and Lutherans on justification by faith."[132] The next section of the response is generally appreciative of the statement, although it urges that in the future an effort be made to produce not only scholarly theological material but "texts more conducive to churchwide study and reaction."

Perhaps the most telling criticism deals with the need to define further the claim that there is "fundamental consensus on the gospel." The response states, "We judge there is more agreement on *sola gratia* (see Common Statement, Paragraph 4) than on *sola fide,* and we believe that more work needs to be done on this important matter. A significant issue in this consideration is the contrast between Roman Catholic teachings and practices that affirm transformation in the justified person and the Lutheran teaching that we always live as *simul justus et peccator.* " In view of the fact that this involves historic differences between Roman Catholics and Lutherans, the evaluation concludes that "testing the consensus on the doctrine of justification will reveal the extent to which there is fundamental consensus on the gospel."

The Lutheran-Roman Catholic dialogues in the United States, of course, should not be viewed in isolation from the international dialogue that had been going on between the Lutheran World Federation and the Roman Catholic Church since 1967. The latest document in this series, *Facing Unity—Models, Forms and Phases of*

Catholic-Lutheran Fellowship, was completed in 1984.[133] The response to this document was drafted by a joint committee from ALC and LCA. It was approved by the LCA Executive Council in July 1987.[134] Although generally commendatory of the document and its proposal of concrete steps for moving toward "structured fellowship," the response suggests a number of points where clarification is needed. It concurs, "As the report *Facing Unity* itself recognizes, it is premature to implement its suggestions for a mutual recognition followed by the common exercise of episcopé."

An Invitation to Action. In the 1960s and 1970s representatives of North American Lutheran and Reformed churches had engaged in two series of dialogues with mixed results. The hope was to resolve differences that had separated the two traditions since the Marburg Colloquy in 1529 when Martin Luther sharply disagreed with Huldreich Zwingli about Christ's Real Presence in the Eucharist. In 1983 participants in a third round of dialogues completed a report, *An Invitation to Action,* that called upon the member churches of LCUSA and the North American Area of the World Alliance of Reformed Churches to "recognize one another as churches in which the gospel is proclaimed and the sacraments administered according to the ordinance of Christ."[135] In addition, the churches were being asked to recognize one another's ordained ministries and one another's celebrations of the Lord's Supper as a means of grace in which Christ grants communion with himself.[136] The 1984 LCA convention proposed an extensive study process and to seek to develop, together with AELC and ALC, a common response for action in 1986.[137]

An AELC/ALC/LCA Committee on Reception of Ecumenical Documents was formed, which set up a joint study process and looked forward to preparing "identical recommendations" for the simultaneous meetings of the three churches in 1986.[138] As work proceeded, however, divergent views began to arise in various quarters, both on theological grounds and in terms of "ecumenical strategy."[139] On January 7, 1986, ALC Bishop David Preus proposed in a lecture at Luther Northwestern Seminary that "U.S. Lutherans enter into altar and pulpit fellowship with the Presbyterian Church (USA), the Reformed Church in America and the Cumberland Presbyterian Church."[140] He went on to indicate that if the ALC Church Council concurred, the ALC convention would be asked to declare fellowship with the Reformed bodies.

What eventually emerged from all the ensuing debate were similar proposals in AELC, ALC, and LCA to recognize the Presbyterian Church (USA) and the Reformed Church in America "as churches in which the Gospel is proclaimed and the sacraments administered according to the ordinance of Christ" and to "recognize as both valid and effective [their] ordained ministries which announce the Gospel of Christ and administer the sacraments of faith as their chief responsibility."[141] AELC and ALC also voted to allow for "sharing of pastors between [the two] traditions" and "occasional joint services" of Communion.[142]

The proposal that the Executive Council brought to the LCA convention was more cautious when it came to Holy Communion.[143] It extended "a special welcome" to members of these Reformed churches to receive Holy Communion in LCA congregations in accordance with the Statement on Communion Practices and encouraged LCA members to do likewise when invited in a Reformed church. The convention also adopted an amendment that would provide "for occasional services of the Lord's Supper where appropriate and desirable, and in accord with the disciplines of our several churches."[144] A "Commentary" on the convention response authorized by the Executive Council explained that "these occasional services are not to be confused with the joint services provided by the Lutheran-Episcopal Agreement. These occasional services are either a Lutheran service of communion presided over only by Lutheran clergy or a Reformed service of communion presided over by Reformed clergy."[145]

Meanwhile, the Commission for a New Lutheran Church had gotten into the act and proposed that the conversations take place involving the ELCA, the Presbyterian Church (USA), and the Reformed Church in America to provide for a study of Lutheran-Reformed relations and that recommendations be voted on at the first regular convention of the new church.[146] This procedure was approved at the constituting convention.

The whole series of events was interpreted in widely different ways. Some saw the various moves and countermoves primarily as ecclesiastical politics at work. Others believed it was a tug-of-war between those who put relations with the "sacramental" churches, notably those in the Anglican, Orthodox, and Roman Catholic traditions, ahead of relations with other Protestants, and those who did not. Still others felt it was a process of addressing anew the genuine theological issues of Reformation times. In any event, it was clear that the LCA was fully in accord with the goal of pursuing closer relationships with the Reformed but was not ready to move as swiftly as its other partners that formed the ELCA.

The Person-to-Person Factor in Ecumenism

Representatives of the LCA and its predecessor bodies had been deeply involved at almost every level in inter-Lutheran agencies such as the National Lutheran Council, LCUSA, and the Lutheran World Federation, and ecumenical bodies such as the National Council of Churches and the World Council of Churches, from their inception. Major assemblies of the Lutheran World Federation and the World Council of Churches deepened the sense of being part of living, witnessing communities that were global in their scope. For those who participated in the WCC Assembly in Vancouver, British Columbia, in 1983, there were dramatic opportunities to struggle together with Christians who faced oppression and suffering daily in their homelands, and then to experience oneness in Christ with them in ecumenical worship.[147] When the LWF Assembly was held in Budapest, Hungary, in 1984, it was the first time the meeting had taken place in a socialist country in Eastern Europe; it marked the end of the term of Josiah M. Kibira, the first Black African president of the Federation; it was the first time a president was elected from an Eastern bloc country; and it was the first time that churches had been suspended from membership.[148]

In the years following the adoption of the statement *Ecumenism: A Lutheran Commitment,* however, a new kind of person-to-person and church-to-church ecumenical contact began to emerge. Taking his cue from the thrust of this statement, Bishop Crumley began a series of ecumenical visits to heads of major world church families in an effort to open doors and strengthen relationships. These trips took him several times to the Vatican to meet with Pope John Paul II and included visits to the Ecumenical Patriarchate in Istanbul, the Archbishop of Canterbury, the Patriarchate of Antioch, the Patriarchate of Jerusalem, the Patriarchate of Moscow, the Patriarchate of Alexandria, and the Orthodox Coptic Church.[149] Although Bishop Crumley and those who accompanied him were always received with great cordiality, the results ranged from the most preliminary of contacts to genuine advances in mutual understanding.[150]

Among the most productive were the visits to the Vatican, which

Bishop Crumley and the Ecumenical Patriarch, Demetrios I (Istanbul)

Bishop Crumley and Pope John Paul II

led to an exchange of letters between the pope and Bishop Crumley and a visit by Johannes Cardinal Willebrands, President of the Secretariat for Promoting Christian Unity, to the 1984 LCA convention.[151] As part of a special ecumenical event, Cardinal Willebrands addressed the convention in great detail regarding the current status of the ecumenical movement. He described, in relation to such documents as those produced by the Lutheran-Catholic dialogues in the United States, the lengthy and complex process of reception with the Roman Catholic Church. He did not avoid reference to obstacles that still lay in the path of full rapprochement between Lutherans and Catholics. "Even though it is not yet possible for us to celebrate the holy eucharist at the same table," he said, "our joint prayer is yet possible and necessary."[152] Both the cardinal and his carefully worded lecture were received warmly by the delegates, although most realized that there was still a long road to be traveled if there was ever to be hope or unity between Roman Catholics and Lutherans.

Another landmark was reached at the 1986 convention in Milwaukee when Robert A. K. Runcie, Archbishop of Canterbury, not

Archbishop of Canterbury,
Robert A. K. Runcie

only participated in the opening Communion services and received the consecrated elements from Bishop Crumley. He also gave the bread and wine to the LCA leader. At the special ecumenical event the next evening, Archbishop Runcie delivered the main address and, as he put it, tried "to express . . . the close Anglican-Lutheran ties" since the Reformation.[153] Of course, he pointed out in a lighter vein that the first interaction between an Archbishop of Canterbury and Lutheran theology was in 1521 during an elaborate ceremony outside Old St. Paul's Cathedral. "There was an inordinately long sermon on the theological opinions of Dr. Martin Luther delivered by the Bishop of Rochester, England," he said. "Then my predecessor, Archbishop William Wareham, sitting under a canopy of gold with the Papal Legate Cardinal Wolsey, solemnly lit a bonfire of all the confiscated books of Martin Luther which could be found."[154]

In his address, Archbishop Runcie observed that "in spite of the differences about episcopacy we have never denied one another the name Church. We have never denied the reality of each other's ministry of Word and Sacrament. Anglicans have never officially declared that the Church cannot exist without the episcopal order—even if we have always insisted on its necessity for unity." He did point out the danger of becoming "so engrossed as ecumenical Christians in our historical and theological arguments that we fail to remember why Our Lord prayed for the unity of his disciples at the Last Supper: 'Father may they all be one; that the world may believe.' An energy absorbing ecclesiastical ecumenism may distract us from the wider ecumenism to which Church unity should be a sign and pointer. . . . Our ecumenism must never lose sight of the goal of the *oikumene*—the original meaning of which is the unity of the whole inhabited earth." His carefully nuanced message was greeted with a standing ovation.

CONGREGATIONAL LIFE ON THE THRESHOLD
OF THE FUTURE

Although what happens on the churchwide scene often commands the headlines, it is in the lives of the people in their congregations that many feel the real story of the church takes shape. It seems obvious that the health of the whole church is intimately tied to the health of congregations spread across the face of a continent who are seeking to carry on their ministry in a bewildering variety of situations. During the final years of the LCA's existence, several studies were done that shed light on what could be learned about its congregations that would not only inform the church's current planning but also provide helpful data for the ELCA in the future.

The Baby-Boomers. One was a research project designed to learn more about the "baby-boomers," the cohort of the population born following World War II who many sociologists assumed had been irretrievably lost to the church during the chaos of the late sixties and seventies.[155] The study showed that this group, which actually comprises about 31 percent of the LCA membership, were deeply interested in religion, but that "denominational pedigree, rightness of doctrine and constancy in piety" were less important than a friendly atmosphere and a "sense of being wanted" as reasons for their being drawn to a congregation.[156]

They were a much more diverse group than their parents, including not only couples but also many varieties of singles. Their pastors characterized them as eager to grow, ready for involvement, open to new ideas, enthusiastic, energetic, capable of leadership, possessing skills needed by the church, and concerned about the Christian nurture of children. At the same time, many had nontraditional life-styles, were overextended financially, lacked follow-through on responsibilities, and were highly mobile.[157] Nevertheless, the baby-boomers provided both new challenges and new potential strengths for congregations.[158]

Congregations in Transition. A surprising response to a simple question on the congregational report form showed that about 20 percent of the parishes in the LCA believed themselves to be located in communities that were changing either racially or economically. This discovery prompted a broad survey and a series of in-depth case studies to learn how congregations were coping with transition in their communities.[159] Among the key findings were the importance of pastoral leadership and the way in which worship life is related to the culture of the community. The study also underscored the importance of a congregation's understanding its community and working closely with agencies committed to serving the area's needs. A practical product of the work is to be a publication, *Congregations in a Place of Transition,* that will be a resource for the new church.

Ministry in Daily Life. During the last few years of the LCA's life, there was a marked upswing of interest in the way a Christian carried out his or her ministry in the normal arenas of everyday life. It was sparked, in part, by the efforts of a special Task Force on the Ministry of the Laity appointed in 1985 by Bishop Crumley, and the work of groups such as LAOS in Ministry.[160] As an aspect of this total concern, DPS conducted a series of case studies of congregations that were regarded as having particularly effective emphases on ministry of the laity.[161] The research showed that most of the members of these congregations felt that they were carrying out a ministry in their daily lives, although they found it difficult to describe theologically or to articulate in specific terms. It was a hope of the Division for Parish Services that its new program, *Connections: Faith and World,* would assist in this educational process.[162]

Parish Program Profiles. Beginning in 1984 the DPS Research and Studies Department conducted a series of studies that sought to identify factors contributing to effectiveness in each program area of parish life. One revealing fact was that worship attendance seems to be the key barometer of congregational health.[163] A high level of worship attendance was frequently related to such factors as congregational climate, personality of the pastor, and quality of preaching. In addition, it was found that effectiveness in the other program areas of outreach, stewardship, youth ministry, educational ministry, and service tends to correlate with vitality in worship. It also confirmed the holistic concept of parish life that is based on the view that all of the programmatic aspects of a congregation should be interrelated and not dealt with in isolation from one another.

Although persons normally find the support for their own lives as Christians within the community of the parish, healthy congregations do not dwell in isolation from the church as a whole. The fifteen years of the existence of the Division for Parish Services have shown that what the church-at-large does has an impact on the congregation in either a positive or negative but seldom a completely neutral way. For this reason, it is useful to scan a few major happenings as DPS sought to deal with needs and issues during its final five years.

Worship

Perhaps nothing was more widely debated during this period than the use of gender-neutral language in worship. The question came to a head with the publication of the NCCCUSA's *Inclusive Language Lectionary: Readings for Year A.* The reaction to the translation itself and the DPS Management Committee's recommendations regarding it tended for many to overshadow other significant projects: the introduction of the *Occasional Services* book; completion of *Liturgia Luterana,* the Hispanic version of *LBW* liturgical materials; testing of a common series of lectionary texts for Lutherans, Roman Catholics, Episcopalians, and other Protestant churches, prepared by the Consultation on Common Texts; an inter-Lutheran Festival of Worship and Witness that brought more than 3,500 persons to Minneapolis-St. Paul in 1983; publication of *Selected Hymns for Singing in Harmony* that supplied familiar settings and tunes to *LBW* hymns; preparation of *Songs of the People,* a collection of hymns reflecting various ethnic and cultural traditions; work on a series of Spanish hymn companions to *Liturgia Luterana;* and a host of other projects.[164]

As the time approached for publication of the NCC inclusive language lectionary translation and its use beginning in Advent 1983, Bishop Crumley asked six LCA biblical scholars to review the manuscript for Series A and advise him regarding its suitability.[165] On October 1, 1983, Bishop Crumley met with the DPS Management Committee to discuss a possible response regarding the document. Two LCA seminary biblical scholars—a man and a woman—were present to share in the discussion. Following a full day of debate, the management committee adopted a minute that reaffirmed its commitment "to the development of the best possible translation of the lectionary which is inclusive of all persons and, at the same time is faithful to the issues of linguistic and historical accuracy."[166] It indicated that anything short of this might be more detrimental than helpful to the cause of inclusiveness in the church. In addition to rejecting a proposal that the LCA withdraw from the project, the committee adopted a two-part resolution that recommended that the translation not be used in corporate worship in the LCA but that it be studied and reviewed.[167]

Publication of the inclusive language lectionary set off a storm of controversy not only in the LCA but also in other Protestant churches. The issues did not revolve so much around substituting words such as "humanity" for "man" in translation of biblical texts. The strongest objections related to the efforts to interpret terms for God and Jesus in non-male-oriented language and to the insertion of the names of women when they were not included in a particular biblical text.[168] There was also strong criticism of the awkwardness of certain passages for public reading. Bishop Crumley felt strongly enough about the issues that he wrote a two-page article for *The Lutheran* explaining his own reservations.[169] It was only one of a barrage of articles and books that have appeared on the subject of inclusiveness in biblical language.[170] DPS did follow through on publishing a study guide and response form to enable congregations and individuals to register their views, but the responses received were too few to be conclusive.[171] The matter of trying to find more inclusive language for scriptural translations was far from dead, however, and several new versions of the lectionary readings and the New Testament appeared in the late 1980s.[172]

Educational Ministry

Although the largest single project during these years was the launching of the "Living Faith Series" for the Sunday church school, the LCA was deeply involved in educational ministry on other fronts.[173] Adult education proved to be one of the growing edges, with the average congregation offering five adult study groups per week.[174] By 1982 over a half million adults were engaged in some type of educational ministry, and the number was continually growing.[175] The settings ranged from Sunday morning classes and forums to breakfast, lunch, and supper groups, work-place discussions, new member classes, and intergenerational groups. For the first time, special adult courses were being prepared where Asian, Black, Native American, and Hispanic writers sought to link their cultural gifts with Lutheran theological roots. Known as the "Living Waters of Faith Series," the first four courses were to be *Eternal River* (Asian), *Let Justice Roll Down* (Black), *Rivers of Living Waters* (Hispanic), and *Running Water—Constant Life* (Native American).[176]

Confirmation ministry was given a boost with the preparation of "The Living Catechism Series." The print materials were supplemented with a videotape and two computer programs, *The Learning Center* and *The 'Lectronic Catechism,* that appealed to young computer fans as a fresh way to engage in individual study. For the first time, a major curriculum was adapted simultaneously for use with the moderately mentally disabled, poor readers, and slow learners. The pupil's books looked exactly like the regular materials but used vocabulary suitable to those with special needs.[177] The "Living Catechism" was also being made available in Braille. With the addition of a full-time editor for Spanish language materials, three confirmation ministry resources were published in 1985: *El Credo Apostolico* (the Apostles' Creed), *La Vida Cristiana* (the Christian Life), and *La Iglesia como Pueblo de Dios* (the Church of the House of God).[178]

Evangelical Outreach

For a full decade, beginning in 1977, Evangelical Outreach was a major emphasis for the Lutheran Church in America. At its 1984 convention in Toronto, the LCA paused to mark what had been accomplished and to issue "A Call to Witness." Emphasizing inclusivity in outreach, the equipping of persons of all ages to witness to their faith, restoration of the inactive, and the nurturing of all members for ministry, the resolution called upon its members, congregations, synods, and leaders to renew their commitment to the seeking, shepherding, and equipping tasks of evangelical outreach and to work cooperatively with the ALC, the AELC, and other churches in accomplishing these goals.[179]

Despite the intense efforts of the church to emphasize the crucial importance of evangelism during these years, the perception in many quarters seemed to be that the LCA was not taking the task seriously. In reality much had been done. More than 65,000 persons were trained in the Word and Witness program; Pastor Evangelists conducted hundreds of events; more than four hundred Growing Church Seminars involving from thirty to a hundred persons each were held; thousands of parish callers were trained; almost every synod had at least one EO emphasis; an average of ten to twelve Koinonia Institutes, often involving as many as 150 persons each, were held annually; hundreds of pastors sharpened their skills in Preaching from Commitment seminars; and literally millions of pieces of material were used in the effort.[180]

While it is difficult to compare statistics for the whole period because of the Canadian merger, which decreased the number of synods by three at the end of 1985, it is clear that the total baptized membership of the balance of the LCA had edged slowly downward during the decade except for a few "up" years, such as 1980, 1982, and 1983.[181] Although "roll-cleaning" had abated somewhat in 1986, there were still 86,796 persons dropped from the baptized rolls for unexplained "other reasons." It would appear that more than a million persons were "lost" in this way since 1977, and the amazing thing is that accessions by Baptism, affirmation of faith, and transfer came as close as they did to offsetting the total losses for all reasons. The heartening side of the picture, however, was that there had been some growth in both confirmed and communing membership during the same period. And even though there were many who insisted that numbers were not the most important criterion of the church's health, the statistics were always examined with great interest as one indicator.

Youth Ministry

There was no slowdown in youth ministry in the waning years of the LCA. In fact, the tempo seemed to increase in many ways, with youth staffers and facilitators at work in synods and youth flocking to regional gatherings, convos, cultural awareness seminars, plus world hunger seminars at the United Nations and in Washington. In addition, twenty-five North American and thirty-five Brazilian youth and their leaders engaged in a work-study program dealing with the hunger crisis in the northeastern part of Brazil. In turn, several Brazilian youth visited the 1986 LCA convention in Milwaukee and addressed the delegates about the situation in their own land.

The highlight of these years, however, was the second LCA Youth Gathering that brought an overflow throng of more than 5,700 young people and adults to the campus of Purdue University in July 1985. For a few brief moments, the gathering theme of "Power in the Cross" was symbolized in a dramatic scene as the youth and their leaders formed a living cross that nearly filled the football field in the huge Purdue stadium.[182] It was the last time that LCA young people would hold their own event. No sooner was it history than leaders of ALC, AELC, and LCA began to plan a huge gathering to be held in the summer of 1988 at San Antonio, Texas, to bring the youth of the three churches into a new community with one another.

Stewardship

When the LCA moved into its comprehensive Stewardship Development Program in 1981, the hope was that by interrelating the basic stewardship work of DPS with Designated Advance Giving, Major Gifts, the LCA Foundation, the Lutheran Laity Movement for Stewardship, the World Hunger Appeal, the synodical consultation process, and congregational fiscal consultations, it would be possible to strengthen Christian giving throughout the church. Although some energies were diverted by necessity to the One in Mission Appeal, the cumulative impact upon giving in the LCA was impressive. Total giving by members had increased from a little over $465 million in 1980 to almost $675 million by 1985.[183] Regular benevolence had climbed from approximately $57.16 million to $69.9 million in the same period.[184] In 1981, congregations had assets of $3.466 billion. By 1985, that had grown to $4.409 billion.[185] Although a sizable part of the total assets in buildings and other real estate would have been affected by inflation, the startling figure was that by the end of 1985 congregations held more than $400 million in cash, bonds, and other types of assets.[186] Obviously, when taken as a whole, the LCA was not on the brink of poverty despite the fact that the church-at-large was continually needing to pare back programs.

Congregational Social Ministry

During the final five years of the LCA's life, there was a heightened sense of the urgency of congregational social ministry that expressed itself in concerns for the elderly, the unemployed, victims of domestic violence and chemical dependency, injustices toward people of color and language other than English, the disabled, the homeless, and the hungry. People sought to understand and deal with issues such as global justice, the need for low-income housing, sponsoring refugee families, providing shelters for battered women, the crisis in many family farms, and the quality of public education. Congregations organized themselves in a wide variety of ways to meet these needs and undergird their members' ministry in the world.[187]

The Division for Parish Services had provided a steady flow of resources and programs to sensitize congregations to the issues and help them in their efforts. Perhaps the most important step during these years, however, was a unique action/research project to develop a systematic strategy of intervention to support congregations in their social ministry.[188] The project involved sixteen synods, 862 congregations, approximately 492 synodical resource team members, sixteen coordinators, and some 8,070 congregational leaders.[189] During the process, the participants developed two powerful visions of the church. One was the vision of a transcultural, inclusive, and diverse church; the other was a vision of a sustainable society. Each of these requires strategies that will link the efforts of individuals, congregations, synods, regions, social service systems, and church-wide agencies as parts of a global network for change. What is envisioned is a long-term effort that long outlasts the LCA, not a simplistic, "quick fix" solution.

MINISTRY AND PROFESSIONAL LEADERS

As was true in most other areas of the church's life, the mid-eighties was a time of intense activity for the Division for Professional Leadership. On the one hand, there was the continuing need to support the work of professional workers and strengthen the institutions that served them, and to complete major assignments such as the study of ministry of the laity. On the other hand, there was the increasing responsibility to work closely with ALC and AELC counterparts to insure a smooth transition into the new church.

Trends in Ordained Ministry

During these years, the number of ordained ministers continued to grow, but the balance was changing in significant ways. The loss of the three Canadian synods, of course, made precise statistical comparisons difficult, but certain trends were clear.[190] The number of ordained women had grown from zero to 484 in sixteen years; but among the active clergy, 12 percent of the women were on leave from call as compared to 5 percent of their male counterparts.[191] Not surprisingly, perhaps, by 1986 there were 135 clergy couples, with 56 of them serving the same congregation.[192] As career change became more a way of life in the United States, the age of those entering the ordained ministry continued to increase, with almost half being over thirty when they completed seminary.

The ordained among persons of color and language other than English leveled off at 150 by 1986, but there were forty-one such persons enrolled in the M.Div. pipeline.[193] One encouraging sign of the times was the growing number of congregations that could afford to have a pastor full-time or a team ministry. In 1973, there were only 81.9 pastors per 100 congregations, but by 1985, that figure had increased to 88.2.[194]

Theological Education

As the LCA moved toward merger, major shifts had been occurring in seminary education. One was the multicultural emphasis that was growing as courses and extracurricular programs were introduced to insure that both students and faculty gained an awareness of Asian,

Native American, Black, and Hispanic traditions.[195] By 1986 theological faculties included three Blacks, one Asian, two Hispanic, and one Native American within their ranks.[196] Both Southern and Philadelphia Seminaries became recognized theological resources for Black denominations. Gettysburg developed a cooperative program with Howard University's School of Religion in Washington, D.C. Pacific Seminary pioneered a multicultural center, and LSTC strengthened its Hispanic ministry program. Luther Northwestern provided a cross-cultural concentration in its first degree program.

All students were being influenced by the increasing number of women on campus. Twenty-four women served on faculties or in administrative posts at LCA-related seminaries. Those involved in teaching brought new insights to theology, the interpretation of Scripture, pastoral care, and parish administration. And the substantial number of women students helped to sensitize males both on the faculty and in the student body to feminine concerns.[197]

Enrollment of LCA candidates in the M.Div. program peaked in the 1983–84 academic year at 1,017.[198] Of these, 372 were women, and 340 out of that number were in LCA-related seminaries. After the merger of the church in Canada, the number of women in LCA schools was 325, but in the 1986–87 academic year, the total for some reason dropped to 288. The decline seemed to be due to fewer women entering seminary rather than dropping out of theological studies.[199] At the same time, male enrollment in LCA seminaries increased from 539 to 555 between 1985 and 1986, after having declined for five years. No one could say whether the overall decline in the number of LCA M.Div. students preparing in the church's own seminaries and the balance between men and women was a temporary aberration or had significance for the future.

God's People in Ministry

Ever since the LCA had adopted its statement on *The Comprehensive Study of the Doctrine of the Ministry* in 1970, the church had laid great emphasis on the fact that "all Christians are ministers."[200] Translating that concept into terms that clarified the relationship between the ordained ministry and the ministry of the laity had proved elusive and difficult to communicate to the constituency. When DPL reaffirmed that "ministry is the work of the whole people of God" in *A Study of Ministry, 1980,* the convention asked that the division prepare a report by 1984 "concerning the ministry of the laity in the world and in the church."[201] This persistent search for clarity ran much deeper than semantics and reflected a growing movement among articulate laity in the church who were concerned about affirmation and support of their own ministry in daily life. It was a concern that would have a strong influence in the work of the Commission for a New Lutheran Church.

A special consulting committee was created to conduct the LCA study. The committee presented a carefully nuanced report, *God's People in Ministry*, to the 1984 convention in Toronto.[202] The document contained an appendix that traced the development of the basic question in the LCA and highlights from a special Lutheran Listening Post survey designed to discover concepts of the ministry of the laity current in the church.[203] The survey had shown that a large percentage of both pastors and lay members had a broad view of ministry as being everything done to serve others in the name of Jesus Christ.[204] Only a tiny minority thought of ministry as limited to activities within the church or the work of the ordained.[205]

The consulting committee's report sought at the outset to define its use of certain terms. "The terms, 'people of God' and 'the Church' are equivalent to the 'one holy, catholic, and apostolic Church.' The word 'church' without the capital letter, refers to the Lutheran Church in America and institutional expressions of the Church." Recognizing the confusion existing over the use of words such as *laos* and laity, it used " 'laos' to mean the whole people of God, and 'laity' to mean Christians whose ministry is expressed in the many ways the church serves the world apart from the Office of Word and Sacrament."[206]

Indicating that ministry is a term rich in meaning, the document states, "At its deepest level, ministry is rooted in the work of God. Ministry embraces both the call of all the baptized and the office of the ordained. . . . Such a broader understanding is not to be viewed as diminishing the work of the clergy. The issue is not one of status and worth, but one of calling and gifts, opportunities, and responsibilities."[207] In speaking of the whole Church as the Body of Christ in the world, it stresses that *"the ministry of Christians in the world is the Church at work. The church can recognize, affirm, equip, support, and hold accountable Christians in their ministries in the world as fully and directly as Christians in their ministry in the church."* [Italics in text]

The major part of the report deals with "A Study of Ministry" related to Luther's catechetical explanation of the three articles of the Apostles' Creed. The First Article on Creation is seen in terms of the arenas for ministry in a world that is fallen but loved by God. It emphasizes ministry in relationships and daily occupation as well as the ministry of justice and peace.[208] The Second Article on Redemption is seen as providing the "shape of ministry." This includes ministries of proclamation and at times of death, loneliness, celebration, and decision making. It also emphasizes that there is a cost to ministry: "When we offer ourselves, in the name of Jesus, to comfort the distressed, care for the needy, befriend the friendless, forgive the offenders, confront the oppressor, and stand by the oppressed, we make ourselves vulnerable. We learn in the services to others, what it is to 'bear the cross.' "[209] The Third Article on Sanctification is related to the ministering community. "Members have their place in this servant company not by their decision but by the Lord's. . . . The agent of this choosing is the Holy Spirit. . . . The sacrament of baptism signifies the Holy Spirit's engagement in our lives."[210] All Christians are given gifts for ministry in and to the world that should be recognized, affirmed, and supported, and for which they are held accountable.

The report continues with a section on implications that includes practical suggestions of ways in which the ministry of the laity can be recognized and supported by the church. It urges changes in attitudes and language so that "ministry" is used more broadly, "minister" is applied to other than the ordained clergy, and "lay" is rescued from its implications of amateur or secondary.[211] The report concludes with a "Declaration of Ministry" for affirmation and commitment that was adopted by the convention and was to be used at all services of worship on November 18, 1984. The recommendations included establishing a Task Force on the Ministry of the Laity that was to report its observations and recommendations to the next convention.[212]

Lay Professional Leaders

During the final years of the LCA's existence, the number of certified lay professional leaders increased rapidly so that by 1987 the total had grown to 580, more than four times the number at the beginning of the decade.[213] Following a 1982 convention action that suggested formation of an association for lay professionals, DPL made an extensive study to evaluate the existing programs to support these workers and to identify their needs. Although the study did not recommend an association specifically, it resulted in a series of steps to deal with such issues as compensation, fringe benefits, working conditions, mobility information, gatherings of leaders for mutual support, role clarification, and opportunities for continuing education.[214] A key tool in the whole process was the *Lay Church Occupations Handbook,* which was thoroughly revised in 1984 to include new standards and procedures to strengthen the program.[215]

A Century of the Diaconate

The Lutheran Church in America paused in its 1984 convention to recognize the one hundredth anniversary of the Deaconess Community. In doing so, it paid tribute to the 565 women who had been "set apart" through the years for lives of service in more than 336 parishes and 221 agencies and institutions.[216] It is difficult to measure the impact that the lives of these dedicated women has had on the LCA and its predecessor churches, but it has been far beyond their sheer numbers. In recent years, the Community has had to struggle at times to maintain its identity in a changing church. The numbers had dwindled to 123 by 1987, of whom forty-seven were on full-time active status, but the total Community will continue to be a resource for the new church.[217]

The Deacon Question Again

The question of whether there should be a male diaconate had been with the LCA off and on since the 1970 Report of the Commission on the Comprehensive Study of the Doctrine of the Ministry had called for closer partnership between lay and ordained persons in ministry.[218] This prompted a series of experiments that were reported upon by DPL in 1976, but any action was deferred until the next convention.[219] When the matter was brought back to the 1978 convention with guidelines to govern two more years of experimentation, the discussion took a surprising new direction. It was argued that encouraging such an office would undermine the broader ministry of the laity.[220] When the proposal was defeated, President Marshall ruled that "the defeat of recommendations regarding churchwide encouragement did not prevent synods and congregations from proceeding with their own deacon programs."[221]

Matters rested there until the 1982 convention instructed the DPL to review the 1978 action and current needs and desires for the service of deacons, and report back in 1984.[222] The division's response to the Toronto convention provided a thorough review of the history of the issue and a report on a survey of approximately two hundred congregations that said they had deacons.[223] About half of these indicated that the deacons performed services similar to other lay members of congregations who act as worship assistants. In other cases they performed broader functions, including taking Communion to shut-ins, teaching, preaching, and community service. Although about three out of five pastors who had deacons felt there was a growing need for the office, DPL recommended that in light of the prospects of merger, it would be best to refer the matter to the Commission for a New Lutheran Church. The recommendation was adopted.[224] Bishop Crumley remarked wryly, "Now we're able to get rid of things we've never been able to settle before!"[225]

WOMEN'S ORGANIZATIONS
AFTER A CENTURY

Although organized women's ministry among Lutherans was well into its second century by the mid-eighties, it had lost nothing of the original vision that had led the pioneers to work to establish the rightful role of women in the mission of the church. If anything, Lutheran Church Women were afforded recognition and were involved in ministry in far-ranging ways that would have amazed their forebears.[226] While the first churchwide women's organization in the General Synod was intended for the support of overseas missionary work, those interests had expanded to the point where the "organization supported women's solidarity and individual talents."[227]

While LCW continued to provide liberal financial support to the church's programs during the final years of the LCA, its own program went far beyond that.[228] Its members were engaged in the study of issues such as racism, inclusive language, building peace, holistic health care, drug abuse, displaced homemakers, women and unemployment, abortion, alcoholism, new frontiers of mission, care of aging parents, child abuse, and poverty.[229] Special attention was given to materials that grew out of Theological Conferences for Women and dealt with the newer concepts of feminist theology and understandings of the Scriptures.[230] Through interdenominational resources, they became aware of the needs of the world's refugees, environmental concerns, the problems faced by Native Americans, technology and human values, and the concerns of Christians in Central America, Korea, Southern Asia, and Africa.[231] LCW worked in close partnership with DPS in producing study materials and with other churchwide agencies in advancing their programs.

Lutheran Church Women were interested not only in studying about problems but also in dealing with them directly. In a nation that ranked forty-ninth in literacy among member countries of the United Nations and where one out of three adults cannot read a book, the LCW continued to be one of the leading organizations dealing with the problem of illiteracy.[232] Its program included training volunteers to work with the illiterate and persons for whom English was a second language, producing "new readers editions" of its own materials and pioneering in the use of computer programs to develop reading skills.[233] The LCW put the same kind of concern in developing a network of "Peace with Justice Enablers" to work on consciousness raising about issues of world peace throughout the church.[234]

"Change was in the air during the past biennium," LCW said in its report to the Milwaukee convention, "and became very real in 1985 when the Canadian LCA synods and LCW synodical units, along with the Evangelical Lutheran Church in Canada and Evangelical Lutheran Church Women, held constituting conventions for a new Canadian church and women's organization.[235] Meanwhile, in the United States LCW was working closely with its counterparts in AELC and ALC to provide a smooth transition into their own new organization, Women of the Evangelical Lutheran Church in America.

PLANNING AND FINANCING THE NOW
AND THE FUTURE

Planning had been a strong concern for the LCA from the seventies onward as it struggled to meet shifting demands and look responsibly toward the future. Inevitably, this meant that program and fiscal planning were inextricably linked to one another. The time was long past—if indeed it ever existed—when across-the-board increases and decreases in spending authorizations could deal equitably and realistically with the vast range of causes in which the church was being asked to invest its resources. How the LCA functioned in the unusual circumstances of the mid-eighties involved some significant changes.

Planning, Research and Evaluation

As late as June 1982, the Executive Council had completed a lengthy process of identifying nine strategy areas that were to be given emphasis in developing the 1983–84 fiscal proposals and to be given first consideration for 1985–86.[236] By March 1983, lower than expected synodical commitments for benevolence created an emergency that required an adjustment in the budget.[237] "Although the needed reductions were approved at the June 1983 meeting of the Executive Council, it had become obvious that the budget development process was inadequate because of its inability to deal with the priorities in a holistic way across agencies, particularly in a time of fiscal shortages."[238] The nine "emphases" were simply too broad for budgeting purposes.

Meanwhile, it had become painfully apparent that a plan for year-by-year increases in apportionment to synods that would have resulted in a 10 percent jump annually by 1987 was much too optimistic, and a cap on increases was set at 6 percent per year.[239] In an effort to stave off further problems, a process was initiated called "Intentional Planning," which presumably was not meant to imply that earlier planning had been unintentional.[240] The purpose was to accomplish three things:

1. Identify areas of churchwide priority and provide increased funding for their support.
2. Identify programs or areas of service which can be maintained at a minimum level, reduced, or eliminated.
3. Provide equity among agencies in administrative and management support at lowest cost possible.

As the process unfolded, three "Central Ministry Emphases" were identified: witness and outreach, justice and peace, and unity in the church. Other programs areas were relegated to a kind of descending order of priority under "organizational requirements," "primary support activities," "ongoing support activities," and "organizational support."[241] The inevitable whittling away at the LCA's ongoing activities and the transition towards a new church had begun, perhaps, earlier than many would have believed.

Research and Evaluation. The role of research in the LCA had come a long way through the years. Initially, only two churchwide agencies, the Boards of American Missions and Parish Education, had research capabilities.[242] In the years following restructuring, much greater emphasis was placed on this function, and there was a blending of efforts of a central staff with those of churchwide agency research staffs and outside consultants. Most of their work could be described as "applied research" to assist in program design and decision making rather than more esoteric "pure research." Even though some reduction in numbers had already begun by 1985, there were still thirteen professional staff plus support personnel working in the area.[243] Few denominations have ever placed this kind of emphasis on research, and it can be argued that the LCA's capacity to meet the needs of its constituency was more effective because of it. During the mid-eighties, the Commission for a New Lutheran Church relied heavily upon these capabilities.

Evaluation is the place where research and planning tend to come together. It is the process of using research tools to discover as objectively as possible what progress has been made toward achieving program objectives. During the last several years of the LCA's life, various churchwide agencies and the central department in the Office of the Bishop carried out extensive evaluation projects to assess what the experience of the LCA had been through the years that could inform the work of the new church.[244] Whether the information will be utilized in this way remains to be seen.

Administration and Finance

Putting the LCA's financial house in order and taking the necessary steps for an orderly transition to the new church were enormous tasks that began as early as 1984.[245] It was also a time when raising the necessary funds for the ongoing work of the LCA, accounting, record keeping, asset management, real estate services, and management of the Church Property Fund of the Board of American Missions, computer services, personnel work, and administration had to continue without interruption.[246]

During this period, certain highlights should be mentioned. In 1987 the Lutheran Laity Movement for Stewardship celebrated eighty years of service in this area that had begun in the General Synod and had spanned the lives of the ULCA and LCA.[247] Its Fund-Raising Service alone raised over $300 million in congregational, synodical, and institutional campaigns since that office was created in 1953.[248]

The World Hunger Appeal garnered $70 million for that cause

since 1974.[249] Since 1972 the Designated Advance Gift program had raised over $27 million.[250] Bequests, gift annuities, memorials, and other types of gifts continued to pour into the church as a result of the efforts of the LCA Foundation.[251] Capping it all was completion of the achievement in 1987 of $36 million in pledges for the One in Mission Appeal for the Church Extension Fund and a Birth Gift for the ELCA.[252]

Pensions and Benefits

One of the most complex operations of the LCA was its Board of Pensions. Not only did it administer fixed income and variable income pension plans for clergy and laity, but it also was responsible for health benefit plans for church employees, death benefits, and minimum pensions for those whose benefits were extremely low for one or more of several reasons.[253]

The fact that the pension portfolios of the church amounted to over $780 million at the end of 1986 created a continual temptation to well-meaning individuals to dictate how these funds should be invested.[254] For example, a memorial was sent to the Executive Council by the Texas-Louisiana Synod in 1981 asking that the Council instruct the board to invest 10 percent of its fixed income resources with the Board of American Missions.[255] Laudable as this might seem, it was established by the Executive Council Committee on Legal Matters that this was not possible under the laws of the State of Minnesota in which the LCA was incorporated.[256] Another issue related to corporate social responsibility in investments, particularly with the regard to South Africa. Although the Board of Pensions did vote for more than fifty shareholder resolutions as recommended by DMNA after 1975, it continued to assert that its fiduciary responsibility compelled the management of assets solely in the financial interests of the plan participants.[257] The difference in view between those who advocated corporate social responsibility as the primary criterion and the board continued unresolved throughout the final years of the LCA's life.

REVOLUTIONS IN COMMUNICATIONS

New technologies that had once been only a gleam in the eyes of church communicators and seemed far beyond the LCA's financial reach only a few years before were becoming commonplace in the mid-eighties. Satellite transmission gave on-the-spot immediacy to key events.[258] Lap-top computers allowed editors to write on-scene reports and transmit them directly to the home office where they were converted immediately to type without all the former time-consuming processes. Networking and easy access to data banks made possible on-line availability of religious news to editors and congregations with the equipment to plug into the system.[259] Digital recording, fiber optics, videotaping, desktop publishing, and a steady stream of technical breakthroughs were revolutionizing the way the church told its story to the world.

There were new problems, however, to go along with the new opportunities. OC reported to the 1986 convention, "The radio and cable-tv ministries of main line denominations have been rendered virtually invisible by the massive 'paid time' broadcast efforts of fundamentalists and independent Christian programmers. The few moments of public and community service time the church bodies have relied upon are no longer available because of federal deregulation of the American broadcast industry."[260] Rather than retreat from the field, however, the Telecommunications Department worked at developing new media contacts and providing consultative services to local groups that still had a wide range of opportunities to utilize.

Patterns continued to change in many areas of communication. OC issued a third edition of *Guidelines for Avoiding Bias* with the new title *Guidelines for Inclusive Language* to help editors, speakers, and illustrators use better terminology and images when referring to various groups. The clamor for full access by the media to church meetings resulted in OC's developing a statement of *Guidelines for Open Meetings*.

Not everything was new, of course. Syndicated programs such as the Lutheran series on "The Protestant Hour" radio program completed forty years of continuing success, although the number of outlets was down from a pre-deregulation high.[261] Even though the "Davey and Goliath" children's television series had been pioneered thirty-five years earlier, and Davey himself should have been pushing forty-five if he had been allowed to age, the weekly viewers still numbered in the millions.[262] One casualty, however, was "Church World News" (renamed "Intersect: World and Religion") that was discontinued after thirty-five years on radio.

The Lutheran

By one reckoning, the predecessor publications of *The Lutheran* in the English language stretched back to 1831. The publication in December 1986 of *Voces Luteranas* (Lutheran Voices), however, marked the first time that the magazine appeared with a section in the Spanish language. The sixty-six LCA congregations that had services in Spanish received the new publication without charge. *Voces Luteranas* was a cooperative effort, with DMNA underwriting the cost of the magazines, DPS providing the salary of the editor, and *The Lutheran* assuming the cost of fonts in Spanish, typesetting, printing, and postage.[263]

During the 1984–86 biennium, *The Lutheran* was redesigned to make use of full-color printing, computer-designed charts, and a number of other changes that gave the magazine a new look.[264] By this time, the publication had moved completely to preparing copy on computers and setting type and designing pages electronically.

Rising expenses meant that by 1987 a single issue of the magazine cost over $55,000 to produce and $41,000 to mail.[265] Circulation, which had peaked at 601,000 a few years before, had dropped slowly until it stood at slightly over 536,000 in August 1987.[266] As the process of preparing for the new church's version of *The Lutheran* in January 1988 absorbed more time and energy, a decision was reached to publish the LCA edition monthly during the last half of 1987. The final issue was to be a commemorative one that would provide pictorial highlights of the past quarter century and seek to portray something of the character of the church that was about to become a part of the ELCA.

Board of Publication

The LCA Board of Publication, which traced its lineage to 1855 when publishing houses were intended primarily to produce catechisms and hymnals, had grown to become a place where pastors and congregations could turn for almost every kind of resource needed for ministry.[267] These ranged from academic books to curriculum materials, worship books, hymnals, periodicals, video and audio materials, computer programs, paraments, vestments, ecclesiastical arts, and a host of other items. All told, sales were expected to top $24 million in 1987.[268]

The mid-eighties was a significant period for the Board of Publication as it rethought its strategy for the future. One of its crown jewels was the highly regarded Fortress Press, which produced an average of seventy new books a year and had agreements where many of its publications were translated and printed in German, Japanese, Italian, French, Swedish, Portuguese, and Spanish.[269] To put it another way, Lutheran theological and other scholarly publications were now flowing steadily into the life of churches throughout the world.[270] "While this is not new, it is relatively new that theology is moving from American scholarship to Europe and other parts of the world."[271]

As marketing moved toward the nineties, the publishing house found that the strategy of expanding its network of stores needed to be reexamined. During the period from 1985, five stores were closed, and the remaining fourteen operated without subsidy. Much of the ordering by customers was now done through WATS lines, which was characteristic of much retailing throughout the country.[272] Even though it was contributing an average of $110,000 to the LCA in royalties, $22,000 for the congregational communication system, and some $33,000 in disaster relief to congregations, the publishing house approached the new church with no long-term debt and an anticipated cash balance.

FAREWELL TO CANADA!

It was a joyous time and a sad time when the Lutheran Church in America convention met in *Tarantou* June 28 to July 5, 1984, for the last time on Canadian soil. It was a joyous occasion because it signaled realization of the long-postponed dream of many Canadian Lutherans that some day they would have their own national church body.[273] It was a sad time because close ties had bound the synods north and south of the border since 1826 when Herman Hayunga was sent by the New York Ministerium to serve Lutheran settlers in the southeastern tip of Dundas County, Ontario.[274] That bond was welded even more strongly in 1849 when Adam Keffer, of the Vaughan congregation in Dundas, walked barefoot to Pittsburgh to plead with the synod for a Lutheran pastor.[275] By 1834 the Indian name of *Tarantou* had been anglicized to Toronto, and it was there that the ULCA had held its 1954 convention and restructured that church in major ways.

After a series of overtures to other Lutherans in Canada, the LCA

Canada Section had finally begun a series of negotiations in 1978 with the Evangelical Lutheran Church of Canada that would eventually lead to merger.[276] Although the final votes of the Canadian synods to join in forming a new church had been conclusive, there were those who were reluctant to sever the binational ties.[277] The United States portion of the LCA was carefully neutral, believing that the decision was properly a Canadian concern. By the time of the LCA convention, however, the die was cast, and on January 1, 1986, the Evangelical Lutheran Church in Canada became a reality. The first bishop of the new church was Donald Sjoberg, who had been bishop of the LCA's Western Canada Synod.[278] The headquarters of the new church was established in Winnipeg.

Loss of the Canadian synods did make a difference in the strength of the LCA. It meant the transfer of some 341 congregations, 397 pastors, and 125,700 baptized members.[279] It also meant that the LCA no longer was directly involved in the two Canadian theological seminaries. In order to assist the ELCIC on its way, the LCA voted to transfer to the new church $4,567,907 as its proportionate share of the assets of the Lutheran Church in America.[280] Although technically the ties had been severed, the bonds that had linked Lutherans in Canada and the United States had lasted too long to be dissolved in an instant or, perhaps, in a lifetime.

SHAPING THE "NEW" LUTHERAN CHURCH

The story of the formation of the Evangelical Lutheran Church in America is one that will be seen more clearly a decade or more from now when there has been sufficient time for reflection on a task that was daunting in its scope and mind-boggling in its complexity.[281] Since the purpose of the present volume is to describe the history of the Lutheran Church in America, it is appropriate to deal here only in the most general way with how the CNLC went about its work, a sampling of salient issues faced, and the shape of the ELCA at its inception.

Almost before the CNLC itself had had a chance to catch its breath, there was intense discussion of every question that might be raised about the merger in all types of conferences, articles in church periodicals, and mailings by special interest groups. One early indication of the high level of interest came at a colloquium on "The New Church and Its Ministry: The Ecclesiological Challenge Facing

LUTHERAN UNITY INCREASES DIVERSITY

These church bodies	Formed more inclusive church bodies	Which formed the ELCA

These church bodies

American Lutheran Church

Evangelical Lutheran Church

Lutheran Free Church

United Evangelical Lutheran Church

Lutheran Church— Missouri Synod*

American Evangelical Lutheran Church

Augustana Evangelical Lutheran Church

Finnish Evangelical Lutheran Church of America (Suomi Synod)

United Lutheran Church in America

Formed more inclusive church bodies

The American Lutheran Church (formed 1960, 2.3 million members)

Association of Evangelical Lutheran Churches (formed 1976, 109,000 members)

Lutheran Church in America (formed 1962, 2.9 million members)

Which formed the ELCA

Evangelical Lutheran Church in America (formed 1988, 5.3 million members)

Major cultural origins
Danish
Finnish
German
Norwegian
Swedish
Other cultural origins

*The Lutheran Church—Missouri Synod, from which the congregations withdrew that formed the AELC, continues as a separate church body.

American Lutheranism" that was held in February 1983 at the Lutheran School of Theology at Chicago. The planners had recruited an
imposing array of speakers and hoped for two hundred registrants.
Actually, more than seven hundred persons flocked to the campus to
discuss questions that would prove nettlesome throughout the process of designing the new church.[282] Such debate would go on
throughout the next four years, and no doubt, will continue in the
future.[283]

**Work of the Commission for a
New Lutheran Church**

During the scant four years of its existence, the CNLC held ten
meetings averaging from three to five days in length. That the members were devoted to their task is evidenced by the fact that attendance of the seventy members at meetings averaged more than 96
percent.[284] In addition, most of them served at one time or another
on special committees and task forces that required many more days
of effort. Early on, the commission determined that its meetings
would be open to the public, and it purposely scheduled the sessions
in various parts of the country to make it possible for interested
persons to attend.[285]

Even a casual reading of the seven progress reports issued, beginning in February 1983, indicates an evolution in the thinking of the
members as ideas were tested and reactions flooded in from the
churches. For example, the idea held by some at the outset that
envisioned a completely new church rather than merging three existing bodies was modified somewhat by the time of the commission's
report to the 1984 church conventions, which said, "The new Lutheran church will be new in some senses but not in others. It will
be new in time but in continuity with our past. It will not be new in
kind but will reflect the age-old newness of God's revelation in
Christ."[286]

At its first meeting, the commission had created two important
task forces that were to deal with theology and society; the task forces
were chaired by Fred W. Meuser and Robert J. Marshall, respectively.[287] The Task Force on Theology Report, which dealt with a
confession of faith, the nature of and membership of the church, and
the mission and ministry of the church, was widely distributed and
studied by congregations of the three churches.[288] The CNLC itself
took action at its September 24–28, 1983, meeting indicating first,

that a new statement of doctrine was not necessary as the basis for union, and second, that certain affirmations could be made regarding the Word of God and Scriptures.[289] For reasons that are not made explicit in the CNLC documents, the Report of the Task Force on Society was regarded as "an internal resource document for the use of the Commission and its Task Forces" and not distributed in a fashion similar to the one on theology.[290]

Another key work group that was formed was the Task Force on New Church Designs, chaired by Franklin D. Fry.[291] In many ways the work of this group was a pivotal step in forming the new church because it was here that the long and sometimes tortuous process of translating theological and ecclesiological issues into an operational structure for the ELCA began.[292] On the basis of this group's report, the commission established eleven other design task forces that were to deal with more limited assignments.[293] The reports of these task forces were reviewed by a Committee on Design, chaired by Dorothy K. Jacobs. This committee continued throughout the various stages of drafting and revising the structural design for the new church.[294]

In the course of the commission's work, a large number of other task forces and committees were created to deal with such matters as purpose, headquarters site, legal matters, synodical boundaries, constitution and bylaws, and the constituting convention. Narrative descriptions of the new church were developed and reviewed in a variety of surveys. Extensive research documents were prepared to assist in different phases of the process.[295] There were troublesome points, however, that continued to be debated at all levels of the churches well into 1986.

Among the more persistent issues faced by the CNLC were the following: the nature of the church under the Lordship of Jesus Christ; whether the church is primarily a federation of congregations or synods that delegate authority to a central body, or whether the church is interdependent in all its parts; whether the ELCA was to be made up of nine or ten powerful regions while the national church had minimal responsibility; the number and responsibilities of churchwide agencies; the size and composition of churchwide staff; the size and number of synods; whether quotas were necessary to insure the appropriate balance among clergy and laity, men and women, and persons of color and language in elective and appointive bodies; the type of church pension plan and the amount of employer contributions; the method of continuing the funding of the LCA health benefit program for retired employees; the relation of the ordained ministry of Word and Sacrament and other types of specific ministries; the role of bishops; the conditions under which a congregation may withdraw from the ELCA and the ownership of its property; membership in ecumenical organizations, particularly the NCCCUSA and WCC; location of the church headquarters; definition of the membership of the ELCA; the question of whether the term *inerrant* should be applied to the Scriptures; and the goal of unity among Lutherans who accept the teachings of the Unaltered Augsburg Confession. While not exhaustive, the list is at least illustrative of the complexity of the negotiations.

In spite of all the CNLC's work and the various attempts to develop consensus, there were some issues that were carried into the new church as subjects for further study.[296] Other questions were not resolved until compromises were struck during the simultaneous church conventions in 1986 when the final details of the merger documents were forged into the form that would finally be adopted by the processes required in the different bodies.[297] The mechanism for ironing out the differences during the three church conventions in August 1986 was a Reception Committee of thirteen persons who conferred by telephone hookup as motions and countermotions were made by delegates as they waded through the 210-page *Report and Recommendations* from the commission.[298]

Finally, the moment came at 10:53 A.M. on August 29, 1986, for the crucial vote on merger. The hope was that the results could be communicated from convention to convention at the same time, but in this case the technology failed. As the delegates waited restlessly for communications to be restored, a former LCA pastor seized a microphone on the rostrum and tried to denounce the merger.[299] The convention quickly recessed, and when it was reconvened in the afternoon, the LCA vote was announced as 644–31 in favor of the ELCA governing documents and 640–29 to approve the legal documents needed to effect the merger. By this time, it was known that the ALC had voted 900–37 and 891–59 in favor of the same documents, and AELC had voted 137–0 in favor on both questions. "My friends," Bishop Crumley said, "there will be a new church!" The convention erupted in cheers, tears, applause, and a spontaneous chorus of "Amen!" The members of CNLC were given a standing ovation.[300]

The New Look of the New Church

The church that was affirmed that August day in 1986 would bring together the various streams of Lutheranism that had been separated so long by ethnic origins, traditions, and theological views. It was a vastly different body from the largely German synod that Henry Melchior Muhlenberg had envisioned in 1748. Within its ranks of more than 5,300,000 members, 11,000 congregations, and 16,600 pastors, there would be persons whose origins were traced to Africans, Asians, Pacific Islanders, Native Americans, Finns, Swedes, Norwegians, Danes, Germans, Hungarians, Slovaks, Eskimos, Hispanics, West Indians, Dutch, Latvians, Estonians, Icelanders, and virtually every other group that had settled in North America.[301]

Congregations related to the ELCA would be in all fifty states, the Caribbean, Bermuda, and several cities in Europe.[302] There would be sixty-five synods working together with churchwide agencies in nine regional centers for mission. The church would relate to twenty-nine colleges, eight seminaries, and some 275 social service agencies and institutions. The churchwide structure provides for administrative units related to the officers of the church, six program divisions, five commissions to provide advice and counsel in specific areas, a women's organization, a youth organization, the possibility of a men's group, a publishing house, a foundation, a pension board, and a conference of bishops.[303] Global mission outreach projects will be carried on initially in sixty countries.[304] The ELCA will be a member of the Lutheran World Federation, World Council of Churches, and the National Council of Churches of Christ in the USA. Lutheran World Ministries and National Lutheran Campus Ministries will be merged into the ELCA.

THE ENDING OF THE BEGINNING

If anyone had expected the long trek that the Lutheran Church in America had made toward unity to end with a flourish, the actual event would have been a disappointment. Instead of the full-blown closing conventions held by the predecessor bodies before the birth of the LCA in 1962, the final convention of the LCA itself was over in little more than an hour. The business was confined to ratifying merger documents.[305] As one observer remarked, "If someone had sneezed, he would have missed it." Instead, in the final acts of the

Barbara K. Lundblad

William A. Kinnison

Communion service in Columbus. Bishops Herzfeld, Chilstrom, Preus, and Crumley at Columbus Convention Communion Service

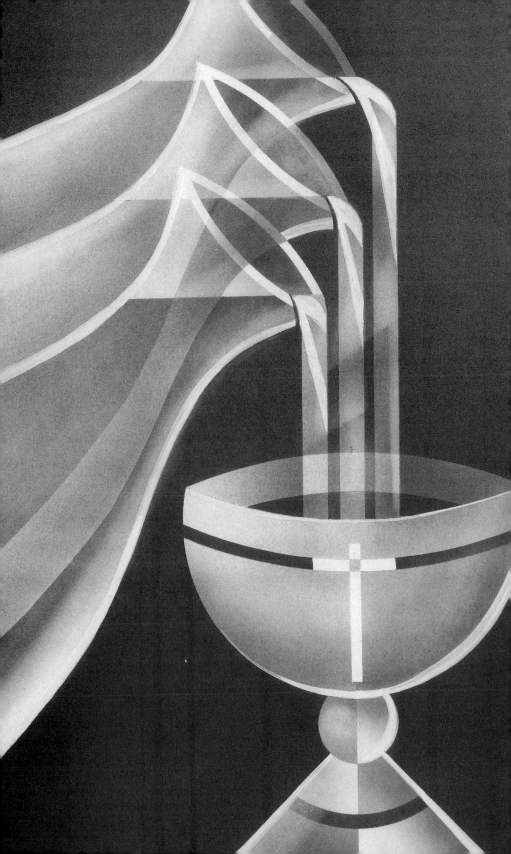

LCA, thoughts were focused on the beginnings of the new church and the crucial election of officers.

The opening service of the Evangelical Lutheran Church in America was an impressive one. Symbolically, the bishops of the merging churches poured water from three vessels into a large font for the remembrance of Baptism in which all had shared. The preacher was the Rev. Barbara K. Lundblad, pastor of Our Saviour Atonement Church in New York City.[306]

Presiding at the business sessions was William Kinnison, who had chaired the CNLC.[307] Finally, the moment came for election of the first bishop. Sixty-eight persons received votes on the first ballot.[308] After the second ballot, the field was reduced to the top eight candidates, and biographical information was distributed before the next vote was taken.[309] Slowly, the process of whittling down the number of candidates went on until the seventh ballot, when David Preus with 340 votes, Herbert Chilstrom with 347, William Lazareth with 197, and Barbara Lundblad with 154 remained.[310] On the next ballot, the field was narrowed to three, with Chilstrom receiving 423 votes, Preus 378, and Lazareth 233. On the ninth and final ballot, Herbert Chilstrom was elected the ELCA's first bishop with 626 votes to David Preus's 411.

When Dr. Chilstrom was called to the podium along with his wife, the Rev. Corinne Chilstrom, they were both greeted with a standing ovation.[311] The new bishop declared, "I feel a tremendous sense of responsibility. I feel like many mantles have been sewn together and placed on my shoulders. . . . I can only thank God and ask you to pray that I bear that mantle well."[312] ALC Bishop Preus asked for the privilege of the floor and graciously pledged his support to Bishop Chilstrom.

The other officers who were elected at the convention were Vice-President Christine Grumm, an AELC lay person from San Francisco, and Secretary Lowell G. Almen, an ALC minister and editor of *The Lutheran Standard.* Edgar R. Trexler, who had been editor of the LCA's periodical, was elected editor of the ELCA's magazine, *The Lutheran.* According to the procedures of the new church, the Church Council elected George Aker, of Reno, Nevada, treasurer and executive director of the Office for Finance.

The climax of the constituting convention came on Saturday evening with a festival Eucharist attended by more than three thousand persons. The presiding minister was Bishop Chilstrom, and the

preacher was Gunnar Staalsett, general secretary of the Lutheran
World Federation. Prayers of intercession were offered in German,
Swana, Zulu, Spanish, Indonesian, Afrikaans, and Norwegian. At the
time of the consecration of the elements for the Holy Communion,
the bishops of the predecessor churches came to the altar and poured
wine from three flagons into the chalice held by Bishop Chilstrom.

When the Lutheran Church in America was formed a quarter of
a century earlier, the union was symbolized by the joining of four
quarter-candles that flamed as one. In the opening service of the
Evangelical Lutheran Church in America, the waters of Baptism
were mingled from three vessels. And in the Eucharist, the wine
borne by the leaders of the three churches was blended in the chalice
as one. In a way, each of these symbols through the years has spoken
to the hearts of the people of their unity in Christ. Just as they have
shared in the gift of the Holy Spirit and have been made one in
Baptism, so they are sustained by the body and blood of the Lord of
the church for the next step in their never-ending journey.

NOTES

1. *CNLC Progress Report 1*, p. 2. By the time of its second meeting, at
least, the commission had indicated, "The commission has not discussed the
content of the papers and therefore has not made any corporate judgment
as to whether it agrees or disagrees with the viewpoints expressed." The nine
papers in question were as follows: Keith Bridston, "The New Church in
Relation to the Church Universal, to Its Antecedent Bodies, and to Other
Churches"; Faith Burgess, "The Church and the Power Structures"; Gerhard Forde, "Declaring Our Faith Today"; Martin Heinecken, "The Gospel
and the Church"; Donald Juel, "The New Testament and Lutheran Ecclesiology"; Martin Marty, "What Does the Lord Require of Us?"; E. Clifford
Nelson, "Ecclesiology: A Review and a Proposal"; Albert Pero, "The
Church's Role in Such Movements as Those Concerning Peace, Justice, Ecology, Nuclear Power, Racism, Sexism"; Walter Stuhr, "The Context as a Factor in Planning the New Lutheran Church."
2. Ibid., 1.
3. *Time* (June 15, 1987):48–49.
4. These figures are based on Bureau of Labor statistics for August 1987.
Hispanics fared slightly better with unemployment hovering around 8%.
5. The anomaly of a shortage of workers and continuing unemployment
is illustrated by two citations in an article in *The Wall Street Journal* (May
27, 1987):62. William Johnston, a Hudson Institute researcher studying the
problem for the Labor Department, is quoted as saying, "The demographics
create an opportunity but don't guarantee it. The shift to higher-skill jobs
creates a huge counter-trend." John Kasarda, a sociologist from the Univer-

sity of North Carolina, stated, "There is a huge deficit in entry-level jobs in the cities where the labor pool is, and a huge deficit of entry-level workers in the areas where the jobs are."

6. Federal Reserve Board statistics indicated, for example, that the dollar in early 1985 was worth over 250 yen, but by June 1987 had dropped to a rate of 144.5 yen. Economists worried that the slide would go even further, and in fact, it did.

7. See Susan Lee and Christie Brown, "Barometer Falling," *Forbes* (September 7, 1987):32. The article dealt with danger signals pointing to an increase in inflation.

8. After climbing as high as 2,722, the Dow dropped sharply to 2,561 by Labor Day. The figures are cited only to indicate the volatility of the stock market that had swings of as much as a hundred points in an hour. There was little agreement among analysts as to what it all meant in the long run.

9. Brazil had the largest foreign debt of any LDC at $107.2 billion; Mexico was second with $105.4 billion; and Argentina, third with $53.8 billion. See *Fortune* (August 3, 1987):74.

10. In the United States, some banks and savings institutions were hit not only by the impact of shaky foreign loans but also by bankruptcies in the farm belt and the oil patch. Extreme pressure was placed on the government's own deposit insurance agencies.

11. The peak of the 1929 market found the Dow at 381.17, but that was only the beginning of the debacle. By July 8, 1932, the average had lost 89.2% and stood at 41.22. See "Market Historians See Parallels with the Past" and "Stock Carnage Extends Worldwide," *USA Today* (October 20, 1987):3B.

12. Major periodicals made careful analyses of the similarities and differences between the 1987 situation and the one in 1929. See "Dow Movements Last Week Mirrored Market 58 Years Ago" and "A Look at Array of Data Shows Some Parallels, Many Differences," *The Wall Street Journal* (October 26, 1987):29; M. S. Forbes, Jr., "1929? or 1962?" *Forbes* (November 16, 1987):24–25. *Time* devoted 34 pages of its November 2, 1987, issue to commentary on "The Crash," pp. 22–55.

13. *New York Times* (June 18, 1987):4.

14. Ibid. The World Food Council estimated that 40,000 children die of hunger-related causes every day.

15. The situation was not true of the United States alone. Most of Western Europe had huge surpluses of such things as dairy products.

16. The problem had so many different forms and causes that no single, simplistic solution could be applied. Studies of the situations of the poor in the United States, for example, indicated that programs intended to remedy their plight sometimes actually worked counter to their purpose. In some cases, public housing projects had to be destroyed because criminals preyed on the occupants, and vandalism made buildings unfit for habitation. This is not to imply that there were not successful programs, nor that society could simply turn its back on the problem.

17. "The Ghetto: From Bad to Worse," *Time* (August 24, 1987).

18. *Time* points to the work of Black scholars, such as sociologist William Julius Wilson of the University of Chicago, who stress the widening social and economic gap between ghetto residents and the rest of American society, both white and Black.

19. An article by Lena Williams, "Shifting Gears in Pursuit of Equality," *New York Times* (July 26, 1987):E7, describes the convergence of objectives within the Urban League and the National Association for the Advancement of Colored People on the importance of Black self-reliance. "They have adopted the thesis that blacks must rely on their own resources to fight poverty, drug abuse, teen-age pregnancy, unemployment and violence."

20. Ibid.

21. Ibid. The N.A.A.C.P. itself was pushing for legislation that would hold parents accountable for the actions of their children and compel absent fathers to assume financial responsibility for their children. The group was also giving qualified support to "workfare" programs to help people move from welfare dependency to employment.

22. The Department of the Interior's 1985 statistics showed that unemployment on the Sioux Rosebud reservation in South Dakota was 82%; the Crow, in Montana, 56%; the Sioux, Pine Ridge in South Dakota, 53%. The tribe with the least joblessness among the ten largest reservations was the Salt River Pimas in Arizona with 23%.

23. See Thomas J. Knudson, "Zoning the Reservations for Enterprise," *New York Times Week in Review* (January 25, 1987).

24. See *New York Times* (April 19, 1987):1.

25. See Meg Dooley, "Bridging the Access Gap," *Columbia* (June 1987):27. The statistics, which are based on those of the American Council of Education, also indicate that the number of Black graduate students fell by 11.9% from 1980 to 1984, and the number of Black faculty members dropped by 4.3% in the same period.

26. The case involved Lillian Garland, a Black worker at a savings institution in California, who had not been allowed to return to her former job when complications arising from delivery of her child prevented her return to work for three months. The court decision required the employer to reinstate her. See *Facts on File, January 23, 1987,* 33.

27. Amy Wilentz, "Garland's Bouquet," *Time* (January 26, 1987):14–15.

28. "The debate over pregnancy leave has created a deep rift among feminists. One side argues that pregnancy leave, even though it benefits individual women, poses a general danger to female workers because it singles them out for special protection. Historically, they point out, such privileged treatment has eventually led to discrimination against women. . . . But other feminists contend pregnancy leave simply acknowledges women's child-bearing function and neutralizes its effect on career advancement." Ibid., 15.

29. See Richard Stengel, "Balancing Act," *Time* (April 6, 1987):18–20.

30. This fact is brought out in an economic study, *The American Woman 1987–88,* issued by the Congressional Caucus for Women's Issues. Entrenched male dominance in major segments of the economy was underscored by the fact that in 1987 men were the chief executive officers of the

world's fifty largest industrial corporations. These companies employed 8.7 million people and had sales of $1.3 trillion, some 50% greater than the gross national product of West Germany. See "The World's 50 Biggest CEOs," *Fortune* (August 3, 1987):23–60. At the same time, *Fortune* pointed out that women were succeeding in "industries rocked by change—computers, telecommunications, financial services—because competition puts a premium on sheer talent. They are also nearing the top in fields like retailing and advertising that traditionally employed lots of women, but held them back" (Anne B. Fisher, "Where Women Are Succeeding," pp. 78–86).

31. Statistics released by the American Institute for Islamic Affairs indicated that there are more than 140 million Muslims (85% of the population) in Indonesia, 92 million in Pakistan (97% of the people), 101 million in Bangladesh (89%), 90 million in India (12%), 49.8 million in the Soviet Union (18%), 43.6 million in Egypt (91%), 42 million in Iran (98%), 40 million in Nigeria (45%), 22.7 million in Algeria (99%), plus additional millions in other countries in the Middle East, Asia, and Africa.

32. Karen Elliott House, "Mosque and State, Rising Islamic Fervor Challenges the West," one of a series of articles in *The Wall Street Journal* (August 7, 1987):1. Although written from the perspective of journalists, the articles in the series were carefully researched and, at the very least, indicated the force of Islam in major areas of the globe at this time.

33. Not only had the movement caused consternation throughout the Middle East and the West, but also in the Soviet Union. The regime of Mikhail Gorbachev had been relatively lenient on religious matters, but in a visit in November 1986 to Tashkent, the capital of heavily Muslim Uzbekistan, Gorbachev called for "a firm and uncompromising struggle against religious phenomena." See "Taking a Firm Stand Against Faith," *Time* (January 12, 1987):60, which describes not only the renewed Soviet concern about Islam but also its severe restrictions on Jews. In contrast, a feature article in the *New York Times Week in Review* (August 23, 1987) reported that the Gorbachev administration was seeking "a new kind of coexistence with religion," which was tolerated as a cultural relic or personal consolation.

34. Although conservatives were not successful in getting "equal time" for creationism in science courses, publishers of public school textbooks did at times go to ridiculous lengths in excluding religion from the content of some subjects. For example, it was reported in *The Philadelphia Inquirer* that one history book spent thirty pages on the Puritans without ever mentioning why they had left England (Dale Mezzacappa, "Striving to Get Texts to Face Up to Religion," (August 9, 1987):A1.

35. For example, it was claimed that some of the TV programs brought receipts of from $129 million to $183 million annually, but that scandals related to one of the enterprises had caused a decline in the number of viewers and funding for several major projects. See "Enterprising Evangelism," *Time* (August 3, 1987):50–53.

36. See "John Paul's Feisty Flock," *Time* (September 7, 1987):46–51, and Joseph Berger, "Being Catholic in America," *The New York Times Magazine* (August 23, 1987):22–27, 64–65.

37. "The Church John Paul Will See in America Is Ever More Hispanic," *The Wall Street Journal* (August 31, 1987):1, 6.

38. Among the most important prior statements were *Church and State: A Lutheran Perspective* (1966), *Conscientious Objection* (1968), *World Community* (1970), *Human Rights* (1978), and *Economic Justice* (1980). In addition, *Peace and Politics* refers to the resolutions of the previous church bodies, particularly *The Problem of Nuclear Weapons*, adopted by the ULCA in 1960. The action of the 1982 convention in ordering the study was a result of twenty-one synodical memorials dealing with questions related to peace and war in a nuclear age, memorials which had precipitated hours of convention discussion (*LCAM, 1982,* 183–89, 204–5, 267–68, 308–12).

39. The DPS research department analyzed the data for DMNA in three separate reports. One dealt with a special sample of congregations recruited for the purpose. The second was made up of congregations that volunteered responses on their own. The comments from these two samples were very similar. The most divergent responses came from individuals and were analyzed in a third document. All three research reports on the *Peace and Politics* study are in the LCA archives.

40. *LCAM, 1984,* 260–76, 312–13, 333–47.

41. Paul Nelson, *A Commentary on Peace and Politics* (New York: DMNA, 1984). Although the publication provides a consensus of persons in the Department on Church and Society and does not purport to be an official judgment on the part of DMNA or the LCA, it is a helpful interpretation of how the policy statement was developed and the original intent of the drafters.

42. For example, such requests had been made by the Illinois, Michigan, and Minnesota Synods in 1978 (*LCAM, 1978,* 52, 72, 105, 113) and the Central Pennsylvania Synod in 1980 (*LCAM, 1980,* 70, 123–24, 239). In the last instance, the request was denied because of the estimated cost of such a study and the pending DMNA study of "Women and Men in Church and Society."

43. *LCAM, 1982,* 60, 315–16. The memorial was one of a number referred to the Executive Council because of lack of time for discussion at the convention.

44. The synodical bishop had sought the advice of the Executive Council after a person who acknowledged being homosexual and living in a covenantal relationship with a person of the same sex had applied for reinstatement. The request had been denied by both the Examining Committee and the full Commission on Professional Leadership. The latter had voted to ask the synodical Executive Board to refer to the Court of Adjudication the question of whether the LCA's documents precluded ordination of persons in such circumstances. The board deferred action and asked the bishop to seek Executive Council advice. The Council voted in light of the discussions with ALC and AELC regarding forming a new church to ask the LCA bishop to explore with the heads of those bodies whether there was interest in pursuing a joint study of the question. See *ECM, June 17–19, 1982,* 594–95.

45. Consideration of the study is reported in *ECM, September 1983*, 334; *December 1983*, 400; *March 1984*, 486; *June 1984*, 667; *September 1984*, 92–94. A full report was also given to the convention in 1984 (see *LCAM, 1984*, 702–6, 688, 818).

46. DPL had considered a study of the ordination issue as inadvisable for several reasons that included the LCA's ecumenical relationships, the preferences of ALC and AELC, the general study already underway on "Women and Men in the Body of Christ," and the fact that the historical practice of the LCA provided the basis for "advice to synods to be interpreted and applied in pastorally responsible ways." See *LCAM, 1984*, 704. The Executive Council in June 1983 had reaffirmed an earlier decision "that a formal study on the subject of the ordination of persons living in a homosexual relationship not be pursued at this time." See *ECM, June–July 1983*, 223–26; and *September 1983*, 335.

47. *ECM, September 1984*, 92–94.

48. An interpretation of the meaning of the Executive Council's suggestions about "comprehensive and participatory" appears in the *LCAM, 1984*, 706.

49. The committee that conducted the study indicated that two factors helped shape its work: one was the Executive Council decision not to include the question of ordination of homosexual persons, and the other was that "the Executive Council did not request a new social statement, nor a reopening of the 1970 social statement 'Sex, Marriage, and Family.'" See *LCAM, 1986*, 580.

50. *LCAM, 1986*, 575–645.

51. Ibid., 644–45. See also *ECM, June–July 1986*, 791–93.

52. The report was published separately as *A Study of Issues Concerning Homosexuality* (New York: DMNA, 1986). One paragraph from the section on "Pastoral Strategies" gives something of the tone of the report. "The church is in an interim situation. Far from being able to instruct the world about the meaning of homosexuality, the church finds itself, with the world, struggling to understand and know where to praise and where to judge. In such a time, it is necessary to ask for self-restraint, understanding, and a venturesome acceptance from all parties. *The advisory committee is convinced that this church can neither condemn, nor ignore, nor praise and affirm homosexuality."* Ibid., 38. (The italics are in the printed text of the report.)

53. *1984 Convention Summary*, 8.

54. *LCAM, 1984*, 446–54, 462–66. For example, Goal 5-C had stated that additional persons be enlisted so that the number of minority persons on the roll of ordained ministers reach 100. By December 31, 1982, there were 130 minority persons on the roll. At the same time the goal of ten persons on the roll of lay professionals and the diaconate had not been met (the figures for 1983 were zero for certified lay professionals and two deaconesses). Goal 2-A of increasing minority membership of the LCA by 15,000 persons per year was missed by a wide margin, although there was a 53.2% increase between 1978 and 1982.

55. *LCAM, 1984,* 208–13, contains the text of the document itself and the convention actions. As preparatory material, DMNA had commissioned a series of five study papers: Arnold L. Tiemeyer, "The Lutheran Church in America: Freed to Be an Inclusive Fellowship"; Paul R. Hinckley, "Racism, a Contemporary Babylonian Captivity of the Church"; Carolyn Green and Albert Pero, "The Church: A Word to and from the People of Language and Color: Brothers and Sisters—Remember or Be Dismembered"; Albert Pero, "Called to a Life Together in One, Holy, Catholic, Apostolic Church"; Julio Quinones, "Inclusiveness: Principles and Goals," in *Study—Inclusiveness and Diversity: Gifts of God* (New York: DMNA, 1985).

56. Ibid. The intentions were to acknowledge and celebrate the diversity in our membership as a gift of God; confront racism as sin and work towards its elimination; increase fellowship among members, congregations, and churches; proclaim and celebrate the gospel to and with God's whole community in the world; pursue racial justice through individual and corporate actions; develop leadership that reflects and responds to the diversity of our membership; organize the church so that all members are represented in and served by decisions made; monitor and be accountable for our life together as an inclusive church that celebrates its diversity. Each of these "intentions" was followed by a list of concrete examples, some of which had not been articulated before, such as engaging in formal and informal dialogue with denominations whose membership is predominantly Black; providing Spanish-language training through all our seminaries.

57. The only amendment was to change the commitment to increase investments in minority-owned banks and development projects by 500% instead of 100%.

58. A final report on the response of the LCA to the intentions set forth in the statement on inclusiveness and diversity appears in the *LCAM, 1986,* 308–39.

59. *LCAM, 1986,* 280–81, 777–91. The DMNA issued a periodical, *Dateline: Namibia,* dealing with the latest information on that troubled area of Southwest Africa. It also published a booklet on *The Church as Shareholder: Socially Concerned Investing for Groups and Individuals.*

60. *LCAM, 1984,* 419–20. Congress finally passed a bill making restitution to internees, and it was signed by President Reagan on August 10, 1988.

61. See *Questions and Answers on Treaty Rights* (Seattle: National Coalition to Support Indian Treaties), distributed by DMNA. In order to provide help to tribal groups in such matters as preparing "acknowledgment petitions" to the federal government, a series of seminars had been set up by NILB that ended in 1983. At that time, an American Indian Research and Resource Institute was established at Gettysburg College to provide as extensive services as possible to tribal groups. Through NILB itself an average of fifty grants of direct assistance to Indian-operated programs were made each year. See *LCAM, 1984,* 632; *1986,* 481–82.

62. *LCAM, 1986,* 484–87. In the years from 1975 through 1985, LIRS relocated more than 80,000 refugees. LIRS also became involved in assisting undocumented persons to obtain legal status under the new United States immigration law that went into effect in 1987.

63. Reports of these conferences, which included recommendations for action by the church, were published under corresponding titles by DMNA in 1984 and 1985.

64. *LCAM, 1984*, 455–61; *1986*, 306–7.

65. See Joy M. K. Bussert, *Battered Women: From a Theology of Suffering to an Ethic of Entitlement* (New York: DMNA, 1986).

66. A summary of the whole sequence of steps in reaching an agreement to have a feasibility study, the goals to be tested, a summary of the report, and the initial recommendation of the Executive Council to the Toronto convention appear in the *LCAM, 1984*, 213–23.

67. The possible causes listed were:
    a. Common to all three bodies:
        1. Capital funds: Church Property Fund (LCA); Church Extension Fund (ALC and AELC).
        2. Start-up costs for a new church, including the costs of terminating the present church structures.
    b. AELC and LCA: theological education.
    c. LCA alone: college—student scholarships and grants.
    d. ALC alone: college endowment, including campus ministry.
See *ECM, June 1983*, 288–89.

68. *ECM, March 1984*, 532. The figures showed that 80% indicated support of a potential appeal, 70% agreed the appeal should be held prior to beginning the new church, 65% would share in the leadership, 90% would give financial support.

69. Ibid., 530–31. Possible overlapping with other synodical appeals was considered a negative factor and made flexibility in timing essential for success. There were several other negative factors, including resentment over the fact that SFM had been promoted as a "once-in-a-lifetime-appeal"; the need to redefine and retitle the Church Property Fund; the lack of detail about the purpose of a transition fund; the perceived need to restructure the seminary system; and worries about the economy, particularly in the agri-business area. The *ECM, March 1984* plus exhibits provide the whole series of developments in the feasibility study and the actions of the Executive Council in far greater detail than could be included in the LCA minutes.

70. *LCAM, 1984*, 222–23.

71. Ibid., 259.

72. *1984 Convention Summary*, 12.

73. *LCAM, 1984*, 320–21.

74. As it turned out, both AELC and ALC had appeals but with somewhat different goals and procedures.

75. *LCAM, 1986*, 709–28, traces the whole procedure followed and the efforts to coordinate as closely as possible with the other church bodies. Further detail is provided in the *ECM, September 1984*, 99–108; *December 1984*, 204–13; *April 1985*, 237–43; *September 1985*, 333–35; *December 1985*, 449.

76. *LCAM, 1984*, 98. The major gifts personnel were assigned to work on One in Mission.

77. *The Lutheran* (August 1987):19. *The Lutheran* had given careful coverage of the appeal. An article in the January 1986 issue on "Seed Money for Planting Churches" is an example of the major thrust of the appeal. It stated, "Lutherans can't afford to enter all worthwhile mission fields. The One in Mission campaign is trying to change that" (pp. 5–7).

78. It should be noted that in June 1985 DMNA had realigned its internal structure so that its units would correspond to the design of the ELCA. The division reported to the 1986 convention that "DMNA's present program and responsibilities fall into the proposed Division for Outreach, Division for Education, Division for Social Ministry Organizations, Commission for Church in Society, Commission for Multicultural Ministries, and the Commission for Women. An office of strategic mission planning was created to see that the current mission responsibilities be carried smoothly into these new units" (*LCAM, 1986,* 271).

79. *LCAM, 1984,* 425. The fact that there is always a time period between entering a field and the actual organization of a congregation complicates the task of projecting existing numbers five years in advance. From 1983 through 1985 there were actually 63 congregations organized (ibid., 426; *LCAM, 1986,* 292).

80. Malcolm L. Minnick, Director of New Ministry Development, explained in an article in *The Lutheran* that church grants for traditional missions to support pastors and programs cost about $62,000 compared to $90,000–$110,000 for minority ethnic situations and $85,000–$100,000 for pioneer-slow growth areas. See "Seed Money for Planting Churches" (January 15, 1986):7. Furthermore, it is typical for traditional missions to require support for five years, while the other types may need assistance for ten.

81. *LCAM, 1984,* 425–26.

82. *LCAM, 1986,* 292–93.

83. Ibid., 296–97.

84. Ibid., 293–94.

85. Ibid., 294–96.

86. The two school years involved were 1981–82 and 1982–83 when the enrollment fell an aggregate of around 4%. In 1983–84 and 1984–85, the figures went up a miniscule amount. See *LCAM, 1986,* 288–89.

87. "LCA College Enrollments Decrease," *The Lutheran* (February 5, 1986):20. The decline was by no means universal, however, for six colleges had reported increases in enrollment.

88. *LCAM, 1986,* 289.

89. Ibid., 682. The latest available figure for synodical support to NLCM, which was in addition to the LCA grant, was $1,731,000 in 1985 (ibid., 340).

90. During the 1800s, which became known as the "great century for missionary outreach," Lutherans in North America had "joined hands with some of the European and American societies in order to bring the gospel to distant countries. . . . The Foreign Mission Society of the Evangelical Lutheran Churches in the United States, formed in 1837, was the first American Society following in the wake of the new mission interest. It joined Moravians, Reformed, and Lutherans, especially in the General Synod. Prior

to this time Lutherans occasionally supported the work of the American Board of Commissioners for Foreign Missions organized in 1810." See August R. Suelflow and E. Clifford Nelson, "Following the Frontier," in *The Lutherans in North America*, ed. Nelson, 200–1.

91. "Starting New Lutheran Church Bodies Overseas," *DWME-MCM, October 1983*, Exhibit C-6, p. 1.

92. Ibid., 1.

93. See *Call to Global Mission* (New York: DWME, 1983), 5, 14–16, and *Ecumenism: A Lutheran Commitment* (New York: LCA, undated), 30, which states, "The Lutheran Church reaffirms its commitment to engage in ministry and mission throughout North America and overseas, *whenever possible* [italics added] in cooperation with other Christian churches or ecumenical agencies."

94. See "Mission in Peru—An Issue Process Paper," *DWME-MCM, March 1986*, Appendix A-2.

95. "Starting New Lutheran Church Bodies Overseas," 3.

96. The consultation sought to build upon the insights of other major conferences on evangelism held by the WCC at Melbourne, Australia, in May 1980; by the Lausanne Committee for World Evangelization at Pattaya, Thailand, in June 1980; and the LWF at Stavanger, Norway, in May 1982. The Jacksonville consultation included not only Lutherans but also representatives of Roman Catholic and ecumenical mission agencies.

97. The topics for six of the work groups were as follows: "Evangelism and the Poor and the Oppressed," "Evangelism and People of Other Faiths," "Doing Evangelism Ecumenically," "Evangelism and the Institutions of Society," "Evangelism and Scientific/Intellectual Change," "Evangelism and Peacemaking." The other two work groups dealt with "Perspectives on Mission and Evangelism" and "Evangelism and the Form of Mission." See *Group Reports: Consultation on Evangelism* (New York: DWME, 1984).

98. Ibid., 4–5.

99. There actually were several spinoffs of this kind from the Jacksonville consultation. One was an effort to develop an LCA position statement on evangelism analogous to *Stewardship and Christian Giving: A Biblical and Theological Perspective*. An interagency task force was formed that produced a study document, *Evangelism Is Christian Witness*, in 1987. In the final stages of development, the ALC Division for Life and Mission in the Congregation also was involved. Although the paper never reached the point of becoming an official LCA statement, it was one of the many resources passed on to the new ELCA Division for Congregational Life.

100. In 1984 the Department of Interpretation prepared a book on *The Continuing Frontier* (New York: DWME, 1984). The division also gathered thirty situation analyses from missionaries and other church leaders around the world. All of this background material was fed into development of a series of policy papers on evangelism that were commended to the new Global Mission agency. Their titles give a clue to their direction: "The Unreached in Rural Settings," "The Unreached in Urban Settings," "Evangelism among Migrants and Refugees," "Communication with Pivotal

Persons," "Evangelism and Women," "Witness to Faith among Youth, Students and Faculty," "DWME's Responsibility to Expatriates," "The Theological Preparation of Leaders in Evangelism." (*DWME Final Report, August 1987*, 3–5, in ms. form.) Appended to the papers were critiques by the DWME Management Committee.

101. A "missionary unit" may be a single person, a married couple, or a family with the same assignment.

102. *LCAM, 1986*, 396. An arrangement had been worked out with the ELCIC that the missionaries could be "secunded" to DWME and continue their existing assignments while maintaining their ties to the Canadian church.

103. *DWME Final Report, August 1987*, 37–38.

104. *LCAM, 1984*, 531. Hundreds of lay women, of course, had served as missionaries through the years, but up to this point, none had been ordained. Since the assignment of Pastors Kreller and Jacobson, other ordained women have joined the ranks of LCA missionaries.

105. *LCAM, 1984*, 526–28; and *1986*, 386–89. During this period DWME was given responsibility for coordinating the allocation of funds for world hunger projects carried on by other LCA and inter-Lutheran agencies.

106. One of the new initiatives taken by ALC and LCA was to bring thirty undergraduate students to the United States for college study during 1986–87 in the hope of developing a core of trained leaders for an independent Namibia. See *DWME Final Report*, 13–14.

107. Ibid., 19. See also *LCAM, 1984*, 387. LCA also found a special opportunity for ministry among refugees and the many Westerners working in Cairo, which is known as a "city of expatriates" (*LCAM, 1986*, 389).

108. Ibid., 27–28.

109. A "Planning Document for ELCA Middle East Ministry" was prepared as a result of two years of work by missionaries and area secretaries of the three merging bodies (see *DWME Final Report*, 20–21).

110. India had played a major role in Lutheran missions for nearly 150 years, but as the ELCA was formed, DWME had only six persons serving there because of the changing situation and the difficulty in obtaining visas for missionaries. A major consultation was held during the last biennium of the LCA to plan with the church in India to develop new priorities for its work in this second largest country in the world. See *DWME Final Report*, 21–22.

111. *LCAM, 1986*, 393.

112. David Vikner describes the three phases as "The Missionary Stage, 1842–1942"; "The Younger Church Stage, 1943–1968"; and "The Independence/Interdependence Stage." For the fullest description of these developments, see "LCA in World Mission 1842–1982," in *Background Papers to the Document—Call to Global Mission* (New York: DWME, 1982), 153–99.

113. The paper, Exhibit A-1 of the *DWME-MCM, October 23–25, 1986*, was adopted as a "planning document" to be forwarded to the new Global Mission unit.

114. Ibid., 3.

115. Ibid., 5–6. The paper points to the fact that there has at times been a separation between two aspects of mission: societal, or structural, on the one hand; and personal, or attitudinal, on the other. Curren's view is that both must be held together in healthy tension for change to be most effective.

116. *LCAM, 1986*, 383.

117. *Lutheran Bishops Call Meeting with Pope "A Symbol, and Much More Than a Symbol,"* LCA News Bureau release, September 14, 1987, p. 2. The 90-minute meeting, which was described as "historic," took place in Columbia, South Carolina. Other Lutheran leaders who attended were LCA Bishop James R. Crumley, ALC Bishop David W. Preus, and LCMS President Ralph Bohlmann.

118. In 1984 the Division for Theological Education and Ministry of the ALC published *Ecumenics and Inter-Lutheran Relationships: An Annotated Bibliography*. This compact listing of resources for pastors and lay leaders points out that the WCC has assembled in Geneva the most complete collection of writings on the ecumenical movement in the twentieth century. It cites a *Classified Catalog of the Ecumenical Movement*, 2 vols. (Geneva: WCC; Boston: G. K. Hall & Co., 1972), as listing holdings through 1971 that included "about 52,000 books and pamphlets plus 1350 periodicals, 750 of them current" (p. 14).

119. *Ecumenism: A Lutheran Commitment*, Commitments 5a and b, p. 30.

120. It should be noted that "dialogue" and "dialog" are spelled differently in various basic documents. Other studies in which the LCA was involved during this period included those with Baptists, Conservative Evangelicals, Methodists, Episcopalians, United Church of Christ, and the Orthodox. In addition, interfaith conversations were going on with Jews and other religious groups. See "Report of LCUSA" in *LCAM, 1986*, 479–80. In many cases, there were parallel discussions going on through the Lutheran World Federation. All of these efforts had produced documents through the years that prompted reaction in one way or another.

121. William H. Lazareth and Nikos Nissiotis, in the "Preface" to *Baptism, Eucharist and Ministry* (Geneva: World Council of Churches, 1982), 5. The Conference on Faith and Order to deal with the input from the churches is tentatively set for 1989.

122. LCA News Bureau release, September 14, 1987, *"Challenging Times" Ahead for Ecumenical Movement, Says Head of Vatican Secretariat*, p. 6.

123. Ibid., 6.

124. *LCAM, 1984*, 277.

125. Ibid., 864. Bishop Crumley appointed a steering committee to oversee the study and begin the development of responses. The committee included Chairperson Franklin D. Fry, H. George Anderson, Karlfried Froehlich, and Martha Stortz.

126. Ibid., 285. As it is stated in the LCA's response to BEM, *reception* "includes all the phases and aspects of a process by which a church makes

the results of an ecumenical dialogue or statement a part of its faith and life. Reception thus is a process involving all parts of the church, all believers. It may take years and it only occurs as Christ graciously accomplishes it by his spirit. This convention is not being asked to 'receive' *Baptism, Eucharist and Ministry* in this sense of the term 'reception.' "

127. The full text of the response, which is so compactly stated that it is difficult to summarize properly, appears in the *LCAM, 1984,* 284–90.

128. The six earlier reports dealt with *The Status of the Nicene Creed as Dogma of the Church* (1965), *One Baptism for the Remission of Sins* (1966), *The Eucharist as Sacrifice* (1967), *Eucharist and Ministry* (1970), *Papal Primacy and the Universal Church* (1974), and *Teaching Authority and Infallibility in the Church* (1980). The first two were edited by Paul C. Empie and William W. Baum; the third, fourth, and fifth by Empie and T. Austin Murphy; the sixth by Empie, Murphy, and Joseph A. Burgess. *Justification by Faith,* Dialogue VII, edited by H. George Anderson, T. Austin Murphy, and Joseph A. Burgess (Minneapolis: Augsburg, 1985), provides not only the text of the statement itself but also sixteen background papers prepared by dialogue participants. The whole group of dialogues has stimulated a large number of articles and books related to the topics.

129. The DPS produced *A Discussion Guide for Congregations* (Philadelphia: DPS, 1985) that provided for a three-session discussion and reaction to *The Common Statement on Justification by Faith,* which was published as a separate document. Once more the Conference of Bishops and other groups were involved.

130. See *ECM, June–July 1986,* 831–36.

131. *LCAM, 1986,* 246. The full text of the response and the amended recommendations appear on pp. 241–46. The practice of referring questions for study in the future by the new church was becoming increasingly prevalent by the time of the 1986 convention.

132. The complete paragraph 4 reads as follows: "We emphatically agree that the good news of what God has done for us in Jesus Christ is the source and center of all Christian life and of the existence and work of the church. In view of this agreement, we have found it helpful to keep in mind in our reflections and affirmations which both Catholics and Lutherans can wholeheartedly accept: *our entire hope of justification and salvation rests on Christ Jesus and on the gospel whereby the good news of God's merciful action in Christ is made known; we do not place our ultimate trust in anything other than God's promise and saving work in Christ.* This excludes ultimate reliance on our faith, virtues, or merits, even though we acknowledge God working in these by grace alone *(sola gratia).* In brief, hope and trust for salvation are gifts of the Holy Spirit and finally rest solely on God in Christ. Agreement on this Christological affirmation does not necessarily involve full agreement between Catholics and Lutherans on justification by faith, but it does raise the question, as we shall see, whether the remaining differences on this doctrine need to be church-dividing. Our intent in presenting this statement is to help our churches see how and why they can and should increasingly proclaim together the one, undivided gospel of God's saving mercy in Jesus Christ."

133. This report of the Roman Catholic/Lutheran Joint Commission is a remarkably concise statement on the developments in this historic interchange. In the preface, the co-chairmen Hans L. Martensen, R. C. Bishop of Copenhagen, and George A. Lindbeck, Professor at Yale University, write, "This document strives for clarity regarding the nature of church unity and a concept of that goal which implies neither absorption nor return, but rather a structured fellowship of churches. The prerequisite is community in confessing the one faith and in sacramental life. A solution must be found for still existing divisive differences." See *Facing Unity—Models, Forms and Phases of Catholic-Lutheran Church Fellowship* (Geneva: LWF, 1985), 6. An informative interview with George Lindbeck that probes his own views on *Facing Unity* and the current status of Catholic-Lutheran relations appeared in *Lutheran Partners* (March/April 1986):8–12.

134. *ECM, July 1987,* 326–31.

135. Originally, the four LCUSA bodies—ALC, AELC, LCA, and LCMS —had been involved in the dialogue. LCMS representatives issued a dissenting minority report that, in effect, meant that the proposal was directed to the other three churches by their participants. Of the Reformed churches involved, the report was acted upon by the Presbyterian Church (USA), which was the result of a merger in 1984 of the "Northern Presbyterians" (UPCUSA) and the "Southern Presbyterians" (PCUSA), and the Reformed Church in America (RCA). The Cumberland Church did not act on the proposals, and the United Church of Christ and Lutheran church leaders agreed that a special dialogue was needed to clarify certain doctrinal matters before closer relations would be possible. The foregoing is based on correspondence between the writer and Robert H. Fischer, an LCA participant in the dialogue.

136. James E. Andrews and Joseph A. Burgess, eds., *An Invitation to Action: The Lutheran-Reformed Dialogue, Series III, 1981–1983* (Philadelphia: Fortress Press, 1984), 4–5. This volume not only contains the agreements of the third dialogue, but the agreements from *Marburg Revisited* (1966), the report of *Lutheran-Reformed Dialogue II* (1974), the Leuenberg Agreement among various Lutheran and Reformed churches in Europe (1973), and the ALC-LCA statement on Communion practices. The first dialogue, reported in *Marburg Revisited,* was judged relatively successful, but the second was not because the participants admitted that they could not make significant progress.

137. *LCAM, 1984,* 314.

138. *ECM, April 1985,* 317.

139. Michael Root, a member of the LCA Executive Council committee on ecumenical relations and an associate professor of systematic theology at Southern Seminary, described some of the basic differences in viewpoints in "Communion with the Reformed," *The Lutheran* (August 1986):16–18. For example, he quotes Walter Wietzke, director of the ALC Division for Theological Education and Ministry, as calling the Reformed "our closest theological kin." Whereas he indicates that Carl Braaten, professor of systematic theology at LSTC, referred to the Reformed tradition as "in many ways the polar opposite of Lutheranism." Root went on to

explain that "such sharply divergent views of the relation of the Lutheran and Reformed traditions is not uncommon" (p. 18). See also Robert H. Fischer's rationale for maintaining that the dialogue proposals were consistent with the LCA's own statement on ecumenism in "Where Do We Go in Lutheran-Reformed Relations?" in *Lutheran Partners* (July/August 1986):12–16. Fischer, who taught historical theology at LSTC, was a participant in the dialogue.

140. See "Preus Asks Reformed Intercommunion," *The Lutheran* (February 5, 1986):17. The article also stated that Bishop Preus favored "a course correction," accepting the view of "unity in reconciled diversity." It indicated that he urged U.S. Lutherans also to—

—continue to practice "interim sharing of the Eucharist with Episcopalians while searching for more complete agreement with them;

—"pursue with patience" the goal of altar and pulpit fellowship with Roman Catholics, and;

—express willingness to explore possibilities of sufficient agreement in the gospel and sacraments with other Christian churches, "mainline or evangelical," that are willing to join in such theological exploration.

141. See "Inching Toward the Reformed," in the summary of the 1986 LCA convention in *The Lutheran* (September 17, 1986):23.

142. Ibid. The *1986 Convention Summary* described the common aspects of the resolutions in slightly different language and indicated that the Reformed and Presbyterian bodies had also accepted them (p. 8). Essentially, the AELC, ALC, PCUSA, and the Reformed Church had adopted the recommendations that had come from the dialogue team.

143. *LCAM, 1986*, 246–47.

144. Ibid., 247–48. The amendment also called for additional dialogue among the churches on the questions of the Lord's Supper, Christology, and predestination.

145. *ECM, December 1986*, 128–29. This procedure of providing a "commentary" on a convention action was quite unusual.

146. *Reports and Recommendations of the CNLC, June 25, 1986*, 191–92. According to Robert H. Fischer, "This procedure was a salutary one, for the situation in the merging churches was anomolous: AELC and ALC now were officially 'in pulpit and altar fellowship' with PCUSA and RCA, while LCA was not." (From correspondence with writer.)

147. One report that gives a sense of these dimensions of the WCC Assembly is by Karl J. Mattson, "The Issue at Vancouver," *LCA Partners* (December 1983):7–11.

148. The African was Bishop Josiah Kibira, who had been elected at the Dar es Salaam assembly; the new president was Bishop Zoltan Kaldy of Hungary; and the two churches suspended were white South African churches that were accused of not ending apartheid practices (the *Minutes of the Seventh Assembly*, 49–52, includes highlights of the debate on the issue). Bishop Kaldy died in 1987, and Bishop Johannes Hanselmann of Bavaria was elected by the LWF Executive Committee to fill his unexpired term. See *The Lutheran* (September 1987):22.

149. Bishop Crumley described the purpose of these visits in an interview by the writer on July 25, 1987, in Philadelphia. Detailed reports were included in *The Lutheran* after each visit.

150. The ecumenical visits became contagious among LCA synodical bishops. During 1985 and 1986, more than half of the bishops visited the Vatican and sites in the Middle East for conversations with heads of churches. Two different groups were guided on their visits by the director of ecumenical relations (see *DWME Final Report,* 40).

151. This exchange of correspondence in 1985 was of significance in relationships between the LCA and Rome. In a preface to a publication of the letters, William G. Rusch states that "a careful examination of history may well disclose that this correspondence is unprecedented. In the form of personal letters, a bishop of a bi-national Lutheran Church and the Pope have shared with each other, and now their churches, their assessment of the present state of ecumenical progress between their churches and their hopes for the future." See *A Correspondence Between Pope John Paul II and Bishop James R. Crumley, Jr.* (New York: LCA, 1985). Dr. Crumley explained the importance of encouragement from Rome in the Lutheran-Roman Catholic dialogues. He noted that "progress has been made, but the relationship which grows so rapidly remains fragile" (p. 8). While extremely cordial in encouraging dialogue, the pope was frank in saying, "It is especially in the light of what unites us that we are able to see the seriousness of what divides us and the urgency of finding the way, in faithfulness to the Word of God, towards that unity which is the will and the grace of the Lord for his Church" (p. 13). The pope pointed to aiming "at making the dawn of the third millennium the beginning of a special time for seeking full unity in Christ" (p. 14). The visit of the pope to the United States in 1987 did nothing to change the impression that the hope for unity of Protestant churches with Rome was something for which to pray but not a probability in the near future.

152. *LCAM, 1984,* 290–99, contains the full text of Cardinal Willebrands' address as well as Bishop Crumley's response.

153. *The Lutheran* (September 17, 1986):21.

154. *LCAM, 1986,* 168–69. The full text of the address and Bishop Crumley's response are on pp. 168–74. There were no less than twenty-two other ecumenical guests present for the event.

155. The study on *The Baby Boom Generation in Congregations of the Lutheran Church in America* (Philadelphia: DPS, 1986) was an inquiry into the participation of persons in this age-group in 111 parishes that reported a larger than average number of members in this category.

156. LCA Office for Communications news release, January 14, 1987, 3. The findings corroborated many of the insights from the earlier LCA study on *Congregations as Nurturing Communities.*

157. See "Doctrine Doesn't Draw Baby Boomers," *The Lutheran* (February 18, 1987):22.

158. Interestingly, the LCA study mirrored in many ways the findings in a more broad-based study by sociologists David Roozen and William McKin-

ney of the Hartford Seminary in Connecticut, reported in "Baby-Boomers Come Back to Church," *The Lutheran* (January 21, 1987):18. The report indicated that regular attendance at worship by baby-boomers increased from 35.5% in 1972–74 to 42.8% in 1984.

159. The findings are reported in the document *Congregations in Transition* (Philadelphia: DPS, 1986).

160. The task force was appointed in response to an action taken by the 1984 convention in adopting the "Declaration of Ministry" and the report "God's People in Ministry" (*LCAM, 1984,* 254; and *1986,* 919). The task force's own report appears as Part III of the Report of the Bishop to the 1986 convention (*LCAM, 1986,* 35–46). It contained a lengthy series of recommendations addressed to churchwide agencies of the LCA and the ELCA regarding strengthening the ministry of God's people in the world.

161. The report is titled *Ministry in Daily Life, A Study of Nine Congregations* (Philadelphia: DPS, 1987).

162. *Connections* was launched in 1986 after an intensive process of pilot testing in 100 congregations. It is designed to help persons in their ministry in daily life by on-site visits to the participants' worlds of work, leisure, home, and outdoor activities. Following the visits, the participants discuss their experience using the language of the Lord's Prayer, Creed, and Luther's Small Catechism. See *LCAM, 1986,* 345, and *DPS Final Report,* 18, in ms. form.

163. The full report and implications appear in *Parish Program Profiles: Worship Attendance* (Philadelphia: DPS, 1986). Other studies completed in 1986 and 1987 included Stewardship, Outreach, Educational Ministry, Service, and Youth Ministry.

164. *LCAM, 1984,* 481–83, and *1986,* 352–54.

165. Special permission was obtained from the NCCCUSA Division of Education and Ministry offices for this review with the clear agreement that no public statement or release of the material be made before the Council's own announcement of the publication. Although the DEM Unit Committee had received periodic reports on the project while work was in progress, there had not been an opportunity for review. Summaries of these progress reports were shared with the DPS Management Committee and appear in its minutes.

166. All citations are from the October 25–27 minutes of the *DPS-MC,* 1–4, which bring together the 1983 action with subsequent steps leading to a study process.

167. The full text of the action was as follows:

WHEREAS, the management committee has carefully reviewed the inclusive language lectionary text, Series A, prepared by the NCCCUSA Division of Education and Ministry, having received advice and counsel from pastors and biblical scholars. The management committee has determined that the translation, as it now stands, inadequately resolves the matter of inclusiveness, that the text contains serious problems at several points, and lacks artistic sensitivity and linguistic flow; and therefore is not appropriate or conducive to public reading in the church.

In light of this, the management committee adopts the following:

RECOMMENDATIONS—

1. That the management committee recommends that the Division of Education and Ministry of the NCCCUSA "Inclusive Language Lectionary: Readings for Year A" not be used in corporate worship within the LCA; and

2. That the management committee considers this lectionary translation appropriate for study and review, together with other documents appropriate to the issue of inclusive language and biblical translation, and requests the staff to prepare study materials.

168. For example, many persons objected to referring to God as "Mother" as well as "Father," particularly in passages such as the Lord's Prayer.

169. See "The Bishop's Turn," *The Lutheran* (November 2, 1983):14–15. The article is a helpful summary of some of the issues raised.

170. For example, Barbara J. MacHaffie lists more than 35 books and articles in a bibliography related to a chapter on "Biblical Images of Women," in *Her Story, Women in Christian Tradition* (Philadelphia: Fortress Press, 1986), 5–22, 166–68.

171. A report was made to the DPS Executive Committee on October 24, 1984, that only nine responses were received. They tended to come down about equally on both sides of the issue.

172. In April 1987, Roman Catholic bishops in the United States announced publication of the Revised New Testament portion of the New American Bible that was originally published in 1970 as the English language version authorized for use in worship and study. The new translation aims at using contemporary language and nonsexist terms relating to persons. It does not go as far as the NCCCUSA lectionary, particularly with reference to terms referring to God and Jesus. See "New Revised Bible Avoids Using 'Man,'" *New York Times* (April 5, 1987):1, 28. A new translation of Series A of the Lutheran, Roman Catholic, and Episcopal lectionaries was published in 1986 by Pueblo Publishing Company in cooperation with Fortress Press. Called *Lectionary for the Christian People,* it was edited by two Lutheran scholars, Gordon Lathrop and Gail Ramshaw-Schmidt. The editors explain the principles followed in an introduction (pp. xi–xv). The goal was a contemporary translation that "is basically conservative in its maintenance of key biblical imagery." According to an LCA Office for Communications release (March 31, 1987), "In some cases the recastings to inclusive language are more in line with the original texts than earlier renditions, the editors say. They report being astounded at 'how often masculine designations have entered the text in English translations' with 'no basis in the original language.'"

173. More than 10,000 persons took part in 254 introductory events in the fall of 1984. The new materials proved popular, and all of the new courses were soon in their second printings. Use of LCA materials in congregations increased by from 10% to 12% in each age-group as the new resources became available. See *LCAM, 1986,* 348–49, 363–64.

174. *LCAM, 1986,* 349–50.

175. *LCAM, 1984,* 476.

176. *DPS Final Report,* 5, 27.

177. Supplementary leader guides were also prepared to help teachers use the special pupil books effectively. See *DPS Final Report,* 15–17.

178. *LCAM, 1986,* 350–51.

179. *LCAM, 1984,* 138–40.

180. Information regarding the EO programs appears in the *LCAM, 1984,* 470–73; *1986,* 346–47; and in the *DPS Final Report,* 20–24.

181. Calculations have been made on the basis of statistical data supplied by the DPS Research Department for 1986. Other data is from the *LCAM, 1978,* 781–89; *1980,* 740–49; *1982,* 827–38; *1984,* 879–87; *1986,* 871–81. The net loss in baptized members between 1977 and 1985 was approximately 65,000, while communing membership remained almost the same. The loss of the Canadian synods by 1986 would skew comparisons for that year with prior years, although it is clear that the baptized membership in U.S. congregations had declined very slightly between 1985 and 1986.

182. *LCAM, 1986,* 342–44.

183. These figures included the Canadian Synods; the 1986 total for U.S. congregations alone amounted to $692.5 million.

184. Regular benevolence for the U.S. congregations topped $70.2 million in 1986. It should be noted that in 1982, for the first time in more than a decade, the increase in regular benevolence was greater than the rate of inflation. The purchasing power of the benevolence monies, however, had actually decreased to the equivalent of $21.54 million by 1982 in terms of 1967 "constant dollars." For programs funded by benevolence to have stayed even with inflation in the 1972–82 decade, the receipts would have had to have been over $101.93 million in 1982. See *LCAM, 1984,* 881.

185. See *LCAM, 1982,* 836; and *1986,* 880.

186. *LCAM, 1986,* 879. This total was equivalent to nearly 60% of congregational annual income.

187. *LCAM, 1984,* 483–84.

188. The project is described in detail in the *LCAM, 1984,* 484–85; *1986,* 354–56; and in the *DPS Final Report,* 40–50.

189. The persons involved included not only people from the LCA but also some drawn from ALC, AELC, ELCIC, and LCMS.

190. See *DPL Final Report, 1987,* 19–20, in ms. form.

191. DPL speculated in 1984 that the significant numbers of persons who had not accepted first calls during the early months following graduation frequently had more to do with the individuals themselves placing greater restrictions on where they would serve than on availability of opportunities. See *LCAM, 1984,* 506.

192. In the case of 33 couples, they were serving different congregations. In 30 instances, one or both of the spouses was not serving in a congregation.

193. *DPL Final Report,* 19, 25.

194. *LCAM, 1986,* 378.

195. *LCAM, 1984,* 498.

196. *LCAM, 1986,* 369.

197. Ibid., 370.

198. All data is from the *DPL Final Report,* 25. The total enrollment includes students in non-LCA schools. Statistics are complicated by the fact that 55 Canadian students were enrolled in 1983–84 and 58 in 1984–85, but it is not clear how many of these may have been in non-LCA schools. Canadians are not included in the totals after the ELCIC was formed at the end of 1985. United States candidates in all theological seminaries numbered 962 in 1983–84; 947 in 1984–85; 943 in 1985–86; and 918 in 1986–87.

199. Interpretation of the changes in the number of men and women enrolled in LCA seminaries was attributed to DPL's director of studies, Martin H. Smith, in an LCA news release, *LCA Seminary Enrollment Drops: Number of Women Students Declines,* November 19, 1986.

200. *LCAM, 1970,* 428–41.

201. *LCAM, 1980,* 140–55. The proposal for the further study actually came from the DPL Management Committee at its meeting of March 27–29, 1980 (see ibid., 155–58, 178). A related action in 1980 asked for the development of a statement on the expectations of the church of its ordained ministers. This document was prepared by DPL and adopted by the Executive Council in June, 1984. Its official title is *Expectations of the Lutheran Church in America of Its Ordained Ministers (LCAM, 1984,* 837–46). It places the exercise of the ordained ministry in the context of the ministry of the whole people of God but clearly delineates the specific nature of the Office of Word and Sacrament.

202. *LCAM, 1984,* 240–57, contains the full text of the report.

203. A *Summary of Results, The Lutheran Listening Post Panel II, Questionnaire 3* was produced by the Department of Planning, Research and Evaluation, Office of the Bishop, March 1983. An earlier study from *Panel I, Questionnaire 4* had dealt with Ministry of the Laity in a much briefer form in 1978.

204. It has been pointed out to the writer that as the questions were worded, it is not entirely clear whether some respondents also regarded serving others as being ministry even when it might not be done in Christ's name.

205. See *LLP Summary,* 2–5; and *LCAM, 1984,* 256. Interestingly, although 91% saw some part of their own life as ministry, more than half felt other members of the congregation would not view the respondent's efforts as ministry, and nearly one-quarter believed the pastor would not do so.

206. *LCAM, 1984,* 240–41.

207. Ibid., 242.

208. Ibid., 243–45.

209. Ibid., 247.

210. Ibid., 248.

211. Ibid., 250–52.

212. The task force report, which was referred to earlier in this chapter, is included in the *LCAM, 1986,* 35–46. An LCA news release commented that the report chided the LCA for not promoting the ministry of the laity adequately. It referred to the task force's conclusion that "the understanding

and support of ministry of the laity has not fully entered the bloodstream of the church." See News of the LCA release, June 16, 1986.

213. See *LCAM, 1984,* 496; and *DPL Final Report,* 15. The *Final Report* stated that "certification as a lay professional in the LCA assures a person of a place on a roster of the ELCA during the course of the six-year study of ministry. . . . Being included on such a roster helps a person qualify for certification as an associate in ministry in the ELCA." (See pp. 14–15.)

214. *LCAM, 1984,* 513–16.

215. *LCAM, 1986,* 375.

216. *LCAM, 1984,* 141, 493–94. A history of the movement by Weiser, *To Serve the Lord and His People,* was published to commemorate the event.

217. "Beginning in January 1988, that community will become the Deaconess Community of the Evangelical Lutheran Church in America." See *DPL Final Report,* 16–19. At that time, there were 24 candidates for the diaconate in various stages of the process of registration, certification, and investiture.

218. *LCAM, 1970,* 428–50.

219. *LCAM, 1976,* 582–86.

220. See "The Form and Function of the Ministry of Deacons," *LCAM, 1976,* 162–73.

221. Quoted from DPL report to the 1984 convention, 510.

222. The motion was actually a substitute response to a memorial from the Nebraska Synod that asked for discussions with the Deaconess community to remove barriers to male service in the diaconate. See *LCAM, 1982,* 52, 160.

223. *LCAM, 1984,* 508–13.

224. Ibid., 258.

225. *1984 Convention Summary,* 10.

226. The writer is indebted for this insight to Kathryn E. Kopf, executive director of LCW, in an interview July 13, 1987.

227. See Lani L. Johnson, *Led by the Spirit,* 14. Initially expected to devote their efforts to fund raising, women's groups in the predecessor bodies soon went beyond that limitation in finding ways to support one another in serving to the best of their ability both in church and society (pp. 16–22).

228. In the 1984–85 biennium, for example, LCW's financial gift to the LCA totaled $1,606,934 (*LCAM, 1986,* 459).

229. These topics are only a sampling of the subjects listed in the *LCW Catalog* and treated in *Lutheran Church Women* from 1983 through 1987.

230. See *Toward a New Creation,* a retreat design published by LCW in 1986.

231. Many of the study materials promoted were developed under the auspices of the NCCCUSA, but others came from women's organizations in other denominations.

232. One book on the shocking rate of illiteracy in the United States and the role of grass-roots organizations in combatting the problem is Jonathan Kozol's *Illiterate America* (New York: Doubleday Anchor Books, 1985).

233. *LCW Board Minutes, October 2–5, 1986*, 38–42, and Exhibit 4A.

234. Ibid., 34–36.

235. *LCAM, 1986*, 462. At the time of the new auxiliary's formation, LCW transferred $35,000 of its assets to the new organization.

236. The nine areas were outreach, theological education, capital financing of congregations, new Lutheran church, stewardship, ecumenism, Christian education, advocacy for justice and peace, and ministry of the laity of the world. Of these, three were considered as priorities: outreach, theological education, and capital financing. See *ECM, June 17–19, 1982*, 681–86.

237. See *ECM, March 3, 1983*, 165.

238. Leonard Sibley, *Planning*, 20.

239. *LCAM, 1984*, 348–49.

240. See *ECM, December 8–9, 1983*, 453–59. The proposal included a long list of areas for possible cuts in programs and services anticipated for the period 1985 through 1987. It was agreed that these three final years of the LCA should be treated together as a single set of fiscal proposals.

241. *LCAM, 1984*, 349–50. Much greater detail about how the process was implemented is provided in Sibley, *Planning*, 21–26. He concludes, "The intentional planning process was, in a sense, forced upon the churchwide agencies by financial stringencies. In another sense, however, it reflects a new and more effective implementation of hopes which have lain behind all of the planning efforts of the LCA: the desire for interdependence and mutual support, participatory decision-making, and flexibility within agreed-upon purposes and priorities."

242. Sibley and Hart, *Research and Evaluation*, 7. This paper is an unpublished summary of the history of these functions in the LCA and some of the most significant studies completed.

243. Ibid., 12.

244. One of the most informative was the evaluation of progress toward a ten-year aim set by the LCA in 1976 (*LCAM, 1976*, 313–14, 438). The aim was that "by 1986, persons within the LCA fellowship will increasingly experience and share their faith and apply that faith to everyday life situations through: an increasing number of opportunities designed to provide mutual support and nurture in the Christian faith; a greater ability to be more articulate in describing, discussing, explaining, and witnessing to that faith; more effective mobilization for service in society." The evaluation indicated that adopting this aim had made a difference in the life and work of the church. In some cases the measurable results had been large, and at other times, slight. The report itself gives an informative overview of what happened (*LCAM, 1986*, 881–92).

Somewhat different but also useful in assessing the life of the LCA during its first twenty years was a study, *Membership and Giving Trends, LCA, 1963–84.* See *LCAM, 1986*, 892–913. It covers such areas as growth and decline in various categories of membership, inclusivity, congregational vitality, membership vitality, evangelism vitality, trends in sources of gains and losses in membership, and trends in congregational giving and expenditures. For those who take the time to read it, the report gives solid analytical data that should dispel much conjecture and rhetoric.

245. *LCAM, 1984,* 403. By 1986, the executive director of OAF was devoting over 60% of his time to these transition-related tasks. See *OAF Final Report,* 4, in ms. form.

246. Records management, which had been a responsibility of OAF, was transferred in January 1985 to the Office of the Secretary, who is the LCA archivist. The official archives of the LCA have been maintained at the Lutheran School of Theology at Chicago. Current records management was handled in a special office at the church headquarters in New York. Despite periodic shipments to the archives and a continuing process of pruning unnecessary material, the New York office had almost one thousand file feet of paper records by 1984 in addition to microfilmed documents and computerized files (*LCAM, 1984,* 542; *1986,* 50–51). Finding a "home" for all that needed to be maintained for legal and historical purposes in the future posed a logistical problem that was only one example of the complex task of transition to a new church.

247. *OAF Final Report,* 24. LLM will continue in the ELCA and has pledged $70,000 annually in support during the first two years of the new church's existence (LCA news release, September 23, 1987, p. 7).

248. *OAF Final Report,* 26.

249. Ibid., 22–23.

250. Ibid., 21.

251. In 1986 alone this amounted to $5,288,000 (ibid., 31).

252. Ibid., 26. In addition, approximately $24 million had been pledged for synodical causes.

253. *LCAM, 1986,* 762–63. For example, pastors who retired before July 1, 1955, and, therefore, were not eligible for Social Security benefits, received $6,888 for the year 1986. It was hardly a livable sum at that time but was as much as the church could make available.

254. Figures are from the *1986 Annual Report* (Minneapolis: Board of Pensions, 1987), 8–9.

255. *LCAM, 1982,* 730–32.

256. *LCAM, 1984,* 798–99.

257. See *Board of Pensions Final Report, 1987,* 13–14.

258. One example was a large-scale evangelism conference, "Together in Witness," where participants in Denver were linked by Westar V satellite to Lutherans gathered in Albuquerque, NM; El Paso, TX; Salt Lake City, UT; Casper, WY, and two other sites in Colorado. See *OC Final Report, 1987,* 7, 9.

259. *LCAM, 1986,* 439. The Office for Communications had, for example, set up its own experiment in producing an electronic newsletter called *Religion-Online.* OC also routinely transmitted news stories directly to *The Lutheran* and news agencies throughout the country without going the paper and postal route.

260. Ibid., 442.

261. Ibid., 443.

262. During 1986–87, there had been an increase of 47 outlets for the program. The series was viewed on 29 broadcast stations, 8 cable systems, 5 cable/satellite systems, and 5 Roman Catholic instructional systems. Broadcasters were now permitted to make their own copies of tapes for later viewing. See *OC Final Report*, 8.

263. *OC Final Report*, 11–12.

264. *LCAM, 1986*, 445.

265. *OC Final Report*, 15.

266. *LCAM, 1984*, 598; and *OC Final Report*, 14.

267. The progenitor of the LCA board had been the Lutheran Publication Society, which was founded in 1855 and became the Board of Publication of the General Synod in 1867. See Suelflow and Nelson, "Frontier," 209.

268. *Board of Publication Final Report, 1987*, 11.

269. Ibid., 4.

270. *LCAM, 1984*, 601.

271. *Final Report, Board of Publication*, 4.

272. Ibid., 6–7.

273. At the time of negotiations in the Joint Commission on Lutheran Unity to form the LCA, the Canadian representatives expressed the hope that when their synods had achieved sufficient strength, an independent church could be formed.

274. Suelflow and Nelson, "Frontier," 202. Some of the earliest Lutheran settlements had been in colonial times in Nova Scotia. A fuller account of the early days may be found in Carl R. Cronmiller, *A History of the Lutheran Church in Canada* (Toronto: Synod of Canada, 1961).

275. At the 1984 convention, the Canadians presented a moving drama about Keffer's pilgrimage and gave a statue of Keffer to the LCA as a memento of their long history together. See *1984 Convention Summary*, 7–8.

276. *LCAM, 1978*, 556–57.

277. *LCAM, 1986*, 465–67, contains the final report of the Canada Section. The largest vote against the merger had been in the Eastern Canada Synod, but even there the tally was 245 for to 81 against. Central Canada voted unanimously in favor, and Western Canada was 155 for and 4 against. The vote in the Evangelical Church of Canada was 355 to 51.

278. Interestingly, it was Bishop Sjoberg who was the preacher at the installation service for the first bishop of the Evangelical Lutheran Church in America on October 10, 1987, in Chicago.

279. See *LCA Yearbook, 1987*, 377–87, for final statistical data.

280. *LCAM, 1986*, 735–53, describes the complex analysis of the funds and other property to be distributed.

281. Much of the responsibility for steering the CNLC through the morass of conflicting views and voluminous detail of work fell on the shoulders of William Kinnison, the chairperson, and Arnold Mickelson, the coordinator. Loretta Walker served as the commission's secretary.

282. Most of the major papers are included in a volume edited by Carl E. Braaten, *The New Church Debate* (Philadelphia: Fortress Press, 1983). The

writers and subjects of the chapters were as follows: Carl E. Braaten, "Introduction: The New Lutheran Church and Its Ministry"; William H. Lazareth, "Evangelical Catholicity: Lutheran Identity in an Ecumenical Age"; Robert W. Jenson, "Sovereignty in the Church"; Walter R. Bouman, "The Identity of the Ordained Minister"; Philip Hefner, "Can We Have Bishops—Reformed and Evangelical?"; Nelvin Vos, "The Vocation of the Laity"; Kathleen S. Hurty, "Embodying the Gospel in an Inclusive Church"; Robert W. Bertram, "Confessing the Faith of the Church"; Timothy F. Lull, "The Catholicity of the Local Congregation"; Elizabeth Bettenhausen, "Missionary Structures and World Struggles"; and Robert Benne, "The Social Sources of Church Polity."

283. A further indication of the degree of interest was that in addition to responses to several surveys and opinion polls, the CNLC office had been inundated with 10,370 letters from individuals; 584 letters from church-related groups; 387 actions taken by boards and commissions of the church bodies; and 1,113 sense motions from the 53 synodical/district conventions and the three churchwide conventions. See *Reports and Recommendations of the Commission for a New Lutheran Church*, June 25, 1986, p. xv.

284. Ibid., xvi.

285. To facilitate reaction to its work, the CNLC's reports were produced in both English and Spanish.

286. *CNLC Progress Report 3*, 4.

287. Members of the task forces are listed in *CNLC Progress Report 1*, 8. Details of their assignments are described on pp. 2–7 of the same report. Members of these groups were drawn from among experts in the particular field in addition to persons on the CNLC itself.

288. *The Report of the Task Force on Theology* (Minneapolis: CNLC, 1983). A study/action guide by Stanley D. Schneider, *Theology and the New Lutheran Church*, was prepared by the Division for Parish Services and LCA Board of Publication to facilitate the study and feedback process.

289. *CNLC Progress Report 3*, 2. This report also contains "A Preliminary Statement of Faith." It is interesting to compare how this initial effort was reworded and sharpened into the more precise language of the chapter on "Confession of Faith" in the ELCA Constitution (*Recommendations and Reports*, p. 13).

290. *Information About Society*, a paper distributed by Arnold R. Mickelson, CNLC Coordinator, September 28, 1983, p. 2. The report itself, which represented the work of eighteen specialists, was 302 pages in length and quite comprehensive in scope.

291. Members of the fifteen-member task force are listed in *CNLC Progress Report 1*, 8.

292. Ibid., 2. The task force's assignment included determining the implications of the church's mission as described in the statement of purpose for the organization of the new church; identifying ecclesiological and organizational issues to be considered in developing a preliminary design; developing an order in which to consider these issues and make decisions about them; and propose task forces, study groups, committees, or hearings to carry out specific assignments.

293. These task forces dealt with ecumenical and interfaith relationships, the church's global mission, development of the church in the United States, specific ministry (lay and ordained), services and resources for congregational ministry, the church and education, the church's social ministry (through homes, institutions, and agencies), the church in society, communication/interpretation, resources (volunteer, personnel, financial, property, and record resources), and pensions, health and related benefits. The commission elected 121 persons to these groups, twelve of whom were commission members. See *CNLC Progress Report 2*, 7–8. For some reason, LCA staff —with two exceptions, one of whom was a replacement for a board member —were not members of these groups, although this limitation was not the case with ALC representation. Names of the representatives were published in news reports.

294. The first of a series of designs was proposed for review by the committee in *CNLC Progress Report 3*, 4–8. As reactions from the churches were received, the design was adapted and expanded until it formed the basis for the structure that was proposed to the churches at their 1986 conventions in the document on *Reports and Recommendations*.

295. For example, the Task Force on Boundaries was assisted by a county-by-county statistical study of all fifty states called *Where Are the Lutherans?* This document, which was based on 1980 data, was compared with an earlier study by H. Conrad Hoyer that had been done for the National Lutheran Council in 1952.

296. These included such things as membership in the NCCCUSA and WCC, relations with the Presbyterian Church (USA) and Reformed Church in America, and a study of theological education in the new church.

297. The constitutions of the AELC and the LCA gave authority to the churchwide conventions to approve the necessary merger documents. The ALC constitution required a vote also by its congregations. Results of this referendum were announced by the ALC General Secretary Kathryn M. Baerwald at a press conference on March 20, 1987. Of the 4,660 congregations voting, 3,752 were in favor of the new church and 863 were opposed. Some 45 ballots were counted as abstentions. The margin for merger was approximately 4 to 1, well above the two-thirds majority required. See *The Lutheran* (April 15, 1987):17.

298. Among the most debated questions were the amount of pension contributions, quotas, headquarters site, and the size of the national body's church council. Although LCA delegates voted 4-1 to raise the pension rate from the proposed 9% to the LCA level of 12%, the change failed when presented to the ALC convention. Opposition to a quota system for representations also did not prevail, so that at least 60% of "assemblies, councils, committees, boards, and other organizational units" are to be lay persons; 50% of the lay persons are to be female and 50% male; and 10% of members of such units are to be persons of color and/or persons whose primary language is other than English. The decision was to have the ELCA headquarters in the Chicago area (an alternate proposal had been Milwaukee). An effort also failed to change the composition of the church council from the four officers plus 33 members chosen by the convention to a plan similar to

the ALC system where there would have been the four officers plus a person chosen by each synod for a total of 69. See *1986 Convention Summary*, 3–5.

299. See "Protest Mars Joint Announcement," *The Lutheran* (September 17, 1986) 18.

300. *The Lutheran* (September 17, 1986):17.

301. A helpful and readable book on the backgrounds of the three groups that formed the ELCA is by Todd W. Nichol, *All These Lutherans* (Minneapolis: Augsburg, 1986). One of a series of videotapes prepared to introduce the new church is *Making History*, available through synodical libraries and the publishing house.

302. The best and most useful book about the ELCA itself is by H. George Anderson, *What's New in the New Church?* (Philadelphia: Parish Life Press, 1987). The accompanying leader guide is by Jutta F. Anderson.

303. The units related to the officers will be the Offices for Ecumenical Affairs; Finance; Personnel; and Research, Planning, and Evaluation. The program Divisions are Congregational Life, Education, Global Mission, Ministry, Outreach, and Social Ministry Organizations. The Commissions include Church in Society, Communication Services, Financial Support, Women, and Multicultural Ministries. The women's organization is called Women of the Evangelical Lutheran Church in America. The youth group's name is Lutheran Youth Organization. The Conference of Bishops will have its own staff in the new church. The church periodical will be called *The Lutheran*. The ELCA Publishing House will have its own board and be separately incorporated. The Board of Pensions will also be incorporated. The ELCA Foundation will have a management committee. Complete details of the structure and responsibilities of various agencies and the roles of the officers are described in *Reports and Recommendations*.

304. ELCA missionaries will be serving in 47 countries, and there will be projects without ELCA personnel in 13 other nations.

305. The *Bulletin of Reports* was all of four pages in length—a far cry from the volumes of papers delegates had been accustomed to in previous conventions.

306. Pastor Lundblad was widely known as one of the Lutheran preachers on the Protestant Hour.

307. The delegates had to juggle several documents in the course of the sessions: *Program and Reports, Reports and Recommendations of the CNLC as Amended by the Delegates of the AELC, ALC, and LCA on August 29, 1986, Pension and Other Benefit Plans, Summary: Pension and Other Benefit Plans*, and *Nominations*. One cloud hung over the proceedings because of threats that had been made by Pittsburgh-based Denominational Ministry Strategy to disrupt the proceedings. See *The Lutheran* (January 7, 1987):18. Security was tight throughout the proceedings, and the protest "fizzled except for a scuffle near a curtained entrance to the delegates seating area." See *The Lutheran* (May 20, 1987):23.

308. The leaders on the first ballot were David Preus, 284; Herbert Chilstrom, 112; William Lazareth, 101; Reuben Swanson, 61; Kenneth Sauer, 56; James Crumley, 55; Barbara Lundblad, 52; Kenneth Senft, 44. All figures are

recorded in the *ELCA Constituting Convention Minutes,* beginning on p. 8 of the manuscript copy.

309. Second ballot: Preus, 294; Chilstrom, 187; Lazareth, 134; Lundblad, 83; Swanson, 79; Sauer, 57; Senft, 43; Crumley, 37.

310. This may well have been the first time in the history of Lutheranism that a woman pastor had been such a serious candidate for bishop of a national church body. To many, it was one of the most significant events at the convention.

311. Bishop Herbert Walfred Chilstrom, 55, was bishop of the LCA's Minnesota Synod at the time of his election. His great-grandparents were among the earliest Swedish settlers in Minnesota. He is a graduate of Augsburg College and Augustana Seminary. He received a master's degree in theology from Princeton Seminary and a doctorate in education from New York University. Corinne Chilstrom was serving as assistant pastor at Bethlehem Church, an ALC congregation in Minneapolis.

312. *The Lutheran* (May 20, 1987):20.

THE CONSTITUTION OF THE LUTHERAN CHURCH IN AMERICA

Including amendments adopted through the 1984 convention of the Lutheran Church in America

PREAMBLE

In the name of the Father and of the Son and of the Holy Spirit. Amen. Remembering the prayer of our Lord Jesus Christ that His disciples might be one as He and the Father are one, and believing that His Spirit is ever leading His people toward unity in the household of God, we of the American Evangelical Lutheran Church, the Augustana Evangelical Lutheran Church, The Finnish Evangelical Lutheran Church of America, and The United Lutheran Church in America, persuaded that the time has come when His unifying power should be manifested through a united profession of faith by these churches and through forms of fellowship which will make for a more effective stewardship of His gifts to us, adopt this constitution to govern our common life in Him and our united witness to Him, praying that He who is the Lord of the Church may thereby lead us toward a more inclusive union of all Lutherans on this continent.

ARTICLE I

Name and Incorporation

Section 1. The name of this church shall be the Lutheran Church in America.

Section 2. The Lutheran Church in America shall be incorporated.

Section 3. For the purposes of this constitution and the accompanying bylaws, the Lutheran Church in America is hereinafter designated as "this church."

ARTICLE II

Confession of Faith

Section 1. This church confesses Jesus Christ as Lord of the Church. The Holy Spirit creates and sustains the Church through the Gospel and thereby unites believers with their Lord and with one another in the fellowship of faith.

565

Section 2. This church holds that the Gospel is the revelation of God's sovereign will and saving grace in Jesus Christ. In Him, the Word Incarnate, God imparts Himself to His people.

Section 3. This church acknowledges the Holy Scriptures as the norm for the faith and life of the Church. The Holy Scriptures are the divinely inspired record of God's redemptive act in Christ, for which the Old Testament prepared the way and which the New Testament proclaims. In the continuation of this proclamation in the Church, God still speaks through the Holy Scriptures and realizes His redemptive purpose generation after generation.

Section 4. This church accepts the Apostles', the Nicene, and the Athanasian creeds as true declarations of the faith of the Church.

Section 5. This church accepts the Unaltered Augsburg Confession and Luther's Small Catechism as true witnesses to the Gospel, and acknowledges as one with it in faith and doctrine all churches that likewise accept the teachings of these symbols.

Section 6. This church accepts the other symbolical books of the evangelical Lutheran church, the Apology of the Augsburg Confession, the Smalcald Articles, Luther's Large Catechism, and the Formula of Concord as further valid interpretations of the confession of the Church.

Section 7. This church affirms that the Gospel transmitted by the Holy Scriptures, to which the creeds and confessions bear witness, is the true treasure of the Church, the substance of its proclamation, and the basis of its unity and continuity. The Holy Spirit uses the proclamation of the Gospel and the administration of the sacraments to create and sustain Christian faith and fellowship. As this occurs, the Church fulfills its divine mission and purpose.

ARTICLE III

Membership

Section 1. This church shall consist at its organization of the congregations and ordained ministers of the American Evangelical Lutheran Church, of the Augustana Evangelical Lutheran Church, of The Finnish Evangelical Lutheran Church of America, and of the constituent synods of The United Lutheran Church in America.

Section 2. Additional individual congregations and ordained ministers may be received into membership as set forth in Articles VI and VII of this constitution.

Section 3. Congregations and ordained ministers when organized into a synod may through such synod unite with this church upon application for membership, subscription to this constitution including its Confession of Faith, and acceptance by a two-thirds vote of the delegates present and voting at a convention of this church.

ARTICLE IV

The Nature of the Church

Section 1. All power in the Church belongs to our Lord Jesus Christ, its head. All actions of this church are to be carried out under His rule and authority.

Section 2. The Church exists both as an inclusive fellowship and as local congregations gathered for worship and Christian service. Congregations find their fulfillment in the universal community of the Church, and the universal Church exists in and through congregations. This church, therefore, derives its character and powers both from the sanction and representation of its congregations and from its inherent nature as an expression of the broader fellowship of the faithful. In length, it acknowledges itself to be in the historic continuity of the communion of saints; in breadth, it expresses the fellowship of believers and congregations in this our day.

ARTICLE V

Objects and Powers

Section 1. This church lives to be the instrument of the Holy Spirit in obedience to the commission of its Lord, and specifically
   a. To proclaim the Gospel through Word and Sacraments, to relate that Gospel to human need in every situation, and to extend the ministry of the Gospel to all the world.
   b. To gather into fellowship those who respond in faith to the call of the Gospel and to nurture them in the faith through that fellowship.
   c. To affirm its unity in the true faith and to give outward expression to that unity.
   d. To safeguard the pure preaching of the Word of God and the right administration of the Sacraments by all its ordained ministers and in all its congregations in conformity with its Confession of Faith.
   e. To strive for the unification of all Lutherans within its boundaries in one church and to take constructive measures leading thereto when such action will extend the mission of Christ's reconciling love.
   f. To foster Christian unity and to serve humanity by participating in ecumenical Christian activities, contributing its witness and work and cooperating with other churches which confess God the Father, Son and Holy Spirit.
   g. To develop relationships with communities of other faiths for dialogue and common action.
   h. To lift its voice in concord and to work in concert with forces for good, cooperating with church and other groups participating in activities that promote justice, relieve misery, and reconcile the estranged.

Section 2. To achieve these ends, this church shall
   a. Establish and receive congregations.
   b. Further missions in America and throughout the world.
   c. Educate and ordain ministers of the Gospel and be responsible for the discipline of the ordained ministers in its membership.

d. Establish and maintain institutions for the education of youth and for training in leadership in this church and in society, and serve the spiritual needs of youth in other schools of higher learning.

e. Provide institutions and agencies to minister to human need in the name of Christ our Lord.

f. Study contemporary society in the light of the Gospel and witness to the truth of God in relation thereto.

g. Issue study materials setting forth Christian truth and disseminate knowledge concerning the doctrine, practice, history and life of the Lutheran church.

h. Cultivate edifying practices of worship, and prepare and publish service books for congregational, family and private use.

i. Decide all questions of doctrine and life on the basis of the Holy Scriptures in accordance with the Confession of Faith of this church.

j. Act in and through the synods for the proper administration of its work entrusted to them.

k. Establish such churchwide structures and agencies as are deemed appropriate to carry out assigned responsibilities.

l. Estimate financial needs for support of approved work of this church and solicit and disburse funds for such work.

m. Enter into relations with other Lutheran church bodies and with other evangelical churches for the furtherance of the Gospel of our Lord.

Section 3. This church carries forward the life and activities of the American Evangelical Lutheran Church, the Augustana Evangelical Lutheran Church, The Finnish Evangelical Lutheran Church of America, and The United Lutheran Church in America. In so doing, this church accepts at its organization and assumes as its own each and all of the commitments of the four predecessor churches: their membership, including congregations and ordained ministers, relationships with institutions, assets and liabilities.

ARTICLE VI

Congregations

Section 1. A congregation of this church is a worshiping, learning, witnessing, and serving community of baptized persons among whom the Word is proclaimed and the sacraments are celebrated according to the Gospel; and whose corporate existence is recognized by the Lutheran Church in America.

Section 2. Congregations of this church retain authority in all matters that have not been committed to the Lutheran Church in America or its synods in this constitution or by subsequent enactments.

Section 3. After the organization of this church, admission of a congregation into its membership shall be by action of the synod on whose territory it is located or of a nongeographic synod whose character and antecedents it shares. Each congregation shall, in its application for admission into this church, covenant to abide loyally by the enactments of this church and those of the synod of which it becomes a member.

Section 4. The lay delegates who represent congregations in conventions of the synods to which they belong shall be chosen by the congregations themselves. Each synod shall act for its member congregations and ordained ministers in electing delegates to represent them in conventions of this church.

Section 5. Congregations shall have the right to petition this church in the following manner. Such petitions shall be addressed to the synod to which the congregation belongs for response by the synod, or, at the discretion of the synod, for forwarding to the convention of this church.

Section 6. All proposed changes in the constitution or incorporation documents of a congregation shall be reported to the bishop of the synod for scrutiny and counsel. Any amendment that would affect the articles on faith or adherence to this church shall require approval by the synod.

Section 7. In cases of strife and division, should any part of a congregation belonging to this church reject the faith as set forth in Article II, or refuse to abide by other provisions of this constitution or by its obligation as a member of this church, that part of the congregation, whether a majority or minority of its membership, which continues in unity with this church and its faith shall be recognized as the lawful congregation and shall continue in possession of all the property of the congregation.

Section 8. A synod may declare a congregation within its jurisdiction defunct if such congregation has disbanded, or if it has ceased to maintain religious services according to the tenets and usages of the Lutheran Church, or if its membership has so diminished in numbers or financial strength as to render it impracticable for such congregation to fulfill the purposes for which it was organized, or to protect its property from waste and deterioration. In such case, or if a congregation departs from membership in this church without the consent of a convention of the synod, all property of the congregation, real, personal and mixed, shall vest in the synod, its successors or assigns.

Section 9. A congregation which desires to sever its relation with this church in order to unite with another Lutheran church body shall make written application to its synod for a proper transfer. The synod may grant such request by convention action.

Section 10. A synod, acting for this church, may exclude a congregation from the membership of this church for proper cause by the disciplinary process prescribed in the bylaws. If a congregation is so excluded, all its property, real, personal and mixed, shall vest in the synod, its successors and assigns.

Section 11. The executive body of the synod to which the affected congregation belongs shall be charged exclusively with the responsibility to make all determinations, whether of a secular, doctrinal or ecclesiastical nature, relevant to the administration of Sections 7 and 8 of this article, and its decision shall be final subject only to the right of appeal to a convention of the synod.

ARTICLE VII

Ordained Ministers

Section 1. This church shall define the standards of acceptance into and continuance in its ordained ministry. These standards shall be applied and administered by the synods.

Section 2. Ordination and reception of ministers shall be a function of the synods, acting in behalf of this church. Synods shall also have prior responsibility for recruiting, approval and supervision of all candidates for ordination. Each applicant for ordination or for reception from another Lutheran church body shall appear before the examining committee of the synod, unless this requirement is waived as provided in the bylaws, and can be ordained or otherwise admitted to membership only upon recommendation by such committee. The majority of the members of the examining committee shall be appointed or elected by the synod; one or more members shall be designated by the appropriate churchwide agency to represent the interest and concern of this church as a whole in the ordination and reception of its ministers. The Division for Professional Leadership shall provide guidelines for examining committees and maintain liaison with them to provide for interpretation and for receiving suggestions for revision of the guidelines.

Section 3. Each minister shall preach and teach in conformity with the Confession of Faith of this church and shall lead a life befitting the holy office of the ministry.

Section 4. After the organization of the Lutheran Church in America no person, who belongs to any organization which claims to possess in its teachings and ceremonies that which the Lord has given solely to His Church, shall be ordained or otherwise received into the ministry of this church, nor shall any person so ordained or received by this church be retained in its ministry who subsequently joins such an organization. Violation of this rule shall make such minister subject to discipline.

Section 5. Each minister of this church, except those who are retired by reason of age or disability, shall be in possession of a call from a congregation, a synod or this church itself. As an exception to this rule, a minister on leave from call may be retained on the roll of ordained ministers from year to year for no more than three years by action of the synod to which such minister belongs, except as provided in the bylaws for graduate study.

Section 6. Each minister who is a member of this church shall be a member of one of its synods and also, unless this requirement is waived in an exceptional case in accordance with the bylaws, on the roll of confirmed members of one of its congregations. Ministers shall be entitled to exercise the full rights of membership, including the right to vote, at conventions of the synod.

Section 7. Responsibility for discipline of ministers and the imposition of penalties up to and including deposition from the ministerial office is vested in the synods, acting in behalf of this church. The majority of the members of the committee on discipline shall be selected by the synod involved; other members shall be designated by the bishop of this church to represent the interest and concern of this church as a whole in the proceedings. An appeal, when permissible, from the findings and recommendation of the committee on discipline shall be heard and adjudicated by an appeal committee constituted as specified in the bylaws.

ARTICLE VIII

Synods

Section 1. This church shall be divided into synods, whose number and boundaries are to be determined by this church in its bylaws. Synods having distinctive linguistic or national characteristics may, at the discretion of the convention, enter this church on a non-geographic basis.

Section 2. Each synod shall be incorporated upon the terms of appropriate documents ratified by this church in convention or by the Executive Council. Amendments thereto shall be subject to like ratification.

Section 3. Each synod shall have a constitution, ratified by this church in convention or by the Executive Council. Amendments thereto shall be subject to like ratification; provided, however, that an amendment which includes no variant from the parallel portion of the Approved Constitution for Synods shall be deemed to have been ratified by the Executive Council upon its adoption, report thereon to be made promptly to the Executive Council.

Section 4. Each congregation, with the exception of those in non-geographic synods, shall belong to the synod on whose territory it is located.

Section 5. The membership of ordained ministers in synods shall be as follows:

    a. A minister under call from a congregation, in the same synod as the parish served.

    b. A minister under call from a synod, in that synod.

    c. A minister under call from this church, in the synod of membership at the time of the issuance of such call unless otherwise assigned by the bishop of this church.

    d. A minister on a synod's clergy roll who is on leave from call as provided in Article VII, in that synod.

    e. A retired or disabled minister, in the synod in which last called or in the synod of current residence.

Section 6. The voting body at the conventions of each synod shall consist of a lay delegate from each congregation and the ordained ministers on its clergy roll. Provision for additional voting delegates from its congregations may be made in the constitution of the synod. By exception, and with the approval of the bishop of the church, a synod may grant voice and vote to an ordained minister of a Lutheran church body outside North America who, by agreement between this church and the other church body, is serving one of the congregations of the synod or in another ministry authorized by it.

Section 7. The function of synods shall be oversight and advancement of the mission of this church within their bounds by propagating the Gospel, conserving unity in the true faith and guarding against any departure therefrom, and encouraging the fuller employment of resources of spirit and means for the furtherance of the Kingdom of God.

Section 8. Specifically, duties and powers of synods shall include:
  a. Care of congregations by
   (1) Organization, reception and approval or disapproval of location or relocation of congregations.
   (2) Counsel and guidance in filling vacancies in pastorates.
   (3) Encouragement and assistance for congregational worship, learning, witness, service, social responsibility and administration.
   (4) Adjudication of appeals from congregational discipline, as provided in the constitution of the synod.
   (5) Intervention and mediation in times of strife and division.
   (6) Discipline of congregations as stated in Article VI.
  b. Counseling and enabling of professional workers by
   (1) Recruitment, assistance in preparatory and continuing education, career guidance and counseling.
   (2) Providing financial assistance to college and seminary students as stated in the bylaws of the Lutheran Church in America. (LCABL, Section III, Item 6)
   (3) Exercise of responsibility for ownership and administration of the theological seminaries of this church, election of their governing boards, and provision of basic financial support for them, with each synod related for this purpose to a single seminary, except that in order to provide for common ownership of a seminary with another Lutheran church body, this church may exercise these responsibilities under specific agreements with the synod or synods involved.
   (4) Ordination and reception of ordained ministers.
   (5) Encouragement to congregations, agencies and institutions concerning proper levels of remuneration.
   (6) Discipline of ordained ministers as stated in Article VII.
  c. Planning, development and supervision of special congregational, institutional and social action ministries by
   (1) Cooperating with the appropriate churchwide agency in developing new congregations and in providing assistance to congregations engaged in special ministries or with special problems.
   (2) Provision of higher education for the members of this church and others and for the involvement of this church in higher education through support of church-related colleges.
   (3) Provision for Lutheran ministry to persons involved in higher education.
   (4) Maintenance and support of social ministry institutions and agencies.
   (5) Participation, including membership in state, regional and metropolitan councils of churches and similar cooperative Christian movements which have been approved by a convention of this church or the Executive Council as adhering to sound principles.
   (6) Lifting its voice in concord and working in concert with forces for good, cooperating with church and other groups participating in

activities that promote justice, relieve misery, and reconcile the estranged.

d. Interpretation and support of the continent-wide and world-wide work of this church by
   (1) Creation and development of means for effective collaboration with churchwide agencies of this church.
   (2) Fostering of relationships of mutual benefit with the synodical units of the official auxiliaries of this church.
   (3) Election of delegates to represent their congregations and ordained ministers in conventions of this church.
e. Administration of the synod as stipulated in its constitution.

Section 9. Every synod shall have the right to memorialize the convention of this church on any subject affecting the welfare of this church. Such memorials must be adopted by the synod in convention.

Section 10. Subject to other provisions of this constitution, each synod shall have jurisdiction in its own affairs. When this church deals with internal matters within a synod, its cooperation and consent must be secured.

Section 11. Any synod desiring to publish books of devotion and instruction, such as liturgies, hymnals and catechisms, other than those provided or authorized by the Lutheran Church in America, shall first receive permission from a convention of this church or the Executive Council.

Section 12. Bishops of synods may be invited to meet as consultants with the Executive Council and shall appear before it when requested to represent their synods. They may also make suggestions to the Executive Council or seek its advice, with respect to conditions and work in their synods.

Section 13. There shall be a Conference of Bishops which shall meet at least once a year with the officers of this church for the discussion of the problems, program and plans affecting the synods and the Lutheran Church in America. The functions of the conference shall be consultative and advisory. Its meetings shall be upon call of the bishop of this church at times determined by the bishop of this church or when written request is received from the bishops of seven or more synods. The bishop of this church shall chair all meetings of the conference, and the secretary shall record the minutes of its meetings and transmit its recommendations to the Executive Council.

ARTICLE IX

Special Interest Conferences

This church shall authorize, as provided in the bylaws, the organization of special interest conferences of ordained ministers and lay persons having a common linguistic, national or cultural heritage. Such conferences may hold periodic meetings for fellowship and discussion of common concerns but shall have no powers of legislation or oversight. Reports of meetings, together with any recommendations arising out of the special spheres of interest, shall be made to the Executive Council.

ARTICLE X

Conventions

Section 1. The convention of this church shall be its highest legislative authority. All congregations, ordained ministers, synods, officers, the Executive Council, and churchwide agencies (except common agencies) shall be bound by all actions pertaining to them taken by a convention in conformity with this constitution.

Section 2. A convention of this church shall be held biennially at such time and place as determined by the Executive Council.

Section 3. Special conventions shall be called for specified purposes by the bishop of this church at the request in writing of two-thirds of the members of the Executive Council or of the bishops of a majority of the synods.

Section 4. The secretary shall publish the time and place of each regular convention at least two months in advance, shall give written notice of a special convention to the bishop of each synod immediately upon the issuance of the call, and shall publish the same at least thirty days prior to the opening date of the convention.

Section 5. The congregations and ordained ministers of each synod of this church shall be entitled to representation through the synod at conventions of the church by an equal number of clergy and lay delegates to a total number as specified in the bylaws, computed on the basis of the number of congregations on the synodical roll, except that additional delegates shall be allocated by the Executive Council to synods which are significantly underrepresented in ratio to their confirmed membership. Each synod shall be entitled to at least one clergy and one lay delegate. The total voting membership of the convention shall consist of the delegates elected by the synods, such delegations to include the bishops of the synods, and, in addition thereto, the constitutional officers of this church who shall serve as delegates ex officio.

Section 6. The delegates at a special convention shall be those who were seated in the preceding regular convention, provided they have not been disqualified by termination of membership in the synod or its congregations, or superseded by the election of new delegates. Vacancies in delegations shall be filled according to the rules of the several synods.

Section 7. A majority of the delegates from a majority of the synods shall constitute a quorum.

ARTICLE XI

Executive Council

Section 1. The Executive Council shall consist of the three officers of this church, together with fifteen clergy members and fifteen lay members who shall be elected at large by the convention for a term of four years. Elected members shall be eligible to serve no more than two terms consecutively, nor shall more than two persons from any synod serve simultaneously as elected members of the Executive Council. A vacancy occurring ad interim shall be filled by the Executive Council until the next regular convention of this church, which shall fill the unexpired term.

Section 2. During the interim between conventions and under the limitations imposed by this constitution and the bylaws, the Executive Council shall carry forward the work and policies of this church and shall act for this church, subject in all matters to review of its actions by the subsequent convention.

Section 3. The duties and functions of the Executive Council shall be to:

   a. Be the board of directors of the corporation and exercise trusteeship responsibilities for this church.

   b. Do long-range planning of the work of this church, with emphasis on spiritual life and growth, for approval by the convention.

   c. Issue letters of call to ordained ministers as authorized by the convention.

   d. Set the salaries of the officers of this church and adopt a compensation plan for its staff and the staff of churchwide agencies.

   e. Prepare the proposed agenda and program for each convention.

   f. Recommend annual program budgets to the regular conventions.

   g. Supervise the expenditure of the funds of the church, subject to the provisions of the bylaws and the program budgets adopted by the convention.

   h. Address and counsel the synods in the interim between conventions for the promotion of intersynodical harmony.

   i. Fill vacancies not otherwise provided for, and determine the fact of the incapacity of an officer of this church.

   j. Be responsible, under the primary authority of the convention, for approving all ecumenical and interchurch relations, except in Canada, of this church, its synods, and its churchwide agencies.

   k. Make official pronouncements on behalf of this church ad interim, under terms and conditions defined in the bylaws.

   l. Fulfill all other obligations assigned to it by this constitution, the bylaws, or the convention.

   m. Report its actions to the convention.

ARTICLE XII

Officers

Section 1. The officers of this church shall be a bishop, a secretary and a treasurer. The bishop shall be an ordained minister of the Lutheran Church in America. The bishop and the secretary shall serve full time in office. The secretary and the treasurer shall each be either an ordained minister of this church or a lay member of one of its congregations. The treasurer may serve full or part time in office.

Section 2. Each officer shall be elected by ballot at a regular convention for a term of four years. No person who has attained the age of sixty-seven years shall be eligible for election. The schedule of elections shall be so arranged that the terms of office of the bishop and the secretary will expire in alternate biennia.

Section 3. The officers shall serve in the same capacities in the Executive Council.

Section 4. The bishop of this church shall be its leader and counselor in matters spiritual and temporal. The bishop of this church shall be its chief executive officer and the president of the corporation. The bishop shall preside at its conventions and make policy recommendations to them, seeing that the constitution is observed and that the enactments of this church are carried out. When serving as presiding officer, the bishop of this church shall conduct worship at conventions and other meetings, or appoint someone to do so. The bishop of this church shall convene and preside at meetings of the Conference of Bishops, shall coordinate the work of the churchwide agencies, nominate executive directors subject to election by the Executive Council, and consult with chief staff officials regarding individual staff appointments. The bishop of this church shall appoint committees not otherwise provided for; shall be ex officio the primary representative of the Lutheran Church in America in all interchurch associations and councils, except in Canada, in which it holds membership; shall discharge such other duties as are delegated to the bishop of this church by the convention or the Executive Council; and shall have oversight of the office of secretary.

Section 5. The secretary, as the recording officer of this church, shall keep the minutes of the conventions and prepare the same for publication, shall have charge of records, registers, and archives, shall attest all documents of this church that require such attestation, and shall be custodian of the seal.

Section 6. The treasurer shall be the fiscal officer of this church, shall receive and disburse all monies and keep an accurate account of all transactions, and shall make full report of the financial affairs of this church to conventions and to the Executive Council.

Section 7. In the event of the death, resignation or incapacity of an officer, the Executive Council shall fill the vacancy until the next convention, which shall elect a successor to fill the unexpired term. In the event of the death, resignation or incapacity of the bishop of this church, the secretary shall call a meeting of the Executive Council as soon as possible. Pending the convening of the Executive Council, and, if it decides not to fill the vacancy, pending the next convention, the secretary shall discharge the duties of bishop as well as those of secretary.

ARTICLE XIII

Churchwide Agencies

Section 1. Churchwide agencies shall include divisions, offices, boards and auxiliaries.

 a. A division shall provide a wide range of services to a particular category of organizational units or persons which have responsibilities of special significance to this church.

  b. An office shall provide designated support services, primarily to other churchwide agencies.

  c. A board, which may be incorporated, shall render services of a specialized nature to the constituency of this church. It reports to the convention and the Executive Council through an office.

  d. An auxiliary shall be an autonomous organization officially recognized by this church and operating within the provisions of this constitution, the bylaws and actions of the convention.

Section 2. Charters, articles of incorporation, constitutions, bylaws or standing rules of procedure for churchwide agencies and amendments thereto shall go into effect after approval by the convention or the Executive Council.

Section 3. Each division and office shall have a management committee, normally consisting of no more than twelve members, and each board normally shall consist of no more than fifteen members. The exact size of each management committee and board shall be determined by the convention which shall elect approximately one-half of the members in alternate years for a term of four years and shall fill all vacancies for unexpired terms, except that in each election year two members of the Board of Pensions and one member of the Board of Publication shall be elected by the Executive Council. No member shall serve more than two terms consecutively. No member shall receive emolument therefrom or shall simultaneously be an officer of the church, a member of the Executive Council, the Court of Adjudication, another management committee, a board, or the board of directors of an auxiliary.

Section 4. Consulting committees, as needed, shall be appointed by the bishop of this church, by an executive director, by a management committee or by a board to serve for such time and for such purpose as specified when appointed. The composition and activities of consulting committees shall be included in the reports of the churchwide agencies which are presented to the convention.

ARTICLE XIV

Common Agencies

Section 1. This church may, by vote of the convention, assign specific functional activities to common agencies in which this church participates in cooperation with other Lutheran church bodies. Such activities while under the supervision and control of such common agencies acting in accordance with their constitutions, shall have the same status in this church as is accorded to work carried on under its direct authority by its other agencies. Such assignments shall continue until terminated by vote of a convention.

Section 2. Common agencies shall report to the regular conventions of this church on their assigned tasks.

ARTICLE XV

Periodical

Section 1. The Lutheran Church in America shall publish a periodical, *The Lutheran.*

ARTICLE XVI

Court of Adjudication

Section 1. There shall be a Court of Adjudication to which shall be referred for decision questions of principle or practice which may arise under this constitution or otherwise within this church, including questions involving disputed jurisdiction or the interpretation of powers claimed or conferred by this church. Referral of such questions shall be by resolution of the convention or the Executive Council, or by a synod or its executive body. The decisions of the court in such matters shall be binding until reversed by vote of the convention on appeal properly taken. The right of such appeal shall always be recognized.

Section 2. Questions of doctrine or conscience may also be referred to the Court of Adjudication for its counsel at the discretion of the convention, which shall be free to use any alternate method to ascertain the right application of the truth of the Gospel to the question at issue. Such opinions of the court shall be submitted to the convention for its scrutiny and decision.

Section 3. The Court of Adjudication shall consist of nine members, six ordained ministers and three lay persons, who shall be elected by the convention for a term of six years. No member shall serve more than two terms consecutively. The consent of at least six members shall always be necessary for a decision. A vacancy occurring ad interim shall be filled by the Executive Council until the next regular convention of this church, which shall fill the unexpired term.

Section 4. The Court of Adjudication shall report all its actions, decisions and opinions to the next regular convention.

ARTICLE XVII

Canada Section

Section 1. The synods of this church located in Canada shall jointly constitute the Lutheran Church in America—Canada Section through which they can speak with a united voice and act together in relationships and areas of church work in which there is a common Canadian concern.

Section 2. The Lutheran Church in America—Canada Section shall have full power, in the name and stead of this church:

    a. To be incorporated under the laws of Canada.

    b. To make approaches to, and have dealings with, the government of Canada and other Canadian authorities.

    c. To form associations with Lutheran church bodies and other churches in Canada, and to elect commissioners or representatives to such associations.

d. To negotiate and consummate union with other Lutheran church bodies in Canada.

e. To form at any time a separate and autonomous Lutheran Church in Canada.

Section 3. The Lutheran Church in America—Canada Section shall have as further powers:

a. To set the ratio of representation for its conventions.

b. To elect officers and establish agencies through which to carry on its activities.

c. To elect or appoint a Standing Committee on Canadian Missions to survey and investigate home mission opportunities and needs in Canada, to initiate proposals arising therefrom, and to coordinate the resultant requests of the Canadian synods to the appropriate church-wide agency, which shall in turn provide mutually agreed staff support to the standing committee and shall grant to its representatives seat and voice in all management committee meetings.

d. To publish a Canadian church paper.

e. To engage in social action programs and projects.

f. To conduct public relations activities in Canada.

g. To advise and make recommendations on distinctive Canadian interests in any other fields of the work of this church, forwarding such advice and proposals to this church in convention or to the Executive Council ad interim.

ARTICLE XVIII
Bylaws and Amendments

Section 1. This church may adopt bylaws not in conflict with this constitution. Such bylaws may be suspended or amended at any convention by a two-thirds vote of the delegates present and voting.

Section 2. Amendments to this constitution must be presented in writing to the convention over the signature of no fewer than twenty delegates representing no fewer than five synods. Following such presentation, they shall be immediately referred for study and recommendation to the Executive Council, which shall make report thereon to the same convention if possible but which shall not be required to do so until forty-eight hours have elapsed following the presentation. Adoption of an amendment shall require passage at two successive conventions by a two-thirds vote of the delegates present and voting, and the full text thereof shall be mailed to each delegate within thirty days after adjournment of the convention first acting favorably thereon.

NOTE: This version of the LCA Constitution is as amended by the 1984 convention. The 1986 convention deleted the article dealing with the Canada Section since the Evangelical Lutheran Church in

Canada had already been formed. Amendments were also made to remove the two-term restriction on election to bodies, such as the Executive Council, in order to permit persons to serve for the duration of the LCA's existence.

Appendix B | BACKGROUND STUDIES RELATING TO
THE HISTORY OF THE
LUTHERAN CHURCH IN AMERICA
AND ITS PREDECESSOR BODIES

There are a number of volumes that provide general background on Lutheranism in North America. References to these appear in the endnotes to each chapter. The most recent comprehensive history is E. Clifford Nelson's *The Lutherans in North America*, rev. ed. (Philadelphia: Fortress Press, 1980).

Among the histories of the predecessor bodies are the following: G. Everett Arden, *Augustana Heritage: A History of the Augustana Evangelical Lutheran Church* (Rock Island, Ill.: Augustana Press, 1963); Jacob W. Heikkinen, *The Story of the Suomi Synod* (originally commissioned by the Finnish Special Interest Conference of the LCA, this volume was published in 1986); Enok Mortensen, *The Danish Lutheran Church in America: The History and Heritage of the American Evangelical Lutheran Church in America* (Philadelphia: LCA Board of Publication, 1967). No complete history of the United Lutheran Church in America has ever been published, but one has been commissioned recently and the writer is to be E. Theodore Bachmann.

The process that led to the LCA merger itself is described in Johannes Knudsen, *The Formation of the Lutheran Church in America* (Philadelphia: Fortress Press, 1978).

HISTORIES OF LCA SYNODS

Many of the synods of the Lutheran Church in America have published their own histories. Since most synods themselves had predecessor bodies, the number of volumes written is large, and the following list provides only a representative selection.

Canadian Synods

The story of the three LCA synods in Canada is for the most part included in more general works about Canadian Lutheran history, such as the following:

Baglo, Ferdinand Eugene. *Augustana Lutherans in Canada.* Saskatoon: Canada Conferences of the Augustana Lutheran Church, 1962.

Cronmiller, Carl R. *A History of the Lutheran Church in Canada.* Toronto: Synod of Canada, 1961.

Eylands, Valdimar J. *Lutherans in Canada.* Winnipeg: The Columbia Press, Ltd., 1945.

Threinen, Norman J. *Fifty Years of Lutheran Convergence: The Canadian Case-Study.* Dubuque, Iowa: William C. Brown Co., 1983.

A history of the Eastern Canada Synod is being written by Roy Grosz and will build upon the earlier work by Cronmiller.

Synods in the United States of America

Central Pennsylvania

Dunkelberger, Harold A. *One Body We, A History of the Central Pennsylvania Synod, 1938–1978.* Harrisburg, Pa.: The McFarland Co., 1978.

Florida

Driscoll, Carl A., et al. *History of the Florida Synod of the LCA.* Tampa, Fla.: Florida Synod, 1978.

Indiana-Kentucky

Waltmann, Henry G., ed. *History of the Indiana-Kentucky Synod of the Lutheran Church in America.* Indianapolis: Indiana-Kentucky Synod, 1971.

Iowa

Larson, Robert, ed. *Iowa Synod of the Lutheran Church in America, 1962–1987.* Des Moines: Iowa Synod, 1987.

Metropolitan New York

There are approximately fifteen books dealing with various phases of the history of the New York Ministerium and its successor synods. These include the following:

Kreider, Harry J. *Beginnings of Lutheranism in New York.* New York: New York Synod, 1949.

Jaxheimer, David C. *The Story of Our Synod.* New York: New York and New England Synod, 1954.

Deitz, Charles E., et. al. *New York Ministerium Legacy.* New York: Northeast Synods, 1986. This volume deals with the histories of congregations of the Metropolitan New York, Upper New York, New England, and New Jersey Synods.

Nebraska

Lund, L. Dale. *Partners in Mission, 1962–1987: The Lutheran Church in America in Nebraska.* Omaha, Neb.: Nebraska Synod, 1987.

New England

See references under Metropolitan New York Synod.

New Jersey

See references under Metropolitan New York Synod.

North Carolina

There are five major histories of the North Carolina Synod, plus a new one projected. The most recent is—

Anderson, Hugh George. *The North Carolina Synod Through 175 Years, 1803–1978.* Salisbury, N.C.: Committee on Historical Work, North Carolina Synod, 1978.

Northeastern Pennsylvania

See references under Southeastern Pennsylvania.

Ohio

Allbeck, Willard. *A Century of Lutherans in Ohio.* Yellow Springs, Ohio: Antioch Press, 1966.

Pacific Northwest

Emerson, Heidi, Milton Nesvig, Philip Nordquist, Roland Swanson, eds. *New Partners, Old Roots: A History of Merging Lutheran Churches in the Pacific Northwest.* Tacoma, Wash.: AELC, ALC, LCA districts and synods, 1986.

Red River Valley

Lund, Gene, ed. *Deep Runs the River, History of the Red River Valley Synod LCA.* Fargo, N.D.: Red River Valley Synod, 1987.

Slovak Zion

Body, John. *History of Slovak Zion Synod LCA.* Slovak Zion Synod, 1976.

South Carolina

McCullough, Paul G., et al. *A History of the Lutheran Church in South Carolina.* Columbia, S.C.: South Carolina Synod, 1971.

Southeastern

Swygert, Alice Lovern. *Twenty Years of Progress, 1962–1982, A History of the Southeastern Synod of the LCA*. Atlanta, Ga.: Southeastern Synod, 1982.

Southeastern Pennsylvania

Pfatteicher, Helen E. *The Ministerium of Pennsylvania, Oldest Lutheran Synod in America, 1748–1938*. Philadelphia, Pa.: Ministerium Press, 1938.

Upper New York

See references under Metropolitan New York Synod.

Virginia

Eisenberg, William E. *The Lutheran Church in Virginia, 1717–1962*. Roanoke, Va.: Virginia Synod, 1967.

Handley, George E. and George A. Kegley. *Lutherans in Virginia*. Vol. 1, *A 25-Year History;* Vol. 2, *Congregational Sketchbook*. Salem, Va.: Virginia Synod, 1987.

The following synods have indicated that synodical histories are projected, and writers who have been commissioned are noted: Indiana-Kentucky, Bernhard Hillila; Metropolitan New York, Robert F. Scholz; North Carolina, Raymond M. Bost; Ohio, Lewis Voight; South Carolina, History of Synod Commission; Texas-Louisiana, Russell Vardell.

Appendix C | OFFICERS OF THE LUTHERAN CHURCH IN AMERICA

Presidents/Bishops

Franklin Clark Fry, 1962–68*
Robert J. Marshall, 1968–78
James R. Crumley, Jr., 1978–87

Secretaries

Malvin H. Lundeen, 1962–68
George F. Harkins, 1968–74
James R. Crumley, Jr., 1974–78
Reuben T. Swanson, 1978–87

Treasurers

Edmund F. Wagner, 1962–66
Carl M. Anderson, 1966–72*
L. Milton Woods, 1972–82
Robert F. Blanck, 1982–87

Assistants to Presidents/Bishops

Ralph E. Eckard, 1962–87
George F. Harkins, 1962–68
Martin E. Carlson, 1962–74
Brady Y. Faggart, 1969–75
Dorothy J. Marple, 1975–85
Albert L. Haversat, 1980–84
Cedric W. Tilberg, 1986–87

*Died in office

Appendix D

SYNODICAL PRESIDENTS/ BISHOPS
OF THE
LUTHERAN CHURCH IN AMERICA

Caribbean Synod

Arnold A. Wuertz, 10/62–9/64
Victor M. Rodriguez, 9/64–1/76
Henry E. Dierk, 6/77–8/81
Edelmiro Cortes, 8/81–12/87

Central Canada Synod[1]

Otto A. Olson, 10/62–4/76
G. W. Luetkehoelter, 8/76–12/85

Central Pennsylvania Synod

Dwight F. Putnam, 10/62–9/66
Howard J. McCarney, 9/66–12/87

Central States Synod

N. Everett Hedeen, 10/62–8/70
Harvey L. Prinz, 9/70–8/78
Roger J. Gieschen, 9/78–12/87

Eastern Canada Synod[1]

Albert W. Lotz, 10/62–7/70
Otto F. Reble, 9/70–8/78
William D. Huras, 9/78–12/85

Eastern Pennsylvania Synod[2]

Samuel E. Kidd, 10/62–11/68

1. The Canadian synods became part of the ELCIC in 1986.
2. The Eastern Pennsylvania Synod was divided in 1968.

Florida Synod

Royall A. Yount, 10/62–12/87

Illinois Synod

Robert J. Marshall, 10/62–8/68
Gerald K. Johnson, 8/68–10/75
Paul E. Erickson, 10/75–12/87

Indiana-Kentucky Synod

Walter M. Wick, 10/62–8/79
Ralph A. Kempski, 9/79–12/87

Iowa Synod

Raynold J. Lingwall, 10/62–6/78
Paul M. Werger, 7/78–12/87

Maryland Synod

J. Frank Fife, 10/62–10/68
Paul M. Orso, 10/68–10/83
Eugene A. Gardner, 10/83–1/84
Morris G. Zumbrun, 3/84–12/87

Metropolitan New York Synod[3]

James A. Graefe, 9/69–12/87

Michigan Synod

Frank P. Madsen, 10/62–9/72
Howard A. Christensen, 9/72–8/80
Raymond A. Heine, 8/80–12/87

Minnesota Synod

Leonard Kendall, 10/62–6/65
Melvin A. Hammarberg, 6/65–9/76
Herbert W. Chilstrom, 9/76–12/87

Nebraska Synod

Alfred W. Young, 10/62–9/64
Reuben T. Swanson, 9/64–10/78
Dennis A. Anderson, 11/78–12/87

3. The New York Synod was divided in 1969.

New England Synod

O. Karl Olander, 10/62–9/70
Eugene A. Brodeen, 9/70–9/82
Harold R. Wimmer, 9/82–12/87

New Jersey Synod

Edwin H. Knudten, 10/62–8/70
Edwin L. Ehlers, 9/70–2/78
Herluf M. Jensen, 3/78–12/87

New York Synod[3]

Alfred L. Beck, 10/62–8/69

North Carolina Synod

George R. Whittecar, 10/62–8/78
Ernest L. Misenheimer, 7/78–9/82
Michael C. D. McDaniel, 9/82–12/87

Northeastern Pennsylvania Synod[2]

Wilson E. Touhsaent, 11/68–8/83
Harold S. Weiss, 8/83–12/87

Ohio Synod

Herbert W. Veler, 10/62–8/66
John W. Rilling, 8/66–8/73
Kenneth H. Sauer, 9/73–12/87

Pacific Northwest Synod

A. G. Fjellman, 10/62–9/83
Thomas L. Blevins, 9/83–12/87

Pacific Southwest Synod

Carl W. Segerhammar, 10/62–6/75
Lloyd L. Burke, 7/75–6/79
Stanley E. Olson, 7/79–12/87

Red River Valley Synod

Walter E. Carlson, 10/62–9/68
Carl W. Larson, 8/68–8/80
Harold R. Lohr, 9/80–12/87

Rocky Mountain Synod

Leeland C. Soker, 10/62–1/70
Franklin C. Heglund, 5/70–12/87

Slovak Zion Synod

John Zornan, 10/62–9/76
Paul L. Brndjar, 6/76–6/81
John Adam, 9/81–12/87

South Carolina Synod

Karl W. Kinard, 10/62–7/71
Herman W. Cauble, 7/71–12/87

Southeastern Synod

Raymond D. Wood, 10/62–7/67
Harvey L. Huntley, Sr., 7/67–7/75
Gerald S. Troutman, 7/75–12/87

Southeastern Pennsylvania Synod[2]

William A. Janson, 12/68–9/83
Lawrence L. Hand, 9/83–12/87

Texas-Louisiana Synod

Philip L. Wahlberg, 10/62–12/87

Upper New York Synod[3]

Edward K. Perry, 6/67–12/87

Virginia Synod

J. Luther Mauney, 10/62–8/76
Virgil A. Moyer, 8/76–12/87

Western Canada Synod[1]

John M. Zimmerman, 10/62–7/70
Donald W. Sjoberg, 9/70–12/85

Western Pennsylvania-West Virginia Synod

William C. Hanke, 10/62–9/74

Kenneth R. May, 9/74–12/87

Wisconsin-Upper Michigan Synod

Theodore E. Matson, 10/62–9/74

Robert S. Wilch, 9/74–12/87

Appendix E | CHIEF EXECUTIVES OF CHURCHWIDE AGENCIES OF THE LUTHERAN CHURCH IN AMERICA

Prior to restructuring: 1962-72

Board of American Missions
Donald L. Houser, 1962–72

Board of College Education and Church Vocations
E. Theodore Bachmann, 1962–64
Francis C. Gamelin, 1964–67
Louis T. Almen, 1967–72

Board of Parish Education
W. Kent Gilbert, 1962–72

Board of Pensions
L. Edwin Wang, 1962–72

Board of Publication
H. Torrey Walker, 1962–66
Frank G. Rhody, 1966–72

Board of Social Ministry
Harold Haas, 1962–66
Carl E. Thomas, 1966–72

Board of Theological Education
Conrad J. Bergendoff, 1962–64
E. Theodore Bachmann, 1964–72

Board of World Missions
Earl S. Erb, 1962–68
Arne Sovik, 1968–71
David L. Vikner, 1971–72

Commission on Church Architecture
Edward S. Fry, 1962–72

Commission on Church Papers (Editor, *The Lutheran*)
G. Elson Ruff, 1962–72

Commission on Evangelism
Reynold N. Johnson, 1962–70
Raymond A. May, 1970–72

Commission on Press, Radio and Television
Charles C. Hushaw, 1962–64
R. Marshall Stross, 1964–72

Commission on Stewardship and LLM
Henry Endress, 1962–63
Thorsten A. Gustafson, 1963–69
William P. Cedfeldt, 1969–72

Commission on Worship
Edgar S. Brown, Jr., 1962–70
Eugene L. Brand, 1970–72

Commission on Youth Activities (Ministry)
Carl L. Manfred, 1962–64
Lawrence E. Nelson, 1964–72

LCA Foundation
Chester A. Myrom, 1968–72

Luther League
Executive of the Commission on Youth Activities served as executive
until auxiliary was discontinued in 1968.

Lutheran Church Men
Jack H. Oetgen, 1962–64
Carl H. Jacobson, 1964–66

Lutheran Church Women
Dorothy J. Marple, 1962–72

Following restructuring in 1972

NOTE: Some previous chief executives continued in similar roles within new agencies.

Division for Mission in North America

Kenneth C. Senft, 1972–87

Division for Parish Services

W. Kent Gilbert, 1972–85
Robert N. Bacher, 1985–June 1987
C. Richard Evenson (acting) 1987

Division for Professional Leadership

Louis T. Almen, 1972–77
Lloyd E. Sheneman, 1977–87

Division for World Mission and Ecumenism

Robert W. Stackel, 1972–74
David L. Vikner, 1974–82
Gerald E. Currens, 1982–87

Office for Administration and Finance

Martin E. Carlson, 1972–74
Ralph P. Brighton, 1974–84
Albert L. Haversat, 1984–87

Office for Communications

Howard E. Sandum, 1973–76
William P. Cedfeldt, 1976–87

Office for Research and Planning (until 1980)

John V. Lindholm, 1972–74
Albert L. Haversat, 1974–80

Board of Pensions

L. Edwin Wang, 1972–March 1987
Robert J. Myers (acting) 1987

Board of Publication

Frank G. Rhody, 1972–79
Robert W. Endruschat, 1979–87

Lutheran Church Women

Dorothy J. Marple, 1972–75
Kathryn E. Kopf, 1975–87

The Lutheran

G. Elson Ruff, 1972–73
Albert P. Stauderman, 1973–78
Edgar R. Trexler, 1978–87

NOTE: The Board of Publication and *The Lutheran* were related to the Office for Communications; the Board of Pensions, to the Office for Administration and Finance following restructuring.

INDEX

Abraham, Emmanuel, 308
ACT Appeal, 142, 215
Adequate Housing for All Canadians, 330
Administration and Finance. *See* Office of Administration and Finance
Advent Day of Prayer, 160
Afro-Americans. *See* Black Lutherans
Aging, 301, 329
"Aging and the Older Adult," 301
Aging Is Everybody's Business, 329
Aging Persons in the Community of Faith, 301
Ahlstrom, Sydney E., xv, 11, 57, 58, 60, 69, 78, 85, 86, 112, 113, 114, 115, 125
Aker, George, 534
Albany, 9
Alleman, Herbert, 83, 84, 114
Allin, J. M., 414
Almen, L. G., 333, 535
Alpha Synod, 19
Althouse, LaVonne, 233, 366
American Board of Commissioners for Foreign Missions, 19
American Evangelical Lutheran Church, 2, 39, 45, 62, 88, 100, 101, 104, 105, 119, 353–55, 444–49

American Home Mission Society, 27
American Indian Movement, 210
American Indians. *See* Native North Americans
American Lutheran Board of Parish Education, 89
American Lutheran Church (1930), 77, 81, 84, 99, 116; predecessor bodies of, 44
American Lutheran Church (1960), 93, 352–55, 445–49
American Lutheran Conference, 77, 81, 95, 100–101, 118
"American Lutheranism," 11, 13, 28, 35
American missions. *See* Board of American Missions; Home missions
Americanism and religion, 86
Andersen, Rasmus, 40
Anderson, Albert E., 447
Anderson, H. George, 8, 18, 58, 60, 358–59
Andren, C. T., 28
Apostles' Creed, 44, 287, 422, 516
Apostolic Lutheran Church, 50
Appel, André, 175
Archbishop of Canterbury. *See* Runcie, R. A. K.
Archives (LCA), 60

Page numbers in **boldface** refer to the principal treatment of a subject. Page numbers in *italics* indicate photographs.

Arden, G. Everett, 29, 34, 61, 62, 78, 113, 114, 116, 117, 118, 119

"Armament or Disarmament," 204

Asian Lutherans, 297, 334, 397–98, 448–49

Assets management, 349. *See also* Board of Pensions; Church Property Fund; Common Investing Fund

Associates in Diaconal Service Program, 337, 427

Association for Evangelical Danes in America, 44

Association of Black Lutherans, 398, *399*

Association of English Churches, 32

Association of Evangelical Lutheran Churches, 175

Augsburg Adult Bible Studies, 156

Augsburg Confession, 3, 10–11, 12, 13, 28–29, 75, 96, 103, 105, 119, 136, 412, 421, 498

Augsburg Publishing House, 320

Augustana, 34, 114

Augustana College, 51

Augustana Evangelical Lutheran Church, 2, **24–35,** 59, 62, 77

Augustana Mission Society, 35

Augustana Seminary, 29, 84, 109, 114

Augustana Synod, 31, 33–35, 70, 76, 80, 99, 100, 101, 104, 105

Authority, centralization of, 12, 59

Auxiliaries, 157–61. *See also* Luther League; Lutheran Church Men; Lutheran Church Women

Bachmann, E. T., 60, 96, 116, 117

Back, Johannes, 53

Backman, A. E., 50

Bagger, Henry, 107

Bainton, Roland, 442

Baltimore Deaconess School, 164, 238

Baltimore Declaration, **82–83,** 84

Baptism, 223, 287–88

Baptism, Eucharist and Ministry, xii, 357, 411, 415, 497–99

Barge, William, 377

Barrus, Kathryn, 119

Baum, W. W., 548

Beck, Vilhelm, 39–40

Becker, C. L., xvi, xix

Beisler, Henry, 115

Benne, Robert, 560

Benson, A. B., 61

Benson, O. A., 88, 99, 101

Bergendoff, Conrad, 61, 84, 101, 105–7, 114, 119, 162

Berkenmeyer, Wilhelm, 5

Bernadotte, J. B. J., 24

Bersell, P. O., 24, 80, 88

Bertram, R. W., 560

Bethany College, 35

Bettenhausen, Elizabeth, 560

Bible interpretation, 41–42, 76–77, 81, 82, 84, 96, 103, 353. *See also* Word of God

Bible reading in public schools, 137–38

Bishops, 262, 420–23

Björk, C. A., 33

Björk, Eric, 3

Black Lutherans, 4, 18–19, 21, 38, 60, 124, 133, 141, 297, 334, 398, 404, 448

Blanck, R. F., *406,* 456

Board of American Missions (LCA), **144–46,** 180, 214–16, 256

Board of American Missions (ULCA), 54

Board of College Education and Church Vocations, 141, 162, 164, 236, 256, 312

Board of Foreign Missions (ULCA), 92, 225

Board of Parish Education (LCA), 169, 180, 320. *See also* Division for Parish Services

Board of Parish Education (ULCA), 89

Board of Pensions, 119, 349–51, 403, 522
Board of Publication, 169, 213, 229, 320, 342, 443, 524–25
Board of Social Ministry, 110, 133, 134, 203–7, 231, 256, 403
Board of Theological Education, 109, 132, 162, 234, 256
Board of World Missions, 147–49, 216–19
Boe, N. E., 50
Bohemian Brethren, 6
Bonnemere, Eddie, *435*, 436
Book of Concord, 17
Bost, L. W., *430*
Bouman, W. R., 560
Braaten, C. E., 549, 559–60
Brandelle, G. A., 62
Brauer, Jerald, 380
Bridston, Keith, 536
Brndjar, P. L., *393*
Brown, E. S., Jr., 115, 226
Budgets (LCA), 344–45. *See also* Stewardship
Buffalo Synod, 76, 77
Bulletin service, church, 343
Burgess, Faith, 536
Burgess, J. A., 548

California Lutheran College, 90
"Call for Lutheran Union," 354, 445. *See also* Commission for a New Lutheran Church; Unity, Lutheran
Call to Global Mission and Ecumenism, 408–9, 493, 495
Calumet, Mich., 50
Campus ministry, 313–14. *See also* National Lutheran Campus Ministry
Canada, 8, 54, 60, 111, 246, 444, 525–26
Canada Conference, 35
Canada Home Missions Conference, 95
Canada Section (LCA), 60, 111, 117, 246, 355, 444, 526

Canadian Lutheran Council, 92, 95, 117, 133
Canadian World Relief, 257
Capers, J. M., 374
Capital punishment, 138
Capital University, 27
Caribbean synod, 4
Caring for the World, 329
Carlson, A. B., 91
Carlson, E. M., 164
Carlson, M. E., 61
Carlsson, Erland, 28, 34, 35
Carthage College, 90
Catechetics, 509–10
Catechism. *See* Luther's Small Catechism
"Catholic spirit," 73, 74
Celebrate, 343
Center for Ethics and Society, 295
Central Pennsylvania Synod, 16, 119, 359
Certified lay professionals. *See* Lay professionals
Charismatic Movement of the LCA, 327
Charleston, S.C., 6, 18
Chicago, 28, 32, 70, 74, 100, 111, 301
Chicago Seminary, 45, 53, 55, 109. *See also* Lutheran School of Theology at Chicago
Chicago Theses, 73–74
Chilstrom, H. W., 359, 449, 488, 496, *533*, 534
Chinese Rhenish Church, 309
Chisholm, Shirley, 233
Christ Seminary-Seminex, 354, 426
Christensen, H. A., 47
Christian education. *See* Parish education
Christian Growth Series, 89, 115
Church: Missions of the, **142–49**, 304–6; nature of the, 75, 105
Church and social welfare, statement on, 139–40. *See also* Social issues
Church and state, 136, 138

Church Mission Society (England), 19
Church Mission Society (USA), 41
Church Property Fund, 216, 284, 311, 349, 489, 521
Church vocations. *See* Board of College Education and Church Vocations; Deaconess Movement; Lay professionals; Ordination
"Church World News," 167, 240, 340, 523
Civil disobedience, 136, 395
Civil religion, 285
Clausen, C. L., 40
Clausen, K. S., 175
Clergy, 119, 355–56. *See also* Ordination
Cleveland, 133
Cobbler, Michael L., xix
Colleges, Lutheran, 17, 109, 312–13, 419, 489, 491–92. *See also* Education, higher; *names of specific institutions*
Columbia, S.C., 497
Commission for a New Lutheran Church, 448–49, 475, 501, 515, 518, 521, **526–30**
Commission for Soldiers' and Sailors' Welfare, 15, 70
Commission of Ecumenical Relations (Augustana), 118
Commission on Architecture, 256
Commission on Evangelism, 157, 229, 256
Commission on Function and Structure, 239, **249–61**, 291, 295
Commission on Press, Radio and Television, 240
Commission on Religion in Appalachia, 216
Commission on Stewardship, 171–72, 256
Commission on Student Service, 93
Commission on the Comprehensive Study of the Doctrine of the Ministry, 142, 238, 420, 423, 514–16, 517

Commission on the Hymnal, 88
Commission on the Liturgy, 88
Commission on the Theology and Practice of Confirmation, 220. *See also* Confirmation
Commission on Worship, 151, 153, 226, 256. *See also* Inter-Lutheran Commission on Worship
Commission on Youth Activities/Ministry, 159, 223–24, 231, 256
Committee of Thirty-four on Lutheran Unity, 95, 99
Committee on Church Unity (Augustana), 78
Committee on Lutheran Unity (Augustana), 100
Committee on Social Trends (NLC), 81
Common Investing Fund, 349
Common Service, 6, 13, 32, 55, 88, 316
Common Service Book, 13
Communication, 166–68, 441–43, 522–23. *See also Lutheran;* Office of Communications; Press, Radio and Television
Communion, first. *See* Commission on the Theology and Practice of Confirmation; Confirmation
Communion practices, **151–52**, 174–75, 355–56, 411, 413–14, 500–501
Community, Communication, Communion, 228
Concordia Seminary, 353, 426
Cone, J. H., 124
Confer, B. A., 93
Conference of Bishops/Synodical Presidents, 260–61, 293, 318–19, 422–23, 433
Conferences, 105. *See also* Synods
Confessio Augustana. *See* Augsburg Confession
Confession of faith, 103
Confessional and representative principle, 98, 172

Confessions, Lutheran, xiii, xvii, 73, 75, 78, 82–83, 100, 102, 103, 213, 287, 412–13, 498. *See also* Augsburg Confession; Ecumenical confessionalism

Confirmation, 132, **220–24**, 328. *See also* Catechetics

Congregational data system, 345–46

Congregations, 34, 142–43, 150–51, 315, 325, 418, 440–41, 505–509, 512. *See also* Home missions; Mission congregations

Congregations as Nurturing Communities, 348

Connections: Faith and World, 507

Conscientious objection, 140

Conservative Lutheranism, 11

Constitution (LCA), 105–10, 293–94, **565–79**

Consultation on Church Union, 153

Consultation with synods. *See* Synods, consultation with

Consulting Committee on Church Cooperation, 352

Consulting Committee on Minority Group Interests, 296

Contemporary Worship, 226–27, 317

Continuing education. *See* Education, continuing

Convention (ALC) at Sandusky (1938), 83

Convention (Augustana) of 1952, 100–101

Convention (LCA): at Detroit (constituting), 118, **127–28**, 153, 220; at Pittsburgh (1964), 135, 137, 150, 152; at Kansas City (1966), 138, 170; at Atlanta (1968), 143, 149, 182, 208; at Minneapolis (1970), 208, 210, 212, 216, 223, 234, 239, 241, 246; at Dallas (1972), 210, 226, 230, 243–44, 251, 254, 258, 260–62, 285–86, 293, 298, 300, 302, 311, 314–15, 327, 342, 344, 403, 423; at Baltimore (1974), 259, 288, 291, 293–94, 297, 298, 302, 305, 327, 330, 333, 352, 354, 356, 423; at Boston (1976), 299, 301, 305, 306, 313, 315, 317, 323, 333, 335, 337, 341, 352, 517; at Chicago (1978), 295, 298, 301, 306, 318, 334, 337, 352–53, 354–55, 423, 427, 430, 445, 517; at Seattle (1980), 401, 404, 408, 420–21, 430, 439, 444, 446; at Louisville (1982), 394, 395, 403, 404, 412, 417, 449, 483, 488, 517; at Toronto (1984), 420, 483, 486, 489, 498, 504, 510, 515, 518, 525; at Milwaukee (1986), 496, 511, 519; at Columbus (1987), 531, *533*

Convention (ULCA): at Washington (1920), 74, 84; at Savannah (1934), 81, 84; at Baltimore (1938), 84; in 1940, 84; in 1944, 87

Conventions, 259, 291

Coordinating Committee on Cooperative Parish Education Projects, 228

Coordinating Committee on Race Relations, 208, 254

Council for Theological Education in the Northeast, 235

Covenant relationships, 237

Crawford, Eugene, 210

Creation, orders of, 178–79, 207, 313, 394–95

Criminal justice, 205–6

Crumley, J. R., Jr., xii, 286, 291, *292,* 359–60, 387, 433, 440, 496, 502, *503,* 508–9, *533*

Cully, K. B., 116

Cults, 482

Currens, G. E., 495

Dan, Adam, 41

Danish Evangelical Lutheran Church in America/of North America, 41, 44

Danish Folk Church, 41, 43

Danish Folk Society, 43
Danish Lutheran Church, 70
Danish Lutherans, 36–47
Danish Special Interest Conference
  (LCA), 62
Danish West Indies, 38
Danske Kvinders Missionsfond,
  46
"Davey and Goliath," 168, 240,
  340, 523. *See also* Press, Radio
  and Television
Deaconess Community, 35, 164,
  165, 332, 337–39, 427, 517
Deaconess movement, 20–21, 60,
  165, 237, 256, 337, 517
Deacons. *See* Diaconate, male
Death and dying, 395–97
Death penalty, 138
Declaration of Principles
  Concerning the Church and Its
  External Relations, 74–75
"Definite Synodical Platform,"
  10
Degler, C. N., 66
Department of Information
  Services, 324
Depression, Great, 78, 80–81
Designated Advance Giving,
  241–42, 324, 432, 522
Detroit, 1, 111, 127
Devotional material, 330
Diaconate, male, 238, 337, 517
Dialogues, interconfessional, xii,
  246–47, 356–57, 497, 499–501,
  504–5
Diehl, Charles F., 21
Discipline, ecclesiastical, 82
Discrimination, racial. *See* Race
  relations
Divestment. *See* Investments
Division for Life and Mission in
  the Congregation (ALC), 320
Division for Ministry. *See* Division
  for Professional Leadership
Division for Mission in North
  America, 256, 295, 301–2,
  310–12, 416–18, 484–85, 487–88,
  490–92

Division for Parish Services, 256,
  300, 302, 314–15, 320–21,
  433–34, 512
Division for Professional
  Leadership, 256, 313, 331–38,
  424–27, 513
Division for World Mission and
  Ecumenism, 257, 261, 306–10,
  410–11
Division of Church Planning, 145
Divorce, 204
Doberstein, J. W., 57
Doctor of Ministry degree, 235,
  337
Dorf, Thyra, 47

Eastern Canada Synod, 237
Eastern Pennsylvania Synod, 150
Eastern Lutheranism, 72, 109, 236
Ebenezer, Ga., 6
Ebenezer Home for Orphaned
  Girls, 21
Ecclesia plantanda, 6
Ecclesiastical arts, 169, 343
Ecclesiastical discipline, 82
Ecology, 201–2, 206–7, 394
Economic justice, 394
Ecumenical confessionalism, 74,
  78
Ecumenism, xii, 104, 172–79,
  244–49, 356–58, 411–15, 440,
  496–505
Education, 17, 35–36, 60, 77,
  228–29; continuing, 426; higher,
  90–91, 109, 164, 234–37, 312–13,
  418–19, 480. *See also* Board of
  College Education and Church
  Vocations; Colleges, Lutheran;
  Long-Range Program of Parish
  Education; Parish Education
Education Fund (LCA), 165, 426
Educational Ministry Program,
  320–21, 431
Eilert, E. F., 59
Empie, P. C., xii, 93, *94,* 173, 218,
  548
Endress, Henry, 171
Engberg, Emmer, 62

English as a second language, 161, 519
English-language question. See Language problem
Engstrom, S. E., 101
Episcopal communion, 413–15, 501, 504–5
Equal Rights Amendment, 300, 330, 390, 401, 480
Erb, E. S., 116, 148, 149
Erickson, P. E., 359
Esbjörn, L. P., 25–26, 29
Ethics. See Social issues
Ethnicity, xvi, 215. See also Consulting Committee on Minority Group Interests; Minorities
Eucharistic hospitality. See Communion practices
Euthanasia. See Death and dying
Evald, Emmy, 35
Evangelical and representative principles, 172, 356
Evangelical Lutheran Church, 89, 98, 100, 116
Evangelical Lutheran Church in America, 355, 475, 526
Evangelical Lutheran Church in Canada, 117, 494, 519
Evangelical Lutheran Church of Canada (ALC), 117, 153, 246, 355, 444, 526
Evangelical Lutheran Synod of North America, 8
Evangelical Lutherans in Mission, 354
Evangelical Movement (Finnish), 50
Evangelical Outreach, 305, 322, 437, 442, 510
Evangelisches Magazin, 17
Evangelism, 156–57, 229, 256, 321–24, 409–10, 437, 493
Every Member Response Growth Program, 325
Exploration in Faith, 287

Faith, confession of, 103
Faith and Life Institutes, 302

Faith and order. See World Council of Churches, Faith and Order Commission of
Faith-in-life dialogues, 157
Falckner, Justus, xvi
Family. See Marriage and family
Fandrey, G. A., 117
Federal Council of Churches, 97
Feminism. See Women's movement
Fevold, E. L., 33, 39, 45, 51, 58
Finances, 170–72, 240–44, 257, 521–22. See also Investments; Office of Administration and Finance; Stewardship
Finck, Theodore, 89
Finck, W. J., 57
Finnish American National Evangelical Lutheran Church, 51
Finnish Apostolic Lutheran Church, 50
Finnish conference, 4, 64
Finnish Evangelical Lutheran Church of America, 2
Finnish Lutherans, 47–56, 64, 119
Finnish Missionary Society, 50
First communion. See Commission on the Theology and Practice of Confirmation; Confirmation
Fischer, R. H., 59, 63, 115, 118, 550
Fisher, W. E., 288, 289, 290
Fjellman, Burnice, 62
Flack, E. E., 84
Flessner, D. A., 117, 118
Fliedner, Theodor, 20
Florida Synod, 170
Forde, Gerhard, 536
Foreign and world missions, 18–21, 35, 54, 77, 91, 147–49, 406–10, 492–96; in Africa, 494; in Argentina, 310; in China, 91, 92, 116, 308, 495; in Ethiopia, 308; in India, 19, 20, 41, 46, 91, 492, 495; in Japan, 116, 495; in Jerusalem, 41; in Sudan, 35; in Tanganyika, 35

Forell-Davis, Mary, 365
foreword, 442
Forman, James, 199–200, 208
Fortress Press, 343, 525
Francis, Sister Emma, 21, 60
Franckean Synod, 12
Frederick, Md., 10
Free Lutheran Diet, 13
Frobisher Bay, 36
Fry, F. C., xii, 46, 59, 84, 87, 93,
    98, 101, 102, 104, 107, 115, 118,
    119, 128, *130–31*, 135, 141, 142,
    153, 158, 175, *176*, 178, **182**,
    249, 358, 496
Fry, F. D., 359, 529
Function and structure. *See*
    Commission on Function and
    Structure
Fundamentalism, 76, 113, 285,
    392, 482, 523
Furer, H. B., 57

Garhart, Marjorie, 334
General Council, 12–13, 14, 15,
    31–32, 35, 59, 70, 160
General Synod, **9–10**, 12–13, 15,
    28, 70, 518
General Synod of the Evangelical
    Lutheran Church in the
    Confederate States of America,
    12
General Synod, South. *See* United
    Synod, South
Gerberding, D. R., 306
German Evangelical Lutheran
    Synod of Missouri, Ohio, and
    Other States, 11
Gettysburg College, 10
Gettysburg Seminary, 10, 12, 17,
    55, 83, 84, 103, 213–14, 234–35,
    425–26, 430
Gilbert, W. K. 116
Giving. *See* Designated Advance
    Giving; Strength for Mission;
    Stewardship; World Hunger
    Appeal
Glen Foerd Center, 172

Global mission. *See Call to Global
    Mission and Ecumenism;*
    Foreign and World missions
Global Mission Events, 307, 416
Glock, C. Y., 439, 380
*Goals and Plans for Minority
    Ministry, 1978–1984*, 298, 397
Gospel Society of Finland, 51
Grand View, Iowa, 44
Grand View College and Seminary,
    44–45, 64, 103, 109
*Greater International
    Responsibility*, 330
Green, Carolyn, 542
Greever, W. H., 115
Gregersen, Mrs. Jens, 46
Gröning, Alfred, 53
Grove-Rasmussen, A. C. L., 40
Growth in Ministry, 335–36,
    426
Grumm, Christine, 534
Grundtvig, F. F., 43
Grundtvig, N. F. S., 39–40, 63
Grundtvigians, 43–44
Gullixson, T. F., 100, 116
Gunn, Lorena, 20
Gunther, J. E., 360–61
Gustafson, T. A., 171
Gustavus Adolphus College, 35
Gutwasser, J. E., 3

Hagerstown, Md., 10
Hahn, A. W., 216
Hakanson, Magnus, 25, 33
Halkola, D. T., 65
Halle, Saxony, 5
Hamma Divinity School, 17, 55,
    84, 235, 333
Hancock, Mich., 53
Handlin, Oscar, xvi, xix, 57
Hansen, Verner, 64
Harjunpaa, Toivo, 55
Harkins, G. F., 118, 127, 182, *183*,
    184, 261, 290
Harms, Oliver, 153, 175–*76*
Harrisburg, 70
Hartwick, J. C., 17

Hartwick College and Seminary, 17, 58, 164, 236
Hasselquist, Tufve, 28–29, 34
Hayunga, Herman, 525
Hazelius, E. L., 18
Health benefits program. *See* Board of Pensions
Health Care for All Canadians, 330
Hedin, Naboth, 61
Hefner, Philip, 134, 560
Heiges, Donald, 93, 163
Heikkinen, J. W., 55, 64
Heilbroner, R. L., 67, 112
Hein, C. C., 82
Heinecken, Martin, 536
Helmuth, J. H. C., 17
Helveg, Thorvald, 43
Henkel Press, 17
Hering, Ambrose, 80
Herzfeld, W. L., *533*
Heyer, John C. F., 19, 492
Hillila, Bernhard, 55
Hinckley, P. R., 542
Hispanic Lutheran Declaration, 210
Hispanic Lutherans, 4, 210–12, 334, 398, 429, 448, 508, 510, 524
Hock, R. L., 374
Hoglund, A. W., 54, 64, 65
Hoikka, J. J., 51
Hollander, Peter, 3
Holston Synod, 15
Holy Communion. *See* Communion practices
Home missions, 73, 77, 80, 87, 144, 214–16, 310–12, 416–17, 490–91. *See also* Board of American Missions (LCA); Board of American Missions (ULCA)
Homosexuality, 484–85
Hong Kong, Evangelical Lutheran Church of, 92
Hooks, B. L., 479
Horn, E.T. III, 88, 115
Houser, Donald, 146
Hudson Bay, 2, 36

"Human Rights, Doing Justice in God's World," 295
Hungarian Conference, 4, 119
Hunger. *See* World Hunger Appeal
Hunt, R. D., 35
Hurty, K. S., 560
Hymnal, common, 88. *See also* *Lutheran Book of Worship*; *Service Book and Hymnal*
Hymnody, 317, 319, 508

Icelandic Lutherans, 59
Icelandic Synod, 4, 16, 99, 105, 119
Illinois State University, 28
Illiteracy, 161
Immigrants, Asian and Hispanic, 310. *See also* Asian Lutherans; Hispanic Lutherans
Immigration, Lutheran, xvi, 1, 11, 38, 40, 61, 117, 417
Inclusive language. *See* Language, inclusive
Inclusiveness and Diversity, 486–87, 510
Index of Studies, LCA, 345
Indians, American. *See* Native North Americans
Inerrancy, biblical, 76, 77, 81, 82. *See also* Bible interpretation
Infant communion, 224, 356, 429–30. *See also* Communion practices
Inner Mission, 39, 41, 44, 63, 77, 80
Inner-city congregations, 86, 146, 418. *See also* Urban concerns; Urban crisis
Institute for Ecumenical Research, 175
Inter-Lutheran Commission on Worship, 153, 226–27, 317–19, 428–29
Inter-Lutheran relationships, 78
Intercommunion. *See* Communion practices
International Consultation on English Texts, 227

"International Development," 204
"International Law and
Institutions," 204
Interreligious Foundation for
Community Organization, 216
Investments, 207, 231, 398, 403–4,
522
Invitation to Action, 500
Iowa Synod. *See* Synod of Iowa
and Other States

Jacobs, C. M., 113, 114
Jacobs, D. K., 529
Jacobs, H. E., 6, 15, 57, 58, 73,
74–75, 82, 84
Jacobs, J. E., 479
Jacobson, Leesa, 494
Jacobson, S. T., 355, 444
Jalkanen, R. J., 64
Japan Evangelical Lutheran
Church, 91, 217, 309
Jefferson Prairie, Wis., 28
Jensen, Alfred, 45, 88
Jensen, Erling, 47
Jensen, Herluf, 47
Jensen, Rasmus, 2, 36
Jenson, R. W., 560
Jesus People, 202
Johnson, Amandus, 64
Johnson, J. C., 60
Johnson, L. L., 60
Johnson, Marvin, 377
Johnson, Miriam, 365
Johnson, R. A., 380
Joint Commission on Lutheran
Unity, 102–4, 118, 129, 422, 443
Joint Committee on Doctrine and
Practice, 74
Joint Committee on Union,
100–101
Joint Strategy and Action
Committee, 216
Joint Synod of Ohio, 25, 70, 77. *See
also* Ohio Synod
Jones, Jehu, 18
Journal of Church Music, 151, 343
Joy of Bach, 442

Juel, Donald, 536
Justice, Peace, and Freedom, 204–5
*Justification by Faith, Common
Statement on*, 499
Jutikkala, Eino, 49, 65

Kalevala, 49
Kallen, H. M., 56, 66
Kantonen, T. A., 55, 65
Kassel, Peter, 25
Keffer, Adam, 21, 60, 525
Keiter, Dr., 15
Keljo, Karlo, 55
Kennard, Massie, 486
Kenosha, Wis., 90
Kero, Reino, 64
Key '73, 229–30, 314, 321, 326
Kibira, J. M., 502
Kidd, S. E., 182
Kierkegaard, Søren, 39
Kildegaard, Axel, 47, 64
King, M. L., Jr., 124
King, M. L., Sr., 141, *143*
Kinnard, Massie, 216, 297–98
Kinnison, William, 235, *532*, 534
Kirkelig Samler, 41, 43
Klick, Laura, 142
Klos, F. W., 222
Knubel, F. H., 15, 59, 70, *71*, 73,
74–75, 81, 82, 83, 87, 96, 97, 115
Knubel, Helen, 115
Knubel-Miller Lectures, 119
Knudsen, Johannes, 38, 41–42, 46,
47, 63, 64, 102, 103, 108, 118,
119
Knutson, Kent, 226, 245
Kocherthal, Joshua, 5
Kohn, W. H., 354, 445–46
Koob, Kathryn, 434
Koontz, D. J., 18
Kopf, K. E., 331
Korteniemi, Salomon, 50
Kraft, Valentine, 6
Krauth, Charles Philip, 10
Krauth, Charles Porterfield, 166
Kreider, H. J., 57, 58
Kreller, Margaret, 494

Krueger, Sister Marie, 21
Krumbholz, Clarence, 93
Krych, Margaret, 299, 365
Kugler, Anna, 20, 60
Kukkonen, Walter, 55
Kunze, J. C., 9
Kurtz, Benjamin, 166

Laestadian Movement, 50
Laestadius, L. L., 50
Laity, 302, 335, 420–21, 507, 513,
  514–16. *See also* Lay
  professionals
Lancaster Compromise, 32
Lane, Marti, *329*
Langsam, W. C., 112, 113, 114
Language, inclusive, 299–300,
  431–31, 508, 523
Language problem, 11, 32, 54, 55,
  59, 144.
Lankenau, J. D., 21
LaRiviere-Mestre, Ivis, 365
Lavin, R. J., 323
Lay Associate Program, 210, 216
Lay ministry, 335
Lay preaching, 40, 50
Lay professionals, 142, 334, 429,
  516–17
Lazareth, W. H., xii, 134, 286, 287,
  291, *292*, 359–60, 412, 415, *435*,
  449, 534, 560
LCA Foundation, 172, 522
LCA Partners, 427
Lectionary, 227, 430–31, 508
Lehre and Wehre, 73
Leipzig Mission Society, 35
Letts, H. C., 115
Lilje, Hans, 96
Lind, Jenny, 27
Lindbeck, G. A. 392, 412, 549
Listening Post. *See* Lutheran
  Listening Post
Liturgia Luterana, 429, 508
Liturgical renewal, 142–44. *See
  also* Worship
Liturgy, common. *See* Common
  Service

"Living Faith Series," 509
"Living Waters of Faith Series,"
  509
Lock, Lars, 3
Lodge question, 31, 75, 76–77, 82,
  104
Lohr, Harold, 377
Long, Ralph, 93, 96
Long-range planning. *See* Research
  and planning
Long-Range Program of Parish
  Education, xiii, 46, 55, 89, 116,
  155, 180
Lonnrot, Elias, 49
Lord's Supper. *See* Communion
  practices
Love Compels Action Appeal,
  303–4
Lull, T. F., 380, 560
Lundblad, B. K., *532*, 534
Lundeen, Lyman, 380
Lundeen, M. H., 103, 111, 127,
  128–29, *131*, 182
Luther League, 157, 158
Luther Northwestern Seminary,
  17, 333, 425, 500, 514
Lutheran, 119, 129, 155, **166–67**,
  239, 257, 324, **341–42**, 442–43,
  509, 524, 534
Lutheran and Home Journal, 166
Lutheran Book of Worship, 227,
  316–19, 343, 428–29
Lutheran Church-Canada, 444
Lutheran Church in America:
  headquarters site of, 111; merger
  origins of, 99–101, 111; name
  choice of, 110–11. *See also*
  Canada Section (LCA);
  Convention (LCA); *names of
  specific boards*
Lutheran Church Men, 129,
  157–58
Lutheran Church-Missouri Synod,
  51, 173, 316, 351–52, 444
Lutheran Church of China, 91
Lutheran Church Quarterly, 83,
  114

Lutheran Church Women, 129, 160–61, **231–33, 328–31,** 400, 437–39, 518–19
Lutheran Companion, 100–101, 118, 240
Lutheran Council in the USA, 133, **174–75,** 210, 213, 216, 246, 351, 354, 400; Division of Campus Ministry and Educational Services of, 314
Lutheran Film Associates, 442
Lutheran Free Church, 77
Lutheran Immigration and Refugee Service, 117, 417
Lutheran Inner Mission Society of New York, 80
Lutheran Laymen's/Laity Movement, 171, 257, 303, 328, 521
Lutheran Listening Post, 347, 515
Lutheran Observer, 166, 341
Lutheran Publication Society, 17
Lutheran Quarterly, 115, 317
Lutheran Refugee Service, 93
Lutheran Resettlement Service, 93
Lutheran School of Theology at Chicago, 17, 45, 109, 163, 218, 426, 514, 528
Lutheran series. *See* "Protestant Hour"
Lutheran Social Service System. *See* Social ministry
Lutheran Society for Worship, Music and the Arts, 228
Lutheran Standard, 442, 447, 534
Lutheran Theological Education in the Northeastern United States, 425
Lutheran Theological Seminary. *See* Gettysburg Seminary; Philadelphia Seminary; Southern Seminary
Lutheran Witness, 81
Lutheran Women, 160, 233, 330
Lutheran World Action, 92–93
Lutheran World Convention, 96

Lutheran World Federation, 91, 92, **95–97,** 117, 132, 147, **175,** 221, 247, 257, 354, 358, 410, 531
Lutheran World Ministries. *See* Lutheran World Federation
Lutheran World Relief, 92–93, 257, 303, 494
Lutheran Worship, 316
Luther's Small Catechism, 3, 17, 96, 103, 155, 287, 328, 516

McCarney, H. J., 359
McCurley, Foster, 374
Making a Global Difference, 329
Malmberg, C. J., 33
Malmin, O. G., 116
Manifesto, 150–51, 224, 250
Marple, D. J., 251, *252,* 299, 331, 360–61
Marriage and family, 136–37, 203–4, 485
Marshall, Alice, 232
Marshall, R. J., xii, 182, *183,* 202, 244, 246, 249, 251, 260–63, 285, 288, 290, *292,* 298, 322, 351, 422–23, 445, 449, 496, 517, 528
Marshall, Wis., 31
Martensen, Daniel, 47
Martensen, H. L., 39, 549
Marty, M. E., 86, 114, 115, 356, 449, 536
Maryland Synod, 214
Maryland-Virginia Synod, 9
Mattson, A. D., 62, 84
Maywood Seminary. *See* Chicago Seminary
Medical Issues of the Seventies, 329
Membership, 229, 324, 436–37, 506; voting (LCA), 108
Men of Color, Men of Faith, 228
Menendez, Peter, 2
Meuser, F. W., 14, 16, 59, 60, 62, 73–74, 112, 113, 528
Michelfelder, S. C., 96–97
Michigan Synod, 423
Midwest Lutheranism, 73, 76

Miller, Dagmar, 46
Ministerial Health Benefit Plan, 351
Ministerium, 119, 355–56.
Ministerium of New York. *See* New
    York Ministerium
Ministerium of Pennsylvania, 6, 8,
    9, 12, 15, 16, 19, 316, 492
Ministers Information Service, 151
Ministry, doctrine of, 290, 507,
    514–16. *See also* Commission on
    the Comprehensive Study of the
    Doctrine of the Ministry; Lay
    ministry; Ordination
Ministry with Older Persons, 301
Minneapolis, 76, 80, 111
Minneapolis Theses (1925), 74,
    76–78, 82, 83, 100, 112, 118
Minnesota Conference, 32, 34
Minnesota Synod, 485
Minnick, M. L., 544
Minorities, 296–98, 334, 397–401,
    416, 425, 486–87. *See also*
    Consulting Committee on
    Minority Group Interests
Minuit, Peter, 3, 57
Mission congregations, 144, 490–91
Mission Development Certificates,
    311, 349, 432
Mission Friends, 33, 62
Mission of the church, 142–49,
    304–6
Mission on Six Continents, 218,
    309, 416
Missions. *See* Foreign and world
    missions; Home missions
Mississippi Conference, 27–28
Missouri Synod, 19, 81, 83, 84, 93,
    99, 101, 112, 133, 245, 246. *See
    also* Lutheran Church-Missouri
    Synod
Modean, E. W., 98, 118
Modernists, 76
Mohawk Valley, 5
Monday's Ministers, 303
Morehead, J. A., 72, 95–96, 117
Mortensen, Enok, 36, 40, 43, 62,
    63, 64, 115, 116, 127

Muhlenberg, Henry Melchior, xvii,
    5, 8, 316, 531
Muhlenberg College, 47, 90, 238
Munk, Jens, 2, 36
Murphy, T. A., 548
Muskego, Wis., 40
Mynster, J. P., 39

National Black Economic
    Development Conference,
    199–200
National Council of Churches, xii,
    92, 98, 133, **176–78**, 248, 330,
    357, 531; Commission on
    Religion and Race of, 159
National Lutheran Campus
    Ministry, 492
National Lutheran Commission for
    Soldiers' and Sailors' Welfare.
    See Commission for Soldiers' and
    Sailors' Welfare
National Lutheran Council, 55,
    70–74, 81, 89, 91, **92–95**, 99–100,
    112, 116, 133, 173
National Lutheran Educational
    Conference, 91
Native North Americans, 1, 146,
    200, 210, 233, 334, 397, 449,
    487, 518
Nebraska Synod, 360
Nelson, E. C., xv, xix, 57, 58, 59,
    60, 61, 62, 73, 77, 87, 92, 98,
    102, 104, 112, 113, 114, 115,
    116, 117, 118, 119, 536
New England Synod, 403
New Hanover, Pa., 5
New Jersey Synod, 485
New Market, Va., 17
New Netherlands, 2, 57
New York City, 9, 111, 119
New York Ministerium, 9, 10, 18,
    525
Newburgh, N.Y., 5
Nichol, T. W., 562
Nielsen, A. S., 40, 41
Nielsen, E. D., 64
Nikander, J. K., 51, 53–54, 65

Nikander, V. K., 55
Non-English-language ministry,
144. *See also* Hispanic Lutherans
Norelius, Eric, 28, 34
Norske Lutheraner, 31
North Carolina Synod, 9, 18
Northern Illinois Synod, 28
Northwest, Synod of the, 32
Northwestern Seminary. *See*
Luther Northwestern Seminary
Norwegian Evangelical Church in
America, 40, 73, 77
Norwegian Lutheran Church, 70,
76, 84
Norwegian Lutheran Free Church,
70
Norwegian Synod, 59
Norwegian-Danish Augustana
Synod, 31. *See also* Augustana
Synod
Norwegian-Danish Conference, 44,
63–64
Nova Dania, 36
Nova Scotia, 8
Nuclear threat, 394, 483
Nygren, Anders, 97
Nyholm, P. C., 63, 64
Nystrom, Daniel, 61, 62, 66

Occasional Services, 428–29, 508
Odman, Charlotte, 61
Offerman, Henry, 84, 114
Office for Government Affairs, 488
Office of Administration and
Finance, 257, 348
Office of Communications, 257,
339–43, 441–43
Office of Research and Planning,
257, 344–47
Ofstedal, R. A., 116
Ohio Synod, 9, 73, 76, 359. *See
also* Joint Synod of Ohio
Olive Branch Synod, 15
Ollila, D. J., 51, 65
Olson, E. W., 61
Olson, O. A., 246
Olson, O. N., 61

Omaha, 35
One in Mission, 488–89, 522
Ontario, 8, 21
Ordination, 108, 213, 420–22, 485,
498, 513, 530. *See also* Women,
ordination of
Orthodox communions, xii, 502,
503
Outdoor ministries, 321

Pacific Lutheran Seminary, 55,
334, 425, 426, 514
Pacific Northwest Synod, 158
Pacific Southwest Synod, 291
Parish and Church School Board,
89
Parish education, **89, 154–56,**
228–29, 320–22, 431–32, 509. *See
also* Long-Range Program of
Parish Education
Parish Education Curriculum
(LCA), 89, 432
Parish Life and Ministry
Development, 224–26, 314–15
Parish services. *See* Division for
Parish Services
Partners. See LCA Partners
Passavant, W. A., 20, 27
Pastor Evangelists, 322–23, 437,
510
Pastor's Desk Book, 119
Patriarch Demetrios I, *503*
Paxton, Ill., 29
"Peace and Politics," 483
Peace and war, 394, 484, 519
Pennsylvania College, 10
Pennsylvania Ministerium. *See*
Ministerium of Pennsylvania
Pensions, 110, 349–51, 522. *See
also* Board of Pensions
Pentecostalism, 202
Pero, Albert, 536, 542
Perry, E. K., 359
Personnel Support Service, 336
Peterman, Richard, 490
Philadelphia, 3, 5, 12–13, 18, 21,
111, 343, 398

Philadelphia Motherhouse, 21
Philadelphia Seminary, 12, 17, 74, 84, 88, 107, 164, 216, 234–35, 238, 286, 424, 425–26, 514
Pichaske, D. R., 151
Pietism, 39, 43
Piety, patriotic, 86
Pittsburgh, 20, 135
Pittsburgh Agreement, 83–84, 114
Pittsburgh Synod, 21
Planning. *See* Division of Church Planning; Research and planning
Platz, Elizabeth, 214
Polity, 34
Pope John XXIII, 126
Pope John Paul II, 392, 482, 496, 502, *503*
Poppen, Emmanuel, 99
Portlock, Carver, 365
Poverty, statement on, 139
Poverty and Youth, 330
Prayer in public schools, 137
Presbyterian churches, 500–501
Press, Radio and Television, 167, 240, 340, 441
Preus, D. W., 445, 447, 496, 500, *533,* 534
Preus, J. A. O., 175, 246, 322, 353, 426
Princell, J. G., 33
Printz, Johan, 3
Priority Program for Justice and Social Change, 208–9
Professional leadership. *See* Division for Professional Leadership
Prosser Trust, 172
"Protestant Hour," 167, 240, 340, 442, 523
Public Policy and Church-Related Higher Education, 237
Publications, 17, 77. *See also* Board of Publication; *Lutheran;* Press, Radio and Television
Pulpit and altar fellowship, 73, 77, 82, 84, 174, 245, 246, 414, 500

Qualben, L. P., 57
Quinones, Julio, 542

Race relations, 135–36, 141, 199–200, 208–9, 297, 391, 403–4, 486–87. *See also* Consulting Committee on Minority Group Interests; Minorities
Racial revolution, 479–80
Racine, 44, 47
Racism, institutional, 297
Radio Voice of the Gospel, 147, 308
Rasmussen, C. C., 103
Rationalism, 38–39
Reading, Pa., 5, 12
Reed, L. D., 88, 115
Reformation anniversaries in 1917, 14–15
Reformed churches, 9, 500–501
Refugees, 391. *See also* Lutheran Refugee Service
Regional units (ELCA), 447
Rejoice with Us, 228
Relief work, 72
Religious liberty, 139
Research and planning, **179–82,** 242–43, 315, 327–28, 345–47, 427, 507, 520–21. *See also* Office of Research and Planning
Resource Mobilization Network, 418
Reu, J. Michael, 77, 83, 114
Reumann, John, 116, 374, 424, 449
Revivalism, 33, 50, 86
Reynolds, W. M., 27
Rhody, F. G., 443
Roanoke College, 72, 95
Rock Island, Ill., 29
Roman Catholic Church, xii, 126, 153, 175, 392, 482, 499
Root, Michael, 549
Rosenius, C. O., 33
Rudman, Andrew, 3
Ruff, G. E., 129, *131,* 166, 239
Runcie, R. A. K., 415, 503, *504,* 505

Rusch, W. G., 117, 411, 458
Ryden, E. E., 101
Rygh, G. T., 117

Sacrament of the Altar. See
  Communion practices
Saint Croix, 21
Salzburg, 6
Sandusky Declaration, 83
Saskatoon Seminary, 425
Sauer, K. H., 359
Savannah Declaration, 81, 84
Scandinavian Conference, 28
Scandinavian Evangelical Lutheran
  Synod of North America, 29
Schiotz, F. A., 93, 175, *176*, 245,
  247, 496
Schmalenberger, J. L., 374
Schmauk, T. E., 15, 70, 74
Schmucker, S. S., 10, 13, 58
School of Missions, Lutheran
  School of Theology at Chicago,
  218
School prayer, 137
Schuh, H. F., 99
Schuh, H. J., 117
Scopes trial, 76
Scripture. See Bible interpretation;
  Bible reading in public schools;
  Word of God
Seaman, W. R., 115
Second Vatican Council, xii, 126,
  356
Secret societies. See Lodge
  question
Secular humanism, 482
Seminaries, location and number
  of, 333, 355
Seminary education, 10, 12, 32, 43,
  53, 77, 80, 109, 132, **162–63**,
  234–35, 256, 332, 425–26, 488,
  513–14, 526
Senft, Kenneth, 489
Service Book and Hymnal, 46, 55,
  88, 115, 135, 317, 429
Sex, marriage, and family, 203–4,
  485

Shell, A. F., 374
Shirey, Sister Miriam, *338*
Sibley, Leonard A., 377
Significant Issues for the Seventies,
  242
Sittler, Joseph, 178, 442
Sjoberg, Donald, 526
Sjöblom, Peter, 34
Slovak Evangelical Lutheran
  Church, 153
Slovak Lutherans, 59
Slovak (-Zion) Synod, 4, 16, 99,
  105, 107
Small Catechism. See Luther's
  Small Catechism
Snellman, J. V., 49
Social Criteria for Investments,
  207, 403. See also Investments
Social issues, 80, **294–304**
Social ministry, 20–21, 80, 115,
  133, 314, 325, 512; institutions
  and agencies of, 109–10. See also
  Board of Social Ministry
Social statements, **134–40**, 203–6,
  295, 301, 394–96, 416, 483
Society for Inner Mission, 39
Solberg, R. W., 60, 61, 62, 63, 64,
  90, 116, 119, 126
Soldiers' and Sailors' Relief, 55. See
  also Commission for Soldiers'
  and Sailors' Welfare
Sørenson, R., 63
South Carolina Synod, 9
Southeast Asians. See Asian
  Lutherans
Southern Christian Leadership
  Conference, 124
Southern Seminary, 17, 323, 374,
  514
Sovik, Arne, 149
Spanish-speaking ministries. See
  Hispanic Lutherans
Special interest conferences, 119
Spiritual awakening, 39
Spitz, C. T., 175
Staalsett, Gunnar, 536
Stackel, R. W., 304

Stadius, Arnold, 53, 65
Stamm, R. T., 84
Stauderman, Albert, 119, 166, 239, 321, 341
Stauffer, S. A., 365
Steimle, E. A., 146
Stendahl, Krister, 380
Stephenson, G. M., 61
Stephenson, J. R., 374
Stewardship, 171, 305–6, 324–25, 432–34, 511–12
Strength for Mission, 305, 310, 322, 324, 417, 432, 488
Structure. *See* Commission on Function and Structure
Stub, H. G., 73, 74
Student Nonviolent Coordinating Committee, 199
Stuhr, Walter, 536
Suburbs, 86
Suelflow, A. R., 58, 60, 61, 62
Sullivan, L. E., 403–4
Sunday schools. *See* Parish education
Suomi College, 53, 65, 109
Suomi Synod, **51–56**, 65, 66, 88, 98, 100, 101, 104, 105, 119
Susquehanna University, 214
Swanson, S. H., 116
Swanson, Reuben T., 359, 360–61
Swede Bend, Iowa, 33
Swedish Evangelical Mission Covenant of America, 33
Swedish Lutherans, 24–35
Swensson, Charlotte, 35
Swensson, Jonas, 28
"Synod Mission Profile," 311–12
Synod of Iowa and Other States, 70, 73, 76, 77
Synod of the Northwest, 32
Synodical Conference, 76, 112
Synods: consultation with, 244, 312; role of (LCA), 105, 107, 255

Taiwan Lutheran Church, 92
Tappert, T. G., 57, 58, 60, 63, 64, 65, 119

Television. *See* Communication; Press, Radio and Television
Tennessee Synod, 9
Texas-Louisiana Synod, 522
The American Lutheran Church (TALC), 89, 116, 155
Theological Basis for Ministry to and with Older Adults, 301
Theological education. *See* Board of Theological Education; Seminary education
Theological Issues Related to Men & Women in the Body of Christ, 300
Theological Statement on Social Ministry, 134
Thomas, Carl, 231
Thomsen, Niels, 41
Thousand Oaks, Calif., 90
Tiemeyer, A. L., 542
Tietjen, J. H., 353
Toward the Development of a United States Food Policy, 303
Town and country ministry, 418
Trappe, Pa., 5
Traver, A. J., 59
Trexler, E. R., 342, 443, 534
Trinity Seminary, 17, 235, 333, 425
Tsan, Sister Margaret, *338*
Tuchman, Barbara, xvii, xix, 197

Unaltered Augsburg Confession. *See* Augsburg Confession
Unionism, 9, 76, 104
United Church Women, 160
United Danish Lutheran Church, 77
United Evangelical Lutheran Church in America, 44, 100, 116
United Lutheran Church in America, 2, 73, 99, 100, 105; origin of, 15–16, 32; Special Commission on Relations of American Lutheran Church Bodies of, 118. *See also* Convention (ULCA)
United Nations, 205

United Synod, South, 13, 15, 59, 70
"United Testimony on Faith and
Life," 100, 101
Unity: Christian, xii, 412, 502;
Lutheran, 16, 81–82, 95, 351–55,
387, 443–49, 502. *See also*
Ecumenism; Joint Commission
on Lutheran Unity
Universal Declaration of Human
Rights, 205
Upsala College, 35, 141
Urban concerns, 115, 145, 491. *See
also* Inner-city congregations
Urban crisis, 142, 208–9
Uthe, E. W., 181

Vatican Council, Second, xii, 126,
356
Verbal inspiration, 81
Vestergaard, Rasmus, 44
V-12 Navy program, 90
Vickner, D. L., 60, 91, 116, 308,
408, 546
Vieth, Paul, 89
Vietnam, 197
Views from the Pews, 347
Vig, P. S., 43–44, 63
Virgin Islands, 21, 36, 297
Virginia Synod, 9
Visser 't Hooft, W. A., 117
Vocations, church, 332. *See also*
Board of College Education and
Church Vocations; Deaconess
Community; Deaconess
movement; Lay professionals;
Ordination
Voces Luteranas, 524
Volunteer Reading Aides Program,
161
Vos, Nelvin, 560
Voting membership. *See*
Membership, voting (LCA)

Wagner, E. F., 129, *131*
Wagner, Joseph, 377
Wagner College, 55
Wahlberg, P. L., 359

Wahlstrom, E. H., 84
Waisenen, C. E., 65
Waldenström, P. P., 33
Wang, L. E., 119
Waniek, Marilyn, 366
War. *See* Peace and war
Wargelin, John, 54, 64, 88
Wargelin, R. W., 54, 65, 66, 88,
103, 119, *130*
Wartburg Seminary, 426
Washington Declaration, 76, 84,
98, 113, 172
Waterloo University, 236–37
Weber, M. C., 380
Wee, Morris, 93
Weeg, Howard, 291
Week of Prayer for Lent, 160
Weenaas, August, 31
Weiser, F. S., 60
Welcome to the Lord's Table, 228
Welfare, Department of, of
National Lutheran Council, 81
Welfare, social. *See* Church and
social welfare, statement on;
Social issues; Social ministry
Weller, Dr., 15
Wentz, Abdel Ross, 1, 8, 11, 15, 72,
77, 80, 84, 93, 97
Wentz, F. K., 112–14, 117, 235
Wesley, L. H., 141, *142*, 209
West Denmark, Wis., 43
West Pennsylvania Synod, 9
Wickey, Gould, 91
Wietzke, Walter, 549
Wilfrid Laurier University, 237
Willebrands, Johannes, 497, 504
Wilmington, 3
Wilson, C. R., 60
Winter, Gibson, 115
Wisconsin-Upper Michigan Synod,
289
Wolf, R. C., 5, 10, 93, 95
Women and Alcoholism, 329
Women: changing role of, 125,
142, 298, 480–81, 514; ordination
of, 142, 328, 330, 334, 400, 444,
513, 514

Women in Church and Society,
Consulting Committee on, 298,
328, 398–400, 416, 487–88
Women Offenders, 329
Women's Missionary Society, 35,
46
Women's movement, 129, 142,
160–61, 200–202, **212–14**,
398–401. *See also* Lutheran
Church Women
Woods, L. M., 290, *292*, 361,
405–6, 456
Woodward, C. V., xvi, xix
Word and Witness, xiii, 323, 374,
437, 510
Word of God, 13, 33, 40, 44, 73,
76, 81, 82, 96, 104, 114
World community, 204–5
World Council of Churches, xii, 92,
97–98, 132, 142, **178**, 249, 257,
356–57, 415–16, 497, 531; Faith
and Order Commission of, xii,
354, 415–16, 497

World Encounter, 148
World Hunger Appeal, 231–33,
303–4, 305, 324, 342,
400–402, 432, 478–79, 494,
521–22
World missions. *See* Foreign and
world missions
Worship, 88, **151–53**, 226–28,
428–31, 507–8. *See also*
Commission on Worship;
Liturgical renewal
Wuorinen, J. H., 47, 64
Wuthnow, Robert, 380

Yearbook, LCA, 346
Youngert, S. G., 117
Youth, 125–26, 158–60, 230–31,
232, 314, 326–27, 434–36, 511.
See also Commission on Youth
Activities/Ministry

Ziehl, W. H., 251, *252*
Zinn, Howard, 113, 114